Edip Yuksel

Peacemaker's Guide to Warmongers:
Exposing Robert Spencer, Osama bin Laden, David Horowitz, Mullah Omar, Bill Warner, Ali Sina and other Enemies of Peace:

ABC
Aegis Defence Serv.
AIPAC
Airal Sharon
AirScan
Alan Dershowitz
Alberto Gonzales
Al-Qaeda
American Enterprise Inst.
Ann Coulter
ArmorGroup
Army of Mahdi
Ayaan Hirsi Ali
Basij-e Mostaz'afin
Benjamin Netanyahu
Beverly LaHaye
Bill Graham
Bill Kristol
Bill Warner
Blackwater (Xe)
Bush Family Co.
Boeing Co.
Brigitte Gabriel
CAMERA
Campus Watch
CBS
CIA
Charles Krauthammer
Christopher Hitchens
CNN
Custer Battles
Daniel Pipes
David Brooks
David Horowitz
Debbie Schlussel
Dick Cheney
Donald Rumsfeld
Doug Feith
DynCorp
Eliot Cohen
Elliott Abrams
Eric Prince
Estee Lauder
Foreign Policy Initiative
FOX News
Fouad Ajami
Geert Wilders

General Dynamics
Glenn Beck
Hal Lindsey
Haliburton
Health Net Inc
Heritage Foundation
Honneywell
Hughes
Ibn Waraq
IDF
IFCJ
IRGC
Iranian Mullahs
Israel Aircraft Indust.
Israel Military Indust.
Israel Weapon Indust.
Jack Hayford
JINSA
John Bolton
John Hagee
John Yoo
Joseph Alois Ratzinger
Joseph Lieberman
Jundullah
Karl Rove
Kimberly Kagan
L-3 Communications
Lashkar-e-Taiba
Left-Behind Crusaders
Lewis Scooter Libby
Lindsey Graham
Lockheed Martin
Mark Steyn
Michael Savage
Michelle Malkin
Mormon Church
Motorola
Mulla Omar
NBC
Neal Boortz
Neocons
New Grounds
Newt Gingrich
The New Republic
Nonie Darwish
Northrop Grumman
Osama Bin Laden

Pat Robertson
Paul Wolfowitz
Peter King
PNAC
Rafael Development Corp.
Raytheon Co.
Richard Armitage
Richard Perle
Rupert Murdoch
Rockxell
Rudy Giuliani
Rush Limbaugh
Sam Harris
Sarah Palin
Science Applications
Shimon Peres
Radovan Karadzic
Religious Right (Wrong)
Robert Kagan
Robert Spencer
Shiites for Sharia Law
Starbucks
Steven Emerson
Sunnis for Sharia Law
Taliban
Textron
Tim LaHaye
Titan Corp.
Tom DeLay
Tony Blair
Triple Canopy
Tzipi Livni
TRW Inc.
United Technologies
USA-MIC
Valayat-i Faqih
Victoria's Secret
Vinnel Corp
Wafa Sultan
Walid Shoebat
Wall Street Journal
Warner Brothers
William Kristol
Xe (Blackwater)
Zionists
And other war profiteers,
fearmongers, warmongers.

brainbowpress

ISBN: 978-0-9796715-3-1

$19.95
ISBN 978-0-9796715-3-1
51995>

9 780979 671531

Cover Design: Uğur Şahin

Printed in the United States of America

10 9 8 7 6 5 4 3 2

EDIP YUKSEL is an American-Turkish-Kurdish author and activist who spent four years in Turkish prisons in the 1980's for his political writings and activities promoting an Islamic revolution in Turkey. He experienced a paradigm change in 1986 transforming him from a Sunni Muslim leader to a reformed muslim, a rational monotheist, or a peacemaker. Edip Yuksel has written more than twenty books and hundreds of articles on religion, politics, philosophy and law in Turkish, and numerous articles and books in English. Edip is the founder of 19.org, the Islamic Reform organization, and co-founder of Muslims for Peace Justice and Progress (MPJP). His personal site is yuksel.org. After receiving his bachelor degrees from the University of Arizona in Philosophy and Near Eastern Studies, Edip received his law degree from the same university. Edip is an Adjunct Philosophy professor at Pima Community College, and teaches various classes at Accelerated Learning Lab. He is fluent in Turkish, English and Classic Arabic; proficient in Persian, and barely conversant in Kurdish, his mother tongue.

Join the Movement; Let the World Know!

The Islamic Reform movement is receiving momentum around the globe. We invite you to join us in our activities locally, internationally. Please contact us through the contact addresses posted at:

www.islamicreform.org
www.free-minds.org
www.yuksel.org
www.mpjp.org
www.19.org

To study the Quran more diligently, you may visit 19.org for links to computer programs, searchable Quranic indexes, electronic versions of this and other translations, and various study tools. We highly recommend you the following sites for your study of the Quran:

www.quranic.org
www.quranix.com
www.openquran.org
www.studyquran.org
www.quranmiracles.org

www.19.org	www.yuksel.org	www.free-minds.org	www.islamicreform.org	www.quranmiracles.org	www.brainbowpress.com	www.deenresearchcenter.com	www.commondreams.org	www.quranbrowser.com	www.openburhan.com	www.studyquran.org	www.quranix.com	www.mpjp.org

The peacemakers of the world should unite their voices and forces against militaristic government policies, nationalism, fascism, military-industrial complex, and they must confront corporations, organizations and individuals that promote wars among the children of Adam.

We should not discriminate among warmongers, the followers of Cain, because of their color, religious or political affiliations, titles, nationalities, or the fashions of their grooming! Warmongers belong to the same pack; they need each other to fan the flames of hate and war.

If we spent a fraction of our money and effort to establish peace on earth, rather than wasting it on war machines, we would have a much better world.

As a muslim (peacemaker), I have dedicated my life to confronting the enemies of peace and I invite you to join our efforts. Peacemakers of the world, must unite for peace, justice, and progress!

Peace, Justice and Liberty in 19 Languages
(The refrain will be repeated in 19 languages as indicated)

Me, you, he, she, white, black or brown
East, west, south, north, up or down
Rich, poor, old, young, low or high
We share the same earth, the same sky
  Peace, justice and liberty
  Blessings in diversity
    (English; Mandarin; Hindi)

With a Big Bang since billions of years
On this blue planet we're forlorn travelers
Surviving hurricanes, plagues, and tribulation
We share the same origin, the same creation
  Peace, justice and liberty
  Blessings in diversity
    (Arabic; Russian; Malay)

After millions of terrestrial revolution
Perfected by a naturally designed evolution
Dancing around the sun in the milky-way
We share the same cosmos, the same human DNA
  Peace, justice and liberty
  Blessings in diversity
    (Bengali; Spanish; German)

Together we invented poetry, numbers and alphabet
Algebra, motor, jet, radio, TV, Internet
Vaccine, A.C., camera, computer, and soon
We were all in Apollo that split rocks from the Moon
  Peace, justice and liberty
  Blessings in diversity
    (Urdu; Turkish; Persian)

Surviving the horrors of wars world wide
Inquisition, slavery, holocaust, genocide
Enduring all sorts of atrocities and aggressions
We see the same light, learning the same lessons
       Peace, justice and liberty
       Blessings in diversity
              (French; Japanese; Portuguese)

We are the generation of information
Transcending borders, we're one nation
Tearing down the walls of repression
We share the same dream; the same aspiration.
       Peace, justice and liberty
       Blessings in diversity
              (Javanese; Swahili; Hebrew, Kurdish)

       Freedom of expression
       Engine of progression
       Peace, justice and liberty
       The song of next generation

PS: If you have a band and wish to sing this
song, please contact me so that we might
modify it together.

CONTENTS

CONTENTS (Continued)

Peacemakers Confront and Expose Warmongers and Torturers

Bible: "Blessed are the peacemakers..." Matthew 5:9

Quran: "O you who acknowledge, join in peace, all of you, and do not follow the footsteps of the devil. He is to you a clear enemy." (2:208)

Quran: "God bears witness that there is no god but He; as do the controllers, and those with knowledge; He is standing with justice. There is no god but Him, the Noble, the Wise. The system with God is peacemaking and peaceful surrendering (islam). Those who received the book did not dispute except after the knowledge came to them out of jealousy between them. Whoever does not appreciate God's signs, then God is swift in computation." (3:18-19)

I have written more than 20 books in Turkish and English, and this is a book with the longest and ugliest title I have ever written. Without the names in the subtitle and the following list, the world would be a much better world. Of course, many would claim the same thing about my name too, since I have offended the religious and political sensitivities of millions, if not billions. However, the people, organizations and corporations in my incomplete and casually compiled list have the following common characteristics: they directly or indirectly support or promote violence, aggressions, occupations, and wars.

We need to act and become catalysts for reform in ourselves and in the political system of our countries, before the religious and nationalist zealots of all colors and creeds hurl humanity towards an irreversible course of self-destruction. There are many evil forces, both in the east and west, which work to inflame animosities and provoke another major calamities. They will not hesitate to engage in covert operations in order to incite hatred and atrocities.

On the other hand, there are bystanders which make up the majorities of people in every country. Yet they can easily be manipulated by warmongering politicians, media, religious leaders and war-profiteering corporations to cheer for bloody wars and atrocities. If they are scared by politicians and provocateurs, they would support every bloody conflict without hesitation, as they did when Hitler or Stalin incited them. The same people and the same Hitler and Stalin are still alive among us. They just come in different colors and shapes, but they think (well, more accurately, they feel) and behave exactly the same. Therefore, it is no surprise to see incarnations of Hitlers and Nazis on the one hand condemning the Holocaust and on the other hand treating other people exactly like Hitler and Nazis did in the past.

> "If these ~~gentlemen~~ *men* have the right to depict Muhammad to be an evil guy and his supporters being as evil or duped, then I should also have the right to expose their so-called scholarly work, which is merely based on hearsay books and distortion and contortion of the Quranic verses by the followers of those hearsay stories. For instance, ~~brother~~ Spencer generously uses the hearsay stories fabricated centuries after Muhammad's life to assassinate Muhammad's character, while he knows well that according to the same sources which he trusts, Muhammad reportedly split the Moon causing half of it to fall in Ali's backyard, or Muhammad reportedly made trees walk, Muhammad ascended to the seventh heaven with his body, and many other stories. Scholarly integrity requires consistency and honesty in using sources in evaluating a historic personality. But, your ~~gentlemen~~ *crusaders* pick and choose from those books as they wish. They take advantage of the crazy noises created by Jingoists, Crusaders and Jihadists, and hideously try to justify a bloody imperial Crusade with its resurrected Spanish Inquisition mentality against Muslims. I consider the work of these gentlemen a dishonest or ignorant attack against one of the most progressive and peaceful leaders in human history."

This is a modified quote from my debate with the most rabid Crusaders, Robert Spencer, Bill Warner, and other allies of the notorious torture-promoter Zionist David Horowitz. I later regretted using kind words to describe them. It was they who first reminded me of my naiveté; they were disturbed by my use of the word "brother" to depict them. In retrospect, I know that I was naïve to consider them "gentlemen" or "brother," as they were a troop of bloodthirsty warmongers with clandestine missions and connections. All they were after was the promotion of a new Crusade through their depictions of all Muslims as threats to civilization (read: Christian hegemony and imperialism!).

Bill Warner is a rabid enemy of peace. In a recent article published at his website under the title Losing Israel, he criticized Israeli Zionists for not fabricating enough propaganda! Israel, doesn't fabricate enough propaganda?! It is like criticizing of a braying donkey for not making a louder noise, or Fox News for not hiring enough rightwing demagogues, or a serial killer for not killing more! Towards the end of the article, Bill ensures his place in the short list of warmongers:

> "Now, which one of the two maintains a stronger position -- peace or victory? Today Israel desires peace and the Palestinians insist on victory. Guess who wins? Peace is for losers. Regrettably, Israelis and American Jews are choosing to be the losers. The consequences however are too dire; ultimately, Israel may get their peace, but it may be the peace after jihad's victory."
> www.americanthinker.com/2009/10/losing_israel_1.html

Ironically, in the very article asking Israel to construct more propaganda, a coded way of asking for production of more lies, Bill Warner demonstrates his skills by subliminally peddling the loudest Zionist propaganda in the century: "Israel desires peace..." Perhaps, the main purpose of the article was to sneak in this bloody lie while diverting the attention of his readers. We may never know. But we know that his readers congratulated him for discovering the formula for victory: No peace! One of his readers commented, "I, for one, will no longer utter the word *Shalom* (peace) when hailing or farewelling Jews. Rather, I will say *Netzah* (victory). Who will join me?!" The fascist propaganda machine is working: it is turning peace into an ugly word and it is making his bigoted and fanatic followers salivate for victory without peace.

Robert Spencer is another member of this bloody cabal. He is one of the most active Crusaders and he has authored a few best-selling propaganda books to justify genocide against Muslims, such as: *The Complete Infidel's Guide to the Koran*, The *Truth About Muhammad: Founder of the World's Most Intolerant Religion, The Politically Incorrect Guide to Islam (And the Crusades)*, and *Religion of Peace?: Why Christianity Is and Islam Isn't.*

Of course, the Horowitzs, Spencers and Bills of the world have a right and even a duty to criticize religious teachings and practices they deem harmful. I too have written numerous books exposing the problems with Sunni, Shiite, Jewish and Christian religions. But their agenda is much beyond an intellectual combat; it is ugly, devious, hypocritical, and bloody.

Modern Crusaders do not directly fight as they used to in medieval times. They now sing peace in their churches while voting for warmongers and promoting militarism. Instead of quoting verses from their holy book that instructs its adherents to burn and stone infidels, destroy cities and kill every living being including babies, they now use modern secular propaganda filled with euphemism and doubletalk. They do not hesitate to establish coalitions with nationalists, capitalists, or Zionists. They have mutated with time and learned how to use secular governments and their militaries as proxy warriors for their bloody crusades. In fact, nothing has changed much: the king and the pope are toasting blood and these stooges are their public relation knights and bishops![1]

---

[1]   As of October 2009, the Iraqi Death Estimator at www.justforeignpolicy.org/iraq estimates 1,339,771 Iraqi deaths due to U.S.-led invasion, which deliberately started a civil war between the Shiite and Sunni Iraqis in order to crush the popular uprising against its brutal invasion, massacres, plundering, rape and torture. This is only Iraq! For the list of other atrocities and war crimes perpetrated by the West and Church see the article *From Wounded Knee To Iraq: a Century Of U.S. Military Interventions*.

Thank God there are reasonable and progressive people who promote peace and stand against the destructive attitudes and actions. For instance, there are numerous religious or non-religious pro-peace organizations in the West such as, Unitarian Universalists, Jehovah Witnesses, Quakers, Jews for Peace, Muslims for Peace Justice and Progress, Progressive Muslims, and Code Pink, just to name a few. They are brave and resolute activists for peace.

I compiled the following list of U.S.-based peace organizations.

- 19 Org
- 20/20 Vision
- Alliance for Justice
- America First Committee
- American Empire Project
- American Friends Service Committee
- American League Against War and Fascism
- American Peace Mobilization
- Americans for Democratic Action
- Amnesty International
- A.N.S.W.E.R.
- Another Mother For Peace
- Antiwar
- Anti-War Committee
- Boston College Center for Human Rights and International Justice
- Campus Antiwar Network
- The Carnegie Endowment for International Peace
- The Carter Center
- Catholic Association for International Peace
- Catholic Worker Movement
- The Center for Global Peace - American University
- Centre for Peace and Conflict Studies
- Center for the Study of Islam and Democracy
- Center on Conscience & War (formerly known as NISBCO)
- Central Committee for Conscientious Objectors
- Christadephians
- The Council for National Interest
- Code Pink: Women for Peace
- Common Dreams
- ChildVoice International
- Democracy Now
- Department of Peace Campaign
- DC Anti-War Network
- Eyes Wide Open
- Friends Committee on National Legislation
- GI Rights Network
- Green Party
- Gold Star Families for Peace
- Growing Communities for Peace
- Historians Against the War
- If Americans Knew
- Institute of Peace & Conflict Studies
- International Peace Bureau
- International Peace Research Association
- International Physicians for the Prevention of Nuclear War
- International Service for Peace
- International Solidarity Movement
- Iraq Action Coalition
- Iraq Peace Action Coalition
- Iraq Veterans Against the War
- Islamic Reform
- Jehovah Witnesses
- Jewish Voice for Peace
- Just Foreign Policy
- Long Island Alliance for Peaceful Alternatives
- M.K. Gandhi Institute for Nonviolence
- Mennonite Central Committee
- Military Families Speak Out
- MoveOn
- Muslims for Peace, Justice and Progress (MPJP)

- National Coordinating Committee to End the War in Vietnam
- National Lawyers Guild
- National War Tax Resistance Coordinating Committee
- Nevada Shakespeare Company
- New Security Action
- Nonviolent Peaceforce
- Not in Our Name
- Nuclear Age Peace Foundation
- Pax Christi USA
- Physicians for Social Responsibility
- Peace Action
- Peace and Justice Studies Assoc.
- Peace Brigades International (PBI)
- Peace Action
- PeaceBuilders
- Peace Resource Center
- Peace Pledge Union
- The Pen
- Physicians for Social Responsibility
- Ploughshares Fund
- Progressive Democrats of America
- Project on Defense Alternatives
- Port Militarization Resistance
- Progressive Democrats of America
- Randolph Bourne Institute
- Save Darfur Coalition
- September Eleven Families for Peaceful Tomorrows
- Student Nonviolent Coordinating Committee
- Students for a Democratic Society
- Teachers for Peace
- The World Can't Wait
- Traprock Peace Center
- Troops Out Now Coalition
- True Majority
- Unitarian Universalist Association
- United for Peace and Justice
- US Labor Against War
- Union of Concerned Scientists
- Veterans for Peace
- Vietnam Veterans Against the War
- Voices in the Wilderness
- VoteVets
- Win Without War
- War Resisters League
- Women's Action for New Directions (WAND)
- Women's International League for Peace and Freedom
- Zaytuna Institute

There are also many activists, authors, artists and thinkers who promote peace. Here is an incomplete list of prominent peacemakers from the West:

Abby Zimet	Alison Bechdel	Bill Moyer
Abdullahi An-Naim	Amy Goodman	Bob Harris
Abdur Rab	Andrea Germanos	Bob Herbert
Aftab Alam	Andrew Bacevich	Bob Somerby
Ahmed S. Mansour	Andy Worthington	Bono
Aisha Jumaan	Anita Roddick	Brandon Toropov
Aisha Musa	Ann Wright	Brian Baird
Al Franken	Antonia Zerbisias	Brian Willson
Al Kamen	Arianna Huffington	Burt Blumert
Alex Falco Chang	Arnold Yasin Mol	Caner Taslaman
Alexander Cockburn	Arundhati Roy	Charles Knight
Alexia Gilmore	Barbara Ehrenreich	Charles Peters
Alfred W. McCoy	Barry Crimmins	Chibuzu Ohanaja
Alan Bock	Bassam Haddad	Chris Hedges
Ali Abunimah	Ben Cohen	Chris Smith
Ali Behzadnia	Bernie Sanders	Christopher Brauchli
Ali Eteraz	Bevin Chu	Christopher Cook

Christ. Montgomery
Cindy Sheehan
Clare Bayard
Colin Hunter
Courtland Milloy
Craig Brown
Cynthia McKinney
Dahr Jamail
DailyKos
Daniel Martin Varisco
Danny Schechter
Dave Lindorff
Dave Zirin
Dave Zweifel
David Bacon
David Cole
David Corn
David Michael Green
David Korten
David Krieger
David Morris
David Zlutnick
Dean Baker
Dennis Kucinich
Dennis Roddy
Derrick Jackson
Diana Allen
Diane Carman
Dilara Hafiz
Donella Meadows
Doug Ireland
Earl Ofari Hutchinson
Eboo Patel
Ed Peck
Eddie Falcon
Edip Yuksel
EJ Dionne Jr
Elizabeth Sawin
Ellen Goodman
Ellen S. Miller
El-Mehdi Haddou
Eman Ahmad
Eric Alterman
Eric Garris
Eric Margolis
Eric Stoner
Eric Zorn
Eugene Kane
Farai Chideya
Farouk Peru

Fereydoun Taslimi
Frank Rich
Frank Smyth
Frida Berrigan
G. Simon Harak
Garry Wills
Gary Younge
George Galloway
George Monbiot
George Will
Gershom Kibrisli
Ghayasuddin Siddiqui
Gideon Levy
Gini Courter
Glen Ford
Glenn Greenwald
Granny D
Greg Palast
Hakham Ezra
Hamza Yusuf Hanson
Harley Sorensen
Harold Meyerson
Harry Kelber
Harvey Wasserman
Hasan Mahmud
Heather Wokusch
Helen Thomas
Holly Sklar
Howard Zinn
Huck Gutman
Hussein Najafi
Imad Ad-Dean Ahmad
Ira Chernus
Irshad Manji
Ivan Eland
Jack Lessenberry
Jamal Barzinji
James Carroll
James Goldsborough
James K. Galbraith
James Ridgeway
Jeanmarie Simpson
Jeff Garrison
Jeff Gates
Jeff Cohen
Jennifer Pozner
Jeremy Scahill
Jerry Brown
Jesse Jackson
Jim Hightower

Jim Lobe
Jimmy Breslin
Jimmy Carter
Joe Conason
Joel Beinin
Johann Hari
John Buell
John Conyers
John Dear
John R MacArthur
John Mearsheimer
John Nichols
John Pilger
John Queally
Jonathan Schell
Joseph Stromberg
Juan Cole
Juan Gonzales
Justin Raimondo
Kani Xulam
Karla Solheim
Katha Pollitt
Katherine Paul
Kathy Kelly
Katrina vanden Heuvel
Kelly Wentworth
Ken Silverstein
Kevin Martin
Khaleel Muhammad
Laura Flanders
Laurel Druley
Lawrence Kaplan
Leonard Pitts Jr
Leora Broydo Vestel
Lewis Diuguid
Linda McQuaig
Llewelyn Rockwell
Lynn Samuels
Lynn Sweet
Madeleine Bunting
Mahmood Mamdani
Manning Marable
Marc Cooper
Marie Cocco
Marjorie Cohn
Mark Ellis
Mark Fiore
Mark LeVine
Mark Morford
Mark Shields

15

Mark Weisbrot
Martin A. Lee
Martin Sheen
Marty Jezer
Mary McGrory
Matt Neuman
Matthew Bargainer
Matthew Edwards
Matthew Capiello
Matthew Rothschild
Max Sawicky
Mel Duncan
Melissa Robinson
Melody Moezzi
Michael Ewens
Michael Lerner
Michael Moore
Michael Parenti
Michael Tomasky
Mike Ghouse
Mohamed Hedjaj
Mokhiber/Weissman
Molly Ivins
Mustafa Akyol
Musin Aslbek
Nahid Taslimi
Nancy Snow
Naser Khader
Naomi Klein
Nayeem Aslam
Nathan Newman
Neal Peirce
Nebojsa Malic
Nicolas J S Davies
Nick Turse
Nir Rosen
Noam Chomsky
Norman Finkelstein
Norman Solomon
Pat Buchanan
Paul Craig Roberts
Paul Krugman
Paul McCartney
Paul Rogat Loeb

Paul Rogers
Peter Laarman
Peter Morales
Pierre Tristam
Polly Toynbee
Radwan Masmoudi
Rahul Mahajan
Ralph Nader
Randal Amster
Rashid Khalidi
Ray McGovern
Raymond Catton
Reggie Rivers
Ren HaCohen
Reza Aslan
Richard Cohen
Richard Silverstein
Richard Falk
Rick Mercier
Riffat Hassan
Robert Borosage
Robert Dreyfuss
Robert Fisk
Robert Koehler
Robert Kuttner
Robert McChesney
Robert Naiman
Robert Reich
Robert Scheer
Robert W. Jensen
Robyn Blumner
Ron Paul
Roy Martin
Ruby Amatulla
Sadruddin Noorani
Safia Ansari
Salam al-Marayati
Sam Husseini
Sara Roy
Sarah van Gelder
Sarah Lazare
Sascha Matuszak
Scott Horton
Scott Ritter

Sean Gonsalves
Shabbir Ahmed
Sheryl McCarthy
Signe Wilkinson
Sophia Catton
Stella Jatras
Stephan Funk
Stephanie Salter
Stephen Zunes
Sukran Kivrak
Taj Hargey
Tad Daley
Tarek Fatah
Ted Rall
T.O. Shanavas
Thanna Rajapakse
Thom Hartmann
Thomas Gumbleton
Tom Andrews
Tom Brazaitis
Tom Engelhardt
Tom Gallagher
Tom Hayden
Tom Tomorrow
Tom Turnipseed
Tom Wicker
Tony Judt
Turki Al-Balawi
Usama Qadri
Walter Shapiro
Wendy Kaminer
Will Durst
William Blum
William Greider
William Raspberry
William Saletan
William Sinkford
Yemin Dickinson
Zaid Shakir
Zeba Khan

And many more

Despite having many peace-promoting organizations and intellectuals, why the USA-Inc is addicted with wars? The answer was given in 1961 by Eisenhower in a prophetic warning against MIC. With the addition of Zionist and Crusader hormones, the coalition for perpetual wars and atrocities has reached its most potent level: Zionists+Crusaders+Military Industrial Complex, or, ZC-MIC! The so-called mainstream media and Hollywood uses the most sophisticated propaganda to promote violence, torture, state terrorism, racism and jingoism. Video games, TV programs, films have already desensitized Americans to great extent, and they are the best recruiting tools for military. Just a few examples out of hundreds of movies that directly or indirectly aids the ZC-MIC agenda:

> **Wanted: Dead or Alive** (1987) Portrays Arabs as thugs who plan to ignite Los Angeles, killing millions.
> **True Lies** (1994) Justifies shooting dead Palestinians like clay pigeons.
> **Rules of Engagement** (2000) Justifies US Marines killing Arab women and children.
> **24 (TV Series):** First aired by Fox in November 2001, the film desensitizes American people and justifies every means possible, including state terrorism and torture, against their declared enemies. Its fictional hero, the counter terrorism agent Jack Bauer, was praised by warmongers to manipulate jingoists and fascists.
> **Inglorious Basterds** (2009) promotes violence and torture.

Many violent video games have been openly or secretly funded by the USA government to increase military recruitment. In 2008, US Army spent at least 21 million dollars on video games that simulate violence and barbarism. By turning violence and murder into an entertainment, government, Hollywood and military industrial complex are promoting murder and torture as an attractive career choice for our children. Our tax money is used to turn our children to become killers, murderers, and mercenaries in the service of corporations and their stooges in the government.

Here is the sample list of some most violent video games that helps create a culture of violence to be exploited by the war profiteers:

- Resident Evil 4
- NARC
- The Warriors
- 50 Cent: Bulletproof
- Condemned: Criminal Origins
- True Crime: New York
- Mortal Combat
- Grand Theft Auto
- The Punisher
- Killer 7
- Soldier of Fortune
- Gears of War
- God of War
- Thrill Kill
- Manhunt

About three years ago, David Horowitz's FrontPage Magazine contacted me for an interview. Yes, I was kindly invited by the notorious cabal that has passionately advocated many wars and issued the Zionist fatwa defending the morality of torture!

Let me have a paragraph of diversion here: as a young activist and author who was tortured in Turkish prisons in 1980's for my published essays and books, I know first hand the character of torturers: they are lower than animals! I know that my educated friends living in ivory towers will frown on my "unkind" words for depicting a reputed Zionist author who made up fictional horror stories to import the practice of torture from Israel to the United States. I have no doubt that if the torturemonger Horowitz and his stooges were the contemporary of Jesus, they would join the Pharisees and Romans to oppose his message of peace and love. Horowitz, Spencer, Warner and their ilk would be rebuked with the harshest words:

> "Woe to you, scribes and Pharisees, hypocrites!... Fools and blind ones!... Serpents, offspring of vipers, how can you escape the condemnation of hell?" (Matt 23).

When I used the word *Nazionists* and *Zionazists* for modern Zionists, aftermath of the Israeli massacre of hundreds of Palestinian babies in Gaza,[2] colleagues of mine asked me to "tone down". Tone down?! I know that they had good intention, but this is exactly what the hypocrites, serpents, pigs and vultures hope for! They want peacemakers tone down so that they can carry out their mischief and crimes against humanity. Regardless of his fancy grooming, education and influence, by promoting wars against innocent people and justifying torture, David Horowitz and his stooges are lowly criminals, enemies of humanity; we should not hesitate to call scoundrels by their real names. The blood of many children is dripping from their Zionist propaganda.

Back to the first paragraph. I did not know that Zionists had some hopes about my utility for their cause of promoting wars and torture against Muslims. Learning about my past and present, they thought they could use me like they have used other apostates and heretics, to justify the ongoing and planned wars, occupations, tortures, atrocities, and oppression against Muslims. But, I disappointed them in the two subsequent debates arranged by them. When David Horowitz and his troops realized that they could not use me for their fascist ideology, they tried to win the debate. Their previous victories against several straw men perhaps had given them false confidence. Instead of winning, they lost big time: their hypocrisy and bloody fascism was exposed.

---

[2]   During the Israeli operation in the last days of 2008 and beginning of 2009, more than 1,400 Palestinians and 13 Israelis were killed. More than 400,000 Gazans were left without running water, while 4,000 homes were destroyed or badly damaged, leaving tens of thousands of people homeless; 80 government buildings were hit.

A Turkish proverb says, kill the brave yet give him the due respect. The Front-Page Magazine published every word I sent to them, without censoring a single word. Unlike, their counter-part ditto-heads Sunni and Shiite warmongers, they showed civil courage to publish them. Perhaps, it was due to their arrogance, sense of invincibility. With their firm control on American media, financial system, politics and academia, they might have considered my voice to be inconsequential to their warmongering activities.

This book comprises of eight sections:

1. An Invitation to Jews, Christians, Muslims, and All, an excerpt from the last section of the *Manifesto for Islamic Reform*.
2. An analysis of selected Quranic verses that are distorted or taken out of context to justify violence and terror, an excerpt from notes of *Quran: a Reformist Translation*.
3. Interview with FrontPage Magazine about my life and cause to promote Islamic reform.
4. A debate between me and Robert Spencer, Bill Warner, and Thomas Haidon, which was organized by and published at FrontPage Magazine.
5. Another debate between me and Khalim Massoud, Thomas Haidon, Abul Kasem, Robert Spencer, and Bill Warner.
6. A lengthy debate between me and Ali Sina, the agitator-in-chief of the faithfreedom.org site. The debate is presented in 16 sessions.
7. Various essays I have written on violence, peace and war.
8. Various related news and essays by other authors.

The royalty from this book will be distributed among the following non-profit peace organizations, and I invite readers to donate to any and all of these and other organizations as long as they promote peace, justice and progress:

- Amnesty International
- Code Pink: Women for Peace
- Common Dreams
- Democracy in Action
- Democracy Now
- If Americans Knew
- Jewish Voice for Peace
- Kucinich.us
- Muslims for Peace, Justice and Progress
- Unitarian Universalist Association
- United for Peace and Justice

Get your peacemaker or warmonger score by recording -1 for every description on the left column that fits you, and +1 from each on the right, and 0 for none. The perfect score is 15. Lower scores are indicative of serious intellectual and psychological problems.

Warmonger, Jingoist, Reactionary, Terrorist, Militarist, Extremist, Bully	Peacemaker, Patriot, Progressive, Rationalist, Fair, Moderate
Might give lip service to Golden Rule, but in reality subscribes to the Iron Rule, that is, the preemptive strike doctrine	Subscribes to the Gold-Plated Brazen Rule: retaliation with occasional forgiveness
Favors either a Big Government or Big Corporations	Favors neither of them; wants both to be smaller
Lacks character, confidence, self-criticism	Introspective, practices critical thinking
Identifies more with Thrasymachus	Identifies more with Socrates
Inclined to support oppressive and corrupt dictators if they are imperialist stooges	Opposes all dictators and oligarchs regardless of their masters
Defends mass murder, use of WMD, terrorism, and torture as long as they are committed by his gang or government	Categorically opposes violence except in the course of self-defense and proportional to the threat
Exaggerates the capabilities of "enemies", imminence of danger, and is ready to manufacture lies to justify violence	Seeks creative and preventive ways to prevent conflicts and establish peace
Paranoid and coward; ready to give up civil rights, privacy, and liberties in exchange for security	Appreciates the importance of freedoms and individual rights, and is averse to governmental or corporate intrusion
Condemns underground terrorism, yet supports state terrorism, or vice versa	Condemns all sorts of terrorism
Unable to think critically	Is a critical thinker
Either is a sheep in a religious community or is an exploiter of the gullible masses	Spiritual, yet suspicious and averse to organized religions
Supports war industry, bigger military	Supports green industry, less military
Worships a flag or heroes and may justify killing millions for their exclusive idols	Considers nationalism a dangerous ideology leading to wars and tragedies
Mocks those who care about environment	Cares about environment and climate
If lived in the past, would most likely join Pharaohs against Jews, Pharisees and Romans against Jesus, Meccan theocracy against Muhammad, Pope against Galileo, and British colonialists against Gandhi.	If lived in the past, would more likely support the peacemakers and truthseekers.

20

An Invitation to Jews, Christians, Muslims, and All

(This is an excerpt from Edip Yuksel's book, *Manifesto for Islamic Reform*, which was also published as one of the appendices of the *Quran: a Reformist Translation*)

In this foreword, we focused on the incredible amount of distortions made in the message delivered by Muhammad. Christianity and Judaism are no different. Today's Christianity, with its dogmas and practices, is far way from the monotheistic teachings of Jesus, the son of Mary.

If Moses, Jesus, and Muhammad were back today, Jews would condemn the first as Anti-Semite, Christians would denounce the second as Anti-Christ, and Muslims would revile the third as the *Dajjal* (The imposter).

Imagine a religion that its members worship the murder weapon, perform rituals to pretend that they are drinking the blood and flesh of their heroic victim, claim that 1+1+1 equals to 1, adopt a word as their name which was used by none of the early followers, misspell and mispronounce the name of their hero, follow someone's teaching who was prophetically condemned by their hero, accept a formula that was coined by a self-appointed commission 325 years after the founder, sing love and peace yet be responsible for most of the blood-shed and weaponry in the world, mobilize even children for centuries of barbarism called Crusades, sell parcels of heaven, excommunicate scientists, burn the first translator of their holy book, burn women in witch-hunt craze, invent ingenious torture devises and torture many in their holy courts, declare the earth as the flat center of the world for more than a millennium, lead and pray for colonialists, defend and practice slavery and racism until the cause was lost, mostly side with kings and the wealthy, deny women from many of their rights, condemn the theory of evolution, support occupations and wars with jingoistic slogans... Yes, how can such a religion, with a fake name, with a fabricated doctrine, with bizarre pagan practices, and with such a miserable historical record and bitter fruits belong to God? How can it be attributed to a philosopher, to a peacemaker, to an advocate of the rights of the weak, to a human messenger of God? (For a more detailed critical evaluation of modern Christianity, see *19 Questions for Christians*, by Edip Yüksel)

Idolization of human beings is the epidemic of all religions, and it is the most common tragedy of human history. According to the original teachings of all God's messengers, idol worship or setting up partners to God is the biggest offense against God. Besides, the idolization of prophets, messengers, saints and the faith of human intercession creates religious abuse, oppression, conflict and fighting between children of Adam, who are servants of God.

When believers start idolizing their previous religious leaders, they develop the tendency to idolize their living religious leaders too. Instead of seeking the truth, they are attracted to names and titles. The clergymen, in order to take advantage of that weakness and gain more power over their subjects, focus their preaching on praising the departed heroes, instead of God.

These clergymen and their fanatic followers killed many people, destroyed many homes in the name of their incarnated gods. They fabricated many rules and prohibitions in the name of God, and with such a complicated religion, they secured their jobs as professional holy men. They made money and fame in the name of those human gods. And they claimed to have the power of intercession in their names--so much so that they sold keys to the heavens, turned temples and churches to big businesses.

If we want to follow the basic principles common among the Old, the New and the Final Testaments, if we want to stop religious exploitations, if we don't want to use our God-given reasoning faculties to its maximum capacity, if we want the unity of all the monotheists of all religions, freedom for everyone, including for non-religious people, and if we want to attain eternal salvation, we must start a "Copernican revolution" in theology. Instead of Krishna-centered, Jesus-centered, Mohammed-centered religions, we must turn to the original center, to the God-centered model. To achieve this revolution, each of us must start questioning the formulas and teachings that have created gods out of humans like us.

In a time where religious fanatics are pushing the world for another Crusade or Holy War, in a time where the words Messiah, Rapture, Armageddon, *Mahdi* invite hostile masses to shed more and more of each other's blood, in a time when those in power and in positions of making profit from curtailing civil liberties, in a time when wars and occupations are playing on jingoistic and religious emotions, yes in such a time, people of intelligence and good intentions should come together and plant the seeds of tolerance, peace, reason, human rights, and unity of humanity.

On Israel, Palestine, Suicide Bombers, and Terror

Compared to their small population, the Jewish influence is immense in the global arena, financially, politically and culturally. Disproportionate to their population, Jews have exhibited astonishing examples in both good and bad, in both success and blunder, and they have enjoyed vivid presence in world politics for millenniums. This explains why the Quran mentions them so frequently. Well, may be it is also true the other way around.

After being subjected to genocide and atrocious tortures by fascist forces, Jews were scattered around the world as immigrants. Yet, they did not disappear from the global scene or take centuries to recover, as many other nations would do. Not surprisingly, with the help of major powers of the time they were able to establish their own independent state in 1948, soon after their almost utter anni-hilation; a state not in Germany, but in their historical land, which has once again become the focal point of a global conflict; stirring the world by showcas-ing human aggression, greed, hatred, cruelty, racism, and terror.

As it seems, victim nations too might repeat the crimes of their predators. One would expect Israel to be the first against racism and colonialism, yet Israel was the last government to cut its relationship with the racist apartheid regime in South Africa, reflecting the depth of its racist policy against Palestinians. One would expect Israel to be the first nation against the weapons industry, yet Israel is one of top weapon manufacturers and exporters in the world. The racist and colonial policy of Israel by no means should be generalized to all Jews. There are more Jews in the world who condemn this policy then those who perpetrate it, and many are ashamed of what is being done in their name. While we should condemn terrorism as a method to get back one's land and independence, we should also mention that there are many Arabs who are hoping for a just solution and peaceful co-existence with their Jewish cousins.

Jews and Muslims lived together in peace for centuries, and their current con-flict is partially due to the early terrorist tactics used by Zionist guerillas, and partially due to a myriad of external forces who are trying to keep the fires burn-ing. These external forces include the ambitions of UK-Inc and USA-Inc, the racist Zionist zealots, corrupt Mullahs, racist Sunni and Shiite zealots, Evangeli-cal Crusaders, Weapon and Oil industries, who make massive amounts of money from the tension in the region. Unfortunately, super powers who medi-ated the negotiations have not honestly sought justice in this conflict. Perhaps, they deliberately wanted a continuous, yet controlled conflict in the region so that they could exploit its rich resources through puppet regimes.

In their pre-emptive war in 1967, the Israeli soldiers carried the verse 2:249 of the Quran over their tanks when they entered Sinai after defeating the Arabs, and their misguided Arab nationalism. Ironically, the evildoers among them pushed for further land-grab in the East, thereby subjecting Palestinian natives to racial discrimination, dislocation, humiliation, massacres, destruction of property/infrastructure, legalized torture, and assassinations. Israel deliberately did not set a border, rather it kept its borders flexible seeking excuses and occasionally provoking its dehumanized subjects so that it could invade new territories and create more settlements. Decades of suffering under the brutal and humiliating fascist occupation destroyed the hopes and aspiration of a Palestinian population and it gave birth to suicide bombers, which in turn provided more excuses for the occupational force to continue its invasion and barbarism. The West's propaganda machine distorts the real picture of the conflict and deceives Christendom by depicting the victimized Palestinians as the aggressor. The numbers speak clearly. The number of Palestinian civilians and children killed by Israeli occupying forces far greater than the number of Israeli civilians and children killed by suicide bombers. Palestinians gave up continuing a hopeless fight with slings and rocks against tanks. The world's indifference against injustice in the region, and on top of that, the support of the super powers of the brutal racist occupation, gave birth to global resentment and hatred among Muslims, triggering a global gang-terrorism challenging the legalized and glorified state-terrorism.

Islam (more accurately, Hislam) has been around for centuries, and compared to other religious groups Muslims do not fare more violent. An objective study of suicide terrorism will inform us that it has more to do with brutal occupations than religions or ideologies. Religion and ideologies are mostly used for justification and propaganda of the political cause. Robert Pape, of the University of Chicago, in his book *Dying to Win: The Logic of Suicide Terrorism*, rightly argues that suicide terrorism is not driven by religion but by occupations. He provides many examples, such as the suicide attacks of Marxist Tamil Tigers organization in Sri Lanka in 1990's that inspired Palestinians who were using slings, rocks and rifles against occupying Israeli soldiers and tanks before the *Intifada* of 2000. In fact, a great majority of suicide-terrorist campaigns carried out in Lebanon, Sri Lanka, Chechnya, Kashmir, and Palestine aimed to compel occupation forces to withdraw. No wonder, Ayman al-Zawahiri and his terrorist organization Islamic Jihad was born after Israel's occupation during the 1967 pre-emptive war. No wonder, Russian invasion and occupation of Afghanistan, together with the legalized US occupation of Middle East through puppet and oppressive kings and emirs gave birth to Osama bin Laden and al-Qaida. No wonder, Russian brutal occupation of Chechnya gave birth to Shamil Basayev and his terrorist organization. Again, it is no wonder that US occupation of Iraq gave birth to Abu Musab al-Zarqawi and hundreds of other suicide bombers. Though compared to rebels or insurgents, occupiers commit much worse acts of barbarism and terrorism on the population of lands they occupy, that state terrorism is cleverly hidden from the world. Ironically, occupiers who create these terrorist insurgents or contribute substantially to their growth, use the terrorist attacks to justify and continue their occupation. Occupying forces cleverly use fear, xenophobia, and patriotic emotions of the taxpayers and take advantage of their ignorance about foreign affairs. Government agencies work cleverly to depict their brutal and bloody occupation as a justified act against evil and barbarism. Secret agencies are showered with money to stage covert operations, flood the world with misinformation and disinformation campaigns. Talking heads in media and academics are secretly hired to promote the policy of occupations. No wonder, despite all the obvious fraud, deception, and lies, the mainstream American media gave green card to the Neocon-Zionist-Crusader coalition to justify their pre-emptive war against Iraq. The pictures of Rumsfeld shaking hands with Saddam at the time Saddam was committing his horrendous atrocities against Kurds and Iran as a puppet of US-Inc, somehow became a footnote, rather than an incriminating headline, demonstrating the hypocrisy of warmongers.

The cycle of violence has since been accelerated by religious fanatics on all sides. The Zionist-Crusader-Capitalist coalition on one side and the Salafi-Mullah-Taliban coalition on the other, each adds more fuel to the fire. Each with their own agendas. Zionists hope to grab more land, Crusaders pray for a bloody Armageddon followed by Rapture, the capitalist salivates for more profit from wars; and the other gang weep for the *Mahdi* to come with its sword to seek out Jews hiding behind rocks. Another aspect of recent conflict between Christendom and Muslims is the empty shoes of "evil" after the demise of communism. Global oligarchs, who strengthen their political and financial capital during conflicts and mass paranoia, were looking for a substitute to communism. With a mixture of covert operations, provocations, unjustified wars, tyrant puppets, the lesser-of-two-evil policy, and training future terrorists, the mission is almost accomplished.

Now, Muslims in general, and Arabs in particular will be christened as the new face of evil. Knowing the history, we should not be surprised to witness another genocide and another use of nuclear weapons, followed by tears of regret, confession sessions, and cry of "Never again!" So long as people do not use their God-given reasoning and follow their clergymen and politicians blindly, Satan will use every tool at his disposal to create artificial divisions, hostility and hatred among the children of Adam. And Satan, who has a successful record of enticing since Cain & Abel, has always found religious clergymen and jingoistic politicians to be his best allies in his acts of corruption, destruction, and bloodshed on earth.

To the East, Muslims, and the Middle East

The following words are not from an enemy of yours, but from someone who shares the same book and the same history. These are the words of someone who cares a great deal about you. Someone who cries at night for your plight, for the tragedies which have befallen you. This is someone who knows your generosity, your sincerity, your unfulfilled dreams, your aspirations, your trage-dies, your fears, your follies and delusions. You should listen, at least once. Enough prejudice and bigotry. Enough paranoia and hatred.

We must acknowledge the truth so that the truth will set us free.

Before looking around to point fingers at the cause of your problems, first look at the mirror. I do not mean that you should ignore the imperialistic ambitions of other nations and their open or clandestine interferences with the politics, econ-omy and culture of your people. But, you cannot change your condition unless you change yourself. You cannot glorify the invasions, aggressions, massacres, and imperialistic policy of corrupt Umayyad, Abbasid, and Ottoman caliphs in your history and at the same time criticize others for doing the same. Had God given you the same superiority, perhaps you would inflict the earth with more corruption and destruction than your current powerful enemies. You cannot kick them out from your home unless you reform yourself and your home. You can-not demand mercy from others if you do not have mercy on yourself.

We must acknowledge the truth so that the truth will set us free from self-righteousness.

Go check the list of patents issued last year. Check and see how many of them belong to a group, nation, religion you identify with. It should tell you a lot you a lot about your position in a world where information and technological pro-gress is so crucial. Go check the list of prosperous countries. Check see how many of them belong to a group, nation, religion you identify with. Centuries ago, you were a role model for civilization, justice, democracy, and freedom; once you were a pioneer in mathematics, astronomy, medicine, and philosophy. Now look around and look at the mirror; who are you? You followed the reli-gious *fatwa* of a *sheikh ul-islam* (highest cleric within the Ottoman Empire) who prohibited the use of printing machine from 1455 to 1727 for 272 years, for 100,000 precious days, in a vast land stretching from North Africa to Iran, from today's Turkey to Arabian Peninsula. While Europe indulged in learning God's signs in nature, shared the knowledge via printing machines, and was rewarded by God with renaissance, reform, technology, and prosperity; you devolved and sunk further in your ignorance. While Europeans engaged in philosophical ar-guments, you recited the holy book no better than a parrot, the book that high-lighted the importance of learning, questioning, discovery, and pursuit of knowledge. You marveled at handwritten books of hearsay and superstition, at the lousy arguments developed by Gazzali who with the full support of a king aimed to banish philosophy. While Europe sought for a better system to save themselves from the tyranny of kings and church, you recited handwritten poems to praise your corrupt kings and idols. No wonder why, your land, your name, your face, your religion is now associated with backwardness, ignorance, oppression, violence, and poverty. You have become the bum of the world.

We must acknowledge the truth so that the truth will set us free from our ignorance.

Once the religious among you hoped that the theocracy of mullahs would fulfill your dream, would bring back the glorious days of your past. They promised "*istiqlal, azadi, hukumat-i islami*" (independence, freedom, Islamic government); yet what you ended up with a swarm of leaches with turbans, repression, and a satanic government. Some of you hoped that a Sunni Taliban in Afghanistan would bring dignity and glory to you. What they brought was worse than the Saudi regime: they put women in black sacks, revived the barbaric stoning practice, regressed to the times of tribalism, denied women education, exponentially increased ignorance, and turned Afghanistan into an international farm for opium. You did not question the religion and sect you inherited from your parents or the teachings of the mullah, the sheikh, or the imam. You little examined the nightmare sold to you as dreams.

We must acknowledge the truth so that the truth will set us free from our own transgression.

God blessed you with crucial natural resources, so that you could utilize it for your prosperity. Yet, their proceeds are wasted by corrupt, hedonistic, short-sighted, backward and oppressive kings, emirs, tribal leaders, and mullahs. Instead of gaining your freedom, instead of establishing the democratic system instructed by the holy book you claim allegiance, you are wasting your time in cafeterias, on the streets, and in rotten offices of antiquity, which produces nothing but zeros.

We must acknowledge the truth so that the truth will set us free from apathy and slavery.

Look at half of your population, your wives, mothers, sisters, daughters. What have you done to them? How can you hope to progress and attain peace, prosperity and God's mercy, while you have buried many of them alive? You cannot expect happiness, while you despise half of God's creation, your wives, mothers, sisters, and daughters; while you deprive them from their human rights given by their Creator, turn them to fractionally humans. You cannot tell God that you did all those evil things to please the idols called Bukhari, Muslim, Tirmizi, Ibn Hanbal, Ibn Maja, Abu Dawud, Malik, Kafi, and a herd of other imams, mullahs and clergymen. None of those idols will save you from God's justice. You are already paying dearly for your misogynistic beliefs and practices. You must

27

apologize to your mothers, wives, sisters, and daughters for treating them like your slaves; you must repent for acting like Pharaohs against them.

We must acknowledge the truth so that the truth will set us free from the dark holes of our deception.

The world knows that Israel has transformed from a victim nation to a racist colonial power. Many progressive Jews too are painfully accepting this fact and they are fighting against it. The world sees and most people acknowledge the fascist policy, occupation, atrocities, massacres, and humiliation committed against the Palestinian people since 1948. The world knows that Israel has killed many more Palestinian children than the Palestinian suicide bombers have done. The numbers and events are out there recorded to prove that Israel has used state terrorism against Palestinian people. The world knows that a coalition of Crusaders, Zionists, and weapon/oil and other interest groups, nested in towers of power are using American tax money, military, and political power to perpetuate this tragedy, hoping for the Armageddon, more land, or bloody profits from wars. Nevertheless, again you must look in the mirror. What have you done, what have you become? You have become as racist as the Zionist you condemn. You condemn Jews without discrimination, Jews that raised many great prophets, philosophers, scientists, and inventors whom you revere and admire. You have become a suicidal nation. Though there were more than mere pacifism into Gandhi's resistance against British colonialism, Gandhi's struggle provided a great example for you. Instead, you followed ignorant leaders, racist and manipulative politicians, terror organizations, misguided religious clerics, and your hormones. If you had taken lessons from modern history and you had used your mind more than your animalistic instincts, if you had followed the Quran rather than the religious teachings that promote violence and racism, by now you would be living next to Israel sharing Jerusalem peacefully as brothers and sisters. You cannot have God's mercy if you respond to hatred with hatred, racism with racism, atrocities with atrocities. You cannot attain freedom and peace without sincerely asking the same thing for your enemies. How can you claim to be muSLiMs, while you have taken SiLM (peace), out of it?

We must acknowledge the truth so that the truth will set us free from violence that has surrounded us.

By continuing along the path of denial and sectarianism, you are risking more than just happiness and dignity in this world, but you also risk shame and retribution in the Hereafter...

> "Those who had rejected will be told: 'God's abhorrence towards you is greater than your abhorrence towards yourselves, for you were invited to acknowledge, but you chose to reject.' They will Say, 'Our Lord,

28

You have made us die twice, and You have given us life twice. Now we have confessed our sins. Is there any way out of this path?' This is because when God Alone was mentioned, you rejected, but when partners were associated with Him, you acknowledged. Therefore, the judgment is for God, the Most High, the Most Great." (40:10-12)

Unless you are willing to take the necessary and painful steps of reform through self-examination and research, you will be led by the mold of complacency and blind followings into the abyss that is becoming your fate. You must turn to the true system of Islam, as revealed by God through His messenger, and stop blindly following your scholars and leaders into distortions and unauthorized teachings. You have been losing continuously because you have abandoned the word of God and replaced it with other religious laws and teachings which in-turn has caused God to abandon you and leave you to your folly.

This life is not just about fun and games…it is about fulfilling our part of the pledge with God and proving that we can serve Him Alone.

> 39:45 And when God Alone is mentioned, the hearts of those who do not acknowledge in the Hereafter are filled with aversion; and when others are mentioned beside Him, they rejoice!

Are you ready to embrace the path of God Alone and abandon all your idolatry? Or, will you continue to lose? We must acknowledge the truth so that the truth will set us free.

To the West, Christians, and Americans

The following words are not from an enemy of yours, but from someone who is a member of your society and cares about your interest as much as you care. These are not the words of a politician either, who is ready to break a world record in somersault to appease you; neither the words of a religious leader who lives in a parallel universe of deception and hallucination. These are the words of a common man who left his country behind to seek peace, justice, and liberty. These are the words of a grateful person who found such a refuge in your midst. So, do not treat these words of advice with prejudice, but with care. Do not be scared to hear the truth about your "way of life" which always highlighted the freedom of expression and justice for all. Do not expect me to count the list of the many good things you have accomplished; you hear them frequently from speeches and news in your media, and you celebrate them in your holidays. Sure, you should remember the good things in your past, present, and remember them, so that you can continue repeating those good things. However, you need to hear the other voice too; the voice that you have not yet allocated a holiday to hear. You should open your ears to what you do not hear from those who have invested interest in caressing your ego, nationalism, patriotism, and feelings. I think you do not wish to be aloof to the facts around you and repeat the pattern of all fallen civilizations in history. Do not be arrogant, aloof, self-righteous, and selfish, since they will only inflict you further harm.

We must acknowledge the truth so that the truth will set us free.

Since you have separated the church from state, since you have appreciated the importance of freedom, God has blessed you with progress, abundance and prosperity. Though your history is tainted with wars, oppression, superstitions, and injustices, such as crusades, inquisition, indulgences, sectarian wars, witch-hunt, holocaust, slavery, racism, colonialism, misogynistic practices, sexual abuse, you seem to have learned from the past mistakes and have come up with a better functioning society that tolerates diversity and respects science. Though your society suffers from a myriad of problems such as promiscuous lifestyle, sexually transmitted diseases, high divorce rate, high crimes, videogames teaching violence, addiction with drugs and alcohol, gambling, greed, big gap between rich and poor, children abused by priests, high number of prisoners per capita, homelessness, waste, pollution, jingoism, apathy, etc., your constitutions, courts, congresses, and academic institutions are still functioning. Freedom has its own side effects, and having the freedom of living one's life according to their own choice, without the fear of government repression is by far the greatest value. The greatest danger to your society is the corruption of the democratic process through the influence of money and lobbies. When big corporations control your finance, media, and congress, your democracy and freedom will be only an illusion. However, there is hope, since you frequently demonstrate the confidence to be self-critical and you are able to acknowledge your weaknesses and shortcomings. You have also demonstrated times and again that you have the ability to find novel solutions for social, economic, and political problems. You have shown grace and generosity against your former enemies.

We must acknowledge the truth so that the truth will set us free from self-righteousness.

The world has shrunk due to increase in population, pollution, economic inter-dependence, mass transportation, and speed and ease in communication; thus, you can no more have a world with half of it eating themselves to obesity while the other half starving to death. You can no more spend billions of dollars on pets, millions of dollars for cosmetic surgeries (including on your pets), gulp world's limited resources to feed your ever-increasing appetite for consuming, and yet expect love and admiration from the rest of the world to your capitalism, the system you adhere to like a religion. How can you convince the world that you are the bastion of liberty while your prison industry is booming and you have the highest number of prisoners per capita in the world? You can no more support cruel, corrupt, regressive puppet regimes and occupying military forces, and expect not being hurt by those who you have deprived directly or indirectly from freedom, education, progress, prosperity and hope. You can no more self-righteously claim to be a free and civilized nation while spending a great portion of your national production on conventional and unconventional weapons, which transforms you into arrogant beasts running from one war to another, from one occupation to another. You can no more fool yourselves to be a peaceful nation while you have been shedding the blood of millions of people around the globe in more than hundred wars, covert operations and occupations in less than a century! You cannot condemn terrorism without apologizing to humanity for destroying not one, but two cities in its entirety as retaliation to an attack of your enemy to your military base. If terrorism means to intimidate the enemy by aiming at civilians, then you should look in the mirror without trying to find justification for your own aggression and acts of terrorism. You cannot talk about a free and better world while you reject banning landmines that kill and maim so many innocent people every day.

We must acknowledge the truth so that the truth will set us free from our own transgression.

Watch out for the right (wrong) wing religious organizations; when they are passionate about a social or political issue think thrice. If their historical record is a measure, they occasionally get it right, but usually they are wrong, very wrong. You cannot let the left-behind fiction fans lead your global policy. However, pay more attention to the other wing, to the other groups, such as Quakers. Their record, their conscience, their heart, their stand for peace and justice, is what you need. We are not telling you to turn your left cheek when you are slapped; but beware of getting intoxicated with power. While you might be pretending to be David, without knowing, your arrogance and transgression might transform you into a Goliath. The change might be slow, so you might not be able to notice it by looking at yourself through the mirror; especially when there are some politician magicians and their entourage whose job is to distort and contort the mirror so that you cannot see yourself as you should.

We must acknowledge the truth so that the truth will set us free from our sins.

You can no more give lip service to the Biblical advice regarding the speck and plank in the eyes. You can no more ignore the fact that those who live by sword are destined to die by the sword. You can no more preach, "Love your enemy" while you are out there trying every means possible to hurt your friends, half-friends, and potential friends. You can no more talk about "the golden rule" while you are working hard to justify the "iron rule" under the euphemistic expression, "preemptory strike." You can no more talk about human rights and freedom while at the same time, you have turned little islands and navy ships

31

into torture centers and you have become the inventors of a diabolic scheme called "offshore interrogation." How come America that once led the establishment of the United Nations and promotion of Human Rights, now has turned torture into an international enterprise and high tech affair? How can you allow the gulags such as, Abu Ghraib and Gitmo happen? Yes, you have not broken the records of Stalin, Mao, Hitler, Pol Pot; but you should not be competing with them. Your founding fathers did not fight for independence and did not draft one of the best legal documents in human history so that you become a super war machine and be the cowboy of the world. You carpet bombed dozens of countries in your short history, destroying hundreds of cities and killing millions of them. You destroyed two big cities with its civilian population as retaliation to losing less than three thousands of your soldiers in Pearl Harbor. As retaliation to losing less than three thousand civilians by a terrorist organization, which once you trained and financed, you started two wars, killed hundreds of thousands, destroyed many cities, and are still looking for more countries to destroy. How can you label your revenge, your aggression, your disrespect to the lives of other people, as "freedom" or "civilization"? You cannot change the reality by fabricating fancy names in your PR rooms and spinning them as the corporate media your accomplice. You cannot fool the world by replacing one puppet regime with another, by supporting oppressive and cruel tyrants in Saudi Arabia, Egypt, Pakistan, Israel, and then congratulate yourselves for being the champion of "freedom" and "democracy." You cannot preach about morality, rights, and God, as long as you do not value the lives of each innocent human being equally, regardless of their religion, nationality and color. You have been taking wars, destruction, death, horror and terror to many nations around the world without even changing your fancy lifestyle at home. Now, you are enraged and you demand justice from the world because you have tasted a small fraction of what others have tasted.

We must acknowledge the truth so that the truth will set us free from the dark holes of our deception.

Why should we treat terrorizing an entire nation, destroying their cities, killing, torturing, and humiliating their children and youth in the name of "democracy and liberty" lightly? Why killing tens of thousands of civilians should be forgiven if the murderers, who are also proven congenial liars, use the magic word "collateral damage?" Why smashing the brains of children with bombs or severing their legs and arms should be considered civilized and treated differently than beheadings? Why destroying an entire neighborhood or city and massacring its population by the push of a button from the sky should not be considered equally or more evil than the individual suicide bomber blowing himself or herself up among his powerful enemies who snuffed out all their hope? Why surviving to push another button to kill more people should be considered a civilized action not the action of those who gave their own lives while doing the killing? Why should the smile of a well-fed and well-armed mass murderer be deemed more sympathetic than the pain and anger of a poor person? How can one honestly call an occupying foreign military force to be freedom fighters? How can one call the native population to be terrorists just because they are fighting against an arrogant and lethal occupation army, which was mobilized against them through lies and deception? Why are the children of poor Americans used to kill the children of poor countries?

We must acknowledge the truth so that the truth will set us free from violence that has surrounded us.

You should not favor one criminal over another because of their religion or nationality. Your media did not depict the Serbian rapists and murderers as Christian Murderers, nor did they label IRA terrorists who engaged in a long sectarian terror campaign that took the lives of thousands, as Christian terrorists. The right wing Christian militia that massacred thousands of Palestinian refugees in Sabra and Shatilla camps somehow lost their religion when they became news on your media. The same with terrorist groups who claimed the cause of Zionism. Furthermore, you should know that state terrorism, regardless of the nationality and religion of the population, is much more cruel, dangerous, and sinister than the group or individual terrorism. In your stand against war, violence, and terrorism, you must be consistent and fair. Peacemakers and promoters must protest and condemn the atrocities regardless as to whether those engaged in atrocities have a uniform on them or not. If military uniform justifies the acts of terror, destruction, or genocide, then Nazi soldiers should receive your sympathy.

We must acknowledge the truth so that the truth will set us free.

One World and Shared Destiny

We must eliminate the nationalistic virus that alienates the children of Adam and turns them into monsters against each other. This does not mean that we should eliminate national borders or abolish the social contracts among groups of people. We must consider the entire world as one community and work accordingly. This is not only morally right, but is the only way we can survive on this little planet. We can no longer be reckless in treating this planet, this precious earth, and can no longer be myopically selfish in our dealings with other nations. Otherwise, we will inhale and poison ourselves with each other's pollution, we will suffer calamities caused by global warming, we will spend a great portion of our national production, we will overpopulate the land, we will shed the blood of many innocent people, and we will lose our individual freedoms for security because of the economic and political problems in other parts of the world. The world has become smaller and troubles are shared more than ever before. We must act now as a world and revive the spirit of the United Nations with a new vision. We can no long afford jingoism, macho attitudes, another world war, always looking for an "evil" outside us, retaliating against violence and terror with our own version of violence and terror. We should not let terrorists or warmongers define our vision, our destiny, since they will only bring more disasters for humanity. We should not allow evil whisperers to dupe us into inflicting another holocaust against another race; we should have learned our lesson. We should not tolerate authoritarian regimes, corrupt leaders, kings, and emirs in our countries; we must be braver than the corrupt bullies. We should be vigilant against the myopic and greedy interest groups that have grown like cancerous tumors in our democracies, infecting legislation, judiciary, executive branches and the mass media.

Hopefully, this century will be the century of unity under the banner of "God Alone," so that the children of Adam will greet each other with peace by saying, "your system/religion is for you and my system/religion is for me." So that, all humanity, including Atheists and polytheists, share this planet in peace and justice.

> "The Lord your God is One God. You shall worship the Lord your God with all your heart, with all your soul, with all your mind, with all your strength." (Old Testament, Deuteronomy 6:4; New Testament, Mark 12:29-30)

> "God bears witness that there is no god but He, as do the angels, and those with knowledge, He is standing with justice. There is no god but Him, the Noble, the Wise." (Quran 3:18)

> "Say, 'O followers of the scripture, let us come to a logical agreement between us and you: that we do not worship except God, that we never set up any idols besides Him, and never set up each other as gods beside God.' If they reject such an agreement, then say, 'Bear witness that we are Submitters.'" (Quran 3:64)

Therefore:

- Let's reject all manmade religious teachings, and let's dedicate the system to God alone.
- Let's stand against marginal elements among us, oppressive puppet regimes, brutal wars, occupations, and clandestine operations.
- Let's topple the oppressive monarchs, and elect our own leaders so that we can have peace, liberty and justice on our own volition.
- Let's fight not with bullets or bombs, but with intelligence and wisdom.

- Let's give up superstitions and medieval culture, and start engaging in scientific enterprise.
- Let's stop subjugating our mothers, sisters, daughters and wives; let's give them back their dignity, equal rights, liberty, and identity.
- Let's unite our voices and prayers with genuine Christians, Buddhists, Jews, Agnostics, anyone who seeks justice and peace, rather than injustice and war.
- Let's organize local and international conferences to discuss this issue. We may invite religious scholars of every sect or cult, but we should not let them run them, since our experience shows that they have not done a good job in leading.
- Let's acknowledge the truth so that the truth will set us free.

Quranic Verses Abused by Sunni and Shiite Warmongers

Below are some excerpts from *Quran: a Reformist Translation*, which will expose the fact that Quran never promotes aggression or terror.

Should Muslims Levy Extra Tax of Non-Muslims?

Verse 9:29 is mistranslated by almost every translator. Shakir translates the Arabic word *jizya* as "tax," Pickthall as "tribute." Yusuf Ali, somehow does not translate the word at all. He leaves the meaning of the word at the mercy of distortions:

Disputed passage: The meaning of the Arabic word *jizya* (reparation/compensation) has been distorted to mean extra tax for non-muslims.

Yusuf Ali	Pickthall	Shakir	Reformed
"Fight those who believe not in Allah nor the Last Day, nor hold that forbidden which hath been forbidden by Allah and His Messenger, nor acknowledge the religion of Truth, (even if they are) of the People of the Book, until they pay the **Jizya** with willing submission, and feel themselves subdued. (9:29).	Fight against such of those who have been given the Scripture as believe not in Allah nor the Last Day, and forbid not that which Allah hath forbidden by His messenger, and follow not the Religion of Truth, until they pay the **tribute** readily, being brought low. (9:29)	Fight those who do not believe in Allah, nor in the latte day, nor do they prohibit what Allah and His Messenger have prohibited, nor follow the religion of truth, out of those who have been given the Book, until they pay the **tax** in acknowledgment of superiority and they are in a state of subjection. (9:29).	**"You shall fight (back) against those who do not believe in God, nor in the last day, and they do not prohibit what God and His messenger have prohibited, and do not abide by the system of truth among those who received the scripture, until they pay the <u>reparation</u>, in humility." (9:29).**

36

Discussion on 9:29

You have noticed that we inserted a parenthesis since the context of the verse is about the War of *Hunain*, and fighting is allowed for only self-defense. See: 2:190-193, 256; 4:91; and 60:8-9.

Furthermore, note that we suggest REPERATION instead of Arabic word *jizya*. The meaning of *jizya* has been distorted as tax on non-muslims, which was invented long after Muhammad to further the imperialistic agenda of Kings. The origin of the word that we translated as Compensation is *JaZaYa*, which simply means compensation or in the context of war it means war reparations, not tax. Since the enemies of muslims attacked and aggressed, after the war they are required to compensate for the damage they inflicted on the peaceful community. Various derivatives of this word are used in the Quran frequently, and they are translated as compensation for a particular deed.

Unfortunately, the distortion in the meaning of the verse above and the practice of collecting a special tax from Christians and Jews, contradict the basic principle of the Quran that there should not be compulsion in religion and there should be freedom of belief and expression (2:256; 4:90; 10:99; 18:29; 88:21,22). Since taxation based on religion creates financial duress on people to convert to the privileged religion, it violates this important Quranic principle. Dividing a population that united under a social contract (constitution) into privileged groups based on their religion contradicts many principles of the Quran, including justice, peace, and brotherhood/sisterhood of all humanity.

Some uninformed critics or bigoted enemies of the Quran list verses of the Quran dealing with wars and declare islam to be a religion of violence. Their favorite verses are: 2:191; 3:28; 3:85; 5:10, 34; 9:5; 9:28-29; 9:123; 14:17; 22:9; 25: 52; 47:4 and 66:9. In this article, I refuted their argument against 9:29, and I will discuss each of them later.

Some followers of Sunni or Shiite religions, together with their like-minded modern Crusaders, abuse 9:5 or 9:29 by taking them out of their immediate and Quranic context. Sunnis and Shiites follow many stories and instructions falsely attributed to Muhammad that justify terror and aggression. For instance, in a so-called authentic (or authentically fabricated) hadith, after arresting the murderers of his shepherd, the prophet and his companions cut their arms and legs off, gauge their eyes with hot nails and leave them dying from thirst in the dessert, a contradiction to the portrayal of Muhammad's mission in the Quran (21:107; 3:159). In another authentically fabricated hadith, the prophet is claimed to send a gang during night to secretly kill a female poet who criticized him in her poetry, a violation of the teaching of the Quran! (2:256; 4:140; 10:99; 18:29; 88:21-22). Despite these un-Quranic teachings, the aggressive elements among Sunni or Shiite population have almost always been a minority.

Beheading?

47:4   So, if you encounter those who have rejected, then strike the control center until you overcome them. Then bind them securely. You may either set them free or ransom them, until the war ends. That, and had **God** willed, He alone could have beaten them, but He thus tests you by one another. As for those who get killed in the cause of **God**, He will never let their deeds be put to waste.

047:004 The expression "*darb al riqab*" is traditionally translated as "smite their necks." We preferred to translate it as "strike the control center." The Quran uses the word *unuq* for neck (17:13,29; 8:12; 34:33; 38:33; 13:5; 26:4; 36:8; 40:71). The root *RaQaBa* means observe, guard, control, respect, wait for, tie by the neck, warn, fear. "*Riqab*" means slave, prisoner of war. Even if one of the meanings of the word *riqab* were neck, we would still reject the traditional translation, for the obvious reason: The verse continues by instructing muslims regarding the capturing of the enemies and the treatment of prisoners of war. If they were supposed to be beheaded, there would not be need for an instruction regarding captives, which is a very humanitarian instruction. Unfortunately, the Sunni and Shiite terrorists have used the traditional mistranslation, and abused it further by beheading hostages in their fight against their counterpart terrorists, Crusaders and their allied coalition who torture and kill innocent people even in bigger numbers, yet in a baptized fashion that is somehow depicted non-barbaric by their culture and media. The Quran gives two options regarding the hostages or prisoners of war before the war ends: (1) set them free; or (2) release them to get a fee for their unjustified aggression. Considering the context of the verse and emphasis on capturing the enemy, we could have translated the segment under discussion as, "aim to take captives."

The Old Testament, on the other hand, contains many scenes of beheadings and grotesque massacres. For instance, see: 2 Samuel 4:7-12; 2 Kings 10:7, and 2 Chronicles 25:12.

The Most Frequently Abused Verses, 9:3-29, and Some Notes

9:1   This is an ultimatum from **God** and His messenger to those who set up partners whom you had entered a treaty.

9:2   Therefore, roam the land for four months and know that you will not escape **God**, and that **God** will humiliate the rejecters.

9:3   A declaration from **God** and His messenger to the people, on this, the peak day of the Pilgrimage: "That **God** and His messenger are free from obligation to those who set up partners." If you repent, then it is better for you, but if you turn

away, then know that you will not escape **God**. Promise
those who have rejected of a painful retribution;

9:4   Except for those with whom you had a treaty from among
those who have set up partners if they did not reduce anything from it nor did they plan to attack you; you shall fulfill
their terms until they expire. **God** loves the righteous.

9:5   So when the restricted months have passed, then you may
kill those who have set up partners wherever you find them,
take them, surround them, and stand against them at every
point. If they repent, hold the contact prayer, and contribute
towards betterment, then you shall leave them alone. **God** is
Forgiving, Compassionate.

Do Not Let Those Who Violate the Peace Treaty Succeed

9:6   If any of those who have set up partners seeks your protection, then you may protect him so that he may hear the
words of **God**, then let him reach his sanctuary. This is because they are a people who do not know.

9:7   How can those who have set up partners have a pledge with
God and with His messenger? Except for those with whom
you made a pledge near the Restricted Temple, as long as
they are upright with you, then you are upright with them.
God loves the righteous.

9:8   How is it that when they come upon you they disregard all
ties, either those of kinship or of pledge. They seek to please
you with their words, but their hearts deny, and most of them
are wicked.

9:9   They purchased with **God**'s signs a small price, so they turn
others from His path. Evil indeed is what they used to do.

9:10   They neither respect the ties of kinship nor a pledge for any
those who acknowledge. These are the transgressors.

9:11   If they repent, and they hold the contact prayer, and they
contribute towards betterment, then they are your brothers in
the system. We explain the signs for a people who know.

9:12   If they break their oaths after their pledge and they taunt and
attack your system; then you may kill the chiefs of rejection.
Their oaths are nothing to them, perhaps they will then
cease.

9:13   Would you not fight a people who broke their oaths and intended to expel the messenger, especially while they were
the ones who attacked you first? Do you fear them? It is
God who is more worthy to be feared if you are those who
acknowledge.

9:14   Fight them; perhaps **God** will punish them by your hands,
humiliate them, grant you victory over them and heal the
chests of an acknowledging people,

9:15	To remove the anger from their hearts; **God** pardons whom he pleases. **God** is Knowledgeable, Wise.
9:16	Or did you think that you would be left alone? **God** will come to know those of you who strived and did not take other than **God** and His messenger and those who acknowledge as helpers. **God** is Expert in what you do.
9:17	It was not for those who have set up partners to maintain **God**'s temples while they bear witness over their own rejection. For these, their works have fallen, and in the fire they will abide.
9:18	Rather, the temples of **God** are maintained by the one who acknowledges **God** and the Last day, holds the contact prayer, contributes towards betterment, and he does not fear except **God**. It is these that will be of the guided ones.
9:19	Have you made serving drink to the pilgrims and the maintenance of the Restricted Temple the same as one who acknowledges **God** and the Last day, who strives in the cause of **God**? They are not the same with **God**. **God** does not guide the wicked people.
9:20	Those who acknowledged, emigrated, strived in the cause of **God** with their wealth and their lives are in a greater degree with **God**. These are the winners.
9:21	Their Lord gives them good news of a Mercy from Him, acceptance, and gardens that are for them in which there is permanent bliss.
9:22	They will abide in it eternally. **God** has a great reward.
9:23	O you who acknowledge, do not take your fathers nor brothers as allies if they prefer rejection to acknowledgement. Whoever of you takes them as such, then these are the wicked.

Dedicate Yourself to Establish Peace and Liberty

9:24	Say, "If your fathers, your sons, your brothers, your spouses, your clan, and money which you have gathered, a trade you fear its decline, and homes which you enjoy; if these are dearer to you than **God** and His messenger and striving in His cause, then wait until **God** brings His decision. God does not guide the wicked people."
9:25	**God** has granted you victory in many battlefields. On the day of Hunayn, when you were pleased with your great numbers but it did not help you at all, and the land became tight around you for what it held, then you turned to flee.
9:26	Then **God** sent down tranquility upon His messenger and those who acknowledge, and He sent down soldiers which you did not see. He thus punished those who rejected. Such is the recompense of the rejecters.

9:27	Then **God** will accept the repentance of whom He pleases after that. **God** is Forgiving, Compassionate.
9:28	O you who acknowledge, those who have set up partners are impure, so let them not approach the Restricted Temple after this calendar year of theirs. If you fear poverty, then **God** will enrich you from His blessings if He wills. **God** is Knowledgeable, Wise.
9:29	Fight those who do not acknowledge **God** or the Last day, they do not forbid what **God** and His messenger have forbidden, and they do not uphold the system of truth; from among the people who have been given the book; until they pay the reparation, in humility.

009:003-029   The verse 9:5 does not encourage muslims to attack those who associate partners to God, but to attack those who have violated the peace treaty and killed and terrorized people because of their belief and way of life.

According to verses 9:5 and 9:11, the aggressive party has two ways to stop the war: reinstate the treaty for peace (*silm*), which is limited in scope; or accept the system of peace and submission to God (islam), which is comprehensive in scope; it includes observation of *sala* and purification through sharing one's blessings. These two verses refer to the second alternative. When, accepting islam (system of peace and submission) as the second equally acceptable alternative and when the first alternative involves only making a temporary peace, then none can argue for coercion in promoting the Din.

The Quran does not promote war; but encourages us to stand against aggressors on the side of peace and justice. War is permitted only for self-defense (See 2:190,192,193,256; 4:91; 5:32; 8:19; 60:7-9). We are encouraged to work hard to establish peace (47:35; 8:56-61; 2:208). The Quranic precept promoting peace and justice is so fundamental that peace treaty with the enemy is preferred to religious ties (8:72).

Please note that the context of the verse is about the War of *Hunain*, which was provoked by the enemy. The verse 9:29 is mistranslated by almost every translator.

Furthermore, note that we suggest "reparation", which is the legal word for compensation for damages done by the aggressing party during the war, instead of Arabic word *jizya*. The meaning of *jizya* has been distorted as a perpetual tax on non-Muslims, which was invented long after Muhammad to further the imperialistic agenda of Sultans or Kings. The origin of the word that I translated as Compensation is *JaZaYa*, which simply means compensation, not tax. Because of their aggression and initiation of a war against muslims and their allies, after the war, the allied community should require their enemies to compensate for

41

the damage they inflicted on the peaceful community. Various derivatives of this word are used in the Quran frequently, and they are translated as "compensation" for a particular deed.

Unfortunately, the distortion in the meaning of the verse above and the practice of collecting a special tax from Christians and Jews, contradict the basic principle of the Quran that there should not be compulsion in religion and there should be freedom of belief and expression (2:256; 4:90; 4:140; 10:99; 18:29; 88:21,22). Since taxation based on religion creates financial duress on people to convert to the privileged religion, it violates this important Quranic principle. Dividing a population that united under a social contract (constitution) into privileged groups based on their religion contradicts many principles of the Quran, including justice, peace, and brotherhood/sisterhood of all humanity. See 2:256. For a comparative discussion on this verse, see the Sample Comparison section under the title, Why a Reformist Translation, in the Introduction.

Moral rules involving retaliation can be classified under several titles:

- **The Golden Rule**: Do unto others as you would have them do unto you.
- **The Silver Rule**: Do not do unto others what you would not have them do unto you.
- **The Gold-plated Brazen Rule:** Do unto others as they do unto you; and occasionally forgive them.
- **The Brazen Rule**: Do unto others as they do unto you.
- **The Iron Rule**: Do unto others as you like, before they do it unto you.

Empirical studies on groups have shown that the gold-plated brazen rule is the most efficient in reducing the negative behavior in a community abiding by the rule, since the rule has both deterrence and guiding components. The Golden rule, on the other hand, does not correspond to the reality of human nature; it rewards those who wish to take advantage of the other party's niceness. Therefore, though the golden rule is the most popular rule in the lips of people, but it is the least used rule in world affairs. It might have some merits in small groups with intimate relations; but we do not have evidence for that.

The Quran is book of reality, and its instructions involving social issues consider the side effects of freedom. Thus, the Quran recommends us to employ the gold-plated brazen rule. "If the enemy inclines toward peace, do you also incline toward peace." (8:61; 4:90; 41:34). Other verses encouraging forgiveness and patience in the practice of retaliation (2:178; 16:126, etc.), makes the Quranic rule a "Gold plated Brazen Rule," the most efficient rule in promoting goodness and discouraging crimes.

Sunni and Shiite mushriks inherited many vicious laws and instructions of violence through *hadith* books, of which scholars trace their roots to Jewish Rabies and Christian priests who supposedly converted to Islam. Here are some samples of terrifying and bloody instructions found in The Old Testament. We recommend the reader to study them in their context:

> "The Lord said to Moses: 'Take the blasphemer outside the camp. All those who heard him are to lay their hands on his head, and the entire assembly is to stone him. Say to the Israelites: If anyone curses his God, he will be held responsible; anyone who blasphemes the name of the Lord must be put to death. The entire assembly must stone him. Whether an alien or native-born, when he blasphemes the Name, he must be put to death.... Then Moses spoke to the Israelites, and they took the blasphemer outside the camp and stoned him. The Israelites did as the Lord commanded Moses." (Leviticus 24:13-16).

> "Now kill all the boys. And kill every woman who has slept with a man. But save for yourselves every girl who has never slept with a man." (Numbers 31:18).

> "And they utterly destroyed all that was in the city, both man and woman, young and old, and ox, and sheep, and ass, with the edge of the sword" (Joshua 6:21).

> "Now go and smite Amalek, and utterly destroy all that they have, and spare them not; but slay both man and woman, infant and suckling, ox and sheep, camel and ass" (1 Samuel 15:3).

> "And as David returned from the slaughter of the Philistine, Abner took him, and brought him before Saul with the head of the Philistine in his hand" (1 Samuel 17:57).

> "Thus the Jews smote all their enemies with the stroke of the sword, and slaughter, and destruction, and did what they would unto those that hated them" (Esther 9:5).

> "Why do the wicked prosper and the treacherous all live at ease?... But you know me, Lord, you see me; you test my devotion to you. Drag them away like sheep to the shambles; set them apart for the day of slaughter" (Jeremiah 12:1-3).

> "A curse on all who are slack in doing the Lord's work! A curse on all who withhold their swords from bloodshed!" (Jeremiah 48:10).

Chapter 20 of LEVITICUS contains a list of very severe punishments for various sins. For instance, cursing one's own father of mother would prompt death penalty. A man marrying a woman together with her daughter must be burned in the fire. Homosexual men must be put to death. Those who commit bestiality, must be put to death together with the animals. And many more death, burning penalties.

Did Muhammad Massacre Jews?

> "There were three Jewish tribes in Medina: Banu Qaynuqa, Banu al-Nadir and Banu Qurayza. They provoked Muslims and the first two tribes were forced to leave the city with their transportable possessions. However, Prophet Muhammad did not forgive Banu Qurayza; their necks were struck and their children were made slaves. Estimates of those killed vary from 400 to 900." (Sunni Hadith and *Siyar* sources)

The Quran refers to the event and never mentions killing or enslaving them, which is in direct contradiction of many verses of the Quran. The Quran, in the Chapter known as Exodus, informs us that a group from "The People of the Book" was forced to leave the territory because of their violation of the constitution and secretly organizing war together with their enemies against muslims (59:1-4). Verse 59:3 clearly states that they were not penalized further in this world.

59:0 In the name of God, the Gracious, the Compassionate.

59:1 Glorifying **God** is everything in the heavens and the earth, and He is the Noble, the Wise.

The Mass Exile

59:2 He is the One who drove out those who rejected among the people of the book from their homes at the very first mass exile. You never thought that they would leave, and they thought that their fortresses would protect them from **God**. But then **God** came to them from where they did not expect, and He cast fear into their hearts. They destroyed their homes with their own hands and the hands of those who acknowledge. So take a lesson, O you who possess vision.

59:3 Had **God** not decreed to banish them, He would have punished them in this life. In the Hereafter they will face the retribution of the fire.

59:4 This is because they challenged **God** and His messenger. Whosoever challenges **God**, then **God** is severe in punishment.

59:5 Whether you cut down a tree or left it standing on its root, it was by **God**'s leave. He will surely humiliate the wicked.

059:002-5   The credibility of the story of Muhammad massacring Bani Qurayza Jews has been the subject of controversy since the time it was published by Ibn Ishaq. Ibn Ishaq who died in 151 A.H., that is 145 years after the event in question, was severely criticized by his peers for relying on highly exaggerated Jewish stories. He was also harshly criticized for presenting forged poetry attributed to famous poets. Some of his contemporary scholars, such as Malik, called him "a liar." However, his work was later copied by others without critical examination. This is an example of a hearsay used by dubious Jewish reporters for propaganda purposes.

Modern scholars found astonishing similarities between Ibn Ishaq and the account of historian Josephus regarding King Alexander, who ruled in Jerusalem before Herod the Great, hung upon crosses 800 Jewish captives, and slaughtered their wives and children before their eyes. Many other similarities in details of the story of Banu Qurayza and the event reported by Josephus are compelling.

Besides, the lack of reference or justification in the Quran for such a massacre of great magnitude and the verses instructing principles for muslims to abide by takes all credibility out of this story (35:18: 61:4). The Quran gives utmost importance to human life (5:32) and considers racism and anti-Semitism as evil (49:11-13).

If They Mock God's Signs...

> **4:140**   It has been sent down to you in the book, that when you hear **God**'s signs being rejected and ridiculed in, then do not sit with them until they move on to a different subject; if not, then you are like them. **God** will gather the hypocrites and the unappreciative people in hell all together.

004:140 We are not permitted to kill or punish people for their insults and mockery of God's revelation and signs. Any aggressive behavior against those people is against God's law that recognizes freedom of choice, opinion and their expression (2:256; 4:90; 4:140; 10:99; 18:29; 25:63; 88:21, 22. Also see: 28:54). In verse 4:140, the Quran recommends us to protest passively those who indulge in mockery of our faith by leaving their presence. Furthermore, it recommends us not to cut our relationship with them; we should turn back in peace and continue our dialogue when they come to their senses and are able to engage in a rational discourse.

Those who react with violence against those who insult the tenets and principles of islam, are not following the very system they claim to defend. The Quran does not recognize the "fighting words" exception recognized by Western juris-prudence. Specific false accusation against a person, however, is not included in expression of opinion, since it is defamation and it can harm a person in many ways. Insult to someone's values or heroes, however, only harms the person who indulges in such an ignorant and arrogant action.

The only unforgivable sin, according the Quran is the sin of associating other partners/idols to God. God allows this biggest sin to be committed in this world. He fulfills his promise to test humans by giving them free choice. He condemns those who deprive others from exercising that freedom of choice. Who then, in the name of the same God, can force others from any expression of their belief or disbelief?

In contrast to how the warmongering Crusaders, Sunnis and Shiites wish to por-tray, Muhammad was not a man of violence but a man of reason and peace. Numerous verses of the Quran and critical study of history will reveal that the portrait of Muhammad depicted in Sunni or Shiite hearsay books is fictional; a fiction created by the propagandists of rulers of Umayyad and Abbasid dynasties to justify their atrocities and aggression! He and his supporters were threatened and tortured in Mecca for their criticism of their corrupt and unjust theocratic system. They were forced to leave everything behind and immigrate to Yathrib (today's Medina). There they established a peaceful city-state, a federal secular democracy, among its multi-religious diverse citizens. Nevertheless, the Meccan oligarchy did not leave them alone to enjoy peace and freedom; they organized several major war campaigns against the coalition of muslims, Christians, Jews and Pagans united under the leadership of Muhammad. In all the wars, including Uhud, Badr, and Handaq, the monotheist reformers fought for self-defense. They even dug trenches around the city to defend themselves from aggressive religious coalition led by Mecca's theocratic oligarchy. Muhammad's message that promoted reason, freedom, peace, justice, unity of children of Adam, appre-ciation of diversity, rights of women and slaves, and social consciousness soon received acceptance by masses in the land. Yet, after ten years in exile, when finally Muhammad and his supporters returned to Mecca as victors, he declared amnesty for all those oppressors and warmongers who inflicted on them great suffering, who maimed and murdered many of their comrades, all because they questioned the teachings and culture they inherited from their parents. However, guided by the teachings of Quran, Muhammad chose forgiveness and peace; he did not punish any of his bloody enemies. After all, he was one of the many messengers of islam, peace and submission to God alone.

From Radical to Reformed Muslim

By Jamie Glazov

FrontPageMagazine.com | 12/4/2007

Frontpage Interview's guest today is Edip Yuksel, a Kurdish-Turkish-American author and progressive activist who spent four years in Turkish prisons in the 1980's for his political writings and activities promoting an Islamic revolution in Turkey. He experienced a paradigm change in 1986 transforming him from a Sunni Muslim leader to a reformed Muslim or rational monotheist.

Edip Yuksel has written more than twenty books and hundreds of articles on religion, politics, philosophy and law in Turkish, and numerous articles and booklets in English. He is the founder of 19.org and the Islamic Reform organization. His personal site is yuksel.org.

After receiving his bachelor degrees from the University of Arizona in Philosophy and Near Eastern Studies, Mr. Yuksel received his law degree from the same university. Today he is an Adjunct Philosophy professor at Pima Community College and teaches various classes at his children's school.

His recent major work, Quran: a Reformist Translation, has been recently published by BrainbowPress, after being canceled by Palgrave-Macmillan, which followed the fatwa of a "very established scholar."

Today Mr. Yuksel is a "dissident" and "ex-prisoner" in the records of the Turkish government, an "apostate" in the fatwas of Muslim clergymen, a "betrayer" in the hearts of his family, and a "reformer" in the minds of progressive Muslims.

FP: Edip Yuksel, welcome to Frontpage Interview.

YUKSEL: Thank you for the invitation.

FP: Tell us a bit about your youth and what influenced you to become a radical Muslim and how this landed you in Turkish prison. Share some of the things you were involved in as a Muslim radical.

YUKSEL: It is a real life story filled with plots and events: activism, religious fanaticism, street fights, detentions, prisons, torture, assassinations, hijacking, secret police, import and export of revolution, fame, excommunication, fatwas, betrayal, paradigm change, religious experience, etc... I am currently trying to finish writing my life story, which is titled, In the Name of God. Let me give you some snapshots from my youth:

I became an active participant in the 1970's political upheaval within Turkey's student intelligentsia. I had front line experiences with the Turkish government's violent repression of protesters in the streets of Istanbul, as we were gassed, beaten, and taken to jail for torture by police, and those events had profound effects on both my country and me.

While a revolution, which had incubated for decades, was intensifying in Iran in 1978 and erupting in early 1979, together with my brother, I led the Raiders organization promoting a religious revolution. I put aside my education at Bosphorus University, as I did before at Middle East Technical University, and got busy to form my own underground teen organization FT-19. After losing my brother to the bullets of Turkish fascists, Gray Wolves, I plunged into political activism and protest meetings; numerous detentions.

Following my brother's assassination by political opponents, I intensified my passionate leadership of my youth group as they promoted outright religious revolt. While jailed for this by state security police, I am held at close quarters in the same prison with the killers who murdered my brother. In one of the failed assassination attempt against me my friend, a fellow inmate, was mistaken for me and knifed nearly to death by a hired prison hitman.

I lectured, wrote articles for Islamists magazines, trained radical militants, organized Muslim youth and staged political events to spur an Islamic revolution envisioned by the founder of Ikhwan-i Muslimin (Muslim Brotherhood) Hasan el Banna (Egypt), Sayyid Qutub (Egypt), Abul A'la al Mawdudi (Pakistan), Said Hawwa (Syria), Ali Shariati (Iran), Khomeini (Iran), and more recently by Blind Sheik Abdurrahman and Osama Bin Laden. I established relationship with Muslim Brotherhood and other underground radical Muslim organizations, such as Hizb-i Islami of Afghanistan and Hizbu al-Tahrir of Iraq.

After the Soviet invasion of Afghanistan, I attempted to commandeer Istanbul's airport with the members of my organization, demanding the Turkish government provide aircraft for more than 200 Muslim radicals volunteering to join the Afghan *mujahideen*. My attempt failed, because I was arrested by police just one day before the scheduled event, which would have high visibility in the media. I later met with Afghan resistance leader Gulbeddin Hikmetyar and gave him thousands of dollars collected from Turkish merchants, who later became notorious for his destruction of Kabul and the brutal killing of thousands of Afghanis from other tribes.

I had zeal, charisma, courage and plenty of stupidity. I was going to make a revolution in my country. Enough was enough for the rule of a secular, oppressive government and its ally the Great Satan, U.S.A. We were going to have an Islamic government that would bring economic and political justice, freedom and peace.

> "Shah, Butto, Hoveyda; which infidel is next to die?"
> "Sharia will chop and aggression will stop!"
> "Down with America!"
> "Allah-u Akbar!"

I was recruited in the late 1970's by Iranian Islamic fundamentalists, who sought to cultivate me as an agent of the same revolutionary movement then sweeping Iran. Nearly seduced into the Ayatollah's inner circle by the promise of exporting the revolution to Turkey, I secretly travel to Tehran for an audience with the leader of Pasdaran (the Revolutionary Guards) and leading Ayatollahs in the ministry of Irshad.

I was disappointed when I learned that my preferred method for bringing about an Islamic revolution in my country was radically different than my Iranian comrades. Though there were violent factions in my organization, even during my heydays as an Islamist leader, I was always for the use of propaganda and other peaceful means for Islamic revolution. Thus, I asked their help to establish a radio and TV station inside the border of Iran to promote a non-violent Islamic mass revolution in Turkey. Yet, the Iranian leaders offered guerilla training for Turkish Jihadies and expected intelligence on Turkish and NATO military basis in turn. The leader of Pasdaran, Abu Sharif, who with his beard, hat and uniform, looked like so much to the young Fidel Castro, asked me to delegate my comrades to gather intelligence regarding Turkish and American military bases in my country. Though I considered the USA as the Big Satan and the Turkish Republic my proximate enemy, I never even imagined myself participating in bloody wars against them.

I spent four years in Turkish jails and prisons and subjected to physical and mental torture for leading and promoting Islamic revolution in Turkey. At age

24, I became the best-selling author in Turkey. Many of my close friends and comrades decades later became congressmen, ministers and even prime ministers. For instance, Turkey's current Prime Minister Tayyip Erdogan was my comrade in 1970's and early 1980's. He even participated in one of my illegal public demonstrations, where 300 Islamists rallied, without the permission of the military government, where I led a congregational prayer in the middle of downtown in Fatih, Istanbul. The following excerpt from a well-known Turkish political figure who summarizes the kind of environment I was in and the kind of people I was in company of (Turkish characters in proper names are converted to the closest characters in Latin alphabet):

> "Year 1979, the chaotic years of martial law in Turkey. A month in summer. We are in a rally protesting the assassination of two Raiders in Kagithane. Our walk started in Aksaray and ended in Fatih. There we are suddenly surrounded by military and police forces and herded to military trucks. Who is not among us! From the leader of the illegal rally Edip Yüksel, to the airplane hijacker journalists Yilmaz Yalciner and Omer Yorulmaz, to Recep Tayyip Erdogan; the famous names of that era. Erdogan was the leader of MSP's Istanbul youth organization. After spending one night at a military base, we are released without being subjected to torture or indignity." Yemyesil Seriat Bembeyaz Demokrasi (All-Green Shariah, All-White Democracy), Mehmet Metiner, Dogan Kitap, Istanbul, 2004, second edition, pp 63-64. Also see: The Portrait of Tayyip Erdogan by His Consultant Mehmet Metiner, Ortak Haber, 08.07.2003. Radikal, a Turkish Newspaper, published an excerpt from the book that contains this section: www.radikal.com.tr/ek_haber.php?ek=r2&haberno=2341

The year that the Islamist excitement reached its zenith… An Islamic revolution had just taken place in Iran. A mujahid resistance started in Afghanistan against the communist occupation. In Pakistan, general Ziya ul Haq had established a so-called Islamist regime after ending the democratically elected Zulfikar Ali Butto's government with a military coup.

The popular slogans frequently chanted by the youth of that era were: "Yesterday it was Iran, Pakistan; now it is your turn Musluman!" and "The non-religious state will be destroyed; Islamic government will be restored!"

These were the slogans that were declaring the faith and enthusiasm of Tayyip Erdogan and ours.

Of course, our purpose was to establish an Islamic government and islamicize the society through the state power. It did not matter whether it was through a mass revolution as it was in Iran, or through a military coup as it was in Pakistan. As long as an Islamic state could be established in a country with a majority Muslim population... But, in Turkey we believed, unlike other countries, that this goal could have been accomplished via a political party.

FP: How long did you spend in Turkish jails and prisons? Share your experience there with us. What kind of physical and mental torture were you subjected to? How did you cope?

YUKSEL: I was arrested on the night of September 12, 1980 Turkish military coup as an alleged seditionist and I would spend about 4 years in prison. I was picked up like a panda from the street in Fatih/Istanbul while walking with an Egyptian and British member of Muslim Brotherhood. I was interrogated for about three weeks in horrible conditions (not much different what we know about Gitmo) by state security police. My lengthy incarceration was made even longer by periodical torture sessions for the crime of being a dissident against a repressive government.

In retrospect, I thank God for the arrest and prison time. I was so busy with the political activities that perhaps I would have never found a chance to sit down and translate the book that would lead to the paradigm change in my religious and political position. Though occasionally there was torture and very strict rules, such as not being allowed to read any book of our choice, there was a period in prison where I could find ample time to examine Deedat's book on the mathematical structure of the Quran and then translate it. My first months in this prison provided me with a great opportunity not only to translate the book, but also to verify many of the Quranic data presented in the book. I employed my comrade inmates for the verification and falsification process. Later, I contributed to the subject matter and became its co-author. I added my studies on the scientific aspect of the Quran, and it was published. It became an instant best-selling book, for about five years crowning the top of the best-selling list in Turkey, until the religious establishment banned it.

Convicted of the charges against me by a kangaroo court for religious and political expressions that would have drawn little if any reproach in the Western world, I was sentenced to six years in prison. During the three and a half years of actual prison term, I experienced systematic torture for about one year. In a story stunningly similar to that of Billy Hayes in "Midnight Express," I enter a terrifying world where I am solitarily confined amongst filth and vermin, routinely beaten and mentally abused, deprived of sunlight and medical care, fed adulterated food, stripped of my individuality, forced to undergo hours of political indoctrination, and, worst of all, set up by my captors as a target for fellow inmates who try repeatedly to harass me.

Let me make a comment about torture. I will never condone torture even to my ardent enemies. I do not think that a terrorist is any different than a soldier or military commander captured in a war. There is no justification in condemning torture against soldiers while justifying it against terror suspects. Torture must be categorically banned and no hypothetical horror stories should be use to justify it.

51

FP: So what led you to your transformation? What exactly did this transformation entail? Crystallize for us what you ended up believing and how it collided with what you once believed.

YUKSEL: While doing the mandatory military service, which was an adventure on its own, I secretly corresponded with the original discoverer of the prophetic numerical structure of the Quran. He was a biochemist residing in America. During our initial correspondence I got disappointed and shocked that he was not the kind of Muslim scholar that I expected him to be. After discussing the issues via snail mail for several months, finally I received his landmark book, "Quran, Hadith, and Islam," which changed my world in several hours in the night of July 1st 1986.

I underwent what a major transformation or paradigm change as a religious and political thinker, ultimately rejecting much of the earlier fundamentalism that had made me so popular and so targeted by the Turkish state. In a period of maturation similar to that of America's Malcolm X, I came to recognize the profound flaws of the orthodoxy I once fervently believed in and promoted. I realized that Sunni and Shiite sects, and their modern offspring the fundamentalist Islam had severely distorted the original message of the Quran transforming it into a concoction of medieval Arab culture with borrowings from Jewish and Christian teachings. I learned that Sunni or Shiite versions of Islam have been shaped by religious and political leaders imposing their will on the masses as a method of repressive socio-political control.

I provide numerous examples and arguments in Manifesto for Islamic Reform, which is published in the end section of the Quran: a Reformist Translation. I recommend the readers to read that article, and they will be surprised to see the incredible distortion in the message of the Quran, which once created a major civilization out of a bunch of superstitious tribes. (The book can be ordered via www.brainbowpress.com or can be downloaded for free at: http://groups.google.com/group/19org/files)

FP: What consequences did you face in the Muslim community after your transformation? What did the radicals think of you after? Were you in danger? How did your family react?

YUKSEL: After finishing my military service, I was detained for the eleventh time, and remained in Turkish prisons for half a year because of promoting Islamic revolution in Turkey. By then, I had no desire in promotion of such a revolution; but I expressed my contempt to the repressive Turkish legal system.

Soon after being freed from prison, I published a new book wherein I publicly renounced my religious and political fundamentalism. This break from my past severely disturbed my father, a renowned Muslim scholar, who just as publicly condemned me as an "apostate" -- a branding that is widely reported in Turkey's religious and secular press.

Following this stunning denunciation, my books were removed by Muslim fundamentalists from bookstores throughout the country and destroyed; and their publishers and retailers were threatened by the perpetrators with violence. I was repeatedly threatened, publicly assaulted and attacked several times by my former comrades and followers who became my most rabid enemies on the streets of Istanbul. Within a week after I was targeted by this campaign of terror, I realized the truth – I was marked for death. Unfairly likened to Salman Rushdie, I disappeared into hiding, and then left all that is important to me to escape to the West. (Ironically, nineteen years later, an American publishing company named Palgrave/Macmillan canceled the publication of the Reformist Translation in last minute, after its announcement in their catalogue. They were scared by a fatwa-review of a prominent Sunni scholar who falsely likened our translation to Salman Rushdie's Satanic Verses. Unfortunately, that shameless political misrepresentation was swallowed as a scholarly review by the board of Palgrave.)

FP: In the end, you had to escape to America, to the land of "The Great Satan", leaving everything behind. This is a bit of an irony, yes?

YUKSEL: Yes, it was more than a mere irony, it was irony squared! With little more than a plane ticket, the clothes on my back, and few hundred dollars in my pocket, I immigrated to the United States, where I was heartily welcomed in Arizona by my spiritual and intellectual mentor, Dr. Rashad Khalifa, an Islamic reformist whose views strongly influenced my transformation in Turkey. Khalifa was himself a controversial figure among Muslims, and had a similar experience. He was too rejected by his father who was a prominent scholar and a leader of a Sufi order in Egypt. He too lost his popularity and reputation and became the target of threats, slanders and numerous false accusations.

Eighteen years ago, when I escaped to America from Turkey to save my life, I thought I knew America. In my teenager years, America was the land of my favorite comic book heroes: Texas, Tom Mix, Captain Swing, Tom Bronx, Red Kit, etc. I was always on the side of white cowboys, hunters, and soldiers who were fighting against bad guys, such as barbaric Indians, lazy Mexicans or stupid British soldiers with funny uniforms. Then, when I became a political activist promoting an Iranian-like revolution, America was transformed into the "Great Satan," the evil imperialist power that exploited the resources of Muslim countries through puppet regimes. I once shouted "Yankee Go Home!" Now, I am in the same home with the Yankees!

My account of first encounters with American culture; I was like Alice in wonderland. Now, I frame my seminal impressions of America in the context of Janus, the two-faced Greek god. America is at once both the land of liberty and that of a burgeoning prison industry; a place of stunning prosperity and of abject

53

poverty; the base of the world's peacekeeping forces and also a global war machine that terrifies it -- a place where heaven meets hell.

FP: Your mentor and the discoverer of the "Secret," Dr. Rashad Khalifa, was assassinated by associates of Osama Bin Laden in 1990. Can you talk a bit about that?

YUKSEL: I came to know Rashad through Ahmad Deedat who had used his computerized studies on the Quran. I witnessed and participated in the unveiling of "The Secret", or the mathematical code of the Quran and the Old Testament, that became controversial all around the Muslim world. After my immigration, I was hosted by Rashad and worked with him in Masjid Tucson for about a year, seven days a week, ten hours every day. (When he was alive, I called him with his first name; so I will respect that memory).

Rashad was an Egyptian-American Biochemist. He worked in the United Nations and for a while he became a science adviser to Muammar al-Qaddafi, the despot of Libya. Rashad became a popular author in Muslim world and later he dared to criticize the orthodox teaching of the Muslim clerics; he promoted a radical reformation in Islam by rejecting all sectarian teachings other than the Quran. In my archive, I have letters written to Rashad from the director of al-Azhar University and many other prominent religious scholars, expressing their disbelief and shock to hear rumors about his rejection of the sectarian teachings called Hadith and Sunna.

By referring to the Quranic verses, Dr. Khalifa demonstrated that today's Islam has little to do with Muhammad's original message, but rather is a religion concocted by scholars using fabricated narration and medieval Arab culture (Hadith and Sunna), and falsely attributing these to Prophet Muhammad. By incorporating their opinions, along with those mediaeval lies, Muslim scholars have created various orthodox sects promoting vicious and oppressive laws, misogyny, hatred, terror and aggression.

In February 19, 1989 a group of scholars met in Saudi Arabia to discuss the issue of Salman Rushdi. Saudi King was competing with Ayatullah's Iran for leadership of the so-called Muslim World, and he felt that he needed to come up with something on that big controversy. When the so-called scholars issued their fatwa (religious decree) it became headline news in Muslim countries, including my homeland Turkey. Their fatwa was: "Both Rashad and Rushdi are apostates!" The world knew Rushdi, but who was Rashad? Rashad, a biochemist resident of Tucson, Arizona, had become a popular figure in Muslim countries after he discovered a secret mathematical system in the Quran via computer analysis. The consequence of the mathematical code was too difficult to be accepted by the Muslim clergymen. Consequently, they issued fatwas calling for his assassination.

In early 1990, Rashad, my friend, colleague, mentor, the discoverer of the "Secret," was stabbed to death brutally in his Tucson mosque by men who, over a decade later, were ultimately revealed by FBI and respected American journalistic sources to be associates of the infamous Usama Bin Laden. A popular reformist Muslim thinker, Rashad dared to criticize the religious orthodoxy of Islamic dogmas, calling for radical change wherein all sectarian teachings would be rejected except for the Quran itself. (I have numerous media clips from several languages regarding the reaction of Muslim Clerics to our reformation movement. The assassination of my mentor and its aftermath was widely covered by Arizona Daily Star and Tucson Weekly and local radio and TV stations. After September 11, the national media picked up the story. For instance, see: CBS Evening News with Dan Rather, on October 26, 2001; cover story of Newsweek, January 14, 2002 , p.44. On March 19, 2002, KPHO-TV at Phoenix , a CBS affiliate, in its evening news, broadcast an interview with me under the headline: Traces of Al Qaeda Cell in Tucson).

I was spending about 12 hours a day at Masjid Tucson, working on my Turkish books and assisting Rashad in his revision of the Final Testament. I had been at Masjid with Rashad the night before his assassination and the following morning I arrived there just two hours after Khalifa's assassination there. As I did several times before in Turkey, -- in a place most Americans would find far removed from the bitter conflicts within Islam – I again barely escaped losing my life over my beliefs.

I differ from Conservative politicians; since I have no doubt that the American foreign policy and sectarian Islam are both incubators of religious terrorism. A campaign against terrorism must have two fronts: reformation in American democracy and reformation in Islamic understanding and practice. Unfortunately, the victims of this conflict, whether they live in skyscrapers or caves, are mostly innocent people.

FP: Tell us about Quran: a Reformist Translation.

YUKSEL: The Reformist Translation of the Quran offers a non-sexist and non-sectarian understanding of the divine text; it is the result of collaboration between three translators, two men (Layth al-Shaiban and I) and a woman (Martha Schulte-Nafeh). It explicitly rejects the authority of the clergy to determine the likely meaning of disputed passages. It uses logic and the language of the Quran itself as the ultimate authority in determining likely meanings, rather than ancient scholarly interpretations rooted in patriarchal hierarchies. It offers extensive cross-referencing to the Bible and provides arguments on numerous philosophical and scientific issues. It is God's message for those who prefer reason over blind faith, for those who seek peace and ultimate freedom by submitting themselves to the Truth alone.

You may find endorsements of numerous authors and academics, and if you wish you may include them here. (Some are published at www.brainbowpress.com). I recently, shared the following announcement with people, under the title, "Following a Fatwa-Review of Establishment, Palgrave/Macmillan Abandoned the Publication of this Book"

In 2004, my colleagues and I signed a contract with Palgrave/Macmillan publishing house for the publication of Quran: a Reformist Translation. The editor and other staff of the publishing house were very encouraging and enthusiastic, and during the summer of 2006, I was personally introduced to the director of the publishing company at its New York headquarters. Palgrave even published an announcement about the upcoming Reformist Translation in their 2006 Fall/Winter Catalogue, which was later postponed to the summer of 2007. The publishing house posted information about the Reformist Translation for pre-orders at Amazon.com and other online bookstores. However, in December 2006, the editor informed me that the board had determined that my manuscript was not acceptable for publication.

Apparently, they were convinced or intimidated by a review (more accurately, a fatwa) of "a very well-established professor," who misleadingly likened our annotated translation of the Quran to Salman Rushdie's Satanic Verses. This was akin to a medieval publishing house turning down Martin Luther's 95 Theses after consulting "a very well-established" Catholic Bishop! It is telling that Palgrave's "very well-established scholar" in his several-page review, had only one substantive criticism, which consisted of our usage of a word, yes a single word in the translation: progressive.

I believe that without hearing my defense against this Sunni version of excommunication in the guise of a "scholarly review," the publishing house committed an injustice against my person and our work. I called the publishing house and asked them to give me the chance to respond to the reviewer and defend myself and work against his disparagement and distortions; I was told he remain anonymous.

We were not surprised to hear negative remarks, insults, or false associations from a reviewer who considers a rejection of backward and bankrupt sectarian dogmas "heresy." However, we were surprised to learn that the board of the publishing house cancelled the publication of a potentially controversial yet crucial book that would introduce the message of the Quran -- the message of peace, justice, reason, and progress -- without the distortion of sectarian teachings. Any scholar who can see beyond his or her office can see the growing reform movement, open or clandestine, particularly in Turkey, Malaysia , Iran, Egypt and Kazakhstan where people take great risks to question the popular sectarian dogmas.

You may visit the following websites for the full text of the letter of the Sunni scholar whose advice was taken at face value by Palgrave/Macmillan, and for our response to the letter. You may also find in the following websites, recent updates, reactions, and feedback from reviewers, our responses, related news in the media, and the activities of the global reformist movement:

www.19.org
www.islamicreform.org
www.progressivemuslims.org
www.free-minds.org

Let the world hear the message. Let the West hear the voice of monotheism, the voice of reason, peace, justice and progress. Let the East and the Middle East hear the clear message of the book that they have abandoned for centuries, despite efforts by their leaders to repress it.

FP: You witnessed and participated in the unveiling of "The Secret", or the mathematical code of the Quran and the Old Testament, that became controversial all around the Muslim world. What is this about?

YUKSEL: The miraculous function of the number 19 prophesized in Chapter 74 was unveiled in 1974 through a computerized analysis of the Quran. Though, in retrospect, the implication of 19 in Chapter 74 traditionally called Hidden One, were obvious, it remained a secret for 1406 (19x74) lunar years after the revelation of the Quran. Ironically, the first words of the Chapter 74, The Hidden One, was revealing, yet the code was a divinely guarded gift allocated to the computer generation; they were the one who would need and appreciate it the most. As we have demonstrated in various books, hundreds of simple and complex algorithms, we witness the depth and breath of mathematical manipulation of Arabic, an arbitrary human language, to be profound and extraordinary.

This is the fulfillment of a Quranic challenge (17:88). While the meaning of the Quranic text and its literal excellence was kept, all its units, from chapters, verses, words to its letters were also assigned universally recognizable roles in creation of mathematical patterns. Since its discovery, the number 19 of the Quran and the Bible has increased the faith of many believers, has removed doubts in the minds of many People of the Book, and has caused discord, controversy and chaos among those who have traded the Quran with men-made sectarian teachings. This is indeed a fulfillment of a Quranic prophecy (74:30-31).

Before the discovery of the 19-based system, we were aware of a symmetrical mathematical wonder in the Quran. For example:

- The word "month" (shahr) occurs 12 times.
- The word "day" (yawm) occurs 365 times.

- The word "days" (eyyam, yawmeyn) occurs 30 times.
- The words "satan" (shaytan) & "angel" (malak), each occur 88 times.
- The words "this world" (dunya) and "hereafter" (ahirah), each occur 115 times.
- I have written several books and dozens of articles on this subject. I have also given lectures in math departments such as University of Arziona, and discussed it on live TV programs in Turkey. When I was under-graduate student in philosophy, as my honor thesis, I discussed it with Carl Sagan as another evidence for God's existence. I am currently work-ing on finishing an English book titled "NINETEEN: God's Signature in Nature and Scripture." If your readers are interested, I can give you a more comprehensive summary, with some background information, than this truncated one. Here are some examples of the numerical structure of the Quran.
- The first verse, i.e., the opening statement "Bismillahirrahmanirrahim", shortly "Basmalah," consists of 19 Arabic letters.
- The first word of Basmalah, Ism (name), without contraction, occurs in the Quran 19 times.
- The second word of Basmalah, Allah (God) occurs 2698 times, or 19x142.
- The third word of Basmalah, Rahman (Gracious) occurs 57 times, or 19x3.
- The fourth word of Basmalah, Rahim (Merciful) occurs 114 times, or 19x6.
- Although this phenomenon (the opening statement consists of 19 letters, and each word occurs in multiple of 19) represents a minute portion of the code, it was described by Martin Gardner in the Scientific American as "ingenious" (September, 1981, p. 22-24)
- The multiplication factors of the words of the Basmalah (1+142+3+6) add up to 152 or 19x8.
- The Quran consists of 114 chapters, which is 19x6.
- The total number of verses in the Quran including all unnumbered Bas-malahs is 6346, or 19x334. If you add the digits of that number, 6+3+4+6 equals 19.
- The Basmalah occurs 114 times, (despite its conspicuous absence from chapter 9, it occurs twice in chapter 27) and 114 is 19x6.
- From the missing Basmalah of chapter 9 to the extra Basmalah of chap-ter 27, there are precisely 19 chapters.
- The occurrence of the extra Basmalah is in 27:30. The number of the chapter and the verse add up to 57, or 19x3.
- Each letter of the Arabic alphabet corresponds to a number according to their original sequence in the alphabet. The Arabs were using this system for calculations. When the Quran was revealed 14 centuries ago, the numbers known today did not exist. A universal system was used where

the letters of the Arabic, Hebrew, Aramaic, and Greek alphabets were used as numerals. The number assigned to each letter is its "Gematrical Value." The numerical values of the Arabic alphabet are shown below: [the table is omitted]

- A study on the gematrical values of about 120 attributes of God which are mentioned in the Quran, shows that only four attributes have gematrical values which are multiples of 19. These are "Wahid" (One), "Zul Fadl al Azim" (Possessor of Infinite Grace), "Majid" (Glorous), "Jaami" (Summoner). Their gematrical value are 19 , 2698, 57, and 114 respectively, which are all divisible by 19 and correspond exactly to the frequencies of occurrence of the Basmalah's four words.

- The total numbers of verses where the word "Allah" (God) occurs, add up to 118123, and is 19x6217.

- The total occurrences of the word Allah (God) in all the verses whose numbers are multiples of 19 is 133, or 19x7.

- The key commandment: "You shall devote your worship to God alone" (in Arabic "Wahdahu") occurs in 7:70; 39:45; 40:12,84; and 60:4. The total of these numbers adds up to 361, or 19x19.

- The Quran is characterized by a unique phenomenon that is not found in any other book: 29 chapters are prefixed with "Quranic Initials" which remained mysterious for 1406 years. With the discovery of the code 19, we realized their major role in the Quran's mathematical structure. The initials occur in their respective chapters in multiples of 19. For example, Chapter 19 has five letters in its beginning, K.H.Y.A'.SS., and the total occurrence of these letters in this chapter is 798, or 19x42.

- To witness the details of the miracle of these initials, a short chapter which begins with one initial, letter "Q", will be a good example. The frequency of "Q" in chapter 50 is 57, or 19x3. The letter "Q" occurs in the other Q-initialed chapter, i.e., chapter 42, exactly the same number of times, 57. The total occurrence of the letter "Q" in the two Q-initialed chapters is 114, which equals the number of chapters in the Quran. The description of the Quran as "Majid" (Glorious) is correlated with the frequency of occurrence of the letter "Q" in each of the Q-initialed chapters. The word "Majid" has a gematrical value of 57. Chapter 42 consists of 53 verses, and 42+53 is 95, or 19x5. Chapter 50 consists of 45 verses, and 50+45 is 95, or 19x5.

- The Quran mentions 30 different cardinal numbers: 1, 2, 3, 4, 5, 6, 7, 8, 9, 10, 11, 12, 19, 20, 30, 40, 50, 60, 70, 80, 99, 100, 200, 300, 1000, 2000, 3000, 5000, 50000, & 100000. The sum of these numbers is 162146, which equals 19x8534.

- In addition to 30 cardinal numbers, the Quran contains 8 fractions: 1/10, 1/8, 1/6, 1/5, 1/4, 1/3, 1/2, 2/3. Thus, the Quran contains 38 (19x2) different numbers. The total of fractions is approximately 2.

- If we write down the number of each verse in the Quran, one next to the other, preceded by the number of verses in each chapter, the resulting long number consists of 12692 digits (19x668). Additionally, the huge number itself is also a multiple of 19.

(Unfortunately, some innumerate zealots are abusing this feature of the Quran through numerous arbitrary and childish numerical juggling. I caution the reader to be critical of claims of numerical discoveries in scriptures. You should not be confusing the statistically impressive examples with human manipulations and arbitrary calculations.)

It is significant that the same 19-based mathematical composition was discovered by Rabbi Judah in the 12th century AD in a preserved part of the Old Testament. Below is a quote from Studies In Jewish Mysticism:

> "The people (Jews) in France made it a custom to add (in the morning prayer) the words: " 'Ashrei temimei derekh (blessed are those who walk the righteous way)," and our Rabbi, the Pious, of blessed memory, wrote that they were completely and utterly wrong. It is all gross falsehood, because there are only nineteen times that the Holy Name is mentioned (in that portion of the morning prayer), . . . and similarly you find the word Elohim nineteen times in the pericope of Ve-'elleh shemot . . . .

> "Similarly, you find that Israel were called "sons" nineteen times, and there are many other examples. All these sets of nineteen are intricately intertwined, and they contain many secrets and esoteric meanings, which are contained in more than eight volumes. Therefore, anyone who has the fear of God in him will not listen to the words of the Frenchmen who add the verse " 'Ashrei temimei derekh (blessed are those who walk in the paths of God's Torah, for according to their additions the Holy Name is mentioned twenty times . . . and this is a great mistake. Furthermore, in this section there are 152 words, but if you add " 'Ashrei temimei derekh" there are 158 words. This is nonsense, for it is a great and hidden secret why there should be 152 words . . ." (Studies In Jewish Mysticism, Joseph Dan, Association for Jewish Studies. Cambridge, Massachusetts: 1978, p 88.)"

I recently discovered a surviving book of Rabi Judah, and it is among the research projects that I will be working on next year.

FP: Share with us your efforts on behalf of an Islamic reformation. Why is it not happening? On what foundations would it be based? Are you optimistic or pessimistic in its possibility?

YUKSEL: To Tell the Truth: It is very difficult to tell the truth in a world where actors are heroes, fiction is the best-selling literature, doublespeak is the lingua franca, and capitalism is the only way of attaining freedom.

As a Reformist Muslim, a monotheist, who continuously receives death threats from Muslim fanatics, a Muslim who lost my closest friend to the knives of Osama Bin Laden's terrorists, a Muslim who has dedicated himself to the promotion of human rights, freedom of expression, democracy and reformation in Islam, I invite Muslims to reform themselves under the light of the Quran alone.

We should seek peace and justice for all. We should attain individual freedom by submitting ourselves to God's laws in nature and His scripture. We should use our reason, rather than submitting to superstition. We should reject the teachings of clergymen, which have doomed us to the darkness of ignorance and to the backwardness of medieval culture.

I argue that the ramifications of following the Quran alone cannot be exaggerated. It provides a paradigm shift regarding the role of women, freedom of speech, democracy, position against science and technology, criminal system, international terrorism, and peace with other nations.

The impediments against Islamic Reform movement are numerous. Let me enumerate the major ones:

1. Sectarian dogmas and practices that have distorted the message of the Quran. It is so ingrained in the culture of Muslims, they are psychologically shocked when their dogmas questioned.

2. Traditional institutions and organizations that has little tolerance to objective and critical scientific research and debate, such as al-Azhar University.

3. Backward authoritarian governments that uses religious teachings as opium of masses, such as Saudi Arabia.

4. Backward authoritarian governments that uses religious teachings as testosterone for masses, such as Iran.

5. Western financial and academic institutions that have vested interest in dealing with backward regimes. For instance, many Middle Eastern Studies at American Universities, including Harvard University.

6. Myopic American foreign policy that has been incubating and spreading the cause of Christianists and Islamists.

As an American citizen, I invite American people to be more attentive towards the foreign policy of our government. The myopic American foreign policy, which primarily serves the interests of corporations, such as the weapon and oil industries, has inadvertently helped the cause of religious terrorists. Recently, I reached the conclusion that the threat and fear "terrorism" provides political and financial benefits for some groups and thus, it is deliberately exaggerated and strengthened through reckless wars and invasions that have been creating millions of orphans, and traumatized angry people in Muslim countries.

Militant clerics, whether they are collaborators with totalitarian regimes or are dissidents, should be taken seriously. Using the language of religion and the proverbs of their forefathers, they can mobilize gullible masses, perpetrating bloody conflicts. The best way to deflate the power of militant clergymen is (1) to support intellectuals, who promote democracy and freedom, and (2) to denounce and punish the oppressive leaders, without favoring one over another, through international legal devices, such as freezing their assets in foreign countries and trying them in international tribunals.

So far, I have authored numerous books on politics, philosophy, religion, and law. Most of my books are published in Turkey, such as: Interesting Questions, Books Are Dangerous, 19 Questions for Muslims, 19 Questions For Christians, Errors in Translations of the Quran, Democracy/Theocracy/Oligarchy, Purple Letters, and The Message: Turkish Translation of the Quran.

As a founder of www.19.org, I have a network of hundreds of young activists who promote reformation in Islam, freedom of speech, democracy and peace all around the world. Together with Layth al-Shaiban, I established www.islamicreform.org to promote a paradigm-changing reform in Muslim countries. My occasional appearances on Turkish TV have created a powerful reformation movement in Turkey, which its ripple effect has been felt from Malaysia to America. Turkish reformists established 114 Organization to promote the message. There are very good news all around the world, but again, against powerful political and religious forces.

I have several unfinished English books evolving or molding in my computer. Years ago, a small British publishing house discovered my websites and offered me to publish all of my books, starting with my autobiography, In the Name of Allah. But, I am reluctant to sign a contract with a small publishing house with British accent. I am working on variety of projects, including a script for an animation movie on Muhammad's life, and another script for a philosophical-religious comedy, titled "12 Hungry Men" I do not have contacts in Hollywood, but I submitted the treatment to a small European film company and they are very interested in producing it. I have yet to reach a decision on it.

My first English book, Quran: A Reformist Translation, is recently published. Besides the translation, it contains a lengthy introduction titled Manifesto for

Islamic Reform, and arguments in footnotes making a powerful theological and philosophical case for a paradigm change in the realm of religions. We are also producing video programs and God willing they will be made available both on DVD disks and youtube.

FP: Well sir, we would clearly disagree about the foreign policy of our government, that it primarily serves, as you say, the interests of corporations and that it has helped the cause of religious terrorists, etc. Much evidence suggests that Bush's foreign policy is legitimate and influenced by a moral clarity that sees the necessity of confronting radical Islam in key parts of the world. But we'll have to debate and discuss this in another forum my friend.

There are also, of course, scholars and critics who would take issue with some of your interpretations of Islam, and they are most welcome to begin a dialogue with you in our pages.

Edip Yuksel, thank you for joining Frontpage Interview.

YUKSEL: Thank you for allowing me to share the views of Islamic Reform movement with the world. The movement that started in 1974 is now getting momentum. Let me finish my words with several verses from chapter 74:

> 74:32 No, by the moon.
> 74:33 By the night when it passes.
> 74:34 By the morning when it shines.
> 74:35 It is one of the great ones.
> 74:36 A warning to people.
> 74:37 For any among you who wishes to progress or regress.

Peace.

Previous Interviews with Islamic Reformers:

> Thomas Haidon
> Khalim Massoud
> Hasan Mahmud

Jamie Glazov is Frontpage Magazine's managing editor. He holds a Ph.D. in History with a specialty in U.S. and Canadian foreign policy. He edited and wrote the introduction to David Horowitz's Left Illusions. He is also the co-editor (with David Horowitz) of The Hate America Left and the author of Canadian Policy Toward Khrushchev's Soviet Union (McGill-Queens University Press, 2002) and 15 Tips on How to be a Good Leftist. To see his previous symposiums, interviews and articles Click Here. Email him at jglazov@rogers.com.

The Fictional Muhammad?

By Jamie Glazov
FrontPageMagazine.com | 3/7/2008

Is the Muslim account of Muhammad valid? To discuss this issue with us today, Frontpage Magazine has assembled a distinguished panel. Our guests today are:

Edip Yuksel, a Kurdish-Turkish-American author and progressive activist who spent four years in Turkish prisons in the 1980's for his political writings and activities promoting an Islamic revolution in Turkey. He experienced a paradigm change in 1986 transforming him from a Sunni Muslim leader to a reformed Muslim or rational monotheist. He is the founder of 19.org and the Islamic Reform organization. His personal site is yuksel.org . His recent major work, Quran: a Reformist Translation, has been recently published by BrainbowPress, after being cancelled by Palgrave-Macmillan, which followed the fatwa of a "very established scholar."

Robert Spencer, a scholar of Islamic history, theology, and law and the director of Jihad Watch. He is the author of seven books, eight monographs, and hundreds of articles about jihad and Islamic terrorism, including the New York Times Bestsellers The Politically Incorrect Guide to Islam (and the Crusades) and The Truth About Muhammad. His latest book is Religion of Peace?

Bill Warner, the director of CSPI Publishing and the spokesman for Political Islam.com.

and

Thomas Haidon, a Muslim commentator on human rights, counter-terrorism and Islamic affairs. He is active in the Qur'anist movement and works with a number of Islamic reform organisations as an advisor. He has provided guidance to several governments on counter-terrorism issues and his works have been published in legal periodicals, and other media. Mr. Haidon has also provided advice to and worked for United Nations agencies in Sudan and Indonesia.

FP: Edip Yuksel, Thomas Haidon, Robert Spencer and Bill Warner, welcome to Frontpage Symposium.

Edip Yuksel, let me begin with you.

I think a good way to begin this discussion is to talk about Muhammad in the context of women's rights. What, for instance, are your thoughts on our video about the violent oppression of women in Islam? Some critics would argue that this reality is the outgrowth of the foundation that Muhammad laid down in terms of his own teachings and also his own actions in terms of women. Do you agree?

YUKSEL: No I do not agree. The video portrays a sickening reality, but if Muhammad came back today, these same people would declare him an apostate and heretic and would perhaps stone him to death.

FP: But just a second, some would argue that the misogynist pathologies in the Islamic world (i.e. female genital mutilation, forced marriages, child marriage, forced segregation, forced veiling, honor killings etc.) are engendered by the second-class status accorded to women in Islam and the demonization of female sexuality that is rooted in Islamic theology.

Are the teachings and actions of Mohammed himself in regards to female equality, rape and sexual slavery, not a part of this issue? Is his life, what he taught, and how he led by example really irrelevant to Muslims who seek to follow their religion in terms of how women are treated?

Mr. Yuksel, what do you make of the track of evidence in terms of Mohammed as demonstrated by Bill Warner? Can you explain how and why it is irrelevant when it comes to Islamic gender apartheid? Please also take a look at how Robert Spencer has documented Mohammed's life in his new book -- and this book is based on Islamic sources.

Are Spencer's and Warner's findings about the Muslims' prophet really irrelevant, especially when they are all based on Islamic sources and agreed to -- and pointed too -- by Muslim clerics and scholars themselves?

YUKSEL: None, yes none of these innovations can be found in the Quran, the only book delivered by Muhammad; they were imported from other cultures and sanctified or they were innovated centuries after the revelation of the Quran. Not only they do not exist in the Quran, they contradict it. Hadith (hearsay narrations falsely attributed to Muhammad and his companions) and their collections have been the prime tool in distorting the progressive message of Islam. The reactionary forces, misogynistic ideas and practices, racism, tribalism, superstitions, despotism, and many other vices of the "days of ignorance" were resurrected and sneaked back into the minds and lives of Muslim communities after they were rejected by the early Muslims at great cost.

Soon after Muhammad's death, thousands of hadiths (words attributed to Muhammad) were fabricated and two centuries later collected, and centuries later compiled and written in the so-called "authentic" hadith books:

- to support the teaching of a particular sect against another (such as, what nullifies ablution; which sea food is prohibited);
- to flatter or justify the authority and practice of a particular king against dissidents (such as, Mahdy and Dajjal);
- to promote the interest of a particular tribe or family (such as, favoring the Quraysh tribe or Muhammad's family);
- to justify sexual abuse and misogyny (such as, Aisha's age; barring women from leading Sala prayers);
- to justify violence, oppression and tyranny (such as, torturing members of Urayna and Uqayla tribes; massacring the Jewish population in Medina; assassinating a female poet for her critical poems);
- to exhort more rituals and righteousness (such as, nawafil prayers);
- to validate superstitions (such as, magic; worshiping the black stone near the Kaba);
- to prohibit certain things and actions (such as, prohibiting drawing animal and human figures; playing musical instruments; chess);
- to import Jewish and Christian beliefs and practices (such as, death by stoning; circumcision; head scarf; hermitism; rosary);
- to resurrect pre-Islamic beliefs and practices common among Meccans (such as, intercession; slavery; tribalism; misogyny);
- to please crowds with stories (such as the story of Miraj (ascension to heaven) and bargaining for prayers);
- to idolize Muhammad and claim his superiority to other messengers (such as, numerous miracles, including splitting the moon);
- to defend hadith fabrications against monotheists (such as, condemning those who find the Quran alone sufficient); and even
- to advertise products of a particular farm (such as, the benefits of dates grown in a town called Ajwa).

In addition to the above mentioned reasons, many hadith were fabricated to explain the meaning of the "difficult" Quranic words or phrases, or to distort the meaning of verses that contradicted the fabricated hadith, or to provide trivial information not mentioned in the Quran (such as, Saqar, 2:187; 8:35…).

In terms of discrimination against women, verse 49:13 unequivocally rejects sexism and racism, and reminds us that neither man nor female, neither this race nor that race is superior over the other. The only measure of superiority is right-

66

eousness; being a humble, moral and socially conscientious person who strives to help others.

> 49:13 O people, We created you from a male and female, and We made you into nations and tribes, that you may know one another. Surely, the most honorable among you in the sight of God is the most righteous. God is Knowledgeable, Ever-aware.

As I have demonstrated in the *Quran: a Reformist Translation* and *Manifesto for Islamic Reform*, the message of the Quran is a liberating and progressive one. I would appreciate if you share the following table from Manifesto regarding some topics involving misogynistic ideas and practices in today's so-called Muslim societies:

Teachings Based on the Man-Made Sources, Such As, *Hadith, Sunna, Ijma*, and *Sharia*	The Quranic Verses Contradicting these Teachings, and Brief Discussions on Their Sources
When Muhammad was 53 years-old, he married Aisha who was only 9 years-old.	This is another lie by the enemies of God and His messenger. They tried to create a moon-splitting, tree-moving, child-crippling superman with the sexual power of 30 males (Verse 24:11-12 with its non-specific language, prophetically addresses this lie too). Muhammad was an honorable person and would not have a sexual relationship with a child (68:4; see 4:5-6). Discrepancies in the historical account show a deliberate attempt to reduce Aisha's age. This lie is perhaps produced to justify the sexual excesses of kings and the wealthy. They tried to justify their violence, oppression, injustice, sexual transgressions, and many other crimes through the fabrication and promotion of *hadith*.
The menstruating women should not touch the Quran, should not pray and should not enter the mosques.	This is based on a misunderstanding of at least two verses. Verse 56:79 is not an inscriptive but a descriptive verse about understanding of the Quran. The only verse mentioning menstruation forbids sexual intercourse during menstruation since it is considered a painful period (2:222), and does not forbid women from praying or reading the Quran. The Quran prohibits sexual relationship with a menstruating woman, not because she is dirty, but because menstruation is painful. The purpose is to protect women's health from being burdened by the sexual desires of their husbands. However, the male authors of the Old Testament exaggerated and generalized this divine prohibition so much so that they turned men-

	struation to a reason for their humiliation, isolation, and punishment. (Leviticus 15:19-33) Despite the Quranic rule, the followers of *hadith* and *sunna* adopted Jewish laws that consider a woman unclean, and treat her like dirt for fourteen straight days of every month. According to the fabricated rules of the Old Testament, a menstruating woman is considered unclean for seven days, and during that period wherever she sits will be considered unclean; whoever touches her or sits where she sits must wash and bathe. After she finishes the menstruation, she has to wait for seven more days to be considered clean for ceremonial purposes. (Leviticus 15:19-33)
Women should not lead congregational prayers, and it is not recommended for them to participate either.	The verse instructing those who acknowledge the truth to gather for congregational prayer does not exclude women (62:9). The Quranic expression, "O you who acknowledge..." includes both men and women. Thank God, we have ended this misogynistic rule since 1999 and women have been leading congregational prayers and giving speeches ever since The end of the world did not come, nor did anything bad happen. To the contrary, we are now blessed with being members of a balanced congregation.
Women are mentally and spiritually inferior to men. If a donkey, a dog, or a woman passes in front of the praying person the prayer is nullified. Hell will be filled with mostly women; women are deficient in intelligence and religion.	These are male chauvinist statements that reflect a diabolic arrogance, and lack appreciation of half of the human population, who are the mothers, sisters, friends, and wives. (9:71; 33:35) This is another misogynistic statement falsely attributed to Muhammad by so-called "authentic" *hadith* books. If we measure the level of intelligence by people's response to those who questioned their dogmas and superstitious beliefs, men have not scored better than women. Most of those who committed violence against the messengers and prophets were the male leaders, and most of those who distorted their message after their departure, again were all male religious leaders. With a few exceptions based on biological differences or special conditions, men and women are considered equal in every aspect. The Quran expressly states the equality of man and woman, by the expression "you are from each other" (4:25). Furthermore, it reminds us of the common origin of both sexes and the purpose of why God created us as male and female, is the purpose being love and care (30:21). *Hadith* sources do not reflect a loving and caring relationship between man and woman, but an arrogant, chauvinistic and patronizing attitude towards women. Unfortunately, when consultation and election was replaced by monarchy and satanic *khilafa* (theocratic

rule), the rights women enjoyed with the revelation of the Quran were taken one by one, and within two centuries after Muhammad, Muslims reverted to the misogynistic attitudes and practices of the pre-Islamic days of ignorance.

The rights of women during the time of prophet Muhammad is reflected with all its power in verse 58:1, where a Muslim woman argues with Muhammad regarding her husband. God does not reprimand that woman; to the contrary, God sides with the grievances of the woman and criticizes the superstition. A critical study of *hadith* and history books will reveal that even those books contain many hints regarding the individual, social and political rights enjoyed by women during the era of revelation and even decades afterwards. History books report that Aisha, Muhammad's wife, in her old age became the leader and commander of a major faction that participated in a civil war that took place thirty years after the departure of Muhammad.

Verse 60:12 informs us of the rights and privileges enjoyed by women in the early Muslim community during the life of Prophet Muhammad. In that verse, the prophet acknowledges women's right to vote, by taking the pledge of believing women to peacefully surrender themselves to God alone and lead a righteous life. The word " *BaYA*" used in the verse implies the political nature of the pledge; they accepted the leadership of the prophet individually, with their free choice. This verse is not about some pagan or *mushrik* women embracing Islam, but rather about a group of Muslim women publicly announcing their allegiance to Muhammad who became a founder of a federally secular constitutional government in central Arabia. This is a historical document that Muslim women were not considered default appendices of their decision-making husbands, brothers, fathers or male guardians, but Muslim women were treated as independent political entities that could vote and enter into social contract with their leaders. Unfortunately, many of the human rights recognized by Islam were later one by one taken away from individuals, especially from women, by the leaders of Sunni and Shiite religions; they replaced the progressive teaching of the Quran and practices of the early Muslims with hearsay fabrications thereby resurrecting the dogmas and practices of the days of ignorance. It took humanity centuries to grant women their God-given rights. For instance, the US recognized the right of women to vote in 1919 by passing the 19th Amendment, exactly, 13 centuries after it was recognized by the Quran. As for the region that once led the world in human rights and freedom, it is more than 13 centuries behind! After women, the men too lost their dignity to elect their leaders. What a regression!

69

According to the Quran, Mary was a sign for the world just as Jesus was (21:91). The Quran reports that Abraham's wife together with her husband welcomed male guests, participated in conversation, and laughed loud in their presence. She was not reprimanded for participating. To the contrary, at that meeting, God blesses her with the good news of pregnancy with Ishaq (11:71).

Verse 49:13 unequivocally rejects sexism and racism, and it reminds us that neither male nor female, neither this race nor that race is superior over the other. The only measure of superiority is righteousness; being a humble, moral and socially conscientious person who strives to help others.

The Quran is filled with verses referring to men and women in a neutral language that treats them equally (3:195; 4:7,25,32,124; 9:68-72; 16:97; 24:6-9; 33:35-36; 40:40; 49:13; 51:49; 53:45; 57.18; 66:10; 75:37-39; 92:3).

The Old Testament and St. Paul's Letters in the New Testament contain many misogynistic instructions. I recommend comparing Torrey's index for entries on 'Man' and 'Woman.' The comparison will show how the Old Testament and St. Paul are biased against women. St. Paul 's misogynistic teaching is a reflection and extension of a historical trend. The Old Testament contains many man-made misogynist teachings. For instance, a woman is considered unclean for one week if she gives birth to a son, but unclean for two weeks if she gives birth to a daughter (Leviticus 12:1-5).

Here are some of the misogynistic Biblical verses that changed Muslims' attitudes towards women centuries after the Quran:

- Woman was created from Adam's ribs (Genesis 2:21-22)
- Woman was deceived by Satan (Genesis 3:1-6; 2 Corinthians 11:3; 1 Timothy 2:14)
- Woman led man to disobey God (Genesis 3:6,11-12)
- Woman was cursed (Genesis 3:16)
- Woman is weaker than man (1 Peter 3:7)
- Woman is subordinate to man (1 Corinthians 11:7)

Women should be covered from head to toe under a veil. Women should be confined in their homes. Women should be segregated	Societies, on certain occasions, times, or places might choose to segregate the sexes, but none can sanctify those decisions in the name of God. After a brief period of freedom and progress women enjoyed during the revelation of the Quran and several decades afterwards, they lost many of their human rights because of the fabricated misogynistic teachings introduced under the title of

in public places.

hadith, sunna, and sharia of various sects (3:195; 4:19, 32; 9:71; 2:228).

The word "*KHuMuR*" in 24:31 is a plural noun that comes from the root word of "*KHaMaRa*" which means, "to cover." It is used for any cover, not exclusively for headscarves. An extensive Arabic dictionary, *Lisan-ul Arab*, informs us that the word was even used for rugs and carpets, since they cover the floor. The singular form of the same word "*KHaMR,*" has been used for intoxicants, which "cover" the mind (5:90). In verse 24:31, God advises female Muslims to maintain their chastity and put their covers on their chests, not their heads! Additionally, the word " *fel yedribne* = they shall put, they shall cover" is significant in that verse. If *KHuMuR* meant head cover, the verb, "*fel yudnine* = they shall lengthen," (like in 33:59) would be more appropriate.

Another distortion involves the word "*ZiYNa*" of verse 24:31. Muslim clergymen have abused this word to cover women from head to toe. They considered almost all parts of female body as *ZiYNa*. Reflecting on the rituals of ablution for the daily prayers, one can easily infer that women can publicly open their faces, hair, arms, and feet as an act of worship (5:6). Therefore, opening their faces and arms is indeed an act of worship; and they are not required to worship in secret or segregated places (17:110). If a man stares at a woman who is taking ablution and is sexually aroused it is not her fault, but it is either a symptom of his psychological problems or an indication of the deep-rooted problems in that society. By requiring women to cover any of these parts of their body, religious scholars have turned a religious ritual into a matter of sexual expression.

It is up to women to cover themselves for their own protection. It is not up to men or moral police to mandate or impose this divine instruction on women, since the instruction is personal and specific to women. Besides, the language of the instruction is deliberately designed to accommodate different cultures, norms, conditions, and individual comfort level. A divine recommendation to protect women from the harassment of unrighteous men should not be abused to justify the harassment and oppression of self-righteous misogynistic men.

Verse 33:52 informs us that Muhammad was attracted to the physical beauty of women. No reasonable man is attracted to the "beauty" of women walking in black sacks. Despite this verse informing us that Muslim women during the time of Muhammad were interacting with men, their faces open. Those who tried to deprive women from social and political life and from their individual and group identity went to the extreme and issued religious fatwas mandating a veil to cover their faces. The veil is a satanic innovation designed to turn women into the slaves of men who claim to be lords and masters.

Verse 60:12 mentions the practice of another role model, prophet Muhammad. Muhammad did not receive any divine warning regarding the danger of the devil during this face-to-face interaction! Furthermore, the Quran permits men and woman to eat together or to help each other (24:61; 3:195; 9:71).

The Quran, for important political reasons, advises to the wives of the Prophet not to mingle with people as they used to (33:32-33). The advice is due to protecting Muhammad and his spouses from the defamation campaign started by the unappreciative crowd (8:30-31; 24:11-20).

Ironically, the followers of *hadith* ignore their own history regarding the condition of women during the time of Muhammad and the four "guide leaders": Aisha, Muhammad's wife, is reported to lead a faction of Muhammad's companions after his departure. How could have Aisha lead men and women, in peace and war, if she did not interact and communicate with them, if she did not have her own identity, if she was imprisoned in her home or in her black veil?

The Quran provides several examples of women being active role models in their societies and interacting with men, such as Abraham's wife (11:69-71; 60:4-6), Muslim women in Madyan with one whom Moses married (28:23-28), the Queen of Sheba who later surrenders to the will of God (27:34:40), and Mary (19:16-30; 3:42-43; 66:11-12). Muslim women were so outspoken that they could engage in debate with Muhammad (58:1), and women pledged allegiance and voted for Muhammad's leadership (60:12).

Therefore, segregating men and women has no Islamic basis; it is a un-Quranic practice imported from misogynistic teachings of St. Paul and the Old Testament.

Segregation in places of worship existed as an innovation among Jews (Exodus 38:8; 1 Samuel 2:22) and reached its zenith with additional condemnation and degradation with St. Paul who condemned women for Adam's sin and silenced them in the public arena.

"Let your women keep silent in the churches, for they are not permitted to speak; but they are to be submissive, as the law also says." (I Corinthians 14: 34)

72

"For a woman is not covered, let her also be shorn. But if it is shameful for a woman to be shorn or shaved, let her be covered. For a man indeed ought not to cover his head, since he is the image and glory of God; but woman is the glory of man. For man is not from woman, but woman from man. Nor was man created for the woman, but woman for the man." (I Corinthians 11:6-9)

"Let a women learn in silence with all submission. And do not permit a woman to teach or to have authority over a man, but to be in silence. For Adam was formed first, then Eve. And Adam was not deceived, but the woman being deceived, fell into transgression. Nevertheless, she will be saved in childbearing if they continue in faith, love and holiness, with self-control." (I Timothy 2:11-15)

The followers of *hadith* and *sunna* adopted the misogynistic teachings of St. Paul, and still many of them clung onto them as their religion, while most of Christendom has meanwhile mutated many times and quietly ignored and abandoned those teachings. In the Christian world, St. Paul's teachings have been partially rejected; women no longer cover their heads, and they no longer stay silent in churches. It is ironic that to-day's Sunnis and Shiites follow more seriously many of the teachings of Judaism and Christianity than the Jews and Christians themselves.

A woman cannot divorce her husband on her own.	Verse 2:228 establishes equal rights to both genders. By associating and even preferring numerous collections of lies and innovations to the Quran, the followers of hadith and sunna denied Muslim women the right to divorce and turned them into slaves of male despotism. Verse 4:19 clearly recognizes the right of women to divorce.
A man can divorce his wife by uttering some words three times.	Sectarian scholars who ignored the Quran and upheld volumes of books of *hadith* and *sunna*, issued laws (*sharia*) allowing the marriage contract to be terminated with several words coming from the husband's mouth. Divorce is an event lasting several months; it is not just an oral declaration of the male spouse. A wife cannot be divorced by announcing, "I divorce you three times." This ease and one-sided divorce created miserable marriages and destroyed many families. Many men, who "divorced" their wives by uttering the magical word *talaq* (divorce) unintentionally or in the heat of anger, desperately looked for a solution (*fatwa*), and found mullahs and religious judges selling *fatwas* to save their marriage! The class that created the problem in the first place became the benefactor of the solution (2:226-230; 9:34-35; 33:49).

	The New Testament takes the opposite direction; divorce is considered a great offense and after the marriage, none should divorce, except for reasons of adultery. Marriage after divorce is committing adultery (Matthew 5:32; 19:9).
Polygamy up to four women is permitted. One can marry four previously unmarried women. Men do not need the consent of his wife(s) for polygamy.	The Quran does not limit the number of women. Though the Quran allows polygamy (4:3), it discourages its practice by requiring certain conditions: a man can marry more than one, only to the widows with children and should try to treat them equally (4:19-20, 127-129). Besides the consent of the former wife(s) is essential since they have the right to object or divorce their husbands. Unfortunately, verse 4:127 has been traditionally mistranslated as to allow marriage with juvenile orphans rather than their mothers. The word *ibkar* in verse 66:5 too has been mistranslated. For discussion on verses, 4:127 and 66:5 please see the notes.

It is an injustice to blame the Quran for advising us to care about the orphaned children and their widowed mothers. These verses primarily advocate the economic interests, psychological and biological needs, and social status of orphans, especially during war. Unfortunately, the enemies of the last prophet who attributed volumes of fabrications to him (6:112-116), have distorted the meaning and purpose of these wonderful divine precepts.

Muhammad's marriages to widows had political and social reasons. Unfortunately, the permission for polygamy was distorted and it became a means to satisfy the libido of the rich and dominant males. The all-male scholars, to achieve their goal used *hadith* and distorted the meaning of verses, such as 4:3-6, 4:127 and 66:5.

Here, we should note that exaggerated examples of polygamy, explicit details of sexual affairs, and stories of incest have been inserted into the Bible. We find much similarity between stories in *hadith* books and those Biblical stories. For instance, 1 King 11:3 claims that Solomon had 700 wives and 300 concubines. Anyone familiar with the current versions of the Bible would know that it contains numerous textual problems, translational errors, and contradictions. Numbers in the Bible are easily subjected to distortion, exaggeration, or simple scribing errors. For instance, we see a big difference in the number of charioteers killed by David. It is 700 according to II Samuel 10:18 and it is 7000 according to I Chronicles 19:18. Note that both numbers are whole numbers and the discrepancy is ten times.

A little attention to the numbers of wives and concubines attributed to Solomon would reveal a deliberate attempt to make |

it as round as possible. 700+300=1000. Total of seven zeroes! Most likely Solomon had a few wives. Contrary to the Quran that exhorts muslims to help widows, the misogynistic Rabbinical teachings inserted to the Old Testament put them in the category of harlots, and finds them unworthy of marriage by the privileged class, priests (Leviticus 21:14).

In terms of male and female circumcision:

Modifying God's creation for religious purposes is considered evil (See 4:119). Obviously, foreskin is not an abnormality in God's creation; it is the norm. Attempting to change such a creation through surgery to attain salvation is superstition (13:8; 25:2; 32:7; 40:64; 64:3; 82:6-9).

Sunni sources report many contradictory stories regarding circumcision. For instance, Ahmed B. Hanbal in his Musnad reports that Usman bin el-As refused to participate in a circumcision ceremony, since he considered circumcision an innovation. The Sunni historian Taberi reports that Caliph Abd al-Aziz rejected the suggestion of his advisors that the people of Khurasan should be circumcised; they were converted to "Islam" to avoid paying extra tax! Bukhari gives contradictory numbers for the year Abraham was allegedly circumcised, 80 versus 120. Bukhari who reports hearsay regarding the circumcision of converts and women, also reports that when Greeks and Abyssinians embraced islam they were not examined at all by Muhammad.

Hadith books, including Bukhari, contain numerous hadiths promoting circumcision including female circumcision, which is a torturous mutilation. However, hadith fabricators somehow forgot to fabricate hadiths about the circumcision of prominent figures during the time of Muhammad. More interestingly, since the practice of circumcision was adopted centuries later, they missed the opportunity to attribute this practice to Muhammad himself. Sunni scholars, therefore, came up with another so-called miracle: Muhammad was born circumcised. This would answer those who wondered about the absence of such an "important" record in the books of hadith and sunna.

The Quran never mentions Abraham practicing circumcision. If indeed Abraham did such a surgery on himself, perhaps he wanted to eliminate some kind of infection, and the blind followers who later idolized him turned his personal deed into a religious ritual. Looking at the history of the Jewish people and their trials and tribulations, it is more likely that this is an invention of Rabbis to mark the endangered race and protect it from extinction. Introducing innovations in religious communities may need some "holy stories" to attribute the innovation to historical idols.

The Quran never mentions the adventures of the Biblical character Samson who had a bizarre hobby of collecting the foreskins of the thousands of people he killed by the jaw of an ass (Old Testament Judges 15:16).

The Old Testament contains hyperbolic exaggerations and bizarre practices. For instance, ignoring the discrepancy in the number of mutilated penises read the following verses from Bible:

> "So David rose and he and his men went and struck down among the Philistines two hundred men, and David came bringing their foreskins and giving them in full number to the king, to form a marriage alliance with the king. In turn Saul gave him Michal, his daughter, as a wife." (1 Samuel 18:27).

> "Then David sent messengers to Ish-Bosheth son of Saul, demanding, 'Give me my wife Michal, whom I engaged to myself for a hundred foreskins of the Philistines" (2 Samuel 3:14).

Using a bundle of foreskins of mutilated genitals of the dead bodies of enemy as the symbolic show of manhood, and literally using them in exchange for a woman is appalling and insulting to women.

In sum:

Men and women, in general, have some differences because of their different biology, and have some different needs and roles. However, some sex roles and inequalities are created by society and exploited by men. In order to let nature and justice prevail over superficiality and injustice, it is imperative to have the following: 1) Equal respect and appreciation of roles regardless of their gender, 2) Equal chance for both males and females to choose their roles freely and responsibly, And 3) Laws to promote and guarantee these two goals.

FP: Thank you Mr. Yuksel. Robert Spencer, go ahead.

SPENCER: All sincere and genuine attempts to reform Islamic theology so as to reinterpret and/or remove violent and supremacist elements are to be welcomed. They are to be welcomed all the more wholeheartedly when they keep a consistent focus on the purpose that all such efforts have or should have in the first place: to convince Muslims that jihad violence and Islamic supremacism are not "pure" and "true" Islam, as the jihadists themselves claim, but that there is another way to live out their faith that is consistent and authentic on its own terms.

Edip Yuksel, when he says that "none of these innovations can be found in the Quran, the only book delivered by Muhammad" and that the Hadith are "hearsay narrations falsely attributed to Muhammad and his companions" that "contradict" the Qur'an, argues for the proposition that the Qur'an alone holds authority for Muslims, and that the Hadith is to be dismissed out of hand. This view is being espoused by an increasing number of reform-minded Muslim thinkers in the West, and there are certainly many immediate apparent merits to this view – stoning for adultery, the death penalty for apostasy and the compulsory covering of all but a woman's face and hands all come from the Hadith, not the Qur'an. A Qur'an-only Islam gives the hope that such practices, and others that have no Qur'anic foundation (although stoning is a bit of a problematic case, since in one Hadith Umar informs us that it was originally in the Qur'an, and should be considered to be from Allah, and some Muslim exegetes see the death penalty for apostasy in Qur'an 2:217 and/or 4:89) could easily be jettisoned.

As comforting as this may be to non-Muslims and Western-minded Muslims, the fundamental question for this and for all genuine reform efforts is: what chance do they have to become widely accepted among Muslims? One way to evaluate this is to examine the obstacles it will face in gaining such acceptance. The chief obstacle that Yuksel's blanket dismissal of the Hadith will encounter among Muslims is the fact that acceptance of ahadith that have been deemed authentic by traditional Islamic authorities is very deeply rooted within Islamic tradition. All Muslims agree that some ahadith were fabricated, but few would agree with Yuksel that all of them are. While he may be able to make a case for this on strict historical grounds, since in reality the historical foundations even for the ahadith that Muslims deem authentic are quite shaky, he will have a harder time compelling Muslims to accept such historical judgments even against ahadith that have been deemed authentic by authoritative Islamic scholars such as the Imams Bukhari and Muslim.

In fact, the acceptance of the Hadith is itself grounded in the Qur'an, in its exhortations to Muslims to "obey Allah and his Messenger" – that is, Muhammad (3:32; 3:132; 4:13; 4:59; 4:69; 5:92; 8:1; 8:20; 8:46; 9:71; 24:52; 24:54; 33:33; 47:33; 49:14; 58:13; 64:12; cf. also 24:47; 24:51; 24:56). Qur'an 4:80 even says, "He who obeys the Messenger, obeys Allah." It is Muhammad who "commands them what is just and forbids them what is evil; he allows them as lawful what is good (and pure) and prohibits them from what is bad (and impure)" (Qur'an 7:157).

How can Muslims obey such emphatic and oft-repeated commands after the death of Muhammad? The traditional answer to this question has been the Hadith. Muslims are told to follow what Muhammad commands, and only in the hadith can those commands be discovered. The Tafsir Anwar ul-Bayan, for example, articulates this traditional view in sharp terms: "Those who reject the Ahadith do not accept the position that Allah accorded to the Holy Prophet... Those who reject the Ahadith seem to object to Allah for conferring this position to the Holy Prophet...In this way, they actually reject the Qur'an since verses like the one above [7:157] clearly reveal that the duty of the Holy Prophet was much more than that of a mere postman." In other words, Muhammad is more than just Allah's messenger: he is, according to Qur'an 33:21, uswa hasana, an excellent example of conduct, the supreme model for emulation. Muqtedar Khan of the Center for the Study of Islam and Democracy explains:

No religious leader has as much influence on his followers as does Muhammad (Peace be upon him) the last Prophet of Islam….And Muhammad as the final messenger of God enjoys preeminence when it comes to revelation – the Qur'an – and traditions. So much so that the words, deeds and silences (that which he saw and did not forbid) of Muhammad became an independent source of Islamic law. Muslims, as a part of religious observance, not only obey, but also seek to emulate and imitate their Prophet in every aspect of life. Thus Muhammad is the medium as well as a source of the divine law. ("The Legacy of Prophet Muhammad and the Issues of Pedophilia and Polygamy," Ijtihad, June 9, 2003.)

This is a traditional and mainstream Islamic understanding. I wish Mr. Yuksel well in its efforts against it, but caution non-Muslim observers against assuming that he will achieve easy or widespread acceptance for his views among Muslims.

Unfortunately, there are also some problems with his analysis on strict Qur'anic grounds alone – problems that will also hinder the acceptance of his reform efforts among Muslims. Mr. Yuksel asserts, for instance, that Qur'an 49:13 "unequivocally rejects sexism and racism, and reminds us that neither man nor female, neither this race nor that race is superior over the other." Qur'an 49:13 says, "O people, We created you from a male and female, and We made you into nations and tribes, that you may know one another." While it would be comforting indeed to see this as a blanket rejection of the male supremacism and commodification of women that mars so much of Islamic tradition and culture, on its face it is nothing of the sort. It merely states that Allah has created people from a male and a female, and says nothing that contradicts Qur'an 4:34 -- which, interestingly enough, in his lengthy exposition Mr. Yuksel does not quote at all. Yet besides its notorious command to beat disobedient women, this verse says: "Men are in charge of women, because Allah hath made the one of them to excel the other…" That doesn't sound like an unequivocal rejection of sexism to me. Nor does the condition of women in the Islamic world in general, expecially where Islamic law is rigorously applied, testify to a widespread understanding that Qur'an 49:13 has established equality between the sexes. Here again, I wish Mr. Yuksel well with his reform efforts, but I suspect that all too many traditional Muslims will quote 4:34 against his views. I look forward to his explanation of how he might respond to them.

Similarly, in his refutation of the proposition that "women are mentally and spiritually inferior to men," Mr. Yuksel never mentions Qur'an 2:282, which stipulates that for testimony," if there are not two men, then a man and two women, such as ye choose, for witnesses, so that if one of them errs, the other

78

can remind her." It was on the basis of this verse that, according to a hadith, Muhammad declared that women are "deficient in intelligence and religion." When a woman challenged him on this statement, he replied: "Is not the evidence of two women equal to the witness of one man? This is the deficiency in her intelligence." Mr. Yuksel may deny the hadith, but the Qur'an verse upon which it rests remains.

In conclusion, I find it unfortunate that Mr. Yuksel so often has recourse to the Bible in his attempts to show the Qur'an and Islam to stand for enlightenment and equality. For whatever the actual barbarity of any of the Biblical verses he quotes may be, the unpleasant fact remains that it is not Jews and Christians, but Muslims, who today are applying teachings that render normative "bizarre practices." Judaism and Christianity have developed interpretative traditions that mitigate the literal understanding of such material, while Islam has not – and no religious reform has ever succeeded when the reformers simply ignored uncomfortable material, as Mr. Yuksel has here so far, rather than confronting it.

HAIDON: The Center's video is a sickening reminder of the nature and foundations of what we are facing. The Muslim account of Muhammad (via the Hadith and Sirah) is replete with references to Muhammad's alleged appetite for tyranny, oppression and violence of the worst kind. Both Mr. Spencer and Mr. Warner's work painstakingly sets out this account in clear terms. I am deeply troubled by much of the Muslim historical account of Muhammad as enshrined in the Hadith and Sirah. While in many instances these sources portray the Prophet as a moral and upright, other instances portray a sinister picture of violence against women, and non-Muslims, and in some cases sexual violence.

Similar to Mr.Yuksel, I advocate a Qur'anist approach to Islam which seeks to marginalise/de-emphasise the so called Sunnah of the Prophet Muhammad towards greater deference to the Qur'an which, in Islam, is divine revelation (whereas the latter sources are not). Although there are some differences in our approaches. I will allow Mr Yuksel to respond to Mr. Spencer's observations about the rationalist movement to de-emphasise the Sunnah. I will say however that there is a growing Qur'an based rationalist movement that is "walking the talk" so to speak by developing intellectual and theological responses to Islam's underlying problems which address and refute Mr. Spencer's concerns. Mr. Yuksel's translation, as well as the work of Ahmed Subhy Mansour, Caner Taslaman and the scholars at www.free-minds.org and www.quranists.org provides a framework for addressing the key issues.

In reality, however, we cannot ignore the entire written account of Muhammad, whether it be enshrined in the Quran, Hadith or Sirah. I would like nothing more than to be able to inform my co-panelists that I have every confidence that Muhammad did not commit any of the atrocities attributed to him. However I think from a practical perspective it is a difficult case indeed to sweepingly disregard the historical account of Muhammad or to categorically say that it is false. It also poses strategic problems. Nonetheless, whether or not the Muslim account of Muhammad is fictional or fact, the reality is that Muslims rely on that history regardless.

FP: Mr. Haidon, if you don't mind me following up with you for a moment in terms of your own faith. If it is a difficult case to sweepingly disregard the historical account of Muhammad or to categorically say that it is false, as you say, how and why do you remain a Muslim? I don't mean this in an aggressive or accusatory way, but more in a hope to open up the discussion and to crystallize, perhaps, what it means to be a Muslim for many Muslims who are ready to be honest about the truth regarding their own Prophet.

HAIDON:

> "The Messenger said 'My Lord, my people have deserted this Qur'an'" (Qur'an, 25:30)

> "Shall I seek other than Allah as a source of law, when He has revealed this book fully detailed? ....The word of your Lord is complete , in truth and justice. Nothing shall abrogate His words; He is the hearer, the omniscient. Yet, if you obey the majority of people, they will take you away from the path of The God. That is because they follow conjecture, and they fail to think." (Qur'an, 6:114-116)

> "And We have sent down the Book to you as a clarity for everything, and a guidance and mercy and good news for those who Submit." (Qur'an 16:89)

> "Allah has revealed herein the best Hadith [the Qur'an]; a book that is consistent, and points out both ways. The skins of those who reverence their Lord cringe there from, then their skins and their hearts soften up for Allah's message. Such is Allah's guidance; He bestows it upon whoever wills. As for those sent astray by Allah , nothing can guide them." (Qur'an39:23)

In summary, I am Muslim and will remain Muslim because I believe in the primacy of the Qur'an and its wisdom. I believe that the Qur'an is complete, and provides comprehensive guidance to Muslims when interpreted contextually. I believe in the principle in the Qur'an that all Prophets are equal, and that Muslims must not distinguish between them. I believe that to blindly follow the Sunnah and place it in close parity to the Qur'an is a form of shirk.

To be clear, I believe that many of the Hadith (and aspects of the Sirah) are fabrications developed in order to help the powers that be (Ummayids and Abbasids) legitimise their power to control Islamic jurisprudence. As a rationalist, I believe that the isnad hadith verification methodology is flawed, and that the real test of whether an ahadith should become a recognised source of Islamic jurisprudence is its overall consistency with the Qur'an. Any Ahadith must be interpreted and understand in light of the Qur'an, not the other way around. The Qur'an is the Criterion in Islam and has ultimate primacy.

To reject all ahadith as false is also impractical because there are a number of early hadith which support our position that the Prophet Muhammad was vehemently opposed to recording his traditions out of a credible fear that they would become, in the eyes of Muslims, equal to the Qur'an ("The prophet said:'Do not write anything from me EXCEPT QURAN. Whoever wrote, must destroy it" (Muslim, Zuhd 72; Hanbel3/12,21,39)) . There is also historical evidence to suggest that the early, so called "rightly guided" Caliphs were opposed to the codification of Hadith for the same reasons. The impact of Muslim adherence to Hadith and Sunnah, as imposed by Islamic rule, has been devastating and has lead to the veneration and de-ification of Muhammad. Ironically, the practice of traditional Islam has almost become a form of shirk. It also contravenes the principle of the equality of the prophets as enshrined in 2:285 and 4:152. However, while I cannot reject the authenticity of all Hadith, I reject their place of authority in the realm of Islamic jurisprudence, because a significant portion of the Hadith are prima facie inconsistent with the Qur'an.

Mr. Spencer has correctly framed the traditional Sunni justification/arguments arguments for the legitimacy of the "Sunnah" as a primary source of Islam. These verses, along with others, have been the primary basis of the Muslim reliance on Sunnah. However, to a rationalist, this view is fatally flawed. I will defer to Mr. Yuksel to provide a more coherent explanation, as his marvelous Translation and accompanying Manifesto for Islamic reform does. Briefly, however the Qur'an is complete and is the culmination of Allah's commandments and injunctions. Mr. Spencer writes: "Muslims are told to follow what Muhammad commands, and only in the hadith can those commands be discovered". This is where we differ: Muhammad's commands and injunctions are derived from the Qur'an. Therefore his commands and injunctions must be consistent with the Qur'an. This is the essential principle which undermines the traditional Sunni view. Again, I will leave it to Mr. Yuksel to provide a more cogent articulation.

I understand where Mr. Spencer is coming from and have every respect for him. However, I am slightly surprised by Mr. Spencer's tone towards Mr. Yuksel. Mr. Spencer has, for many years exhorted Muslims to provide a practical and sustainable framework for reform. Well, its here. I would hope that Mr. Spencer would, instead of merely citing/parroting the traditional Sunni critique of the Qur'anist/rationalist movement, view it for what it is; a comprehensive, rational and practical framework for reforming Islam. That does not mean he should not challenge it of course, but I would hope that he will closely evaluate all sides of the argument.

81

Mr. Yuksel, nor anyone in the Qur'anist movement said that convincing Muslims will be easy. This is not because any lack of soundness in the Qur'anist approach, but again because the approach challenges Islamist power and places the powers and freedoms into the hands of individuals. Mr.Yuksel or Qur'anists cannot be faulted for not yet being able to convince the massive swarms of Muslims who believe in traditional approaches. Efforts are being made however, that go beyond rhetoric and double-speak. Mr. Yuksel's work and the work of others in the Qur'anist movement illustrate this. The rationalist movement however, as Mr. Spencer points out, represents a minority of Muslims. Much more work will need to be done to challenge the status quo. Non-Muslims, who are legitimate stake-holders to Islamic reform, should not be diluted that full scale reform will happen any time soon. However progress is being made.

WARNER: I do not find the reform ideas here to be either comprehensive or rational. All of my comments are from the standpoint of the unbeliever, the kafir. I have no interest, whatsoever, in religious Islam. My interest is only in how Islam treats the "other" or political Islam.

The amount of the material in the Trilogy (Koran, Sira and Hadith) about the kafir is considerable. About 67% of the Koran written in Mecca is about the kafir, 51% of the Koran written in Medina is about the kafir. About 75% of the text in Ishaq's Sira is about the kafir and 20% of the Hadith (Bukhari) is about the kafir.

Every mention about the kafir is negative. "Kafir" is usually translated as unbeliever, but this is wrong. The word "unbeliever" is neutral. The Koran defines the kafir by its usage and says that the kafir can be killed, hated, punished, raped, mocked, enslaved, plotted against, beheaded, tortured, insulted, condemned, stolen from, deceived, kidnapped, humiliated and on and on. The Hadith and Sira follow in the same vein. There is no word in the English language that has the negativity of the word kafir.

As a measure of the negativity it is interesting to observe the Jew hatred. The hatred of Jews accounts for 10.6% of the text written in Medina . As a comparison, 6.8% of the text in Mein Kamph is about Jew hatred.

Even Hell is political. Only 6% of the people in Hell are there for moral failings—theft, lying and so on. The majority, 94%, of the people in Hell are tortured for the simple reason of not believing Mohammed. That is a political and intellectual disagreement, not a moral failing. Allah's Hell is a political prison for kafirs.

So when the gentlemen in this symposium say they reject the violence and hatred against the kafir found in the Sira and Hadith, I applaud them. However, they are wrong about the reason to reject it. They argue that Mohammed was a wonderful man and did not do those horrible things in the Sira and Hadith. We have a way to measure the truthfulness of the Sira and Hadith regarding Mohammed.

Mohammed left four very close friends and students, the "rightly guided" caliphs. No men were as intimate with Mohammed and his teachings as these men. They carried his teaching forward into history where their actions are recorded. Abu Bakr killed thousands of Muslims who wanted to leave Islam, apostates. Umar brought jihad to the kafir world and killed, raped, stole and tortured the Christians, Jews and Zoroastrians of the Middle East . Uthman was assassinated and Ali died in an Islamic civil war. Any coach will tell you—you play like you train. The rightly guided caliphs practiced what they were taught by the master—jihad and kafir hatred.

These men lived their lives just as Mohammed taught them. The teachings are portrayed in the Sira and Hadith. They did what we would expect. Now, if Mohammed was a wonderful man, why did his best students annihilate the kafir civilization? We do not have to speculate about the "real" Mohammed, he is found in the Sira and Hadith. History proves this.

The second reason to accept the Sira and Hadith as a good portrayal of Mohammed (I am not referring to the excessive detail in them, an obvious story-telling technique) is the integrity of the Trilogy. The Koran, Sira and Hadith are a seamless fabric of ideas. The Koran is the warp and the Sira/Hadith is the weft. All three of them are based upon submission and duality. They relentlessly advance the dominance of Islam over all kafirs. They form an integral whole, a unified ideology.

Having said that, I want to help with Islamic reform. If we decide to divide the Sunna into good Sunna and bad Sunna, how do we do it? We need a rational method, not whim, taste or like/dislike.

If we take an overview of the Trilogy, we find two organizing principles— submission and duality. The Koran is a text devoted to submission and duality. Submission is straightforward enough, but duality is not as familiar. Part of the Koran's dual nature is seen in the Meccan Koran and the Medinan Koran. They contain contradictory principles.

The Koran gives a method to resolve the contradictions—abrogation. But since every word in the Koran is from the perfect god, both sides of the contradiction are true. It is just that the later verse is better than the earlier verse, but the earlier verse is still true.

This establishes an Islamic dualistic logic, which can accept both sides of a contradiction as being true.

As an example of this dualism, the nice Muslim practices the Meccan (early) Koran. Osama bin Laden practices the Medinan (later) Koran. Both are "good" and "real" Muslims, but Osama is the better Muslim.

The dualism is further seen in Islamic ethics. A Muslim must not kill another Muslim; a kafir may be killed, or not. A Muslim must not lie to another Muslim, but a kafir may be deceived, or not. A Muslim is not a friend to the kafir. So Islam has one set of rules for Muslims and another set of rules for the kafir. This is dualistic ethics.

As an aside, the word "kafir" is pure dualism.

There is no universal view of humanity in the Trilogy. It always has a dualistic view of Muslim and kafir. The closest thing to a universal view is that all of humanity must submit to Islam.

Dualism and political submission is the divide between Islam and the rest of the world. There is one principle which will heal this division. All of the world cultures, except Islam, have the ethical principle of the Golden Rule: treat others as you would be treated. The Golden Rule establishes a unitary ethical system. All people are treated the same. Our civilization includes this unitary ethic. Women's rights, ending slavery, and the Declaration of Independence, were based upon this unitary ethic. We fall short of this unitary ethic on a daily basis, but we use it as a principle to judge and correct our actions. The Golden Rule is a goal and operating principle, not always an achievement.

Unitary ethics is a rational basis for reforming political Islam and its dualistic ethics. A comprehensive reform of Islamic politics must reform the Koran as well as the Sira and Hadith.

What happens if we apply the Golden Rule to the Trilogy? All of the hurtful, negative and harmful words about the kafir disappear. The Sira is reduced in size by 75%. Only 20% of the Hadith vanishes. The Koran is reduced by 61%. But that is not the only reduction. The Golden Rule will also eliminate the prejudice about women and this will reduce the texts even more.

The way to reform Islam is to add the missing ethical principle—the Golden Rule.

But here is the problem. Not even Mohammed could make the religion of Islam a success. He preached the religion of Islam for 13 years and garnered only 150 Muslims. But when he turned to politics and jihad in Medina , he conquered all of Arabia in his last 9 years. He averaged an event of violence every 7 weeks for those 9 years, not including assassinations and executions. Political violence against the kafir succeeded, when preaching failed. Dualism and political submission worked.

My point is: why would Islam drop what has brought it success? Political submission and duality work for political Islam. Everyone fears political Islam and does what it demands due to its doctrine of political submission and duality. No one quits a winning strategy for a losing strategy. The Center for the Study of Political Islam could easily produce a Koran, Sira and Hadith based upon the Golden Rule. It would be a thin book, but who would accept it?

[A technical note: the percentages of text used here are not based upon counting verses. Verses limit an idea to one sentence. What you want to measure is ideas, not verses. See A Simple Koran for a detailed discussion.]

YUKSEL: Our effort is to reform our minds, attitude, actions and culture according to monotheistic precepts, which require rational approach. We know that only truth will set us free. Thus, the Islamic Reform movement will only contribute in making this world better for all, including, Christians, Jews and Muslims; Atheists and Polytheists; Edip and Haidon; Spencer and Warner.

I find Spencer's and Warner's understanding of the Quran heavily distorted by the teachings of Sunni or Shiite sects. I do not blame them for this. Had they studied the Quran without the distortion of Hadith, Sunna and sectarian fatwas, they would find out that the address of their criticism and concern is wrong. I invite them to study our exposition of sectarian distortions. I invite them to reflect on the translation of those verses and our arguments in the Quran: a Reformist Translation.

If Spencer and Warner learn the historic distortions committed centuries after the revelation of the Quran, they might regret for attacking Prophet Muhammad and his message, the Quran, because of those who have deserted and betrayed it (Quran 25:30; 10:100; 6:22-24; 6:112-113; 45:6-11; 31:6-7; 68:35-38). Perhaps, one day they will hear the message of the Quran without the backward background noises and will submit themselves to God alone.

I invite both to participate in our next conference on celebration of heresy and reform in Atlanta this spring. We will, God willing, have open debates on these and other controversial issues. We invite those who wish to participate to come to the Celebration of Heresy Conference: Critical Thinking for Islamic Reform, 28-30 March 2008, Atlanta, Atlanta Perimeter Holiday Inn. Join our low activity emailing list at http://groups.google.com/group/19org or visit http://www.hereticmuslims.com and www.19.org for information.

Spencer is right that majority of Sunni and Shiite masses are not receptive to the message at this point. But, the situation is changing dramatically. When I first rejected Hadith and Sunna in 1986 and invited Turkish Muslims to reform themselves by following the Quran alone, I was a young author with a few supporters. Then, I declared jihad against powerful Sunni and Islamist organizations, foundations, sects and orders with millions of followers and billions of dollars.

After about thirty years, dozens of books, thousands of emails and forum discussions, hundreds of articles, and numerous live TV debates, now there are tens of thousands of Turkish people accepting this message. The message is now receiving the attention of especially the educated Muslims all around the world.

There are threshold points in history of nations and the world; I do believe that the time has come. Muslims are getting ready for extraordinary social and political change. Despite the obstacles we encounter, from Christianists to Islamists, we are witnessing a global interest in the message of Quran alone, especially among the youth. You will hear much better and surprising news within a few years, God willing.

FP: Mr. Yuksel, just as follow-up, you say that perhaps one day Mr. Spencer and Mr. Warner "will hear the message of the Quran without the backward background noises and will submit themselves to God alone." Just wondering, how is it that you presume that they do not have, in their own way, a belief in and relationship with God? There is the implication here that you somehow have access to the truth, or some kind of relationship with a true God that they do not have. Is this by any chance connected to the fact that you are Muslim and they are not? Are you implying here that this is a bad thing for them and that they must, in the end, come over to your religion? How come they haven't made any such comments in your direction? And what does this signify?

And if you are here to argue that the true Islam is one that does not and should not see its believers as superior to non-Muslims and that non–Muslims should not be subjugated, why do you make comments here suggesting the superiority of your beliefs and the inferiority of the beliefs of others? Surely you are aware that this in the fertile ground on which Islamism and Islamic jihad finds its inspiration? Please explain why you assume that Spencer and Warner somehow need to start believing what you believe.

I am also interested about you mentioning "Christianists" and Islamists in the same sentence and in the same context -- as if there is some kind of moral equivalency between the two (and I am still not completely certain what exactly a "Christianist" is, but that is beside the point). There have been more than 10,000 deadly terrorist attacks carried about Islamist jihadists worldwide since 9/11. How many have the "Christianists" perpetrated? Would you yourself rather be found stuck in an environment filled with Islamists or "Christianists"? In which group do you think you would remain alive for more than five minutes? How many "Christianists" have blown themselves up lately, in a crowd of innocent people, in their effort to get to paradise? How many "Christinaists" kill non-Christians and do so by pointing to the New Testament verses to legitimize their acts? Who are these Christianists and what verses are they pointing to? Why would you even make a moral equivalency in this regard, Mr. Yukself, when you know very well that Islamism is the totalitarian and terrorist ideology that poses a monstrous threat to the world today and that "Christianists" are completely benign in comparison?

YUKSEL: I will attempt to clarify my statement. I meant what I said. Either Muhammad was one of God's messengers or he was an impostor. Since, I am convinced because of substantial evidence that the Quran is the word of God; it follows that I should consider those who have devoted themselves to distort the truth about the Quran and its messenger, to be on the wrong path. Unlike Sunni or Shiite Muslims, I support their freedom to choose any path they wish and express their faith or conviction without fear. I will side with them against any group that would try to deprive them from their God-given right to freedom.

So, if these gentlemen have the right to depict Muhammad to be an evil guy and his supporters being as evil or duped, then I should also have the right to expose their so-called scholarly work, which is merely based on hearsay books and distortion and contortion of the Quranic verses by the followers of those hearsay stories. For instance, brother Spencer generously uses the hearsay stories fabricated centuries after Muhammad's life to assassinate Muhammad's character, while he knows well that according to the same sources which he trusts, Muhammad reportedly split the Moon causing half of it to fall in Ali's backyard, or Muhammad reportedly made trees walk, Muhammad ascended to the seventh heaven with his body, and many other stories. Scholarly integrity requires consistency and honesty in using sources in evaluating a historic personality. But, your gentlemen pick and choose from those books as they wish. They take advantage of the crazy noises created by Jingoists, Crusaders and Jihadists, and hideously try to justify a bloody imperial Crusade with its resurrected Spanish Inquisition mentality against Muslims. I consider the work of these gentlemen a dishonest or ignorant attack against one of the most progressive and peaceful leaders in human history.[3] I would like to repeat my invitation to Spencer to discuss his book about Muhammad at the Celebration of Heresy Conference, which we are organizing in Atlanta by the end of March. See: www.hereticmuslims.com.

---

[3]   [In less than two years after we debated in a symposium, Robert Spencer came up with a book titled *The Politically Incorrect Guide to Islam (and the Crusades)*, in which he mixes truth with falsehood and engages in deliberate distortions. In order to promote the wars and tortures of the ZC-MIC alliance, Spencer uses hideous and heinous tactics. Here is one of the blogger's reaction to the chapter entitled *Islam oppresses women*: "Of course the reality is that Spencer has spoken a half-truth, which is what he normally does. Spencer's modus operandi is simple: he presents the absolutely most conservative view as if it is not only the most authoritative one but also the only one. He then compares this ultraconservative Islamic opinion with the most liberal Judeo-Christian view, and then says aha!" *Robert Spencer Rapes the Truth, Part 1: Does Sharia Reject the Testimony of a Rape Victim?,December 19, 2009, by Danios]*

As for the charge of superiority, I am not morally relativist nor do I find subjectivist epistemology to be accurate. I do argue that in the court of reason and evidence, Muslims (not Sunnis or Shiites, but anyone, including Christians and Jews, whoever peacefully submit themselves to the laws and message of their Creator) are indeed superior over those who are willing to discard rational thoughts or confuse fake evidences from the genuine ones to join a religious or political bandwagon. People do not need to call themselves Muslim to become muslims (with miniscule). Ironically, most of those who call themselves Muslims are not muslims according to the Quran. The flowers, insects, trees, animals, planets, stars, galaxies, everything in the universe, with the exception of human mind, are entirely muslim, since they follow God's law without deviation. So, superiority is only through righteous acts that follow right thoughts and ideas (See Quran: 49:13).

Arguing for the superiority of some maxims or actions does not necessarily lead to suppression or oppression of others. Does your belief in democracy being superior over monarchy transform you into a democratic bully? (Don't ask me the Thrasymachusian bullies exploiting the good name of democracy). Does a Christian's belief in "salvation-through-Jesus-only" necessarily turn them to torturers and bloody Crusaders? I do not believe so. I would like, however, to remind the reader that I do not glorify "faith" as it is used by adherents of religions. We, the monotheist reformists, have a problem with even the definition and implication of the word "religion." We consider faith without reason to be fakery or delusion. Appreciation and acknowledgement of God starts with questioning everything, and after rejection of all gods and religious power-brokers, including nationalistic and religious dogmas, we can reach the Truth or God.

As for morally equivocating Christianists to Islamists, you are right. They are not morally equal. The line between morality and immorality is not always categorically clear and sometimes there are grey areas. Unfortunately, the language of propaganda ignores the many important subtle details. The ethical question is a bit deeper than the propaganda language of both parties. For instance, none questions the immorality of killing innocent people for the fun of it? This is surely reprehensible. But, what about killing innocent people to save the lives of many more innocent people, as it is used for justification of the nuking the two Japanese cities and killing hundreds of thousands of civilians and injuring millions? Is this as reprehensible as the killing of a few innocent people for fun? Perhaps, not. What about killing innocent people by sacrificing one's life in order to fight against a fascist invasion and oppression? What about killing innocent people while targeting terrorists or aggressor invaders? What about not directly killing but financially or politically supporting the terrorists or the military aggression of a government? What about voting for a fascist or warmongering government and using the children of the poor people to kill the poor children of other nations for unjustified wars? What about calling for jihad against imperialists and their supporters, or calling for pre-emptive strikes against jihadists and their supporters?

You are right, that Muslims have unfortunately adhered to many hearsay fabrications that promote intolerance, violence and aggression. It is also true the New Testament, (of course not the Old one) promotes a peaceful message that usually promotes the Golden Rule. But, despite those books we have seen mixed results. There have been periods in history where the followers of Hadith and Sunna have been more peaceful and tolerant than the followers of the Gospels, and vice versa. So, we cannot just focus on the theology alone to address the problem properly. There are more than one reason for the level of violence and anger among Muslims at our time, and without honest diagnosis we will never be able to prescribe a proper set of solutions. Weeks after the 9/11 attack, I remember Dan Rather telling David Letterman with a straight face that the reason they attacked us was because "we were number one!" Dan knew better than that, but he wanted to please the crowd and unfortunately misled them. When intellectuals play for the tribune, the truth becomes the first victim and the price can be very costly. The Islamist terrorism has ecology, and the imperialist policy of the western world is an important contributor and incubator in its emergence and continuation. Just knowing that bin Laden was trained by the CIA and was once our ally against Russians, should inspire a wider angle and better vision to address this problem.

As for the 10,000 fatal terrorist acts… My ethical standard does not discriminate between on life or thousands of lives. Each human life is as important as the entire humanity. If we do not respect a single life then why should we respect the second one? So, a single terrorist act should be enough for us to seek justice on behalf of the victim. You should also know that I do not discriminate between gang terrorists and state terrorists, my dear friend. Both are evil. If gangs of terrorists are danger for humanity, just look at Iraq alone. More than a million Iraqi lost their lives[4]; millions were injured and became orphans, because of the unjustified war waged by the politicians elected by the votes of "peaceful" Christians against a country led by their former monster. I know you will try to blame the victim by telling us about Sunni and Shiite division in Iraq, but if a bigger bully invaded the USA and employed provocations and covert operations to win a victory over the American freedom fighters, that super-duper bully could have easily created multiple civil wars in the USA by exploiting her ethnic and religious fault lines. In short, I condemn every terrorist act, regardless of their religious affiliation, nationality, and color.

---

[4]   [As of October 2009, the Iraqi Death Estimator at www.justforeignpolicy.org/iraq estimates 1,339,771 Iraqi deaths due to U.S.-led invasion, which delibaretly started civil war to crush the uprising against the brutal invasion, massacres, and torture.]

In my youth, I did not lick the boots of Turkish generals nor kissed the beards of the Muslim clergymen, which led me to find freedom in the land of free that is established not by Evangelical Christians, Sunni or Zionist fanatics, but by open-minded rational humans, such as Thomas Jefferson or Ben Franklin, whom I consider Muslims (submitters to God/Truth in peace) or very close to that description according to the definition of the Quran. Any person who believes in one God, engages in good deeds, and acknowledges the Day of Judgment is a Muslim (Quran 2:62). Thus, I will not abandon my spirit of dissent against criminal politicians and corporations in my second country either. We need to save the planet from the crazy battle between the "coalition of evil" between religious zealots, jingoist nationalists and big corporations.

FP: I find it interesting that the forces that you demonize are the forces that you have sought refuge in to save your life. And due to the protection and freedom they grant you, you can say anything you want – even condemning them -- knowing nothing will happen to you. . . .not a luxury you could afford living anywhere where Islam has taken control of the state.

Needless to say, there is such a thing a thing as a just war, and the war against Fascism and Communism was just, just as our war is today against Islamo-Fascism. There is no morally equivalency between those who want to impose tyranny through terror and those free states who must engage in war to defend liberty. Muslims who engage in jihad can find the legitimacy to do so in the Quran. Christians who engage in any violence are betraying Christianity's teachings and can find no legitimacy to do what they do in the New Testament.

SPENCER: Thomas Haidon says,

> "I am slightly surprised by Mr. Spencer's tone towards Mr. Yuksel. Mr. Spencer has, for many years exhorted Muslims to provide a practical and sustainable framework for reform. Well, its here. I would hope that Mr. Spencer would, instead of merely citing/parroting the traditional Sunni critique of the Qur'anist/rationalist movement, view it for what it is; a comprehensive, rational and practical framework for reforming Islam. That does not mean he should not challenge it of course, but I would hope that he will closely evaluate all sides of the argument."

I am slightly surprised in turn that Mr. Haidon, for whom I have great respect, would take issue with my "tone" after I repeatedly wished Mr. Yuksel well with his reform efforts, and explained that I was only raising questions about them because if attempts at Islamic reform fail to be internally consistent and coherently argued on Islamic grounds, they will fail to convince any Muslims of their truth – which is the point of them in the first place. If Mr. Yuksel's version of Qur'an-alone Islam is neither traditional nor mainstream, nor even consistent on Qur'anic grounds, as I have shown above, then it is important for non-Muslims to be aware of that, so that they can realistically assess its prospects for success.

As such I make no apologies for pointing it out. My position on this has always been consistent. In May 2005, after another self-proclaimed reformer, Khaleel Mohammed, made a similarly flimsy presentation amid similar false charges about my own work, I wrote:

> "I am all for supporting moderate Muslims, but I am not for getting my intellectual pocket picked. I don't care one bit about how good any given moderate speaker can make non-Muslims feel about Islam and the war on terror. All I care about is: can this moderate's arguments from the Qur'an and Sunnah convince jihad terrorists to stop waging war in the name of Islam? If it looks as if they can, I will support the moderate wholeheartedly. But if it looks as if they can't, then I wish someone would tell me why such moderates are even worth supporting."

I stand by those words.

Mr. Yuksel, meanwhile, claims that if Mr. Warner and I had "studied the Quran without the distortion of Hadith, Sunna and sectarian fatwas, they would find out that the address of their criticism and concern is wrong." While that may be true, he ignores the fact that hundreds of millions of Muslims have likewise studied the Qur'an as "distorted" by the Hadith and Sunnah, and they will think of the same Qur'an verses that contradict his Qur'anic arguments that I referred to above. It is unfortunate, but revealing, that he did not deal with those points at all, thus leaving the weaknesses of his presentation exposed and making Mr. Haidon's objection to my "tone" even more bizarre, as if I should simply be abjectly and uncritically grateful for any attempt to reform Islam, no matter how much of a farrago or how tissue-paper-thin it may be.

Mr. Yuksel also complains that Mr. Warner and I "depict Muhammad to be an evil guy and his supporters being as evil or duped" in my "so-called scholarly work, which is merely based on hearsay books and distortion and contortion of the Quranic verses by the followers of those hearsay stories." One who is not reading closely may miss the fact that the "followers of those hearsay stories" constitute the great majority of Muslims around the world today, and that in my biography of Muhammad I was merely depicting Muhammad as he appears in texts written by pious Muslims and accepted by most Muslims as authoritative. But for Mr. Yuksel, "scholarly integrity requires consistency and honesty in using sources in evaluating a historic personality," and Mr. Warner and I have fallen short of this, daring to "pick and choose from those books as [we] wish."

Of course, if a book is not simply going to reproduce another book in its entirety, some picking and choosing is necessary, and Mr. Yuksel unfortunately provides no examples of what he finds so objectionable about the choices I made in my book, except that I rely on early Islamic traditions about Muhammad – traditions that he rejects. But for this also I make no apologies, as I was trying simply to illuminate some elements of mainstream Islamic belief about

Muhammad as he is depicted in mainstream Islamic texts. If this makes Mr. Yuksel regard me as irresponsible and unscholarly, I trust he has the same view of the multitudes of Muslim biographers of Muhammad, such as Muhammad Husayn Haykal, Safi ur-Rahman al-Mubarakpuri, and Yahiya Emerick, as well as non-Muslim Islamic apologists such as Karen Armstrong, who rely on the same sources.

But in this Mr. Yuksel accuses me of dark motives, saying that Mr. Warner and I "take advantage of the crazy noises created by Jingoists, Crusaders and Jihadists, and hideously try to justify a bloody imperial Crusade with its resurrected Spanish Inquisition mentality against Muslims" and says that he considers "the work of these gentlemen a dishonest or ignorant attack against one of the most progressive and peaceful leaders in human history." Now we have entered the realm of fantasy, since in reality I have repeatedly called on Islamic spokesmen to acknowledge the elements of Islam that jihadists use to recruit terrorists, repudiate those elements, and formulate some way to combat the jihadist challenge within Muslim communities, so that non-Muslims and Muslims may coexist as equals on an indefinite basis. That Mr. Yuksel would take this as heralding some "bloody imperial Crusade" casts yet more doubt upon the seriousness of his reform efforts. In that light, while I am grateful for his invitation to attend his Atlanta Conference, and am always open to discussion and debate (and am quite prepared to defend my work), I am unsure if he is inviting me to speak, or simply to be the target there of more insults and smears on my work and my integrity as a human being. If the latter, I must respectfully decline.

HAIDON: I must apologize up front for contributing to any hostilities in the debate. Invariably, as often happens in these kinds of debates, we have returned to the question of Islamic reform. While I want to address some of the points raised by the co-panellists here, I hope that my response will help bring us closer to the theme of this discussion: the validity of the Muslim account of Muhammad. There is much to comment on, however, I have limited my responses in the interest of time and space.

I've read Mr. Warner's response with interest. I think his views are representative of a growing number of non-Muslims who are simply tired of atypical Muslim responses to the Islamist problem. What I find particularly interesting about Mr.. Warner's responses is that he speaks in certitudes and absolutes. I think that Mr. Warner needs to carefully read my rejoinder above. I did not state that Muhammad was a "was a wonderful man and did not do those horrible things in the Sira and Hadith". In fact, I stated that I could not categorically say that Muhammad did not do the things he was accused of. To say, without qualification, that Muhammad did not commit any of the dreadful acts accredited to him in the Sunnah is disingenuous, because we simply do not know. Mr. Spencer, in his initial comments, appears to recognise that there may very well be historical grounds to cast doubt on the veracity and validity of the hadith and Sunnah. This view is also shared by many non-Muslim and Orientalist scholars, including Ibn Warraq and Joseph Schact. Within this historical backdrop, the political context, and the motivations of the Ummayid and Abassid rulers who used Sunnah to consolidate their power, is a key consideration. For Mr. Warner to say with such certainty that Muhammad did what he did, while ignoring the historical and political arguments which challenge the veracity of hadith and the Muslim record of Muhammad, is rather weak.

But it is unlikely that the entire body of hadith are prima facie invalid. This may be a point of departure between myself and Mr. Yuksel. To be sure, many of the hadith arecan be viewed as perfectly innocuous and relate to ritual and manners. Simply casting away all hadith, is not realistic and would also remove this class of "good" hadith. I subscribe to the great Qur'anic scholar Kassim Ahmad's view that true test of authenticity of a specific ahadith lies in its consistency with the Qur'an, not in the flawedisnad chain methodology.

The real question then becomes, what is the methodology for determining consistency of ahadith with the Qur'an? Most traditional Muslims would argue that all sahih hadith are prima facie consistent with the Qur'an. Indeed, proponents of the insnad chain methodology would argue that this is a key component of that approach. This is a key challenge/question to proponents of the Qur'an alone and Qur'anist approaches.

For purposes of clarity, I would like to draw upon Kassim Ahmad's articulation of five key principles that, at a high level, provide the foundation of the Qur'anist approach[1] (the book, contains the enumerable Qur'anic references, to support each principle):

> · The Qur'an is complete, perfect and detailed. It is the fundamental law and the basic guidance for mankind .
>
> · The sole mission of the Prophet Muhammad was to deliver the divine message, the Qur'an. His other roles were secondary.
>
> · The hadith compiled by hadith scholars consists of reports of alleged sayings of the Prophet and cannot be absolutely guaranteed as to their authenticity. Those hadith that conform to the Qur'an are acceptable, while those that conflict with it are automatically rejected.
>
> · Religious duties of prayer, fasting charities and optional pilgrimage were not delivered by way of hadith, but were religious practices handed down through generations from the time of the Prophet Abraham.
>
> · Besides being prophet and messenger of God, Muhammad was also a leader of the medina city state and the later Arab nation state. In that

93

role he implemented the divine imperatives of the context of the 7th century Arabia. It is impossible that he would have done anything contrary to God's commandments.

Underlying the Qur'anist approach is the core assumption that the Prophet could never issue an injunction that contradicted the Qur'an. In the context of this symposium, further discussions on the validity of the Qur'an alone/Qur'anist approach are probably unhelpful. The traditionalist view is prevalent, and widely held by Muslims across the world. Whether Mr. Yuksel and I believe in the validity of the Muslim record is irrelevant for the moment. The bleak picture painted by Robert Spencer in his autobiography of Muhammad, is not conjecture, but based exclusively on Muslim sources, and is supported by the majority of ulaema, worldwide. Mr. Spencer nor Warner cannot be blamed, or derided, for merely spelling out what this historical record is, and what potential barriers exist for reformers.

So, the answer to the question about whether or not the account of Muhammad is fictional is irrelevant in this context. For all intents and purposes, the account is real because it is drawn upon and relied upon so heavily by jihadists and Islamists. Perception, unfortunately, is everything.

WARNER: This symposium started with the question: who is the "real" Mohammed? Why do we need to keep asking this question? After September 11, 2001, we heard that the Muslims who committed that act of horror were not "real Muslims" and that the real Islam is the "religion of peace". What is there about Islam that makes us keep trying to figure out what is the real Islam?

In the same way, is the religious Koran of Mecca the real one? Or is it the political Koran of Medina? Said in another way, is the real Mohammed the preacher or the jihadist?

Duality is one of the two Islamic fundamental principles. Submission is the other. Duality means that Islam holds two contradictory views on all subjects. Thus, asking the question about which view is the real one is like asking which end of the magnet is the real magnet. Is it the north end or is it the south end? At least we can agree that both poles are just different ends of the same magnet.

Just like the magnet, the "complete, perfect and detailed" Koran is both religious and political and the real Mohammed is the jihadist and the preacher. Islam uses each one when it is needed. Yuksel and Haidon need the "good" Mohammed. But the Taliban and the Muslim Brotherhood presently are using the jihadist Mohammed. North pole. South pole. Same magnet. Preacher Mohammed. Jihadist Mohammed. Same Mohammed.

So this symposium is based on the false premise that Mohammed must be one or the other, when he is both sides of the contradiction.

It is this dualism that lets Islam deceive the kafir. When talking to kafirs and dhimmis, Islam presents a saintly man. The apologist dhimmis say, "Well, if Mohammed was such a nice guy, the other Mohammed must be false." The shape-shifting dualism fools the dhimmis.

Which brings us to the Koran. Haidon and Yuksel think that if we didn't have to deal with the "false" jihadist Mohammed, Islam would be acceptable. However, the Koran says over 30 times that Allah wants every human to be just like Mohammed. Then it says over 40 times, that if we aren't like Mohammed, we burn in Hell. Islam has to have Mohammed. Without him, a Muslim does not know how to fulfill any of the Five Pillars. To be generous, the Koran is an incomplete document. Without Mohammed's life there is no Islam.

Also the actions of Mohammed show up constantly in the Koran. Mohammed the jihadist shows up at the battles of Badr and Uhud. Mohammed the politician shows up in the Victory sura. Islam has to have Mohammed even if there were no Sira or Hadith.

All of the mentions of Mohammed in the Koran are seamless with the Hadith and Sira. That is one of the reasons that the Sira and Hadith cannot be dismissed. The Koran, Sira and Hadith are a unified intellectual work.

But let's go along with the argument that without the Mohammed of the Sira and the Hadith, a good Islam would be a Koran-only Islam. Mr. Haidon and Mr. Yuksel are so immersed in dualism of believer/kafir that they cannot see what a dreadful document the Koran is for the kafir. They love it when the Koran says that they are the "best of people", but they cannot see how horrible it is that I and all other kafirs are called the worst things in Allah's creation.

The Medinan Koran has brought political misery to the kafirs for 1400 years. There is not one good statement in the Koran and Islam for us. It says that we can be tortured, beheaded, crucified, robbed, raped, enslaved, mocked, and humiliated. These are political actions and they define the Islamic worldview. Why does any Muslim think that I get a warm feeling and a smile when I am told that Allah plots against me and hates me?

A reformed Islam based upon the Koran without Mohammed is still an Islam where the kafirs are political second class citizens to be abused. The only reform that is good for kafirs is the removal of the negative language. The application of the Golden Rule to the Koran will do this, but over half of the Koran would vanish. Only a Koran with a Golden Rule and without kafirs is a reformed Koran.

I can give a criteria for a reformed Islam. Can I hear a good Mohammed joke after reform? I am very serious. There are jokes about Jesus, Noah, Adam and Moses (all supposed Islamic prophets of Allah). Why not Mohammed?

I cannot help but notice that no Muslim can discuss Islam without criticizing Christianity. The reason for this is found in the "complete, perfect and detailed" Koran. The Koran is vicious about all other religions. Due to its dualism, it has a good word in the beginning about the Jews and Christians, but in the end, the dualism prevails and the Koran's second view is brutal. It demands that it, and it alone, determines the truth of all other religions. But the Koran does not stop with religious criticism, but it always includes political persecution of other religions. The "complete, perfect and detailed" Koran also dictates that all other religions must politically submit in this world. Islam is not just about religion, but politics. The Koran is a political text that contains only negative, pejorative, hurtful, insulting words for the kafir.

The "complete, perfect and detailed" Koran of Medina contains more Jew hatred than Hitler's Mein Kamph. A detailed statistical analysis of Mein Kamph shows that 6.8% of the paragraphs are Jew hatred. The same analysis of the Koran written in Medina shows that 10.6% of the material is about Jew hatred.

To conclude, like Mr. Spencer, I note that Mr. Yuksel has called me to Islam. Let me use this example to show the dualism of Islam. This "call" has two meanings. The first meaning is that Mr. Yuksel has an actual concern for my well being and does not want me to be one of the citizens of Hell who is being mocked by the Muslims in Paradise as I burn with my shirt of fire and drink my molten brass. I like that interpretation.

But there is a second meaning to the call. When Mohammed attacked the Jews of Khaybar (an event referred to in the Medinan Koran) he first called them to Islam. When they rejected this call they were attacked, crushed and made dhimmis. It was in this vein that bin Laden called America to Islam before he attacked on September 11, 2001 .

So the call to Islam can be from care and concern or it can be a prelude to death by jihad. Such is the dualistic nature of political Islam and the Koran.

This makes me very sad. I wish that I could believe that Islam can be reformed and that Muslims could be convinced to stop imitating the jihadist Mohammed, obeying the Medinan Koran and killing kafirs. Look at the results. Mao was responsible for the deaths of 77,000,000 people, Stalin killed about 62,000,000 and Hitler was responsible for the deaths of 21,000,000. And for the last 1400 years those who imitate Mohammed and follow the Koran of Medina, have killed over 270,000,000 kafirs. If you could bring about a reform that would negate this effect, you and your work would be the greatest blessing to humanity in written history.

HAIDON: After serious reconsideration, I wish to withdraw my comment about Mr. Spencer's "tone". I believe my remarks are an unfair characterisation of Mr. Spencer's rejoinder. Mr. Spencer was merely challenging the points put forth by

Mr Yuksel, and responding with reasoned arguments (firmly rooted in Islamic history and theology) as to why Mr. Yuksel's points about Muhammad, the Sunnah and the Quran were flawed. In criticising Mr. Spencer's tone, I inadvertently adopted a common tool of Muslim apologists when confronted by legitimate questions about Islam. It was wrong of me to do so.

> Mr. Spencer, in this symposium (and through his wider work in general), has presented well constructed arguments that are firmly rooted in traditional Islamic teachings, to highlight the troubles facing traditional Islam . In many ways, Mr. Spencer is carrying out the work that genunie reforrmers need to carry out, in terms of identfying problems, and gaps (and shortcomings) of reform efforts. Instead of maligning scholars like Mr. Spencer, we need to answer the hard questions, with well developed answers, not accusations of Islamaphobia or weak accusations. As a Muslim, I firmly believe in the Qur'anic injunction: "O you who believe! Stand out firmly for justice, as witnesses to Allah, even if it be against yourselves, your parents, and your relatives, or whether it is against the rich or the poor..." (Quran 4:135).

FP: Edip Yuksel, Thomas Haidon, Robert Spencer and Bill Warner, thank you for joining Frontpage Symposium.

Jamie Glazov is Frontpage Magazine's managing editor. He holds a Ph.D. in History with a specialty in U.S. and Canadian foreign policy. He edited and wrote the introduction to David Horowitz's Left Illusions. He is also the co-editor (with David Horowitz) of The Hate America Left and the author of Canadian Policy Toward Khrushchev's Soviet Union (McGill-Queens University Press, 2002) and 15 Tips on How to be a Good Leftist. To see his previous symposiums, interviews and articles Click Here. Email him at jglazov@rogers.com.

A New Koran?

By Jamie Glazov
FrontPageMagazine.com | 4/18/2008

The organization Muslims Against Sharia is creating a new Koran with the violent verses removed. How legitimate and wise is this action? There is an effort in Turkey, for instance, to also revise Islamic texts. What real hope can these acts offer to bring Islam into the modern and democratic world? To discuss this issue with us today, Frontpage Symposium has assembled a distinguished panel. Our guests are:

Khalim Massoud, the president of Muslims Against Sharia, an Islamic reform movement.

Edip Yuksel, a Kurdish-Turkish-American author and progressive activist who spent four years in Turkish prisons in the 1980's for his political writings and activities promoting an Islamic revolution in Turkey. He experienced a paradigm change in 1986 transforming him from a Sunni Muslim leader to a reformed Muslim or rational monotheist.

Thomas Haidon, a Muslim commentator on human rights, counter-terrorism and Islamic affairs. He is active in the Qur'anist movement and works with a number of Islamic reform organisations as an advisor. He has provided guidance to several governments on counter-terrorism issues and his works have been published in legal periodicals, and other media. Mr. Haidon has also provided advice to and worked for United Nations agencies in Sudan and Indonesia.

Abul Kasem, an ex-Muslim who is the author of hundreds of articles and several books on Islam including, Women in Islam. He was a contributor to the book Leaving Islam – Apostates Speak Out as well as to Beyond Jihad: Critical Views From Inside Islam.

Robert Spencer, a scholar of Islamic history, theology, and law and the director of Jihad Watch. He is the author of seven books, eight monographs, and hundreds of articles about jihad and Islamic terrorism, including the New York Times Bestsellers The Politically Incorrect Guide to Islam (and the Crusades) and The Truth About Muhammad. His latest book is Religion of Peace?

and

Bill Warner, the director of the Center for the Study of Political Islam (CSPI) and spokesman for politicalislam.com. CSPI's goal is to teach the doctrine of political Islam through its books and it has produced an eleven book series on political Islam. Mr. Warner did not write the CSPI series, but he acts as the agent for a group of scholars who are the authors. The Center's latest book is The Submission of Women and Slaves, Islamic Duality.

FP: Khalim Massoud, Abul Kasem, Edip Yuksel, Thomas Haidon, Bill Warner and Robert Spencer, welcome to Frontpage Symposium.

Khalim Massoud, let's begin with you.

Your group Muslims Against Sharia is creating a new Koran with the violent verses removed. Tell us about this effort and what you hope to achieve and how realistic you think it is.

MASSOUD: Thank you Jamie.

We don't look at it as a new Koran, but rather a reversion to the original. We base it on three premises:

* God is infallible
* God is the Most Merciful, the Most Compassionate
* The Koran contains contradictory verses

We believe that unless you are a fundamentalist Muslim, a pagan or an atheist (and there is nothing wrong with being a pagan or an atheist), you would agree with all three premises.

If two verses in the Koran contradict each other, then at least one of them could not have possibly come from God because it would contradict the doctrine of God's infallibility. And because God is the Most Merciful, the Most Compassionate, the peaceful verse could come from God and the violent could not.

If you are a Muslim and you follow our logic, you would agree with us. So what we are trying to achieve is to educate Muslims that the doctrine of Islamic supremacy is not divine, but rather a perversion put in the Koran by nefarious people to fit their agendas. Once we get rid of Islamic superiority doctrine, which is the cornerstone of all evil in Islam, Islam once again could become peaceful, loving, enlightened religion as we believe God has intended.

As to how realistic it is, it really depends on how many Muslims we can reach and on the position, which will be taken by non-Muslims. Unfortunately Western governments and media chose to embrace Western Muslim establishment, which overwhelmingly comprised of Islamists masquerading as moderates, thereby ignoring true moderates by default. It is beyond me why most of the Westerners ignore Islamists' terrorist ties and believe their words that clearly contradict their actions. The latest example of this madness is URJ-ISNA alliance. If this is the direction the West is heading, no matter what we do will fail.

FP: Sorry, with all due respect, I am a bit confused about the business of humans moulding God into their own image. Who says that contradictory messages can't come from God? Who says that peaceful verses have to come form God and not the violent ones? What human is the arbiter of these things? What's the process here? You leaf through the Koran and on your own whim say: "No God could have possibly said that, so I'll just strike that out." etc.?

And if God is only peaceful in your view, and therefore incapable of making violent commands, then how do you explain the life of Muhammad? Are you going to strike the proven facts of Muhammad's life out of the historical record like you are doing with the verses of the Koran?

I ask the panel, and our readers, to look at the historical records outlined by Bill Warner and Abul Kasem about Muhammad's life. I would like you, Mr. Massoud, and then the rest of the panel, to explain how this fits with reversing the Koran to its "original" -- or to the reality of a peaceful Allah. If the Koran was intended to be peaceful from the very beginning, then how do we explain these aspects of Muhammad's life?

MASSOUD: Contradictory messages cannot come from God (the God, not a God), because God is infallible. If we assume that God is fallible, then he ceases to be a Supreme Being.

We believe that God is a loving God, that's why we believe that only peaceful verses can come from him. Jihadis believe that violent verses come from him. That's the difference between us and Jihadis. We love our God and they are terrified of theirs.

In regards to proven historical facts about Prophet Muhammad's life, let's consider this. We all know, or at least we think we do, that Muhammad was illiterate, therefore he did not write anything himself. The Koran, the Sira, and the Ahadith were written by people, most of whom weren't even Muhammad's contemporaries. So we are talking about oral tradition that went from one person to another for dozens, and in some cases hundreds of years before it was actually put in writing. Then, there was more than a millennium for those writings to be changed.

Now, let's consider the events of September 11, the most documented event in the history of humanity. Just several years after the events, it is quite easy to find many different "historical" versions of what "really" happened, including some versions that are diametrically opposed to each other. So the statement like "proven historical facts" is at the very least a stretch. Having said that, I would like to emphasize that we believe that Muhammad was God's messenger, which does not make him a perfect human being. It is quite possible that he did all the things that he is accused of. We also need to consider that norms of today's society are very different from the norms of many centuries ago. Slavery, polygamy, pedophilia, gender discrimination, etc., are not unique to the Seventh century Arabia. We can find all of that in the religious texts preceding the Koran.

FP: I don't know, perhaps maybe I am missing something here, but I don't understand how people can arrogate the authority to themselves to explain who God is, what he is and how he behaves and how he thinks. Contradictory messages cannot come from God? Really? Who decides this exactly? What happens if they can and they do? What happens if our minds are so tiny that we interpret something to be a contradiction which in God's grand design is not a contradiction at all?

In terms of Muhammad, I don't get it either: so now Islam's prophet may have very well engaged in slavery, polygamy, pedophilia, gender discrimination, murder, rape etc., as the historical record suggests he did (click here and click here), but it's ok because such acts were not in conflict with the norms back then? So there's not a timeless and universal morality? I thought the idea was that God disapproves of that kind of behavior because he is peaceful and just and incapable of contradiction? Therefore his prophet wouldn't engage in those acts right? Or is there some kind of thinking that since the prophet is a messenger and not a perfect human being, it is ok that he engaged in all of those acts? Or, as it appears to be also implied by you Mr. Massoud, since it all happened so long ago, and we can't really trust any accounts about anything, we can just attribute to Muhammad any and every quality we simply wish him to have?

In any case, Thomas Haidon go ahead.

HAIDON: Thank you for inviting me to partake in this discussion Jamie.

At the outset, I will categorically state that I find Mr. Massoud's approach to "Islamic reform" to be ludicrous. While I accept that he may be a progressive/or moderate Muslim, I find his thesis, which lacks any clear rationale or methodology, to be disingenuous. If Mr. Massoud were basing his arguments in a similar fashion to the late reformer Mohammed Taha, who argued from a historical and theological perspective that the Meccan verses of the Qur'an should effectively

101

be removed, I would be more attentive. Not only has Mr. Massoud failed to provide any intellectually persuasive arguments (so far) in this symposium, he has failed miserably to do so on his own website, which sets out his organisation's ideas and mission statement. Ideas that are bereft of any substance are meaningless, and potentially harmful. We must support our arguments with ideas, and not merely emotions.

Mr. Massoud correctly points out the dangers of Islamists masquerading as moderates. I would further state that Muslims who make incomplete and incompetent arguments for reform also do harm, particularly when non-Muslims are lulled into a false sense of security and hope. "True moderates" (the term that Mr. Massoud uses) must not only talk about Islam's problems, but must develop responses that are rooted in Islam, and have some probability of success.

While I am supportive of attempts to modernise and contextualise the hermeneutics of the Qur'an, I am opposed to the removal of parts of the Qur'an. In other words, I am supportive of a new understanding of the Qur'an, not a new Qur'an itself. There is no debate among Muslims that the Qur'an is the "Criterion", and represents the culmination of Allah's revelations to Muhammad. The Qur'an, on a number of occasions, affirms its primacy and completeness (Qur'an, 6:114-116, 16:89 39:23, et al.). To argue therefore, that parts of the Qur'an should simply be removed is fatally flawed. Mr. Massoud offers no insight into how he would address this core issue. This is the primary doctrinal obstacle, and there are others as well. From a practical perspective, I think it is relatively clear that Muslims will never accept, on any level, removal of parts of the Qur'an. There is virtually no internal debate or discourse on the whether the Qur'an is complete or "perfect".

I am conscious that this symposium, given the topic, could shift to a discussion on the fundamental question of Islamic reform, or whether there is any capacity for this to happen within Islam. I suspect we will find little consensus between the Muslims and non-Muslim panelists. However, in response to Mr. Massoud's ill-conceived approach I will say that the key to reforming Islam is not abandoning the Qur'an, but returning to a modern, contextual understanding of it, and rejecting man made traditions that are a primary source for what Islam has become.

Mr. Massoud apparently assumes that the Qur'an is only capable of being interpreted as ulaema have traditionally interpreted it. Mr. Massoud uncritically accepts the concept of abrogation in the Qur'an, and the historical record of Muhammad. I find this perplexing. My colleague on this panel, Edip Yuksel, has authored (along with other scholars) a modern, contextual interpretation and translation of the Qur'an which seeks to confront the very verses that Mr. Massoud wishes to toss out. I will leave it to Mr. Yuksel to further address the fallacy of Mr. Massoud's approach from this perspective.

In summary, Mr. Massoud's "Islamic reform movement" is not a movement at all. Mr. Massoud's thesis is intellectually bankrupt and lacks any methodology or substance, and has no prospects of being accepted on any scale among Muslims. I suspect that Mr. Spencer and Abul Kasem will agree with me, albeit for contrasting reasons.

The public debate on Islam and its role in terrorism, human rights abuses and oppression, suffers significantly from political correctness, disinformation and obfuscation. We need to strip down this discourse to its bare bones and ugliness, in order to move forward. Genuine reformers have an obligation to contribute to this through open discussion, and practical solutions. We cannot distil and whitewash the Islamic record, we must confront it, especially the unattractive elements. Genuine reformers also need to contribute to this debate by not raising expectations. Wide-scale reform unfortunately aspirational, and while yes, there is some good work being done, we have not scratched the surface.

FP: Bill Warner?

WARNER: Thank you Jamie for this opportunity to discuss the reform of Islam.

First, let me establish the basis for my logic with regards to Islam. To Mr. Massoud, I say: I have no interest in whether there is no god, one god or a million gods. I also have no interest in whether the texts of Islam—Koran, Sira and Hadith (the Islamic Trilogy)—are accurate or false. For over a billion Muslims, the Trilogy is the basis of the doctrine of their life, politics and civilization. They believe the Trilogy to be true and live their lives by it.

The Koran, the Sira and the Hadith are of one cloth. They form an integrated and complete ideology. The logical perfection of the Trilogy is the reason that it has lasted so long.

The other basis for my logic is that the reform be comprehensive and logical. We must have principles, not beautiful opinions.

One of those opinions was stated by Mr. Massoud, "God is a loving God." I don't know anything about Allah, but I do know what the Koran says. While there are over 300 references in the Koran to Allah and fear, there are 49 references to love. Of these love references, 39 are negative such as the 14 negative references to love of money, power, other gods and status.

Three verses command humanity to love Allah and 2 verses are about how Allah loves a believer. There are 25 verses about how Allah does not love kafirs.

This leaves 5 verses about love. Of these 5, 3 are about loving kin or a Muslim brother. One verse commands a Muslim to give for the love of Allah. This leaves only one quasi-universal verse about love: give what you love to charity and even this is contaminated by dualism since Muslim charity only goes to other Muslims.

So much for love. Fear is what Allah demands.

Mr. Haidon says, "…we need to strip this discourse down to its bare bones and ugliness." I agree and the ugliest parts of Islam are the concepts of the kafir, political submission and duality.

My only concern is how Islam treats me and my people, the kafirs. How Islam views and deals with the kafir is political Islam. The Trilogy determines the political doctrine and practice of relating to the kafir. The Koran says that the kafir may be murdered, tortured, plotted against, enslaved, robbed, insulted, beheaded, demeaned, mocked and so forth. The Hadith and Sira agree. That's ugly.

The Trilogy establishes the fundamental principles of Islam—political submission and duality--the basis of dualistic ethics. The Trilogy advances one set of ethics for the Muslims and another for the kafirs. A Muslim is not to lie to another Muslim; a Muslim may lie to a kafir, or not. A Muslim is not to kill another Muslim; a Muslim may kill a kafir, or not. And so forth.

The word "kafir" is pure dualism.

The Trilogy also establishes a dualistic logic. The early (Meccan) Koran and the later (Medinan) Koran frequently contradict each other, but since they are both the words of Allah, both sides of the contradiction are true. It is just that the later Koran is better and can "abrogate" the earlier Koran. Western logic says that if two things contradict, then one of them is false—a unitary logic. Dualism is the heart of the Trilogy's logic.

Dualism explains the two types of Muslims and which one is the "real" Muslim. The "nice" Muslim and the Taliban-type Muslim both follow a dualistic Koran and are both "real" Muslims. Dualism gives the "nice" Muslim plausible deniability. They can say that those jihadists are not "real" Muslims.

There can be an infinite number of reforms, but the only reform that matters to the kafir is ethical reform. That removes the principles of political submission and duality. There is a very easy way to see the problem and its solution. Go back to how the Koran defines the kafir and what can be done to them. No one wants to be insulted, raped, robbed, killed, threatened or tortured. No one wants to be treated badly. No one wants to be rejected as the "other", the kafir.

I propose a rational reform based upon how to treat the "other"--the Golden Rule: treat others as you wish to be treated.

The Golden Rule is centered on ethics, not god, and is universal to all cultures, except Islam. Indeed, the whole Islamic Trilogy denies the truth of the Golden Rule. Therefore, the Golden Rule reform has to be applied to the Koran, Sira and Hadith. Only then will the reform be comprehensive. Mr. Haidon says, "Muslims will never accept, on any level, removal of parts of the Koran." To just reform the Sira and the Hadith is petty change. I want ALL of the ugliness towards the kafir removed. That means that the Koran must also be subject to analysis.

The Golden Rule removes the brutality, insults and prejudice directed at the kafir. The constant attacks would disappear. The Rule is very simple and logical to apply to the texts.

What is amazing is how much the Golden Rule removes from the Trilogy. About 61% of the Koran vanishes, 75% of the Sira and 20% of the Hadith also go away. As I said, I only care about Islam treats the kafir, but the Golden Rule also removes all of the dualistic rules about women. So the reductions will be even greater when the material about the treatment of women is removed.

The Golden Rule even changes Hell. Islamic Hell is primarily political. Hell is mentioned 146 times in the Koran. Only 9 references are for moral failings— greed, lack of charity, love of worldly success. The other 137 references to Hell involve eternal torture for not agreeing that Mohammed is right. That is a political charge, not a morals failure. Thus 94% of the references to Hell are as a political prison for dissenters. The Golden Rule would empty Islam's political prison.

The Golden Rule annihilates the cruelty of dualistic ethics. Golden Rule Islam would be a reformed Islam that the kafirs would not fear and dread. We are tired of living in fear of political Islam. We have suffered enough and would welcome an Islam that did not argue, demand, pressure, dhimmize, threaten, deceive and destroy kafirs and their civilization.

However, all of Islam's success has been based upon political submission and dualism. Mohammed preached the religion of Islam for 13 years in Mecca and converted 150 Arabs to Islam. When he went to Medina he became a politician and a warrior. In the last 9 years of his life he conquered all of Arabia. In those 9 years Mohammed was involved with a violent event on the average of every 7 weeks. The violence destroyed the native Arab culture of tolerance. Political submission and duality triumphed.

But even if this symposium group could change the ideology of political Islam by integrating the Golden Rule, who would follow Golden Rule Islam? Islam is like the Internet; it has no central ruling body. Islam is a distributed network with the Trilogy as the operating system. An upgrade is not possible. But if

Muslims want to show me to be wrong, the only reform worth anything to a kafir is an ethical reform based upon the Golden Rule.

[A technical note: I use Ishaq for the Sira and Bukhari for the Hadith. Ibn Sa'd, al Tabari, Muslim and Dawud add little additional information. The percentages stated above are not based upon verses. Analyzing the Koran only by verses amounts to analysis by sentences. Who would analyze Plato or Kant by sentences? We want to measure ideas, topics and concepts; not just sentences. See the Epilogue in A Simple Koran for details.]

FP: Mr. Yuksel?

YUKSEL: This is an exciting symposium. Thank you for having me and get ready for a good fight. Mr. Warner is summarizing the problem well with the Trilogy of traditional Islam and yet at the same time he is indulging in intellectual acrobatics with jaw-opening contortions and distortions against the Quran. Meanwhile, the FP moderator is introducing the Sunni hearsay stories like a CNN news report about current events, and he is promoting assumptions and false accusations like the Laws of Thermodynamics. A careful reader will notice that the entire symposium is designed to promote the "click-here and click-there" propaganda activities of a cabal. Let me first start with Mr. Massoud's claims and then respond to the claims of Mr. Walter and his tennis partner, Mr. Glazov, FP moderator.

I nominate Khalim Massoud, whoever he is and wherever he is, for the Ignoble Prize for his theologically inconsistent, logically Swiss-cheese, practically useless, objectively insincere, substantially oldie-moldy, academically elementary, mathematically innumerate, Quranically unacceptable, and politically neoconning project. I also acknowledge that it has some merits as Thomas Haidon indicated: it is entertaining and ludicrous.

Now let me support each of my characterization:

It is THEOLOGICALLY INCONSISTENT, since it does not address many important theological and philosophical problems, such as Socrates' question, "Is it good because God says so, or God says so therefore it is good?" Sure, it could be both. But Mr. Massoud is even unaware of the existence of such an important question. If the Quran is the word of God, then whom am I to "correct" or "censor" his words? Massoud thinks he has an answer for that. Whichever he dislikes, or whichever does not agree with his current culture, or whichever does not please the FrontPage, or whichever he cannot comprehend, it cannot be from God. That is so simple. Just give him a pair of scissors and he will reform the Muslim world. Archimedes needed a fulcrum to move the world; our friend just needs a pair of scissors. A sharp scissoring reform. In other words, he devolves God to his level or evolves himself to become a god. He has nothing to learn from God; to the contrary, he wishes to teach God.

106

If Massoud lived in medieval times, and had a scissors in his hand, he would end up with a very different Quran that he envisions now. He would cut off verse 21:30 and 51:47 since they did not make any sense: how could the space and earth be one single body and then explode and expand? He would perhaps have problem with a round earth since he would never feel upside down wherever he traveled; so to bestow some reason and common sense to his Wise God he would cut off verses 10:24; 39:5; and 55:33. He would find the idea of egg-shaped earth ridiculous, so, he either would toss out the egg in the verse 79:30 (indeed, his contemporaries with no scissors would try to interpret the egg as a metaphor for a flat nest). He would find verses suggesting an evolutionary method of creation to be unfit to the wisdom of his Omnipotent God and would save his Quran from 7:69; 15:28-29; 24:45; 32:7-9; and 71:14-17. He would find equality of man and women bizarre and unfit to a Just God, so he would slash 3:195; 4:124; 9:71; 16:97; 33:34; 49:13; 60:12, and many other verses. He would have problem with too much freedom of expression of "evil ideas" and would like to save his Almighty God from allowing the expression of blasphemous ideas; so he would discard 2:226; 18:29; 10:99; and 88:21-22. He would find the verses promoting peace unrealistic and would chop 60:8-9; 8:60 and many others. Verses abolishing slavery (3:79; 4:3,25,92; 5:89; 8:67; 24:32-33; 58:3-4; 90:13; 2:286; 12:39-42; 79:24), verses promoting public elections and consultations (42:38; 5:12; 4:58; 58:11), verses condemning profiteering from religion and rejecting clergymen and religious intermediaries (2:48; 9:31; 9:34; 2:41,79,174; 5:44; 9:9) and hundreds of other verses promoting progressive ideas would get eliminated by Mr. Massoud.

It is LOGICALLY SWISS-CHEESE. I do not mean offence to Swiss cheese since I enjoy it, but this Quran-with-a-Scissors package has too many holes in it. Mr. Massoud appears to be engaging in a logical activity. Since I teach logic and philosophy classes at college, I cannot ignore it. He asserts three premises to reach his conclusion:

> (1) God is infallible
> (2) God is the Most Merciful, the Most Compassionate
> (3) The Koran contains contradictory verses

> Thus, WE need to conduct a surgery on the Koran!

But wait. What about questioning the third premise? What about modifying it this way?

> (3) It appears to me that the Koran contains contradictory verses.

> Thus, I need to improve my knowledge and comprehension skills in studying the Quran, OR I need to ask those real reformists who do not distort the message of the Quran through hearsay stories. AND, IF I

still see contradictions in the Quran, then I need to conduct a surgery on my Koran.

It is PRACTICALLY USELESS, since if we can subject our holy book to such a personal cut-and-discard operation, we would not need to have a leader like Massoud. In fact, any person can grab a marker and cross out the verses they do not like. Even if I lost my mind for a moment and followed the suggestion of Massoud, I would never purchase his version of the Quran, since I am not his clone. So, all what Massoud is telling people is this: "cross out the verses you think that are contradictory!" So, why anyone should follow a version published by Massoud or any other person? If I were going to write a blurb for the book, it would be the following: "This is an infidel-friendly, neoconized lite-version of the holy book with zero cholesterol. Yet, it contains plenty of turn-your-left-cheek-and-behind attitudes against imperialistic invasions and aggression. Three thumbs up Massoud & Co!"

It is OBJECTIVELY INSINCERE, since Massoud should know that no teacher would ask students to tear the pages of a text book if they thought it contains wrong or contradictory ideas. No text book would survive such a collective task of weight-reduction! And no author would like to see a reader like Massoud mobilizing others to cut the statements, paragraphs and pages off his book and republish it in his or her name! If Massoud really believes that there is an original Quran hidden inside the circulated Quran, he cannot be sincerely hoping to discover it by the votes of a particular group of unidentified people in a particular time. So, either he does not really believe the divinity of the Quran, or he has no clue about what he is saying.

It is SUBSTANTIALLY oldie-moldy, since already skeptics have done a great job in annotating the Quran, and indicating the "perceived" contradictions. Though I disagree with their (mis)understanding, but I find their work thought-provoking and very useful. Skeptics provide their critical arguments. All what Massoud suggests is to delete those arguments together with the verses they address! And for this ingenious idea he is now participating in a symposium organized by FP!

It is ACADEMICALLY ELEMENTARY, since it does not provide a methodology to accomplish the task. Since the Quran is an interconnected book, where each verse is etymologically and semantically connected to many other verses, any modification will cause the need for another series of modification. The number of combinations is enormous and so is the potential chain reaction and unintended consequences. I could give dozens of examples but I have limited room here.

It is MATHEMATICALLY INNUMERATE, since the Quran is not only a literary prose, but it is also a numerically structured book (83:7-21), it is the most interesting book in the world. For instance, 29 chapters of the Quran start with combination of numbers and letters, such as A1L30M40, or K20H5Y10A70S90, or Q50. For instance, the frequency of the word ShaHR (Month) in singular form is exactly 12, the frequency of the word YaWM (Day) is exactly 365, and there are many more interesting nu-semantic examples. For instance, the numerical structure of the Quran based on the number 19 is so extensive that it involves every element of the Quran, the count and order of letters, words, sentences, verses, and chapters. They fill volumes of books. (You may find a good summary of the Code 19 in the Appendix of the Quran: a Reformist Translation). Thus, Mr. Massoud's project is aimed to destroy such an incredible structure that bears witness to the divine nature of the Quran.

It is QURANICALLY UNACCEPTABLE, since numerous Quranic verses reject the very same attempt. Here is a sample:

15:90   As We have sent down on the dividers.
15:91   The ones who have taken the Quran apart.
15:92   By your Lord, We will ask them all.
15:93   Regarding what they used to do.
15:94   So proclaim what you have been commanded and turn away from those who set up partners.
15:95   We will relieve you from the mockers.
15:96   Those who sat up with God another god; they will come to know.
15:97   We know that your chest is strained by what they say.
15:98   So glorify with the praise of your Lord, and be of those who prostrate.
15:99   Serve your Lord until certainty comes to you.

Most likely Massoud would chop these verses too, by an additional maxim: "Delete all the verses that rejects our deleting activities!" Ironically, Massoud is not suggesting something new. Sunnis and Shiites already disregard many verses of the Quran: they do not hear nor understand them. Furthermore, their sectarian teachings contain a rule called "abrogation" thereby they reject the decree of the many verses of the Quran, while at the same time they declare their belief in every letter of the Quran. I have discussed this issue in detail in the endnotes of the QRT.

And it is POLITICALLY NEO-CONNING, since it serves the policy of Neo-con-led coalition of warmongers. I do not know whether Massoud is a hired petty officer for this agenda or just a naive person, but, it is clear that his project will only irritate and provoke Muslims who are frustrated and traumatized under cruel military invasions and occupations (such as Palestine, Iraq, Afghanistan, and Chechnya), or suffering under USA-supported oppressive regimes (such as Egypt, Saudi Arabia, and Pakistan). When a few angry and pathetic Muslims engage in some stupid and violent action, the Western media will salivate and rush to focus their cameras on the ugly faces of "barbarians", while the American capitalists will continue their racket by transferring billions and billions of our tax money to the accounts of war industry and its sub contractors.

IN SUMMARY, I am astounded that FP is taking this ridiculous idea seriously. If we are going to take any idea published on the web seriously, then we will be volunteering for an alien abduction adventure. I feel like I am talking in a symposium organized by the flat-earth society. Sir, do you also discuss cubic meteorites with avocados in their center?

Since I do not have space for more words, I would like to say a few words about the claims of FP moderator. His depiction of Muhammad is based on unreliable hearsay stories, yet he craftily sandwiches the "proven historical facts" into his complex question. If he introduced those accusations as "according to Sunni or Shiite story books written centuries after Muhammad" then it would be an accurate depiction. I challenge the integrity of each of the story books he is peddling as "historical fact." Where did he find those "proven historical facts"? As for brother Massoud's response, well, there is no surprise: he is receiving a "proven" false accusation from the moderator and after putting a petty spin on it he passes it back to him: intact!

As for brother Warner, he is perhaps doing statistics on Thalmud or Old Testament. His claim is far from truth. The most repeated and most highlighted Quranic verse that opens every chapter, except one, is *Bismi Allah al-Rahmani al-Rahim*, which means "In the name of God, Gracious, Compassionate." Let me give you the attributes of God most frequently mentioned in the Quran (The following list does not include the frequencies of the attributes in unnumbered 112 opening statements mentioned above). The Quran contains about 114 attributes for God. The most frequently used attributes of The God (Allah repeated 2698 times) are:

- Lord/Sustainer/Nourisher (Rabb): 970
- All-Knowing (Alim): 153
- Loving/Caring/Compassionate (Rahim): 114
- God (Elah): 93
- Wise (Hakim): 91
- Forgiving (Ghafur): 91
- Honorable (Aziz): 88
- Gracious (Rahman): 57
- Hearer (Sami): 45
- Planner (Qadir): 45
- Knower (Khabir): 44
- Seer (Basir): 42

These most frequent attributes of God, which are used in semantically relevant contexts, depict a very different Quran than Warner wishes us to believe. Perhaps, the Quran, like beauty, is in the eye of the beholder.

As for Warner's assertion about the Golden Rule removing 61% of the Quran, I am glad to hear that. This shows that the Quran is a book of reality, not a book of fairy tales. First, the so-called Golden Rule is not a realistic rule and it is very rarely used, usually among family members and close friends. In fact, experiments show that the Golden Rule promotes immorality and crimes in real life. In my ethic classes, I have repeated the experiments and reached the same conclusion. I recommend Carl Sagan's article, titled "The Rules of the Game," where Sagan quotes the verse of the Quran, "If the enemy inclines toward peace, do you also incline toward peace," concluding that the best rule is not the golden rule but the gold-plated brazen rule, that is, retaliation with occasional forgiveness, which is exactly what the Quran promotes (See Quran 42:20; 17:33).

The irony is not in Warner's lack of knowledge; the irony is in the iron. Warner is aligning with those who promote and practice the Iron Rule (pre-emptive strike), and yet he bashes Muslims for not abiding by the Golden Rule. Perhaps this is the rule of double standard in generosity: iron for us, gold for you. No my dear: I cannot enjoy gold while you have the iron.

FP: Well Mr. Yuksel, you are astounded that I am taking a "ridiculous idea serious" but nowhere did I say I am taking it seriously. As a matter of fact, all my comments so far reveal that I don't know how it could be taken seriously. But the idea needs to be put on the table because it is one of the efforts being made right now by a Muslim reformer and his organization to try to bring Islam into the modern and democratic world – if that is at all possible.

And a discussion of an issue like this can bring a very important dialogue to the table. I find it a bit strange that you affirm that you are "astounded" that I am taking this "ridiculous idea" seriously and yet you yourself have agreed to join a panel to discuss it. Perhaps you see no point to your own contribution to this symposium, even though you have spent quite a bit of energy and time to offer it.

I also remain a bit confused as to how American "warmongers" are behind taking violent verses out of the Quran. And I am yet still to hear what you yourself think of the violent verses and the problem that jihadists point to them as their inspiration.

Also, calling me and other people names is, unfortunately, no way to delegitimize the aspects of Mohammad's life that people like Warner, Kasem and Spencer have pointed to.

Abul Kasem, go ahead.

KASEM: I appreciate that Khalim Massoud understands there are problems with the Koran.

Khalim Massoud writes that Allah is infallible. Then he writes that the Koran contains contradictory verses. How is it possible for an infallible God (Allah) to contradict Himself? Here Massoud is playing the role of another God to correct Allah. Isn't this quite bizarre that a human being, such as Massoud, has to correct Allah?

Massoud confounds us further when he says:

'If two verses in the Koran contradict each other, then at least one of them could not have possibly come from God because it would contradict the doctrine of God's infallibility. And because God is the Most Merciful, the Most Compassionate, the peaceful verse could come from God and the violent could not.'

Who says Allah is always compassionate and merciful? He is certainly not, as can be demonstrated from many other verses in the Koran. Allah has peculiar temperament, to say the least. Under this circumstance why must we accept that Allah only sends the merciful verses? Who inserted those unkind, hateful, belligerent and barbaric verses? Without identifying these people, Massoud calls them nefarious. Why does he not identify these people? Could it that they were Muhammad and his coterie of power hungry people who surrounded him for a share of Islamic loot and plunder?

If we were to accept that the Koran is the absolute words of Allah, then how could Allah allow such calumny as tampering with the Koran?

Massoud says: If we assume that God is fallible, then he ceases to be a Supreme Being.

I simply do not get it. The Koran says clearly that Allah is the Supreme Being. Massoud further contradicts himself.

It appears that Massoud has accepted the truth that the Koran contains the words of humans, such as Muhammad, and possibly others. This completely breaks down Massoud's logic that the infallible Koran is the authorship of Allah.

In this context, Thomas Haidon is correct when he says: From a practical perspective, I think it is relatively clear that Muslims will never accept, on any level, removal of parts of the Qur'an. There is virtually no internal debate or discourse on whether the Qur'an is complete or "perfect".

I agree that the vast majority of Muslims hold the Koran as the incorruptible, unchangeable words of Allah, valid for eternity.

It is important to comprehend that Islam derives its mighty power not only from the Koran but also from ahadith and sirah. How about these important sources of Islam? Will Massoud edit these sources, especially those blood-thirsty, barbaric, inane ahadith? Will Massoud go ahead with the task of purgation of Muhammad's sirah to remove the unsavory, cruel, and inhuman disposition of Muhammad?

One important point: if Massoud agrees that parts of the Koran are human-created, why does he not abandon the Koran itself? Why he wants to mess with the task of editing the Koran with his own hand which, will cast him as an apostate and render him liable to severe Islamic punitive measures?

It appears that Massoud has forgotten that the Koran says that none can change the words of it (6:34, 6:115, 10:64, 18:27, 27:6). Verse 10:15 clearly says even Muhammad could not change a single word in the Koran. Thus, according to the Koran, Massoud's act will be the greatest of all Islamic crimes. Massoud should not forget the fate of Rashad Khalifa who attempted to do similar acts of revising the Koran, but paid a heavy price. Zealot Islamists murdered him while he prayed in his mosque. To day, Rashad Khalifa's minions are known as 'Submitters' or the Qur'an-only Muslims. Needless to say, most of them live in the western countries, for had they expressed their views in an Islamic paradise they would be certainly killed for tampering with the Koran.

Nevertheless, I appreciate the efforts of Massoud and Thomas Haidon who sincerely want to reform Islam and bring it to conform to the current civilized world. They are genuinely appalled at the barbaric, cruel and inhuman aspects of Islam, largely emanating from the application Koran and ahadith. Unfortunately, history of Islam demonstrates that many such attempts in the past had been dismal failures, and there is very little prospect that such current attempts or future attempts will succeed. I might sound pessimistic, but Islamic history uncannily confirms that playing with Koran and ahadith is a dangerous game that is destined to failure.

I agree with Bill Warner when he says: The Koran, the Sira and the Hadith are of one cloth. They form an integrated and complete ideology.

This means if one edits the Koran he must also edit the other two sources of Islam. Is Khalim Massoud willing to do this job? Will the Muslims, by and large, will agree with Khalim Massoud's versions of Sira and Hadith? I doubt they will.

What I disagree with Bill Warner is that, while he accepts that the Koran is reformable, I do not. I have already stated my reason/s why this is just not possible—the Koran completely forbids its reformation, and whoever attempts to do so will be murdered, Islamically.

There is only one choice left, to abandon the Koran, totally.

I find quite hilarious Edip Yuksel's discovery of numerical miracles in the Koran. This is akin to Rashad Khalifa's discovery of miracle of the number 19 in the Koran. I doubt if any mathematician will agree with Edip Yuksel's discovery.

Yuksel chastises Bill Warner for exposing the Korans' inanities and its stipulations to extirpate un-Islam by killing infidels, if need be. Unfortunately, Yuksel cannot refute Warner's allegation that the Koran commands Muslims to kill the Kafirs. Yuksel simply avoids this important topic by alleging that Warner is resorting to word gymnastics. It is interesting that Yuksel himself indulges in the intellectual gymnastic just to avoid the truth: the Koran has barbaric provisions for those who do not accept Islam.

It is sad to note that Yuksel has hurled vitriolic attack on both Khalim Massoud and Bill Warner. Instead of refuting/and/or arguing their cases in a dignified manner, Yuksel simply resorts to personal attack and logical fallacies. He indulges in irrelevant topics, America's foreign policies, Palestine issues and so on. This demonstrates his attempt to 'flight' from the burning issues of Islam and whether it is reformable.

We must appreciate that Massoud and Thomas Haidon have, at least, have plans to reform Islam—no matter how much we might disagree with their methods.

I find it very unbecoming of an Islamist scholar like Yuksel to reprimand the FP editor for opening a dialogue session with people of contrasting views.

Finally, here are a few suggestions, which, to my mind, will be of help not only to Massoud and Haidon, but to the entire world.

We need to expose Islam, the truth about it, and nothing but the truth. The world must pay heed to the fundamental messages of the Koran which is to conquer (by sword) the entire world and enforce sharia laws.

The infidel world must digest the fact that Islam wants to obliterate un-Islam, replace the western/un-Islamic civilization with Islamic/ Arabic civilization.

It is important that all infidel leaders must have a working knowledge of the Koran and Islam, and understand the language of the Islamists, which is anything but peaceful.

SPENCER: Khalim Massoud is correct that the "Islamic superiority doctrine" is "the cornerstone of all evil in Islam," or at least of the evil that some Muslims perpetrate in the name of Allah against unbelievers. Bill Warner is right: reform should eradicate Islamic supremacism and the institutionalized mistreatment of women and non-Muslims sanctioned by Islamic law. The rest is just window dressing. But how that doctrine can be removed or reformed, and whether or not it can be accomplished by a drastic re-editing of the Qur'an, as proposed by Mr. Massoud, is another question.

Thomas Haidon is clearly right when he says that "from a practical perspective, I think it is relatively clear that Muslims will never accept, on any level, removal of parts of the Qur'an." This is true regardless of whatever logical or theological merits the plan may or may not have. Abul Kasem also raises an important conceptual question for Mr. Masoud: "If we were to accept that the Koran is the absolute words of Allah, then how could Allah allow such calumny as tampering with the Koran?"

So how, then, can it be done, if it can be done at all? It is noteworthy that Mr. Haidon says that he would be "more attentive" to Mr. Massoud's arguments if they more closely resembled those of Mahmoud Mohammed Taha, "who argued," says Mr. Haidon, "from a historical and theological perspective that the Meccan verses of the Qur'an should effectively be removed." Mr. Haidon clearly has in mind the Medinan verses, which Taha actually targeted, not the Meccan ones, but the main problem here is that for his views Taha himself was executed by the Sudanese government in 1985. Abul Kasem is correct that most of the Qur'an-only Submitters "live in the western countries, for had they expressed their views in an Islamic paradise they would be certainly killed for tampering with the Koran." Nothing is more certain than that those who attempt reform of Islamic doctrine in Muslim regions take their lives into their hands. One notorious example is that of Suliman Bashear, who "argued that Islam developed as a religion gradually rather than emerging fully formed from the mouth of the Prophet." For this his Muslim students in the University of Nablus in the West Bank threw him out of a second-story window.

Western non-Muslim analysts need to have a steady and sober awareness of these realities. Mr. Haidon is absolutely right that "Muslims who make incomplete and incompetent arguments for reform also do harm, particularly when non-Muslims are lulled into a false sense of security and hope." But those suffering from that false sense of security are legion. Numerous Western analysts, policymakers, and even law enforcement officials are so anxious not to appear "anti-Muslim" that they embrace any self-professed reformer, and have been gulled many times. They should bear in mind that Mr. Haidon is also correct when he says that "we cannot distil and whitewash the Islamic record, we must confront it, especially the unattractive elements," and that "genuine reformers have an obligation to contribute to this through open discussion, and practical solutions." But so far this has not been done, despite many loud proclamations to the contrary from many quarters.

And as an example of a Muslim who, in Mr. Haidon's words, makes "incomplete and incompetent arguments for reform," we have here with us Mr. Yuksel, whose bluster and abuse of other Symposium participants may be entertaining, but only exposes the bankruptcy of his arguments. He accuses Jamie Glazov of relying on "unreliable hearsay stories" for information about Muhammad, but fails to inform us that the great majority of Muslims around the world rely on those same "unreliable hearsay stories," and offers no program for convincing those hundreds of millions of Muslims of the historical weakness of these stories.

Mr. Yuksel's presentation likewise suffers from inaccuracies that will it extremely unlikely that it will ever be accepted by large numbers of Muslims. To take just one of many possible examples, he asserts that in the Qur'an "the frequency of the word YaWM (Day) is exactly 365." But another Muslim writer has noted that Yuksel only arrived at this total by not counting many forms of the word, including every time it appears as "that day" rather than "the day" or "a day." When Mr. Yuksel's fellow Muslims so readily notice such inaccuracies in his presentation, it's unlikely that many will accept his program for reform.

MASSOUD: Mr. Glazov states, "the idea was that God disapproves of that kind of behavior because he is peaceful and just ... [t]herefore his prophet wouldn't engage in those acts."

Not necessarily. God gave people, including Prophet Muhammad, Free Will. I do not claim that evil deeds attributed to the Prophet are false. I am not justifying rape and murder as acceptable practices of medieval times. What I'm trying to do is to raise the possibility of the historical record being incorrect. We also need to consider things like polygamy in historical perspective. When the female/male ratio is roughly 1/1, polygamy is a clear form of gender discrimination. But when half of the men are killed in a war and the ratio becomes 2/1, polygamy becomes a practical solution. When life expectancy is 75, marrying a young teenager is clearly inappropriate, but what if the life expectancy is 20? All I'm saying is that the Prophet Muhammad should not be looked at from black-and-white perspectives. He was not the perfect human, but he was not pure evil either.

Mr. Haidon finds our approach disingenuous, ludicrous, and lacking any clear rationale or methodology. I believe that Mr. Haidon refuses to see what is right in front of him, i.e., the contradictions in the Koran. The question is: does Mr. Haidon believe that the Koran contains contradictions? If so, our rationale should be pretty clear, if not, how can you explain something to a person who refuses to accept reality?

Mr. Haidon is proposing a new understanding of the Koran. I find that approach disingenuous and ludicrous. Attempts to reinterpret verses like 2.191 or 9.5 are simply pathetic. It is nothing more than whitewashing of genocide.

> "The Qur'an, on a number of occasions, affirms its primacy and completeness (Qur'an, 6:114-116, 16:89 39:23, et al.)."

Should I remind Mr. Haidon that the Koran also affirms Islamic supremacy on a number of occasions? If he thinks that "kill them [infidels] wherever you find them" (2.191) means something other than what it says, why "there is none who can change His words" (6.115) cannot mean something else? Or what if someone already disregarded 6.115 and added 2.191?

Mr. Haidon keeps referring to "modern, contextual understanding" of the Koran. How can one possibly interpret "slay the idolaters wherever you find them" (9.5) other than "you must kill the infidels whenever you can"? Or does Mr. Haidon's "modern, contextual understanding" refer to simply ignoring the violent verses? If so, I believe removing the verses rather than ignoring them is a more practical approach.

> "Mr. Massoud apparently assumes that the Qur'an is only capable of being interpreted as ulaema have traditionally interpreted it."

Apparently. Every single non-Muslim layman that we discussed the Koran with interpreted the Koran exactly the same way, which leads us to believe that the problem is not with interpretation, but with the source.

Mr. Haidon states that our "thesis is intellectually bankrupt and lacks any methodology or substance, and has no prospects of being accepted on any scale among Muslims." Neither I, nor any other member of Muslims Against Sharia (which is a movement, even if Mr. Haidon does not consider it such) claim that our proposal to reform Islam is perfect. As a matter of fact, we believe that there are no good solutions to reform Islam; there are bad and worse. We believe that our solution is most practical, and therefore, the best. Or the least bad, if you want to call it that. There are three points of view: Islam is perfect, Islam needs to be eradicated, and Islam needs to be reformed. If you believe that Islam needs to be reformed and could offer a more effective solution than ours, we'll support you all the way.

Mr. Warner's argument is based on his belief that "The Koran, the Sira and the Hadith ... form an integrated and complete ideology." We believe that anything except for the Koran is pure hearsay. Some of the ahadith are so vile that if there is an argument for book burning they should be prime examples together with Mein Kampf. As many Westerners, Mr. Warner fails to separate Islam, the religion, from Islamism, the political ideology. In regards to the concept of dualism, it stems from the concept of Islamic supremacy. We believe that our proposal, however ludicrous Mr. Haidon might find it, is the only one on the table that completely eliminates the doctrine of Islamic supremacy, and with it, concepts of dualism, infidel, and every other concept that Westerners and moderate Muslims find objectionable.

Mr. Warner states, "I propose a rational reform based upon how to treat the "other"--the Golden Rule: treat others as you wish to be treated." This idea is practically identical to the paragraph in our manifesto (www.reformislam.org) titled "Equality."

I see no reason to address Mr. Yuksel's diatribe. Any Muslim who considers liberations of 50+ million Afghanis and Iraqis "cruel military invasions and occupations" by "Neocon-led coalition of warmongers" or believes that the Prophet or the Koran is above criticism is a radical. And I have zero interest in arguing with Islamic extremists. I wanted to address Mr. Yuksel's hypocrisy of participating in a "ridiculous" forum, but Mr. Glazov already did that.

Next, I will address Mr. Kasem's analysis. He writes: "Khalim Massoud writes that Allah is infallible. Then he writes that the Koran contains contradictory verses. How is it possible for an infallible God (Allah) to contradict Himself?"

It is impossible. That's why we believe that the contradictory parts of the Koran did not come from God.

> "Who says Allah is always compassionate and merciful? He is certainly not, as can be demonstrated from many other verses in the Koran. Allah has peculiar temperament, to say the least."

Again, we believe the verses Mr. Kasem is referring to did not come from Allah.

> "Who inserted those unkind, hateful, belligerent and barbaric verses? Without identifying these people, Massoud calls them nefarious. Why does he not identify these people?"

Anyone who was involved in a chain of custody of the Koran could have changed it. People who write new copies, people who kept the Koran in oral form, and maybe the Prophet himself. I wish I could give a more specific answer, but I cannot.

> "How could Allah allow such calumny as tampering with the Koran?"

People have Free Will.

> "Massoud says: If we assume that God is fallible, then he ceases to be a Supreme Being. I simply do not get it. The Koran says clearly that Allah is the Supreme Being. Massoud further contradicts himself."

Let me clarify it. God is infallible. If he were fallible, he wouldn't be God.

> "It appears that Massoud has accepted the truth that the Koran contains the words of humans, such as Muhammad, and possibly others. This

118

completely breaks down Massoud's logic that the infallible Koran is the authorship of Allah."

I never claimed that the Koran is infallible and that Allah is the sole author of the modern Koran.

"From a practical perspective, I think it is relatively clear that Muslims will never accept, on any level, removal of parts of the Qur'an."

Our poll contradicts that "practical perspective." Almost a quarter of Muslim responders either agrees with our plan or thinks that our reforms do not go far enough.

"There is virtually no internal debate or discourse on the whether the Qur'an is complete or "perfect"."

Isn't that the more reason to start one?

"I agree that the vast majority of Muslims hold the Koran as the incorruptible, unchangeable words of Allah valid for eternity."

And what of those Muslims who disagree with that? Should we just kill them off?

"Will Massoud edit these sources, especially those blood-thirsty, barbarous, inane ahadith?"

I believe I addressed this earlier.

"One important point: if Massoud agrees that parts of the Koran are human created, why does he not abandon the Koran itself?"

Because if we remove the human-created parts, we'll give the Koran back its divine nature.

"Verse 10:15 clearly says even Muhammad could not change a single word in the Koran."

We are not trying to change the Koran, we are trying to un-change it.

There is no reason to bring up fates of some Muslim reformers. We are quite aware of the dangers.

I agree that "history of Islam demonstrates that many such [reformist] attempts in the past had been dismal failures", but it does not mean that "there is very little prospect that such current attempts or future attempts will succeed." Past attempts to reform Islam were made inside Islamic world when reformers were greatly outnumbered. Now we have many non-Muslims on our side.

Mr. Haidon says (and Mr. Spencer agrees) that "from a practical perspective, I think it is relatively clear that Muslims will never accept, on any level, removal of parts of the Qur'an." I would have to disagree. Our experience shows that an average open-minded Muslims is likely to be receptive to the idea that the Koran has been corrupted and that the corrupted parts must be removed. We firmly believe that while the concept of Islamic supremacy is enshrined in the Koran, Islam cannot be reformed. Interpreting violent verses as non-violent is the same as calling terrorist acts 'freedom fighting' or 'God's will'.

HAIDON: There are a number of divergent views emerging from this symposium. I think what we need to reinvigorate this discussion with a little bit of good old fashioned reality. As Muslims on this panel, I think we have an obligation to be forthright and honest about the Qur'an and potential solutions for addressing its core problems. Mr. Massoud has been forthright about identifying the problems of the traditional, literalist understanding of the Qur'an, but has provided an illogical and incoherent solution to address it. While I agree on some points with Mr. Yuksel makes about the primacy and inviolability of the Qur'an, and his identification of problems with the Muslim tradition. I strongly disagree with his characterisation of Mr. Glazov, Mr. Spencer and Mr. Warner. Mr. Glazov, Mr. Warner and Mr. Spencer are merely stating the positions of traditional Islam. Given that millions upon millions of Muslims rely on the traditions of Muhammad and associated commentaries, it is only right that our panellists point this out. I also am perplexed about his characterisation of the United States, which is locked in a battle with traditional Islamic extremists.

I stand by my strong criticism of Mr. Massoud, and his ill-conceived approach to reforming Islam. Mr. Massoud has once again missed a golden opportunity to explain the methodology of his approach to unilaterally remove parts of the Qur'an. In response to Mr. Massoud's initial question, I do believe that there are, at face value, contrary verses in the Qur'an. I do believe however that these verses can be rationalised, when read in a contextual manner. Recent translations of the Qur'an published by Mr. Yuksel, Amina Wadud, and the Progressive Muslims provide a new framework of thinking about these verses. Mr. Massoud's assertion that if I recognise that there are contradictions in the Qur'an, I should automatically subscribe to his approach is pure absurdity.

Mr. Massoud is welcome to consider my argument that the Qur'an must be reinterpreted, as equally ludicrous and disingenuous. Fair enough. The reality is, however, there is a body of literature, and scholarly material which supports my arguments. There is an emerging body of literature from Muslim scholars, including Ahmed Subhy Mansour, Abdulahi Na'im, Kasem Ahmed, Amina Wadud, and others who have sought to challenge classical translation and interpretation of the Qur'an. These scholars have not attempted to "whitewash geno-cide", but to end genocidal understandings of the Qur'an. Unfortunately, the same cannot be said for Mr. Massoud. Mr. Massoud's has expressly rejected the work of Mahmoud Mohammed Taha, leaving him with no support from Islamic literature or scholars. In other words, Mr. Massoud's approach lacks any theo-logical support. Further, it is over-inclusive and ignores the entire body of Qur'anist literature. This is another reason why I consider Mr. Massoud's ap-proach to lack any intellectual rigour. My question to Mr. Massoud is, why have you ignored this body of literature and what is your response to their arguments for re-interpreting the Qur'an differently?

Despite Mr. Massoud's continued insistence that his approach is both logical and practical, he has failed to demonstrate the case for either. Muslims are unlikely to accept an approach that lacks no methodology, or theological basis. If Mah-moud Mohammed Taha's well crafted and hermeneutical approach can be re-jected, I suspect that Mr. Massoud's approach will garner no support among tra-ditional Muslims. I have to admit, I am sceptical about Mr. Massoud's claims of support among Muslims. I would hardly consider Mr. Massoud's "online poll" to be empirical evidence of a paradigm shift among Muslims towards acceptance of his views. For him to attempt to use the results of this poll to demonstrate his point is misguiding, and dangerous. This relates to my earlier point that pseudo-reformers can be dangerous because they tend to build false expectations, and lull non-Muslims into a false sense of security.

I do not consider Mr. Massoud's organisation to constitute a movement. For Mr. Massoud to say so is disingenuous. I would suspect that Mr. Massoud's organi-sation contains not more than a handful of actual and committed members. This is hardly enough to be considered a movement at the cusp of challenging the traditional Islamic establishment. To conclude, my apparent hostility towards Mr. Massoud's approach does not stem from my contempt of the notion of re-moving parts of the Qur'an, it stems from Mr. Massoud's ineptness in being able to articulate an adequate rationale.

WARNER: I would like to thank Mr. Yuksel for restating my thesis. The "beauty of the Koran is in the eye of the beholder". There are three kinds of eyes that look at the Koran—the kafir, the dhimmi and the believer. Restated, all scholarship in Islam is either from the viewpoint of the kafir (kafir-centric), the dhimmi (dhimmi-centric) or believer (believer-centric).

For the believer, Allah is wise, forgiving, knowing, and so forth. But for the kafir, Allah is a hater, a torturer, a plotter, a sadist, and an enemy. Allah makes us kafirs. Then he goes ahead to tell the Muslims what filthy scum we are. The word "kafir" is the worst word in the human language. No other pejorative is so cruel, demeaning, bigoted, insulting, and hateful as kafir. Why? It is not just the Muslim who believes this, but Allah, himself.

121

From the kafir-centric point of view, the Koran is not remotely a holy book. For the scholar, who sees the Koran as simply another old text, the Koran is a derivative work, taken from the Torah, heretical Christianity, Zoroastrianism and the aboriginal Arabic religions. The only new ideas in the Koran are jihad and that Mohammed is the "messenger" of Allah.

Mr. Yuksel calls me, "brother Warner". But, according to some 14 verses in the Koran a Muslim is not the friend of a kafir. Therefore, I cannot be your brother. And since you agree with my thesis that Islam does not use the Golden Rule, but instead uses "retaliation" (pure submission and duality), you cannot be my friend.

This is the saddest part of Islam. Islam rejects the bond of love between humans and substitutes submission, retaliation and other forms of dominance by the "best of people". The Koran, Sira and Hadith say that you are better than me in every way, and that I am an enemy of all Muslims. It also says that Islam must destroy my civilization over time. The Trilogy says that that if you want to be my brother and friend then you are an apostate.

I also appreciate Mr. Yuksel giving us a perfect example of Islamic logic with his insults. This is pure Islam since the Koran is filled with insults. Mohammed insulted the kafirs as well. But Mr. Yuksel goes further and gives us an example of dualism. He says that he teaches logic and philosophy, so he knows insults are an example of the "ad hominem" fallacy, attacking the person, instead of the idea. Mr. Yuksel is a Western logician who uses Islamic insults as ad hominem attacks. This is contradictory. He holds two opposite "truths" in his mind at the same time. He does not see the compartmentalization and dualism of his own mind.

The divided Koran, the Koran of Mecca and the Koran of Medina, is the foundation of dualism. The two Korans are in contradiction, but Islam considers them both to be true. Dualism creates a mental barrier that compartmentalizes the mind and allows the Muslim to never be bothered by the contradictions, such as those stated here.

Dualism affects all Muslims. It creates a lack of empathy with the suffering of the kafir and an inability to see how the Koran is filled with hate for them. Kafirs are not really humans in the eyes of Islam. This is supported by the dualistic ethics of Islam. In Islam all Muslims are brothers and sisters, but the kafir may be treated well or murdered, robbed, raped…. When these things happen to us, Muslims never really take responsibility. The closest Islam gets to acknowledges our suffering, is to say, "Well, that … is not really Islam." This is a total lack of empathy.

The gentlemen address the contradictions in the Koran and the nature of god. But they overlook the obvious. Allah is dualistic—he contradicts himself, but he is a perfect god. Therefore, the Koran is filled with contradictions and both sides of the contradiction are true.

Here we see the foundation of the Islamic doctrine of dualistic logic. Kafir logic is based upon eliminating contradictions. A contradiction in an argument shows that the argument is false. Islamic logic is based upon accepting contradictions as truth. It is a dualistic logic.

The genius of Islam is that it defines a dualistic morality and a dualistic logic that creates a civilization that is completely outside of kafir civilization. To try to apply kafir logic to eliminate contradictions about the Koran and Mohammed is to miss the point. Islam is inherently contradictory, that is its nature. There is no compromise or resolution between the two civilizations. We live in parallel universes.

Let's take the concept of integrity. In kafir ethics integrity is a high measure of character. It means that our words and actions are consistent at all times. Integrity is a measure of unity and lack of contradictions. You can trust a man with integrity.

But, Islamic ethics allow the Muslim to lie or tell the truth to the kafir. [Mohammed consistently told his jihadists they could lie and deceive the kafirs to advance Islam.] Islam's ethical values do not even allow a definition of integrity, since it permits deceit. The most common Islamic deceit is to only speak of the Koran of Mecca and equivocate about the Koran of Medina. Speaking half-truths is a lack of integrity, but it is not a fault in Islam. Mohammed had no integrity with respect to the kafirs, only with Muslims.

Kafirs see a contradiction in Mohammed being such a violent man and yet being called a prophet of a loving god. Muslims see this as a bountiful generosity of ethical choices Allah sets forth. They can be violent and peaceful. Muslims can have their cake and eat it too. They can choose peace and war and both are sacred choices. Islam offers a bounty of moral choices in its dualistic ethics.

I sense a need in our Muslim scholars to try to create an Islamic integrity that would be the same as the kafir is. But there is no bridge between unitary kafir ethics and dualistic Islamic ethics.

When Mr. Kasem says that I believe that the Koran can be reformed, I think that I did not pose my argument well enough. I argue that if the Koran is to be reformed, the only reform that matters to the kafir is to remove the kafir hatred. If you reform the text this way, 61% is eliminated. Of course that destroys the Koran. My argument is to assume it can be reformed and when we see the result, it is absurd. Reform leads to absurdity. Mr. Kasem and I agree, the Koran cannot be reformed; or if it is reformed, it is no longer the Koran.

Islam is a political and religious doctrine found in three books--Koran, Sira and Hadith. Those books are posited to be complete, eternal and perfect. They are all based on the principles of submission and duality. They form a unified whole. To reform one is to reform the others. So how is the reform of Islam possible? The Mohammed of Medina cannot be thrown out. The Koran of Medina cannot be deleted. The texts cannot be altered.

And there is no mechanism for reform. Our results--good, bad or indifferent— do not make any difference. There is no body or group that could vote or agree on any change. Islam is like wild yeast. There is no way to control it. It has no center.

The only reform that matters is the reform of the dhimmis into kafirs. Only as kafirs can we survive. We are a civilization that has been dhimmified. We refuse to acknowledge the 270 million killed and the enslavement of all races of humanity for 1400 years, the Tears of Jihad. We won't teach about the dreadful spread of Islam that annihilated kafir culture in Egypt, North Africa, Anatolia (Turkey) Iraq and the Middle East. We won't acknowledge that Islam has always annihilated all kafir civilizations.

The very idea of needing to take the time to argue about of the reform of Islam shows how we are a dhimmi civilization. A kafir civilization would have taught the doctrine and history of political Islam to us as children. We would know with whom we were dealing and why Islam does what it does. All of the knowledge of the Tears of Jihad, the suffering of the dhimmi and the doctrine of political Islam would have come in our mother's milk.

Since we did not get this wisdom from our ancestors, we must teach ourselves the political nature of the Koran, Sira and Hadith. We must honor our dead by learning the stories of their suffering. Our reform efforts must not be directed towards Muslims. We must reform ourselves, stop being dhimmis and become kafirs.

Instead of reasoning with believers, we should reason with our dhimmi leaders, our near enemies. We should aggressively call them out and challenge politicians, ministers, rabbis, and media types who apologize for Islam. We should use our time more productively.

As a political goal, kafirs must demand that the history of the dhimmi and the Tears of Jihad—the 270,000,000 dead and the enslavement of the European, African and Hindu—must be taught in all levels of our public schools. The survival of our civilization depends upon it.

YUKSEL: I would like to thank FP moderator for reminding the contradiction in my joining a panel that I accused of taking a ridiculous project seriously. I confess my guilt for becoming an accomplice with FP in discussing a silly agenda. However, a silly agenda can become a seriously silly agenda if it receives the attention of a serious media, like Frontpage. Regardless of the degree of my fault in this, I am going to let Masoud alone with his project. So, I will focus on other issues.

Kasem's argument has some problems. He asks, "Who inserted those unkind, hateful, belligerent and barbaric verses?" I challenge him to quote verses fitting those descriptions from the Reformist Translation of the Quran without taking them out of their context. As for removing *hadith* and *syra*, we have already a powerful theological and historical argument for that. I invite Kasem to read the Manifesto for Islamic Reform.

As for Kasem's invitation to "reform Islam and bring it to conform to the current civilized world," I have to defer. What does "current civilized world" refer to? If it is referring to the practices of super duper powers that are major parties of the two world wars and responsible of numerous invasions, massacres, genocides, and atrocities that have caused the death and suffering of tens of millions, then such a "civilized world" is not worth conforming. However, if he is referring to the expressed ideals and the democratic practice of the civilized world, then it is a different story. Sure, I would also correct the "reforming Islam" to "reforming Muslims" or "Islamic reform".

Kasem continues: "Unfortunately, Yuksel cannot refute Warner's allegation that the Koran commands Muslims to kill the Kafirs." Well, this symposium has limitations and I cannot properly answer all the laundry lists of accusations and distortions hurled by Kasem and Warner. If he is honest in his belief in Warner's accusations, I recommend him to see my translation of those verses and my arguments in the endnotes, especially in the endnote for verse 9:29. He will learn that the Quran justifies fighting against aggressor and violent Kafirs, that is warmongering ingrates, not peaceful ingrates like Kasem and Warner. [At this point, I was still hoping that these two ingrates were not warmongers.]

Let me briefly deal with Warner's complaint about the horrible descriptions of hell, which are clearly metaphors. A dash of logic, I believe, will save Warner from his nightmare. If the Quran is not word of God, then he does not need to worry, since all those consequences will never happen. However, if the Quran is the word of God, then he should either save his complaint for the Day of Judgment to God and ask for forgiveness for his wrongdoing, or he should just accept the truth and set himself free from incubating false ideas. Thus, Warner has no good reason to fear ending up in hell. Perhaps, Warner's complaint is less philosophical: "You see me deserving hell and you masochistically enjoy it." No sir, just to the contrary. Otherwise, I would not have invited you to study the Quran without distorting it with false ideas borrowed from fabricated Sunni liturgy.

As for the America's militaristic foreign policies and the Jewo-fascist aggression against Palestinians being "irrelevant topics," no sir. We cannot discuss today's reactionary Islamist movements and their fascist and violent organizations without considering their causes, effects, ecology and their opponents.

It is simply dishonest and foolish to focus on violence committed by Muslims but ignoring the much greater violence they have been subjected to by the so-called "civilized world" that does not terrorize but "shocks and awes", does not torture but does "water-boarding", does not kill civilians and children but turns millions of them into "collateral damage," does not support dictators, but supports the oppressive and corrupt Leaders, Kings and Generals. There were no suicide bombers among Muslims until the Second *Intifada*, which started at a time when for every 1 Israeli soldier 25 Palestinians, mostly teenagers, were killed before year 2000. There was no al-Qaida until Afghanistan became the battle ground of the clashing "civilized world" in 1980s. There were little prospects of the so-called Islamic Republic in Iran, until the CIA planted back its dictator, Shah Reza Pahlawi, by toppling Iran's elected prime minister in 1950s. There was no Hamas, until the Zionist regime destroyed Palestinian cities, massacred them in their tents and towns, and treated them like animals. Sure, there are Sunni and Shiite teachings justifying violence, but there are similar and even more violent teachings (and their historic practices) in Christian and Jewish liturgy. So, you cannot ask us to close our eyes to the super barbarism and violence of the "civilized world", and give all our attention to the barbarians among Muslims.

No sir; only those who sold their sense of justice will buy your double standard. If we are for a peaceful world, we should show the wisdom, the honesty and bravery to denounce all parties promoting violence and atrocities. I have yet to hear a word from you condemning the atrocities committed against Muslims by Christian and Jewish soldiers. That is telling.

And Kasem manages to sneak in the "Islamist scholar" title while describing me. I think that it is not an innocent slip of tongue; it is a calculated and pathetic threat. Why? Because I do not use a double standard in condemning all sorts of terrorism and barbarism? Because I stand for justice and peace for all humanity? The adjective Islamist is used by the media for a group of reactionary forces that is intolerant of diversity, freedom and peaceful co-existence. Kasem intends to make me the target of his "civilized world" with its invasions, destructions, carpet bombing, "harsh interrogation techniques," Gitmos, Abu Ghraibs, millions of orphans, widows, and displaced people in just last few years.

I do not believe that Kasem is using that adjective by accident, since by now, he knows that I am one of the organizers of the Celebration of Heresy Conference, I am the author of Quran: a Reformist Translation, and he knows that I have brave standing against the Islamists, and my mentor and colleague was the first

126

victim of Islamist terrorists in the USA. Despite all these facts, he attributes to me an adjective that describes my enemies. I understand his message very well: "Edip, if you continue exposing the violence and hypocrisy of my allies, then I will brand you with a title so that our civilized world will take care of you." My only response to Kasem is this: a monotheist is the ultimate free person and cannot be hushed by implicit or explicit threats. We will see each other in the Day of Judgment, where God will be the only judge.

Kasem continues: "He accuses Jamie Glazov of relying on 'unreliable hearsay stories' for information about Muhammad, but fails to inform us that the great majority of Muslims around the world rely on those same 'unreliable hearsay stories,' and offers no program for convincing those hundreds of millions of Muslims of the historical weakness of these stories." Wrong, again. If you had read the Reformist Translation or Manifesto for Islamic Reform you would learn that we offer a theologically consistent and very powerful argument to trash all those hearsay stories. No wonder, with little effort, our message is welcomed by many around the world.

Kasem also finds the mathematical structure of the Quran hilarious, yet he does not provide a single substantial argument for his position, except claiming that some people reject it: "To take just one of many possible examples, he asserts that in the Qur'an 'the frequency of the word YaWM (Day) is exactly 365.' But another Muslim writer has noted that Yuksel only arrived at this total by not counting many forms of the word, including every time it appears as 'that day' rather than 'the day' or 'a day.' When Mr. Yuksel's fellow Muslims so readily notice such inaccuracies in his presentation, it's unlikely that many will accept his program for reform."

I am glad that he brought that up. Well, if he looked at the entire argument, which is posted at my website, he would learn that my opponents finally accepted their error. See: http://www.yuksel.org/e/religion/365days.htm

As for Massoud, I will briefly mention his distortion of the Quranic verse 2:191. To serve his agenda, he plucks and chops the verse from its context. It is a primitive and yet a very common ploy used by intellectually bankrupt warmongers who push for another holocaust, this time against Muslims. Let's read the verse together with its context from QRT:

2:190 Fight in the cause of God against those who fight you, but do not transgress, God does not like the aggressors.*

2:191 Kill them wherever you find them, and expel them from where they expelled you, and know that persecution is worse than being killed. Do not fight them at the Restricted Temple unless they fight you in it; if they fight you then kill them. Thus is the reward of those who do not appreciate.

2:192   If they cease, then God is Forgiving, Compassionate.

2:193   Fight them so there is no more persecution, and so that the system is God's. If they cease, then there will be no aggression except against the wicked.*

ENDNOTES:

002:190 War is permitted only in self-defense. See 9:5; 5:32; 8:19; 60:7-9.

002:193 God's system is based on freedom of faith and expression. God's system recommends an egalitarian republic, and a federally secular system that allows multiple jurisdictions for different religious or non-religious groups. See 58:12 and 60:8-9.

Now let's look at Massoud's quotation of the verse. He shows the audacity to expunge the verse which he just distorted by plucking and chopping it!:

"kill them [infidels] wherever you find them".

Massoud reminds me of the anecdotal would-be businessman whose brilliant plan for a glass repair company is no more than breaking the glasses of windows in the neighborhood by giving slingshots to some brats. Distort the verses of the Quran through mistranslating, chopping and slicing, and then promote your crusade to save the world from those verses. And the success is guaranteed.

Massoud does his chopping and distortion in this very symposium on my own words. Let's see how he distorts my position. "I see no reason to address Mr. Yuksel's diatribe. Any Muslim who considers liberations of 50+ million Afghanis and Iraqis 'cruel military invasions and occupations' by 'Neocon-led coalition of warmongers' or believes that the Prophet or the Koran is above criticism is a radical."

I have not opposed the invasion of Afghanistan, since I believe the USA was justified to attack there. Though, its conduct of war has been harshly criticized by human rights agencies, the USA had a legitamate reason for invading Afghanistan: al-Qaida. But, the same cannot be said about Iraq, and today the majority of American public has finally came to agree with my position, that war against Iraq had nothing to do with liberating Iraqies or fighting against terrorists, but a lot to do with oil, imperialistic agenda, and profit for war industry.

Massoud, deliberately distorts my position by mixing Afghanistan with Iraq, so that his audiance will have a knee-jerk reaction to whatever I may say. Massoud must be one of the few gullible people out there still buying the "liberating Iraq" mantra. That is his choice, but he has no right to distort my position about Afghanistan. Bill Moyer, in his recent film exposed the series of lies and scams played by the Bush's neocon administration to lead the nation to an unnecessary war. The cost of this unjust war is enourmous: 4,000 dead Americans, tens of thousands injured, one million dead Iraqies, millions more injured... About 600 billion dollars have been wasted for this attrocious destruction and annihilation.

I have also, since 1986, never claimed that the Prophet of the Quran to be above criticism. To the contrary, in my books and articles, I emphasized his human side and vulnaribility to commit errors. Only God can be immune of errors and sins. Thus, in one sentence, Massoud manages to fabricate and attribute two false ideas to me, while I am still alive. If he lived centuries ago, perhaps he would be among those narrators who fabricated numerous hadiths in the name of the Prophet Muhammed. I will leave the rest of his aruguments, since it will take too much space to correct so many factual and logical errors he is commiting. Interestingly, he managed not to address any of my criticism to his project.

Now let me finish this round with Warner. . "Then he goes ahead to tell the Muslims what filthy scum we are. The word 'kafir' is the worst word in the human language. No other pejorative is so cruel, demeaning, bigoted, insulting, and hateful as kafir. Why? It is not just the Muslim who believes this, but Allah, himself."

Here is the allegory for Warner: A hiker is attacked by a dozen hungry and angry javelinas and he starts throwing rocks at them while cursing at javelinas. After javelinas escape, he hears another hiker behind him complaining: "you are a bigoted, insulting, and hateful man. I am a javelina and you hurt my feelings." Warner is proudly volunteering for the title kafir (ingrate, unappreciative, aggressor) as it is described in the Quran, and at the same time he is complaining about its meaning! Kafirs are described by the Quran to be active opponents of monotheists who are unappreciative and aggressive, oppressive, misogynistic, racist, or hypocritical. Furthermore, there is variety of kafirs (ingrates) and each treated according to the severity of their hostility, aggression and crimes. For instance, the Quran condemns the ingrates (kafirs) for attacking weak men, women and children (4:75-76), and Warner's feelings are hurt because we are asked to stand against those Kafirs.

No wonder Warner has blinded himself to the progressive message of the Quran and sees nothing novel in it but "Jihad and Muhammad." I would invite him to see the list of verses in the beginning of the Reformist Translation describing Muslims, Islam and the Quran, but with this attitude he might have handicapped himself to appreciate the wisdom in the Quran.

As for me calling him "Brother Warner." The Quran calls all humanity as the "children of Adam," in other words, sisters and brothers. "O children of Adam enter the peace all together." However, now learning that Warner is a hostile opponent, an ingrate activist against the message of the Quran which promotes peace, freedom and justice, I cannot call him "brother" in this context. So, his system is to him, mine is to me.

Warner complains about me insulting him through ad hominem attacks. I will leave it to the reader to compare my statements critical of Warner's position with the definition of ad hominem. What Warner does is called projection, and I confess he is very good at it. If anyone is defaming and attacking a historical character based on selective hearsay sources, my pointing at the contradiction and dishonesty in such a tactic cannot be considered ad hominem, since it is perfectly relevant.

Warner accuses the Quran for condemning the Kafir (the unappreciative, the aggressor opponent): "Dualism affects all Muslims. It creates a lack of empathy with the suffering of the kafir and an inability to see how the Koran is filled with hate for them." Well, I invite the readers to read all the verses that describe and define Kafirs and then ask themselves whether anyone who acts as such is worthy of empathy. According to the Quran Kafirs kill and evict people because of their beliefs, Kafirs violate the treaties, Kafirs kill children and women, Kafirs engages in slavery, Kafirs do not appreciate God's blessings, Kafirs considers women lower than man, Kafirs do not help the poor, etc.

Warner continues his diatribes and vitriolic attacks: "But, Islamic ethics allow the Muslim to lie or tell the truth to the kafir. [Mohammed consistently told his jihadists they could lie and deceive the kafirs to advance Islam.] Islam's ethical values do not even allow a definition of integrity, since it permits deceit." The real deceit is committed by Warner, since he knows that I do not subscribe to hearsay stories about Muhammad, to the contrary that I reject all. He is implicitly attacking my integrity by referring to the sources that ironically neither of us trusts. I challenge him to find a single verse in the Quran permitting Muslims to lie. The Quran, however, is a realistic book and do not promote the Kantian principle of categorical imperative. For instance, if one fears of injury or death because of his opinion and conviction, that person might choose to hide his opinion to avoid harm to his or her person. If Warner is imprisoned by Taliban, perhaps he would act the same way to avoid harm to his person. Warner is so biased and hostile; he has blinded himself to hundreds of verses advising people to be honest, truthful even if it is against their interest and family members.

Furthermore, the Quran advises Muslims not to defend a group of Muslims who violated the treaty between Muslims and non-Muslims, thereby putting the rule of law above religious affiliation.

Warner might defend his position by pointing at Shiite and Sunni liturgy. Then, he should also declare Christians and Jews too with lack of integrity and honesty, since the Bible and Talmud contain numerous verses encouraging deceit and double standard. If I had no integrity and honesty, as Warner suggest, I would be acting as a stooge of the powerful. But, anyone familiar with my struggle since my youth will know that Warner's attack to my integrity and honesty is a pathetic lie. Ironically, he is the one who is attacking my person rather my position, and he is using falsehood. He is the one who is making a diabolic accusation, since his accusation is not falsifiable. Whatever I do, whatever I say, Warner's accusation regarding my intention will remain unchallenged.

Warner is rightly critical of Muslim invasions and occupations in the past. I condemn all aggression regardless of the religion or tribe of the culprits. In my articles and books I have promoted the Quranic position clearly. However, Warner, unable to face me and my reformist theology, is resorting to punching the straw man in his pocket. Well, he does not only punch the straw man, he attempts to eat it. For instance, he puts the following words in my mouth in an accusatory tone: "We won't acknowledge that Islam has always annihilated all kafir civilizations." ALWAYS? Well, surprise: Though I question the Islamic identity of the empires he is alluding to, yet I accept that statement in general, since history contradicts what Warner wants us to believe.

Muslims had invaded Spain and ruled there for about five hundred years. But, for the most part, Jewish and Christian population found justice and peace in Muslim Spain. Furthermore, when Muslims were forced out from Spain, we know what they left behind: a Christian population, libraries, universities, civilization, seeds of reform and renaissance in Europe. The same with the Ottoman Empire. They invaded south eastern part of Europe for a long period of time, and we know what they left behind. Compare those two great empires, which I am fond of neither, and their evil deeds during the course of 1000 years to the destruction and atrocities of the USA-Inc led by a born-again Christian president overwhelmingly supported by evangelical Christians just in Iraq alone during the course of just 5 years. Warner has never condemned the atrocities of the USA-Inc, but I have in my writings condemned the atrocities committed by Muslim kings, caliphs, and empires numerous times. Who has honesty and integrity? I will not ask Warner from which hat has he pulled out the 270,000,000 dead, since I know if he can get the ALWAYS despite several hundreds years of exception, I am surprised that he did not get 27 billions dead.

FP: There is so much rhetoric here that I wouldn't even know where to start. Suffice it to say that when America liberated Iraq it freed 25 million Muslims from a Fascist dictator. The destruction and atrocities there are not the result of what the U.S is doing; they are the result of Islamist violence and Islamic sectarian violence. If the jihadists never waged war in Iraq, if they didn't intend to build a caliphate, and the Sunnis and Shiites never massacred each other, there would have been no destruction and atrocities; there would be a building of a civil, democratic and modern society, which is what the U.S. objective is.

There were no suicide bombers among Muslims until the Second Intifada because the Palestinians had not reached the zenith of their genocidal program against Israel. The death cult had not completely manifested itself until then. And what triggered the Second Intifada? Israeli Prime Minister Barak offered the Palestinians their own state and the possibility of peace at Camp David in July 2000. It was an extraordinarily generous offer. But because the Palestinians lust to kill Jews more than to have their own state, they punished the Israelis severely for this offer and began to kill not only Jews but also themselves and their own children -- by strapping them up with bombs and sending them into Israeli restaurants and cafes.

Mr. Yuksel, I am shocked at the equivalency you apply to Islamic and Judaic and Christian teachings. Surely you know that when Christians have behaved in aggressive ways, their acts were not based on Christian teachings; their acts were un-Christian. The same cannot be said for Muslims when they engage in aggression and intolerance, since such behavior is a fulfillment of their theological mandates. All the schools of Islamic jurisprudence teach that it is part of the responsibility of the umma to subjugate the non-Muslim world through jihad. There is nothing in the New or Old Testament that teaches any such thing.

KASEM: I thank Robert Spencer for pointing out the gross inanities in the arguments of Mr. Khalim Massoud and for admonishing the very angry and belligerent tone of Mr. Yuksel's red herring fallacies. Robert Spencer has correctly identified the true problem with the Koran. Like him, I agree that the efforts of either Mr. Massoud or Mr. Yuksel to tamper with the Koran with their own version of interpretations and/or contextual relevance will be of little importance to the vast majority of the Muslims.

Mr. Massoud relapses to contradictory statements, again and again. It is difficult to proceed with dialogue with such absurd arguments and statements. For example: when I posed the question: How is it possible for an infallible God (Allah) to contradict Himself? Mr. Massoud's answer was:

> "It is impossible. That's why we believe that the contradictory parts of the Koran did not come from God."

Then in other parts Mr. Massoud writes:

> "Let me clarify it. God is infallible. If he were fallible, he wouldn't be God."

I never claimed that the Koran is infallible and that Allah is the sole author of the modern Koran.

There is virtually no internal debate or discourse on the whether the Qur'an is complete or "perfect".

We are not trying to change the Koran, we are trying to un-change it.

Past attempts to reform Islam were made inside Islamic world when reformers were greatly outnumbered. Now we have many non-Muslims on our side.

Honestly, Mr. Massoud, I do not get what is the true message you want to convey to your readers. Do you want to reform the Koran with such convoluted and hard-to-understand statements?

Just like Mr. Thomas Haidon, I do not at all trust your poll. Firstly, the sample size is too small to have any statistical significance, secondly, when I added up the figures you quoted for the Muslim response it was merely 10 percent and not 25 percent that you claimed. Correct me if I am wrong in interpreting your statistics.

Mr Warner grasped the essence of Islam when he wrote:

> "Islam is inherently contradictory, that is its nature. There is no compromise or resolution between the two civilizations. We live in parallel universes."

It is true that there cannot be any compromise with Islam. In Islam, it is either submission or annihilation. Thus, currently, we have two worlds, confronting each other: the world of Islam and the world of un-Islam. This state of perpetual confrontation is stated in a number of verses in the Koran (such as: 4:76, 3:175, 40:51-52, 47:7, 58:19, 58:21). This state of everlasting altercation precludes any reformation of the Koran and Islam.

Mr. Warner wrote further:

> "If you reform the text this way, 61% is eliminated. Of course that destroys the Koran. My argument is to assume it can be reformed and when we see the result, it is absurd. Reform leads to absurdity. Mr. Kasem and I agree, the Koran cannot be reformed; or if it is reformed, it is no longer the Koran."

I thank Mr Warner for stating the reality about the futility of creating a new Koran a-la Khalid Massoud and Mr. Yuksel.

In passing, it will be interesting to note the fate of another reformist of the Koran in our time, Rashad Khalifa.

Mr. Yuksel is very fond of throwing challenges. He writes:

> "I challenge him to quote verses fitting those descriptions from the Reformist Translation of the Quran without taking them out of their context."

How nice of Mr. Yusel to ask me to meet his challenge by using his version of the Koran. Even the dumbest person will know the trap you have set. Why must I trust your version of the Koran when the age-old, and the most eminent translators are there? Mr. Yuksel, please tell me why must I not trust the most celebrated exegetes of the Koran, such as Jalalyn, ibn Abbas, ibn Kathir, Maududi and so on? Are you claiming they are inferior to you, or that they did not understand the Koran?—rather you are the only person who correctly understands the Koran? I could easily challenge you to prove these eminent scholars of the Koran to be wrong. But I shall refrain from this, as this will simply render me as a person bent on vengeance.

Having said this, let me provide just one example of how the Koran commands the Muslims to fight and kill the infidels.

Mr. Yuksel, I am certain you have heard about the verse of the 'sword'. Let us read what the eminent exegetes of the Koran has to say on this verse

After the four sacred months (Rajab, Zulqad, ZulHajj, Muharram) have passed, slay (fight and kill) the pagans wherever (that is, the earth in general—ibn Kathir) they are found. (Do not wait until you find them, seek and besiege them in their areas and forts, gather intelligence about them in various roads and fairways and force them to Islam. If they do not embrace Islam, then kill them. This verse allowed Muslims to fight the non-Muslims until they embrace Islam. These verses allowed fighting people unless and until, they embrace Islam and implement its rulings and obligations. Allah mentioned the most important aspects of Islam here, including what is less important—ibn Kathir, Jalalyn, ibn Abbas. Also see 2:190, 2:194, 5:2, 8:39, 9:36); if they repent and become believers then forgive them. (Note: This verse is called the verse of the sword. This verse abrogates all verses of forgiveness to the pagans. i.e., this verse cancels about 124 verses that espouses mercy, tolerance and forgiveness to the pagans)...9:5

I am certain Mr. Yuksel will deny the tafsirs of ibn Abbas, Jalalyn, and ibn Kathir. But please tell us who understood the Koran better—those who were close to Muhammad (such as ibn Abbas), and those earlier Islamist scholars, or the 21st. century scholar such as you?

Mr. Yuksel then advises me to read his tafsir of verse 9:29. As mentioned previously, what is wrong with the tafsirs of the most eminent Islamic scholars?

Mr. Yuksel writes:

> "He will learn that the Quran justifies fighting against aggressor and violent Kafirs, that is warmongering ingrates, not peaceful ingrates like Kasem and Warner."

This seems fair enough. If we extend the logic of the Koran to justify war and killing against the warmongering then why should Mr. Yuksel blame the West for what it is doing? They are simply responding to the armed insurgency of the Islamist terrorists. Why is it that only Islam has the inalienable right to fight oppression and injustice and not the others? Surely, you are now caught in your own logic. Do you not think that countries such as India, Egypt, Turkey, Tunisia have the right to invade Saudi Arabia and exact reparation for what the Arab invaders did to these lands? Do you not agree that the Jews and the Christians have the right to settle in Medina, in their ancestral lands, from where they had been forcibly evicted by Caliph Umar? Be fair, and let us know.

Mr. Yuksel even issued a challenge to Mr. Warner. He wrote: "I challenge him to find a single verse in the Quran permitting Muslims to lie."

Well, Mr. Yuksel, here are a few verses for you to peruse, of course they are not your translation. If you do not trust the most eminent translators, why must we trust your translation?

Allah judges you by your innermost intentions not by your swearing by Allah (Foundation of Islamic taqiyya and kitman; telling lies and adopting deception for the sake of Islam is permissible; also see 3:28, 40:28, 16:106, 66:2)...2:225

Do not take unbelievers as friends; caution is necessary to befriend the unbelievers (the foundation of Islamic taqiyya and kitman;). (Do not befriend the deniers, even if they are among the closest relatives. In case of danger, Allah allows Muslims to show friendship to the disbelievers outwardly, but never inwardly. The taqiyya is allowed until the Day of Resurrection. Allah has reserved unremitting torment for those who give their support to His enemies, and those who have enmity with His friends.—ibn Kathir; it is all right to tell lies/ adopt deception (taqiyya and kitman) for the sake of Islam. Maududi 3/25: This means that it is lawful for a believer, helpless in the grip of the enemies of Islam and in imminent danger of severe wrong and persecution, to keep his faith concealed and to behave in such a manner as to create the impression that he is on the same side as his enemies. A person whose Muslim identity is discovered is permitted to adopt a friendly attitude towards the unbelievers in order to save his life. If he considers himself incapable of enduring the excesses to which he may be subjected, he may even state that he is not a believer.)...3:28

A believing man among the Pharaoh, who hid his faith (He was the paternal cousin of Pharaoh—Jalalyn), defended Moses, but Pharaoh said that he (that is, Pharoh himself) holds the supreme authority. (This believing man was an Egyptian Copt, a cousin's son the paternal uncle of Pharaoh; only Pharaoh's wife and this man were the believers. They concealed their faith from the Egyptians—ibn Kathir; foundation of Islamic taqiyya and kitman; telling lies and adopting deception for the sake of Islam is permissible)...40:28-29

Allah's wrath is for the apostates; apostasy under duress is forgiven (foundation of Islamic taqiyya and kitman; telling lies and adopting deception for the sake of Islam is permissible; otherwise, there is a dreadful punishment for an apostate)...16:106-107

Muhammad (Muslims) is allowed to break oaths in certain cases (not specified); Allah is Muhammad's protector (it meant that Muhammad is allowed to break his vows to his wives or others; foundation of Islamic taqiyya and kitman; telling lies and adopting deception for the sake of Islam is permissible.)...66:2

To duck the main issue Mr. Yuksel the resorts to America, Palestine, Afghanistan, and so on. This tactic is nothing new, whenever Islam is scrutinized, the Islamists often bring in such red herrings to divert the attention. Nevertheless, we can defeat Mr. Yuksel's diatribe by simply saying that whatever the Americans and the non-Muslim world is doing is just to protect their interest. Why must the world be apologetic to Islam? Why does the Islamic world think that the world owes it a living, that they have the right to fight 'injustice' and 'oppression'?. When America does not act to remove an Islamic despot, she is criticized for supporting a tyrant. But when America deposes a brutal dictator like Saddam, she is chastised for invading Iraq and killing innocent people.

Currently, in Iraq, the major fighting is between various factions of Islam. In Pakistan, Egypt, Thailand, Bangladesh, Indonesia, there are no American soldiers, yet what do we read in the newspapers? Amazingly, Mr Yuksel is completely coy on this.

Mr Yuksel chastises me for having called him an Islamist scholar. I have no intention to hurt you, neither do I attack you personally. Because you have such an impressive background in the knowledge of the Koran and Islam, is not this fair to call you a scholar of Islam? You even translated the Koran (in your own way). Only people who have unparallel knowledge of the Koran and Islam could do such a feat. So, is it wrong to say that you are an Islamist scholar? If you are perturbed with the epithet 'Islamist' then let us know what would be the best way to describe you.

Mr Yuksel wrote:

Kasem intends to make me the target of his "civilized world" with its invasions, destructions, carpet bombing, "harsh interrogation techniques," Gitmos, Abu Ghraibs, millions of orphans, widows, and displaced people in just last few years.

This is just a fib. I never issued any threat to Mr Yuksel. Please show me a single sentence where I have done this.

Mr Yuksel continues:

I do not believe that Kasem is using that adjective by accident, since by now, he knows that I am one of the organizers of the Celebration of Heresy Conference, I am the author of Quran: a Reformist Translation, and he knows that I have brave standing against the Islamists, and my mentor and colleague was the first victim of Islamist terrorists in the USA. Despite all these facts, he attributes to me an adjective that describes my enemies. I understand his message very well: "Edip, if you continue exposing the violence and hypocrisy of my allies, then I will brand you with a title so that our civilized world will take care of you." My only response to Kasem is this: a monotheist is the ultimate free person and cannot be hushed by implicit or explicit threats. We will see each other in the Day of Judgment, where God will be the only judge.

Again, this is a very old game of playing victim. Mr Yuksel, I wish you all the best. Despite our differences, I have great respect for your scholarship and for your courage to proceed with the reformation of Islam. I have no personal enmity with you, rest assured on this.

FP: Mr. Kasem, why do you call Mr. Yuksel an "Islamist scholar"? Surely you see why he has taken offense to this. He says he is not an Islamist and he appears to be fighting Islamism and this is why he has been threatened by Islamists. Why don't you just call him an "Islamic scholar."? Surely you see the difference here?

KASEM: All right, if Mr Yuksel is offended by the term 'Islamist' then I do apologize. Yes, I have no objection in calling him an Islamic scholar.

The reason why I thought that he might be an Islamist scholar, is the manner, in which he attacked America and the non-Islamic world, holding them responsible for all the ills of the Islamic world. This is quite simlar manner in which the Islamists often attack the non-Islamic world, to justify their jihad and terrorism.

Now that Mr Yuksel has clarified himself, I would recognise him as a scholar of Islam rather than an Islamist scholar. Hope this should suffice.

FP: Thank you Mr. Kasem.

Mr. Yuksel, Mr. Kasem has a point does he not? If you are really part of the anti-Islamist agenda and are on the side of the West, why do you spend so much of your time and energy in this symposium attacking America and the non-Islamic world, blaming them for Islam's tyranny and failures? Why do you apply moral equivalency in the terror war? Why do you attack the noble members of this panel that have the courage to point to the ingredients of Islam that fertilize Islamic terror? They have put their lives on the line to tell the truth. Surely you are aware that your words and stances on many of these realms serve the Islamist agenda, no?

And Mr. Kasem has made an apology in terms of the label "Islamist" in being applied to you, despite the doubts you put in peoples' minds with some of your positions and attacks. You have made some attacks in the symposium as well. Do you think you owe anyone an apology of any kind?

Because this symposium has become way too long and you are getting an extra turn, kindly try to be brief.

YUKSEL: Since I am asked by the FP Moderator to be brief I will not be able to respond to all the spins and distortions. I will only address briefly to a few points and will post my response in detail later at 19.org. Mr. Glazov asserts, "All the schools of Islamic jurisprudence teach that it is part of the responsibility of the umma to subjugate the non-Muslim world through jihad. There is nothing in the New or Old Testament that teaches any such thing."

Our school of Islamic jurisprudence does not teach such a thing. To the contrary, we consider such an belief and practice to be anti-Quranic and Satanic. (I know, the modern inquisition court will continue accusing me and the Quran with the contrary).

As for FP moderator's second assertions: The Old Testament contains numerous instructions for violence and terror, which cannot be attributed to a benevolent and just God. They are mixed and introduced together with beautiful and constructive instructions:

> "Joshua and his men utterly destroyed all that was in the city, both man and woman, young and old, ox, sheep and ass, with the edge of the sword." (Joshua 6:20-21).

> "Now go and smite Amalek, and utterly destroy all that they have, and spare them not; but slay both man and woman, infant and suckling, ox and sheep, camel and ass." (1Samuel 15:3)

> "Israel's God will direct his jealous anger against Babylonians, Chaldeans, Pekod, Shoa, Koa, and the Assyrians, and they will be dealt with in fury. Their noses and ears will be cut off, and they will fall by the sword. Their sons and daughters will be taken, and those who are left will be consumed by fire." (Ezekiel 23:25)

In the Manifesto for Islamic Reform, I have listed several dozens of Biblical verses expressing the cruel, violence, racist and misogynistic teachings of the Old Testament, which pales compared to Thalmud.

The New Testament, however, contains a different teaching. Nevertheless, since the New Testament relies on many verses of the Old Testament and there are ambiguities regarding the degree of its validity for Christians, Christians have justified many barbaric acts, atrocities, and torture by using and abusing the verses of both Old and New Testaments. For instance, see:

- Mat 5:17-19, 29-30;
- Mat 10:34;
- Mat 19:12;
- Mat 21:19;
- John 15:6 (was abused by the church and used together with Exodus 22:18 to burn witches)
- 1 Peter 2:13-14 (following this instruction, many atrocities and wars were committed by Christians)

As for Kasem's question: "Mr. Yuksel, please tell me why must I not trust the most celebrated exegetes of the Koran, such as Jalalyn, ibn Abbas, ibn Kathir, Maududi and so on? Are you claiming they are inferior to you, or that they did not understand the Koran?"

This is a fair question, yet it also tells me that Kasem has no idea about our translation and our arguments. He is just happy to classify me with his stereotypes and criticize me with no knowledge at all. Since I have to cut this short, I will invite the reader to check my translation and find the my answer to this question, which initially sounds reasonable.

I would like to end this section with the following verses:

2:109   Many of the people of the book have wished that they could return you to being unappreciative after your acknowledgment, out of envy from themselves after the truth was made clear to them. You shall forgive them and overlook it until God brings His will. God is capable of all things

2:110   Observe the Contact prayer, and contribute towards betterment, and what you bring forth of good for yourselves, you will find it with God. God sees what you do.

Eternal Salvation is not Exclusive to a Race or Sect

2:111   They said, "None shall enter paradise except those who are Jewish or Nazarenes;" this is what they wish! say, "Bring forth your proof if you are truthful."

2:112   No, whosoever peacefully surrenders himself to God, while being a good-doer; he will have his reward with his Lord. There will be no fear over them, nor will they grieve.

3:84   Say, "We acknowledge God and what was sent down to us and what was sent down to Abraham, Ishmael, Isaac, Jacob, the Patriarchs, and what was given to Moses, Jesus and the prophets from their Lord. We do not discriminate between them, and to Him we peacefully surrender."

FP: Well, Mr. Yuksel, you say, "Our school of Islamic jurisprudence does not teach such a thing." I am a bit confused. What is the name of your madhhab (school of Islamic jurisprudence)? I have never heard of it. Who established it and when? How many adherents does it have? How do you propose to convince Muslims to forsake the traditional view and follow yours?

Again, one can find quotes in the Old Testament that are violent, but the key distinction is that there is no equivalent teaching of subjugating by force the world of the unbelievers.

The Qur'an clearly teaches that Muslims are the "best of peoples" (3:110) while the unbelievers are the "vilest of creatures" (98:6). And these vilest of creatures must be converted, killed or subjugated. There is no equivalent in Christian or Judaic teachings in terms of this theme. And that is why there are no armed Jewish or Christian groups anywhere in the world today who are committing acts of violence and justifying them by referring to any of their religious texts. And throughout history, the texts, for instance, that Mr. Yuksel has pointed to, have never been taken as divine commands that either must be or may be put into practice by believers in a new age. And this is the key: all these passages are descriptive, not prescriptive. None of these scriptures amount to any kind of marching orders for believers. They nowhere command believers to imitate any kind of described violent behavior, or to believe under any circumstances that God wishes them to act as his instruments of judgment in any situation at any time.

And this is why Jews and Christians haven't formed terror groups around the world that quote these Scriptures to justify killing civilian non-combatants. And this is why violent jihad is a constant of Islamic history – and why violent warfare in the name of Christianity is not a constant of Christian history. There was never a consensus among Jews or Christians that their religious texts justified violence and none of their sects of any significance ever taught that they did.

In any case, it is noted that Mr. Kasem found something to apologize for, but that Mr. Yuksel did not.

Robert Spencer, your turn.

SPENCER: Nothing I have read in this elephantine and contentious exchange has led me to modify my view that, as Mr. Haidon has said, "Muslims will never accept, on any level, removal of parts of the Qur'an." Not only are large num-

140

bers of Muslims ever likely to accept a drastically edited Qur'an, but they are also unlikely ever to flock to a wholesale reevaluation of Islamic theology involving the dismissal of the Hadith and Sira as "hearsay stories."

Mr. Warner is correct: "And there is no mechanism for reform. Our results-- good, bad or indifferent—do not make any difference. There is no body or group that could vote or agree on any change." Many strange things have happened in history and I would never say that Islamic reform is absolutely impossible, but Westerners are extraordinarily foolish when they harbor any hopes of it actually happening on a large scale. We need instead to focus on efforts to defend ourselves both militarily and culturally from the jihadist challenge, and to continue to call the bluffs of pseudo-reformers who intend ultimately only to deceive Western non-Muslims – many of whom are quite anxious to be deceived.

Because of the entrenched nature of Islamic orthodoxy, and its willingness to commit violence to enforce conformity, I am skeptical of the claims put forward by both Mr. Massoud and Mr. Yuksel to the effect that Muslims are flocking to their reform efforts.

Mr. Warner's insight is excellent -- that "all scholarship in Islam is either from the viewpoint of the kafir (kafir-centric), the dhimmi (dhimmi-centric) or believer (believer-centric)." In a world in which dhimmi-centric and believer-centric studies dominate the universities and media treatments of Islamic issues, Mr. Warner and others have stepped into the breach and begun to provide kafir-centric analyses to help non-Muslims understand exactly what we are dealing with. I myself have tried to fill a gap in kafir-centric scholarship on Muhammad with my book The Truth About Muhammad, and on the Qur'an in my Blogging the Qur'an series at hotair.com. At this point, which such a fog of ignorance and propaganda enveloping us and impeding our understanding of the jihad threat, to be informed is an essential first step.

And Mr. Warner is also quite right, of course, that "for the believer, Allah is wise, forgiving, knowing, and so forth. But for the kafir, Allah is a hater, a torturer, a plotter, a sadist, and an enemy. Allah makes us kafirs. Then he goes ahead to tell the Muslims what filthy scum we are." This dualism is deeply rooted in the Qur'an, which tells Muslims to be merciful to one another but harsh or ruthless to unbelievers (48:29), and tells them that they are the "best of people" (3:110) while the unbelievers are the "vilest of created beings" (98:6). Even worse, unbelievers have no control over their fate – while there are many verses in the Qur'an that assume that human beings have free will, early in Islamic history the proponents of this idea, the Qadariyya, were defeated, and human free will was declared a heretical infringement of Allah's absolute sovereignty.

The guiding principle on this issue in Islamic theology has been Qur'an 10:99-100: "And if thy Lord willed, all who are in the earth would have believed together. Wouldst thou (Muhammad) compel men until they are believers? No soul can believe, except by the will of Allah, and He will place doubt (or obscurity) on those who will not understand." Allah even boasts that he could have made everyone a believer, but instead will fill hell with humans and spirit beings: "If thy Lord had so willed, He could have made mankind one people, but they will not cease to dispute, except those on whom thy Lord hath bestowed His Mercy, and for this did He create them. And the Word of thy Lord shall be fulfilled: 'I will fill Hell with jinns and men all together.'" (11:118-119).

This put the unbeliever in the position of being a victim of Allah's decision not to make him a believer – a decision over which the unbeliever has no control, but for which he will suffer. This only reinforces the idea that the unbeliever – hated by Allah, more vile than any other creature, is not to accorded basic human respect. The presence of such material in the Qur'an first demonstrates, along with the Islamic supremacist and violent material that is also in the Qur'an, that a Qur'an-only Islam would not necessarily be an Islam in which Muslims respect and live in peace with their neighbors as equals

When, however, Mr. Warner makes his excellent observations about the position in which Islam puts the kafir, the inimitable Mr. Yuksel responds by scratching his head in wonder that anyone would want to be classed as an unbeliever. "There is variety of kafirs (ingrates)," he informs us, "and each treated according to the severity of their hostility, aggression and crimes. For instance, the Quran condemns the ingrates (kafirs) for attacking weak men, women and children (4:75-76), and Warner's feelings are hurt because we are asked to stand against those Kafirs." But unless Mr. Yuksel is postulating that anyone who doesn't believe in Islam will inevitably attack weak men, women and children, he is putting the cart before the horse.

The fundamental reason why the Qur'an demonizes kafirs is because they are kafirs, and any evil they do other than disbelieve in Allah flows from that disbelief. This is the sort of attitude, as Mr. Yuksel's demeanor here abundantly demonstrates, that militates against establishment of the basic respect that is required for people of differing views to live together in peace. For orthodox Muslims, and even unorthodox ones like Mr. Yuksel, to be able to have that respect would require that they first reject all this demonization. But it is deeply embedded in the Qur'an.

Mr. Yuksel errs when he attributes to the estimable Abul Kasem this statement: "He accuses Jamie Glazov of relying on 'unreliable hearsay stories' for information about Muhammad, but fails to inform us that the great majority of Muslims around the world rely on those same 'unreliable hearsay stories,' and offers no program for convincing those hundreds of millions of Muslims of the historical weakness of these stories." Actually, I said that, and I stand by it. Mr. Yuksel responds to this by saying, "If you had read the Reformist Translation or Manifesto for Islamic Reform you would learn that we offer a theologically consistent and very powerful argument to trash all those hearsay stories."

That's great, if it's true, but that's only part of what I said. Since Mr. Yuksel doesn't deign to share his "theologically consistent and very powerful argument" with us, but only asserts that it exists, I can't evaluate the chances of its gaining wide acceptance among Muslims worldwide, but that remains the key question. I haven't heard of any of the established Islamic sects or jurisprudential schools or the ulama of any Muslim country embracing his vaunted Reformist Translation. Perhaps Mr. Yuksel would be so kind as to provide us with a list.

Mr. Yuksel again errs by attributing to Abul Kasem my objection to his Qur'anic numerology. I pointed out that another Muslim writer had noted the forced and artificial character of Mr. Yuksel's apologetic, and concluded that "When Mr. Yuksel's fellow Muslims so readily notice such inaccuracies in his presentation, it's unlikely that many will accept his program for reform." Mr. Yuksel, however, now tells us that his "opponents finally accepted their error." In this, however, he did not simply ask us to take his word for it, but gave us a link – and I went there, only to find the Muslim source to which I had referred earlier saying this about Mr. Yuksel: "He is the man who published a list, supposedly of all occurrences of the word 'day' in the Qur'an, and this list was false on its face, and even more false when examined in detail. If I have erred in my publication, I invite correction, something Yuksel does not do; in fact he hates it."

This is Mr. Yuksel's opponent eating crow? It is in fact illustrative of a trait Mr. Yuksel shares with the Islamists he abhors: an inability to engage in self-criticism, and the displacement of one's own faults onto another, as in his complaint about Mr. Warner's alleged "diatribes and vitriolic attacks," when he himself is the only one who has actually engaged in such attacks. I am not saying, after all the squabbles above, that Mr. Yuksel is an Islamist; however, his attitudes are still redolent of the supremacism and contempt that characterizes Islamists. I respectfully suggest that his reform efforts would find better reception were he to rid himself of such attitudes.

Finally, he tells us that in his Reformist Translation we will "learn that the Quran justifies fighting against aggressor and violent Kafirs, that is warmongering ingrates, not peaceful ingrates like Kasem and Warner." Unfortunately, given the widespread Muslim belief that a resistance to or even a simple rejection of Islamic proselytizing constitutes "aggression," or that non-Muslims are aggressors against Allah for having rejected Islam, this is not enough to establish a framework for peaceful coexistence between Muslims and non-Muslims as equals on an indefinite basis.

Finally, Abul Kasem's question is highly pertinent and brilliantly put: "Mr. Yuksel, please tell me why must I not trust the most celebrated exegetes of the

Koran, such as Jalalyn, ibn Abbas, ibn Kathir, Maududi and so on? Are you claiming they are inferior to you, or that they did not understand the Koran?"

To this, Mr. Yuksel answers only by telling us that he has answered this question elsewhere. Great. But in a symposium discussing the reform of Qur'anic ideas and Islam in general, it would have been nice if he had deigned to favor us with his wisdom on this all-important question. And his ridiculous finger-pointing Bible quotes, which are used today by no Jewish or Christian group to justify violence, have already been well answered by Jamie Glazov. But they put the coup de grace to any hope I might have had that we will see any real reform effort coming from such quarters.

FP: Khalim Massoud, Abul Kasem, Edip Yuksel, Thomas Haidon, Bill Warner and Robert Spencer, thank you for joining Frontpage Symposium.

Jamie Glazov is Frontpage Magazine's managing editor. He holds a Ph.D. in History with a specialty in U.S. and Canadian foreign policy. He edited and wrote the introduction to David Horowitz's Left Illusions. He is also the co-editor (with David Horowitz) of The Hate America Left and the author of Canadian Policy Toward Khrushchev's Soviet Union (McGill-Queens University Press, 2002) and 15 Tips on How to be a Good Leftist. To see his previous symposiums, interviews and articles Click Here. Email him at jglazov@rogers.com.

To the Factor of 666

Edip Yuksel v Ali Sina

Dear Ali Sina, faithfreedom.org:

Regardless of your intention or motivation, I believe that your site is serving a great mission: people are provoked to think and question the claims made in the name of God, gods, or about God, gods.

I was told by a participant of 19.org/forum that you are challenging Muslims for debate and you also have expressed your intention to debate with me.

Here is my situation:

I am currently working on the *Reformist Translation of the Quran* with two colleagues of mine and busy with several other projects. With so much on my plate, I will not be able to engage in lengthy internet discussion with anyone. (For instance, years ago, I engaged in a lengthy debate with Abdurrahman Lomax on Code 19, the mathematical structure of the Quran. Our debate was later published as Running Like Zebras and available on the net).

HOWEVER,

I would be willing to engage in a face to face debate that could be recorded. I invite you to Arizona for such a debate; we can hold it at an auditorium at the campus of the University of Arizona or Pima Community College. If you accept this invitation then I will organize the debate. But, if you wish, we might meet at a university campus of your choice. Then, you should take the responsibility to organize and publicize it.

The debate must be public and must be one-to-one. We should agree on a moderator and also decide the topics or the outline of the debate. Later, the transcript of the debate could be posted on the internet and its video recording could be made available for public after we sign a contract.

I do not want you or others consider this as a CHALLENGE, but a friendly invitation to discuss the theological, philosophical, social, political and psychological aspects and ramification of faith in general and islam in particular.

Peace,

Edip Yuksel

Edip Yuksel Accepts Ali Sina's Challenge

Dear Susan and Omen:

I understand Susan's frustration and anger and I understand Omen's taking verses out of their context to demonize muslims.

In a century where Christians have fought two world wars therby killing millions, where Christians committed history's biggestt terrorist acts against two Japanese cities, where Crusaders have been destroying cities and massacring tens of thousands, where Isareli occupying forces have been torturing, killing and terrorizing the Palestinian population, the Christian-Zionist propaganda machine is working hard to depict their victims as monsters and terrorists. I understand that.

But, I am not here to debate with everyone, especially with the ones who appear to be screaming while their ears closed. I wish I had time and energy to respond to every one of you individually, even to those who have no patience to hear the opposing point of view.

I think Ali Sina will represent many of you in your cause against the Quran. If Ali Sina uses the same arguments, then I will respond them, God willing.

I thought that I received an invitation from him for a debate. If I am mistaken, or mislead by one of his fans, then I will continue what I need to do: finish my projects and enjoy my vacation with my family.

Peace, Edip

Then, let's do it in writing.

Dear Ali: Please read my second posting and let me know what is your answer. I will be leaving to California next Sunday and I will spend my time with extended family untill the beginning of the new year. So, I mihgt not be able to access internet...

If you wish, we may start our debate after the new year. Or, if you wish we may start now and continue after a one week holliday break.

As for reform: apparantly you misunderstood what I mean by this phrase. If you check my web site, you will find that your criticism is irrelevant.

Peace, Edip

Ok. Let's Start after the New Year

This is a challenging and colorful forum and without censorship like our forum at 19.org. There are many issues to be discussed and many deep emotions to be dealt with. I hope, when Ali and I start our debate in a restricted forum we will deal with most of these issues. After we settle our debate, hopefully the readers will post their reaction and fill the gaps in our arguments.

I urge you and myself to consider the possibility that there is an alternative way. That the truth may not be in either Christian, Muslim or Atheist side. For instance, when I criticized the wars and aggression of the modern Zionist-Crusader alliance, I did not intend to condone or support the violence conducted or dreamed of by some Muslims. Unfortunately, many were conditioned to assume that position for me with the "either-or" fallacy.

Personally, I suffered the most from the second violence: I had to leave my country, my family, my career, and everything behind to save my life from Sunni radicals! My struggle is well known in Turkey and I have shared with English speakers some of my personal experience at my website, http://www.yuksel.org. So, I think I am justified to demand a fair criticism, since I am not coming here with a mask on my face, but a person who is known by millions of people and who is not shy or scared to share his opinions and personal experience with others.

Unlike Ali Sina, my criticism and rejection of Sunni or Shiite version of Islam did not lead me to rejection of God or the Quran. Though there were times I contemplated such possibilities, but my faith in God and the Quran became much stronger after my rejection of the religion or sect of my parents falsely called Islam. Either I was not intellectually and emotionally as strong as Ali Sina, or I knew things that Ali did not know. Here, by God's will, we will debate these issues and we will find out which one of us is closer to the truth. I hope that you will not watch us like spectators in a football stadium or boxing ring, but with open mind and heart for what both people have to say. I want to remind people that on many issues I agree with Ali Sina, but on some crucial points I disagree and we will try to separate the hay from he grain.

Regardless of Ali's criticism and insults levied against what I consider dear and truth, I respect his courage to challenge Muslim scholars. I assume that he is honest too. His intelligence level is obvious from his writing. I consider honesty, courage, and critical approach to extraordinary claims as prerequisite qualities in the search of truth. And it seems that Ali Sina have all of them.

But, I am hurt by his remarks regarding my intentions. I did not rush to make such a judgment about his and I will try to control my primitive urge to judge his intentions. If Ali had taken a few minutes and asked people who know me, including my enemies, he would have found out that I gave up too many things for what I came to believe to be true. Most of my Sunni enemies, especially those who know me in Turkey, acknowledge the fact that I am honest and courageous. They shared this perception with public on TV debates, articles and books. I have changed my positions on many issues without thinking the social, political and economic consequences to my person. This principled attitude is evident even after my immigration to the United States. I left the Submitters organization when I found them becoming cult members trapped in hero-worship.

So, before attacking my honesty, I expect Ali to check my background. I treat truth above everything. If today I am convinced by a rational argument or by empirical evidence that the Quran is a man-made book, I would not hesitate to reject my present conviction. I do not make money from my books published on religion; I donate them. I am not getting salary to be an imam. I do not expect people to respect me because I am a holy man or the descendent of this or that dead holy man. To the contrary, I advice people who call me with titles such as "hodja", "Dr." or "efendi" to stop calling me with titles, especially when we have discussion or dialogue on religious matters. I deliberately sabotage my perceived charisma in many ways just to allow impressionable people to be able to think for themselves, without being influenced by my title, reputation, etc.

> "Whether Edip accepts the truth or not is not our concern. It would be naïve to expect those who have made a name for themselves and enjoy a position of respect within their community be so honest to give up all that just because they find out that they have been mistaken. In fact such people will never find out that they have been mistaken because they will not even consider the possibility."

Thus, I consider Ali's comment above to be an attack to my core value. I might have false ideas and opinions, but I am honest in perpetual pursuit of truth and appreciation of it. Ali does not need to apologize for his prejudice about me. During the upcoming debate with me, I believe he will recognize how unfair assessment and prejudice it was. However, I think he is right in general. Those who have vested interest in a particular religion or political ideology have invisible walls erected between them and the truth.

I am not seeking your votes. In fact, I believe that majority of people will neither like nor accept what I will say here. So, I hope my arguments will be evaluated separate from presumed negative and positive speculations about my personality or intention. Hopefully, Ali will compile a list of QUESTIONS expressing his reasons for rejecting Islam and we will start discussing them on a new forum.

Peace, Edip

Using Hearsay of Hearsay as History

Ali Sina

12-21-2004

I went to your site and read your views on hadith:

http://www.yuksel.org/e/religion/trash.htm

So you prefer to use the books of history to learn about Muhammad. That is fine with me. I will rely on history when I talk to you. However let us talk about hadith for now.

Your position is that all hadiths should be scrapped because a lot of them are fabricated. Lomax, your opponent in that debate, made a valid observation. He said: "The bound collection of testimony from any court is certain to contain some lies and some errors. The reliability of any piece of evidence remains debatable….And if a collector collects a thousand hadith and makes a few errors neither is he to be condemned as unreliable."

You rebutted his statement and said: "Not a single court will accept the testimony of Bukhari who collected contradictory hadiths about the Prophet Muhammad, narrated from generation to generation 200 years after his departure."

On this issue I side with Lomax. Let us make this clear with an example. The police department of a city is trying to solve a case and asks for tips from the public. Thousands of tips pour in. Most of them are completely unrelated, but among those thousands a few corroborate a story and based on those related tips the detectives will be able to solve the case. It would be unconscionable to through away all the tips because most of them are incorrect.

In our case we want to know about Muhammad and how he lived his life. We have tens of thousands of tips in the form of narrations of his followers. Many of them are weak leads and many of them are fabricated. We know also that the believers tend to exaggerate and aggrandize the virtues and attribute miracles to their beloved prophet. So when it comes to these particular hadiths we should take them with a grain of salt. However when we put all these tips together the picture of a man emerges. We separate those tips that corroborate each other and based on them we sketch the profile of our suspect. Can we be 100% sure that this is how he looked? Maybe not! But because these tips come from a variety of sources and despite the differences in detail they tell us the same story we can be fairly sure that we have a good idea of how our suspect looked and what he did.

So if I were a responsible detective, I would not discard all the tips simply because some of them are fabricated, especially when there is no other source to depend on. However, what if the picture emerging of the suspect portrays my beloved father? What would be my natural reaction? I would probably want to scrap all the tips and discredit them. This is dishonesty. But hey, you are talking about my father. You are asking me to choose between filial piety and honesty. That is a tough choice. Not everyone can pass that test. I would do everything to cover up my father's crime and protect him. That is how I see you and all other hadith deniers. You do not like what you see in the hadith. They embarrass you. You find Muhammad torturing his victims, beheading them, gauging their eyes, raping them and doing all sorts of despicable acts and all that hurts. So instead of being honest and admit that you were wrong and the man whom you worship is a psychopath criminal, you try to dismiss all the hadiths. You think if you put your head in the sand and pretend you do not see; the problem will go away. The despicable lawyers of O.J. Simpson did that and they won. But does that mean that Mr. Simpson is innocent? Even if you win this case based on discrediting the evidence and technicalities, can you still live with your conscience?

Can we use these hadiths in an actual court of law to incriminate Muhammad? I think we can. You may argue that they are circumstantial and try to discredit them. But they are so many of them that any sane jury will find it difficult to dismiss them. Muhammad is guilty as charged.

However, our goal is not to take legal action against Muhammad. He is dead. We want to find out the truth. We may never be able to find the truth one hundred percent. But we can get a fairly good idea of it. What you have now is absolute lie.

Nonetheless, we have enough evidence in the Quran, in the books of history and in the hadith to become certain that Muhammad was not a messenger of God but a cult leader like Jim Jones and David Koresh and this I will prove to you in our discussions.

Muslims have fallen in love with Muhammad because they have been shown a picture of him which portrays him as a holy man, a perfect human being, an example for all to follow, the mercy of God for all the creation, etc, etc. That image is false. According to our tips, and his own book, he was far from being a good man. How did the Muslims get that false picture in their minds? …Because they were fed with lies! It certainly does not match the picture we get from our tips and from our thorough investigation. So which picture is more accurate? The one that is based on the fantasies of his followers or the one that emerges from the tips?

This is just to show the weakness of the position of the Quran only Muslims. Apart from the fact that this is a fallacious way of thinking, it leaves Islam indecipherable.

P.S. I was about to post this that I found you have posted the above message. So I will read and respond to your message in another posting

---

I see in this letter you say that you don't even acknowledge the biography of Muhammad as recorded by Ibn Ishaq, Tabari and Waqidi. I understood this differently when I read your debate with Lomax but now it is clear.

If that is your position and you are adamant to deny all the historic evidences relating to Muhammad, I deny even the existence of Muhammad. I claim that he was the fabrication of Arab rulers who needed a religion to justify their imperialistic ambitions (See Crone and Cook). You are a lawyer. You know that the burden of proof is on the person who is making the positive assertion, i.e. you. It is you who must prove that Muhammad actually existed and was not just a fictitious personage, a figment of the unknown real author/s of the Quran. Anything you say must be documented. However you can't use the hadith or the Sira to make your case. If you deny these books you can't use them.

I do not think that you are relying on every historical report of the syrah books, such as Tabari or Waqidi. I will treat each historical anecdote on ad-hoc basis and evaluate it critically with a healthy dose of suspicion.

So what is your position exactly? Are you saying that part of the history is acceptable? I perfectly understand looking at the history and hadith with a healthy dose of suspicion. That is my position too. The reason I bring this up is to know which documents are admissible in our discussion and which ones are not and whether your rejection of haidth and Sira is categorical or you are open to accept them with a healthy dose of suspicion. Are you willing to use the same criteria also for the hadith or hadith is definitely out?

I asked on what you base your knowledge of Muhammad and you responded:

> "I mostly rely on the narration of the Quran. If the Quran's account contradicts the account of a particular narration I chose the narrative of the Quran."

That is okay with me. If a hadith or a narration contradicts the Quran or the spirit of it we will reject it.

So let me recapitulate what I understood from your position. You would look at hadith and the biography of Muhammad, provided they do not contradict the Quran or the spirit of it. You are willing to consider them as sources of information for their historic value, although with some reservation.

151

If that is your position I am with you. That is how I look at those sources too. But if I have misunderstood you please correct me.

If that is the case, I will make my case against Muhammad using the hadith and Sira as well as the Qurn. You are of course free to dispute the accuracy of each document I present based on the above mentioned criteria. i.e. if they contradict the Quran, we will discard them but if they don't we keep them, not as absolute truth but as a probable.

In other words, we will not discard a hadith or a story just because it incriminates Muhammad. After all that is what I want to prove. If I am not even allowed to present my evidence against him then what is the point of the trial?

I agree not to present any evidence that is against the explicit or implicit teachings of the Quran. You are entitled to question the validity of my exhibits but if you can't demonstrate that they are unauthentic we are not going to discard them. We leave them there as probable. It is my conviction that the weight of these probable documents and that of the Quran will be so overwhelming that I will win the case against Muhammad and will prove to you and the world that he was an impostor and not a prophet. Scott Peterson's lawyer argued that all the evidences against his client are circumstantial. He was right! But they were so many that the Jurry had no problem convicting him. We have a lot more evidence against Muhammad.

Edip Yuksel v. Ali Sina (3)

Palmreader Finds Dirty Character

Edip Yuksel

12-22-2004

> "That is how I see you and all other hadith deniers. You do not like
> what you see in the hadith. They embarrass you. You find Muhammad
> torturing his victims, beheading them, gauging their eyes, raping them
> and doing all sorts of despicable acts and all that hurts. So instead of
> being honest and admit that you were wrong and the man whom you
> worship is a psychopath criminal, you try to dismiss all the hadiths.
> You think if you put your head in the sand and pretend you do not see;
> the problem will go away. The despicable lawyers of O.J. Simpson did
> that and they won. But does that mean that Mr. Simpson is innocent?
> Even if you win this case based on discrediting the evidence and tech-
> nicalities, can you still live with your conscience?"

Dear Sina:

I was denied access to this forum as Edip Yuksel. So, I re-registered under the
username www.19.org and was able to access again. I would prefer to use Edip
Yuksel consistently here. I hope you will correct the technical problem.

This reminded, let's continue our discussion:

Once I was a believer and defender of hadith. However, when I studied the history of hadith, its collection, procedures of its collection, and problems with
their authenticity and the profound difference between hadith and the Quran, yes
when I witnessed that, I gave up from following hadith and sunnah.

I understand why you want me to drag to a source that I have come to refute at
the cost of risking my life. You want me to revert back to my old days and start
believing those sources that are mere hearsay. Here is my answer:

I WILL NOT ACCEPT YOUR INVITATION TO DIG INTO A LITERARY
GARBAGE AND CHOOSE AND PICK WHATEVER WE LIKE AMONG
THE THOUSANDS Of CONTRADICTORY AND OCCASIONALLY
RIDICULOUS NARRATION.

It appears that you are not able to criticize the Quran without the help of adding some garbage from collections of hearsay. Muslims and non-Muslims, all agree that the historical authenticity of the Quran is far beyond the authenticity of hadith. Thus, your insistence to rely on hadith, by a biased criterion of "if it says something good about prophet we will reject it but if it says bad things about him we jump over and accept it" is unacceptable. It is unfair; it is dishonest.

How can you rely on Bukhari who came from Bukhara to the scene 200 years after Muhammad and started collecting anything he heard and liked?

How can you rely on Bukhari who in the beginning of his collection is not even ashamed of insulting MONKEYS by reporting that a companion of the prophet saw monkeys stoning an adulterous monkey to death? According to your suggested criterion of sifting the garbage, we should accept this report since it does not praise Muhammad! Or you have another criterion that you forgot to communicate to me? You may end up with hundreds of arbitrary criteria to be able to justify your picks and rejects!

How can you invite me to speculate on Bukhari who confesses of collecting 700,000 hadiths and accepting only about 7000; rejecting 99 percent of them? Don't you see the exaggeration? Had Muhammad talked every minute of his life after claiming messengership, his words could have hardly added up to 700,000 hadiths.

How can you take Bukhari serious who justifies the abrogation of a Quranic verse after Muhammad's departure by none other than a holy goat that ate the skin where the alleged verses issuing the stoning-to-death for adulterers written? Should we accept that report? In order to add another insult to Islam you would like to have it. But you cannot have it both ways. You have to also believe the "holy goat":)

Bukhari had a very different idea of islam than Muhammad. Bukhari was an ignorant idol worshiper and had no respect for the Quran. Besides, he sided with the oppressive rulers. For instance, he found Marwan, the drunk and murderer governor. to be a credible person and narrating "sahih" hadiths from him, while he declined accepting any hadith from a brave student of the Quran, Abu Hanifah who suffered in the jails of Umayyad and Abbasid dynasties for rejecting to sell his soul! Bukhari was not an objective hadith collector; he was on the side of murderers and agressors.

We can write volumes of books listing the contradiction between the teaching of Bukhari and the Quran, the only book delivered by Muhammad. Then, how can a sound person claim Bukhari to be a friend of Muhammad? To me, he was a real enemy of Muhammad (6:112-116), like St. Paul was the real enemy of Jesus, since he too distorted another messenger's message beyond recognition.

Let me little side track here. For instance, Jesus never silenced women and put them down with xenophobic teachings but St. Paul asked women to submit to men and hush: (1Ti 2:7-15; 1 Corinthians 14:34-35; 1 Peter 3:7). Jesus never asked for money for preaching but St. Paul asked for money shamelessly and likened his audience to flock of sheep to be milked by the holy sheperd! (Who goeth a warfare any time at his own charges? who planteth a vineyard, and eateth not of the fruit thereof? or who feedeth a flock, and eateth not of the milk of the flock? 1Co 9:7). He was a successful Machiavellian (before Machiavelli was born!) as opposed to Jesus who did not twist the truth to gain people: "To the weak became I as weak, that I might gain the weak: I am made all things to all men, that I might by all means save some." (1 Corinthians 9:22).

How can you trust Bukhari who narrates the LAST HADITH while prophet Muhammad in his death bed, rejecting the recording of any hadith through a decleration from the mouth of Omar Bin Khattap and the acquiescence of all prominent muslims that "*Hasbuna kitabullah*" (God's word is sufficient for us)? Will your suggested criterion to sift through the garbage pile help us to decide the authenticity of this hadith and reject all the rest? Which one do you believe? Was the Quran deemed sufficient by early muslims or they too needed hearsay reports to understand the Quran? What is the meaning of protecting the Quran from tempering while making it needy of volumes of dubious and fabricated stories?

How can you trust hadith books that report THE MOST WITNESSED HADITH, or THE MOST AUTHENTIC HADITH and yet manage to confuse the most crucial words, THE LAST WORDS in that hadith? The hadith about the last sermon, which was claimed to be witnessed by more than hundred thousand believers, has three different endings: (1). Follow the Quran. (2). Follow the Quran and my Sunnah. (3). Follow the Quran and my family. Should we pick and choose! Throw dice? How will your criterion help us to pick the accurate version?

How can you invite me to take Bukhari a serious source of history while in its LONGEST HADITH it narrates the story of Miraj in which poor Muhammad goes up and down between 6th and 7th heavens trying to reduce the number of daily prayers? In that hadith, Muhammad is like an innumerate and gullible union leader bargaining for some break time on behalf of his people against a merciless boss (*hasha* God!) who tries to impose 50 prayers a day, that is, a prayer for every 28 minutes, day and night! In that narration Moses is the wise guy and he coaches Muhammad in this hard task of negotiation with God! According to your suggested criterion, we should accept this hadith because Muhammad is depicted as an idiot who cannot even calculate the impossibility of performing 50 prayers (not unit) a day without the help of Moses who resides just one heaven below God? Even if one tried at that time they could not have divided the day to 50 periods of 28-minutes! Since, this hadith insults the intelligence of

155

Prophet Muhammad according to your garbage-sifting criterion, should we believe this story?!

How can you trust the account of hadith books, which unanimously claim that Muhammad was an illiterate man? Based on your criterion, we should swallow this lie because it does not praise Muhammad, since it depicts him an illiterate man who was not capable of learning 28 letters while dictating a book for 23 years! Or should we reject it because while insulting Muhammad it praises the literary excellence of the Quran?

Idiot or ignorant friends can harm a person more than wise enemies. Hadith and siyar books are products of ignorant friends who insulted and defamed the men they idolized. Besides, we should not ignore the possibility of some converts with agenda to distort the message. For instance, many Jewish stories and practices were imported to "islam" via "convert" Jewish and Christian scholars, such as belief in the coming of Mahdi and second-coming of Jesus, and practice of circumcision, stoning to death for adultery, etc. Kab bin al Ahbar is one of those influential converts. The story of Muhammad massacring Bani Qurayza Jews is another fabricated story by Jewish converts; unfortunately they were able to insert such lies into hadith and siyar books, which provided every clever fabricator access to a holy mass propaganda.

Hadith books contain almost anything you want. You may find an extremely kind and nice Muhammad besides a cruel torturer one. You may find Muhammad to be a person with great morals on one page, and on the next page you may see him a pedophile. You will find Muhammad pointing at the moon and splitting it into two pieces letting one piece falling into Ali's backyard, and on the other page you will find Muhammad incapable of reading a simple letter. Now, you want us to enter this Muhammad-in-the-Wonderland story books and separate truth from falsehood. And without looking in my eyes, you are suggesting me to pick the bad and reject the good ones. You cannot be serious!

> "Can we use these hadiths in an actual court of law to incriminate Muhammad? I think we can. You may argue that they are circumstantial and try to discredit them. But they are so many of them that any sane jury will find it difficult to dismiss them. Muhammad is guilty as charged."

It is evident that you have no knowledge of modern rules of evidence in justice system. I challenge you to find a single judge in America that would find those hearsay reports credible for character assassination. If you find one, I promise that I will petition to the bar to take away that judge's license by using similar hearsay statements to depict him as a drunk child molester! Yes, go find a single judge in a secular country accepting the garbage you are inviting me to.

156

> "However, our goal is not to take legal action against Muhammad. He is dead. We want to find out the truth. We may never be able to find the truth one hundred percent. But we can get a fairly good idea of it. What you have now is absolute lie."

As I gave a few examples out of many, it is not possible to get a fair and objective idea by using hadith and siyra books. But, your insistence on this issue gives away your weakness. You are not able to discuss Islam based on the most reliable historic document, the Quran. You had perhaps great time in constructing arguments against Sunni or Shiite Muslims who are mislead by those sources. As you know, I follow the Quran alone, like Muhammad himself did. There are now, thank God, tens of thousands of Muslims all around the world discovering this truth.

> "This is just to show the weakness of the position of the Quran only Muslims. Apart from the fact that this is a fallacious way of thinking, it leaves Islam indecipherable."

Interesting. How in the world you can construe our rejection of hearsay and silly reports as weakness? The real weakness is in your argument, since you mix garbage in your arguments. I did not come here to speculate on books that NEITHER OF US TRUST. Bukhari could not survive five minutes in the witness stand and he would be rejected by every decent court of justice. But, your hatred against Muhammad or Islam, as it seems, has made you care less about truth and justice.

> "If that is your position and you are adamant to deny all the historic evidences relating to Muhammad, I deny even the existence of Muhammad. I claim that he was the fabrication of Arab rulers who needed a religion to justify their imperialistic ambitions (See Crone and Cook). You are a lawyer. You know that the burden of proof is on the person who is making the positive assertion, i.e. you. It is you who must prove that Muhammad actually existed and was not just a fictitious personage, a figment of the unknown real author/s of the Quran. Anything you say must be documented. However you can't use the hadith or the Sira to make your case. If you deny these books you can't use them."

Why do you think that the books collected centuries after Muhammad are more reliable sources regarding the words and deeds of Muhammad? Why rejecting those books should undermine the HISTORIC value of the Quran? I find no connection. Let's say I reject the claims of a biography of Jefferson written by a contemporary author and you tell me: "Well, if you reject this book then how can you prove that Jefferson was indeed a real person who drafted the constitution of the United States?"

I am not sure how serious you are in your denying the historic reality of Muhammad. You are right that I cannot PROVE his existence to you, neither you can prove to me that there was Jesus or Socrates. But, you are missing the entire point.

I follow the Quran. Whether Muhammad existed or not is really a side issue in the context of the message of the Quran. I am not following Muhammad; I am following the message of the messenger. I am here to defend the principles and teachings of the Quran. The questions such as "Did Muhammad really exist or not?", or "Was Muhammad a good guy or not?" are not relevant right now.

Again, I invite you to tell me which verses of the Quran you have problems with and why. Please be as specific and concise as possible. Let's discuss the real issues. I hope we will not be distracted by secondary issues.

PS: I believe and argue that the Quran is the word of God and the information containing there is authentic. Inshallah, when we get over this procedural issues I will share you my REASONS why I believe in the divine nature of the Quran.

Peace,

Edip

Edip Yuksel v. Ali Sina (4)

Sample Discussion with Audience

Edip Yuksel

12-22-2004

Kufr0929:"Edip, I don't believe there was a muhammad, he was invented 50-100 years after his supposed death. Initially arabs used to say muhammad rasoul alla, which also means praised be the messenger of alla, they might have been talking about abraham or ishmael. My question to you is about koran, which I think is the source of hate and fascism: go , pick up a Quran and read the following verses: 2:191,3:28,3:85,5:10,5:34,9:5,9:28,9:29,9:123,14:17,22:9,25: 52,47:4, and 66:9, you will get your answer. They all promote hatred and violence against non-muslims. A person who believes the Quran to be God's words, and has read and believes in, these verses, is thus a terrorist , atleast in mind, if not in practice. It is another matter that most muslims are totally ignorant of what is really in their scriptures and their history books. They continue to believe that Islam is a peaceful religion ; and the knowledgable religious leadership wants it that way because exposing them to the reality will result in losses in mosque attendance and fund collection from gullible muslims. Most effective way to fight this islamic terrorism , instead of spending billions in wars and weapons, is exposing the truth to the world and stop being politically correct. Please support courageous people like Taslima Nasrin, Ali Sina (faithfreedom.org) and Ibn Warraq (secularislam.org)."

EDIP: Dear Kufr0929, I answered Ali Sina regarding his conspiracy theory of the fictional Muhammad. You can even claim that Muhammad was an E.T. So what? One can speculate in infinite ways, as long as he does not think that he needs evidence for his wild assertions.

I would like to keep this discussion between me and Ali Sina, since it will be impossible for me to answer every criticism directed to me regarding my faith. I was hoping that I would discuss this and similar verses with Ali Sina, and we agreed to keep this debate restricted. So, I might be going against our agreement, perhaps justified by your access to this so-called restricted forum.

I am a student of the Quran and I have translated the Quran to Turkish and currently working on its English translation together with native speakers. I understand and relate to you why you could reject those verses. If I (mis)understood them like you and majority of muslims do, then I would too have problems with them.

Here is why I think you do not understand the verses the way I understand:

1. You are taking them out of their Quranic context.

Following your method, I could easily depict Jesus, one of the messengers of peace (islam), as a divider and a trouble maker, rather than uniter and peace-maker:

> "Suppose ye that I am come to give peace on earth? I tell you, Nay; but rather division: For from henceforth there shall be five in one house divided, three against two, and two against three. The father shall be divided against the son, and the son against the father; the mother against the daughter, and the daughter against the mother; the mother in law against her daughter in law, and the daughter in law against her mother in law." (Lu 12:51-53).

But reasonable people will consider this an injustice to Jesus and his message.

2. You rely on distorted translations by sectarian clergymen:

You are relying on the translation of scholars who follow the diabolic teachings of hadith and sunnah. They try hard to distort the meaning or implication of verses to make them compatible with those teachings.

3. You are ignoring many other verses that compliment these verses and clarify the rules of engagement.

4. You falsely assume that the practices of Sunni or Shiite khalifs and kings were in accordance with the Quran.

God willing, I will later deal with each verse you listed here. But, I expect this debate to be done between me and one person, presently Ali Sina.

Here, I just want to briefly express my opinion on the verse number that you have attached to your user name, 9:29:

The verse is mistranslated by almost every translator. The correct translation of it should be:

9:29   "You shall fight (back) against those who do not believe in God, nor in the last day, and they do not prohibit what God and His messenger have prohibited, and do not abide by the system of truth among those who received the scripture, until they pay the COMPANSATION, in humility."

You have noticed that I inserted a paranthesis since the context of the verse is about the War of Hunain, and fighting is allowed for only self defense. See: 2:190-193, 256; 4:91; and 60:8-9.

Furthermore, note that I suggest COMPENSATION instead of Arabic word Jizya. The meaning of Jizya has been distorted as tax on non-Muslims, which was invented long after Muhammad to further the imperialistic agenda of Kings. The origin of the word that I translated as Compensation is JaZaYa, which simply means compensation, not tax. Since the enemies of muslims attacked and agressed, after the war they are required to compensate for the damage they inflicted on the peaceful community. Various derivatives of this word are used in the Quran frequently, and they are translated as COMPANSATION.

I hope you will forgive my lack of opportunity and time to engage in lengthy discussion with you.

armour_piercing_bullets: "Anyone who believe in koran and allah-false god is a terrorist. no need to waste our time on these terrorists. let him prove how his terrorist god/allah created man from mud/clay."

EDIP: Dear Armour: You should be respectful to your creator, who created you from clay (not mud). Several years ago, the Scientific American had a cover story about the origin of life. The scientists were claiming that life must have started from geodesic structure of clay, since its loose layers create a perfect environment for incubation. We are the latest product of evolution that started from the layers of clay. Thus, my understanding of the word FROM is different than the common understanding. I consider it indicating space rather than substance.

> "let him prove how noah took 2 animals each and these later repopulated the world."

The flood related to Noah was not worldwide. The Quran never claims such a world-wide fload. Rather, it was limited to Noah's community around Dead Sea. Noah took pairs from his farm animals to a boat made of logs.

> "let him prove how the stone in kaba is given by allah to ismeal/abraham."

That volcanic stone is not sacred; though Muslims worship that black stone. I guess it might have been used to indicate the starting point of circumbulation during the time of prophet. But, later when Muslims turned back to the days of ignorance they idolized many things including the black stone and Muhammad's grave.

> "there r 100 other things in koran that r false."

Hopefully, Ali Sina will bring these allegations up and I will inshalah deal with each of them. Please remind Ali Sina about these 100 false things.

> "this guy is a fundamentalist muslim,and a threat to peace, secularism and freedom. he is an islamic nazi."

What can I say? It is unfortunate that you falsely depict a man who has been promoting peace against the agents of hatred. May God give you sense of fairness and justice.

> "religion especially judeo christianity islam is a disease and truth is the only cure"

I do agree with the real implication of this statement. I find most of the religious organizations to be manipulated by politicians. However, humans have abused many other institutions. Secular governments spend too much resources to manufacture weapons and kill people of other countries. Communism too was used to suppress and oppress people. Now we see "democracy and liberty" has been abused by an evangelist US-Inc president to invade and destroy other countries.

Shake Down: "Now if the debate continues to use hadiths as a source Ali will win. There is no defense against hadiths. It has long been my view that Sunnis and anti-Islam types both love hadiths but for very different reasons. Sunnis love them because they can find anything they want to support their corrupt beliefs. Anti-Islam folks love them because they can use hadiths to show that Muhammad was an awful person."

EDİP: Thank you Shake Down for this insightful assessment.

Denis Giron: "The first objection I have is that Dr. Sina seemed to avoid the issue of hearsay, which is precisely what the ahaadeeth are comprised of. It is one thing to have witnesses, but it is wholly another to have people saying: "I heard from so-and-so that so-and-so heard from so-and-so that somebody else witnessed person X perform action Y." Mr. Yuksel is right, this would not stand up in court. Rather it would be struck down with a single word objection: hearsay."

"Now, I agree that it might be absurd to say every single claim in the ahaadeeth is unreliable (I find that to be analogous to those who attempt to reject the entire New Testament in toto). Nonetheless, it seems that Dr. Sina considers an uncomfortable amount of the ahaadeeth reliable, and I suspect that he does this only because it provides him with an easier stick with which to beat Islam. I find the attempt to force Yuksel to accept the ahaadeeth as a straw man approach, analogous to trying to force a Protestant to accept Catholic beliefs before disproving Christianity."

162

EDIP: Excellent points Denis. I checked your website, http://www.geocities.com/freethoughtmecca/ and I liked your work. I would like to get to know you further. If you accept, I might invite you to review and participate in our translation of the Quran. It will contain a lot of side notes with philosophical and theological arguments. You may contact me via my cell phone: 520 xxx xxxx..

IDF: "Fine, Yuskel Should be a little more accurate instead of "hinting" the Quran approving the stories before it. Its not making sense that his readers need to "interpret" what Yuskel really meant. Also, how can one re-write something that claimed to be complete anyway? Yuskel doesnt have to use that of a high **language** to express more in less words."

EDIP: You are right IDF. I was not careful in my language. The Quran "narrates" some events that allegedly happened centuries ago. What I meant was the events that happened during the revelation of the Quran. Thank you for this correction.

> "Its funny that I see arabic names like 'JIBREEL', 'YUSUF', 'MUSA', or 'ISMAIL'. I see that and think, do they even know they actually name their kids in hebrew? (only with some arabic accent). I could totally be apathetic towards it, but we all know how arabs/muslims hate jews/americans to no end and call to ITBAH them 'wherever/whenever' they are."

Hebrew and Arabic languages are very close to each other. For instance Salam or Shalom. They are twin languages. An Arab might claim that Hebrew language was derived from Arabic. I consider both claims to be unsubstantiated. Besides, I do consider Jewish race as a prototype of humanity. Their accomplishments and blunders are incredible compared to their population ratio. Besides, I do not consider Arabic holier than Hebrew or any other language...

Farside: "The magical numbers of Islam hold a special place my heart."

EDIP: I loved that picture! But, I could not post it here; and I do not have much time to find a way to do that. Can you please visit 19.org/forum and post it there so that with your permission we can use it.

Peace, Edip

163

Edip Yuksel v. Ali Sina (5)

"Muhammad was illiterate and cruel"

Ali Sina

12-22-2004

> "Dear Sina:
>
> "Once I was a believer and defender of hadith. However, when I stud-
> ied the history of hadith, its collection, procedures of its collection, and
> problems with their authenticity and the profound difference between
> hadith and the Quran, yes I witnessed this, I gave up from following
> hadith and sunnah."
>
> "I understand why you want me to drag to a source that I have come to
> refute at the cost of my life. You want me to revert back to my old days
> and start believing those sources that are mere hearsay. Here is my an-
> swer:"
>
> "I WILL NOT ACCEPT YOUR INVITATION TO DIG INTO A
> LITERARY GARBAGE AND CHOOSE AND PICK WHATEVER
> WE LIKE AMONG THE THOUSANDS Of CONTRADICTORY
> AND OCCASIONALLY RIDICULOUS NARRATION."
>
> "It appears that you are not able to criticize the Quran without the help
> of adding some garbage from collections of hearsay."

On the contrary! I will show that the Quran is full of errors and absurdities and it
can't be a book of revelation unless the revealer was Satan. The reason I want to
clarify the question of hadith is to demonstrate the fallacy of the position of
those who totally deny them. Once that is established I will have no need for
hadith.

Muslims and non-Muslims, all agree that the historical authenticity of the Quran
is far beyond the authenticity of hadith.

It is not true that everyone agrees that the Quran is more authentic than the
hadith. Here is a study that disagrees with that claim:

http://www.derafsh-kaviyani.com/english/quran1.html

> "Thus, your insistence to rely on hadith, by a biased criterion of 'if it
> says something good about prophet we will reject it but if it says bad

things about him we jump over and accept it.' is unacceptable. It is un-fair; it is dishonest."

I already responded to this in my example of police and tips from the public. It would be dishonest to disregard all those tips. No investigator would do such thing unless he is trying to cover up.

You want us to throw all the incriminating evidence against Muhammad just because some of those stories my not be true. The mere fact that some of them are fabricated is not enough reason to discard all of them. You have to do more than that to discredit them all. For example let us talk about the motive.

People do not lie unless there is a motive. What was the motive of those who reported these hadiths?

Sycophantism is a motive. People lie to endear themselves. They falsely attrib-ute miracles to their cult leader because they find receptive audience among fel-low believers. This makes them feel important and validates their ego. This is very typical in cults where the cult leader is elevated superlatively by his cronies and each tries to fabricate a lie to make the cult leader look bigger and holier, both during his life time and after his death. A good example is John de Ruiter, the self appointed "Messiah" who has orgies with two young sisters with the consent and gratitude of their parents even though he is married.

A few years ago in my neighborhood market, I saw his flyer pinned to the bill-board. It was an invitation to his conferences with these words:

> "John de Ruiter: Master of transformation; living embodiment and teacher of Truth."

And;

> "Through the living essence of Truth emanating from his words and from his presence, John de Ruiter awakens what our hearts most long for…"

Any sane person can see that this self proclaimed "guru of the gurus" is insane. But that is not what his followers see. I can bring multitude of examples such as these where the followers of cults become blind and try to fabricate an unreal image of their leader. The point here is that such narrations from the befogged followers of cults should not be taken seriously. So when we see hadiths that attribute miracles to Muhammad we should discard them or at least the part con-taining the miracles. Also attributing miracles to Muhammad contradicts the Quran.

165

We see Muhammad shrugging his shoulder when people ask for miracles. He said "There came to you messengers before me, with clear Signs and even with what ye ask for: why then did ye slay them, if ye speak the truth?"3:138 Or: "Glory to my Lord! Am I aught but a man,- a messenger?" Q.17:93. We see this denial that he can perform any miracles in many verses of the Quran (25:7,8 17: 95) People called him mad and possessed and asked "Why do you not bring to us the angels if you are of the truthful ones? Q15:7 His response was: "We send not the angels down except for just cause Q.15:8 In another place we read ""And the Unbelievers say: "Why is not a sign sent down to him from his Lord?" But thou art truly a warner, and to every people a guide." Q.13:7 His contention was that even with clear signs people rejected the prophets so the miracles are useless. Q.3:184

Therefore if the Quran is right then all the miracles attributed to Muhammad in the hadiths are fabricated.

It is clear why the believers fabricate false stories to make their cult leader look grand. But why would they lies to make him look like a villain? We have stories about Muhammad raiding innocent unarmed people with no warning, massacring and looting them, enslaving their wives and children and raping them, torturing people to make them reveal the whereabouts of their treasures, branding their eyes with hot red iron and then raping their wives on the same day. There are stories about him beheading in cold blood 750 innocent men who had surrendered to him without a fight when he blockaded their quarter and diverted the flow of the water to their town. We have hadiths that say he assassinated his opponents including a 120 year old man and a mother of five small children only because they composed poetries criticizing them.

These hadiths are confirmed in the books of history (Siras). They come to us from a variety of sources. They vary in detail but are consistent in the main theme which is normal when a story is reported by several people. There are names of the people involved. They do not seem to be fabrications because of the amount of details.

The main question is WHY? Why would devout followers who loved their prophet report so many false stories about him that portray him as a criminal, mass murderer, rapist, pedophile, assassin, deceiver, and a highway robber?

The motive is important. We can see a clear motive why people fabricate lies to make their prophet look holy but what motive could they have to lie about their prophet and make him look so evil?

We could also overlook such hadiths if they were just a few. Someone could have been an enemy in disguise and might have lied. But we have thousands upon thousands of hadiths that tell the same tale of brutality and portray Muhammad as a criminal. At the same time we have no other version of the same events. If Muhammad actually did not raid the innocent populations how they converted to Islam? Do we have a different version of how Islam expanded? Why would so many devout believers who waged wars for Islam and gave their lives fabricate so many falsehoods against their prophet? Why would dedicated scholars such as Ibh Ishaq, Tabari, Waqidi, Ibn Sa'd, Ibn Hisham, Bukhari, Muslim, Abu Dawud, Malik or others spend an entire life writing books based on nothing but lies? What happened to the "real" history of Muhammad? How come not a single version of that was ever written? And all what is survived are lies? If all these people were liars, where were the truthful scholars of Islam? How can it be that for 1300 years all the Muslims were lying and suddenly when they came in contact with the West and were embarrassed to see their religion is barbaric in comparison to the humanistic values of the Westerners they discovered that the history of Muhammad that they have is all lies?

Your position of denial is absurd and untenable. You are shocked by the sheer inhumanity of Muhammad, but you are not capable to let go. You try to cling to him desperately but you mask the truth, lie to yourself and cocooned in your leis you feel safe. By these denials you are not changing the truth. You are simply sugarcoating the bitter truth so you can swallow it easier. You are simply beguiling yourself.

> "How can you rely on Bukhari who in the beginning of his collection is not even ashamed of insulting MONKEYS by reporting that a companion of the prophet saw monkeys stoning an adulterous monkey to death?"

If you want to discredit Bukhari and other biographers on the basis of the absurdity of their thinking then why you do not look at the absurdity of Muhammad's thinking?

Muhammad's ignorance is obvious from what he wrote in the Quran. He thought that Jews were transformed into apes and swine. Is that logical? Who is more ridiculous? Bukhari who thought monkeys practice Sharia or Muhammad who thought Jews were transformed into monkeys? 2:65 5:60 7:166

But that is not all. There are numerous ridiculous statements made by Muhammad in the Quran. We will come to that when we come to the Quran.

> "According to your suggested criterion of sifting the garbage, we should accept this report since it does not praise Muhammad! Or you have another criterion that you forgot to communicate to me? You may end up with hundreds of arbitrary criteria to be able to justify your picks and rejects!"

No this hadith should not be accepted. It belongs to that category of hadiths that were invented by Muslims to make their religion look universal. We can see why a zealot Muslim would fabricate such ludicrous hadith. We can also easily see it is false because we know monkeys are not as savage as Muslims to stone their kind. Like all other hadith talking about miracles, this hadith is irrational and hence should be discarded. But when we read Muhammad took a bunch of Arabs and cut their extremities, gouged their eyes and left them to die in the desert for stealing his camels, we have no reason to doubt this is untrue because this heinous act is doable and it fits the character of Muhammad. From the Quran, from thousands of hadiths and from the siras we can see that Muhammad was a violent, unforgiving and ruthless man. There is nothing extraordinary in this hadith for us to doubt it. It is likely that this hadith is true.

- It is repeated in several sources
- It is not contrary to the explicit or implicit teachings of the Quran, in fact it is in unison with it.
- It is not contrary to logic. It is possible to cut the hands and feet of people, gouge their eyes and leave them die in the desert sun.
- It is consistent with the character of Muhammad
- There is no reason to believe why so many believers would fabricate such story
- It is detailed.

Based on all the above this hadith is very likely to be true. And since we have thousands of hadiths like this, it really does not matter even if some of them are not true. We get the picture of Muhammad when we read all of them.

> "How can you invite me to speculate on Bukhari who confesses of collecting 700,000 hadith and accepting only about 7000; rejecting 99 percent of them? Don't you see the exaggeration? Had Muhammad talked every minute of his life after claiming messengership, his words could have hardly added up to 700,000 hadiths."

This is not a valid argument at all. Suppose Bukhari was exaggerating, this does not invalidate his work. Talking hyperbolically is part of the Persian psyche. If only you could see the kind of hyperbole they they use in their poetry! The number 7 and its multiples of ten were the favorite number of the ancient people and we see Muhammad also using it often. As in the example of police and tips brought earlier, sometimes tens of thousands of tips could be reported. The sheer enormity of the false tips should not invalidate the good ones.

> "How can you take Bukhari serious who justifies the abrogation of a Quranic verse after Muhammad's departure by none other than a holy goat that ate the skin where the alleged verses issuing the stoning-to-death for adulterers written? Should we accept that report? In order to add another insult to Islam you would like to have it. But you cannot have it both ways. You have to also believe the 'holy goat'"

I haven't seen this hadith. It could be false but it is not illogical. Goats are known to eat papers and books. The only reason you are so shocked is that you think those writings were revelations from God and if so they could not have been destroyed. Since your premise is wrong your conclusion is wrong too.

> "Bukhari had a very different idea of islam than Muhammad. Bukhari was an ignorant idol worshiper and had no respect to the Quran. Besides, he sided with the oppressive rulers. For instance, he found Marwan, the drunk and murderer governor. to be a credible person by narrating "sahih" hadiths from him, while he declined accepting any hadith from a brave student of the Quran, Abu Hanifah who suffered in the jails of Umayyad and Abbasid dynasties for rejecting to sell his soul! Bukhari was not an objective hadith collector, he was on the side of murderers and aggressors."

> "We can write volumes of books listing the contradiction between the teaching of Bukhari and the Quran, the only book delivered by Muhammad. Then, how can a sound person claim Bukhari to be a friend of Muhammad? To me, he was a real enemy of Muhammad (6:112-116), like St. Paul was the real enemy of Jesus, since he distorted his message beyond recognition."

> "Let me little side track here. For instance, Jesus never silenced women and put them down with xenophobic teachings but St. Paul asked women to submit to men and hush: (1Ti 2:7-15; 1 Corinthians 14:34-35; 1 Peter 3:7). Jesus never asked for money for preaching but St. Paul asked for money shamelessly and likened his audience to flock of sheep to be milked by the holy shepherd! (Who goeth a warfare any time at his own charges? who planteth a vineyard, and eateth not of the fruit thereof? or who feedeth a flock, and eateth not of the milk of the flock? 1Co 9:7). He was a successful Machiavellian (before Machiavelli was born!) as opposed to Jesus who did not twist the truth to gain people: "To the weak became I as weak, that I might gain the weak: I am made all things to all men, that I might by all means save some." (1 Corinthians 9:22)."

> "How can you trust Bukhari who narrates the LAST HADITH while prophet Muhammad in his death bed, rejecting the recording of any hadith through a decleration from the mouth of Omar Bin Khattap and the acquiescence of all prominent muslims that "Hasbuna kitabullah" (God's word is enough for us)?"

I think you are confusing the facts. This hadith that BTW might be apocryphal reports that Muhammad asked for pen and paper to write something and Omar said Hasbuna Kitabullah. Muhammad did not say that. It was Omar who said it in defiance of Muhammad's order and Muhammad was upset and motioned everyone to leave the room. I say it might be apocryphal because a) Muhammad could not write b) it is highly unlikely that Omar would be so disrespectful to him at the moment of his death and c) even if Omar said such thing others who were present would have obeyed Muhammad and not Omar. This hadith could have been invented by a follower of Ali to stain Omar. But whatever it is it has nothing to do with rejecting the hadith. Muhammad claimed to have sublime morals 68:4 and ordered the Muslims to follow his "good example". 33:21 How would you know about his examples if not through the narrations left by his companions? The Quran is allegedly the word of God and not a collection of the examples of Muhammad.

Furthermore isn't this story you are telling us a hadith? So you are trying to discredit the hadiths on the authority of another hadith? And you call that honesty?

> "Will your suggested criterion to sift through the garbage help us to decide the authenticity of this hadith and reject all the rest? Which one do you believe? Was the Quran deemed sufficient by early muslims or they too needed hearsay reports to understand the Quran"

The early Muslims did not need narrations about him because they had seen him themselves. But soon after he died, they went to Aisha and others asking about him so they could emulate him. There is no logical reason to believe that his companions started lying from day one and never said a word of truth. Yes exaggerations happen, memories fail and stories get twisted, but despite all that it is not difficult to find an approximation of what actually happened, especially on major events like wars and mass murders. If we had a different version completely opposite to what we have, you would have a point. But what we have is all there is. There is no other version of the history of Islam and Muhammad.

> "What is the meaning of protecting the Quran from tempering while making it needy of volumes of dubious and fabricated stories?"

How do you know that the Quran has not been tampered, especially when the same Muslims who were so dishonest as to fabricate thousands of hadiths on Muhammad and were left unchecked were the very ones who transmitted the Quran? In fact, even your mentor Rashed Khalifa admitted that the Quran has been tampered.http://www.submission.org/tampering.html

If the Quran has been tampered it throws out the claim that God has promised to preserve it. 15:9 The myth of inviolability of the Quran has been shattered. What guarantees we have that it has not been tampered more than once?

> "How can you trust hadith books that report THE MOST WITNESSED HADITH, or THE MOST AUTHENTIC HADITH and manage to confuse the most crucial words, THE LAST WORDS in that hadith? The hadith about the last sermon, which was claimed to be witnessed by

more than hundred thousand believers, has three different endings: (1). Follow the Quran. (2). Follow the Quran and my Sunnah. (3). Follow the Quran and my family. Should we pick and choose! Throw dice? How will your criterion help us to pick the accurate version?"

No two people will tell you exactly the same story after witnessing the same event. If we have three different versions of this hadith, it shows that such sermon did take place and Muhammad made a plea at the end of his sermon. What did he exactly say? We may never be able to know 100%. But we can say he recommended his followers to follow the Quran with great certainty and possibly his sunna and or his family. But this we can't say with certainty. We can only speculate. In the Quran he says follow my example. 33:21.This is sunna. So the version 2 could be true. It does not contradict the Quran and it ratifies it. What about the family? Muhammad had only one daughter left alive who was married to Ali. So it is very unlikely that he recommended people to follow his family. Can this be a fabrication? If so who would have benefited by fabricating such lie? Well, Shiites would have benefited. So it is highly probably that the version 3 that says follow my family is apocryphal.

You see? Not a big deal at all! We can easily solve most of these problems and sieve the authentic hadith from the false ones once we look at them objectively and not through the lens of a believer who has his responses already made before even asking the question.

If we ask the opinion of a Quran only Muslism about the above hadith, he will chose the version 1. A Sunny will only accept the version 2 and a Shiite will only agree with the version 3. Only an unbiased person like me can see the truth. You can't be a judge and the interested party at the same time.

If we leave our faith and look at the hadith objectively we will find the truth. We may not be one hundred percent right but we can get close. After all our objective is not to follow blindly and religiously these hadiths. They are not sacred to us. We want to use them as sources of information to learn about Muhammad. These are the ONLY sources of information about Muhammad available to us. The Quran does not talk about Muhammad, it is allegedly the message of God to mankind. In that message he says follow the examples of the prophet but those examples are not there in the Quran. They are in the traditions.

"How can you invite me to take Bukhari a serious source of history while in its LONGEST HADITH it narrates the story of Miraj in which poor Muhammad goes up and down between 6th and 7th heavens trying to reduce the number of daily prayers? In that hadith, Muhammad is like an innumerate and gullible union leader bargaining for some break time on behalf of his people against a merciless boss (hasha God!) who tries to require 50 prayers a day, that is, a prayer for every 28 minutes, day and night! In that narration Moses is the wise guy and he coaches

171

Muhammad in this hard task of negotiation with God! According to your suggested criterion we should accept this hadith because Muhammad is depicted as an idiot who cannot even calculate, without the help of Moses who resides just one heaven below God, the impossibility of performing 50 prayers (not unit) a day? Even if one tried at that time they could not have divided the day to 50 periods of 28-minutes! Since, this hadith insults the intelligence of Prophet Muhammad according to your garbage-sifting criterion, should we believe this story?!"

The story of Miraj is ridiculous. But it was a story told by Muhammad himself. Why would you disparage only the bargaining part of this story? Is the very idea of going to heaven not ridiculous? Isn't the story of Miraj in the Quran? 71:1 Muhammad claimed that he traveled from Mecca to Masjd Al Aqsa and from there to the seventh heaven in one night. Isn't this claim more ridiculous? Muhammad bargaining with Allah about the number of prayers is just comic. But the claim that he had such trip is unscientific and absurd. By the way can you tell me where is Majid al Aqsa without referring to hadith? You can't. When we start our discussion of the Quran, I'll show you that the Quran is indecipherable without the hadith.

"How can you trust the account of hadith books, which unanimously claim that Muhammad was an illiterate man? Based on your criterion, we should swallow this lie because it does not praise Muhammad, since it depicts him an illiterate man who was not capable of learning 26 letters while dictating a book for 23 years! Or should we reject it because while insulting Muhammad it praises the literary excellence of the Quran"

That is a valid argument. In fact Ali Dashti asks the same question. He wonders why Muhammad, if he really could perform miracles, did not perform the most practical and easiest miracles and learn how to read and write? Obviously whoever said Muhammad was illiterate said a lie to make him look a prodigy. But who really promoted such lie? It was actually Muhammad himself who said it.

62:2   "It is He Who has sent amongst the Unlettered an apostle from among themselves,"

So I do not understand why you vilify the poor Bukhari who simply reported what Muhammad claimed and say nothing Muhammad who said that lie in the first place.

"Idiot friends can harm a person more than wise enemies. Hadith and siyar books are products of ignorant friends who insulted and defamed the men they were trying to worship."

172

I agree, If they were not idiot they would not have followed a crazed man such as Muhammad. But didn't Islam have any wise person to write the correct history of Islam?

"Besides, we should not ignore the possibility of some converts with agenda to distort the message. For instance, many Jewish stories and practices were imported to "islam" via "convert" Jewish and Christian scholars, such as belief Mahdi and practice of circumcision, etc. Kab bin al Ahbar is one of those influential converts. The story of Muhammad massacring Bani Qurayza Jews is another fabricated story by Jewish converts; unfortunately they were able to insert such lies into hadith and siyar books, which provided every fabricator access to a holy mass propaganda."

Yes also the holocaust is a lie fabricated by the Jews. In fact everyone knows that Osama Bin Laden is a Jew working for CIA who is trying to give a bad name to Islam.

So you want to make us believe that a story reported with so much detail by several historians, containing so many names and data was a total fabrication, that it never happened, that is was a lie concocted by Jews who were exterminated by Muslims but mysteriously reappeared and took control of the Ummah and started writing falsified history of Islam and secretly put those books into the shelves of the Muslims' libraries without anyone noticing the plot, to give a bad name to Islam and there was not a single Muslim coming forth saying hey, this is not what happened the real story is this? No wonder Muslims still believe in Jinns?

The story of Bani Quraiza is recorded by all the Muslim historians. It is not the only disturbing story of crime of Muhammad. What happened to Bani Nadir, Bani Qainuqa, the Jews of Kheibar, the bani Mostaliq, the Hawazin and countless other tribes who became victims of Muhammad's marauding gangs? They were slaughtered, enslaved, banished, looted and subdued. Is the entire history of Islam a fabrication? In that case what proof we have that Muhammad himself was not a fabrication? If the entire history of Islam is false, then what makes you believe that Muhammad ever existed? The whole thing could have been made up. Your first duty is to prove the very existence of Muhammad.

"Hadith books contain almost anything you want. You may find an extremely kind and nice Muhammad besides a cruel torturer one. You may find Muhammad to be a person with great morals and on the other page you will see him a pedophile. You will find Muhammad pointing at the moon and splitting it into two pieces letting one piece falling into Ali's backyard, and on the other page you will find Muhammad incapable of reading a simple letter. Now, you want us to enter this Muhammad-in-the-wonderland and separate truth from falsehood. And without

173

looking in my eyes you are suggesting me to pick the bad and reject the good ones. You cannot be serious!"

It is good that you see these contradictions. However these stories originate from the Quran. The claim that Muhammad was illiterate is in the Quran and the claim that he split the moon asunder is also in the Quran.

54:1-2   "The Hour (of Judgment) is nigh, and the moon is cleft asunder. But if they see a Sign, they turn away, and say, "This is (but) transient magic."

What you should know is that many hadiths were fabricated by zealot believers to back up and justify the claims made in the Quran. But this story is made by Muhammad. He claimed to have ascended to Heaven and this made Abu Bakr waiver for a while doubting the sanity of Muhammad until his blind faith overcame his reason and he succumbed again into ignorance.

"It is evident that you have no knowledge of modern rules of evidence in justice system. I challenge you to find a single judge inAmerica that would find those hearsay reports credible for character assassination. If you find one, I promise that I will petition to the bar to take away his license by using similar hearsay to depict him as a drunk child molester! Yes, go find a single judge in a secular country accepting the garbage you are inviting me to."

That won't be a bad idea. I don't know whether we can prosecute a dead man. But this surely would make a sensational trial. If it can be done and if a lawyer is willing to joins me, it would be a great idea to take Muhammad to court. Or at least try to ban Islam under the anti hate law.

"As I gave a few examples out of many, it is not possible to get a fair and objective idea by using hadith and sira books. But, your insistence on this issue gives away your weakness. You are not able to discuss Islam based on the most reliable historic document, the Quran. You had perhaps had very good time in constructing arguments against Sunni or Shiite Muslims who are mislead by those sources. As you know, I follow the Quran alone, like Muhammad himself did. There are now, thank God, tens of thousands of Muslims all around the world reaching the same conclusion."

Don't be impatient my friend. One thing at a time! First I'll pull the stool from beneath your feet. Once that is done I will move to discredit the Quran and use nothing but the Quran. In fact I left Islam only after reading the Quran. I only became familiar with the hadith afterwards.

174

"Interesting. How in the world you can construe our rejection of hearsay and silly reports as weakness? The real weakness is in your argument, since you mix garbage in your arguments. I did not come here to speculate on books that NEITHER OF US TRUST. Bukhari could not survive five minutes in the witness stand and he would be rejected by every decent court of justice. But, your hatred against Muhammad or Islam, as it seems, has made you care less about truth and justice. Peace,"

On the contrary, the very fact that you prefer to deny the hadith and so desperately reject the evidences that incriminate Muhammad is the sign of the weakness of your position. You perfectly know he can't be defended if those evidences are brought to the light. The books of Bukhari is not one person's opinion. They are collections of thousands of tips. I have never heard a judge throw out the theory presented by the prosecutors on the basis that some of the tips they had received could be false. As long as the theory is not based on false leads, it stands. Just as the police can construct a theory of how the crime happened based on a few tips among many false ones and with that they can prosecute and convict their accused, we can easily construct the profile of Muhammad based on the hadiths that we have even though some of them may not be reliable. It is not impossible or difficult to separate the true hadiths from the false ones.

Going through Rashid Khalifa's claim another fact became apparent. That you do not reject all the narrations but simply those that you do not like.

The above link states:

> "Nineteen years after the Prophet Muhammad's death, during the reign of Khalifa `Uthman, a committee of scribes was appointed to make several copies of the Quran to be dispatched to the new Muslim lands. The copies were to be made from the original Quran which was written by Muhammad's hand. This committee was supervised by `Uthman Ibn `Affaan, `Ali Ibn Abi Taaleb, Zeid Ibn Thaabet, Ubayy Ibn Ka`ab, `Abdullah Ibn Al-Zubair, Sa`eed Ibn Al-`Aas, and `Abdul Rahman Ibn Al-Haareth Ibn Heshaam...."

How do you (or RKh) know that? You are expecting others to believe in that story and not in the story of Bani Quraiza or other stories about Muhammad? Where is the honesty here?

Edip Yuksel v Ali Sina (6)

Addicted to the Smell of Hearsay Trash

Edip Yuksel

12-23-2004

Take your shaky stool away, Ali

A participant of the forum, Mirror of Truth, in another threat answered your argument. You were urging me to join you in using hadith as a reliable evidence to incriminate Muhammad. I am quoting his answer, since I agree it, and it will save me time. I will answer some of other arguments of yours after this excerpt from Mirror of Truth, whose answer is distinguished with five asterisks:

*****

I'm writing my first post regarding the actual debate and I note that some classic AS double talk is beginning to creep into the flow of debate.

On the one hand - AS bluffs his hand by stating:

> "On the contrary! I will show that the Quran is full of errors and ab-surdities and it can't be a book of revelation unless the revealer was Sa-tan. The reason I want to clarify the question of hadith is to demon-strate the fallacy of the position of those who totally deny them. Once that is established I will have no need for hadith."

Well he launches into an awful lot of pre-amble if he has no need for hadith. Edip has made it explicit that he does not need nor has any desire to discuss the hadith.

During this pre-amble AS lists two possibilities as the motives for the fabrica-tions which I accept. These are namely:

1. Glorification of an idolized leader. This would explain hadiths for example that report that Muhammad's manliness was equivalent to 30 men or whatever number it was. In trying to make their hero macho they do not realize the ab-surdity they create - and the inadvertent slander they commit.

2. The fabrications of enemies whether they be hypocrite 'believers'/converts or or open enemies. This explains a great many hadiths that are covert digs at Mu-hammad. An example is the cherished hadith of the 'miraj' where Moses acts as the wiser guide to Muhammad's alleged negotiations with God. Obviously this is

the fabrication of a Jewish convert who asserts the superiority of Moses' bargaining/knowledgeability.

What Ali Sina discounts and does not mention at all is that there is another group of hadiths that were introduced (or supported) in the folklore in order to support the actions of corrupt leaders. If corrupt leaders/mullahs could justify their pedophilia or desires to rape and pillage by introducing or supporting such hadiths then having the absolute power there would be little reason for them to reject such hadith. **Thus the hadith that obviously makes Muhammad look evil/wicked/stupid etc. become canonized because it meets the secondary need of the corrupt leaders.**

Thus there are motives for these hadith that AS has completely ignored.

The sum of it is that whatever the motive for ahadith - none are required for the purposes of following God's system - not one.

AS has stated he has no requirement for them. None of us are shocked and the position to go on sans ahadith is very tenable. They are fabrications. The absurdity they contain is enough to convince the free-thinker of that. I would advise that AS lets go of his love for the hadith that I'm sure rivals the mullahs in order to make a real contribution to the debate. Let's move on from the nonsense of ahadith and see what arguments he has left now.

*****

I want to elaborate little bit more about motivation in fabrication of hadiths. Ali Sina is treating hadith sources in a simplistic way. I recommend him to read Mahmud Abu Rayya's book *Adwa' 'ala al-Sunna al-Muhammadiya* (Cairo: 1377/1958). It is one of the best criticism of history of hadith collection and procedures. The book allocates 60 pages to motives for fabricating hadith. People fabricated hadith to even advertise the dates of a particular town, Ajwa. They fabricated hadiths to promote submission to the rule of Kings. They fabricated hadith to justify the massacres and tortures of Umayyad or Abbasid kings.... Ali Sina ignores all these motives and wants us to believe that any hadith depicting Muhammad as a violent person must be accepted without question! One of his suggested criteria for accepting hadith is if "It is consistent with the character of Muhammad" found in his hostile imagination or in other dubious hadith books! As circular as it could be! Accepting this offer is more difficult than to swallow the prophecies of his favorite psychics.

> "Muhammad's ignorance is obvious from what he wrote in the Quran. He thought that Jews were transformed into apes and swine. Is that logical? Who is more ridiculous? Bukhari who thought monkeys practice Sharia or Muhammad who thought Jews were transformed into monkeys? 2:65 5:60 7:166"

177

Holy cow! Is this your level of reading a literary test that contains metaphors? Your hatred against Muhammad and islam has reduced your literary skills to elementary level. When your friends tells you "Ali don't have a cow" do you chastise them by saying, "When did I want to have a cow? Are you hallucinating?" When someone labels another person "pig!" does he really mean that the other was transformed to a pig or he really means that the person acted like a pig. The verses you refer are metaphors that use the Arabic language and culture. It likens the acts of a particular group of Jews to the behavior of monkeys and pigs. Please check Arabic language for the implication of such metaphors.

> "I haven't seen this hadith. It could be false but it is not illogical. Goats are known to eat papers and books. The only reason you are so shocked is that you think those writings were revelations from God and if so they could not have been destroyed. Since your premise is wrong your conclusion is wrong too."

I do not have such ideas about revelation. You are making up ideas in my name. I do not blame you for this since you have encountered so many Sunni Muslims or Shiite Muslims you may be excused to confuse a "muslim muslim" with them.

> "I say it might be apocryphal because a) Muhammad could not write b) it is highly unlikely that Omar would be so disrespectful to him at the moment of his death and c) even if Omar said such thing others who were present would have obeyed Muhammad and not Omar."

You are accepting one of the biggest lies about Muhammad. Muhammad was literate. He wrote the Quran with his own hands. The Arabic word UMMY does not mean illiterate, it means gentile. For my logical and scriptural reasons for literacy of Muhammad please visit my website at:http://www.yuksel.org/e/books/rtq.htm

Second, if Omar supported Muhammad for 23 years of his messengership he must have known that Muhammad prohibited his companions from writing his hadith all his life. He must have known that the Quran was the only source to be followed and associating man-made teachings to it was another form of polytheism. If I were in Omar's sandals, I would too reject Muhammad's request to prescribe another source for our guidance, especially knowing that he was terminally sick and had high fever.

Third, you are confusing the early believers with later Sunni and Shiite Muhammad-worshipers. They were free minds. They did not follow Muhammad as a cult leader, but they accepted his message by using their God-given reason. As you are confusing me or wish to confuse me with a blind follower of a particular sect or cult, you are also confusing or wish to confuse those brave and progressive souls, those freedom fighters with them.

"But whatever it is it has nothing to do with rejecting the hadith. Muhammad claimed to have sublime morals 68:4 and ordered the Muslims to follow his "good example". 33:21 How would you know about his examples if not through the narrations left by his companions? The Quran is allegedly the word of God and not a collection of the examples of Muhammad."

You share a strikingly similar poor knowledge of the Quran with Sunnis and Siites. You use the same lousy arguments. If you were able to read the Quran without smelling the garbage of hadith, you would easily notice that 33:21 had preceding and succeeding verses and the example of prophet was his bravery in defending Muslims against the aggressor army of Meccan oligarchy. If your knowledge of the Quran was a little bit beyond the surface, you would also notice that verse 60:4 uses exactly the same description, "good example", for Abraham and his supporters. Using your logic Muslims should have had the hadith of Abraham and his supporters too! Perhaps, you will find the story of another hungry holy goat eating those hadith collections too to be "not illogical."

"Furthermore isn't this story you are telling us a hadith? So you are trying to discredit the hadiths on the authority of another hadith? And you call that honesty?"

I use that hadith to show a conspicuous internal contradiction in hadith books. I say, "if you believe this hadith, you must reject all other hadiths. If you accept other hadiths, then you must reject this one. You cannot believe all to be authentic!" I am surprised that you did not understand this common and simple rhetorical device.

"If we had a different version completely opposite to what we have, you would have a point. But what we have is all there is. There is no other version of the history of Islam and Muhammad."

Do you really hear what you are saying? What about the Quran? The book that preceded the hadith books by centuries! The Quran refers to all major wars and conflicts and even generously quotes the allegations and accusations of opponents. But, you are addicted with the stinky smell of hadith narrations and you try hard to engage me in a wrestling match in that location. No, my dear friend. I had been there and I am grateful to God for saving me from that. You might, however, continue enjoying your mud-slings with Sunni and Shiite opponents there. If I have time, I will be watching you with a smile on my face.

"How do you know that the Quran has not been tampered, especially when the same Muslims who were so dishonest as to fabricate thousands of hadiths on Muhammad and were left unchecked were the very ones who transmitted the Quran? In fact, even your mentor Rashed

Khalifa admitted that the Quran has been tampered.
http://www.submission.org/tampering.html

If the Quran has been tampered it throws out the claim that God has promised to preserve it. 15:9 The myth of inviolability of the Quran has been shattered. What guarantees we have that it has not been tampered more than once?"

Finally, a good question, a fair criticism. I would like to reserve a separate discussion on protection of the Quran via its numerical structure.

"Is the entire history of Islam a fabrication? In that case what proof we have that Muhammad himself was not a fabrication? If the entire history of Islam is false, then what makes you believe that Muhammad ever existed? The whole thing could have been made up. Your first duty is to prove the very existence of Muhammad."

Again, you are confusing me with your Sunni friends! If I were in an island and found the Quran there among other books, and if I were able to understand its message and blessed to witness its scientific accuracy, prophecies and mathematical structure, I would not need anything else to believe in its accuracy. Do you hear me? Do you understand me? Besides, I am not a Muhammadan. Islam, as the system of peace and submission to God alone, existed long before Muhammad and will continue to exist as a path for the truth-seekers long after him.

"Yes also the holocaust is a lie fabricated by the Jews. In fact everyone knows that Osama Bin Laden is a Jew working for CIA who is trying to give a bad name to Islam."

No, I do not consider holocaust a lie fabricated by Jews. To the contrary, I consider it one of the most diabolic disasters caused by racism and religious bigotry. Even if the number of massacred Jews has been exaggerated, it does not change this fact a bit. To me, the life of a single human being, be a Jew or Arab, is infinitely important. Killing a single human being unjustly, without self-defense is equivalent of killing all humanity, since if one loses his respect to the life of one human being will lose his respect to the basic principle of brotherhood of humanity (See Quran 5:27-32).

As for Ben Laden being a CIA agent... No, I do not believe that either. CIA might have in the past supported and collaborated with bin Laden, but they parted their ways after Russia left Afghanistan. CIA supported Saddam for long time, when he was killing Iranians and gassing Kurds, my people, to death. But, they parted their way too when Saddam invaded Kuwait, after reading the USA's reaction before the invasion as a "yes". To concoct a new scenario in the region, the USA tricked her former puppet-dictator to invade Kuwait ...

180

> "It is good that you see these contradictions. However these stories originate from the Quran. The claim that Muhammad was illiterate is in the Quran and the claim that he split the moon asunder is also in the Quran."

The Quran does not claim that Muhammad was illiterate, but only illiterates of the Quran claim such. Quran claims that Muhammad was not reading any scripture, in other words, he was a gentile. Muhammad was a literate gentile, like many of his contemporary prominent Meccans. The Quran does not claim that Muhammad split the Moon, but only the splitters of holy lies claim as such. The Quran refers to the end of the world and gives the splitting of the Moon as a sign for its coming close. I understand it as reference to the splitting of the Moon's surface by Apollo astronauts in 1969 when they took rocks from the Moon. I have a detailed argument on this in my Turkish books and inshallah you will find it in our upcoming Reformist Translation of the Quran.

> "That won't be a bad idea. I don't know whether we can prosecute a dead man. But this surely would make a sensational trial. If it can be done and if a lawyer is willing to joins me, it would be a great idea to take Muhammad to court. Or at least try to ban Islam under the anti hate law."

Only an Inquisition or Taliban court would accept your evidence as credible. But, in case you find such a court in Texas or Saudi Arabia, please let the judge appoint me as Muhammad's attorney! I would be glad to represent him against Bukhari, Tirmizi, Ibni Majeh, Ibni Hanbal, Taberi, Waqidi and Ali Sina, combined.

> "Don't be impatient my friend. One thing at a time! First I'll pull the stool from beneath your feet. Once that is done I will move to discredit the Quran and use nothing but the Quran. In fact I left Islam only after reading the Quran. I only became familiar with the hadith afterwards."

Now this is really funny. I never stood on that stool or wanted in the first place. You are the one trying to push it under my feet, and each time I kick it you try harder. Now, you are taking credit for your failure to insert that stinky stool under my feet? What kind of logic are you using? In my first letter to you, I invited you to discuss the Quran and you managed to extend the introduction with silly arguments from silly books.

So, it should be the last round that we discuss hadith. We should now move to the real argument. Are you ready for that, or you want to dwell more on hadith? You will not receive any response from me if you continue your bizarre insistence to force me to accept hadith. Then, you may claim your victory and continue your debates based on hearsay and ignorance.

I hope you will kick that stinky stool under your feet. As it appears, it is the only stool keeping you standing

A PERSONAL NOTE

(Ali, take a deep breath, sit down, take prozac or medication of your choice, and then read it. I do not want to be the cause of your heart attack—Muslims needs to hear your voice and your baby followers need nourishment--but I want to share with you my honest thoughts about you. If my thoughts about you are wrong, please correct me. I assume that I will deserve a personal retaliation. So feel free to express your thoughts about me!).

When I accepted your challenge to debate on Islam, I had no knowledge about your philosophy or political position. All I knew was that you were very aggressive enemy of Islam. During the three days I had chance to browse some of your writings and learn a little about you, as you have been doing the same about me. I cannot claim that I know your philosophy or religion well; but I learned a few things about you that mostly fascinated and occasionally surprised me:

1. You have access to volumes of religious classics and you know well how to navigate among them.

2. You are curious about modern science, you read and you are able to construct some philosophical arguments based on most recent scientific findings or theories. It is a risky business, but hey, intellectuals are entrepreneurs. However, I warn you against taking risks with theories and speculations and by speculating over speculations.

3. You have great aversion, to the degree of hatred, against the religion falsely introduced as Islam.

4. Your aversion and hatred against the corrupt Islam, which I call Hislam, I think, have led you to lose the diamond (the Quran) in the garbage. (I have read some of your criticism directed to the Quran, and inshallah I will demonstrate the problems with MOST of your arguments).

5. Your fight against false ideas and terrorism is somehow focused on Muslims alone, while a segment of Christendom, especially millions of fanatic evangelists and crusaders, equipped with big financial resources and powerful propaganda machines, are propagating similar false ideas, supporting and encouraging state terrorism, occupations, dictatorial governments, military coups, wars, crusades and destruction around the world; yet, you do not show similar aversion and hatred towards them.

As for me, while I condemn Ben Ladin for killing innocent people, I also condemn the evangelical president of the USA-Inc who has terrorized an entire nation based on lies, deception, and has killed many times more civilians, and destroyed many times more buildings in a poor country that had no connection with Ben Laden. (See: www.yuksel.org/e/law).

So, if you call Muslims terrorist because they killed several thousand people in last decade, you must call Christians "terrorists to the factor of 666" since they killed hundreds of thousands in Hiroshima, Nagasaki, Vietnam, and just recently they killed tens of thousands Iraqi civilians, and wounded even more.

Why terrorizing an entire nation, destroying their cities, killing, torturing, raping and sadomizing their children and youth in the name of "democracy and liberty" should be treated lightly? Why killing tens of thousands of civilians should be forgiven if the murderers, who are also proven congenial liars, use the magic word "collateral damage?" Why smashing the brains of children with bombs or severing their legs and arms should be considered civilized and treated differently than beheadings? Why destroying an entire neighborhood or city and massacring its population by a push of button from the sky should not be considered equally or more evil than the individual suicide bomber blowing himself or herself among his powerful enemies who snuffed away all his or her hope? Why surviving to push another button to kill more people should be considered a civilized action not the action of those who gave their own lives while doing the killing? How can one honestly call an occupying foreign military force to be freedom fighters? How can one call the native population to be terrorists just because they are fighting against an arrogant and lethal occupation army which was mobilized against them through lies and deception?

If you read my books, articles, and listen to my speeches, you will find that I do not favor one criminal over another because of their religion or nationality. However, I consider state terrorism, regardless of the nationality and religion of the population, to be much more cruel, dangerous, and sinister than the group or individual terrorism. I expect similar consistency and fairness from you. I expect you to PROTEST and CONDEMN the atrocities conducted by Evilgelical-Zionist coalition in Chechnya, Iraq, Palestine, etc., as you rightly condemn the atrocities committed by Hislamic radicals in Afghanistan, Sudan, Saudi Arabia, etc.

Otherwise, your biased stance against Muslims alone might support the speculations that you are used by Evangelical Christians. I do not know and cannot speculate that there is such a connection, but I found your position intellectually problematic and dishonest.

6. Your belief in paranormal was a surprise, though. You might have already read several of my articles on paranormal. My stance on paranormal is somewhere between yours and skeptics'. I do not want to distract our current debate with this subject, so I will just touch the surface.

I found some entertaining writings about you (See the excerpt below). It seems that some people are taking you too serious and considering you together with Van Praagh (a charlatan who fools gullible people on TV) as the founders of a new religion: Rational Spirituality. I do not know whether you take Van Praagh serious, but getting to know you little bit, I will not be surprised if you do so. You might be one of those people with multiple personalities: genius on one page, gullible on the other; against the Muslim terrorist on one page; for the Christian or Jewish terrorists on the other page!

Regardless, I enjoy reading your writings, including your silly and utterly false or nonsense claims. I respect intelligence and revere it as a divine gift. You are gifted in that sense, and you will have equal responsibility. I hope your ego will allow you to control and check yourself. Be reminded that extreme points might be dancing on a circle, the farthest they go away from each other the closest they might get to each other, and the barrier separating both extremes may collapse occasionally. Here is the funny excerpt by one of your "followers":

> "My fellow friends, we must rally behind Ali and Van Praagh et al. to establish this fledgling religion firmly on earth. I am encouraged by a few converts already joining hands. We must win this battle against the skeptics who destroy people's lives. Remind you- they never build lives; they only destroy. Think about this: the skeptics' camp dominated by the Scientists, Rational Humanists, leading Philosophers etc. have done nothing, absolutely nothing to build people's lives. They have only brought about all scientific progress; they have contributed enormously for the comfortable, easy and just life in this world. Those are just material things – those contributions don't build people's life but instead destroy people's life and destroys people's hope. Of course, the skeptics never kill people in great numbers; still we must believe that they destroy people's life. Although, we rational spiritualists just "do twaddles" by means of our new religion but they still build people's life, bring hopes to people. One may wonder if we destroy the skeptics; who is going to keep the wheel of progress of human life rolling. I don't think we have any problem there at all. Do we remember the fire-ball Ali witnesses in his sister bed room? Ali says that was clearly an intelligent being. It can be presumed that those intelligent beings may be huge gold-mine of genius and intelligence. Once we have established our new religions by destroying the skeptic scientists, philosophers etc., we can replace them with those intelligence beings and the progress of our Spiritual world can even move forward faster." (Alamgir Hussain)

Peace.

184

Edip Yuksel v Ali Sina (7)

Christian, Agnostic, Muslim Audience ...

Edip Yuksel

12-23-2004

HECTOR: Merry Christmas Edip Yuksel, What is your view on my proposition that the Quran is also hearsay because of the evidence chain: Allah to Jibril to Muhammad to verse memorizer to verse scribe?

Merry one-month-after Ramadan Hector:)

EDIP: First, we need to shave the unnecessary part. Since, we have strong evidence that Muhammad was literate and wrote the Quran with his own hand, the physical representation of the Quran came into existence at that point. You have a very good point, but for a slightly different reason. The suspicion, I believe, would not be the reliability of transmission, since one can assume angels to be following God's order verbatim and they are designed to perform their jobs, etc. In other words, if the receiver of the revelation is sure that what is he receiving is a revelation from God; he does not have much reason to worry about the veracity of its transmission, since God should be capable of ensuring a reliable communication. However, the big philosophical problem with receiving revelation involves the question whether the revelation is coming from God or not and this issue was well expressed by the existentialist philosopher Sartre. Sartre questioned Abraham's conviction regarding the divine order sacrificing his son. Sartre asked, "How could Abraham be sure that it was God not Satan who inspired him such an idea?" I have written a short article on this issue and it is available at my personal website under the category: Philosophy.

MR HAPPY: Perhaps you missed my question first time round Edip, briefly, what are your thoughts on the Sharia law, particularly the punishments such as stoning, lashings, amputation etc.

EDIP: I reject any Sharia law made by clergymen. Stoning to death, according to the Quran, was practice of Jews and pagans. It was imported to Islam long after the departure of Muhammad and many lies were fabricated to link it to Muhammad. One of the well-known basis for that is the fabrication of verse that does not exist in the Quran but believed to have the authority of the Quran. The fabricated verse ordering the stoning penalty for married adulterers was allegedly eaten and abrogated by a hungry holy goat! Since that hungry holy goat of hadith books have not eaten my brain Ironically, Ali Sina wished me to believe-Jyet I do not believe such nonsense that nonsense so that he could declare an

185

easy victory after goring me from . But, instead he adopted and gave shelter to the poor goat and called itLbehind "not illogical".

As for lashing, it is in the Quran, and it can be applied to those who freely admit the jurisdiction of Quranic law if they are proven to commit adultery, that is betraying the contract with their spouses. It is in reality a public shame, rather than a harsh physical punishment, since the word used for lash is JiLD, derived from the same root used for skin. We are culturally biased in favor of prison system. I recommend you an excellent book on the origin of prison system and abandonment of corporal punishment in the West. The title of the book is Discipline and Punish, authored by Michael Foucault. It is a very interesting historical, social and legal account of of evolution of western criminal system. As for amputation, it is one of the meanings out of three alternatives. I think amputating the hands of the thieves is a very harsh punishment and it contradicts my sense of justice. Yes, MY sense of justice. So, I prefer the other two alternative understanding, which I have discussed in the short introduction section of my upcoming Reformist Translation of the Quran.

PEACEONEARTH: Having denounced Hadith and Siras, with no historical basis to go by, who is to determine what the right spirit is? Edip will want to give the benefit of doubt to Quran. Arabic is full of ambiguities and Edip will choose to assign the appropriate meaning on the basis of "right spirit".

That in essence is his approach. Am I right, Edip? Did I capture the essence of your approach?

EDIP: It is called the good spirit dear JPeace. Does "in the right spirit" mean "the most likely meaning" or the "meaning that puts Quran in the best light".

Replacing the ambiguity in the book with the ambiguity of "in the right spirit" does only one thing - transfer the right to interpret to the one wanting to define what the "right spirit" is.

Now, is the approach of "right spirit" that is defined by someone in 21st century better than the context provided in Hadith or Siras? I beg to differ

If you are hundred percent convinced by reason and personal experience that the Quran is indeed word of God, then you treat ambiguities also as intentional way of divine communication with generations of humans to come. So, if a word or verse has multiple meaning, I will take the one or the ones that do not contradict other clear verses and spirit of the scripture, the laws of nature. I have some examples at my website.

???: First, a positive: I commend Edip on his intention to reform Islam as we know it. It would be a welcome change if Edip can successfully get Islam to ban

Hadith & Sira and use Edip's translation of Quran. That would be a great change for Islam as we know it. But will it happen?

EDİP: Thanks for this good wish. More accurately stated, we are trying to have an islamic reform according to the teaching of the Quran alone.

??? Such "inspired translation", even as they appear far fetched, are going to be common-place in this debate. This is the "in spirit" translations that one has to believe to make Quran appear to be a book of God.

Does the following seem reasonable to any one other than Edip and his ilk? "Splitting of the moon surface" = "Apollo astronauts taking rocks from the moon". Sigh ... Such rationalization to forward one's own faith ... such a pity

EDİP: Perhaps, I did not use the right English word. The Arabic word SHAQQA perhaps cannot exactly be translated with the word "split" since it is also used to describe the split opening or cracking the soil after rain (Quran 80:26). I would appreciate if you help me find a better English translation, if there is, that can both mean splitting apart AND split opening, cracking (the ground). I have not yet discussed this verse with my co-translators. Since, they are native English speakers and professors of linguistics, I think they will help. (BTW, English is chronologically my fifth language.)

JAK: Escape routine as usual, when get cornered use Christianity as a shield. Hey Edip, your discussion with Ali Sina is about Islam, Christian have nothing to do with it. Use Quran alone in your defend to Islam. You said it yourself that you are "Quran only" man.

EDİP: Are you offended with one paragraph referring to three facts about St. Paul? I did not use it in the context of justifying anything wrong in Islam. The Biblical references were about xenophobia, milking the church goers, and hypocrisy. We have not yet discussed these topics in relation to Islam. I gave it as a parallel example how clergyman of all religions distort the message of messengers after they are transformed to idols. So, your accusation fails to make a case for "red herring" fallacy. If the examples of corruption I gave are part of your religion, then you should try to defend it, or give up from that part of your religion, or take your time and do some research. But, you are filing a trivial procedural complaint about it. The examples were relevant to the argument and they were correct. So, your objection is denied

MIRROR OF TRUTH: However the truth is that man made religions are what this word refers to. Any division created between mankind to break apart the unity of God's system is forbidden by the Quran.

EDIP: Thus the breaking into religions is forbidden. The system of God is outlined within the Quran and a person either chooses to follow it - absolutely without the intervention of any intermediaries - or not. That's the choice - not secularism vs religion.

EDİP: Muhammad was not illiterate. This is a slander generated by traditionalist islamists. In their zeal to 'enhance' the literary miracle of the Quran they most likely assumed that by making the messenger illiterate that it would make things more impressive. However it is quite clear that the word "ummy" means Gentile - and not illiterate as traditionalists hold. Thank you Mirror for these beautiful comments.

FARSIDE: Did Muhammad stand out brilliantly?

EDIP: You are a breeze in dessert blowing from Farside. Thanks:)

IDOLFREE1: ISLAM is NOT a RELIGION. Human beings have taken DIVINE WISDOM and turned it into yet another religion.

The Title "Muslim" is not something that you give yourself and that is it, one is only a "muslim" (lower case) when they submit to righteousness.

EDIP: Wow, three in a row… Thanks for this comments, idolfree1

JUAN: Well, Mr. Edip seems to have a problem with some of the hadiths that depict Muhammad as a criminal. Nevertheless, in my opinion, he is not being clear about the criteria he uses to categorise what haditsh are authentic and which ones are not. When he says that the Quoran should be the only source of guidance, then one has to assume that the Quarna itself provides with the sufficient context for some particular and key issues. For instance, in terms of the wagging war against enemies, could Mr. Edip shows us that the sword verses are indeed intended only for defensive wars? From what I have read in the Quoran, and please correct me if I am wrong, nowhere can I find a single paragraph/context/situation in which it is clearly shown that Muslims were firstly attacked, and that they only retaliated. Another good example concerns the beating of wives in surah 4:23 if I am not mistaken. Can Mr. Edip shows us the paragraph/context/situation in the Quaron in which Muhammad put into practice such commands from Allah? As I said, I stand to be corrected in those two issues. However, if Mr. Edip has to recur to the haditsh to prove and show the context of some verses in the Quaoranm, the he definitely has to show us the criterion he used to say those hadiths are consistent with the message of the Quopran, and why other not of his liking are not consistent !

EDIP: Dear Juan: The Quran does not promote war; but encourages us to stand against aggressors on the side of peace and justice. War is permitted only for self-defense (See: 2:190,192,193,256; 4:91; 5:32; 60:8-9). We are encouraged to work hard to establish peace (47:35; 8:56-61). The Quranic precept promoting peace and justice is so fundamental that peace treaty with the enemy is preferred to religious ties (8:72). As for your second criticism, please visit the BOOK section of yuksel.org and there you will see an introductory section of our upcoming translation. You will find my translation and comments on 4:34 (not 23) there.

JUAN: Mr. Edip, I surely hope you can read me. If you indeed have been doing some ground-breaking research regarding the mathematical miracles in the Quaron and its origins, I will pay attention only until after you have successfully defended your book and theories in front of experts in history, mathematics, linguistics, etc. LISTEN, I AM NOT ASKING YOU TO PROVE THE EXSISTENCE OF GOD. I am just asking you to prove to world-class experts in the relevant areas that you indeed have the correct translation of the Quaraon, that the mathematical miracles in the Quaron can only be found in the Quoran and in no other book or document, etc, etc, etc.

So the challenge for you is Mr. Edip, go and argue with the experts in Cambridge, Harvard, Oxfords regarding your "ground-breaking" research. Once you have convinced the experts that 1400 years of tradition and hadiths are pure garbage and that your new Quoran is the correct one, that it is mathematically inimitable, then you can come here and teach a lesson to us mere mortals. Who knows, you might even be remembered very fondly in the future as the intellectual giant who saved humanity from discarding the "miracle" of the Quaran!!

EDIP: I have already given several lectures on this in Near Eastren Studies, Philosophy and Math departments at the University of Arizona. In math department, more than 30 professors and graduate students attended the speech. I received not a single objection. Here are some possible reasons: (1) they did not understand me; (2) they found the case so hopeless that they did not want to waste their time on it; (3) they were cautious since they needed to study it for themselves and they were not ready to challenge the examples; (4) they were frozen speechless miraculously… My my one to one conversation with them after the lecture showed that the third option was true; at least for the some.

I debated this issue on Turkish TV two years ago against a professor of mathematics at Bosphorus University, Istanbul; a prestigious university in Turkey. The other opponent was Turkey's former Chief of Religious Effairs. Millions of people watched that debate. The debate was in Turkish and is now available as a video stream at 19.org. You may ask a Turkish (preferably, a non-religious one) who watched the debate either live in Turkey/Europe or at my web site.

About a decade ago, when I was student at philosophy department, I engaged in a two-round debate on the numerical structure of the Quran and its implications with Carl Sagan, late astronomer and agnostic. (By the way, I highly recommend his book, The Demon Haunted World, Science as a Candle in the Dark, to everyone, especially to Ali Sina and his followers). Our debate is available on the internet under the title The Prime Argument.

189

I had some communication via mail and phone with Martin Gardner, the famous mathematician and philosopher, on the subject. But, he was merely asking some questions and stayed away from discussing the issue. He wrote several articles on this topic, mostly informative, yet with a little dose of his usual sarcasm.

Inshallah, when I finish the translation I will finish an English book on the mathematical structure of the Quran. Then, I will be challenging all these mathematicians.

JUAN: Mr. Edip, could you please show me the verses in the Quoran where it is clearly explained that the wars the muslims emarked on were only defensive? If you can not and have to recur to the hadiths, could you please show me the methodology that you used to choose those verses?

EDIP: Juan, I listed some references above when you first directed this question. If you missed it, please go back and read my response again.

JUAN: Mr. Edip wrote: "I follow the Quran and whether Muhammad existed or not is really a side issue in the context of the message of the Quran. I am not following Muhammad; I am following the message of the messenger. I am here to defend the principals and teachings of the Quran. Did Muhammad really exist or not, was Muhammad a good guy or not, is not relevant right now."

This is the stupidest thing I have ever read in my life !!! .... so basically, this guy has said that even if Muhhamad was a pedophile, murderer, robber, etc, etc, ALL OF THIS WOULD BE OF NO IMPORTANCE, HE'D STILL BE A MUSLIM !!!

My gosh, I have seen some stupid garbage posted by Muslims, but this one definitely takes the cake !!! ......

MR. GIRON: Well, let's be honest here. Edip is attempting to derive his theology entirely from the Qur'an, and if we're honest about this issue, we will admit that the Qur'an does not tell us a great deal about Muhammad or his role in the revelation of the Qur'an. In fact, were we not carrying the baggage that is a natural result of centuries of Muslim exegesis, we could read the Qur'an in a vacuum and not come to any conclusion about any man named Muhammad (it simply mentioned a man who is praised, and whose name shall be commendable, laudable, praise worthy). The veracity of the Qur'an can actually be discussed regardless of whether there ever was an historical Muhammad or not.

Well, if we reject the ahaadeeth as a reliable source of information, what kinds of conclusions can we really reach about Muhammad? It seems the character of Muhammad becomes almost irrelevant to Mr' Yuksel's interpretation of Islam.

And that's exactly the issue with Mr. Edip's stance. I am catholic, and of course I believe in God. Mr. Edip also believes in his god allah. I think Mr. Edip and I would agree that God has revealed the way in which He wants His children to "act", "behave", so to speak. That's why it is utterly CRITICAL for God that in His revelation, the ultimate example of how to "act" and "behave" is also included! .... so if "allah" had wanted the Quoran to be his ultimate and final revelation, where's that ultimate "role model"/character in the Quoran??!?!? .... again, if one has to go to the haditsh in order to have a picture of who Muhhamad was (if god really intended Muhhamad to be his finest example for humanity), then Mr. Edip has to show why the "nice" haditsh have to be accepted as original, and why the "not so nice" hadiths about Muhhamad have to be rejected because they are corrupted??

And again, I say that it is too bad that the all powerful and wise allah forgot to include all those critical details and examples in his "perfect" "complete" and miracolous book known as the Quoran, but on the other hand, allah made sure to include stupidity and garbage such as 19 codes, seven heavens, sun setting in mud, etc ...

EDIP: I thank Giron for his voice of reason. Juan have misread my words. I was talking about ontological issue not moral one. The key word was EXIST. It was my response to a ridiculous conspiracy theory.

Juan is thinking exactly like Sunnis. One really does not need role model if the rules are clear. For instance, if there is a rule telling you not to lie, you do not need a role model to understand it or practice it.

I have a question to Juan who claims to be a Catholic and presumably believes all the stories in the Old Testament: Many prophets and messengers in the Old Testament are depicted to be less than role models. They committed incest, got drunk, lied, had slaves, had hundreds wives and concubines, massacred their enemies together with their women and babies.... I do not believe that any messenger of God would commit these lowly and horrendous acts.

The same evil people who fabricated those lies about Noah, Abraham and many other prophets, were at work when muslims turned their back to the Quran and paid attention to stories and hearsay attributed to their new idols: Muhammad and his companions. The same criminals, the same evil people attributed evil deeds to Muhammad. The motive: to justify their own sins, corruption, oppression, and aggression.

So, I wonder your motive for insisting that I should believe in those mishmash collection of hearsay and gibberish. I wonder, why you cannot handle Quran alone. Peace.

XXXX: Actually you are called in the muslems sight as (quranni).. we don't consider those kind as Muslems... I wanted to read the full debate.. but your sunna insulting with no clear reason or evidence.. made me not continue.. I think you don't know so much about Hadith .. and its science and how muslems deal with it and clasify it... you (quraanis) just wanted to make things easy for just personnel benefits without any fair. I suggest you go to saudi arabia or egypt to and have a study about the Hadith science... you will never be able to ignore it any more

EDIP: I formally studied hadith and usulu alhadith for ten years, and unfortunately, during the days of my ignorance, I wrote books and articles defending hadith.

The reason you will not see me discussing the details of hadith, because this is not its place. When I debate this issue with believers of hadith and sunnah, then I use the so-called science of hadith. And I hit them with their own science! Millions of Turkish speaking people know my live TV debates with top religious leaders in Turkey. In fact, the audio and video records of several debates are currently available at the Turkish section of 19.org.

If you are too eager organize a debate between me and your top expert in "Science of Hadith" Let him be the graduate of your al-Azhar! Let him have the title "great alim" before his name, a long beard on his face, and a turban on his head. Do you hear me? Then, you will be able to listen to both sides and make your own mind.

If you really want to know what kind of "science" is the "science of hadith," I recommend you to read Muhammad Abu Rayya's defense of Hadith and Sunnah, *Udwa Ala Sunna*. You will be educated and very surprised. But, if you want an entertaining book on this subject, then I recommend you Ibn Qutayba's defense of Hadith, *The Science of Resolving Conflictis among Hadiths*.

In fact, o reasonable person may not need to know the SCIENCE of COLLECTING and EVALUATING hadith (*Jarh and Tadil*), since the outcome is out there! Read Bukhari, Muslim, Timizi, Nasai, Ibn Majeh, Ibn Hanbel and other numerous hadith collections and you will find that this science is very good in only producing trash and losing some precious diamonds among its piles. Peace.

Edip Yuksel v Ali Sina (8)

A Revolution Led by Muhammad
Edip Yuksel

In our previous rounds of debate, Ali Sina used his favorite fabricated hadiths to insult and condemn Muhammad. His zeal in relying on hadith was no less than of a fanatic Sunni. Before starting discussing the Quran, I decided that it would be unfair and unjust to Muhammad, the last prophet of islam, to leave his name and message be stained by those trashy narrations and allegations. So, here I post an excerpt from the beginning of my upcoming book, **"Code 19"**,[5] which summarizes Muhammad's struggle against ignorance, arrogance, selfishness, violence and injustice. Here is the true account of Muhammad's character and mission:

A Revolution Led by a Gentile against the Mollarchy of Medieval Arabia

It was 570 years after Christ when Muhammad was born in Mecca. At the age of 40 he made a declaration that shocked his people. During the month of Ramadan of 610, he claimed that he was visited by Holy Revelation (a.k.a. Jibreel or Holy Spirit) delivering him a message from God. This claim was first kept secret; he shared it only with a few close friends and relatives. A few years later he publicly declared his messengership and his opposition to the religious and political establishment of Mecca. An era of revolution and reformation that would change world history had started.

Muhammad, a member of a powerful tribe and a successful international businessman, was not an ordinary citizen of Mecca. With his sound judgment and trustworthy personality, he had won the respect of the theocratic oligarchy. His uncles were the leaders of one of the prominent tribes and were active in social, political, economic, and religious affairs.

Arabs living in the Hijaz region were brethren of the Jews, and Abraham was their common forefather. Mecca or Bacca was the valley where Abraham had immigrated, after his exile from Babylon.[6] There is only one reference to this important city in the Old Testament:

---

[5]   The title of the book is *NINETEEN: God's Signature in Nature and Scripture.*

[6]   There are some critics who argue that *Baca* or *Becca* is different than *Mecca.*

193

> "Blessed is the man whose strengths in thee; in whose heart are the ways of them. Who passing through the valley of Baca make it a well; the rain also fills the pools. They go from strength to strength, every one of them in Zion appears before God. O LORD God of hosts, hear my prayer: give ear, O God of Jacob." (Psalms 84:5-8)

Meccan Arabs had deep respect for the struggle of Abraham whose courageous stand for his monotheistic belief was legendary. Therefore, they were very protective of his reputation, religious practices, and the Kaba. Knowing that Abraham rejected worshiping the statutes besides God, Arabs never worshiped statues or symbolic objects.[7] Nevertheless, they had holy names, such as Al-Lat, Al-Uzza, and Manat from whom they would ask intercession and help. Their association of other authorities and powers to God and their fabrication of myriad prohibitions and laws in the name of God is called *shirk*[8] and the Quran repeatedly criticizes this mindset and practice as polytheism, the source of all evil.

> 53:19-26 What do you think about Allat (The Goddess), Al-Uzza? And Manat, the third one. Do you have sons, while He has daughters? What a fraudulent distribution! These are but names that you made up, you and your forefathers. God never authorized such a blasphemy. They follow conjecture, and personal desire, when the true guidance has come to them herein from their Lord. What is that the human being desires? To God belongs both the Hereafter, and this world. Not even the angels in heaven possess authority to intercede. The only ones permitted by God are those who act in accordance with His will and His approval.

> 39:43-45 Have they have invented intercessors to mediate between them and God? Say, "What if they do not possess any power, nor understanding?" Say, "All intercession belongs to God." To Him belongs the kingship of the heavens and the earth, then to Him you will be re-

---

[7] The common belief among Muslims is to the contrary. To distinguish themselves from the Meccan mushriks, clerics and scholars fabricated stories about statues. There are dubious narrations that Muhammad broke statutes occupying Kaba. However, the Quran that occasionally refers to the statues of previous communities (see: 6:74; 7:138; 14:35; 21:57; 26:71),never mentions the statues or icons of Meccan mushriks. Furthermore, there is no archeological evidence to support the claims of Muslim scholars. Besides, the classic book about statues, Al-Kalbi's KITAB UL ASNAM (The Book of Statues), contains many contradictory descriptions of the so-called Arabian statues. Muslim historians who were disturbed by lack of material evidence for the allegedly abundant Arabian statues came up with a "cookie" theory: Meccan idol-worshipers were making their statues from cookies and when they got hungry they used to eat them. That should explain why archeologist cannot find statues in the region for that era! Phew!

[8] Shirk is described by the Quran in various contexts. Setting up partners with God, or accepting prophets, clergymen and scholars as **authorities** in God's religion is considered as an unforgivable sin. See 42:21; 9:31; 3:18; 2:48; 6:21; 6:145; 7:17-37; 17:46; 45:6; 16:89; 6:112-115; 19:82; 46:6; 25:30; etc.

turned. When God alone is mentioned, the hearts of those who do not believe in the Hereafter shrink with aversion. But when others are mentioned besides Him, they rejoice.

However, those who accept other authorities besides God, never accept their crime. They vehemently deny their shirk. Though the majority of "believers" follow the teachings of their clergymen and assign divine authority to others besides God, they usually do not accept that they are committing shirk; they claim to be monotheists. If you question a Hindu who worships hundreds of gods and goddesses, you will learn that he or she is really a monotheist! A Christian who puts his full confidence in St. Paul's polytheistic teaching which was formulated in 325 CE by the Nicene Council as the Doctrine of Trinity (i.e., God with three personalities) will still claim to be a monotheist![9] Muslims who elevated Muhammad to the level of God by making him the second source of their religion and by putting his name next to God in the Statement of Testimony will also insist that they are monotheists.

6:22-23　On the day when we summon everyone, we will ask the mushriks, "Where are those whom you claimed partners?" Their only response will be, "By God our Lord, we never were mushriks."

16:35　Those who commit shirk say, "Had God willed, we would not have worshiped anyone besides Him, nor would our parents. Nor would we have prohibited anything besides (what was prohibited by) Him." Those before them have done the same. Can the messengers do anything but deliver the message?

Arab mushriks (those who accept other authorities besides God) never claimed that those holy names were gods, they were merely praying for their intercession. They believed that the saints and angels were mediators between them and God.

39:3　The system absolutely shall be devoted to God ALONE. Those who set up masters besides Him say, "We worship them only to bring us closer to God; they are in a good position!" God will judge them regarding their disputes. God does not guide any liar, unappreciative.

The Quran clearly rejects association of any authority besides God, whether in making religious laws or providing eternal salvation.

42:21　They follow those who decree for them religious laws never authorized by God. If it were not for the predetermined decision, they would have been judged immediately. Indeed, the transgressors have incurred a painful retribution.

9:31　They have set up their religious leaders and scholars as lords, instead of God. Others deified the Messiah, son of Mary. They were all

---

[9]　See *19 Questions for Christian Clergy* by Edip Yuksel.

commanded to worship only one God. There is no God except He. Be He glorified, high above having any partners.

According to the information given by the Quran, Meccan Mushriks preserved their forms of religious practices while losing its monotheistic and spiritual meaning. They were praying, fasting, and performed pilgrimage.[10] It was the most popular religious practice.

Mollarchy in the City State of the Arabian Peninsula
There were some characteristics of Mecca that distinguished it from other Arabian towns and cities. Mecca, with Abraham's temple, was the center of religion, politics and business. Abraham's temple, the Kaba, is described by the Quran as "People's House" or "Sacred Place of Prostration." Abraham, as I mentioned above, was a legendary ancestor for both Arabs and Jews. During the four consecutive sacred months,[11] Arabs dwelling in the region would visit Mecca for pilgrimage. Meanwhile, the occasion was also used for an international trade fair. Merchants from neighboring countries would participate in a lengthy business and cultural activity. During these religious months, besides trading, cultural and athletic competitions such as poetry and wrestling would take place. Mecca was the center for economic, political, and cultural activities of a vast land.

Prominent tribal leaders like Abu Hakem (a.k.a., Abu Jahel), Abdul Uzza (a.k.a., Abu Lahab), Abu Sufyan, Umayy Ben Halef, Nadr Ben Haris, and Valeed Ben Mugiyra, could not tolerate any reformation movement that would change the status quo and risk Mecca's crucial position in the political and economic landscape. They were determined to follow the traditional religion they inherited from their ancestors who had distorted Abraham's monotheistic system to shirk. Preservation of the traditional religion and the status quo was vital for the theocratic government of Mecca. Questioning the orthodox belief system and the common practice could be interpreted as a foreign attack on the unity of Mecca or as a betrayal to the fabric of its society.

A teaching that rejects the idea of intercession and the sacred role of professional clergymen, a teaching that promotes the human rights of slaves and the oppressed, that seeks economic justice by objecting to monopoly and usury, that is concerned about the poor, that condemns ethnic and racial discrimination, that protects the rights of women, that advocates democratic governance through consultation, and encourages people to use their reasoning and questions tradition, surely, such a system would pose a serious threat to the economic and political interest of the ruling elite.

---

[10]   The detailed argument on this subject can be found in author's Turkish book, *Kuran Çevirilerindeki Hatalar (Errors in the Translations of the Quran)*, Ozan Yayıncılık.

[11]   They were originally Zilhija, Muharram, Safar, Rabi 1, and later their order was changed by mushriks.

Social, Economic, and Political Structure Criticized

It is a well-known fact that the early revelations of the Quran use strong language in criticizing the theocratic oligarchy, which did not care about the poor, orphans and aliens; did not free the slaves; did not treat women as equal to men; and did not consult people in public affairs.

107:1-7   Do you know who rejects The System of God Alone? That is the one who mistreats the orphans. And does not advocate the feeding of the poor. And woe to those who observe the contact prayers, Who are totally heedless of their prayers; they only show off. And they forbid charity.

89:17-20   Wrong! It is you who brought it on yourselves by not regarding the orphan. And not advocating charity towards the poor. And consuming the inheritance of helpless orphans. And loving the money too much.

90:6-20   He boasts, "I spent so much money!" Does he think that no one sees him? Did we not give him two eyes? A tongue and two lips? Did we not show him the two paths? He should choose the difficult path. Which one is the difficult path? The freeing of slaves. Feeding, during the time of hardship. Orphans who are related. Or the poor who is in need. And being one of those who believe, and exhorting one another to be steadfast, and exhorting one another to be kind. These have deserved happiness. As for those who disbelieved in our revelations, they have incurred misery. They will be confined in the Hellfire.

16:58-59   Thus, when one of them gets a baby girl, his face becomes darkened with overwhelming grief. Ashamed, he hides from the people, because of the bad news. He even debates: should he keep the baby grudgingly, or bury her in the dust. Miserable indeed is their judgment.

42:38   And they respond to their Lord by observing the contact prayers and by deciding their affairs on the basis of consultation among themselves, and from our provisions to them they give.

4:1-5   O people, observe your Lord; the one who created you from one being and created from it its mate, then spread from the two many men and women. You shall regard God, by whom you swear, and regard the parents. God is watching over you. You shall hand over to the orphans their rightful properties. Do not substitute the bad for the good, nor shall you consume their properties by combining them with your properties. This is a gross injustice. If you deem it best for the orphans, you may marry their mothers—you may marry two, three, or four of them. If you fear lest you become unfair, then you shall be content with only one, or with what you already have. This way, you are more likely to avoid inequity. You shall give the women their due dowries, fully. If they willingly forfeit anything, then you may accept it graciously. Do not give immature orphans the properties that God has entrusted you as guardians. You shall provide for them therefrom, and clothe them, and talk to them nicely.[12]

59:7   Whatever God restored to His messenger from the (defeated) communities shall go to God and His messenger (in the form of a charity). You shall give it to the relatives, the orphans, the poor, and the traveling alien. Thus, it will not remain monopolized by the strong among you. You may keep the spoils given to you by the messenger, but do not take what he enjoins you from taking. You shall reverence God. God is strict in enforcing retribution.

Life Style and Harmful Tradition Criticized

The population of Mecca was afflicted with many social problems caused by individual abuses of time, money, brain, body and exploitation of God's name.

For instance, gambling was transferring money from the poor to the wealthy, thereby creating financial nightmares for many families. Alcohol was the cause of many personal and social problems such as domestic violence, inefficiency, loss of intellectual capabilities, alcoholism, rape, criminal activities, accidents and a myriad of health problems. The Quran, though acknowledging some financial and personal benefits of gambling and alcohol, encouraged believers to abstain from these addictions without criminalizing them via a penal code.

2:219   They ask you about intoxicants and gambling: say, "In them there is a gross sin, and some benefits for the people. But their sinfulness far outweighs their benefit." They also ask you what to give to charity: say, "The excess." God thus clarifies the revelations for you, that you may reflect.

4:43   O you who believe, do not observe the Contact Prayers (Salat) while intoxicated, so that you know what you are saying....

---

[12]   The purpose and practice of polygamy is another distorted issue in islam (submission). Though the Quran discourage polygamy with two verses (4:3 and 4:129), it allows it as a social and economic institution to take care of orphans in a family environment. The Quran allows polygamy with widows who have children. This permission allowed those who could afford to marry with widows to provide a father figure to their children and take care of their needs. Interestingly, the verse clarifying this limited permission is traditionally mistranslated despite its clear grammatical structure. The correct translation of the verse:

"They consult you concerning women: say, as recited for you in the scripture, God enlightens you regarding the rights of orphans of women whom you deprive of their dowries while seeking to marry them, regarding the disadvantaged children: you shall treat the orphans equitably. Whatever good you do, God is fully aware thereof." (4:127).

Unfortunately, Muslim scholars abused this limited permission and justified marrying with four women at a time even without the permission of the first wife who was deprived her right to divorce!

5:90   O you who believe, intoxicants, and gambling, and the altars of idols, and the games of chance are abominations of the devil; you shall avoid them, that you may succeed.

16:67   And from the fruits of date palms and grapes you produce intoxicants, as well as good provisions. This should be (sufficient) proof for people who understand.

Sexual promiscuity or adultery were contributing to the destruction of families and was a major health threat for the public by transmitting sexual diseases. The Quran encouraged men and women to be loyal to their marriage contract. Though polygamy is permitted to take care of fatherless children and their widowed mothers, monogamy was encouraged.

17:32   You shall not commit adultery; it is a gross sin, and an evil behavior.

4:3   If you deem it best for the orphans, you may marry their mothers— you may marry two, three, or four. If you fear lest you become unfair, then you shall be content with only one, or with what you already have. Additionally, you are thus more likely to avoid financial hardship.

A lengthy list of dietary prohibitions concocted in the name of God was wasting many food resources. The Quran prohibited only four items related to animal products and considered any additional religious prohibitions to be fabrications and shirk.

6:145-151 Say, "I do not find in the revelations given to me any food that is prohibited for any eater except: (1) carrion[13,] (2) running blood, (3) the meat of pigs, for it is bad,[14] and (4) the meat of animals blasphemously dedicated to other than God." If one is forced (to eat these), without being deliberate or malicious, then your Lord is Forgiver, Most Merciful. For those who are Jewish we prohibited animals with undivided hoofs; and of the cattle and sheep we prohibited the fat, except that which is carried on their backs, or in the viscera, or mixed with bones. That was a retribution for their transgressions, and we are truthful. If they disbelieve you, then say, "Your Lord possesses infinite mercy, but His retribution is unavoidable for the guilty people." The idol worshipers say, "Had God willed, we would not practice idolatry, nor would our parents, nor would we prohibit anything."

---

[13]   The examples of this category are listed in verse 5:3.

[14]   Many speculations made by Muslims to provide medical reasons for prohibition of *meat* of pig. Though, I consider it as a divine commandment to be followed for just the sake of obeying the Creator of the Universe, I think one of the reasons might lay in the waste of resources and environmental pollution. It is a well-known fact that pigs produce six times more waste than other domestic animals. Pig farms have caused serious environmental problems in some States, such as in North Carolina. Besides emitting disturbing smells, pig waste has contaminated the underground water in many nearby towns.

Thus did those before them disbelieve, until they incurred our retribution. Say, "Do you have any proven knowledge that you can show us? You follow nothing but conjecture; you only guess." Say, "God possesses the most powerful argument; if He wills He can guide all of you." Say, "Bring your witnesses who would testify that God has prohibited this or that." If they testify, do not testify with them. Nor shall you follow the opinions of those who reject our revelations, and those who disbelieve in the Hereafter, and those who stray away from their Lord. Say, "Come let me tell you what your Lord has really prohibited for you: You shall not set up idols besides Him. You shall honor your parents. You shall not kill your children from fear of poverty—we provide for you and for them. You shall not commit gross sins, obvious or hidden. You shall not kill—God has made a person's life sacred - except in the course of justice. These are His commandments to you,that you may understand."

The Quran dealt with many other issues such as protection of the environment and ecological balance and protection of God's creation from unnecessary mutilation. For instance, the Quran prohibited hunting during pilgrimage (5:95-96). It also criticized Meccan Arabs for cutting the ears of animals for religious reasons, which has a negative implication regarding the custom of circumcision.

4:119   "I will mislead them, I will entice them, I will command them to (forbid the eating of certain meats by) marking the ears of livestock, and I will command them to distort the creation of God." Anyone who accepts the devil as a lord, instead of God, has incurred a profound loss.

The chapter "Ben Israel" (Children of Israel) contains a series of commandments aiming to change the mindset, attitude, and actions of individuals:

17:23-39 You shall not set up any other God beside God, lest you end up despised and disgraced. Your Lord has decreed that you shall not worship except Him, and your parents shall be honored. As long as one or both of them live, you shall never say to them, "Uff" (the slightest gesture of annoyance), nor shall you shout at them; you shall treat them amicably. And lower for them the wings of humility, and kindness, and say, "My Lord, have mercy on them, for they have raised me from infancy." Your Lord is fully aware of your innermost thoughts. If you maintain righteousness, He is Forgiver of those who repent. You shall give the due alms to the relatives, the needy, the poor, and the traveling alien, but do not be excessive, extravagant. The extravagant are brethren of the devil, and the devil is unappreciative of his Lord. Even if you have to turn away from them, as you pursue the mercy of your Lord, you shall treat them in the nicest manner. You shall not keep your hand stingily tied to your neck, nor shall you foolishly open it up, lest you end up blamed and sorry. For your Lord increases the provision for anyone He chooses, and reduces it. He is fully Cognizant of His creatures, Seer. You shall not kill your children (infanticide) due to fear of poverty. We provide for

200

them, as well as for you. Killing them is a gross offense. You shall not commit adultery; it is a gross sin, and an evil behavior. You shall not kill any person—for God has made a person's life sacred—except in the course of justice. If one is killed unjustly, then we give his heir authority to enforce justice. Thus, he shall not exceed the limits in avenging the murder; he will be helped. You shall not touch the orphans' money except for their own good, until they reach maturity. You shall fulfill your covenants, for a covenant is a great responsibility. You shall give full measure when you trade, and weigh equitably. This is better and more righteous. You shall not accept any information, unless you verify it for yourself. I have given you the hearing, the eyesight, and the mind, and you are responsible for using them. You shall not walk proudly on earth - you cannot bore through the earth, nor can you be as tall as the mountains. All bad behavior is condemned by your Lord. This is some of the wisdom inspired to you by your Lord. You shall not set up another God beside God, lest you end up in Gehenna, blamed and defeated.

The Quran aimed to reform both society and the individual. The Quran invites individuals to undertake a substantial reformation. The description of believers in the last verses of chapter "Al-Furqan" (The Distinguisher) reveals the desired characteristics of Muslims:

25:58-77 You shall put your trust in the One who is Alive—the One who never dies - and praise Him and glorify Him. He is fully Cognizant of His creatures' sins. He is the One who created the heavens and the earth, and everything between them, in six days, then assumed all authority. The Gracious; ask about Him those who are well founded in knowledge. When they are told, "Fall prostrate before the Gracious," they say, "What is the Gracious? Shall we prostrate before what you advocate?" Thus, it only augments their aversion. Most blessed is the One who placed constellations in the sky, and placed in it a lamp, and a shining moon. He is the One who designed the night and the day to alternate: a sufficient proof for those who wish to take heed, or to be appreciative. The worshipers of the Gracious are those who tread the earth gently, and when the ignorant speak to them, they only utter peace. In the privacy of the night, they meditate on their Lord, and fall prostrate. And they say, "Our Lord, spare us the agony of Hell; its retribution is horrendous. "It is the worst abode; the worst destiny." When they give, they are neither extravagant nor stingy; they give in moderation. They never implore beside God any other God, nor do they kill anyone—for God has made life sacred—except in the course of justice. Nor do they commit adultery. Those who commit these offenses will have to pay. Retribution is doubled for them on the Day of Resurrection, and they abide therein humiliated. Exempted are those who repent, believe, and lead a righteous life. God transforms their sins into credits. God is Forgiver, Most Merciful. Those who repent and lead a righteous life, God redeems them; a complete redemption. They do not bear false witness. When they encounter vain talk, they ignore it. When reminded of their Lord's revelations, they never react to them as if they were deaf and blind. And they say, "Our Lord, let our spouses and children be a source of joy for us, and keep us in the forefront of the righteous." These are the ones who attain Paradise in return for their steadfastness; they are received therein with joyous greetings and peace. Eternally they abide therein; what a beautiful destiny; what a beautiful abode. Say, "You attain value at my Lord only through your worship. But if you disbelieve, you incur the inevitable consequences."

Meccan Leaders are Losing Their Sleep

Mecca could remain an independent center of commerce because of its unique geopolitical situation. Mecca was located in a region where the influence of the two super powers of that era, Byzantine and Persian Empires, collided. This balance of powers created such a vacuum that Mecca could survive without submitting herself to either hegemony. Mecca was a default capital of the Arabian Peninsula. The population of Mecca and surrounding towns did not follow any scripture, but only oral traditions and practices. Religion and politics were inseparable affairs. Though Meccan population had many literate people, they were considered "UMMY" (gentiles) for not having a scripture or a written law as their Christian and Jewish neighbors. Muhammad was a literate gentile.[15]

When Muhammad declared that he had received a message from God, the Meccan oligarchy first did not take him seriously. They just ignored him. However, when they noticed the potential power of his message and the rate of the new converts, their reaction varied between mockery and insinuation. Soon their reaction escalated to slander and threat of eviction and death. Though Muhammad's personal history and his tribal relationship was providing a kind of protection against physical attacks, some of his followers did not have tribal support. For instance, among those who were subjected to torture was Bilal, an Ethiopian slave who was freed by one of Muhammad's friends. The first convert[16] who

---

[15]   Muslim scholars, among many facts, have distorted this one too. They fabricated and narrated stories claiming that Muhammad was an illiterate man and maintained his illiteracy until his death. This claim not only contradicts the Quran and the historical facts, but it is also an insult to Muhammad. Was the prophet who brought a book and dictated it for 23 years not able to recognize the 28 letters of Arabic alphabet? How come a prophet who brought a scripture, which its first revelation starts with the word "READ," did not try to learn how to read? Why a prophet who encouraged his friends to learn how to read and write himself did not practice what he preached to others? If Muhammad was illiterate, then he was either a crook trying to fool people that he could not read (which is impossible since there were literally thousands of people who knew him since his childhood) or he did not have the intelligence to learn how to read and write! To support their claim of "Literal Miracle" Muslim Scholars resorted to this obvious lie and interestingly reached consensus on it! For a detailed argument on this subject see *Quran: a Reformist Translation*.

[16]   Meccan Arabs initially called Muhammad and his followers, "Sabeen" meaning "followers of other religions."

202

was killed was Sumayya, a woman. Slaves and women: victims of racist and misogynistic laws and religions.

Having economic and political interest in man-made religious teachings, clergymen augmented and manipulated the religious fanaticism of ignorant masses. The fatal combination of ignorance and arrogance, which in the past had taken the lives of many messengers and prophets, from Socrates to Jesus, was again at work. The words uttered against previous messengers were repeated against Muhammad, this time in Arabic. Muhammad's situation was no different than of Saaleh, a messenger to a community which perished a long time ago.

> 11:62   They said, "O Saaleh, you used to be popular among us before this. Are you enjoining us from worshiping what our parents are worshiping? We have a lot of doubt concerning everything you tell us.

Muhammad's message was focused on monotheism (tawheed), which is the main theme of Mosaic teaching that crowns the Ten Commandments.

> And God spoke all these words, saying, I am the LORD thy God, which have brought you out of the land of Egypt, out of the house of bondage. Thou shall have no other gods before me. Thou shall not make unto thee any graven image, or any likeness of any thing that is in heaven above, or that is in the earth beneath, or that is in the water under the earth.... Thou shall not take the name of the LORD thy God in vain; for the LORD will not hold him guiltless that takes his name in vain. (Exodus 20:1-4, 7)

Ironically, despite the popularity of Ten Commandments among Jews, Christians and Muslims, the faith and practices negating and defying the first two commandments have become their basic dogmas.

Muhammad delivered the words of the Quran critical of the traditional religion of Meccan people who had transformed Abraham's monotheistic system into polytheism by blindly following their ancestors, inheriting innovations, superstitions, numerous cleric-made religious laws falsely attributed to God, and the belief of intercession.

> 6:161   Say, "My Lord has guided me in a straight path: the perfect system of Abraham, monotheism. He never was an idol worshiper."

Flocking on the Glorious Path of their Ancestors
Mushriks, be it of ancient times or modern times, attempt to justify their religions by the number of their members, by the glory of their ancestors and by the fame of their "saints." In arguments based on logic, scientific investigation and analysis of historical documentation, their common defense is the miserable argument from authority: "this and that holy clergymen said this," or "most of our ancient scholars have decided this way."

203

43:22-24 Instead, they said, "We found our parents carrying on certain practices, and we are following in their footsteps. Invariably, when we sent a warner to a community, the leaders therein said, "We found our parents following certain practices, and we will continue in their footsteps." He would say, "What if I brought to you better guidance than what you inherited from your parents?" They would say, "We are disbelievers in the message you brought."

31:21-22 When they are told, "Follow these revelations of God," they say, "No, we follow only what we found our parents doing." What if the devil is leading them to the agony of Hell? Those who submit completely to God, while leading a righteous life, have gotten hold of the strongest bond. For God is in full control of all things.

Idolizing their ancestors under different titles and following the dogmas and superstitions that are attributed to them as a religion are the universal characteristics of mushriks. Religious idols vary according to religions and languages. For instance, idols in America are Jesus, Mary, or Saints; in Turkey are Ata, Evliya, Sheik, or Hazrat; in India Mahatma; in Pakistan Maulana; in Iran Imams Hussein and Ehl-i Bayt. Religious masses do not seek the truth by using their brains or senses. Instead, they blindly follow the teachings bearing sanctified signatures. Mushriks are like parrots; they repeat words without understanding their meaning.

2:171 The example of those who disbelieve is like those who parrot what they hear of sounds and calls, without understanding. Deaf, dumb, and blind; they cannot understand.

Ironically, it is the religious leaders who promote blind imitation. By institutionalizing ignorance through religious terms, the diabolic saints lead astray masses from Truth.[17] The messengers and prophets, who invited people to question their popular religion and traditions, almost invariably found the clergy fighting and plotting against them.

Nevertheless among the chief rulers also many believed on him; but because of the Pharisees they did not confess him, lest they should be

---

[17] The famous atheist philosopher, Friedrich Nietzsche, was so fed up with the abuse and exploitation of the Church, he opened a scorching attack on clergymen. He wrote, "As long as the priest is considered a higher type of man—this professional negator, slanderer, and poisoner of life—there is no answer to the question: what is truth? For truth has been stood on its head when the conscious advocate of nothingness and negation is accepted as the representative of "truth." ... In Christianity neither morality nor religion has even a single point of contact with reality.... This world of pure fiction is vastly inferior to the world of dreams insofar as the latter mirrors reality, whereas the former falsifies, devalues, and negates reality. Friedrich Nietzsche, *The Antichrist*, in *The Portable Nietzsche*, ed. and trans. Walter Kaufmann (New York: Viking, 1954).

put out of the synagogue: For they loved the praise of men more than the praise of God. (John 12:42-43)

> 38:6-8   The leaders announced, "Go and steadfastly persevere in worshiping your gods. This is all you need. We never heard of this from the religion of our fathers. This is a lie. Why did the message come down to him, instead of us?" Indeed, they are doubtful of My message. Indeed, they have not yet tasted My retribution.

The Black Campaign Waged by Those with White Turbans

The message delivered by Muhammad baffled and bewildered the bearded and turbaned Meccan clerics. They first tried to attack his character. They accused and insulted him labeling him a "wizard," a dreaming "poet," or "a crazy man."

> 51:51-53   Do not set up besides God any other God. I am sent by Him to you as a manifest warner. Consistently, when a messenger went to the previous generations, they said, "Magician," or, "Crazy." Did they make an agreement with each other? Indeed, they are transgressors.

> 37:35-36   When they were told "La Elaaha Ella Allah [There is no other God besides God]," they turned arrogant. They said, "Shall we leave our gods for the sake of a crazy poet?"

> 68:51-52   Those who disbelieved show their ridicule in their eyes when they hear the message and say, "He is crazy!" It is in fact a message to the world.

The Quran encourages Muhammad not to give up against this negative propaganda. Muhammad's mission was to deliver the message at the cost of losing his popularity.

> 52:29-33   You shall remind the people. With your Lord's blessings upon you, you are neither a soothsayer, nor crazy. They may say, "He is a poet; let us just wait until he is dead." Say, "Go on waiting; I will wait along with you." Is it their dreams that dictate their behavior, or are they naturally wicked? Do they say, "He made it all up?" Instead, they are simply disbelievers.

The Reaction and Plans of Disbelievers

Tyranny and terror is a prevalent characteristic of mushriks. Terror and violence is a defense mechanism of many who prefer not to use their brains. The polytheistic elite of Athena convicted Socrates to death for questioning the absurdity of their religion. Persian priests tried to get rid of Zoroaster. Jewish clerics conspired with Romans to kill Jesus for his threat to their abuse of religion. In defense of his theocratic and oppressive regime, Pharaoh mobilized his generals and religious leaders to eliminate Moses. Shuayb's life was threatened by his people. Noah was stoned. Abraham was rejected by his own father and was thrown into a fire. Some messengers were evicted and others were killed. Muhammad, who declared intellectual war against slavery, subjugation of women, racism, superstitions, ignorance, illiteracy, ancestor-worship, and exploitation of religious beliefs, would not be treated differently.

> 8:30-31 The disbelievers plotted and schemed to neutralize you, or kill you, or banish you. However, they plot and scheme, but so does God. God is the best schemer. When our revelations are recited to them, they say, "We have heard. If we want to, we can say the same thing. These are only tales from the past."

The forerunners, who took all kinds of risks by siding with Muhammad, encountered difficult tests. They were excommunicated. They were rejected by their families and relatives. They experienced economic hardship. They were subjected to insult and torture of mushrik Arabs. They were oppressed, banished from their land, and were viciously attacked. Many were killed; but they did not give up their conviction and cause.

> 9:97 The Arabs are the worst in disbelief and hypocrisy, and the most likely to ignore the laws that God has revealed to His messenger. God is Omniscient, Most Wise.[18]

Muhammad was the main target of mushrik Arabs. Not only had he lost his popularity among his people; his life was also in danger. However, he was ordained by the Lord of the Universe. He was commissioned to deliver the Message without compromise. He became the recipient of the greatest possible honor, receiving revelation from God.

> 4:113 God has sent down to you the scripture and wisdom, and He has taught you what you never knew. Indeed, God's blessings upon you have been great...

While the multifarious aggressive campaign of the Meccan government and its allies in the region continued, Muhammad and his comrades promoted the freedom of expression and religious beliefs.

> 109:1-6 Say, "O you disbelievers. I do not worship what you worship. Nor do you worship what I worship. Nor will I ever worship what you worship. Nor will you ever worship what I worship. To you is your system, and to me is my system."

The leaders, whose political and economic interest was at risk, and the ignorant followers, whose conformity was disturbed, responded to this message of "leave us alone" with violence. But, their bloody terror and noise could not prevent the light from piercing and destroying the layers of darkness.

---

[18] The following verse, 9:99, makes an exception of this statement.

To the Factor of 666

Edip Yuksel

If Muslims are Terrorists, then Jews and Christians are Terrorists to the Factor of 666! The Diabolic Coalition Exposed: Evilgelical Crusaders, Fascist Zionists, and Fanatic Sunnis and Shiites are Following Six Steps to Discredit the Quran

The verse 9:5 does not encourage Muslims to attack those who associate partners to God, but to attack those who have violated the peace treaty and killed and terrorized people because of their belief and way of life. The Quran does not promote war; but encourages us to stand against aggressors on the side of peace and justice. War is permitted only for self-defense (See: 2:190,192,193,256; 4:91; 5:32; 60:8-9). We are encouraged to work hard to establish peace (47:35; 8:56-61; 2:208). The Quranic precept promoting peace and justice is so fundamental that peace treaty with the enemy is preferred to religious ties (8:72).

The verse 9:29 is mistranslated by almost every translator. The correct translation of it should be:

> 9:29　　You shall fight (back) against those who do not believe in God, nor in the last day, and they do not prohibit what God and His messenger have prohibited, and do not abide by the system of truth among those who received the scripture, until they pay the COMPANSATION, in humility.

You have noticed that I inserted a parenthesis since the context of the verse is about the War of Hunain, and fighting is allowed for only self defense. See: 2:190-193, 256; 4:91; and 60:8-9.

Furthermore, note that I suggest COMPENSATION instead of Arabic word Jizya. The meaning of Jizya has been distorted as a perpetual tax on non-Muslims, which was invented long after Muhammad to further the imperialistic agenda of Sultans or Kings. The origin of the word that I translated as Compensation is JaZaYa, which simply means compensation, not tax. Because of their aggression and initiation of a war against muslims and their allies, after the war, the allied community should require their enemies to compensate for the damage they inflicted on the peaceful community. Various derivatives of this word are used in the Quran frequently, and they are translated as COMPANSATION for a particular deed.

Unfortunately, the distortion in the meaning of the verse above and the practice of collecting a special tax from Christians and Jews, contradict the basic principle of the Quran that there should not be compulsion in religion and there should be freedom of belief and expression (2:256; 4:90; 10:99; 18:29; 88:21,22, and 4:137). Since taxation based on religion creates financial duress on people to convert to the previliged religion, it violates this important Quranic principle. Dividing a population that united under a social contract (constitution) into previliged groups based on their religion contradicts many principles of the Quran, including justice, peace, and brotherhood/sisterhood of all humanity.

Some uninformed critics or bigoted enemies of the Quran list verses of the Quran dealing with wars and declare islam to be a religion of violence. Their favorite verses are: 2:191; 3:28; 3:85; 5:10,34; 9:5; 9:28-29; 9:123; 14:17; 22:9; 25: 52; 47:4 and 66:9. In this article, I refuted their argument against 9:29, and I will discuss each of them later.

Some followers of Sunni or Shiite religions, together with their like-minded modern Crusaders, abuse 9:5 or 9:29 by taking them out of their immediate and Quranic context. Sunnis and Shiites follow many stories and instructions falsely attributed to Muhammad that justify terror and aggression. For instance, in a so-called authentic (or authentically fabricated) hadith, after arresting the murderers of his shepherd, the prophet and his companions cut their arms and legs off, gauge their eyes with hot nails and leave them dying from thirst in the dessert, a contradiction to the portrayal of Muhammad's mission in the Quran (21:107; 3:159). In another authentically fabricated hadith, the prophet is claimed to send a gang during night to secretly kill a female poet who criticized him in her poetry, a violation of the teaching of the Quran! (2:256; 4:137; 4:140; 10:99; 18:29; 88:21-22). Despite these un-Quranic teachings, the aggressive elements among Sunni or Shiite population have almost always been a minority.

Six Diabolic Steps to Distort and Discredit

The following six steps are cleverly utilized over and over by the enemies of islam, including Christian missionaries, to discredit the Quran. For the 3rd and 4th steps they find great ammunition inside the volumes of hadith and sectarian jurisprudence books. (No wonder they like those books very much). For the 5th and 6th steps they find many allies among Sunni or Shiite versions of Hislamics who are extremely intoxicated by those anti-islamic sectarian teachings.

Before exposing this unholy alliance let me quote several war related instructions from the so-called authentic hadith books:

> Narrated As-Sab bin Jaththama: The Prophet passed by me at a place called Al-Abwa or Waddan, and was asked whether it was permissible to attack the pagan warriors at night with the probability of exposing their women and children to danger. The Prophet replied, "They (i.e. women and children) are from them (i.e. pagans)." I also heard the Prophet saying, "The institution of Hima is inva-

208

lid except for Allah and His Apostle." (Bukhari (Jihad) Volume 4, Book 52, Number 256)

It is reported on the authority of Sa'b b. Jaththama that the Prophet of Allah (may peace be upon him), when asked about the women and children of the polytheists being killed during the night raid, said: They are from them. (Muslim Book 019, Number 4321)

It is narrated by Sa'b b. Jaththama that he said (to the Holy Prophet): Messenger of Allah, we kill the children of the polytheists during the night raids. He said: They are from them. (Muslim Book 019, Number 4322)

Sa'b b. Jaththama has narrated that the Prophet (may peace be upon him) asked: What about the children of polytheists killed by the cavalry during the night raid? He said: They are from them. (Muslim Book 019, Number 4323)

Here are the repeated sixes:

1. Ignore the fact that the Quran is a self-sufficient, self-explaining and detailed book, and destroy its semantic network by deliberately disconnecting its verses. Take a portion of the Quran and ignore all other verses that explain, supplement or bring limitation to that verse. If this is not enough to make it ugly or scary, then;

2. Reduce your reference to a smaller portion; take a Quranic verse or part of it out of its immediate context. If this is not enough to make it ugly or scary, then;

3. Twist the meaning of some words. You may even find a sectarian book or a website that has done that before you. If this is not enough to make it ugly or scary, then;

4. Refer to the mishmash collection of fabrications called hadith and sunnah; there you will find a treasury of trash to stink an entire city. Claim that the Quran is useless and unintelligible without these sources. Some Hislamic people will be confused by your love of those "holy" teachings! That is a good sign. If you cannot convince, you must confuse… But, your goal is to convert as many as possible. So, find as much as garbage out of the Hislamic sources and introduce it as Islamic. If this is not enough to make it ugly or scary, then;

5. Pick some examples of Sunni or Shiite idiots or terrorists, from among more than a billion Muslims, and generalize it to all Muslims. Especially, choose your examples from traumatized populations that have been abused and oppressed under the occupation of USA, UK, Israel, or Russia, or under the tyranny of a puppet dictator supported by one of these nations. While doing this, you must entirely ignore all the wars,

209

destructions, massacres, tortures, and terrorist acts committed by the Judeo-Christian forces. If this is not enough to make it ugly or scary, then;

6. Exchange words of hatred and bigotry with some intoxicated Sunni or Shiite Hislamics. Then go to your church, sing songs about love and Jesus, and do not forget asking forgiveness for your sins. You will start your next day clean and ready to commit more sins. Your Hislamic partner (!) will be waiting for you since they do not have confession sessions. If this is not enough to make it ugly and scary, then you have picked a very wrong verse. Choose another verse from the Quran, and go back and start from step one!

Let's apply it to the Bible:

"Jesus and His Disciples were a warmongering gang!"

Almost any big size book can be discredited by this dishonest and deceitful method; any book! By following these steps, I could easily depict Jesus, one of the messengers of peace (islam), as a divider and a trouble maker, rather than a peacemaker. Let's take one example from Bible:

> "Suppose ye that I am come to give peace on earth? I tell you, Nay; but rather division: For from henceforth there shall be five in one house divided, three against two, and two against three. The father shall be divided against the son, and the son against the father; the mother against the daughter, and the daughter against the mother; the mother in law against her daughter in law, and the daughter in law against her mother in law." Lu 12:51-53

> "Think not that I am come to send peace on earth: I came not to send peace, but a sword." Matthew 10:34

By using the Evilgelical's own methodology of treating the Quran, I came up with a peace-hating, anti-family, troublemaker called Jesus! All I did was to take the verse out of its context. I did not even resort to twisting its words or adding some trash from secondary sources, or giving some examples from crusades, inquisitions, slavery, or irritate and provoke some crazy people among Evilgelical Crusaders.

By using the first two of the six steps, I could claim that the disciple of Jesus were, in fact, a dangerous gang who were planning to shed blood in that peaceful region. They were savages who cut the ears of their opponents:

210

And, behold, one of them which were with Jesus stretched out his hand, and drew his sword, and struck a servant of the high priest's, and smote off his ear. (Mt 26:51. Also see: Mark 14:47 ; Lu 22:50; John 18:10)

I could depict Jesus and his disciples as a gang of blood-thirsty troublemakers, by adding verses justifying violence, blood-shed, massacres and tortures from the Old Testament, which was heavily relied by Jesus and his supporters for their mission. I could even reasonably speculate that Jesus and his few followers were planning a huge massacre in the region, but the Roman Empire stopped them before the cult reached to a dangerous number (Luke 21:24);. Knowing that they were provoked prematurely, Jesus reminded Peter:

> "Then said Jesus unto him, Put up again thy sword into his place: for all they that take the sword shall perish with the sword." (Mt 26:51).

I could reasonably ask a Christian who claims his religion to be the religion of peace: "You will agree that this event happened in the last days of Jesus. Why then did Jesus never tell his disciples not to carry SWORDS before one of them cut off the ear of the servant of the high priest? Or, do you want us to believe that Peter, who was putting his life at risk by trying to defend Jesus did not give a hoot to the instruction of his leader? Was Peter carrying the sword to peel cucumbers? Obviously, Jesus had seen that his disciple(s) were carrying swords and he did not mind. However, here he knew that tactically using sword would not save them from the Roman army and it would be a futile and premature fight." Perhaps, my argument to depict Jesus as another potential Samson who killed a thousand men with the jaw of an ass (Jg 15:16) would receive cheers from the enemies of Jesus.

To depict Jesus as a rebel who planned a bloody revolution, I could cite Mt 21:12; Mr 11:15; Jo 2:19 and claim that he attacked the temple and destroyed its properties. I might have even continued the attack by quoting him:

> "But those mine enemies, which would not that I should reign over them, bring hither, and slay them before me." (Lu 19:27).

> "Then said he unto them, But now, he that hath a purse, let him take it, and likewise his scrip: and he that hath no sword, let him sell his garment, and buy one." (Luke 22:36)

However, if I had done this it would be unfair to the teaching of Jesus, one of the messengers of islam (peace and submission to God), delivered by the New Testament. It would be unfair because I would be taking them out of their context. Without even mixing them with the verses of the Old Testament that usually published in the same volume and frequently referred by the New Testament.

Modern Crusaders, Allied with Big Corporations are Orchastrating a Deceptive Propaganda and Misinformation Campaign to Promote their Bloody Cause to Colonize New Lands and Convert More People

Modern Crusaders distort verses of the Quran, exaggerate the deeds of terrorists and even attribute some events motivated by nationalism or other motives to islam. Their propaganda machine never referred to the Serbs as Christian Rapists and Christian Terrorists. Their propaganda machine never referred to the torturer and murderer Zionist occupying forces as Jewish Terrorists, or Jewish Murderers. Their propaganda machine never acknowledge the Christian faith and zeal behind Nazi crimes. But, they frequently associated any act of terrorism to Islam and Muslims. Furthermore, they cleverly managed to depict the freedom seeking victims of brutal occupying forces as agrressors in conflicts such as Chechenya, or Palestine.

They try to depict islam as a violent religion, thereby seeking to justify their own terror, massacres, pre-emptive wars, which are cunningly promoted in a euphemistic language through their propaganda machines. They don't kill and terrorize civilians; they just produce collateral damage and they just perform colorful shows of "shock and awe." They do not torture prisoners; they either interrogate them or turn them to anecdotals. They do not destroy cities; they do surgical and smart operations. They do not occupy others' lands; they liberate them. They do not take revenge; they take justice to their enemies. Thus, media is cleverly used to hypnotize masses and get their support for neo-colonialism. The ruling class in democracies use media to "manifacture concent." In order to plunder the resources of other countries, greedy corporations and their unholy allies replace one dictator after another, create wars and conflicts, undertake covert operations, and if they are bored, they play liberation games for fun and profit, big profit.

Crusaders have directly participated or supported many atrocities and wars in the last millennium; they have killed many more innocent people than their counterpart Sunny or Shiite warmongers. Inquisition, crusades, witch-hunt, World War I and II, holocaust, Hiroshima, Nagasaki, Phillipines, Korea, Vietnam, Nikaragua, Arjantine, Iraq are just few words in the long list of wars and massacres that are committed or supported by those who call themselves Christians. Nazis used the traditional Christian hatred of Jews as fuel and a twisted Cross (swastika) as the symbol for their racist ambitions. The list of British and American wars, occupations, massacres, slavery, covert operations that were conducted with the approval and support of the Christian church or masses is too long and too gruesome. You can still find many Christians justifying the biggest terrorist attack in the history, the destruction of two big cities with their hundreds of thousands civil population, as a retaliation to the Japanese attack to an American military base. American government has not apologized humanity for this horrific and cowardly act of terror. The mentality of these Crusaders is no different than those of al-Qaida militants who justified the destruction of the World Trade Center as retaliation to the American support for the Israeli's racist policy of occupation, massacres and terror in Palestine.

Modern Crusaders Use Proxies for their Bloody Cause

Right-wing Christianity, which I call Evilgelicalism, is a growing radical movement in Christendom, officially known as Evangelical Christians. They are also known as Left-behind Rapture Freaks. Here, we will refer them by mutating several letters in their name so that their name will fit their deeds: Evilgelicals. Yes, Evilgelicals have recently mobilized all their sources to launch a campaign against the Quran in order to convert Muhammad-worshipers to Jesus-worshipers. Though there won't be much difference, since both populations are like identical twins, but the plan is to start a new era of colonialism and slavery through holy Trojan horses.

Bishop Desmond Tutu, the South African civil right leader, once articulated the method of colonialist Evilgelicals in nutshell: "When the missionaries came to Africa, they had the Bible and we had the land. They said: "Let us pray." We closed our eyes. When we opened them we had the Bible and they had the land."

But, Crusaders are no more relying on prayers or the closed eyes of their victims to grab their lands. Many people nowadays are no more closing their eyes while praying, especially when there is a priest around. Since public learned that some priests grab other things besides lands, there is more reluctance to close eyes. So, the priests and their followers have mutated since last century and have transformed to modern Evangelicals.

This new strand of crusaders use all kinds of media for propaganda, combining their mesmerizing effect with the devastating impact of smart and dumb bombs and modern weapons. They call themselves pro-lifers, but they are always for increase in military budgets, they chant "God bless America" whenever USA-Inc invades a country and kills tens of thousands of its population, and they are more likely support capital punishment. Though they claim that "it is easier for a camel to go through the eye of a needle, than for a rich man to enter into the kingdom of God" (Mt 19:24; Mr 10:25; Lu 18:25), in reality they support poli-cies that make rich richer and poor poorer.

They no more adhere the highest ethical standars thought by Jesus. To the con-trary, for centuries they made a travesty out of it. Before they suck the blood of their victims, they no more use the pain-reducing and sleep-inducing formulas, such as, "right-cheek, left-cheek" or "coat after cloke" (Mt 5:39; Lu 6:29). They claim to bring peace and liberty to barbarians by invading their lands through proxy fighters, such as the armies of corporate-nations. While barbarians terror-ize, they do awing and shocking. They destroy their homes, smack their heads, kill their children, torture, rape, and sodomize those they have captured. They

213

further justify their method by comparing their action to the ones committed by the "few thugs" who were ironically their former allies in their preivous operations, and they look adamant to outdo those barbarians in the acts of shedding blood and inflicting pain.

Repeating the Old Habits

In the lands they occupy they kill 666 times more innocent people than their counterpart Hislamic barbarians. They excuse themselves by babtising those dead and mutilated bodies with the holy word "collatoral damage." If one of them or an innocent person is beheaded by Hislamic radicals by sword, they complain from barbaric nature of this and go on killing spree and shatter their heads together with the heads of many collatoral lambs.

Evangelical Christians have last year got a great doze of virtual blood and passion by watching several hours of brutal beating of their idol on the screens. While their mouth uttered peace songs, they dreamed blood and more blood. They drank wine pretending to be the blood of their sacrifical lamb, they ate bread pretending to be the flesh of their idol, but pretence was not satisfying them like actual blood and flesh. They are now determined to direct their anger away from Jews to Arabs. Sucking the blood from Jews is no more feasable since Jews have cleverly taken the top seats almost everywhere. For its unending apetite to suck more semitic blood, this dangerously mutated strand signed a contract with a newly mutated blood-sucking strand of Children of Israel.

Sure, on the other hand, there are many peacemaking Christians who follow the teaching of Jesus in this regard (Matthew 5:9), such as Jehovah Witnesses and Quakers, who have consistently and bravely opposed aggression and unjustified wars. Similarly, among the Jews too there are many peaceful people bravely condemning Israel's fascist policy. Nevertheless, the Old Testament, which is accepted by most Christians as verbatim word of God, is filled with horrific and racist instructions to commit terror, massacres and genocide that cannot be attributed to a Caring and Merciful Lord of all people. It is a great wonder that those Christians and Jews, who take this and few other Quranic verses out of their context in the hopes of misrepresenting the peaceful message of islam, do not see the sword in their own bloody eyes. I do not think that any contextual argument would be able to transform the following blood-sucking beasts to the knights of peace:

> And they utterly destroyed all that was in the city, both man and woman, young and old, and ox, and sheep, and ass, with the edge of the sword. (Jos 6:21).

> And Judah went up; and the LORD delivered the Canaanites and the Perizzites into their hand: and they slew of them in Bezek ten thousand men. And they found Adonibezek in Bezek: and they fought against

him, and they slew the Canaanites and the Perizzites. But Adonibezek fled; and they pursued after him, and caught him, and cut off his thumbs and his great toes. And Adonibezek said, Threescore and ten kings, having their thumbs and their great toes cut off, gathered their meat under my table: as I have done, so God hath requited me. And they brought him to Jerusalem, and there he died. Now the children of Judah had fought against Jerusalem, and had taken it, and smitten it with the edge of the sword, and set the city on fire. And afterward the children of Judah went down to fight against the Canaanites, that dwelt in the mountain, and in the south, and in the valley. And Judah went against the Canaanites that dwelt in Hebron: (now the name of Hebron before was Kirjatharba:) and they slew Sheshai, and Ahiman, and Talmai.And from thence he went against the inhabitants of Debir: and the name of Debir before was Kirjathsepher: And Caleb said, He that smiteth Kirjathsepher, and taketh it, to him will I give Achsah my daughter to wife. (Jg 1:4-12).

And the haft also went in after the blade; and the fat closed upon the blade, so that he could not draw the dagger out of his belly; and the dirt came out... And they slew of Moab at that time about ten thousand men, all lusty, and all men of valour; and there escaped not a man. (Jg 3:22,29)

Then I shall make the heavens shudder, and the earth will be shaken to its foundations at the wrath of the Lord of Hosts, on the day of blazing anger. Like a gazelle pursued by a hunter or like a flock with no shepherd to round it up, every man will head back to his own people, each one will flee to his own land. All who are found will fall by the sword, all who are taken will be thrust through; their babies will be battered to death before their eyes, their houses looted and their wives raped (Isaiah 13:13-15).

Now go and smite Amalek, and utterly destroy all that they have, and spare them not; but slay both man and woman, infant and suckling, ox and sheep, camel and ass. (1Sa 15:3).

But the LORD is the true God, he is the living God, and an everlasting king: at his wrath the earth shall tremble, and the nations shall not be able to abide his indignation. (Jer 10:10).

Why do the wicked prosper and the treacherous all live at ease?... But you know me, Lord, you see me; you test my devotion to you. Drag them away like sheep to the shambles; set them apart for the day of slaughter (Jer 12:1-3).

Then shalt thou say unto them, Thus saith the LORD, Behold, I will fill all the inhabitants of this land, even the kings that sit upon David's throne, and the priests, and the prophets, and all the inhabitants of Jerusalem, with drunkenness. And I will dash them one against another, even the fathers and the sons together, saith the LORD: I will not pity, nor spare, nor have mercy, but destroy them. (Jer 13:13-15)

They shall die of grievous deaths; they shall not be lamented; neither shall they be buried; but they shall be as dung upon the face of the earth: and they shall be consumed by the sword, and by famine; and their carcases shall be meat for the fowls of heaven, and for the beasts of the earth. (Jer 16:4)

A curse on all who are slack in doing the Lord's work! A curse on all who withhold their swords from bloodshed! (Jeremiah 48:10)

The LORD hath brought forth our righteousness: come, and let us declare in Zion the work of the LORD our God. Make bright the arrows; gather the shields: the LORD hath raised up the spirit of the kings of the Medes: for his device is against Babylon, to destroy it; because it is the vengeance of the LORD, the vengeance of his temple. Set up the standard upon the walls of Babylon, make the watch strong, set up the watchmen, prepare the ambushes: for the LORD hath both devised and done that which he spake against the inhabitants of Babylon.O thou that dwellest upon many waters, abundant in treasures, thine end is come, and the measure of thy covetousness. The LORD of hosts hath sworn by himself, saying, Surely I will fill thee with men, as with caterpillers; and they shall lift up a shout against thee. He hath made the earth by his power, he hath established the world by his wisdom, and hath stretched out the heaven by his understanding. When he uttereth his voice, there is a multitude of waters in the heavens; and he causeth the vapours to ascend from the ends of the earth: he maketh lightnings with rain, and bringeth forth the wind out of his treasures. Every man is brutish by his knowledge; every founder is confounded by the graven image: for his molten image is falsehood, and there is no breath in them. They are vanity, the work of errors: in the time of their visitation they shall perish. The portion of Jacob is not like them; for he is the former of all things: and Israel is the rod of his inheritance: the LORD of hosts is his name. Thou art my battle axe and weapons of war: for with thee will I break in pieces the nations, and with thee will I destroy kingdoms; And with thee will I break in pieces the horse and his rider; and with thee will I break in pieces the chariot and his rider; With thee also will I break in pieces man and woman; and with thee will I break in pieces old and young; and with thee will I break in pieces the young man and the maid; I will also break in pieces with thee the shepherd and his flock; and with thee will I break in pieces the husbandman and his yoke of oxen; and with thee will I break in pieces captains and rulers. And I will render unto Babylon and to all the inhabitants of Chaldea all their evil that they have done in Zion in your sight, saith the LORD. (Jer 51:10-24)

And to the others he said in mine hearing, Go ye after him through the city, and smite: let not your eye spare, neither have ye pity: Slay utterly old and young, both maids, and little children, and women: but come not near any man upon whom is the mark; and begin at my sanctuary. Then they began at the ancient men which were before the house. (Eze 9:5-6).

And I will set my jealousy against thee, and they shall deal furiously with thee: they shall take away thy nose and thine ears; and thy remnant shall fall by the sword: they shall take thy sons and thy daughters; and thy residue shall be devoured by the fire. (Eze 23:25).

Therefore he brought upon them the king of the Chaldees, who slew their young men with the sword in the house of their sanctuary, and had no compassion upon young man or maiden, old man, or him that stooped for age: he gave them all into his hand. (2Ch 36:17).

Let the high praises of God be in their mouth, and a twoedged sword in their hand; To execute vengeance upon the heathen, and punishments upon the people; To bind their kings with chains, and their nobles with fetters of iron; To execute upon them the judgment written: this honour have all his saints. Praise ye the LORD. (Ps 149:6-9)

Therefore wait ye upon me, saith the LORD, until the day that I rise up to the prey: for my determination is to gather the nations, that I may assemble the kingdoms, to pour upon them mine indignation, even all my fierce anger: for all the earth shall be devoured with the fire of my jealousy. (Zep 3:8)

Despite their bloody and horrific religious teachings, and despite their practice of colonialism, slavery, discrimination, occupations, destructions, covert operations, productions of weapons of mass destruction, making great profits from production and sales of weapons, plunder of natural resources of earth, terrorizing nations, and massacring poor populations, Modern Crusaders and their allies are successful in portraying one billion Muslims as terrorists and themselves as people of peace and freedom!

Terrorists to the Factor of 666!

Why terrorizing an entire nation, destroying their cities, killing, torturing, raping and sadomizing their children and youth in the name of "democracy and liberty" should be treated lightly? Why killing tens of thousands of civilians should be forgiven if the murderers, who are also proven congenial liars, use the magic word "collateral damage?" Why smashing the brains of children with bombs or severing their legs and arms should be considered civilized and treated differently than beheadings? Why destroying an entire neighborhood or city and massacring its population by a push of button from the sky should not be considered equally or more evil than the individual suicide bomber blowing himself or her-

217

self among his powerful enemies who snuffed out all their hope? Why surviving to push another button to kill more people should be considered a civilized action not the action of those who gave their own lives while doing the killing? How the smile of a well-fed and well-armed mass murderer be deemed more sympathetic than the pain and anger of a poor person? How can one honestly call an occupying foreign military force to be freedom fighters? How can one call the native population to be terrorists just because they are fighting against an arrogant and lethal occupation army which was mobilized against them through lies and deception? Why the children of poor Americans are used to kill the children of poor countries?

We should not favor one criminal over another because of their religion or nationality. However, state terrorism, regardless of the nationality and religion of the population, is much more cruel, dangerous, and sinister than the group or individual terrorism. In our stand against war, violence, and terrorism we must be consistent and fair. Peacemakers and promoters must also PROTEST and CONDEMN the atrocities conducted by the Evangelical-Zionist coalition in Chechnya, Iraq, Palestine, etc., as they condemn the atrocities committed by Sunni or Shiite radicals in Afghanistan, Sudan, Saudi Arabia, etc.

So, if Muslims are called terrorists because they killed several thousand civilian people in last decade, Christians, Jews and capitalists must be called "terrorists to the factor of 666" since they killed hundreds of thousands in Hiroshima, Nagasaki, Vietnam, and just recently they killed tens of thousands civilians in Iraqi, and wounded even more.

Hadith, Sunnah, and Islamic Scholars

Ali Sina

1-3-2005

Dear Edip,

You started your argument by saying I use hadith to insult Muhammad. Can you please show one instance of that?

In this debate with you, knowing perfectly that you deny the legitimacy of hadith, I have refrained bringing the hadith as the evidence of my claim against Muhammad. When I use hadith it is in support of the verses of the Quran.

I started my debate with you showing that the Quran and Islam cannot be understood without any reference to hadith and sira.

The proof of that is in this last long response of yours. Here you went off tangent and instead of answering any of my points you started copy-pasting from one of your books, giving details of the life of Muhammad without attempting to counter my claim that the Quran without haidth cannot be understood and Islam without the biography of Muhammad is meaningless. Since you completely neglected the topic at hand and contended yourself with copy-pasting your book, I am inclined to believe you truly have no answer to the points I raised.

However, despite your claim that the Quran is self-sufficient, you made statements that are not in the Quran.

You wrote:

> "It was 570 years after Christ when Muhammad was born in Mecca. At age 40 he made a declaration that shocked his people. During the month of Ramadan of 610, he claimed that he was visited by Holy Revelation (a.k.a. Jibreel or Holy Spirit) delivering him a message from God. This claim was first kept secret he shared only with several close friends and relatives. A few years later he publicly declared his messengership and his opposition to the religious and political establishment of Mecca . An era of revolution and reformation that would change world history had started."

Muhammad, a member of a powerful tribe and a successful international businessman, was not an ordinary citizen of Mecca . With his sound judgment and trustworthy personality, he had won the respect of the theocratic oligarchy. His uncles were the leaders of one of the prominent tribes and were active in social, political, economic and religious affairs.

Arabs living in the Hijaz region were brethren of Jews, and Abraham was their common forefather. Mecca or Bacca was the valley where Abraham had immigrated, after his exile fromBabylon . There is only one reference to this important city in the Old Testament:

How do you know all these things? This information is not given in the Quran. It can only be found in the hadith and the Sira. But you say that your Islam does not have any need for these "garbage" and the Quran is enough. Then how do you know Muhammad was born in 570 A.D. in Meccaand at the age of 40 he made his declaration, etc. etc.?

In this book that you are writing, you are providing a lot of information about Muhammad, about Mecca , about his uncles and you even name his enemies. You know exactly at what age and in what year Gabriel paid him a visit. You said Abraham was the legendary ancestor of Jews and Arabs. How do you know that? This information is only available in the Bible and haidth. But you said hadith is a load of garbage that would sink a city. Do you accept the Bible? You talked in detail about the costumes of the Arabs in those days and the fact that the time of pilgrimage was also used for trading purposes. You said these occasions were used for cultural and athletic competitions such as poetry and wrestling and that Mecca was the center of economic, political and cultural activities of a vast land. You even talked about Bilal and the fact that he was saved by "one of Muhammad's friends" and you rehashed the apocrypha hadith that Summayyah was the first Muslim martyr. There is a wealth of information in this book you are writing that is not available in the Quran. Where did you get that information?

You sneaked into the books of hadith and Sira didn't you? You naughty little devil you! You shouldn't have done that, you know that. You waddled into that load of garbage to find the goodies for us and save us from seeing that fetid pile of filth accumulated on top of the prophet. How nice of you! You are really the savior of Islam.

Apparently you say something and do something else. Is that a good thing? So you do not reject the hadith and Sira entirely. You simply reject the part that does not suit your agenda. None of these info you are giving away are in the Quran and you keep telling me the Quran is sufficient? If the Quran is sufficient why did you have to dig into the garbage of hadith to write your book?

Why not be honest here? Let us say that you agree with the part of the hadith that is not embarrassing and incriminating but when a hadith becomes too scandalous then that is garbage. The fact that Muhammad was born in 570 A.D. is not embarrassing, so you have no problem with that. But when the same sources say that he massacred the Bani Qurayza or raped a 9 year old child then that is all fabrication and garbage. Thank you for teaching us Islamic honesty.

In round III and IV I raised a series of questions. You did not even touch them. Here is a list of them:

1- How can Muhammad's character be irrelevant to his claim? How can we be sure that he was not a liar? What if he lied for the same reason Jim Jones and thousands of other charlatan, impostor cult leaders lie manipulate and control the foolhardy?

2- Muhammad made so many bogus claims about being the best of the creation, and a perfect example to follow. How can we verify these self adulating claims? And how are we supposed to follow his examples as Allah asked us to do in the Quran if we are not allowed to read his history or believe it? You reject his biography in its entirety (except the part that is not incriminating) so can you tell us how else can we know him to comply with the Quranic injunctions and follow his examples? Or are you saying those verses where he said follow my example and I mentioned before are all later day fabrications? Are we supposed to take those verse and the verse 33:21 that says "Ye have indeed in the Messenger of Allah a beautiful pattern (of conduct)" seriously or not?

3- I asked you to explain the meaning of Sura 111 and Sura 38:41-44 without referring to hadith, tafseer and Sira, by merely trying to decipher their meanings from the Quran. Can you do that? These are just two examples. Most of the Quran is incomprehensible without hadith and tafseer and I will keep pointing them out as we touch them.

4- We also talked about the Quran's claim that God transformed the Jews into apes and swine (5:60) and said "Be ye apes" (2:65, 7:166). These are not metaphors. No scholar has understood them as metaphors because the texts make it clear that they are not metaphors. Can you explain to us how this absurdity is possible? How come such an amazing phenomenon was not recorded in any book prior to Muhammad saying such thing? How can such a ridiculous statement be compatible with science? Remember, it was you who said "We will get to the scientific accuracy... of the Quran". Explain this please scientifically.

5- You claimed Muhammad wrote the Quran with his own hand. I asked how do you know that. Where is your source? Why should we believe you when he himself claimed to be illiterate and unable to read. 7:157 , 6:22

6- You made the claim that ummi does not mean illiterate but gentile. I quoted the verse 2:78 were Muhammad alludes to the Jews and calls them ummayoon أُمِّيُّونَ because they can't read their book. What is your response?

7- We talked about sura 33 and I said this sura is not self explanatory. I asked you to tell us who are the "confederates" mentioned in verse 20 and from where they did not withdraw. Explain that without any reference to hadith or tafseer.

[Re: To the Factor of 666]

What is happening dear Edip? Why is it that I feel like talking to an answering machine? You have completely neglected my questions and like all your fellow co-religionists resorted to copy-pasting. What is the relevance of these to our discussion? Where are the answers to my questions?

Now you start with a new topic. That is okay. I will dance along with all your beats. Let us talk about the verse 9:29 in its context.

You claim that all the translators were drunk when translating this verse or did not know proper Arabic but you, who have decided to become the Martin Luther of Islam and have embarked in writing a "reformist" translation of the Quran", can translate it better.

According to Dictionary.com reform means: "To improve by alteration, correction of error, or removal of defects; put into a better form or condition."

Can you please tell us by what authority are you trying to "alter, correct the errors or remove the defects" of the Quran? If the Quran is perfect, why it needs to be reformed? Are you claiming to be superior in rank and knowledge to the original author of the Quran? Do you know more than Allah? Or, are you the new Mahdi?

Since by your own admission, your translation of the Quran is reformist, it is logical to conclude that it is the least accurate of all the existing ones. You are deliberately trying to alter, correct the errors and remove the defects of the Quran according to your understanding and not translate it faithfully. You want to intentionally change the meaning of the Quran to suit your "reformist" agenda. Please tell us, why should we not read the Quran in Arabic directly or in one of its more faithful non-reformist translations and why should we rely on your "reformist" translation which is twisted and altered?

Now let us study the Sura 9. The first 29 verses of this Sura were written by Muhammad a couple of years after he conquered Mecca and they are allegedly his last "revealed" words. He did not go to Hajj that year but he sent Abu Bakr in his place. Then he dispatched Ali to follow Abu Bakr and publicly announce these injunctions to the pilgrims who were composed of Muslims and pagans.

This Sura is called Bara'at or "declaration of immunity". In this Sura he claimed Allah allowed him to break all his treaties with the Pagans. He gave the pagans four months of grace or immunity to go to their homes and after that they would be fair game for the Muslims. After these four months, they must accept Islam and pay the tithes or they would be hunted wherever they are found and put to death.

As for breaking his oaths, Muhammad had never shown any scruples. He broke his oaths any time it suited him. To justify his own treachery he would often claim that others would break their oaths and hence he is justified to do that pre-emptively.

8.56   "They are those with whom thou didst make a covenant, but they break their covenant every time, and they have not the fear (of Allah).

If thou fearest treachery from any group, throw back (their covenant) to them, (so as to be) on equal terms: for Allah loveth not the treacherous." 8.58

This is the typical mindset of the pathological narcissist who projects his own lack of honor on others and then feels justified to avenge for the breach of an agreement that has occurred only in his paranoiac mind.

In this Sura Muhammad said that if one among the pagans asks for asylum it should be granted so he can convert to Islam. Therefore victims of Islam cannot ask for asylum and live their lives freely. They should only be given asylum provided they convert to Islam and pay zakat or become dhimmis and pay jizyah.

In verse 7 he makes a pledge to spare the lives of those who still had not be-lieved in him for a period of four months. In the verse 8 he tries to justify his treachery by blaming the victims and claiming that they would have done the same. But do we have any proof that the pagans ever broke their treaties with Muhammad? None! The history, written by Muslims, only shows that Muham-mad was the one who broke all his treaties and yet in every occasion he blamed his victims accusing them of "plotting" and "contemplating" to break the treaties and thus leaving him no option but to breach his treaties and attack them pre-emptively.

In verses 9 and 10 he accuses the pagans of not respecting even kinship. This is utterly a lie. The pagans loved their own sons and daughters who had fallen prey to the cult of Muhammad. They did not want to kill them and this was their vul-nerability and weakness. This gave Muhammad extra power who told his fol-lowers that they should shun their own fathers and brothers who do not believe and even kill them.

Today this very dynamism is the cause of the weakness of the civilized world. While the civilized world is unwilling to deal with Muslims harshly and tries to respect their human rights, Muslims have no such twinges and are ready to kill any number of non-Muslims with total ease of mind. `

A good example of that is the Battle of Badr. Abu Sufyan was forewarned of Muhammad's plan to attack the caravan under his leadership. He asked for help from the Quraish. However he managed to escape by rerouting the caravan. When he reached Mecca he learned that the Quraish had already left to confront Muhammad. He sent an emissary asking them to return. The men of the army debated and many of them returned. But encouraged by Abul Hakam and weary of Muhammad's constant taunts, some of them proceeded forward. Before squaring off with the Muslims, again another group of them, headed by Haakim ibn Hizam, the nephew of Khadija (who supplied food to Muhammad and his party when shut up with Abu Talib a few years earlier) is mentioned as urgent in offering this advice: "When we have fought and spilled the blood of our brethren and our kinsmen," said he, "of what use will life be to us any longer? Let us now go back, and we will be responsible for the blood-money of Amr, killed at Nakhlah." Amr was killed by Muhammad's marauding gang a few months earlier and he was the first blood spilt in Islam. Abul Hakam demanded that the army should advance. "If we turn back now" he said, "it will surely be imputed to our cowardice."

So you can see that despite the fact that Muslims had killed a Meccan, the Meccans still did not want to kill the Muslims for these benighted men were their own sons and brothers and this was really the main cause of their defeat in Badr. They were hesitant to kill their own kin while Muslims had no such compunction.

Interestingly Haakim ibn Hizam was captured in the battle of Uhud and despite his previous services to Muhammad was ungratefully slain.

Compare the attitude of the Meccans to what Muhammad told his followers about how they should treat their non believing kin. The Quraish, goaded as they were by the repeated attack of their caravans, and the blood shed at Nakhlah, were yet staggered by the prospect of the battle, and nearly persuaded by their better feelings to return to Mecca. The Muslims on the other hand, though the aggressors, were hardened by the memory of former injuries, by the maxim that their faith severed all earthly ties without the circle of Islam, and by a fierce fanaticism for their Prophet's cause.

Waqidi (p.89) states that Muhammad led the Muslims in prayers and after rising from his genuflexion, called down the curse of Allah upon the Meccans and prayed: "O Allah! Let not Abu Jahl (Abul Hakam) escape, the Pharaoh of his people! Lord, let not Zamaa escape; rather let the eyes of his father run sore for him with weeping, and become blind!" Muhammad's hate was unrelenting, and his followers imbibed from him the same inexorable spirit.

A story is told of Abu Hodhaifa, a young Meccan believer who participated in the battle of Badr and his father was in the rank of the Quraish. It is said that when Muhammad instructed his followers to spare Abbas, his own uncle, who was also among the Quraish, Hodhaifa raised his voice, "What? Are we to slay our fathers, brothers, uncles, etc., and to spare Abbas? No, verily, but I will slay him if I find him." Upon hearing this impertinent remark, Omar, in his usual sycophantic gesture of loyalty, unshielded his sword and looked at the Prophet for his signal to behead the ill-mannered youth at once. [Waqidi p. 75]

This threat had immediate effect. A dramatic change happened in the behavior of Hodhaifa and we see him after the battle, a completely subdued and different person. When he found his father slain and his corpse being unceremoniously dragged to be dumped into a well, he was overwhelmed and started crying. "What?" asked Muhammad, "Are you saddened for the death of your father?" "Not so, O Allah's Prophet!" responded Hodhaifa, "I do not doubt the justice of my father's fate; but I knew well his wise and generous heart, and I had trusted that the Lord would lead him to the faith. But now that I see him slain, and my hope destroyed! ---- it is for that I grieve." This time Muhammad was pleased with his response, comforted Abu Hodhaifa, blessed him; and said, "It is well." [Waqidi, p. 106; Sira p. 230; Tabari, p. 294]

The displeasure of Muhammad at Hodhaifa's irreverence in defying his word and the swift reaction of Omar threatening to slay him on the spot, were such powerful stimuli that Hodhaifa immediately changed his demeanor and a day later he even saw the "justice" in his father's murder. Once Hodhaifa lost his father, in whose killing he had conspired by ganging up with his murderers, then there was no going back for him. He had to justify what he had done and rationalize the slaying of his father. Coming to his senses and facing his own guilty conscience would have been painfully mortifying. He had to continue in the path that he had taken to justify his actions.

As these historic evidences demonstrate, Muslims were the aggressors not the pagans and it was Muhammad who told his benighted followers to hate and kill their own kin and not the other way round. After 9/11 the world was stupefied to see how unabashedly Muslims commit the crime and blame their victims. However this is a sunna set by their prophet. This is the way the Muslim mind works.

But of course since all these historic facts do not conform to your self-made "religion of peace" you prefer to deceive yourself and ease your conscience by denying their validity. Yet what would you say to the following verses of the Quran that confirm the above and the fact that Muhammad told his followers to hate even their own fathers and brothers if they do not believe?

9:23   "O ye who believe! take not for protectors your fathers and your brothers if they love Infidelity above Faith: if any of you do so, they do wrong"

9:113   Muhammad repeatedly instructed his followers not to seek the companionship of the unbelievers 31:15 and even made his imaginary deity say: "It is not fitting, for the Prophet and those who believe, that they should pray for forgiveness for Pagans, even though they be of kin, after it is clear to them that they are companions of the Fire."

4.89   Muhammad's paranoia was so intense that he told his followers "those who believed but came not into exile, ye owe no duty of protection to them until they come into exile;" 8.72 and he went as far as telling them that if some of the believers return renegades "seize them and slay them wherever ye find them; and (in any case) take no friends or helpers from their ranks;"

You have chosen the path of self deception and denial of the historic facts. You reject wholesale all the incriminating tales about Muhammad, (yet keeping the ones that are not incriminating) but what do you say to these hate mongering verses of the Quran?

Continuing with Sura Bara'at, verses 11and 12 say that only if the unbelievers convert to Islam they should be taken as brethrens (in faith) but if they decide to exercise freedom of belief they should be fought and restrained. The verse 13 spews more hate and goads the believers to be resolute in their enmity to the unbelievers and the verse 14 makes it clear that the unbelievers should be fought and punished by the hands of the Muslims. This is the verse that OBL and other terrorists use to justify their crimes against humanity. This verse make clear that the punishment for disbelief is no more left to God but rather it should be meted by the Muslims. This answers all the hypocrite apologists of Islam who come to the West and deceitfully try to portray Islam as a religion of peace, claiming that the terrorists are misinterpreting the Quran.

In the verses 17 to 19 Muhammad prohibits the pagans to visit or maintain the grand Mosque of Ka'ba. This is the first time in the history of that temple were religious apartheid is ordained. For thousands of years, the Meccans had allowed the followers of all faiths to come to Ka'ba and worship together their own gods in amity. That changed when Muhammad came to power and inaugurated an era marked by religious bigotry and hate, which has lasted up to this day.

The verses 25 and 26 talk about the defeat of the Muslims in Hunain, despite their great numbers and then their victory, the details of this event is in sira and really does not belong to this Sura. How would we know what happened in Hunain and with whom Muslims fought without consulting the sira? Isn't this another proof that the Quran without hadith and sira is incomprehensible?

Here is the entire Sura Bara'at. The rest of the Sura is called Tauba and it refers to another unrelated event. [Because of its length Ali Sina's quotation of the entire chapter is not displayed here, since it can be found at various internet sites, including this one: http://19.org/km/RK/9]

226

Fight those who believe not in God nor the Last Day, nor hold that forbidden which hath been forbidden by God and His Apostle, nor acknowledge the religion of Truth, (even if they are) of the People of the Book, until they pay the Jizya with willing submission, and feel themselves subdued.

Now let us discuss the verse 9:29

9:29   Fight against those who believe not in Allah, nor in the Last Day, nor forbid that which has been forbidden by Allah and His Messenger, and those who acknowledge not the religion of truth among the People of the Scripture, until they pay the Jizyah with willing submission, and feel themselves subdued.

You wrote:

"Furthermore, note that I suggest COMPENSATION instead of Arabic word Jizya."

Who are you to "suggest" such thing? How can you suggest that one word should mean something else? You obviously have taken the entire Quran as a book of jokes and you allow yourself to "suggest" meanings that are not there.

To justify your twisted translations you wrote:

"The meaning of Jizya has been distorted as a perpetual tax on non-Muslims, which was invented long after Muhammad to further the imperialistic agenda of Sultans or Kings."

On what you base such claim? How do you know that Muhammad did not exact Jizyah tax on his subdued victims? The hadith and sira tell us Muhammad levied heavy Jizyah on his victims. We are told that for example in Kheibar he usurped their land and allowed the survivors to stay, provided they work the land and pay 50% of the proceeds to him. You deny all these because they do not validate your fantasies about Muhammad. How can you prove to me that Muhammad did not demand Jizyah and all that was invented by the Sultans or Kings? When I say Muhammad charged Jizyah I quote various books of history written by Muslim scholars. Tell me on what you base your wanton claim? Why should we reject the historians of Islam and accept your fantasies? You want us to throw out all the books of hadith and history because they were written a hundred or two hundred years after Muhammad but you expect us to believe in your words 1400 years later?

The verse 29 starts with قَٰتِلُوا This can only be translated as fight and not fight (back). It is an offensive order and not defensive. It is qatilu not dafeu. The verse goes on to say fight them until they pay الجِزْيَة Jizyah. This word derives from

227

Jaza. It means fine and punishment the plural of that is Mojazat. It does not mean compensation. The correct word for compensation is Mokafat.

Your "Reformist Translation of the Quran" is not translation but "reformation" or in other words misrepresentation of the facts and soft selling of the Quran by twisting the truth.

According to wikipedia.org Jizyah is the Arabic language translation of Poll tax or "head tax", a tax imposed on male individuals of other faiths living under Muslim rule.

Jizyah was applied to every free male member of the People of the Book, non-Muslim communities living in lands under Muslim rule. The jizyah was levied in the time of Prophet Muhammad on vassal tribes under Muslim protection, including Jews in Khaybar, Christians in Najran and Zoroastrians in Bahrain .

Give me one reason why should we reject all these historic facts and explanations and accept your claims? Obviously you want to rewrite the history by reinventing it. And your only sources are your fantasies.

The verse 28 of this sura says:

9:28   O you who believe! Verily, the Mushrikin are impure. So let them not come near Al-Masjid Al-Haram after this year; and if you fear poverty, Allah will enrich you if He wills, out of His bounty. Surely, Allah is All-Knowing, All-Wise.)

Can you tell us how are you going to translate this in your "Reformist Translation"? The meaning of this verse is obvious. Please let us see how you twisted it in your version of the Quran.

After mistranslating the word Jizya you made the following statement:

> "Unfortunately, the distortion in the meaning of the verse above and the practice of collecting a special tax from Christians and Jews, contradict the basic principle of the Quran that there should not be compulsion in religion and there should be freedom of belief and expression (2:256; 4:90; 4:137; 10:99; 18:29; 88:21,22). Since taxation based on religion creates financial duress on people to convert to the previliged religion, it violates this important Quranic principle. Dividing a population that united under a social contract (constitution) into previliged groups based on their religion contradicts many principles of the Quran, including justice, peace, and brotherhood/sisterhood of all humanity."

What you have failed to see is the fact that the Quran was written over a period of 23 years and the early writings of Muhammad are very distinct from latter ones. When Muhammad started his prophetic career, he had no earthly powers and the verses that he wrote during that period are all conciliatory and tolerant. During the early phase of his mission, he sounded almost like Christ.

In the verse 2.256 he says:

2:256   "Let there be no compulsion in religion: Truth stands out clear from Error"

And

10:99   "If it had been thy Lord's will, they would all have believed,- all who are on earth! wilt thou then compel mankind, against their will, to believe!"

Or

18:29   "The truth is from your Lord": Let him who will believe, and let him who will, reject (it)"

But these are the Meccan verses. He wrote these verses when he was weak. It would have been impossible for his handful of followers to wage war against thousands of unbelievers and win. In these verses the cunning prophet contented himself by telling his followers that the unbelievers will be severely punished in the afterlife as the verse 18:29 makes it clear where he tries to impress and frighten his gullible followers with his bogus lies about hellfire and his bugabear deity.

18:29   "We have prepared a Fire whose (smoke and flames), like the walls and roof of a tent, will hem them in: if they implore relief they will be granted water like melted brass, that will scald their faces, how dreadful the drink! How uncomfortable a couch to recline on!"

How can any sane person believe that the maker of this universe is a sadist with this much insanity and penchant for torture is beyond comprehension!

However when Muhammad became powerful and managed to fool a sizable number of ignorant men who rallied around him and who were ready to kill at his behest, his so called "revelations" underwent a new twist and he took it upon himself to bring upon those who denied his claim the severest punishments.

So while in Mecca he said "Speak good to men... " 2:83, "be patient with what they say" 20:103 , 73:10 , and preached about the virtues of Abel saying to Cain: "If thou dost stretch thy hand against me, to slay me, it is not for me to stretch my hand against thee to slay thee: for I do fear Allah, the cherisher of the worlds" 5:28, when he went to Medina and became powerful he revealed his true self and a different kind of message. There he wrote: "Oh ye who believe! Murder those of the disbelievers and let them find harshness in you" 9:123 ; "I will instill terror into the hearts of the unbelievers: smite ye above their necks and smite all their finger-tips off. " 8:12 , "Whoso desires another religion than Islam, it shall not be accepted of him" 3:85 , "Strive against the disbelievers and the hypocrites, and be stern with them" 66:9 , "When you meet the unbelievers, strike off their heads; then when you have made wide slaughter among them, carefully tie up the remaining captives" 47:4 , "rouse the Believers to the fight" 8:65, "Against them make ready your strength to the utmost of your power, including steeds of war, to strike terror into (the hearts of) the enemies, of Allah and your enemies". 8:60.

In fact most of the Quran is filled with such violent verses. Definitely the verses written in Medina contradict those written in Mecca. Which ones should we take? Logics says that if I tell you one thing now and another thing the next day, you should follow my last instructions. The latest verses of the Quran are those written in Medina and they are the harsh and violent ones. The very last sura of the Quran is Sura 9, the sura we discussed above. This sura is basically the Will and Testament of Muhammad. If any part of the Quran is in contradictions with what this sura says, it is obvious that the latest words of Muhammad (i,e. sura 9) should override the previous ones.

Dr. Muhsin Khan the translator of Sahih Bukhari and the Quran into English writes:

> "Allah revealed in Sura Bara'at the order to discard (all) obligations (covenants, etc), and commanded the Muslims to fight against all the Pagans as well as against the people of the Scriptures (Jews and Christians) if they do not embrace Islam, till they pay the Jizia (a tax levied on the Jews and Christians) with willing submission and feel themselves subdued (as it is revealed in 9:29). So the Muslims were not permitted to abandon "the fighting" against them (Pagans, Jews and Christians) and to reconcile with them and to suspend hostilities against them for an unlimited period while they are STRONG and have the ability to fight against them. So at first "the fighting" was forbidden, then it was permitted, and after that it was made obligatory "[Introduction to English translation of Sahih Bukhari, p.xxiv.]

Q 9:5 reads: "Slay the idolaters wherever you find them"

According to Dr. Khan in 9:5 Allah ordered Muhammad to cancel all covenants and to fight the pagans, the Jews even the Christians. This is in contrast to what Muhammad wrote earlier.

5:82   "Thou wilt find the nearest of them in love to the believers [Muslims} are those who say 'We are Christians'"

Dr. Khan continues:

The "Mujahideen who fight against the enemies of Allah in order that the worship should be all for Allah (alone and not for any other deity) and that the word is Allah's (i.e. none has the right to be worshipped but Allah and His religion Islam) should be upper most."

So first it was "There is no compulsion in religion" (2:265) and then

61:10-12"O who believe! shall I direct you to a commerce that which will save
   you from a painful torment? That you believe in Allah and His Apostle
   (Mohammad), and that you strive hard and fight in the cause of Allah
   with your wealth and your lives. That will be better for you, if you but
   knew. If you do so He will forgive you your sins, and admit you into
   gardens of Eternity - that is the great success"

Dr. Sobhy as-Saleh, a contemporary academic, does not see in 2:256 and 9:73 a case of abrogation but a case of delaying or postponing the command to fight the infidels. To support his view he quoted Imam Suyuti the author of Itqan Fi 'Ulum al- Qur'an who wrote:

   "The command to fight the infidels was DELAYED UNTIL THE
   MUSLIMS BECOME STRONG, but when they were weak they were
   commanded to endure and be patient. [Sobhy as_Saleh, Mabaheth Fi
   'Ulum al- Qur'an, Dar al-'Ilm Lel-Malayeen, Beirut , 1983, p. 269.]

Dr. Sobhy, in a footnote, commends the opinion of a scholar named Zarkashi who said:

   "Allah the most high and wise revealed to Mohammad in his weak
   condition what suited the situation, because of his mercy to him and his
   followers. For if He gave them the command to fight while they were
   weak it would have been embarrassing and most difficult, but when the
   most high made Islam victorious He commanded him with what suited
   the situation, that is asking the people of the Book to become Muslims
   or to pay the levied tax, and the infidels to become Muslims or face
   death. These two options, to fight or to have peace return according to
   the strength or the weakness of the Muslims."[ibid p. 270]

And Nahas writes:

   "the scholars differed concerning Q. 2:256. (There is no compulsion if
   religion) Some said: 'It has been abrogated [cancelled] for the Prophet
   compelled the Arabs to embrace Islam and fought them and did not accept any alternative but their surrender to Islam. The abrogating verse
   is Q. 9:73 'O Prophet, struggle with the unbelievers and hypocrites, and

231

be thou harsh with them.' Mohammad asked Allah the permission to fight them and it was granted. Other scholars said Q. 2:256 has not been abrogated, but it had a special application. It was revealed concerning the people of the Book [the Jews and the Christians]; they can not be compelled to embrace Islam if they pay the Jizia (that is head tax on free non-Muslims under Muslim rule). It is only the idol worshippers who are compelled to embrace Islam and upon them Q. 9:73 applies. This is the opinion of Ibn 'Abbas which is the best opinion due to the authenticity of its chain of authority."[al-Nahas, An-Nasikh wal-Mansukh, p.80. See also Ibn Hazm al-Andalusi, A-Nnasikh wal-Mansukh, Dar al-Kotob al-'Elmeyah, birute, 1986, p.42.]

Ibn Hazm al-Andalusi writes:

"Fight in the way of God with those who fight with you, but aggress not: God loves not the aggressors (2:190)" On the authority of Ga'far ar-Razi from Rabi' Ibn 'Ons, from 'Abil-'Aliyah who said: This is the first verse that was revealed in the Qur'an about fighting in the Madina. When it was revealed the prophet used to fight those who fight with him and avoid those who avoid him, until Sura 9 was revealed. And so is the opinion of 'Abd ar-Rahman Ibn Zayd Ibn 'Aslam who said this verse was cancelled by 9:5 "Slay the idolaters wherever you find them"[bn Hazm al-Andalusi, An-Nasikh wal- Mansukh, Dar al-Kotob al-'Elmeyah, birute, 1986, P.27]

Now what these eminent scholars of Islam say make sense. Logically the latter revelations override and cancel the previous ones if they contradict each other. But what you say make completely no sense. Your claim is informed by your zealotry and blind faith and not by facts.

You also copy pasted an argument you had with Christians. Although I find it irrelevant to our debate, I would like to point out the fact that you yourself are guilty of the same sins you blame your Christian opponents. Let us go over the six points you raised:

1) You are the one who denies the fact that the Quran is NOT self-sufficient. I asked you a few questions about the Quran. Explain them without referring to haidth. Explain how do you know Muhammad was born in 570 A.D. and declared his message at 40 without referring to haidth. You can't do that without the aid of the hadith and sira and therefore your claim that ALL the haidth is garbage and the Quran is self-sufficient is fallacious.

2) It is you who reduce your references to smaller portion, take a few abrogated verses and disregard the rest of the Quran where it clearly calls for blood and violence. It is you who are scared to show the ugly part of the Quran for the fear of being shown that the man you have accepted to be a prophet was a psycho-

232

path. Let us say the Quran has also a good part. Is there a book, including Mein Kampf, that is completely bereft of any good part? What you fail to see is that a few allegedly "good" verses in the Quran are not enough to call it a divine book. A book of a perfect God should not have even one ugly or imperfect verse in it. And yet we find hundreds of ugly and terrible verses in the Quran.

3) It is you who twist the meaning of some of the words and "suggest" that they should be interpreted differently to suit your "reformist" agenda. To fulfill your agenda, what you have sacrificed is the truth.

4) It is you who selectively deny some of the hadith but cling to others because you realize without them you can't even establish the existence of Muhammad.

5) The argument used in point 5 is a logical fallacy called tu quoque. By using this fallacy you try to justify the crimes perpetrated by Muhammad and his followers with the wrongs committed by the followers of other religions. Followers of other religions were mere followers. Their actions should not reflect on their religion just as the action of the Muslims should not reflect on Islam. The followers could be misguided. We are not blaming the Muslims but Muhammad himself. If Muhammad was a prophet of God indeed, he should have known better.

6) In point 6 again you are attacking the Christians and their conducts. Even if your accusations are proven to be true, how with this, you can justify the crimes of Muhammad or the violence and absurdities of the Quran?

The rest of your message, is a misplaced copy-paste. It has nothing to so with our discussion. It is a discussion you had with Christians. Why you bring that up here is not clear to me. But since you mentioned it let me dismiss it as another tu quoque fallacy. Here you are trying to vilify Christianity and Judaism to get away with the sins of Muhammad. Suppose whatever you say about these religions is true. Would that prove that Muhammad was a prophet of God? Wouldn't this be another proof that he was not a messenger of God? Muhammad said Jesus and Moses were prophets of God. If you show they were not, then doesn't this automatically make Muhammad a liar? Irrespective of the fact that you succeeded or not, by simply questioning their prophethoood you have challenged Muhammad and his authority and you are not a Muslim.

At this stage, I request you to please come back and debate the points that I am discussing, in the same way I am debating the points that you raise. If all you can do is copy paste irrelevant articles and rehash what you wrote in other occasions, I don't see any debate and wonder what we are doing here. This is supposed to be a debate. If you are reluctant even to engage with me, if all you can do is copy paste irrelevant material and expect me to answer them without you contesting my points, is there any point in continuing? Weren't you the person who accused the Christians of "parroting"? Aren't you doing the same here?

233

You seem to have run out of arguments before we even engage and hence with these tedious copy pasting and filibustering tactics you try to bore the readers and find your way out of this discussion. Please prove to us this is not the case.

If this is what you intend, I suggest you would be saving face more by not responding at all. Dr. Zakir Naik, Prof. Michael Sells and Prof. John Esposito are far better now for not responding to me than if they did and failed to engage in coherent arguments. If you are gasping for relief, you may stop, but if you truly want to debate please do not burden me and the readers with long tedious and irrelevant copy pastes.

Finally I would like to speak to your heart. If you can't defend Islam, why you cling to this sinking ship? Islam is a lie and this I have proven here in numerous articles time and again. Why hang to a doctrine that is so evil and so false? I earnestly urge you to leave Islam. You can't save Islam nor can you reform it. Islam is based on total lies. It is not a religion of God but a cult created by a psychopath to control and dominate the gullible. Its fruit speaks for itself.

I call upon all the Muslims to leave Islam. Islam is a lie. The sooner we face this truth the sooner we save our own souls and this battered world. By adhering to this cult we are lending our tacit support to the terrorists. We are committing a sin against our own souls and against our own children. You are responsible for what you believe. Do not be an instrument of hate and destruction. Be an instrument of love and unity of mankind. Let us rebuild this wrecked world together. Let us mend our tattered brotherhood. We are all brothers and sisters in Humanity. You know the maxim of "divide and rule". How can you let yourself to become a victim of this evil ploy? The world is not divided between Muslims and Kafirs. It is not created as dar al Harb and dar al Islam. This is one planet for all of us to share, to cherish and to love.

Enough with insanity! Enough with hatred. Muhammad lied to us. Let us wake up from our slumber. Let us leave this doctrine of hate aside and let us step into the world of love and light. Let us do it now for tomorrow is too late.

11. Chit-Chat

Jan 5, 2005

Dear Ali Sina:

I will, inshallah, answer your most recent posts this weekend. But, before answering your claims, accusations, and false arguments, I would like to express my disappointment in how you handle your debates:

> "You may also tell Dr. Naik that as of 2005 I am offering $50,000 U.S. dollars of my own money to anyone who can refute my charges against Muhammad and prove that he is a prophet of God."

Well, it seems you are really being carried away. I hope that you will give up from these cheap promotional gimmicks. Yes, this is just a deceptive and empty promise. I know this, since I studied law, and reading books on advertising is one of my hobbies.

I had ignored your silly promise of closing your website if you were proven wrong. However, now you need some reality check and a reminder

If any decent person is proven wrong regarding his claims in his website, closing or changing the content of that website must be a next step expected from that person. In other words, your promise is just an empty promise. It is like, "if you prove me wrong, I will act as a decent man and acknowledge that you proved me wrong!" Or little like, "if you prove that I sleep naked in my bed, then I will give you the cloth I am wearing in my bed!"

To top your empty promise, here I am also going to give several empty promises: If anyone proves me wrong regarding my position on Quran and its mathematical structure, I will close the www.19.org and discontinue the publication of more than a dozen Turkish books promoting the message of monotheism. Furthermore, I will resign from participating in Reformist Translation of the Quran!

As for your new empty offer of 50,000 US dollars, well here is why it is empty, deceptive, and pathetic:

> **Alperenaslan**: "I thought you had no Money Ali! You were crying and talking about $300-$400 site ads income."

Ali Sina: "Well, that is my present income. But I had a business before dedicating myself to this cause. Have a house and have some equity. Why, do you think I can survive with $400 dollars income per month?"

Even if one day you miraculously accept to be proven wrong, I will never demand that money from you for a couple of reasons. First, I am not debating with you to get your money. I am not gambling in Las Vegas. Second, I will never accept that money from a person who has such a little income; I am a person with conscious and I cannot doom someone to poverty; especially as a price of him finding and acknowledging the truth! It is just absurd. No decent human being will accept such an offer. However, with your offer you are tacitly insulting our intention for debating you and insulting our sense of justice. You are too gullible if you do not have such an agenda!

Another problem with your money offer is that it is not actionable; it is an empty promise: Without depositing that money in an escrow account and proving that to your opponent, without appointing a team of judges equally selected by you and your opponent, this offer is empty squared!

To top your worthless money offer, here I am going to announce even a bigger worthless money offer: "I am offering $114,000 U.S. dollars of my own money to anyone who can refute my charges against enemies of islam (not hislam!), and prove that Muhammad was not a prophet of God."

I do still believe that you are honest in your offers and you have not thought about their empty and worthless nature. You just wanted to demonstrate how serious and committed you were to find the truth of the matter. Or perhaps, you thought you could draw the attention of those who are easily duped by empty promises. So, I demand you to retract these offers since they are not only empty and worthless, as I said above, they are implicit insults to the intention of all those who debate against you.

Let me make it clear: I am here not because of you or your money; you will most likely not see many of my points in my arguments; but I am here for those who are following and will be following this debate. And, they are not limited with the visitors of your website...

See you this weekend!

Peace,

Edip Yuksel

*****

Jan 5; 2005

Dear Edip

Please get back to your debate, you are wasting your time and people are waiting to see your responses. So far you have not responded to any of my charges.
The last round was just copy paste and had nothing to do with what we discussed in previous rounds.

As for the offer of $50,000 don't worry, I am not going to lose that money. If I
had any doubt in my mind that I could lose, I would not have started this website
and risk being tortured by the savage god of Islam for eternity. What is more
important? Losing $50,000 dollars of being burned for eternity?

Furthermore, if for the sake of argument I lose and have to pay that $50,000
dollars I would go to my own profession and would make at least twice that
amount in one year alone. So financially I would be better off. The reason I decided to dedicate myself to this cause is because I see this is such an important
cause, unique in history. I just could not miss the chance to by part of this great
event in human history and not have a piece of it. Also, I am not planning to live
on the advertisements and donations alone for ever. I believe once my books are
out they will generate enough money to compensate what I lost during these
couple of years. I have built up a good readership and they are supportive of me.
If the movie project becomes a reality then of course the financial rewards
would be substantial. I expect this movie to be a blockbuster. Just the controversy it generates would make it a hit.

Now as your claim that the offer is cheap, I don't see it that way. I believe it
would generate some interest and highlight the fact that the challenge is not yet
met. This has its psychological effect and would help promote our cause.

As for putting the money in a screw, oh please get real. You have not even attempted to respond to my charges and you want the guarantees now? First win
the debate and if I don't pay, then you can trumpet it wild and far that I have
reneged to comply.

As for your "worthless [sic] money offer of $114,000 U.S. dollars to prove that
Muhammad was not a prophet," I take it. I have already proven that Muhammad
was not a prophet. Any reasonable person reading my articles will come to that
conclusion. However I am not going to ask you to read what I wrote. I will
prove also to YOU that Muhammad was not a prophet and will make it clear
like the sun. If at the end you agree and leave Islam you can keep your money
and join me so together we get rid of this curse affecting humanity. Don't worry
about the lost royalty of the books that you have already written. You can start
writing books to prove Islam is false and make an honest living by telling people
the truth. In fact thanks to your fame, your apostasy will make you instantly

237

famous and you may sell your anti Islamic books by millions. You have to sacrifice in the cause of truth and you will be rewarded by the universe. I have done my sacrifice by quitting my own professional practice. You can do that too.

But if I prove that Muhammad was not a prophet, which you can bet your life I will do, and you try to sabotage the debate by, for example, withdrawing from the debate and starting to post huge amounts of unrelated copy-pastes to bore the readers and end the debate, then I expect you to pay what you offered. Of course I am not going to ask you to put the money in screw. I hold you responsible against your honor. You are not going to pay because you are not going to admit defeat, but that is okay. My goal, as I said at the very begging of this debate, is not to convince you but our readers. I want intelligent people who think they are Muslims see that Islam is a failed paradigm and it is hopeless.

You are just one person. It really does not matter to me if you accept the truth or not. But our debate is read by thousands of people and many of them are Muslims. They will see the truth and it is them that I really care for. If you read the recent testimonies and comments, you can see this site is having its intended effect. People ARE leaving Islam.

It is like, "if you prove me wrong, I will act as a decent man and acknowledge that you proved me wrong!" Or little like, "if you prove that I sleep naked in my bed, then I will give you the cloth I am wearing in my bed!"

Obviously truth for you is just a joke that depends on ones whims and wanton interpretation. I think differently and I am sure our readers can see the difference too. Truth can be unraveled. Just as it is possible to prove $2 + 2 = 4$ it is possible to prove Islam is not from God and Muhammad was an impostor. Demonstrating the truth is not difficult, sometimes accepting it is difficult.

See you this weekend!

Hey cheer up. Don't frown at me. Don't take it personal. I am not your enemy but your best friend, if only you could know it. I am the enemy of that cult that has taken you and your brain as hostage. I am not here to hurt you but to set you free.

Ali Sina.

*****

January 5, 2005

> "But if I prove that Muhammad was not a prophet, which you can bet your life I will do, and you try to sabotage the debate by, for example, withdrawing from the debate and starting to post huge amounts of unrelated copy-pastes to bore the readers and end the debate, then I expect you to pay what you offered. Of course I am not going to ask you to put the money in screw. I hold you responsible against your honor. You are not going to pay because you are not going to admit defeat, but that is okay. My goal, as I said at the very begging of this debate, is not to convince you but our readers. I want intelligent people who think they are Muslims see that Islam is a failed paradigm and it is hopeless."

Dear Ali:

In psychology, this is called projection. Accuse me of doing things that you are committing! That might work for a short term propaganda, but hey, I will be here as long as you can endure me. The jury will see the flawed patterns of your modus operandi.

BTW, I enjoy debating with you. I do not get angry with you, since if you are sincere in your cause, which I do not have reason to believe otherwise, you need the light of the truth that will help you to distinguish Islam from Hislam. To humble yourself in front of God and ask forgiveness for your aggression and false accusations.

Though you are still hoping that you will indulge me in debating on the garbage pile of fabricated narrations, your favorite place of wrestling, I will try my best to snatch you from there and put you in a clean agora this weekend, by God's will. For a while, it will be a yo-yo exercise, but eventually, you will be ending up discussing ISSUES and PRINCIPLES, rather than adhominem attack based on hearsay of hearsay on a historical figure.

One of the reasons I enjoy debating with you is because you are an intelligent grumpy old man

By the way, you "screw"ed up the escrow! See you MORUK!

Peace,

Edip Yuksel

12. Evangelical Connection Exposed

Edip Yuksel – Ali Sina

Posted: Thu Jan 06, 2005 4:56 am
Subject: Faith Freedom Foundation Address & Telephone number.
Author: MirrorOfTruth

Peace all,

Just wondering why Ali Sina hasn't put the postal address or telephone number for his organisation on his web site. I believe it is:

> Faith Freedom Foundation
> P.O Box 664
> Amherst, NY, 14226
> United States of America

or the phone number:

> Telephone: +1 - 2516664567

Surely he'd like to hear from his supporters and receive the odd card, or courtesy call now and then ?

Regards.

EDIP: "Exposing" or more accurately unveiling the identity or whereabouts of a person who is out there not to create a personal cult, but to debate important theological issues with great political and social ramification is irrelevant.

But, it is more than irrelevant, it is irresponsible and even evil, since it may jeopardize the live of a person whose all crime is to express his faith and opinion. Putting the life of such a person at risk contradicts diametrically with what I stand for. I stand for freedom of faith and expression. If God Almighty let even Satan express himself and let people choose whatever religion, opinion, philosophy, or faith they want, then it would be against God's system and will to create a hostile environment and conditions that would suppress dissent and oppress some people because of their belief or disbelief.

So, I condemn the acts of those who want to indulge in detective or police work, rather than intellectual debate.

If I want freedom and security for myself, I have to want the same thing for others, including my enemies who are not in act and mindset of physical hostility. To do the opposite is hypocrisy.

I believe that Ali Sina's voice, regardless of its truth-value, is precious and should be protected. We cannot find truth without people like Ali Sina.

Personally, I do not care a bit, whether Evilgelical organizations, Zionist organizations, CIA, or any other power pays or uses Ali Sina. To me, it is not relevant and important, since Ali Sina is raising important issues, and voicing important problems with a religion that is followed by more than a billion people.

We are all brothers and sisters from Adam and Eve. We cannot be muslims (submitters to God alone, and men of peace) if we do not act like humans. To be a human, and care about the life of every single human being is a prerequisite of being a muslim. I have no connection with those who ignore and violate this sacred bond among human beings, a bond that was established by our Lord and Creator in the moment and fabric of our creation.

Peace

Edip yuksel

Thank you Edip,

You wrote that three times already. I think we got the message.

Ali Sina

Jan 09, 2005

Dear Ali Sina:

I got very angry when I noticed such postings, so I reacted with emotions. There are two reasons for my strong reaction to such an act:

1. Submission to God (or Truth) ALONE frees a person. Truth sets a person free. So, freedom of belief and disbelief and their expression is the number one requirement of my belief system.

2. I myself experienced attacks to my life, safety, and my integrity. Hislamics fabricated many lies about my connections. They claimed that I was a Bahai, a follower of Moon cult, a CIA agent, etc. So, far none has yet claimed my being a

Martian agent But, after exhausting their fabrication some of them may come up with that allegation.

So, please feel free to delete the two of the three postings from this forum. But, I want you to keep the one I posted in our main debate threat and page: Edip Yuksel v. Ali Sina. I want people read my position, which I argue with passion that it is also the position of the Quran, regarding the freedom of faith, opinion, philosophy, etc, and their expression.

Peace,

Edip Yuksel

MOT

Thank you for unmasking the true nature of the submitters. Everyone knows your intention has been to put my life in danger. This is a great proof that these so called "reformists" are Muslims after all and Muslims will do what Muslims are supposed to do and that is lie, deceive and murder.

Now for your information, that address is the address of a humanist organization. This is the same address used by Ibn Warraq to register his site. I figured out if have to receive anything in the mail I can trust these guys so I used that address. They do not have my address. Actually no one has my address.

So I am sorry, your plot is frustrated and you'll have to eat your heart knowing I will continue to live. Now do you really think you are the smartest Muslim? Don't you think that is the first place your terrorist brothers would check to learn about me?

To save you the trouble, let me tell you that I have never given any information to anywhere or anyone that may somehow lead to me. For example I could make more money by becoming an affiliate of amazon.com but amzon.com pays only by check and I can't accept checks because this could lead to my address. My information at my host are false, the payment is done through bank draft. So basically there is nothing on the net that could lead to me. I am sorry to disappoint you but thanks for showing the world that submitter or not submitter a Muslim is a Muslim.]Let us make this clear. Although I have said I do not believe in a god or a religion, I have no problem with any of the present religions. My fight against Islam is not because it is a religion but because it is not. It is fascism disguised as religion.

Now, I have been saying all along that all the people of the world must unite to fight Islam. This means as a secularist I see the Jews, the Hindus, the Christians

242

or the Atheists as my comrades in this war. I am very grateful to followers of other religions who have supported me either with their literary contribution to this site or with their donations.

I am a freethinker. Nonetheless I do not want to impose my way of thinking on anyone. Faithfreedom means freedom from and of faith. I believe in diversity and happily will work with any organization or group that shares my goals as long as it is not another racist hatemongering group like Islamists. My goal is not to create yet another group and divide the already divide people but rather bring everyone together and create a common front composed of all the people of the world against Islam. So if Christians or Jews or Hindus or communists want to help in any way, I will accept that help with gratitude and will work with them. In fact four years ago it was Golshan.com that hosted my site and they are Iranian communists. I am entirely anti communist yet I did not allow my personal disagreement with them come in between our common goal. The goal is to eradicate Islam and all of us humans must work together to achieve that goal.

Think if an alien species attack the Earth, wouldn't all of us with all our differences unite to combat them? Well the humnity is under attack by a barbarian cult and we and we must unite to destroy it.

Ali Sina

EDIP: Dear Ali Sina: It seems that your hatred and emotions have turned you to those who you claim to hate.

Here is the difference between you and me:

I do not ally with a vampire or vampires to kill another vampire. I do not ally with Evilgelical Christians (you know which Christian groups I am referring to) who are supportive of wars and invasions that has been taking the lives of so many innocent people. I cannot. Throughout history they have been on the wrong side; they have been involved in many bloody and dirty tragedies in history.

But, it seems that you are following the Machiavellian path of St. Paul and you will accept any alliance to dehumanize all Muslims and making them the subject of another Holocaust. Your mindset and mission is no different than of Hitler.

The guy who posted information allegedly proving your connection with Christians might have endangered your life, but with your propaganda of hatred and general condemnation, you are putting the lives of millions and perhaps billions of people at risk. You even show the audacity to put me in the same category of terrorists! I very rarely use this word. But, I think you deserved until you notice your problem: "shame on you, Ali Sina!"

243

It is hypocritical to applaud the massacres, terrorism, occupations, exploitations, covert operations around the world supported by super powers and its supportive Evilgelical Christian organizations, while condemning the terrorism, violence committed by a group of Sunni or Shiite extremists. This is a diabolic double standard!

If you are a humanist as you claim, you should join me to fight ANY act of terrorism, violence, injustice, regardless the identity or religion of the criminal.

Justice and peace cannot be accomplished by holding one hand of the Devil against another hand. You become just a pawn. I condemned the action of the person who tried to "expose" you, and similarly I condemn the actions of USA-Inc's secret agents that have secretly kidnapped and tortured many innocent people in Guatanamo Bay, Iraqi Abu Ghraib, Egyptian or Saudi prisons used by the USA-Inc.

Jan 9, 2005

Apology to MOT (Mirror of Truth):

Without knowing the real nature of your so-called "exposition", I reacted immediately and condemned your action with strong language. When I first read the reactions of others, I thought that you had indeed announced privately held information about Ali Sina and thus endangered his safety and security.

However, now, I learn that what you posted was available for public. If it is the case, which now it seems that it is the case, then you did nothing wrong, and I apologize for condemning that action.

Though your posting did nothing to endanger the life of Ali Sina, since it was himself who publicized that fake, yet revealing address in the first place, I still believe that it was an irrelevant posting. You gave an excuse to some trolls who took advantage of your posting; they twisted and depicted it differently. They created a storm in an empty teaspoon. I am learning more about the nature of this site and its fanatic supporters and actors. They are just making too much noise...

Ali Sina, by acknowledging today that he is open to make alliance with ANY group against Hislam and islam, did not surprise me. Just by looking at the position of his supporters one must be stupid not to understand where he is standing. He has no integrity in his position, since he justifies some atrocities, terror, murder, deception and opposes some based on the identity or religion of their doers. So, he already lost his claim of being a HUMANIST; he is an Evangelical Crusader!

244

God willing, tonight or tomorrow night I will rebuttle his latest allegations and distortions. The noise of his Evilgelical comrades may provide some comfort for him, but eventually their darkness will be exposed by the light of reason and honesty.

Peace,

Edip Yuksel

Later when I checked Alexa toolbar, I found out that the visitors of faithfreedom.org were also the common visitors of the following sites:

1. http://exmuslim.com, which promotes itself as Muslims For Christ; and

2. http://born-again-christian.info

Thus, the connection between Ali Sina and Evangelical organizations has been established without doubt, since they were sharing the same address, most of the visitors of their websites, and they were also sharing the same twisted mindset and hostility against muslims. However, Ali Sina, even fell lower in hypocrisy by trying to hide his Christian link and agenda.

Edip Yuksel

13. Low foot, high foot; true foot, lie foot; here comes...

Edip Yuksel

Jan 13, 2005

> "How do you know all these things? This information is not given in the quran. It can only be found in the hadith and the sira. But you say that your islam does not have any need for these "garbage" and the quran is enough. Then how do you know muhammad was born in 570 a.d. in mecca and at the age of 40 he made his declaration, etc. Etc.?"

You fell for it, Ali Sina. Indeed, I posted that article to provoke you to make such an attack; a knee-jerk attack. You demonstrated that I did not underestimate your "mistunderestimation". Let me explain and offer you first-aid:

<u>Now identify all those extraneous information that do not exist in the Quran, and take them out of my article, and you will see that nothing would be lost</u> regarding my claims and arguments about the last prophet's character, mission and message. If I do the same thing to your previous claims and arguments about Muhammad's character, mission and message, <u>nothing would stand</u>. That is a big difference. How could I have accomplished something like this? What are you missing so that you are confusing knick with knack? Why you are not able to distinguish the hay from grain? Discard the eyeglass of hatred and fanaticism and this simple issue will become as clear as Tucson's sky.

Let me put in other words so that some of your fans too will understand: Replace 570 with any other date, or replace Mecca with any other city name, or even replace Muhammad's name with any other name. Yes, not a single personal, moral, and legal principle advocated in my article would change or lose its Quranic foundation and truth-value.

As for your assertion that I could not have known that Abraham was a legendary ancestor of Jews and Arabs from any other source besides Bible and Hadith. Well, somehow you forgot the Quran, as you cunningly and frequently do so. See the Quran: 2:132; 22:78…

> "You sneaked into the books of hadith and sira didn't you? You naughty little devil you! You shouldn't have done that, you know that. You waddled into that load of garbage to find the goodies for us and

246

save us from seeing that fetid pile of filth accumulated on top of the prophet. How nice of you! You are really the savior of islam."

You still do not get it, do you Ali? You use THE STINKIEST SUBSTANCE out of the Sunni holy trash as the MAIN MENUE in your round table. As for me, I arguably picked some material too from the same can; but they were CLEAN PLASTICS; I used them as ORNAMENTAL or STYLISTIC COSMETICS on my round table. I can easily trash them if my guests dislike their color, as I did it right now; but if you discard those stinky items from your table, you and your beloved friends will starve to death. Do you smell and see the difference dear Ali? Do you understand metaphors? I bet you do. But, you may act as if you do not understand or hear me.

> "Apparently you say something and do something else. Is that a good thing? So you do not reject the hadith and sira entirely. You simply reject the part that does not suit your agenda. None of these info you are giving away are in the quran and you keep telling me the quran is sufficient? If the quran is sufficient why did you have to dig into the garbage of hadith to write your book?"

Perhaps you are still confusing me with some of your Hislamic opponents. Or, you are praying that I would just devolve to one of them so you could pull my beard, smack my medieval head with those volumes of religious trash! Bad luck! When I say the Quran is sufficient, I say it within the context of the Quran's mission, which is to guide us to eternal salvation. When I say the Quran is sufficient, I do not mean that I do not need or enjoy salt or pepper for my food, car for my transportation, plastic for wrapping, or other sources of information. I do not mean that. I simply mean that anyone who follows the instructions and principles of the Quran ALONE will be guided to the straight path and will attain eternal salvation. I do also believe that people do not need even to know the Quran to free them from the hypnosis of devil by submitting themselves to God--who is the Truth, lead a righteous life and believe in the Day of Judgment (2:62).

None needs to know the birth year or place of Muhammad, nor the name of his enemies, etc, to be a muslim, that is, submitter to God alone and promoter of peace; they are trivial information. Even if those information were wrong, it would not change any tenet of my faith or practice. Are you following me?

> "Why not be honest here? Let us say that you agree with the part of the hadith that is not embarrassing and incriminating but when a hadith becomes too scandalous then that is garbage. The fact that muhammad was born in 570 a.d. is not embarrassing, so you have no problem with that. But when the same sources say that he massacred the bani qurayza or raped a 9 year old child then that is all fabrication and garbage. Thank you for teaching us islamic honesty."

247

The birth year of Muhammad has no substantial contribution to my argument, but your arguments are based on dubious sources with numerous contradictions and ridiculous stories. Besides, reasonable people--not fanatic skeptics or evilgelicals--would easily concede that there is no a reasonable and actual motive behind distorting the birth year of Muhammad, but there are many reasons and motives to fabricate lies about Muhammad's personal life, about his treatment of women, or his treatment of a tribe banished from Medina because of their betrayal during a war of self-defense. There are plenty of motives for those who reverted to the days of ignorance and established kingdoms in the name of God to distort the original message to justify their corrupt acts in public.

I gave some examples of such motives but you ignored them by a silly Martian remark. Soundbites might save ones career in political arena, church, or mosque but not in the market place of ideas. You ignore the fact that many Islamic and Hislamic scholars have written volumes of books to identify and expose the piles of stories imported from Jewish Mishna, Gamarra and Old Testament, which were called ISRAILIYAT. Sunni and Shiite Muslims adopted many Jewish stories and practices via those imported Jewish and Christian fabrications. Knowingly or out of ignorance, you wish to blame Muhammad and Quran for the deeds of their enemies, that is the fabricators and followers of hadith (6:112-115)!

For instance, the Quran does not contain STONING TO DEATH as punishment for adultery. Guess what we discover when we search the source of this punishment? We learn that it was the practice of Jews and ancient pagans. The so-called converted Jewish scholars inserted their distorted Biblical practice into Islam by fabricating hadith and fictional chains of narrators. In order to defend that hadith against the objections of early muslims, they even went further by fabricating Quranic verses that do not exist in the Quran.

How a verse instructing such a big punishment would be removed from the Quran? Well, there is no limit for imagination of clergymen, and there is no shortage of gullible people. The "authentic" hadith books justify the so-called "literal-but-not-legal" abrogation of the stoning verses by the following story: "After the Prophet Muhammad's departure, a hungry holy goat ate the skin where those verses were written on!"

Now, you would like us to believe the first half of this Jewish story and ignore the other half! Circumcision is another of numerous Jewish practices that were centuries later imported to islamic faith, after the fertile era of hadith fabrication ended. They imported that bloody Jewish practice via sectarian jurisprudence. But, you wish to take Muhammad and Quran responsible for this unnecessary and harmful Jewish practice that has survived until modern times.

> "In round iii and iv I raised a series of questions. You did not even touch them. Here is a list of them:

248

"1. how can muhammad's character be irrelevant to his claim? How can we be sure that he was not a liar? What if he lied for the same reason jim jones and thousands of other charlatan, impostor cult leaders lie manipulate and control the foolhardy?"

Here, I am going to touch them with my fingers by tickling the twenty-six letters and punctuation marks of the loyal keyboard of my muslim laptop. I hope some of these letters will touch your heart, if you have any, and mind too, and perform some remote healingJ

I am not an Evilgelical Christian or a Hislamic who believe blindly (euphemistically: on faith) in the claims of someone because they just trust that person or the chain of trust that goes back for many generations. If I were a comrade of Muhammad, I would perhaps have some idea about his character and intelligence, but hey, I came to the world centuries after him and I am not even an Arab. I cannot trust any person whom I have not seen and lived together especially in a matter that involve my eternal salvation. I may not even be hundred percent sure about the trustworthiness of any person, even if I share the same room with them for all my life. Even if I trust someone hundred percent, that does not mean whatever that person is claiming is true. Many people whose honesty we may not reasonably doubt, yet they may honestly assert nonsensical claims, believe in their hallucinations, superstitious and false ideas.

So dear Ali: as a philosopher, I demand extraordinary evidence for extraordinary claims. If trusting Muhammad's character were the only thing I could have as evidence, I would not be considering myself of having even an ordinary evidence for Muhammad's ordinary claims, let alone an extraordinary one. I would not be a muslim. So, go and ask me the follow up question! Need a clue? Well, it starts with the following phrase: "Then why do you believe in…."

2. "muhammad made so many bogus claims about being the best of the creation, and a perfect example to follow. How can we verify these self adulating claims? And how are we supposed to follow his examples as allah asked us to do in the quran if we are not allowed to read his history or believe it? … are we supposed to take those verse and the verse33:21 that says *"ye have indeed in the messenger of allah a beautiful pattern (of conduct)"* seriously or not?"

It seems either you have amnesia or you do not really read my answers. I had, in the past, answered the same question of yours. Let me cut and paste my answer here, again. (Well, I confess that I made two minor changes in spelling and grammar. This will leave something for those Christian detectives who have ample time and curiosity for the frivolous; they will find the corrected words and will accuse me in other threads of this forum for changing my past answers to their guru! Seriously, Ali, how could you attract so many followers with such a hobby and so much time?). Yes, here is the answer:

You share a strikingly similar poor knowledge of the Quran with Sunnis and Shiites. You use the same lousy arguments. If you were able to read the Quran without smelling the piles of hadith, you would easily notice that 33:21 had preceding and succeeding verses and the example of prophet was his bravery in defending Muslims against the aggressor army of Meccan oligarchy. If your knowledge of the Quran were a little bit beyond the surface, you would also notice that verse 60:4 uses exactly the same description, "good example", for Abraham and his supporters. Using your logic, Muslims should have had the hadith of Abraham and his supporters too! Perhaps, you will find the story of another hungry holy goat eating those hadith collections to be "not illogical."

Let me add this too: according to the Quran, Muhammad could never have claimed to be the best of the creation, since as a muslim, he was ordered not to distinguish among God's messengers (2:285), and be humble (32:11-20). This is a lie fabricated by Muhammadans in their polytheistic competition to top the idols of Christians. In thear zeal to turn Muhammad into a holy superman, ignorant Hislamic scholars even fabricated many miracles, from siplitting the moon to jumbo sexual powers for Muhammad.

> 3. "I asked you to explain the meaning of sura 111 and sura 38:41-44 without referring to hadith, tafseer and sira, by merely trying to decipher their meanings from the quran. Can you do that? These are just two examples. Most of the quran is incomprehensible without hadith and tafseer and I will keep pointing them out as we touch them."

Now it is clear that your Hislamic disease is still in your heart and mind. Your approach to the Quran is exactly similar to of the Sunni or Shiite ones. Without being brainwashed by these teachings, any reasonable person would and should understand the meaning and message of those verses. Sure, we can ask more questions regarding the details WE WISH to see, but there is no end of demands for more details, especially irrelevant details. Bring me any explanation, and I bet that I will shower you with too many questions that you will never be able to satisfy my demand for more details. Here is the translation of these verses from the translations of Rashad Khalifa and Layth of Progressive Muslims, respectively:

Remember our servant Job: he called upon his Lord, "The devil has afflicted me with hardship and pain." "Strike the ground with your foot. A spring will give you healing and a drink." We restored his family for him; twice as many. Such is our mercy; a reminder for those who possess intelligence. "Now, you shall travel the land and preach the message, to fulfill your pledge." We found him steadfast. What a good servant! He was a submitter. (38:41-44) http://19.org/km/RK/38

And recall Our servant Job, when he called upon his Lord: "The devil has afflicted me with an illness and pain." "Strike with your foot, here is a cold spring to wash with and to drink." And We restored his family to him along with a group like them, as a mercy from Us; and a reminder for those who possess intelligence. "And take in your hand a bundle and travel with it, and do not break your oath." We found him steadfast. What a good servant! He was obedient. (38:41-44) http://19.org/km/PM/38

I do not understand which part you do not understand. Since the followers of hadith and sunnah blindly accept the lies of their clergymen, they do not trust the Quranic verses asserting that the Quran was detailed, complete, easy-to-understand, and should be the only authority (12:111; 45:6; 39:23; 30:28; 16:89; 7:2-3; 17:46; 27:6; 11:1; 75:19; 54:17,22,32,40; 5:48-49; 6:112-115; 18:109; 10:15; 6:159; 19:64; 10:15; 41:3; 25:30; 17:39; 36:2; 5:101; 42:21; 33:38; 35:43.). To prove their point, they asked numerous IRRELEVANT questions or the questions where they found their answers in mishmash collection of Hadith and Sunnah. As an ex Sunni or Shiite, you have not yet washed your brain from the pollution inflicted by these sects.

Ali, which part of these verses you do not understand? Perhaps, like your Sunni and Shiite evil twins you are wondering with which foot Job hit the ground. The followers of hadith and Sunnah take the right-hand and left-hand, right-foot and left-foot issue more seriously than Dr. Seuss had taken. They try to enter bathroom with left foot, clean themselves with left, and eat with right. Right foot, left foot. Wet foot, dry foot. Low foot, high foot. True foot, lie foot. Here comes the Evilgelical-Sunni sly soot!

4. "We also talked about the quran's claim that god transformed the jews into apes and swine (5:60) and said "be ye apes" (2:65, 7:166). These are not metaphors. No scholar has understood them as metaphors because the texts make it clear that they are not metaphors. Can you explain to us how this absurdity is possible?"

Turning to monkeys and swines is an allegory indicating their spiritual and intellectual regression. Similar allegorical language can be found in the New Testament. For instance, Jesus likens his own people figuratively to swine and dogs (Matthew 7:6; 2 Peter 2:22). Swine was regarded as the most filthy and the most abhorred of all animals (Le 11:7; Isa 65:4; 66:3,17; Lu 15:15-16). TheTalmudic liturgy contains narrations about people who transformed into apes because they attempted to build thetower of Babel.

As for your claim that "no scholar has understood them as metaphors" is simply false. Though my understanding of the Quran does not depend on this scholar or that scholar or the number of their votes, I will give some examples to demonstrate that you frequently make false claims with hyperbolic pontifications.

251

For instance, Muhammad Asad, in his renowned translation of the Quran, The Message, makes the following comments on verse 7:166:

"According to Zamakhshari and Razf, the expression 'We said unto them' is here synonymous with 'We decreed with' regard to them' - God's 'saying' being in this case a metonym for a manifestation of His will. As for the substance of God's decree, 'Be as apes despicable', the famous tabi'i Mujahid explain it thus: '[Only] their hearts were transformed, that is, they were not [really] transformed into apes: this is but a metaphor (mathal) coined by God with regard to them, similar to the metaphor of `the ass carrying books' [62: 5]' (Tabari, in his commentary on 2 : 65; also Mandr I, 343; VI, 448; and IX, 379). A similar explanation is given by Raghib. It should be borne in mind that the expression 'like an ape' is often used in classical Arabic to describe a person who is unable to restrain his gross appetites or passions."

5. "You claimed muhammad wrote the quran with his own hand. I asked how do you know that. Where is your source? Why should we believe you when he himself claimed to be illiterate and unable to read.7:157 , 6:22"

6. "You made the claim that *ummi* does not mean illiterate but gentile. I quoted the verse 2:78 were muhammad alludes to the jews and calls them ummayoon أمِّيُّون `because they can't read their book. What is your response?"

I did not know that you were also illiterate, more accurately a selective illiterate, since in my previous answer I made my case clear from the Quran that UMMY means gentile, not illiterate. In case you missed by accident, here is a more detailed argument on this case. I will copy and paste from the samples of our upcoming Reformist Translation of the Quran[19]. You do not have the right for complaining from my copying and pasting, since I do not need to re-invent the same medicine for the same allergy:

During the month of Ramadan, every evening, after the lengthy congregational prayers, millions of Muslims crowding the mosques ask God to bless the soul of his "Nabbiyy-il Ummy" with the orthodox interpretation "illiterate prophet" In their minds. "Illiterate" (or "unlettered") is one of the most common titles used by Muslim clerics and imams to praise Muhammad, deliverer of the Quran.

The Arabic word "ummy," however, describes people who are not Jewish or Christian. The meaning of this word, which occurs six times in the Quran, has nevertheless been rendered as "one who can neither read nor write." This delib-

---

[19]   [Two year after this debate, the RTQ was published by Brainbowpress and it is available at brainbowpress.com, amazon.com and quranix.com]

erate manipulation by Muslim scholars has become widely accepted as the true meaning of the word. For example Yusuf Ali, in his translation, follows this pattern:

> "... So believe in God and His Apostle, the unlettered Prophet,...."

Marmaduke Pickthall's translation also reflects the same manipulation:

> "... So believe in Allah and His messenger, the prophet who can neither read nor write,..."

Our translation of 7:158:

> "... So you shall believe in God and His messenger, the Gentile prophet..."

COMMENTARY ON 7:158

The Quran itself provides guidance for the true meaning of "ummy". If we reflect on the verse 3:20 below we will easily understand that "ummy" does not mean an illiterate person:

> 3:20   "And say to those who received the scripture, as well as those who did not receive any scripture (ummyyeen)..."

In this verse the word "ummy" describes Meccan idol worshipers. It is obvious that "ummy" does not mean illiterate because it has been used as the counterpart of the people of the scripture. If the verse was " ... And say to those who are literate and illiterate", then the orthodox translation of "ummy" would be correct. According to the verse 3:20 the people of Arab peninsula were two main groups:

1. The people of the scripture, i.e., Jews and Christians
2. Gentiles, who were neither Jewish nor Christian.

If the people who were neither Jews nor Christians were called "ummyyeen" (3:20; 3:75), then the meaning of "ummy" is very clear. As a matter of fact, the verse 3:75 clarifies its meaning as Gentile.

Mecca was the cultural center of the Arabs in the 7th century. Poetry competitions were being held there. It is a historical fact that Meccans were not familiar with the Bible, thus they were gentiles. So the verse 62:2 describes Meccan people by the word "ummyyeen":

He is the One who sent to the Gentiles (ummyyeen) a messenger from among them, to recite to them His revelations, purify them, and teach them the scripture and wisdom. Before this, they had gone far astray. (62:2)

253

The disbelievers claimed that Muhammad was quoting verses from the Old and New Testaments (25:5; 68:15). The verse below refutes their accusation and gives the answer:

You did not read any previous scriptures, nor did you write them with your hand. In that case, the objectors would have had reason to harbor doubts. (29:48)

This verse tells us that Muhammad did not read nor write previous scriptures. The word "*min qablihi*" (previous) suggests that Muhammad *did* read and write the final scripture.

Muhammad was a literate gentile (ummy)

After this examination on the true meaning of the word "ummy", here are the reasons and proofs for the fact that Muhammad was a literate Gentile:

- To magnify the miraculous aspect of the Quran, religious people thought that the story of illiteracy would be alluring.

- The producer(s) of the illiteracy story found it relatively easy to change the meaning of "ummy." Nevertheless, the word appears throughout the Quran, and consistently means "Gentile" (2:78; 3:20; 3:75; 62:2). In verses 3:20and 3:75, the Quran uses the word "ummy" as the counterpart of the "ehlil kitab" ("People of the Book," a phrase that in both of these verses equates with "Jews and Christians").

- The Quran describes Meccan people with the word "ummyyeen" (Gentiles). (62:2). According to the orthodox claim, all Meccan people must have been illiterate. Why then were the poems of pre-Islamic Meccan poets hung on the walls of the Ka'ba (the ancient monotheistic shrine of Abraham)?

- The Arabs of the 7th century were using letters as numbers. This alphabetical numbering system is called "Abjad." The merchants of those days had to know the letters of the alphabet to record their accounts! If Muhammad was a successful international merchant, as is universally accepted, then he most probably knew this numbering system. The Arabs stopped using the "Abjad" system in the 9th century when they took "Arabic numbers" from India.

- The different spelling of the word "bism" in the beginning of the Basmalah and in the first verse of chapter 96 is one of the many evidences supporting literacy of Muhammad. It is not reasonable for an illiterate to dictate two different spellings of the same word which is pronounced the same.

254

- The very first revelation from the Angel Gabriel was, Muslims believe, "Read!" And the first five verses of that revelation encourage reading and writing (96:1-5). The second revelation was "The pen and writing" (68:1). These facts compel some questions that orthodox scholarship would rather avoid. Does God command an illiterate man to "read"? If so, could Muhammad read *after* Gabriel's instruction to do so? The story told in Hadith books about the first revelation asserting that Muhammad could read only after three trials ending by an angelic "squeeze" contradicts the other stories claiming that Muhammad died as an illiterate!

- Traditional history books accept that Muhammad dictated the Quran and controlled its recording. Even if we accept that Muhammad did not know how to read or write before revelation of the Quran, we cannot claim that he preserved this illiteracy during the 23 years while he was dictating the Quran! Let us accept, for the sake of argument, that Muhammad was illiterate before the revelation of the Quran. Why then did he insist on *staying*illiterate for 23 years after the first revelation: "Read !"? Did he not obey his Lord's command? Did he receive another command forbidding him from reading and writing?

- Was it so difficult for Muhammad to learn to read and write? If a person still does not learn to read and write after 23 years of careful dictation of a book, what kind of intellect is that?

- If Muhammad was encouraging his followers to read and write (which he did when he recited 2:44 to them), then why should he have excluded himself?

Muslim scholars, who are in disagreement on a bewildering array of subjects, somehow have managed to agree on the story of Muhammad's illiteracy. Perhaps the glorification of illiteracy, using it as a positive attribute of a worshipped figure, is one of the causes of the high current level illiteracy in Muslim communities.

     7. "We talked about sura 33 and I said this sura is not self explanatory. I asked you to tell us who are the "confederates" mentioned in verse 20 and from where they did not withdraw. Explain that without any reference to hadith or tafseer."

Why should I care what was the name of that group. I find no relevancy for the lesson I get from the verse. Let's say the tribe's name is "Ibn Fulan" or "Abu Falan" what would it change? First, the Quran is not a history book. Yes, it refers to historical events, but does not narrate them as a chronological story, or like Hadith books or the Old Testament does by giving pages and pages of names, number of mules and horses… The Quran uses snapshots of history or events to drive and convey lessons for those who have intelligence and good faith. But people like you (this include your twins, Sunnies and Shiites) miss the main point of the story in search for irrelevant details, for goose eggs.

To create an excuse and to mix pages of garbage to distort the meaning of a clear verse you asked the NAME OF A TRIBE. How clever you are! "Edip, your Quran does not tell me the name of the enemy tribe, so, I will go dig the mishmash collection of contradictory narrations and pig all the garbage I can, and use it to cover and distort the truth in the Quran."

This is a very cheap game Ali. It might have so far worked against those who considered your pile of historical trash as their holy books, but you are still in denial: YOU ARE DEBATING WITH EDIP YUKSEL founder of 19.ORG, A MUSLIM, not A SUNNI OR SHIITE MUSHRIK. Why are you still trying to pretend that your filthy weapons are still efficient in this battle-ground is a subject I leave to psychologists. You PROMISED me several times that you would not use hadith and other dubious sources, but each time you sought a silly excuse to bring a truck-load of them.

Now let me play the game you are begging me to play. Just recently, a sunni posted an article at 19.org/forum asking us where in the Quran we could find how to sleep! He was living in another universe as you do, and could not fathom the simple concept of following the Quran alone to attain eternal salvation. Here are four of his seven challenging questions:

> What are the Quranic ruling on the following things:
> What is the punishment for having sex with an animal?
> Will you loose ablution if you touch a dog?
> Does the Quran tell us how to sleep?
> What are the words most beloved to Allah?

When I hear a Sunni asking me to provide irrelevant or stupid details to challenge the sufficiency of the Quran alone, I remind them the story of Heifer or Cow mentioned in the Quran. When God asked Jews to sacrifice a heifer, rather than obeying God's commandment, they asked irrelevant questions like you and Sunnis do. They asked more details about the heifer's color, its age, etc. (See the Quran 2:67-71).

Some of his great scholars of the past even wondered about the name of the dog, which was the companion of the so-called seven sleepers of the cave. Not finding the name of the dog, they decided that the verses 18:9-27 were not detailed enough to be understood! So they went a head and fabricated a name for the dog: *Qitmeer*. With the name and color of the dog, the names of the youngsters and more similar details, now the story of the People of the Cave and Numbers was finally detailed and comprehensible! Though your curiosity regarding the name of the aggressive tribe is one grade above than your Sunni or Shiite ditto-heads, unfortunately you suffer from the same disease. To understand, and hopefully to appreciate MONOTHEISM, you need to cleanse yourself from the logical fallacies which somehow you retain from your Hislamic past. You came to hate Hislam, but unfortunately, you hate it with similar logical fallacies that had led you to love it in the first place. Thus, you replaced Hislam with Evilgelical Christianity or Spiritual Humanism that is dedicated to promotion of hate, misinformation, and dehumanization of more than a billion Muslims, which may lead to genocide.

Please don not tell me that you cannot see those viruses; I know, they are too little to be seen. Well, when you called me "little devil" you were under the influence of those little devils. So, you should think nineteen times before hurl someone, especially a monotheist, such a label. You need a philosopher, a logician, a monotheist, a miracle, or another act of God, to help you find and delete them. If you cannot delete them from hardware and software system that makes up your personality, then the Ali Sina of FFF may end up in the Creator's depository of "infected free-will programs" or "infected beta programs" and be deleted for eternity.

I almost forgot the game I promised to play against you. The name of the game is called BUMERANG or MIRROR since it mirrors the fallacious logic of the opponent and exposes the absurdity of their argument. Here we go:

Okay, you are right Ali Sina, that the Quran does not contain the details you are asking for, and to understand the Quran we need hadith and tafseer (commentary) books you are so fond of. Now can you please tell me, how can I understand those books, since they do not contain many details that I AM CURIOUS about? For instance, which hadith or tafseer gives the numbers of those people? Which hadith or tafseer describes the flag of the Confederates? In which hadith or tafseer can you find me the temperature of that day? Don't tell me that these are not important information, since you have not claimed to be an authority or the only authority in defining what is important or not. Thus, you have to find another source besides hadith and tafseer to find answers for my questions. If you lived in those times, you had the choice just to fabricate one with a chain of narrators. Otherwise, you have to say exactly the same thing about hadih and tafseer books: 'We cannot understand them.'

> "What is happening dear edip? Why is it that I feel like talking to an answering machine? You have completely neglected my questions and like all your fellow co-religionists resorted to copy-pasting. What is the relevance of these to our discussion? Where are the answers to my questions?"

I know, after receiving all my answers you will be repeating this. You know that if you repeat something many times you will find enough people to believe whatever you are saying. A working political campaign!

> "According to dictionary.com reform means: "to improve by alteration, correction of error, or removal of defects; put into a better form or condition.""

> "Can you please tell us by what authority are you trying to "alter, correct the errors or remove the defects" of the quran? if the quran is perfect, why it needs to be reformed? are you claiming to be superior in rank and knowledge to the original author of the quran? do you know more than allah? or, are you the new mahdi?"

You got it all wrong, Ali. Go ask someone who knows English better than you the difference between "Reform in Islam" and "Islamic Reform." You indicated that you have read some of my articles at my website. If you have done so, you should have learned that I do not suggest what you are trying to put in my mouth. Perhaps, you are deliberately trying to misrepresent my position to divert from the main issues. You have somehow succeeded many times by resorting to your favorite silly storybooks, and copying and pasting them here.

> "The verse 29 starts with قتلوا this can only be translated as fight and not fight (back). It is an offensive order and not defensive. It is *qatilu* not*dafeu*. The verse goes on to say fight them until they pay الجزية jizyah. This word derives from jaza. It means fine and punishment the plural of that is *mojazat*. It does not mean compensation. The correct word for compensation is *mokafat*."

After another lengthy diversion with a load of trashy references and lies, you finally make an argument, though a funny argument. First, the word *MOKAFAT* is modern Arabic and is not used in the Quran and hadith books. You are confusing a Modern Arabic word with classic Arabic. Second, the *JAZA* means recompense, reward. In fact, in haste I missed a better English term for *Jizya*: reparation. Various nouns and verbs derived from the same root, JaZaYa is mentioned in the Quran 118 times. If we exclude the *JiZYa* of verse 29 for the sake of the argument, NOT IN A SINGLE occurrence it has anything to do with TAXation. Furthermore, in dozens of verses this word is used to describe REWARD and COMPENSATION.

Here are some verses that falsify your claim regarding the modern Arabic word MOKAFAT: 3:144-145; 10:4; 12:22; 12:74-75; 14:51; 18:88; 20:76; 28:14; 33:24; 37:80,105,110,121,131; 39:34; 55:60; and more.

> "According to wikipedia.org jizyah is the arabic language translation of poll tax or "head tax", a tax imposed on male individuals of other faiths

living under muslim rule. ... Give me one reason why should we reject all these historic facts and explanations and accept your claims? Obviously you want to rewrite the history by reinventing it. And your only sources are your fantasies."

First, your linguistic sources are little better than your hadith sources, but it is still the third rate source. Any person can go write an article and definition in wikipedia.org, including you and any of your followers. From your *MOKAFAT*, now your of knowledge of classic Arabic become suspect, and from using wikipedia.org I know your level of academic gullibility becomes an issue.[20] Please be serious Ali.

Besides, no scholar who is familiar with transformation of language, will put his or her full trust in a dictionary, even if it is the most reputable dictionary. There are some Arabic words whose meanings have changed through time and it does not take to be a rocket scientist or a monotheist to notice the traces of such change. We have many examples of such a semantical mutation in English too. For instance, you cannot claim that a renaissance poet was homosexual because in his poems he called himself GAY several times. Wikipedia.org indeed does a good job in listing the early meaning of the word GAY. However, it fails to define word ELOI or ELI one of the few Aramiac words used in English translation of the Bible (Mat 27:46; Mrk 15:34). If I claim that the etimological origin of Arabic Elahi (my god) is the same with Aramaic Eloi (my god) or the origin of Allah (the god) is the same as the Aramiac Alohim (the god), you may refute me by referring to wikipedia.org, which defines Eloi as of the two post-human races mentioned in the novel The Time Machine. Of course Jesus was asking help from Eloi not Marlocks who lived in the year 802701 AD!

The Devil's Califs of Umayyad and Abbasid dynasties had too much interest and motivation to change the meaning of a Quranic word and they had many hadith and sunnah fabricators under their service. So, changing the meaning of JIZYA from reperation to tax perhaps took some time, but considering their success in changing much important principles and practices it was not that difficult.

> "In the verse 2.256 he says: *"let there be no compulsion in religion: truth stands out clear from error"*. And *"if it had been thy lord's will, they would all have believed,- all who are on earth! Wilt thou then compel mankind, against their will, to believe!"* 10:99 or *"the truth is from your lord"*: let him who will believe, and let him who will, reject

---

[20]   [I do not wish to be misunderstood, since Wikipedia.org is an impressive site containing so much valuable information. I use it all the time. Though the information there is usually reliable, its use for proving a point in an academic debate is limited and cannot be relied on without critical evaluation or corroborative research. In pursuit of knowledge in serious matters, Wikipedia might be a good starting point, but not the last station.]

(it)" 18:29.   But these are the meccan verses. He wrote these verses when he was weak. It would have been impossible for his handful of followers to wage war against thousands of unbelievers and win."

First, I do not separate the verses of the Quran as Meccan on Medinan verses. Again, you are confusing me with Sunnis. The Quran does not contain such a distinction, and a believer must follow ALL the verses of the Quran. You are a disbeliever of the Quran and you do not care about its internal consistency and integrity. You will divide and chop, mix and twist, take verses out of their context and do all the SIX STEPS to fulfill your agenda until you reach TO THE FACTOR OF 666! You, your Sunni and Shiite partners are warned by the following verses:

15:90 As We have sent down on the dividers.
15:91 The ones who have taken the Quran apart.
15:92 By your Lord, We will ask them all.
15:93 Regarding what they used to do.
15:94 So proclaim what you have been commanded and turn away from those who set up partners.
15:95 We will relieve you from the mockers.
15:96 Those who sat up with God another god; they will come to know.
15:97 We know that your chest is strained by what they say.
15:98 So glorify with the praise of your Lord, and be of those who prostrate.
15:99 Serve your Lord until certainty comes to you.

Second, the trashy sources you are so fond of using against my faith, yes your favorite sources are reporting differently regarding the first verse in your reference: **Verse 2:256 is listed as Medinan verse by the sources you wish me to believe.** Again, you mix truth with falsehood, pieces of glass with diamond, poison with candies… Exactly like hadith narrators and collectors had done.

> "Now what these eminent scholars of islam say make sense. Logically the latter revelations override and cancel the previous ones if they contradict each other. But what you say make completely no sense. Your claim is informed by your zealotry and blind faith and not by facts."

The idea of abrogation is Satanic, and it was fabricated by Sunni and Shiite mushriks who had problems with some verses when they tried to twist others. Ironically, your mentality is not much different. It seems that you have rejected the substance of your religion but you are keeping its mind set, its fallacious reasoning methods intact. No wonder, the Sunnis who are following our argument have found you much closer to themselves!

> "You seem to have run out of arguments before we even engage and hence with these tedious copy pasting and filibustering tactics you try

260

to bore the readers and find your way out of this discussion. Please prove to us this is not the case."

You made me smile. Thanks. Do you remember the words PROJECTION?

"If this is what you intend, I suggest you would be saving face more by not responding at all. Dr. Zakir Naik, prof. Michael Sells and prof. John Esposito are far better now for not responding to me than if they did and failed to engage in coherent arguments. If you are gasping for relief, you may stop, but if you truly want to debate please do not burden me and the readers with long tedious and irrelevant copy pastes."

Copy paste what? So far, I copied and pasted only ONE article of MINE to TRICK you in order to expose the real reason behind your indulgence in loads of trashy hearsays of hearsays of hearsays… You are the one who is continuously copying and pasting the hearsay books and you have the audacity to blame me for what you have been doing since the beginning of our debate. More than half of what you have included in your answers were COPY and PASTE from story books.

"Finally I would like to speak to your heart. If you can't defend islam, why you cling to this sinking ship? Islam is a lie and this I have proven here in numerous articles time and again. Why hang to a doctrine that is so evil and so false? I earnestly urge you to leave islam. You can't save islam nor can you reform it. Islam is based on total lies. It is not a religion of god but a cult created by a psychopath to control and dominate the gullible. Its *fruit* speaks for itself."

Dou you have heart Ali Sina? Then why are you playing as a pawn of Crusaders for their new colonialism plans? Why do you distort facts, you introduce hearsays of hearsays as facts, and dehumanize the entire muslim world? Don't you know that your hatred might justify a genocide against muslims in the minds of some of your followers? I wish you could be brave enough to stand against the terror, destruction and massacres inflicted by evilgelical crusaders and their Zionist allies as you demonstrate bravery to stand against the terror, destruction and massacres inflicted by taliban and mullah hislamics. I invited you to condemn ANY ACT OF AGGRESSION, TERRORISM, ATROCITIES, VIOLENCE, and HUMAN RIGHTS VIOLATION regardless of the religion or nationality of the perpetrator. You should join me in using one standard if you have dignity and sense of justice.

Despite this bitter-tasting debate with you, I still pray for your guidance and I hope that one day you will see the truth that well set you free.

I challenge you to use scientific evidence and reason for your cricticsm of the Quran. I will NOT continue debating with you if ONE MORE TIME

you refer to or quote from hadith, syra or tafseer books that I have rejected vehemently since 1986. If you cannot criticize the Quran without referring to hearsays of hearsays, then you will be proving to the entire world that you lost this debate against someone who followed the Quran alone.

Finally, I would prefer that you post my responses all together, rather chopping them and using them in your complete articles. You had eliminated some of the quotation in my responses and thus making it difficult for the readers to follow my response to each point. If you visit the forum of 19.org you will see how I respected the integrity of your responses and learn learn how to be fair.

Peace,
Edip

14. The Evangelical Faschism

Edip Yuksel

Jan 13, 2005

> "If edip agrees I am ready to change the tone of this debate and instead of being confrontational we both become inquisitive. In other words instead of defending and attacking we discuss this matter like two scientists conducting a research. Let us be open to whatever the study throws at us. Let us accept the facts with open mind. Present them and move on. This debate has a court format; it is litigious. Let us convert it into a lab format. So instead of arguing, we do research. The subject of study would be primarily the Quran and then muhammad and his claim. It is okay if we see things differently. After all even scientists don't agree all the time. Theories are presented, discussed, critiqued and even criticized until a consensus is reached. I am willing to change gear if edip is ready too. After all we are all after the truth. I think if we give up all our preconceived ideas and investigate this matter impartially, we both will find out the truth. Our beliefs act as prejudices and prejudices are veils between us and the truth.

> "So here is my offer to edip. If he does not want to answer the issues that I raised in previous rounds, let us forget about them. Let us start talking about the Quran and see whether this book stands the litmus test of reason and commonsense."

Wow. That means you can do that too. I now take back my judgment regarding your heart, Ali.

Okay, if you wish, you may respond the above-posted response of mine. You do not need to respond every paragraph. Or if you wish, you may just apologize for using wrong weapons and style against me and let's start discussing the Quran alone by applying scientific method with an inquisitive tone.

I already spent too many hours writing a long response to you. I am working more than full time, and it seems that I will have problem in putting up with you. In accepting your challenge I never indented to debate you in writing, but I was carried away. Now, it stuck with me like a triple-mint gum:)

Inshallah, I will be able to continue debating this issues if you post short articles, each not exceeding 1000 words, preferably even shorter than that. The same should apply to mine.

Since I am working more than 60 hours a week on multiple projects, the delay in my responses should not be considered as justifications for your allegations and criticism. If one day I find myself intellectually unable to answer your allegations, I will be the first one denouncing my faith, and you would hear it from my own websites. So, please remind your people, as you have wisely reminded them above, not to make up stories on my behalf.

But, if one day I suddenly disappear, either it is because I had been killed by a crazy Hislamic, or I am kidnapped by patriotic USA-INC forces to be tortured at Guatanomo Bay under the melodious prayers of evilgelical priests, or divorced and made homeless by my wife who is fed up with my lack of getting enough sleep and risking my jobs ☹

Ali Sina, if you will be one of causes of these tragedies in my life; then don't come to heaven next to me ☺

Peace,

Edip

The Fascist Crusader Advocates Genocide Against Muslims

"You may say but Muslims are humans too. Is having the human appearance enough to make us humans? The sign of humanity is in our humanness. No person who believes in those inhumane teachings of the Quran that calls for killing and murder of innocent people deserves to be called human. Therefore, this is a war between humanity and a spiritually underdeveloped subhuman species. The actions of Muslims are barbaric. Their thoughts are beastly. They have no human conscience and they are preying on us humans. So this is a war between humans and Muslims."

Ali, someone posted the above excerpt in another site claiming that Ali Sina wrote it. I know that your mouth is filled with foam and venom against Muslims, but I do not expect you to be using the exact language of Fascists and Nazis. In case you have not written the above-qouted idiotic statements, which I hope that you have not, then ignore these words and let the real source get my message.

To the coward vampire who is instigating wars and genocides:

You are the real subhuman, you are a vampire who is thirsty to suck the blood of more than a billion humans on this planet. If this is an irrational reaction to a terrorist event that killed several thousand people, then you should demonstrate many times more hatred and irrational reaction to the terrorism, atrocities, murders, and massacres committed by USA-INC, UK, USSR, and Israel; in the last century alone, in which they killed MILLIONS of PEOPLE and destroyed countries and annihilated entire cities! By calling destruction of entire cities, together with families and children, with the word WAR does not make a bit difference.

Though I condemn a warmongering group of hypocrite Christians by calling their name Evilgelical, I never justify killing Evilgelical Christians, let alone all Christians, or killing Zionist Jews, let alone all Jews. You are a monster using the mask of humanism. You cannot be a human; you are a hatemonger and blood-thirsty creature. I do not condone killing animals like you; but I might approve of putting a leash around your dirty neck.

Peace is our weapon against fascist warmongers. Yes, PEACE!

Edip

Addendum:

A forum participant accused me of accusing Ali Sina based on hearsay. Ironically, he quoted the part, in which I expressed my doubts regarding its source and I simply lamented to the author of the excerpt whomever he was. Despite this request for clarification in the beginning of the article and my friendly wish, how a person with a gram of fairness would blame me of accusing Ali Sina based on hearsay. The language of the excerpt was close to Ali Sina's, though its Hitler-style thirst for the blood of the followers of a particular religion was something I have not heard before, so I asked his clarification regarding the authorship.

I am waiting for Ali Sina's answer for this matter, ASAP. This excerpt is not something simple to get away with it. I will explain after Ali Sina's rejection or admission. And I hope he will reject or rescind it. I will accept his denial even if he was the one who had written in a moment of irrationality and rabid insanity.

Today I found the same paragraph posted at:

> http://www.faithfreedom.org/debates/EdipYukselp19.htm

> "You may say but Muslims are humans too. Is having the human appearance enough to make us humans? The sign of humanity is in our humanness. No person who believes in those inhumane teachings of the Quran that calls for killing and murder of innocent people deserves to be called human. Therefore, this is a war between humanity and a spiritually underdeveloped subhuman species. The actions of Muslims are barbaric. Their thoughts are beastly. They have no human conscience and they are preying on us humans. So this is a war between humans and Muslims."

So, Ali Sina, if it is not you who has written the above Neo Nazi remarks then who is posting articles together with you? If it is you, be brave and come out of your cave.

Tell me whether it is indeed NOT you who have declared himself to be a promoter of genocide by dehumanizing all muslims. Tell me that a TALIBAN or a NEONAZI hacker hacked your website and wrote that paragraph in your name. I would be glad to accept this senario. Because, I cannot believe that a person who is smart enough to engage in intellectual debates, though frequently sniffing and stuffing himself with holy trash, could be the author of such rabid and diabolic words!

SALAM, that is PEACE

From: MirrorOfTruth

Dear Edip,

The paragraph is in ROUND VI:

> http://www.faithfreedom.org/debates/EdipYukselp19.htm

> "Edip is absolutely right. I am not only willing but striving to bring all the people of the world together and make them see that humanity is under attack by an alien enemy who does not see us as Christians, Jews, Hindus, Atheists, Agnostics, or Animists but merely as kafirs and as such deserving to die. Their enmity is with Mankind.

> "You may say but Muslims are humans too. Is having the human appearance enough to make us humans? The sign of humanity is in our humanness. No person who believes in those inhumane teachings of the Quran that calls for killing and murder of innocent people deserves to be called human. Therefore, this is a war between humanity and a spiritually underdeveloped subhuman species. The actions of Muslims are barbaric. Their thoughts are beastly. They have no human conscience and they are preying on us humans. So this is a war between humans and Muslims."

He has edited portions of that round before so please download these posts he made and post these as soon as possible on your thread - to make his weasel tactics ineffective. I believe he may remove that section as it has just incriminated him if you are not quick. I have saved the page in question just in case. Peace.

266

15. Closing, Analysis, and Surprise

Edip Yuksel

January 17, 2005

On January 14, 2005 I wrote the following:

> "What are you saying Ali Sina? Was it your other personality who for
> about three weeks has been scavenging among the piles of hadith and
> syra books?
>
> "In your attack to the Quran so far you have not been able to get your
> nose out of those trash; you always followed the "Six Steps to the Fac-
> tor of 666" methodology. It would be perhaps a much better argument
> if you could give up from your hadith treasure and focus on that book
> alone. But, deep in your heart you know that you cannot criticize the
> Quran against someone like me; so you tried to delay such a debate. So
> far, all your accusations have been thrown into where they belong.
> With the exception of the few troll who will clap you even if you
> sneeze, people will see it.
>
> "I will post a brief analysis of your site, your cause and I will present
> you a little surprise. Hopefully, before the next week starts."

Well, now it is time for the ANALYSIS and the SURPRISE note. However, first
I will explain what led me to end this debate:

About a month ago, I accepted Ali Sina's invitation to debate on Islam. I had
limited time, so I invited him to debate face-to-face in public. I told him that I
could arrange such a debate at the University of Arizona or Pima College. I was
working to finish important projects such as the *Reformist Translation of the
Quran*; a script for a political comedy; animation school; and establishing an
alliance with other organizations under the name Islamic Reform; and teaching
philosophy.

But, Ali Sina rejected to debate in public claiming security and his need for research; so, we ended up debating on Islam at his website, which took about a
month. Despite my repeated reminder to debate on the Quran, Ali was obsessed
with using hearsays of hearsays in his arguments. I was glad that finally Ali Sina
was offering to debate in a nicer language and focus on the Quran, and I congratulated him for that decision. Nevertheless, my happiness did not last long.

On January 13, 2005, Ali posted a paragraph exposing his real face. I read the paragraph first at free-minds.org then I saw it published at his website, faithfree-dom.org. I reacted to that in a language that it deserved. Here is the merged version of my successive two reactions. Note that for the first time I did not feel free to call Ali with the word "dear":

> "You may say but Muslims are humans too. Is having the human appearance enough to make us humans? The sign of humanity is in our humanness. No person who believes in those inhumane teachings of the Quran that calls for killing and murder of innocent people deserves to be called human. Therefore, this is a war between humanity and a spiritually underdeveloped subhuman species. The actions of Muslims are barbaric. Their thoughts are beastly. They have no human conscience and they are preying on us humans. So this is a war between humans and Muslims. Ali Sina."

> Ali, I know that your mouth is filled with foam and venom against Muslims, but I do not expect you to be using the exact language of Fascists and Nazis. In case you have not written the above-quoted idiotic statements, which I hope that you have not, then ignore these words and let the real source get my message.

> To the coward vampire, who is instigating wars and genocides:

> You are the real subhuman, you are a vampire who is thirsty to suck the blood of more than a billion humans on this planet. If this is an irrational reaction to a terrorist event that killed several thousand people, then you should demonstrate many times more hatred and irrational reaction to the terrorism, atrocities, murders, and massacres committed by USA-INC, UK, USSR, and Israel; in the last century alone, in which they killed MILLIONS of PEOPLE and destroyed countries and annihilated entire cities! By calling destruction of entire cities, together with families and children, with the word WAR does not make a bit difference.

> Though I condemn a warmongering group of hypocrite Christians by calling their name Evilgelical, I never justify killing Evilgelical Christians, let alone all Christians, or killing Zionist Jews, let alone all Jews. You are a monster using the mask of humanism. You cannot be a human; you are a hatemonger and bloodthirsty creature. I do not condone killing animals like you; but I might approve of putting a leash around your dirty neck.

> Peace is our weapon against fascist warmongers. Yes, PEACE

I am waiting for Ali Sina's answer for this matter, ASAP. This excerpt is not something simple to get away with it. I will explain after Ali Sina's rejection or admission. And I hope he will reject or rescind it. I will accept his denial even if he was the one who had written in a moment of irrationality and rabid insanity.

So, Ali Sina, if it is not you who has written the above Neo Nazi remarks then who is posting articles together with you? If it is you, be brave and own your words.

Tell me whether it is indeed NOT you who have declared himself to be a promoter of genocide by dehumanizing all Muslims. Tell me that a TALIBAN or a NEONAZI hacker hacked your website and wrote answer in your name. I would be glad to accept this scenario. Because, I cannot believe that a person who is smart enough to engage in intellectual debates, though frequently sniffing and stuffing himself with holy trash, could be author of such rabid and diabolic words! SALAM, that is PEACE

On January 14, 2005 Ali Sina responded to my query as follows:

> "Looks like you took that personally. Does that description describes you too? If not then why you get so worked out and if yes what else do you want me to call you when all you think is killing innocent human beings? "

> "Make your position clear Edip, do you approve of terror and murder of innocent people or not. Is this talk about reformation and humanization nothing but cheap propaganda? Which side you are standing anyway? If you are on the side of humanity why you get so upset and if you are on the site of the savage terrorists then why pretend to have been reformed. Is there an third position that I am not aware of?"

Ali Sina after condemning and convicting the entire muslim world to death and then as the judge of his court now he is contemplating to forgive my life if I can prove to him that I am not guilty, or subhuman. Though he had visited my personal website (yuksel.org), my organization's website (19.org), read my life story, and learned my uncompromising standing against violence, terror, wars, human rights violation and suppression of freedom... Knowing that I had to flee my country because of my rejection of traditional corrupt Islam, knowing that my mentor and close friend was the first victim of al-Qaida terrorism in the USA, and witnessing that the rabid Sunnies and Shiites participating at his forum sided with him against me, knowing all of these, his majesty is not yet clear whether to distinguish me from other Muslims who are condemned to death by his "humanistic" decree of genocide. He needs more evidence, perhaps, me publicly begging for my life in his court of inquisition!

269

Thank God, this so-called Hislamic apostate who is openly supported by Evilgelical Christians does not have power. He would be worse than Hitler, Stalin, Pol Pot, or his like-minded Taliban.

I am glad that I am in a country established by deists, monotheists, and muslims (submitters to God alone and promoters of peace), who escaped from religious persecution. The constitution of the United States is mostly in harmony with Quranic principles. I am blessed for not living in a country ruled by Pope, Rightwing Evangelical Christians, Talibans, Mullahs, or fascist cult of Ali Sina. Though the USA government is currently infiltrated by Evangelical Christians and Zionists, there are still many institutions and majority of Americans still appreciate justice, equality, liberty, and the separation of church and state. I will fight against organized religion influencing the government of my country.

Thus, Ali Sina's theo-fascist remarks declaring ALL Muslims being "subhuman species" made me decide to discontinue the debate with him. His "subhuman" remark was the last, but a venomous drop that filled his cup of hatred and bigotry. He is not a person to reason with, since his mind is filled with toxic hate and his stomach is thirsty for fresh blood. I now regret calling him with the word "dear," since he does not deserve even its first letter.

Those who are curious about my response to Ali's "6-Step" criticism of the Quran will find our answer to his and many other criticism at the side notes of the Reformist Translation of the Quran, which will be published in the end of the year, inshallah.

As I promised, I am posting my analyses of the leader of this small cult. A SURPRISE note will follow these analyses:

POSITIVE ASPECTS:

1. Ali Sina is a smart, articulate and well-versed in classic Hislamic liturgy. Thus, I do not think that he was originally a Christian introducing himself as a former Muslim.

2. Ali Sina's website, though frequented by cheerleaders and hatemonger drunkards, is indeed an open forum with no censorship, like our forum at 19.org. I have not yet seen a Hislamic or Evilgelical website with such an open door policy.

3. Ali Sina, though chopped some of my arguments by integrating/devouring them within his arguments, he demonstrated acceptable degree of fairness in posting them.

4. Ali Sina, having full control on the website, could have distorted my responses and he even could have posted some outrageous statements under my

name. (This happened in an atheist Turkish forum several years ago!). Ali Sina seems to have integrity in this regard.

5. Ali Sina, though misguided, has complete dedication to his cause. (Since we do not know about his identity, we cannot verify nor falsify claims about his getting financial aid from Rightwing Evangelical organizations or from CIA for his job to promote hate and genocide.).

6. Though Ali Sina appears to be thirstier for the blood of innocent people than his Hislamic clones, such as members of Taliban and Al-Qaida, he has a mediocre sense of humor that others lack. His sense of humor might be an indication that there is hope for his recovery from hatemongering.

7. Using his old sunni mentality, though Ali frequently confuses the Quran with books of hearsay, Ali Sina does an excellent job in exposing the numerous problems in teachings of hadith, sunnah, and sectarian jurisprudence.

NEGATIVE ASPECTS:

1. **Ali Sina follows the Evilgelical-Sunny methodology of Right foot, left foot. Wet foot, dry foot. Low foot, high foot. True foot, lie foot. Here comes the Evilgelical-Sunni sly soot!**

Ali Sina shares a strikingly similar poor knowledge of the Quran with Sunnis and Shiites. He uses the same lousy argument. He uses THE STINKIEST SUBSTANCE out of the Sunni holy trash as the MAIN MENUE in his round table. He is not able to read the Quran without smelling the piles of hadith. Now it is clear that his Hislamic disease is still in his heart and mind. His approach to the Quran is exactly similar to of the Sunni or Shiite ones.

Without being brainwashed by these teachings, any reasonable person would and should understand the meaning and message of verses. Sure, we can ask more questions regarding the details WE WISH to see, but there is no end of demands for more details, especially irrelevant details.

The idea of abrogation is a Satanic idea, and it was fabricated by Sunni and Shiite mushriks who had problems with some verses when they tried to twist others. Ironically, his mentality is not much different. It seems that he has rejected the substance of his religion but he is keeping its mind set, its fallacious reasoning methods exactly. No wonder, the Sunnis who are following our argument have found Ali Sina much closer to themselves!

Ali Sina repeatedly claimed that the Quran was not detailed because it did not provide the real identity of person in chapter 111; he wondered about Abu Lahab and claimed that Quran is meaningless without hadith and other storybooks, since they provide much detail about that character. Well, I he just proved the

Quran, since according to the Quran fanatic disbelievers will never understand the Quran (17:45-46). The believers of the Quran finds Abu Lahab (Father of Fire) a universal character. For instance, with his promotion of hate and violence against one fifth of humanity, Ali Sina is an example of prototype Abu Lahab, he is the Father of Fire. He will end up in his own hell together with his supporters who carry fuel for his fire.

2.   Ali Sina frequently makes false claims with hyperbolic pontifications.

For instance, he claimed that verse 7:166 claims that God "literally" transformed Jews to monkeys and pigs and continued by saying that "no scholar has understood them as metaphors." I quoted from Muhammad Asad's translation, The Message, and proved that he was simply wrong.

Another example is his assertion regarding the Quranic verses promoting freedom of religion and expression. He claimed that all belong to Meccan era when Muhammad was weak. The trashy sources he was so fond of using against my faith, yes his favorite sources are reporting differently regarding the first verse in his reference. Thus, he misrepresented his own trashy sources. Verse 2:256 is listed as Medinan verse by the sources he wished me to believe. Again, he mixes truth with falsehood, pieces of glass with diamond, poison with candies… Exactly like hadith narrators and collectors had done.

3.   Ali Sina has the habit of putting words in his opponent's mouth.

For instance, regarding my promotion of Islamic Reform, either from ignorance or by a deliberate choice, he switched my words around and described it as Reform in Islam.

I told him to go ask someone who knows English better than him the difference between "Reform in Islam" and "Islamic Reform." He indicated that he has read some of my articles at my website. Has he done so, he should have learned that I do not suggest what he is trying to put in my mouth. Perhaps, he is deliberately trying to misrepresent my position to divert from the main issues. He has somehow succeeded many times by resorting to his favorite silly storybooks, and copying and pasting them here.

4.   Ali Sina lacks academic rigor, and when it is in his advantage, he confuses modern Arabic with classic Arabic, or uses third class unreliable sources.

His suggesting *MOKAFAT* in our debate on *Jizya* was interesting: After another lengthy diversion with a load of trashy references and lies, he finally made an argument, albeit a funny one. First, the word *MOKAFAT* is modern Arabic and is not used in the Quran and hadith books. He is confusing a Modern Arabic word with classic Arabic.

Ali's linguistic sources are little better than his hadith sources, but they are still third rate sources. He referred to vikipedia.org regarding our discussion on the word *Jizya* of verse 9:29. Any person can post an article or definition in wikipedia.org, including him and any of his followers. From his *MOKAFAT*, his knowledge of classic Arabic became suspect, and from using wikipedia.org, his level of academic gullibility became an issue.

Another example: He criticizes the Quran for being unscientific by reading the verses of the Quran like a third grader. For instance, he refers to verse 18:86 and understand it as "Koran teaches us that the Sun sets in a muddy spring." He ignores the fact the verse is not describing an astronomic event, but the PERCEPTION of Zul Qarnain (the one with two generations), since he verse introduces the perception as "HE FOUND". I urge anyone to search google by putting the following words in quotation "sun set behind" and they will find that more than ten thousand sites, including astronomy sites of modern universities "teaches us that the Sun sets" behind the mountains, clouds, trees, etc. If you wish you may type the following terms in the search box exactly: "sun sets in" OR "sun set in."

5.   **Ali Sina, instead of accepting his opponent as he is; he pretends what he should be and he debates with the imagined "little devil" character in his mind. He is like a cheap spelling program that cannot distinguish between screw and escrow, between hislamic and Islamic, between hadith and Quran!**

In our one-month debate, he confused me with some of his Hislamic opponents. Or he prayed that I would just devolve to one of them so he could pull my beard smack my medieval head with those volumes of holy trash! Bad luck!

For instance, I do not separate the verses of the Quran as Meccan on Medinan verses. Again, he was confusing me with Sunnis. The Quran does not contain such a distinction, and a believer must follow ALL the verses of the Quran.

Ali Sina uses the common 6 STEPS to reach TO THE FACTOR OF 666, which I have explained in an article published at 19.org.

6.   **Ali broke his promises frequently.**

Ali Sina PROMISED me several times that he would not use hadith and other dubious sources in his criticism of the Quran, but each time he sought a silly excuse to bring a truck-load of them. He was like an obese person breaking his diet not to eat junk food.

Though he knew that I would not continue this debate if he continued to break his promise of not copying and pasting from the hearsay sources, yet he went a head and filled his latest response with those trash. I finished my previous response with the following challenge:

"I challenge you to use scientific evidence and reason for your cricticsm of the Quran. I will NOT continue debating with you if ONE MORE TIME you refer to or quote from hadith, syra or tafseer books that I have rejected vehemently since 1986. If you cannot criticize the Quran without referring to hearsays of hearsays, then you will be proving to the entire world that you lost this debate against someone who followed the Quran alone."

7.   Ali Sina is unaware that he might be heading to Prison:

Ali Sina should be glad that he is in a free and secular country that people are not penalized because of their opinion or belief, how outrageous and stupid they might be. Ali Sina is thinking that he can hide his identity behind the computer screens and continue spew the message of hatred and genocide against Muslims. However, things might change. What goes around will come around.

He has already mesmerized some impressionable imbeciles and they might soon start following his advice and committing acts like Nazi or KKK members. They will kill innocent Muslims and their children in the name of "spiritual humanism." Ali Sina then will find himself in the defendant seat rather than covering his face behind computer screens. I will be there to present the jury with his "subhuman" remarks. I hope this will never happen, but if history any indication, Ali Sina's bloody dream might become his nightmare.

8.   Ali Sina is a modern crusader, masquerading as a humanist.

Ali has a double standard. While he exaggerates and generalizes the atrocities committed by Hislamic fanatic terrorists, he bypasses the bigger atrocities committed by Evilgelical Christians and Zionist Jews (I exclude some of the early Zionists) and their proxy forces.

I wish Ali Sina could be brave enough to stand against the terror, destruction and massacres inflicted by Rightwing Evilgelical crusaders and their Zionist allies as he stands against the terror, destruction and massacres inflicted by Taliban and Hislamic mullahs.

In his latest answer, he briefly stated that he was against all violence and terrorism; but that was it. So far, he has never condemned a single concrete example of violence, torture, terror, occupations, unjustified wars, and atrocities conducted by Evangelical-Zionist alliance or their proxies.

Modern crusaders, allied with big corporations are orchestrating a deceptive propaganda and misinformation campaign to promote their bloody cause to colonize new lands and convert more people.

Modern Crusaders distort verses of the Quran, exaggerate the deeds of terrorists and even attribute some events motivated by nationalism or other motives to Islam. Their propaganda machine never referred to the Serbs as Christian Rapists or Christian Terrorists. Their propaganda machine never refers to the torturer and murderer Zionist occupying forces as Jewish Terrorists, or Jewish Murderers. Their propaganda machine never acknowledges the Christian church and zeal behind Nazi crimes. However, they frequently associate any act of terrorism to Islam and Muslims. Furthermore, they cleverly manage to depict the freedom-seeking victims of brutal occupying forces as aggressors in conflicts such as Chechnya, or Palestine.

They try to depict islam as a violent religion, thereby seeking to justify their own terror, massacres, pre-emptive wars, which are cunningly promoted in a euphemistic language through their propaganda machines. They don't kill and terrorize civilians; they just produce collateral damage and they just perform colorful shows of "shock and awe." They do not torture prisoners; they either interrogate them or turn them to anecdotals. They do not destroy cities; they do surgical and smart operations. They do not occupy others' lands; they liberate them. They do not take revenge; they take justice to their enemies. Thus, media is cleverly used to hypnotize masses and get their support for neo-colonialism. The ruling class in democracies use media to "manifacture concent." In order to plunder the resources of other countries, greedy corporations and their unholy allies replace one dictator after another, create wars and conflicts, undertake covert operations, and if they are bored, they play liberation games for fun and profit, big profit.

Crusaders have directly participated or supported many atrocities and wars in the last millennium; they have killed many more innocent people than their counterpart Sunny or Shiite warmongers. Inquisition, crusades, witch-hunt, World War I and II, holocaust, Hiroshima, Nagasaki, Phillipines, Korea, Vietnam, Nikaragua, Arjantine, Iraq are just few words in the long list of wars and massacres that are committed or supported by those who call themselves Christians. Nazis used the traditional Christian hatred of Jews as fuel and a twisted Cross (swastika) as the symbol for their racist ambitions. The list of British and American wars, occupations, massacres, slavery, covert operations that were conducted with the approval and support of the Christian church or masses is too long and too gruesome. You can still find many Christians justifying the biggest terrorist attack in the history, the destruction of two big cities with their hundreds of thousands civil population, as a retaliation to the Japanese attack to an American military base. American government has not apologized humanity for this horrific and cowardly act of terror.

The mentality of these Crusaders is no different from those of al-Qaida militants who justified the destruction of theWorld Trade Center as retaliation to the American support for the Israeli's racist policy of occupation, massacres and terror inPalestine. If Ali Sina lived in Afghanistan, with is hatemongering and pro-genocide mentality, he would be a Taliban or Al-Qaida leader.

I defended Ali Sina:

Someone who supported me in debates with others, posted information about Ali Sina's website and his affiliation with FFI, an Evangelical organization. Not knowing that the information was available in public, I condemned his action with harsh words:

"Exposing" or more accurately unveiling the identity or whereabouts of a person who is out there not to create a personal cult, but to debate important theological issues with great political and social ramification is irrelevant.

But, it is more than irrelevant, it is irresponsible and even evil, since it may jeopardize the live of a person whose all crime is to express his faith and opinion. Putting the life of such a person at risk contradicts diametrically with what I stand for. I stand for freedom of faith and expression. If God Almighty let even Satan express himself and let people choose whatever religion, opinion, philosophy, or faith they want, then it would be against God's system and will to create a hostile environment and conditions that would suppress dissent and oppress some people because of their belief or disbelief.

So, I condemn the acts of those who want to indulge in detective or police work, rather than intellectual debate.

If I want freedom and security for myself, I have to want the same thing for others, including my enemies who are not in act and mindset of physical hostility. To do the opposite is hypocrisy.

I believe that Ali Sina's voice, regardless of its truth-value, is precious and should be protected. We cannot find truth without people like Ali Sina.

Personally, I do not care a bit, whether Evilgelical organizations, Zionist organizations, CIA, or any other power pays or uses Ali Sina. To me, it is not relevant and important, since Ali Sina is raising important issues, and voicing important problems with a religion that is followed by more than a billion people.

We are all brothers and sisters from Adam and Eve. We cannot be muslims (submitters to God alone, and men of peace) if we do not act like humans. To be a human, and care about the life of every single human being is a prerequisite of being a muslim. I have no connection with those who ignore and violate this sacred bond among human beings, a bond that was established by our Lord and Creator in the moment and fabric of our creation.

I Scolded Ali Sina

But, after learning that the information was public and no additional harm could be done by something already given to the public by Ali Sina himself, I criticized Ali Sina and his attack dogs for accusing and insulting the person who posted that information:

Dear Ali Sina:

It seems that your hatred and emotions have turned you to those who you claim to hate.

Here is the difference between you and me:

I do not ally with a vampire or vampires to kill another vampire. I do not ally with Evilgelical Christians (you know which Christian groups I am referring to) who are supportive of wars and invasions that have been taking the lives of so many innocent people. I cannot. Throughout history they have been on the wrong side; they have been involved in many bloody and dirty tragedies in history.

However, it seems that you are following the Machiavellian path of St. Paul and you will accept any alliance to dehumanize all Muslims and making them the subject of another Holocaust. Your mindset and mission is no different from Hitler.

The guy who posted information allegedly proving your connection with Christians might have endangered your life, but with your propaganda of hatred and general condemnation, you are putting the lives of millions and perhaps billions of people at risk. You even show the audacity to put me in the same category of terrorists! I very rarely use this word. But, I think you deserved until you notice your problem: "shame on you, Ali Sina!"

It is hypocritical to applaud the massacres, terrorism, occupations, exploitations, covert operations around the world supported by super powers and its supportive Evilgelical Christian organizations, while condemning the terrorism, violence committed by a group of Sunni or Shiite extremists. This is a diabolic double standard!

If you are a humanist as you claim, you should join me to fight ANY act of terrorism, violence, injustice, regardless the identity or religion of the criminal.

Justice and peace cannot be accomplished by holding one hand of the multy-handed Devil against another hand. You become just a pawn.

I condemned the action of the person who tried to "expose" you, and similarly I condemn the actions of USA-Inc's secret agents that have secretly kidnapped and tortured many innocent people in Guatanamo Bay, Iraqi Abu Ghraib, Egyptian or Saudi prisons used by the USA-Inc.

Edip Yuksel

My answer to a Christian supporter of Ali Sina:

First, NOT A SINGLE VERSE of the QURAN calls for killing and murdering of INNOCENT people. This hallucination of Ali Sina is embedded as a fact in his allegation. With this cheap twist, he wants to condemn any Muslim who confesses belief in the Quran.

To make it clearer for you let me, with a little modification translate it to a language that you will understand better:

> "You may say but the supporters of FFF are humans too. Is having the human appearance enough to make us humans? The sign of humanity is in our humanness. No person who believes in those inhumane teachings of ALI SINA that calls for killing and murder of innocent people deserves to be called human. Therefore, this is a war between humanity and a spiritually underdeveloped subhuman species. The mission of FFF is barbaric. Their thoughts are beastly. They have no human conscience and they are preying on us humans. So this is a war between humans and FFF."

Did you like this as a supporter of FFF (reminds me KKK)? Though the Quran (not hadith and other trashy story books) NEVER calls for killing the innocent, but here Ali Sina called for the killing of ALL those who believe in the Quran.

Obviously, here you outnumber me, and you will repeatedly post what you are instructed to do by your cult leader, but a ray of fact will destroy your darkness!

PS: A proverb states that if you want to know someone look at his friend. Interestingly, the Sunni who posts messages under the nickname *sbwus* is siding with you against me; whenever he sees you attacking me he is joining you with his saliva leaking from his mouth. This is another evidence that you are dancing on the same circle, that while you are trying to put as much distance between each other, whenever you see me, you meet each other at one point of THAT CIRCLE. When a monotheist delivers the message all idolworsihpers join their forces. Like your Sunni evil twins, your circle is made of the same ingredients: ignorance, fanaticism, hatred and self-deception.

What others say about Ali Sina and his cause?

Finally, I would like to finish this last article with a potpourri of impression by various visitors of faithfreedom.org. You will find the SURPRISE NOTE in the end of these excerpts:

A review from a seasoned visitor:

Over the years, as both a non-muslim participant in the forum and an avid reader, I have watched this site evolve. It began as a rationalist critique to LITERAL readings of the Quran, originally derived from one man's journey out of Islam - Ali Sina, the sites founder - to a compendium of contributions arraigned against Islam from "ex-muslims", religionists of various hues, Atheists, Agnostics, Humanists etc etc. While some of the better critiques are well constructed on a reading of the associated texts, none of the arguments are really informed by a believers SEMANTIC on the texts proferred. Such treatments, in the final analysis, must be considered faulty, for they do not admit an adherents view to "breathe life" into the texts concerned. There have been numerous debates on the forum of this site between muslims and non-muslims, but the modus of the dialogue is to hammer the muslim opposition into a corner on some issue of contention and then to discredit them as "inhuman" etc if they have a view that differs from the prevailing view on the forum. The dialogue is forced down to the lowest common denominator and does not emerge from there. Psychologically manipulative tools of mockery, contempt, shaming and thinly veiled hate are employed to batter dissenters. The site has decayed down to a one-point agenda, that of being ideologically opposed to Islam. Thus, it is not what it claims to be - rationalist - but really, an ideological site of it's own, defined in anti-thesis to Islam. And while it is denied by participants, the site has become a conduit for jaundiced views and hate towards Islam and it's adherents.

This review is an honest appraisal of how I view the site as an ongoing, non-muslim, agnostic participant. The site, while still containing a large amount of rationally well argued treatises against Islam, appears to have succumbed to an ideological fanaticism of it's very own. Even sympathetic dissent is dismissed as "PC" or being the product of "weak-mindedness" and ridiculed without examination. Such are the trademarks of a cult in methodology. I remain a participant, to study what I consider to be the interesting phenomenon of an internet site being the core of the formation and reinforcement of a cultish mentality. Take note of this if you wish to visit or participate in this site.

A Pioneer site:

faithfreedom.org is a very honest web site telling the whole truth about islam and it's violent teachings. Most islam apostates lives is threatened by fanatics.

279

This site gives them a chnace to speak out for their rights and tell the true story of oppressions of islam as it is.

Nursery of Fascism: Disguised Voice of Christian Far Right

Faith Freedom International (FFI) , a self-styled "rationalist" website, preaches: "A good Christian becomes Mother Teresa; but a good Muslim becomes Khomeinii and Osama." What a facile analogy! Let someone enlightern FFI that a "good" Christian can also become Adolf Hitler. Adolf Hitler was faithful Catholic after all and wanted all women to attend Church punctually(a historical fact). Adolf Hitler did not exist in isolated continuum of European history. The Jewish holocaust of Nazi Germany was merely rerun of systematic pogrom of Jews conducted by pious Christians for two millenia. All of these Christians were also "good and faithful" Christians. It is the Christian holy figures like "Saint" Augustine and Martin Luther (founder of Protestantism) who had written testaments of santimonious hate against Jews that led to genocides against them by pious lay Chrisitans. So FFI's claim that Islamic piety only produces evil like Osama and Christian piety produces good like Mother Teresa is not only ignorant but entirely stupid in light of recorded history. In Pakistan there is one Maulana Edhi, a pious Muslim, whose humanitarian work has earned him recognition the world over much on the lines of Mother Teresa. He is often referred by media as "Islamic Mother Teresa". Obviously , FFI has got it all wrong! Christian piety also produces Martin Luthers, Hitlers, Pat Robertsons and Jerry Falwells of the world and Islamic piety is also capable of producing Maulana Edhis, Rumis and Shams, etc. Things in the real world do not exist in such black and white oversimplification as FFI is propagating.

Please do not take me to be some disgruntled Muslim. I am not even remotely Islamic to have any soft corner for it. I am normal 43 year old agnostic person (with Western ethnic background) who happens to have travelled and read a lot. FFI is no rationalist website but a rather motley collection of self-seeking third world "intellectuals" and elements of Christian far right in West who have happened to become bedfellows for political reasons. This website's agenda stands diametically opposite to the minority interests in Western countries (let all blacks, Jews, Hindus,Sikhs and New Agers who visit this site be cautioned along with Muslims). FFI is firmly against religious and ideological pluralism in politics as well as culture. The heavy element of Christian apologists, and people with evangelical leanings disguised as "rationalists", make this website suspicious to its core. One would not be surprised if FFI's connection with Christian Coalition or a similar lobby would be fully exposed. FFI is catering to the agenda of the malevolent right wing forces in America who want to designate all non-Christian ideologies (that also includes all New Age movements) as cults and thus prepare a fabricated case for their marginalization in the Western world. If you are not a Christian with a Western ethnic background, please be extremely wary of this website. This is a site for Pat Robertsons of America where they can pretend to be "rationalists" to fool the gullible multitudes. Quite unsuccessfully , alas! Almost all of FFI's cheerleaders , supposedly "rationalists", are derived from Christian far right and similar backgrounds. This website is a nursery of fascism on the web. Don't trust its pretensions to the contrary. Stay away from this hate trap! Today Muslims are its targets. Tommorrow, all other minorities would be on its hit list. You don't have to be a rocket scientist to perceive this. So beware!

This site has it all!, December 14, 2003

Faithfreedom should continue its journey: I am a secular humanist. Though I do not subscribe with Ali's view, I think Fithfreedom should continue it's jourey. It is indeed a very rare and couageous effort from muslim comunity.

We should be grateful that Ali Sina exists:

This site, to the contrary of the other reviewers, is one of the only accesible resources that people can access by former Muslims. The articles go through various aspects of Islam, Islamic countries, and Islamic life as experienced by people. I forone am glad that this site exists because there is a forum where views can be aired without fear, daily updates with news articles on the web, and op-eds on important issues that concern everybody. Ali Sina is not out to kill people or hurt anybody, as some other reviewers have claimed. It is a small and growing community of people from Muslim origin (by birth) and converts who have left.

This site is very important because they are not allowed to live in Muslim countries because they are supposed to be killed. They can only live safely in the Western countries where their rights are protected and their lives. We should be grateful that Ali Sina and others like him exist otherwise we would not know the danger we are in.

Cheap attention seeker:

I honestly believe that Ali(as) Sina has a personality disorder in which he collects contact with famous people and he gets off on this. He immediately publicises his contact with those of high reknown or high repute. He has debated/interviewed the younger Pahlavi, James Randi, etc and I believe that he is just a cheap attention seeker.

His arguments are on the whole weak, and he is completely insincere... Here is an excerpt that i found amusing - Ali(as) Sina is telling a 'friend' :

"I told him about a strange incidence that happened to myself when I was a university student. One summer night I was reading a book while my sister was sleeping in the adjacent room. I heard noises coming from her room. She was groaning as if having a nightmare. I went to her room to wake her up. What I saw took me by surprise. I saw a globe of orange light about three feet in diameter suddenly moving away from my sister's bed and hovering in the middle of the room. I stood at the door watching this strange thing. I got the impression that this thing was also startled. This thing seemed to have a thought of its own. For a moment we both were paralyzed gazing at each other. Then the thing zoomed out of the window and disappeared in the adjacent field practically in thin air. I woke up my sister and told her what I saw. She said she was having a bad dream and in her dream a bad being wanted to hurt her while someone good had come to her rescue. Well, people have dreams and nothing is strange about that. However, what to me seemed to be strange is that I possibly saw one of the protagonists of my sister's dream. Even if that is not the case, that thing was strange on its own. "

Seeing orange balls of light after hearing his sister moan in the next room... hmmm.

The SURPRISE NOTE and THE GREAT PROPHECY:

I recommend every person who followed my debate with Ali Sina (which is available at both 19.org and faithfreedom.org) to share this note and this instruction under the "The Surprise Note and The Great Prophecy" with as many people as possible. You may share this encoded message with your friends via email or you may post it in other forums.

As the audience knows, Ali Sina has finally unveiled his real mission; promoting genocide against ALL Muslims, in a much bigger scale than even Hitler or Stalin had envisioned.

I will declare the KEY of the coded note, and decode it on February 19, 2005 at 19.org/forum. With the original text unveiled, you will witness a fulfillment of a great prophecy regarding Ali Sina and ditto-heads. The issue will not end with the fulfillment of the prophecy; in fact, it will just start.

If Ali Sina is scared from this message, his fear will not help him. Even if he hires several bodyguards and inform FBI, CIA, al-Qaida, Taliban, or his Evilgelical friends; he will still not be able to escape from the fulfillment of this prophecy! He and his cult members might speculate with paranoia and fabricate any lie they want. Their deception and lies will be exposed one more time the day of the prophecy: February 19. Wait and I am too waiting.

Here is a portion of the great prophecy:

U-N-D-P-R-W-J-Q-Q-W-G-U-A-B
A-N-V-B-Q-P-B-U-R-F-F-G-F-M
R-W-Z-F-W-G-W-A-N-V-B-Z-M-D
N-A-J-P-J-M-S-G-U-Q-I-H-E-F
V-M-"L-I-L-E-N-F-K-M-U-F-X-J
I-N-J-N-D-S-N-P-C-Z-J-V-U-X
U-D-E-B-Q-Y-F-Q-N"-A-X-L-X-Q
P-X-E-N-L-F-M-V-V-L-P-U-Q-Y
E-R-T-V-W-U-T-A-F-Z-B-W-D-J
G-A-A-C-X-F-N-B-W-L-I-R-D-T
H-P-Z-B-Q-P-H-B-V-H-S-H-T-J
A-B-A-W-H-A-G-I-R-G-V-V-F-T
N-U-D-U-K-Q-U-R-X-H-M-H-A-A
R-A-A-U-L-E-S-V-W-W-U-H-Q-S

Peace,

***

Decoding the great prophecy on February 19, 2005 through the key, MIRACLE (13, 9, 18, 1, 3, 12, 5):

He looked
He frowned and whined
Then he turned away arrogantly
He said "This is but clever magic
This is human made"
I will commit him to retribution
What retribution
Thorough and comprehensive
Obvious to all the people
Over it is nineteen (74:21-30)

283

21	14	4	16	18	23	10	17	17	23	7	21	1	2
13	9	18	1	3	12	5	13	9	18	1	3	12	5
8	5	12	15	15	11	5	4	8	5	6	18	15	23
h	e	l	o	o	k	e	d	h	e	f	r	o	w
1	14	22	2	17	16	2	21	18	6	6	7	6	13
13	9	18	1	3	12	5	13	9	18	1	3	12	5
14	5	4	1	14	4	23	8	9	14	5	4	20	8
n	e	d	a	n	d	w	h	i	n	e	d	t	h
18	23	26	6	23	7	23	1	14	22	2	26	13	4
13	9	18	1	3	12	5	13	9	18	1	3	12	5
5	14	8	5	20	21	18	14	5	4	1	23	1	25
e	n	h	e	t	u	r	n	e	d	a	w	a	y
14	1	10	16	10	13	19	7	21	17	9	8	5	6
13	9	18	1	3	12	5	13	9	18	1	3	12	5
1	18	18	15	7	1	14	20	12	25	8	5	19	1
a	r	r	o	g	a	n	t	l	y	h	e	s	a
22	13	"12	9	12	5	14	6	11	13	21	6	24	10
13	9	18	1	3	12	5	13	9	18	1	3	12	5
9	4	8	8	9	19	9	19	2	21	20	3	12	5
i	d	"t	h	i	s	i	s	b	u	t	c	l	e
9	14	10	14	4	19	14	16	3	26	10	22	21	24
13	9	18	1	3	12	5	13	9	18	1	3	12	5
22	5	18	13	1	7	9	3	20	8	9	19	9	19
v	e	r	m	a	g	i	c	t	h	i	s	i	s
21	4	5	2	17	25	6	17	14"	1	24	12	24	17
13	9	18	1	3	12	5	13	9	18	1	3	12	5
8	21	13	1	14	13	1	4	17	9	23	9	12	12
h	u	m	a	n	m	a	d	e	i	w	i	l	l
16	24	5	14	12	6	13	22	22	12	16	21	17	25
13	9	18	1	3	12	5	13	9	18	1	3	12	5
3	15	13	13	9	20	8	9	13	20	15	18	5	20
c	o	m	m	i	t	h	i	m	t	o	r	e	t
5	18	20	22	23	21	20	1	6	26	2	23	4	10
13	9	18	1	3	12	5	13	9	18	1	3	12	5
18	9	2	21	20	9	15	14	23	8	1	20	18	5
r	i	b	u	t	i	o	n	w	h	a	t	r	e
7	1	1	3	24	6	14	2	23	12	9	18	4	20
13	9	18	1	3	12	5	13	9	18	1	3	12	5
20	18	9	2	21	20	9	15	14	20	8	15	18	15
t	r	i	b	u	t	i	o	n	t	h	o	r	o
8	16	26	2	17	16	8	2	22	8	19	8	20	10
13	9	18	1	3	12	5	13	9	18	1	3	12	5
21	7	8	1	14	4	3	15	13	16	18	5	8	5
u	g	h	a	n	d	c	o	m	p	r	e	h	e
1	2	1	23	8	1	7	9	18	7	22	22	6	20
13	9	18	1	3	12	5	13	9	18	1	3	12	5
14	19	9	22	5	15	2	22	9	15	21	19	20	15
n	s	i	v	e	o	b	v	i	o	u	s	t	o
14	21	4	21	11	17	21	18	24	8	13	8	1	1
13	9	18	1	3	12	5	13	9	18	1	3	12	5
1	12	12	20	8	5	16	5	15	16	12	5	15	22
a	l	l	t	h	e	p	e	o	p	l	e	o	v
18	1	1	21	12	5	19	22	23	23	21	8	17	19
13	9	18	1	3	12	5	13	9	18	1	3	12	5
5	18	9	20	9	19	14	9	14	5	20	5	5	14
e	r	i	t	i	s	n	i	n	e	t	e	e	n

284

No Contradiction in the Quran

Verse 4:82 of the Quran claims that the book remains free of contradictions. Any internal contradictions between the Quran and God's laws in nature falsifies the claim. I found the following claims for contradictions posted on an evangelical site disguised as "humanist." Below, you will find the 10 charges with my answers.

QUESTION 1: What was man created from — blood, clay, dust, or nothing?

1. "Created man, out of a (mere) clot of congealed blood," (96:2).

2. "We created man from sounding clay, from mud molded into shape, (15:26).

3. "The similitude of Jesus before Allah is as that of Adam; He created him from dust, then said to him: "Be". And he was," (3:59).

4. "But does not man call to mind that We created him before out of nothing?" (19:67, Yusuf Ali). Also, 52:35).

5. "He has created man from a sperm-drop; and behold this same (man) becomes an open disputer! (16:4).

ANSWER 1: Human beings were created from earthly materials and water according to divinely guided evolution.

The criticism presented above serves as a classic example of an EITHER-OR fallacy, or the product of a mind that does not consider or perceive time and evolution as reality. If he uses the same standards, the critic of these verses will find contradictions in almost every book. If he looks into biology books, he will similarly get confused. In one page he will learn that he is made of atoms, in another cells, in another DNA, and sperm, egg, embryo, earthly materials, etc. He would express his disbelief and confusion with a similar question. A careful and educated reading of the Quran reveals the following facts about creation:

1. There were times when man did not exist. Billions of years after the creation of the universe, humans were created. In other words, we were nothing before we were created:

"Did the human being forget that we created him already, and he was nothing?" (19:67).

2. Humans were created according to divinely guided evolution:

"Have they not seen how GOD initiates the creation, and then repeats it? This is easy for GOD to do. Say, 'Roam the earth and find out the origin of life.' For GOD will thus initiate the creation in the Hereafter. GOD is Omnipotent." (29:19-20).

"He is the One who created you in stages. Do you not realize that GOD created seven universes in layers? He designed the moon therein to be a light, and placed the sun to be a lamp And GOD germinated you from the earth like plants." (71:14-17).

3. Creation of man started from clay:

"We created the human being from aged mud, like the potter's clay." (15:26).

Our Creator began the biological evolution of microscopic organisms within the layers of clay. Donald E. Ingber, professor atHarvard University, published an article titled "The Architecture of Life" as the cover story of Scientific American. He stated the following:

"Researchers now think biological evolution began in layers of clay, rather than in the primordial sea. Interestingly, clay is itself a porous network of atoms arranged geodesically within octahedral and tetrahedral forms. But because these octahedra and tetrahedra are not closely packed, they retain the ability to move and slide relative to one another. This flexibility apparently allows clay to catalyze many chemical reactions, including ones that may have produced the first molecular building blocks of organic life."

Humans are advanced fruits of organic creation, initiated millions of years ago from layers of clay.

4. Human beings are made of water:

"Do the unbelievers not realize that the heaven and the earth used to be one solid mass that we exploded into existence? And from water we made all living things. Would they believe?" (21:30).

The verse above not only emphasizes the importance of water as an essential ingredient for organic life, it also clearly refers to the beginning of the universe, or what we now call the Big Bang. The Quran's information regarding cosmology remains centuries ahead of its time. For instance, verse 51:47 informs us that the universe is continuously expanding. "We constructed the sky with our hands, and we will continue to expand it." Furthermore, the Quran informs us that the universe will collapse back to its origin, confirming the closed-universe model: "On that day, we will fold the heaven, like the folding of a book. Just as we initiated the first creation, we will repeat it. This is our promise; we will certainly carry it out." (21:104).

"And GOD created every living creature from water. Some of them walk on their bellies, some walk on two legs, and some walk on four. GOD creates whatever He wills. GOD is Omnipotent." (24:45).

Bipedal motion on two legs serves as a crucial point in the evolution of humanoids. Walking on two feet may initially appear to be insignificant in the evolutionary process, but many scientists believe that walking on two feet made significant contributions to human evolution by enabling Homo Erectus to use tools and gain consciousness, thereby leading to Homo Sapiens.

4. Human beings are made of dust, or earth, containing essential elements for life:

"The example of Jesus, as far as GOD is concerned, is the same as that of Adam; He created him from dust, then said to him, "Be," and he was." (3:59).

5. Human beings are the product of long-term evolution, and when human sperm and egg, consisting of water and earthly elements, meet each other in the right condition, they evolve to the embryo, the fetus, and finally after 266 days, into a human being:

"Was he not a drop of ejected semen?" (75:37).

"He created the human from a tiny drop, and then he turns into an ardent opponent." (16:4).

"He created man from an embryo." (96:2).

" O people, if you have any doubt about resurrection, (remember that) we created you from dust, and subsequently from a tiny drop, which turns into a hanging (embryo), then it becomes a fetus that is given life or deemed lifeless. We thus clarify things for you. We settle in the wombs whatever we will for a predetermined period. We then bring you out as infants, then you reach maturity. While some of you die young, others live to the worst age, only to find out that no more knowledge can be attained beyond a certain limit. Also, you look at a land that is dead, then as soon as we shower it with water, it vibrates with life and grows all kinds of beautiful plants." (22:5).

As you noticed, we do not translate the Arabic word "Alaq" as "clot." Since neither in interspecies evolution nor in intraspecies evolution does a stage exist where human beings are clots, this is a traditional mistranslation of the word, and the error was first noticed by medical doctor Maurice Bucaille. Any decent Arabic dictionary will give you three definitions for the word "Alaq" — (1) clot;

287

(2) hanging thing; (3) leech. Early commentators of the Quran, lacking the knowledge of embryology, justifiably picked the "clot" as the meaning of the word. However, the author of the Quran referred to the embryo through this multiple-meaning word, as it hangs to the wall of the uterus and nourishes itself like a leech. In modern times, we do not have an excuse for picking the wrong meaning. This is one of the many examples of the Quran's language in verses related to science and mathematics. While its words provide understanding to former generations, its real meaning shines with knowledge of God's creation and natural laws.

QUESTION 2: Is there or is there not compulsion in religion according to the Qur'an?

1. "Let there be no compulsion in religion: Truth stands out clear from Error: whoever rejects evil and believes in Allah hath grasped the most trustworthy hand-hold, that never breaks. And Allah heareth and knoweth all things," (2:256).

2. "And an announcement from Allah and His Messenger, to the people (assembled) on the day of the Great Pilgrimage,- that Allah and His Messenger dissolve (treaty) obligations with the Pagans. If then, ye repent, it were best for you; but if ye turn away, know ye that ye cannot frustrate Allah. And proclaim a grievous penalty to those who reject Faith," (9:3).

3. "But when the forbidden months are past, then fight and slay the Pagans wherever ye find them, and seize them, beleaguer them, and lie in wait for them in every stratagem (of war); but if they repent, and establish regular prayers and practice regular charity, then open the way for them: for Allah is Oft-forgiving, Most Merciful," (9:5). "Fight those who believe not in Allah nor the Last Day, nor hold that forbidden which hath been forbidden by Allah and His Messenger, nor acknowledge the religion of Truth, (even if they are) of the People of the Book, until they pay the Jizya with willing submission, and feel themselves subdued," (9:29).

ANSWER 2: Yes, there is no compulsion in religion according to the Quran, and Muslims are permitted to defend themselves against aggressors and murderers.

The Quran promotes freedom of opinion, religion, and expression. The critic takes the verses from Chapter 9 out of context and presents them as a contradiction with the principle expressed in 2:256 and other verses. Chapter 9 starts with an ultimatum for Meccan mushriks who tortured, killed, and evicted muslims from their homes, and who also mobilized several major war campaigns against them while they established a peaceful multinational and multi-religious community. The beginning of the chapter refers to their violation of the peace treaty and provides them with an ultimatum and four months to stop the aggression.

288

Thus, the verses quoted from Chapter 9 have nothing to do with freedom of religion. They are a warning against aggressive and murderous fanatics.

I discussed this subject extensively in my first debate, and I argued that Sunni tyrants distorted the meaning of the word JIZYA as a taxation against non-muslims, while the word more accurately means "compensation" or "war reparations" which were was levied against the aggressor parties that initiated the war. My argument on Quran's position regarding war and peace is posted at the Articles section of 19.org under the title "To the Factor of 666."

QUESTION 3: The first Muslim was Muhammad? Abraham? Jacob? Moses?

1. "And I [Muhammad] am commanded to be the first of those who bow to Allah in Islam," (39:12).

2. "When Moses came to the place appointed by Us, and his Lord addressed him, He said: "O my Lord! show (Thyself) to me, that I may look upon thee." Allah said: "By no means canst thou see Me (direct); But look upon the mount; if it abide in its place, then shalt thou see Me." When his Lord manifested His glory on the Mount, He made it as dust. And Moses fell down in a swoon. When he recovered his senses he said: "Glory be to Thee! to Thee I turn in repentance, and I am the first to believe." (7:143).

3. "And this was the legacy that Abraham left to his sons, and so did Jacob; "Oh my sons! Allah hath chosen the Faith for you; then die not except in the Faith of Islam," (2:132).

ANSWER 3: Many prophets and messengers were the first muslims in their time and location.

If we check Google.com with the search tag "Olympic first place 100-meters + running," we will find many names for athletes who received first place. If we use the critic's logic, we would think that great confusion and contradictory claims exist regarding the first-place winner for the 100-meter race. What is wrong with that logic? Obviously, we need to consider time and space! Abraham was first muslim (submitter and promoter of peace) in his time and location. Similarly, Moses and Muhammad were also pioneer muslims in their times.

QUESTION 4: Does Allah forgive or not forgive those who worship false gods?

1 "Allah forgiveth not that partners should be set up with Him; but He forgiveth anything else, to whom He pleaseth; to set up partners with Allah is to devise a sin Most heinous indeed," (4:48 ; Also 4:116).

2 "The people of the Book ask thee to cause a book to descend to them from heaven: Indeed they asked Moses for an even greater (miracle), for they said: "Show us Allah in public," but they were dazed for their presumption, with thunder and lightning. Yet they worshipped the calf even after clear signs had come to them; even so we forgave them; and gave Moses manifest proofs of authority," (4:153).

ANSWER 4: God does not forgive those who associate other powers or gods to Him, if they do not repent on time.

The Quran contains numerous verses regarding idol-worshipers or mushriks accepting the message of islam.

"He is the One who accepts the repentance from His servants, and remits the sins. He is fully aware of everything you do." (42:25).

Most supporters and companions of messengers and prophets associated part-ners to God before they repented and accepted the message. For instance, the Quran informs us that Muhammad was a polytheist before he received revela-tion, but after his acknowledgement of the truth he repented regarding his igno-rance and God forgave him.

"Say, 'I have been enjoined from worshiping the idols you worship beside GOD, when the clear revelations came to me from my Lord. I was commanded to submit to the Lord of the universe.'" (40:66).

"Thus, we inspired to you a revelation proclaiming our commandments. You had no idea about the scripture, or faith. Yet, we made this a beacon to guide whomever we choose from among our servants. Surely, you guide in a straight path." (42:52).

"He found you astray, and guided you." (93:7).

"Whereby GOD forgives your past sins, as well as future sins, and perfects His blessings upon you, and guides you in a straight path." (48:2).

QUESTION 5: Are Allah's decrees changed or not?

1. "Rejected were the messengers before thee: with patience and constancy they bore their rejection and their wrongs, until Our aid did reach them: there is none that can alter the words (and decrees) of Allah. Already hast thou received some account of those messengers," (6:34).

2. "The word of thy Lord doth find its fulfillment in truth and in justice: None can change His words: for He is the one who heareth and knoweth all, (6:115).

3. "None of Our revelations do We abrogate or cause to be forgotten, but We substitute something better or similar: Knowest thou not that Allah Hath power over all things?" (2:106).

4. "When We substitute one revelation for another,- and Allah knows best what He reveals (in stages),- they say, "Thou art but a forger": but most of them understand not," (16:101).

ANSWER 5: God's decrees do not change.

This is a valid criticism against those who do not follow the Quran alone, since they have distorted the meaning of 2:106 and 16:101 through fabricated hadiths. Quran's definition of "does not change" refers to Sunnatullah (God's law) and Kalimatullah (God's word), as in 6:34 and 6:115. Verses 2:106 and 16:101 contain neither of these words; they describe God's AYAT (Sign; miracle) given to prophets and messengers. The translation the critic uses contains a translation error, with grave theological ramifications.

According to the official faith of "Hislam," some verses of the Quran abrogate other verses, and even some hadith abrogate some verses as supported by distortion of the meaning of this verse. The Quran has a peculiar language. The singular word "Ayah" occurs 84 times in the Quran, and nowhere it is used for the verses of the Quran; rather, it is always used to mean "sign, evidence, or miracle." However, the plural form of this word, "Ayaat," is additionally used for verses of the Quran. The fact that a verse of the Quran does not demonstrate the miraculous characteristics of the Quran supports this peculiar usage of the word. For instance, short verses existed that were comprised of only one or two words, and they were most likely used in frequent daily conversations, letters, and poetry. For example, see: 55:3; 69:1; 74;4; 75:8; 80:28; 81:26. Furthermore, we are informed that the minimum unit demonstrating Quran's miraculous nature is a chapter (10:38) and the shortest chapter consists of 3 verses (103; 108, 110). The first verse of the Quran, commonly known as Basmalah, cannot be a miracle on his own, but it gains a miraculous nature with its numerical network with other letters, words, verses, and chapters of the Quran. By not using the singular form "Ayah" for the verses of the Quran, God made it possible to distinguish the miracles shown in the text and prophecies of the scripture from the miracles shown in nature. See 4:82 for further evidence that the Quranic verses do not abrogate each other.

QUESTION 6: Was Pharaoh killed or not killed by drowning?

1. "We took the Children of Israel across the sea: Pharaoh and his hosts followed them in insolence and spite. At length, when overwhelmed with the flood, he said: 'I believe that there is no god except Him Whom the Children of Israel believe in: I am of those who submit (to Allah in Islam).' (It was said to him): 'Ah now!- But a little while before, wast thou in rebellion!- and thou didst mischief

(and violence)! This day shall We save thee in the body, that thou mayest be a sign to those who come after thee!' But verily, many among mankind are heedless of Our Signs!" (10:90-92).

2. "Moses said, 'Thou knowest well that these things have been sent down by none but the Lord of the heavens and the earth as eye-opening evidence: and I consider thee indeed, O Pharaoh, to be one doomed to destruction!' So he resolved to remove them from the face of the earth: but We did drown him and all who were with him," (17:102-103).

ANSWER 6: Pharaoh was killed by drowning and his body was saved via mummification.

Verse 10:92 does not say that God will keep Pharaoh alive; it informs us that God will preserve his body after drowning him.

QUESTION 7 Is wine consumption good or bad?

1. "O ye who believe! Intoxicants and gambling, (dedication of) stones, and (divination by) arrows, are an abomination,- of Satan's handwork: eschew such (abomination), that ye may prosper," (5:90).

2. "(Here is) a Parable of the Garden which the righteous are promised: in it are rivers of water incorruptible; rivers of milk of which the taste never changes; rivers of wine, a joy to those who drink; and rivers of honey pure and clear. In it there are for them all kinds of fruits; and Grace from their Lord. (Can those in such Bliss) be compared to such as shall dwell for ever in the Fire, and be given, to drink, boiling water, so that it cuts up their bowels (to pieces)?" (47:15).

3. "Truly the Righteous will be in Bliss: On Thrones (of Dignity) will they command a sight (of all things): Thou wilt recognize in their faces the beaming brightness of Bliss. Their thirst will be slaked with Pure Wine sealed," (83:22-25).

ANSWER 7: Consumption of wine is bad in this world.

The Quran strongly rebukes the consumption of intoxicants for believers. This is not an enforced legal prohibition; but left for individuals to decide. The reason for this prohibition is obvious: intoxicants, though may provide some social or psychological benefits to the consumer, impair judgment and intelligence and cause too many problems for the individual and for society. The Quran prohibits intoxicants to individuals due to various moral reasons (the designer and creator of your body and mind asks you not to intentionally harm the body lent to you for a lifetime), intellectual reasons (the greatest gift you have is your brain and its power to make good judgments, so do not choose to be stupid or stupider than already you are) and pragmatic reasons (you and your society will suffer grave loss of health, wealth, happiness, and many lives, so do not contribute to the production and acceleration of such a destructive boomerang).

This said, let me suggest a correction. The verses 83:22-25 does not mention wine; thus, the translation is erroneous. The only verse that uses intoxicants (KHAMR) in a positive context is 47:15, and interestingly it is about paradise, or the hereafter. A quick reflection on the reason for prohibition of intoxicants explains the apparent contradiction. Harm from intoxicants, such as drunk driving, domestic violence or alcoholism, may not occur in another universe where the laws and rules are different. In other words, a person rewarded by eternal paradise will not hurt himself or herself or anyone else through intoxication (See 7:43; 15:47; 21:102; 41:31; 43:71; 2:112; 5:69).

QUESTION 8: Has the Quran been abrogated?

No, the Quran is perfect and can never be abrogated. However, some verses have been abrogated.

"There is none to alter the decisions of Allah." (6:34).

"Perfected is the Word of thy Lord in truth and justice. There is naught that can change His words." (6:115).

"There is no changing the Words of Allah." (10:64).

"And recite that which hath been revealed unto thee of the Scripture of thy Lord. There is none who can change His words." (18:27).

Yes, some verses have been abrogated.

"And when We put a revelation in place of (another) revelation, - and Allah knoweth best what He revealeth - they say: Lo! thou art but inventing. Most of them know not." (16:101).

"Nothing of our revelation (even a single verse) do we abrogate or cause be forgotten, but we bring (in place) one better or the like thereof." (2:106).

ANSWER 8: No, there is no abrogation in the Quran.

This question received its answer when I answered Question 5 above.

QUESTION 9: Who chooses the devils to be friends of disbelievers?

Allah?

"We have made the devils protecting friends for those who believe not." (7:27).

293

Or the disbelievers?

"A party hath He led aright, while error hath just hold over (another) party, for lo! they choose the devils for protecting supporters instead of Allah and deem that they are rightly guided." (7:30).

ANSWER 9: Disbelievers choose evil and devils in accordance to God's law which tests us on this planet.

While the Quran states that every event happens in accordance to God's design and permission (8:17; 57:22-25), the Quran also informs us regarding our freedom to choose our path (6:110;13:11; 18:29 42:13,48; 46:15).

QUESTION 10: Will all Jews and Christians go to hell?

Yes, all Christians will go to hell.

"Whoso seeketh as religion other than the Surrender (to Allah) it will not be accepted from him, and he will be a loser in the Hereafter." (3:85).

"They surely disbelieve who say: Lo! Allah is the Messiah, son of Mary. ... Lo! whoso ascribeth partners unto Allah, for him Allah hath forbidden paradise. His abode is the Fire. For evil-doers there will be no helpers." (5:72).

No, some will not.

"Those who are Jews, and Christians, and Sabaeans - whoever believeth in Allah and the Last Day and doeth right - surely their reward is with their Lord, and there shall no fear come upon them neither shall they grieve. (2:62).

"Lo! those who believe, and those who are Jews, and Sabaeans, and Christians - Whosoever believeth in Allah and the Last Day and doeth right - there shall no fear come upon them neither shall they grieve." (5:69).

ANSWER 10: Some Jews and Christians will go to hell.

First, the Quran terms the followers of Jesus using the word Nazarenes. Second, the word Sabaean is not a proper name referring to a particular religion. Rather, it is a verb meaning "those who are from other religions."

The critic assumes that surrender to God is only possible if someone utters a magical Arabic word. Islam is not a proper name, neither did it start with Muhammad, nor did it end with Muhammad. Any person who dedicates himself or herself to God alone, believes in the day of judgment, and lives a righteous life — regardless of the name of their religion — is considered muslim. There are many people among Christians and Jews who fit this description.

Zionism 101

After reading the following quotes — not from this unknown Jew or that ob-
scure Zionist, but from the founders and leaders of Israel — you will have no
doubt that Zionism is a cancer against humanity, like its father, Nazism. Starting
as an innocent quest to find a secure place for displaced Europian Jews, Zionism
soon transformed into a cancer and planted the seeds of hostily and hatred
among the children of Adam more successful than Hitler attempted to do. If not
confronted by peacemakers, Zionism will ultimately lead us to another World
War and another holocaust against races and countries. To remind people this
proven fact, I suggest using the words Zionazist or Nazionist instead of Zionist.
This is by no means an insult, since this is a fact that has been hidden from gullible masses of individuals through powerful propaganda machines. It is our
duty to expose the enemies of peace and of humanity, and modern Zionists are
some of the frontrunners. Let us first start with quotes from a few Wikipedia
paragraphs under the title "Zionist Political Violence."

> Irgun was described as a terrorist organization by the United Nations, British,
> and United States governments, and in media such as the The New York Times
> newspaper,[21] and by the Anglo-American Committee of Enquiry.[22] In 1946 The
> World Zionist Congress strongly condemned terrorist activities in Palestine and
> "the shedding of innocent blood as a means of political warfare". Irgun was
> specifically condemned.[23]

> Menachen Begin was called a terrorist and a fascist by Albert Einstein and 27
> other prominent Jewish intellectuals in a letter to the New York Times which
> was published on December 4, 1948. Specifically condemned was the partici-
> pation of the Irgun in the Deir Yassin massacre:

---

[21]   Pope Brewer, Sam. IRGUN BOMB KILLS 11 ARABS, 2 BRITONS. New York
       Times. December 30, 1947. Also see: IRGUN'S HAND SEEN IN ALPS RAIL
       BLAST. New York Times. August 16, 1947.

[22]   W. Khalidi, 1971, 'From Haven to Conquest', p. 598.

[23]   ZIONISTS CONDEMN PALESTINE TERROR New York Times. December 24,
       1946.

"terrorist bands attacked this peaceful village, which was not a military objective in the fighting, killed most of its inhabitants - 240 men, women and children - and kept a few of them alive to parade as captives through the streets of Jerusalem."

The letter warns US Jews against supporting Begin's request for funding of his political party, and ends with the warning:

"The discrepancies between the bold claims now being made by Begin and his party and their record of past performance in Palestine bear the imprint of no ordinary political party. This is the unmistakable stamp of a Fascist party for whom terrorism (against Jews, Arabs, and British alike), and misrepresentation are means, and a "Leader State" is the goal."[24]

Lehi was described as a terrorist organization[25] by the British authorities and United Nations mediator Ralph Bunche.[26]

***

David Ben Gurion
Prime Minister of Israel
1949 - 1954, 1955 - 1963

"We must expel Arabs and take their places." -- David Ben Gurion, 1937, Ben Gurion and the Palestine Arabs, Oxford University Press, 1985.

"There has been Anti-Semitism, the Nazis, Hitler, Auschwitz, but was that their fault? They see but one thing: we have come and we have stolen their country. Why would they accept that?" -- David Ben-Gurion, quoted by Nahum Goldmann in Le Paraddoxe Juif (The Jewish Paradox), pp. 121-122.

"Jewish villages were built in the place of Arab villages. You do not even know the names of these Arab villages, and I do not blame you because geography books no longer exist. Not only do the books not exist, the Arab villages are not there either. Nahlal arose in the place of Mahlul; Kibbutz Gvat in the place of Jibta; Kibbutz Sarid in the place of Huneifis; and Kefar Yehushua in the place of Tal al- Shuman. There is not a single place built in this country that did not have a former Arab population." -- David Ben Gurion, quoted in The Jewish Paradox, by Nahum Goldmann, Weidenfeld and Nicolson, 1978, p. 99.

---

[24]   New Palestine Party - Visit of Menachen Begin and Aims of Political Movement DiscussedNew York Times. December 4, 1948.

[25]   "Stern Gang" A Dictionary of World History. Oxford University Press, 2000. Oxford Reference Online. Oxford University Press.

[26]   Ralph Bunche report on assassination of UN mediator 27th Sept 1948, "notorious terrorists long known as the Stern group"

"Let us not ignore the truth among ourselves ... politically we are the aggressors and they defend themselves... The country is theirs, because they inhabit it, whereas we want to come here and settle down, and in their view we want to take away from them their country." -- David Ben Gurion, quoted on pp 91-2 of Chomsky's Fateful Triangle, which appears in Simha Flapan's "Zionism and the Palestinians pp 141-2 citing a 1938 speech.

"If I knew that it was possible to save all the children of Germany by transporting them to England, and only half by transferring them to the Land of Israel, I would choose the latter, for before us lies not only the numbers of these children but the historical reckoning of the people of Israel." -- David Ben-Gurion (Quoted on pp 855-56 in Shabtai Teveth's Ben-Gurion in a slightly different translation).

***

Golda Meir
Prime Minister of Israel
1969 - 1974

"There is no such thing as a Palestinian people... It is not as if we came and threw them out and took their country. They didn't exist." -- Golda Meir, statement to The Sunday Times, 15 June, 1969.

"How can we return the occupied territories? There is nobody to return them to." -- Golda Meir, March 8, 1969.

"Any one who speaks in favor of bringing the Arab refugees back must also say how he expects to take the responsibility for it, if he is interested in the state of Israel. It is better that things are stated clearly and plainly: We shall not let this happen." -- Golda Meir, 1961, in a speech to the Knesset, reported in Ner, October 1961

"This country exists as the fulfillment of a promise made by God Himself. It would be ridiculous to ask it to account for its legitimacy." -- Golda Meir, Le Monde, 15 October 1971

***

Yitzhak Rabin
Prime Minister of Israel
1974 - 1977, 1992 - 1995

"We walked outside, Ben-Gurion accompanying us. Allon repeated his question, What is to be done with the Palestinian population?' Ben- Gurion waved his hand in a gesture which said 'Drive them out!" -- Yitzhak Rabin, leaked cen-

297

sored version of Rabin memoirs, published in the New York Times, 23 October 1979.

"[Israel will] create in the course of the next 10 or 20 years conditions which would attract natural and voluntary migration of the refugees from the Gaza Strip and the west Bank to Jordan. To achieve this we have to come to agreement with King Hussein and not with Yasser Arafat." -- Yitzhak Rabin (a "Prince of Peace" by Clinton's standards), explaining his method of ethnically cleansing the occupied land without stirring a world outcry. (Quoted in David Shipler in the New York Times, 04/04/1983 citing Meir Cohen's remarks to the Knesset's foreign affairs and defense committee on March 16.)

***

Menachem Begin
Prime Minister of Israel
1977 - 1983

"[The Palestinians] are beasts walking on two legs." -- Israeli Prime Minister Menachem Begin, speech to the Knesset, quoted in Amnon Kapeliouk, "Begin and the 'Beasts,'" New Statesman, June 25, 1982.

"The Partition of Palestine is illegal. It will never be recognized.... Jerusalem was and will for ever be our capital. Eretz Israel will be restored to the people of Israel. All of it. And for Ever." -- Menachem Begin, the day after the U.N. vote to partition Palestine.

***

Yizhak Shamir
Prime Minister of Israel
1983 - 1984, 1986 - 1992

"The past leaders of our movement left us a clear message to keep Eretz Israel from the Sea to the River Jordan for future generations, for the mass aliya (=Jewish immigration), and for the Jewish people, all of whom will be gathered into this country." -- Former Prime Minister Yitzhak Shamir declares at a Tel Aviv memorial service for former Likud leaders, November 1990. Jerusalem Domestic Radio Service.

"The settlement of the Land of Israel is the essence of Zionism. Without settlement, we will not fulfill Zionism. It's that simple." -- Yitzhak Shamir, Maariv, 02/21/1997.

"(The Palestinians) would be crushed like grasshoppers ... heads smashed against the boulders and walls." -- Isreali Prime Minister (at the time) Yitzhak Shamir in a speech to Jewish settlers New York Times April 1, 1988

298

***

Ehud Barak
Prime Minister of Israel
1999 - 2001

"The Palestinians are like crocodiles, the more you give them meat, they want more".... -- Ehud Barak, Prime Minister of Israel at the time - August 28, 2000. Reported in the Jerusalem Post August 30, 2000

"If we thought that instead of 200 Palestinian fatalities, 2,000 dead would put an end to the fighting at a stroke, we would use much more force...." -- Israeli Prime Minister Ehud Barak, quoted in Associated Press, November 16, 2000.

"I would have joined a terrorist organization." -- Ehud Barak's response to Gideon Levy, a columnist for the Ha'aretz newspaper, when Barak was asked what he would have done if he had been born a Palestinian.

***

Ariel Sharon
Israeli Prime Minister
2001 - 2006

"It is the duty of Israeli leaders to explain to public opinion, clearly and coura-geously, a certain number of facts that are forgotten with time. The first of these is that there is no Zionism, colonialization, or Jewish State without the eviction of the Arabs and the expropriation of their lands." -- Ariel Sharon, Israeli For-eign Minister, addressing a meeting of militants from the extreme right- wing Tsomet Party, Agence France Presse, November 15, 1998.

"Everybody has to move, run and grab as many (Palestinian) hilltops as they can to enlarge the (Jewish) settlements because everything we take now will stay ours...Everything we don't grab will go to them." -- Ariel Sharon, Israeli Foreign Minister, addressing a meeting of the Tsomet Party, Agence France Presse, Nov. 15, 1998.

"Israel may have the right to put others on trial, but certainly no one has the right to put the Jewish people and the State of Israel on trial." -- Israeli Prime Minister Ariel Sharon, 25 March, 2001 quoted in BBC News Online, Palestine Monday 31 October 2005.

***

Benjamin Netanyahu
Prime Minister of Israel
1996 – 1999, 2009-

"Israel should have exploited the repression of the demonstrations in China, when world attention focused on that country, to carry out mass expulsions among the Arabs of the territories." -- Benyamin Netanyahu, then Israeli Deputy Foreign Minister, former Prime Minister of Israel, speaking to students at Bar Ilan University, from the Israeli journal Hotam, November 24, 1989.

More Zionist Quotes
Inhuman Racist Ideology

"Spirit the penniless population across the frontier by denying it employment... Both the process of expropriation and the removal of the poor must be carried out discreetly and circumspectly." Theodore Herzl, founder of the World Zionist Organization, referring to the Arabs of Palestine, Complete Diaries, entry for June 12, 1895 .

"In our country there is room only for the Jews. We shall say to the Arabs: Get out! If they don't agree, if they resist, we shall drive them out by force." Professor Ben-Zion Dinur, Israel 's First Minister of Education, 1954, from History of the Haganah, 1956.

"We must use terror, assassination, intimidation, land confiscation, and the cutting of all social services to rid the Galilee of its Arab population." Israel Koenig, 'The Koenig Memorandum,' 1976.

"We have to kill all the Palestinians unless they are resigned to live here as slaves." Chairman Heilbrun of the Committee for the Re-election of General Shlomo Lahat as mayor of Tel Aviv, 1983.

"We declare openly that the Arabs have no right to settle on even one centimeter of Eretz Israel ..... We shall use the ultimate force until the Palestinians come crawling to us on all fours ... When we have settled the land, all the Arabs will be able to do will be to scurry around like drugged roaches in a bottle." -- Israeli Chief of Staff Rafael Eitan, Gad Becker, Yediot Ahronot, 13 Apr 83 and New York Times, 14 Apr 83 .

"I did nothing for the last 20 years. For Jewish Jerusalem I have done things. For East Jerusalem ? Nothing! Absolutely nothing! Actually, we did build the sewerage system and improve the water system. And do you know why? I'm sure you think we did it for their benefit. No way! We did it because we heard about cholera cases, and the Jews feared the spread of an epidemic." -- Teddy Kollek, former mayor of Jerusalem .

"One million Arabs are not worth a Jewish fingernail." -- Rabbi Yaacov Perin in his eulogy at the funeral of mass murderer Dr. Baruch Goldstein, cited in the New York Times, 28 Feb 94 .

Rabbi Yitzhak Ginsburg, head of the Kever Yossev Yeshiva in Nablus , stated: "The blood of the Jewish people is loved by the Lord; it is therefore redder and their life is preferable." The killing by a Jew of a non-Jew . . . is considered essentially a good deed, and Jews should therefore have no compunction about it. Yitzhak Ginsburg, "Five General Religious Duties Which Lie Behind the Act of the Saintly, Late Rabbi Baruch Goldstein, May his Blood be Avenged."

Israeli Minister Rechavam Ze'evi will push for the invasion of Palestinian-ruled towns to end the resistance. He "wants to cleanse the West Bank of Palestinians. The Arabs living in the West Bank and Gaza have to be transferred..." He also wants the army to unleash attack dogs on Palestinian demonstrators. Source: Suzanne Goldenberg, The Guardian, March 7, 2001

During a sermon, the influential Israeli Rabbi Ovadia Yosef exclaimed: "May the Holy Name visit retribution on the Arab heads, and cause their seed to be lost, and annihilate them." He added: "It is forbidden to have pity on them. We must give them missiles with relish, annihilate them. Evil ones, damnable ones." Source: Ha'aretz April 12, 2001

Deputy-Minister Boim and Knesset-Member Hazan declared: "All Muslims are murderers by birth. It is in their genes."

If this had been said about the Jews on any TV program in Europe or America, the station chief would have been fired. If this had been said about the Jews in any parliament in Europe or America, the member would have been forced to resign. Only in Israel does such racist talk pass almost without reaction. In the State of "the Survivors of Racism", racism has now become routine. Gush Shalom advert in "Haaretz," 27 Feb 04.

What has become of the originally noble aspiration?

"The state of Israel will . . . foster the development of the country for the benefit of all its inhabitants; it will be based on freedom, justice and peace as envisaged by the prophets of Israel; it will ensure complete equality of social and political rights to all its inhabitants irrespective of religion, race or sex . . . ; and it will be faithful to the principles of the Charter of the United Nations." (Paragraph 13 of Israel's Declaration of Independence)

"The displacement of one people by another in Israel/Palestine, involving shooting deaths, home demolitions, land confiscation, impoverishment, and retaliatory suicide bombing, is taking place day by day. And yet the rest of the world makes no effective protest. World opinion is potentially a powerful force for change and has contributed to the resolution of other recent conflicts." Elizabeth Barlow in 'Speaking the Truth About Zionism,' ed Michael Prior, 2004.

For more information about Zionism, you may visit the following sites. I do not endorse all the content of the sites below; you should use critical thinking skills and verify the claims for yourself.

> http://www.ifamericansonlyknew.org/
> http://www.occupation101.com
> http://www.monabaker.com/quotes.htm
> http://tonydavies.me.uk/cl6_5a31.htm

Progressive and Peaceful Jews against Zionizm

There are many brave Jewish intellectuals and scholars with sense of justice who have denounced Israel's Zionist policy. They are usually ignored by the Zionist-controlled media. For instance, Noam Chomsky, the world-renowned scholar with brilliant political analysis, is invisible through the so-called mainstream American media.

The following Jewish peacemakers have been attacked by Horowitz and his nefarious cabal. They are accused of being "self-hating Jews," and have been targetted as Collaborators by the rabid Zionist media, Frontpage Magazine.

- Sarah Roy, Professor at Harvard's Center for Middle Eastern Studies
- Howard Zinn, Professor of History at Boston University
- Joel Beinin, Professor of History at Stanford University
- Mark LeVine, Professor of History at University of California at Irvine
- Neve Gordon, Professor of Politics at Ben Gurion University
- Norman Finkelstein, Professor of Political Science
- Tony Judt, Professor of History at New York University
- Michael Lerner, Rabbi and Editor of Tikkun
- Marc H. Ellis, Professor of Theology at Baylor University

Poor Cohen versus Bad Ahmad

Edip Yuksel

The common theme among Islamists around the world involves the demise of old glory after the disintegration of the Ottoman Empire, along with the Western aggression towards Muslims all around the world. I do not mourn after the demise of the Ottoman Empire; to the contrary, I celebrate it. They should have disappeared a long time before 1923. However, I agree with their complaint regarding the second part. The Western civilization is not as humane as its propaganda machine claims to be. In fact, the West has a monstrous record. Setting aside the wars and atrocities committed by Western powers against one another, let's briefly review the suffering of Muslim masses brought about by Western civilization.

For instance, European states invaded, colonized, and ruled most of the countries with considerable Muslim populations, such as India (including Pakistan and Bangladesh), dozens of countries in the Middle East, and most of Northern Africa, which also had a substantial Muslim population. These invasions were considered another wave of the Crusades, and Muslims fought back for their freedom and dignity. The cost of freedom in some places, such as Algiers, was horrific. However, when they thought they had won bloody wars of independence and kicked the colonialists out the door, it did not take them too long to find out that the colonialists had in fact never left their countries; they had just changed their clothes, climbed the wall, and entered through the chimney. They weren't Santa Claus, they were proxy rulers — almost invariably corrupt and despotic. Middle Eastern countries ended up with ruthless kings and monarchs in cahoots with their master Western powers. Colonialists succeeded at drawing artificial borders in order to serve their geopolitical interests. They planted and crowned their puppets as kings, presidents, and other magistrates. They killed any hope of democracy through covert operations and military coups.

Then, when Germany, a predominantly Christian nation, committed genocide against the Jews and massacred them in large numbers, the West granted surviving Jews around the world land — not in Germany, not in Italy, not in Russia, nor in any other European country with a large Jewish population. They carved out a land inhabited by Palestinians. After their horrific experience in Europe, with the help of the UN, the Jews declared the land-grab justice and baptized it as international law. Here is what happened in a parallel cartoon universe:

303

– Ouch! Help me, help me; Shultz is trying to take my seat.
– What?
– Ouch! Help me, help me; Shultz is bullying me!
– What are you mumbling Cohen? I do not understand you!
– Ouch! Help me, help me! Shultz is kicking me and slapping me!
– What?
– Ouch! Help! Help! Help! Shultz is out of control. He is now throwing the books around!
– Shultz stop throwing the books around; it almost hit me. Hey Cohen, did Schultz take your seat?
– Yes, teacher, Schultz took my seat. He is now sitting on both seats. He also slapped me in the neck and kicked me in the back.
– Schultz is a bully, a bad, a really baaaad bully. Don't worry Cohen, we will slap him and spank him!

After slapping and spanking Schultz, the aloof teacher who transformed into a boot camp sergeant turns to Ahmad who is playing with other kids far away next to a not-yet-burned bush.

– Hey, you Ahmad, move away and share your seat with your relative Cohen!
– Why my seat, teacher? My seat is barely enough for me.
– Well, because his ancestors shared that seat with your ancestors two thousand years ago! In fact, three thousand years ago, their ancestors kicked your ancestors' butt and took their seat away! Remember the great Jewish hero Samson who killed a thousand Philistines with the jaw of an ass and collected the foreskins of your ancestors as his wedding present? So, it is time to give their seat back to them, again. They are Samson's poor grandchildren. Besides, look at Cohen; he is crying. Do not let Cohen become Samson incarnate! Then, the skins of no part of your body will be safe.
– But, we never had problems with Cohen's father Moshe. He left here, this old moldy corner, to find a better deal there. He enjoyed his life over there as a banker and successful businessman until the Germans turned against him. If Cohen wants, we may share this seat as our parents had done for centuries in peace. But I do not want to give away half of my seat for good. I love this seat, this desk. Cohen has not been playing with us for long time, neither around the burned bush or the not-yet-burned ones. He has changed. He looks snobbish. He no longer wears a turban on his head or even speaks Hebrew; he now prefers European names. He now makes fun of our turbans and our names. He speaks in European languages and he wears their hat and pants. So, he belongs there now. Besides, why don't you share one of your many chairs

304

with him? You have too many chairs and many of them are not even used. Why should I give away my chair to Cohen?

–   Well, because I say so! Because my friends say so. Haven't you heard of Thrasymachus, you ignorant child? Don't beat around the bush; and give the best half of your seat to Cohen.

–   Teacher; I like Ahmad's seat. I really liked that. It reminds me my grandpa. My poor grandpa was kicked by that bully so bad that he could not sit on the chair for days. Pleeeeeeeeeeeeeease help me get that seat; at least half of it for now. Ouch! My toes are hurting! Schultz was a bad bully, a really baaaad bully! I love you teacher, I love you very much! Thank you for letting me sitting on your desk! This is a much better place! But, I really want that seat at the old moldy corner more than anything else!

–   Cohen is right! Do you hear the principle Balfour? He just called your name through the loudspeaker and told you to immediately follow the decision. You better share your seat now; otherwise you will lose more. Do you hear me Ahmad?

–   But, what about Cohen's seat? It was taken by the bully who kicked his butt! Besides, the bully has more than one seat and his seats are bigger than mine. The bully is now crawling on the ground kissing your boots. So why not just take Cohen's chair from him?

–   Ahmad, you never miss an opportunity to miss an opportunity. If you do not listen to me, I will let Cohen take the other half of your seat too. Besides, I will give him a ruler to slap you in the face, and a pointy shoe to kick you in the ass! Don't force me to declare you to be the next bully, you son of an Arab!

–   Yeaaaaaaaaaah! You bad cousin! Give me my seat! It is my seat! Go somewhere else!

–   Ouch! Teacher, Cohen is kicking me in the ass, punching me in the nose! Cohen is pushing me to the corner! Ouch!

–   Ahmad, you better give your seat to Cohen now and have a peace with him. Otherwise, I cannot help you! Let's have peace in the middle of the room.

–   Ouch! I am hurt teacher! Cohen is bullying me! Help classmates, help me!

–   Ouch! I am hurt. Ahmed is holding on his seat! I need help! Help me!

Cohen has done a great job since he knows how to cry and how to make others cry for him; he has become an expert in this affair. Though there were other victims of the bully, and many other victims of other bullies, Cohen always managed to keep himself as the top victim in the entire school. Not only the top victim, but also a perpetual victim... Cohen wrote several poems and even several

305

short films to keep the mistreatment of him alive in the mind of his schoolmates. Cohen even managed to make any negative remarks about him considered illegal or immoral. Cohen also did not forget about the teachers. He somehow found pens and books and gave them as presents. On the other hand, unlike Ahmad, Cohen worked very hard. Cohen used his mind, while Ahmad asked help from psychics and clowns. Cohen became the best student in his class; getting straight A's. Cohen also got involved in sports and extracurricular activities, and he received many awards including the admiration of the many in his classroom. As for Ahmad, he failed in almost all his classes and did not care about his grooming either. Ahmad also ended up befriending bad and lazy students. Worse than that, Ahmad was filled with hatred and tried to do very bad things to Cohen. He was even tempted to deny the fact that Cohen was bullied by Shultz and justified the bad treatment of Cohen by the bully. Ahmad made some stupid, stupid decisions, while his cousin Cohen, allied with his adopted Uncle Sam, cleverly calculated his next moves.

As a result, after losing half of his seat, Ahmad lost half of the remaining half of his seat to Cohen. Ahmad is pushed to the wall and is getting slapped and kicked almost every day, while Cohen still cries louder for help from the teacher. Somehow Ahmad's cry for help fades away before it reaches the teacher's ears. Recently, with the approval of the teacher, Cohen, who now rules the moldy oldie corner, decided to put Ahmad in a cage for anger management. Ahmad is bad, a very bad kid, a troubled and dangerous seat-less kid in the corner! Since Ahmad now has nothing much to lose, he entertains the idea of hurting himself. But how?

Ahmad is now tied to the wall, perching on the one third of his seat, one foot awkwardly forced to step backward. Poor Cohen is very scared of Ahmad and he has now several metal rulers, pointed shoes, a Swiss knife, a bat, a pepper spray, pliers, a screw driver, tweezers, a rifle, a gun, and a set of shish kebab skewers... Some of those were generously given to him as birthday gifts by his benevolent teacher or uncle. Ahmad too got some stuff. He has several fingers with long nails, a broken pencil and a few marbles in his hand, threatening Cohen with them. Though Cohen and his adopted uncle occasionally feel sad about Ahmad's bad fortune, they will be happy if he just turned into a sheep or dropped dead into the sea. Ahmad is a very dangerous animal, especially with his long nails, those marbles in his mouth, and the broken pencil in his hand.

You would Probably Join the Mob to
Lynch Socrates, Crucify Jesus and Stone Muhammad

Edip Yuksel

Yesterday in one of my Philosophy classes, we discussed Plato's The Apology, the trial and defense of Socrates...one of my favorite books!. To demonstrate the feelings of Athenians against Socrates, I asked the class a provocative question. I asked them about their position against flag burning.

"If someone burns an American flag in public to express his or her dissenting political views, what should be done? Those who burn the flag (a) must get six months in prison; (b) must be banished from country for six months; (c) must publicly apologize and recite the national anthem in front of a flag and jury; (d) pay a fine equivalent to the market value of the flag; (e) receive no punishment. Please discuss your reason."

Some students wished to impose penalties while others did not. I claimed that those who picked a punishment as their option were not much different than the jury members who condemned Socrates, or the Pharisees that condemned Jesus to death, or the Meccan mullahs that evicted Muhammad and waged several wars against him.

I dramatized my point by creating a scene, a frame in which they would hate to see themselves: "If you lived during those historic events, you would be among the mob that lynched and oppressed those brave philosophers." Each mob had (and has) different idols, symbols, and sensitivities, and they would not tolerate anyone who did not show respect to them. The idols and symbols might change, but bigotry, oppression and suppression may not. Ironically, the victims of a previous violence of idol-worship may become the symbols of a new generation of idol-worshipers, who feel justified to victimize others who do not respect their idols.

My provocation worked well, but some students got more excited than I hoped for. One student, whose father was reportedly a veteran, ended up crying. :(On the one hand, I felt bad for allowing the discussion leading to such emotional confrontation among the students. But on the other hand, I am glad that I thought them through their own personal experiences, and helped them to realize that they MAY NOT be much different than the people of the past they feel at liberty to criticize. In other words, the colors of some high horses were noticed not to be so white after all.

I asked them to never let their emotions and sentimental feelings cloud their judgment and guide their actions. Never put the cart (emotions) before the horse (reason). I defended the wisdom of the US Supreme Court (though it was by a small margin) for not justifying the penalty for burning the flag. The consistency in theories of liberty and in pragmatic considerations should lead mature societies to tolerate "annoying" and "fringe" individuals and groups.

Debate With an Evangelist Supporter of Nazionists

(Regarding my article, poor Israel defends itself again)

28 December 2008 to Jan 9, 2009

CHRIS CHRISSMAN: Dear Edip, As one who truly wants Peace in the Middle East, I was disappointed that this year will be ending with another conflagration instead of a lasting treaty establishing a two state solution to the Israeli-Palestinian situation. You lay the blame for this on Israel. It is encouraging that more and more Muslims in the Middle East are actually calling HAMAS and its sponsor country Iran to task for the continuing misery. Egypt is fed up, as is Saudi Arabia, because of HAMAS' continual refusal to sit down and discuss a peaceful solution. Here is what Tariq Alhomayed of Ashark Alawsat had to say today in response to HAMAS' appeal to Arab nations to rally behind them, "What we need is not an emergency summit but a decisive Arab stance, a position that will bring the responsible party to account. If this current escalation was caused by HAMAS and Iran to prevent the expected negotiations between Syria and Israel, then let us call a spade a spade. . . Israeli's obvious crimes must not blind us to what HAMAS did and is still doing to he people of Gaza, and to the Palestinian cause as a whole, otherwise we have become false witnesses in the glorification of [HAMAS'] bloody positions. . . . The Arabs must call a spade a spade so long as HAMAS and those who stand behind the HAMAS movement do not hesitate to make accusations and bring charges of treason against the Arab world. Let them bear the responsibility [of their own actions], if only once."

Your statement in *opednews* could have just as justifiably been with my revisions in *Italics*:

The *HAMAS* regime has imprisoned millions of people in their land, subjugating and treating them like animals. For its menacing role in the Middle East, it is receiving billions of dollars every year from *Western* tax money, as well as military and political support *from Arab nations* to continue its terror, occupation, and fascism in the region.

Here are some facts to consider:

1. The Qassam rocket barrage preceded the Israeli response. Here is the monthly rocket score-card before, during, and after the "lull" which lasted from June 19 to December 17: May -- 149, June -- 87, July -- 1, August -- 8, September -- 1, October -- 1, November -- 126, December (thru 12/21) -- 98. No sovereign nation would allow daily barrages of unguided missiles aimed at populated civilian areas. No responsible government would allow its citizens to "make war" on its neighbor unless it was also willing to take the consequences for their actions. Clearly, HAMAS was able to prevent (or significantly reduce) these rocket attacks when it agreed to do it. To condone the Qassam rocket attacks is to condone government terrorism.

2. Israel lived up to its agreement to allow aid to pass into Gaza, and only shut the borders when there were rocket attacks. For example, during the four day period from December 14 - 17, Gaza received 123 truckloads of humanitarian aid amounting to 3,124 tons. The Israelis also released hundreds of Palestinians from prison as a gesture of good will.

3. While HAMAS attacks civilians with rockets and suicide bombs, Israeli forces are trying very hard to hit only HAMAS military sites. This is an important distinction in warfare. Targeting civilians is a violation of international law, and any country or party that supports such action is condoning war crimes.

4. Since the attack, neighboring countries like Saudi Arabia and Egypt have offered medical help to the people of Gaza, but HAMAS has refused to allow the injured to be picked up at the Egyptian border. Why? The suspicions are that a) the casualties are principally HAMAS militants which would not draw much sympathy from the world, or b) the civilian casualties would testify that they were deliberately put in harms way to increase the apparent atrocity of the attack. This was done in Lebanon in 2006.

5. HAMAS has never abandoned its Charter which is dedicated to destroying Israel. There are two possible avenues for reaching peace in the Middle East -- the Quranic peace which is really submission per Surah 9:29 or the Judeo-Christian peace as reflected in Isaiah 2:4 "[God] will settle disputes among great nations. They will hammer their swords into plows and their spears into pruning knives. Nations will never again go to war, never prepare for battle again." I and many others are hoping and praying for the latter peace to be established and for all parties to abandon war as a means of resolving disputes.

Peace!

EDİP: Dear Chris: You are recycling a bunch of propaganda to justify occupation, terror and fascism committed by a racist regime. You are blaming the victim for throwing rocks and primitive rockets against its mighty, arrogant, and brutal enemy.

Before year 2000, people like you did not blame Israel when it was killing 25 Palestinians, mostly children and teenagers, for every 1 Israeli, mostly occupying soldiers killed by Pals. Then, there was no intifada, no suicide bombing, no rockets, and no Hamas! You had other trivial excuses to defend Israeli's atrocities to grab more land.

As Jimmy Carter rightly diagnosed, Israel is an apartheid regime. He is a true Christian with sense of justice. History will convict the rightwing evangelical Christians again, as it did it in the past. You never fail to pick the wrong side.

You are so delusional that you can justify all the atrocities committed by the USA and Israel. You cannot be the follower of Jesus. It is sad, but it is the truth.

People like you always find justification for mass murdering, occupation committed by the biggest terrorists, the super terrorists. The god in your imagination is a jingoist American or a Zionist Jew. You have no sense of justice or peace.

I am not sure that you will ever seek the truth about this matter; but looking at warmongering Christians who are applauding every massacre and terror committed by Israel and USA-Inc, I have little hope.

Peace AND Justice

CHRIS: Hi, Edip, You didn't read my response very carefully. I was quoting an Arab Muslim columnist. I was quoting statistics, which can be verified. Count how many times you used the word "you" in your email. (12) I'm afraid your hatred for anyone -- even an Arab Muslim -- who criticizes HAMAS got the best of you.

EDİP: Hi Chris: I read the article. But, I found that the facts were so much distorted that was not worth responding point by point. Please check this website for the truth.

http://www.ifamericansknew.org/

If you reside in the United States, you will learn the hidden side of the story in the following video clip, in which Hashim Ahlbarra, the reporter of Al-Jazeera interviewed Hamas' leader Khaled Meshaal is talking about the conflict (5 March 2008):

http://www.youtube.com/watch?v=O8TTjb54GzM&NR=1

Peace and Justice,

CHRIS: Dear Edip, We certainly have different points of view. I'm sure you can even find some Jews who oppose the current fighting, just as I showed you that Arabs are saying that HAMAS should be held responsible. Still, I feel no animosity toward you just because we disagree.

Just so you know that I am not completely in the dark about what HAMAS is up to, here is an interesting article that documents how HAMAS is using this current crisis to eliminate Fatah foes. Nice guys, those HAMAS freedom fighters.

Still more Palestinians executed by Hamas

Source: http://ronmossad.blogspot.com/2009/01/still-more-palestinians-executed-by.html

Our sources disclose that the Hamas extremists are finding time for the brutal persecution of their rivals, the Palestinian Fatah. Under cover of the general mayhem, Hamas gangs are kidnapping Fatah operatives and executing them. Their bodies are tossed onto the mountains of uncollected garbage and their kinsmen informed where to find them. Hamas leaders are convinced their rivals are plotting to exploit the fighting to overthrow their regime.

Uncollected garbage. Well they are Fatah "operatives" after all. Lest we forget who these people are exactly, prior to the apologists' revisionist history of the post-Hamas-rise-to-power era, Fatah was responsible for no less than two intifadas and dozens of hijackings, murders, suicide bombings, shootings, knife attacks and thousands of dead and injured Jews. So while we at the ronmossad blog don't feel TOO bad for these guys, they are the allegedly more "moderate" of the terrorist factions. See they at least PRETEND there might be hope, while Hamas tells it like it is. Which I GUESS is progress.

In any case, these Hamas saints, that are busily butchering their own fellow Palestinian Arabs, are the people the United Nations expects Israel to trust when they passed Resolution 1860 - which "stresses the urgency of and calls for an immediate, durable and fully respected ceasefire, leading to the full withdrawal of Israeli forces from Gaza."
Right. A "durable ceasefire" - with THESE people:
No mention of illegal weapons smuggling.
No mention of Hamas brutality against its own people.
No mention of violation of Israeli soverignty to kill and kidnap Israeli soldiers.
No mention of this guy:
No calls for Hamas to recognize Israel's right to exist.
No mention of Hamas at all.
It would be unbelievable if it wasn't so par for the course.

Thanks for the advice UN, but I think we'll continue taking care of our own business.
Bring back Gilad!

EDİP: Chris, this will be my last mail, until Palestinians are safe from the Nazi-onist atrocities:

You end your first paragraph by telling me, "Still, I feel no animosity toward you just because we disagree." What an honor! Thank you for sparing me from your animosity! Otherwise, I would be declared terrorist by you and your masters and get raped and murdered as you have done thousands of times through your proxy murderers around the world.

Who are you kidding Chris? Do you think I will swallow your lip-service to peace? You are supporting the biggest terrorist state, the fascist killing machine in the Middle East, and now you have the audacity to pretend to be a peaceful Christian! No, Chris. Either you are a very gullible and delusional Christian or you are hypocrite beast. I find no third option.

Here is what I see without sugar-coating or twisting the truth:

Hamas, the presently democratically elected representative of the people in con-centration camps where families are starved by the gestapo, have killed 3 Is-raelis in 16 years with those peanut rockets, and your Nazionist killed almost 1000, and injured more than 5,000 Palestinians of which a third are children, in just 13 days! And you are asking us to feel pity for Israel. Poor Jews, they are attacked, they are scared!

Let's think about that the Israeli solder whose picture you have attached to your email with the following complaint: "No mention of this guy:" Let's assume that Israeli soldier with a beautiful smile on his face and allegedly "kidnapped" by Hamas was just a "kid" shoveling soil to plant a tree for poor Palestinians and was in Gaza concentration camp just to buy some candies and a can of soda. Let's assume that that "guy" was not drafted by fascist IDF that has killed tens of thousands Palestinians, destroyed their homes, crippled tens of thousands, and grabbed their lands for more settlements... Let's assume that the smiling soldier was not trained to kill Palestinians, like Columbus and his men killed American Indians for land and gold... Let's assume that the "guy" was not a Nazionist. Well, then you score 1 against Palestinians, perhaps against a small group among them.

But, what about more than 10,000 Palestinians tortured "legally" in Israeli pris-ons? If the word "kidnap" should be used, this is exactly the right place to use it. They were kidnapped in their homeland by an occupying terrorist military that has confisticated their land, treated them like animals and legalized torturing them. For decades. With the support of the world's superman that has killed millions of people in five continents with its mighty military industrial complex.

But, your delusional mind, your sponge-of-propaganda brain will justify this 1 versus 10,000 injustice with "The USA and the Israel declared them terrorist!" You think that when your masters label people who are fighting for their lives, for their freedoms and for their dignity with the word "terrorist" they really become terrorists. You think when you swallow a piece of crap as a fact, everyone in the world must swallow it too. You think by being called Chris you will really make the heaven! You think that your masters are gods on this earth! You think that you can fool all the people all the time!

Let's check the other point in your Nazionist propaganda. Let's assume that your report is right. Let's assume that indeed Hamas killed dozens of collaborators in Gaza! If indeed they were collaborators of this genocide, they deserved death. If they were not collaborators, then damn Hamas. Here again: DAMN HAMAS!

Here is now your turn. Can you say DAMN ISRAEL, which deserves damnation thousands of times more, since it has the bloodiest hand and teeth in that region and it is the cause of emergence of Hamas from the ashes of the massacres in Lebanon. But, if you are one of those end-timers, if you are one of those Armageddon-freak delusional Christians, you will never be able to condemn Nazionists, regardless how much atrocities they commit. You will praise them and justify their horrendous crimes with diabolic excuses.

Before I responded this email, you sent me another email with a link to a propaganda video made up by MOSSAD and foolishly expecting me to support the Nazionist murderers. Well, an American visitor to that video has already written for me:

> "If hamas is terrorist, I dont know what word should I use for Israeli army who are killing hungry, sleepless and tired women, elderly and children without any mercy. Killing red cross and UN drivers. Putting people into a building asking them to stay inside for safety and next day bombing that building. Seriously I dont have a word for that kind of state & its army!"

Those Christians who voted for a liar warmonger president are big liars in their claims of being pro-peace. What else should we expect from people who sip wine pretending to be the blood of their savior and eat cookies pretending to be the flesh of their saviors?! What else should we expect from people who believe in modern versions of fictional stories made out of older fictional stories! They are fiction-squared and their brains are messed up.

I agree with an American atheist physicist who once said, "There are good people and bad people. But it takes religion to turn good people into bad people."

You are still trying to justify the massacre of about 1400 Palestinians, whose great majority were innocent civilians imprisoned in concentration camp called Gaza and about 30 percent are children...

The world is waking up to the facts in the Middle East, and you should be ashamed of your support of the biggest terrorist organization, the Nazionist Israeli government.

Go fool yourself as a peace-loving Christian, like your predecessor slave-owner, inquisitor, torturer, crusader, witch-burner medieval Christians had done. You only give lip-service to peace, but in reality you are a monster. You voted for a warmonger to become American president and he used the children of poor Americans to kill more than a 1,000,000,000 children of a poor country and injured many more. And like all delusional murderers, your favorite leader has the audacity to blame his victim for his war crimes.

I am not a religious person. I am a rational monotheist. And I see no difference between you and those murderers, since you are intentionally supporting them with your words, money and prayers to your distorted imaginations.

I have no doubt, Jesus will reject bloodthirsty Nazionists and their so-called Christian supporters in the Day of Judgment as he will reject all those Christians of the past who aided and abetted all atrocities of the past in his name.

Palestinians have been massacred by Zionist Goliath for decades.

May God save you from Satan's polytheistic hypnosis, which is called TRINITY. Anyone who can believe that $1+1+1$ equals 1, has a major problem with sound judgment on any issue that involves religions and politics.

Peace and Justice,
Edip

The Naked Pope in a Glass House
By a Child in the Crowd with a Slingshot
2006

"The emperor comes to speak about the issue of jihad, holy war," the pope said. "He said, I quote, 'Show me just what Mohammed brought that was new, and there you will find things only evil and inhuman, such as his command to spread by the sword the faith he preached.' " -- *Pope: Conversion by Violence not of God*, September 12, 2006, Associated Press, and CNN.

(The full text of the speech can be found at Vatican's official page: http://www.vatican.va/holy_father/benedict_xvi/speeches/2006/september/documents/hf_ben-xvi_spe_20060912_university-regensburg_en.html)

"The divinity of Jesus is made a convenient cover for absurdity. ... As I understand the Christian religion, it was, and is, a revelation. But how has it happened that millions of fables, tales, legends, have been blended with both Jewish and Christian revelation that have made them the most bloody religion that ever existed?" **John Adams**, American Statesman.
http://www.burningcross.net/crusades/famous-quotes-christianity.html

Let me start with a clarifying headnote. In this article, I use the words Western, Christian, Christendom, Muslims, and Muslim World loosely and in a general sense, since there are many sects and shades of each and it is not the topic of this paper to clarify this ambiguity. I consider Jesus and his message as a message of peace and reason and I acknowledge that most of the Gospels promote such a message. However, I cannot say the same for many verses of the Old Testament which promotes violence and cruelty and I cannot accept them as the instructions of a Benevolent and Just God. Furthermore, when I refer to America, I mostly refer to the American governments, or the US-Inc, which usually do not represent the will of American people but the will of big corporations and influential lobbies such as AIPAC. If you are not a fan of the Pope, this article should not be considered an offensive to your religious sensitivities, since the Pope's attack on Islam was not just a religious or theological criticism but a cunning political provocation that came when the invading forces of the US-Inc supported by right-wing Christian voters caused a civil war in Iraq, and so far led to the death of about 600,000 Iraqis and millions of orphan children and wounded members of the population.[27] You should also consider that at the same time, the same forces committed and justified all kinds of torture in open and hidden prisons and gave the green light to its most favored ally in the Middle East for invasion and destruction of Lebanon's infrastructure, resulting in killing of thousands

---

[27]   [As of October 2009, the Iraqi Death Estimator at www.justforeignpolicy.org/iraq estimates 1,339,771 Iraqi deaths due to U.S.-led invasion, which delibaretly started civil war to crush the uprising against the brutal invasion, massacres, and torture.]

of Lebanese civilians, mostly children. You should know that this child does not always scream in the crowd while aiming his slingshot towards priests' glass houses. But, this time the Emperor and his top clergyman declared war against truth, peace, and justice in heinous and hypocritical ways, forcing the child to yell to the crowd, Yes, both the Emperor and his Pope are naked. And on top of that, they live in glass houses!

I do not know whether you are among those who are impressed by individuals who wear ostentatious clothes and pretend to carry halos on their heads. I am not. I am neither impressed by the long beards of mullahs and their turbans, nor by the dots on the foreheads of monks and the mantras on their lips. I am not awed by any holy-shmoly person, especially those who show off with funny and colorful hats, zucchettos, stoles, palliums, chasuble, and cassocks while maintaining straight faces. I cannot decide whether to laugh or cry when I see an old guy waving a smoke-generating device or spraying "holy water" by shaking a bulbous object called aspergillum on a crowd denigrated to the level of a flock of sheep. I get nausea when I witness a pretentious cannibalistic ceremony, in which pastors serve wine and bread in a chalice, paten, and ciborium while asking their flock to pretend that these objects are really the flesh and the blood of their savior.

I lose my hope in humanity when I see almost a quarter of the human population revering a man who pretends to be infallible, a man who follows a chain of many "infallible" others who burned people on stakes, led witch hunts, tried to stop the earth from rotating around the sun, sold indulgences, issued edicts for bloody crusades, baptized slavery and racism, all while playing the tune of imperialism. I lose my hope in the honesty of humanity when a man arrogates himself to be called the "Holy Father" (Christian title for God), and claims the right of forgiveness for people in the name of the "Holy Father," and yet does not make it in the Guinness Book of World Records as the world's greatest imposter and charlatan.

No wonder Thomas Jefferson, a rational monotheist and a peacemaker, likened popes and their entourage to darkness:

> "I abuse the priests, indeed, who have so much abused the pure and holy doctrines of their Master, and who have laid me under no obligations of reticence as to the tricks of their trade. The genuine system of Jesus, and the artificial structures they have erected, to make them the instruments of wealth, power, and preeminence to themselves, are as distinct things in my view as light and darkness; and while I have classed them with soothsayers and necromancers, I place Him among the greatest reformers of morals, and scourges of priest-craft that have ever existed. They felt Him as such, and never rested until they had silenced Him by death." (Thomas Jefferson, Letter to Charles Clay, Jan 29, 1815).

So, when I heard a papal incarnation of historical absurdity and violence preaching to the world about reason and peace, my initial reaction was a smile on my face, since that kind of contradiction would perfectly fit the entire theatrical absurdity. It is as absurd as the Sunni Usama Bin Laden or his Evangelical counterpart George W. Bush preaching to the world about peace and reason. However, when I remembered that about a billion people take this guy's word seriously, and that the world's only super-duper power is run by an idiot evangelist who thinks that he is a messenger of God, then my smile faded. It must be the another sign of the end of the world! Take notice, dear Jehovah's Witnesses! This time you might have a hit!

The Pope's recent depiction of Islam and Muhammad reminded me of Karl Marx and his famous statement, "Religion is the opium of masses." Marx described only one face of the holy Janus. But the mess the Pope produced with his speech attacking Islam served as no opium for masses. It was holy fuel added to the fire created by a coalition of Evangelical Crusaders, Neocons, Zionists, Sunni and Shiite extremists, and the Taliban. It was the Pope's way of baptizing another holocaust, the Third World War, the Tenth Crusade. It was the Pope's style of joining the Left-Behind Christian's self-fulfilling prophecy of Armageddon. It was not an inconsequential holy blunder, but a calculated and cunning political wink to the global hegemony.

I have met hundreds of Catholic students in my philosophy and logic classes. I do not recall any negative incident with them. I have many close friends affiliated with many different religions, including Catholicism. I like and respect them, yet I do not act as a hypocrite by declaring my respect to their nonsensical beliefs if they try to preach to me. I consider myself a rational monotheist (a redundancy), and I have little respect for organized religions that have produced human idols and preached irrational dogmas, thereby causing many miseries and tragedies in human history.

Thus, I consider the moral and intellectual integrity of religious power-brokers such as brahmas, mullahs, ayatollahs, gurus, rabbis, pastors, priests, bishops, and of course the Pope, below used car salesmen; since polytheistic clergymen of all hats and robes — and all turbans and beards — rape the minds of masses and exploit the wealth of nations. A deal with a used car salesman may get you a pricey used car, but a deal with a priest will most likely get you a bunch of lies about God, life, and death, along with mind-torturing contradictions, complicated silly rituals, anti-scientific and irrational dogmas, and occasionally bloody jihads and crusades…

Of course, there are exceptions among organized religions, such as the Amish, Quakers, Uniterian Universalits, and Jehovah Witnesses, or such as Bahais and Sufis. These might have redeeming social and political factors. There are exceptions even among the ranks of Catholic Church; some clergymen might indeed honestly believe in their mission and they might have admirable social and political positions, such as the Anglican Bishop Desmund Tutu of South Africa who quoted Jomo Kenyatta who profoundly depicted the role of clergymen in the troubles inflicted on his country and the continent:

> "When the missionaries came to Africa, they had the Bible and we had the land. They said: 'Let us pray.' We closed our eyes. When we opened them we had the Bible and they had the land."

As the members of institutions that usually peddle the most absurd lies and useless rules in the name of our Creator, clergymen present themselves as the gatekeepers for eternal salvation. Ironically, according to the Pope's own book, the man who he worships also shared with me the same aversion towards clergymen:

> "Woe unto you, scribes and Pharisees, hypocrites! For ye devour widows' houses, and for a pretence make long prayer: therefore ye shall receive the greater damnation. Woe unto you, scribes and Pharisees, hypocrites! For ye compass sea and land to make one proselyte, and when he is made, ye make him twofold more the child of hell than yourselves. Woe unto you, ye blind guides, which say, Whosoever shall swear by the temple, it is nothing; but whosoever shall swear by the gold of the temple, he is a debtor! Ye fools and blind: for whether is greater, the gold, or the temple that sanctified the gold?" (Matthew 23:14-17)

As a rational monotheist, I consider God and the truth sanctified above everything including Pope's hat. Because of my aversion to logical contradiction and to hypocrisy, I generated many enemies among the religious crowd, including my father, a prominent Sunni mullah, who disowned me when I rejected my religious faith. This story is expressed in my best-selling books from the country of my birth. I am still a child in the crowd who announces the nakedness of the king, the sultan, the pope, and the caliph with no inhibition:

> "And ye shall know the truth, and the truth shall make you free." (John 8:32).

> "Most of them only follow conjecture. While conjecture does not avail against the truth in anything. God is knower of what they do." (Quran 10:36).

So upon his invitation for dialogue, I decided to start an honest dialogue with the guy who calls himself a title stolen from his God Holy Pope (Holy Father), with a straight face. This guy is the only man with hundreds of millions of followers who pretends to be "infallible," along with his predecessors. I can accept a priest or bishop to be an honest person who honestly yet ignorantly peddles lies and false stories, but I cannot accept the Pope's personal honesty and sanity as long as he claims "infallibility" since every honest and sane person, by age five, should know that he or she is not infallible. It is not a metaphysical mystery to

319

know that you are limited in your knowledge, and that you make mistakes, lots of them.

Before directing my questions to the Pope, let me share with you one of the few poems I have written in English, my fifth language:

Smile to the Child in You

Shunning mature eyebrows nearby,
I smile to the child in me, I smile conspicuously.
Peter Pan is jumping around with his little sword.
Paying my friends no special attention:
Trifling with traditions and taboos;
Prickling the illusive mask of social convention.
Ticklish questions hop from his sling:
       Whizzing "why"s, buzzing "how"s
       Jolt and pester sacred cows
Stunning jittery faces nearby,
I cheer the child in me, I cheer joyously
I won't hush him if he shouts,
       When kings are naked in the crowd,
       When priests are telling stories on God!
Scaring travelers in bandwagons nearby,
I give candies to the child in me, I give generously.
Each time you blink at a "what" or a "how" or a "why "
       I think of the child in you, I think anxiously.
       I wink at the child in you, I wink curiously.

THIRTEEN QUESTIONS FOR POPE OR MR. RATZINGER ON VIOLENCE AND PEACE

In the end of Manifesto for Islamic Reform, I extended an invitation to Muslims, Christians and Jews. Well-versed in their histories, theologies, and good and bad deeds, I looked in their eyes and took the mirror to their faces. The section related to Christianity started with the following paragraphs.

> If Moses, Jesus, and Muhammad were alive today, Jews would condemn the first as Anti-Semite, Christians would denounce the second as the Antichrist, and Muslims would revile the third as the Dajjal (The Great Imposter).

> Imagine a religion in which its members worship the murder weapon, perform rituals to pretend that they are drinking the blood and flesh of their heroic victim, claim that $1+1+1$ equals to 1, adopt a word as their name which was used by none of the early adherents, misspell and mispronounce the name of their hero, follow someone's teachings that were prophetically condemned by their hero, accept a formula coined by a self-appointed commission 325 years after the founder, sing love and peace yet remain responsible for most of the bloodshed and weaponry in the world, mobilize children for centuries of barbarism termed the Crusades, sell parcels of heaven, excommunicate scientists, burn the first translator of their holy book, burn women in witchhunt crazes, invent ingenious torture devices and torture many in their holy courts, declare the earth as the flat center of the world for more than a millennium, lead and pray for colonialists, defend and practice slavery and racism until they were unable to, side mostly with kings and the wealthy, deny women many of their rights, condemn the theory of evolution, support occupations and wars with jingoistic slogans, etcetera etcetera. Yes, how can such a religion with a fake name, with a fabricated doctrine, bizarre pagan practices, and such a miserable historical record and bitter fruits belong to God? How can the religion be attributed to a philosopher, to a peacemaker, to an advocate of the rights of the weak, to a human messenger of God? (Here, I should exclude the "theory of evolution" from my indictment of the Catholics, since they have finally conceded it to science. I will discuss these and many other issues in the upcoming revised version of "19 Questions For Christian Clergy")

Now, after hearing the Pope's criticism directed at Islam for being violent and irrational, add another question to the end of the paragraph above: How does the top promoter of such a religion retain the audacity to talk in the name of peace and reason?

Dear Mr. Ratzinger, I will not call you "Dear Holy Pope" for the reasons that I explained above, but I will call you "dear Joseph" or "Mr. Ratzinger." I do not think that you use drugs, but I am sure that you are one of the biggest drug dealers in the history of the world, the drug that intoxicates normal rational people and transforms them into Crusaders, Talibans, Witch-hunters, Inquisitors, Torturers, Armageddonites, Suicide Bombers, Zionists, Fascists, Bigots and Hypocrites, depending on their nationality or the flavor of the drug. I agree with Physicist Steven Weinberg who once wrote, "With or without religion, you would have good people doing good things and evil people doing evil things. But for good people to do evil things, that takes religion." I would also add political dogmas to religion.

Most likely you did not hear the Turkish proverb: "Tencere dibin kara; senin ki benden kara!" Or its English version, "Pot calls the kettle black." Neither did you heed a Biblical maxim: "Who have glass houses should not cast stones to others." Thus, your glass house is now going to suffer from the many stones of your own casting, and the bottom of your pot will be exposed with all its smoke and dirt. I call it the Boomerang Rule, the Pot Rule or the Glass House Effect.

I will ask you 13 questions on violence and reason. I expect answers from you or from anyone from the list of your ostentatious and complicated hierarchy such as cardinals, primates, metropolitan archbishops, titular archbishops, coadjutor archbishops, emeritus archbishops, ordinary bishops, auxiliary bishops, coadjutor bishops, titular bishops, and bishops emeriti, promontories, apostolic monsignors, prelates of honor of his holiness monsignors, chaplains of his holiness pastors, all the troops of priests, deacons, parishes, and Roman Curia. To fulfill your invitation for dialogue, I would be glad to answer your questions in return. You are also welcome to poke fun in my hat if you find one on my head, or to question my claim of infallibility if you smell any.

1. Did Muhammad Promote Islam through Swords and Violence?

Ironically, to falsely portray the birth of Islam and to accuse Muhammad of this crime, you resort to a quotation NOT from Gandhi, Mandela, Jimmy Carter, or another accepted man of peace, but from a Byzantine Emperor. I believe that you chose a bad person and a bad argument to hatch your provocative and false accusations of Muhammad, as we will discuss.

A critical examination of the history of Muhammad will reveal an abundance of evidence that he was a man of peace. When Muhammad escaped to Medina, many of his close friends were tortured and killed. Yet when he entered Mecca, he gave up his sword. He declared amnesty for all those leaders who mobilized wars against him. Not a single one was punished. He was a man of peace, in contradiction to what you wished us to believe in your speech:

> "The emperor certainly knew that Sura 2, 256, reads 'No force in matters of faith.' It is one of the early suras, from a time — as experts say — in which Mohammed himself was still powerless and threatened."

322

What is your evidence for such a remark? This is an utter lie and a false statement. Though I consider the Quran alone as a book in divine matters and I do not rely on external hearsay sources about the chronology of revelation, the experts you refer to consider Sura (Chapter) 2 to be revealed after immigration to Medina, where Muhammad was an elected leader of a diverse group consisting of Christians, Jews, Pagans and Muslims. So I demand the name of your experts! I hope they are not Taliban and their like-minded tyrants who wish to justify their atrocities. There is no other verse in the Quran contradicting the universal principle stated in verse 2:256. The Quran permits fighting only for self-defense (See the Quran: 2:256; 4:140; 10:99; 18:29; 88:21-22; 60:7-8. Also, see the Introduction of the upcoming Quran: A Reformist Translation).

I think you and your followers need to be educated regarding the true message of Islam, beyond the ignorant remarks of a Byzantine emperor or the distortion of Sunni or Shiite extremists. Since the Quran was the only book delivered by Muhammad, since all other sectarian books were hearsay fabrications compiled centuries after the revelation of the Quran, since we have powerful empirical and mathematical evidence confirming the Quran's claims about its authenticity as God's protected word, and since all muslims regardless of their sects agree on the Quran, here is a brief description of Islam according to the Quran. ISLAM:

- is not a proper name, but a descriptive noun coming from the Arabic root of surrendering/submission/peace, used by God to describe the system delivered by all His messengers and prophets (5:111; 10:72; 98:5), which reached another stage with Abraham (4:125; 22:78).
- involves surrender to God alone (2:112,131; 4:125; 6:71; 22:34; 40:66).
- is a system with universal principles which are in harmony with nature (3:83; 33:30; 35:43).
- requires objective evidence in addition to personal experience (3:86; 2:111; 21:24; 74:30).
- demands conviction not based on wishful thinking or feelings but based on reason and evidence (17:36; 4:174; 8:42; 10:100; 11:17; 74:30-31).
- esteems knowledge, education, and learning (35:28; 4:162; 9:122; 22:54; 27:40; 29:44,49).
- promotes scientific inquiry regarding the evolution of humankind on earth (29:20).
- rejects clergymen and intermediaries between God and humans (2:48; 9:31-34).
- condemns profiteering from religion (9:34; 2:41,79,174; 5:44; 9:9).
- stands for liberty, accountability, and defiance of false authorities. (6:164).
- stands for freedom of expression (2:256; 18:29; 10:99; 88:21-22).
- requires consultation and representation in public affairs (42:38; 5:12).
- promotes a democratic system where participation of all citizens is encouraged and facilitated (58:11).

- prohibits bribery and requires strict rules against the influence of interest groups and corporations in government (2:188).
- requires election of officials based on qualifications and principles of justice (4:58).
- promises justice to everyone regardless of their creed or ethnicity (5:8).
- acknowledges the rights of citizens to publicly petition against injustices committed by individuals or the government (4:148).
- encourages the distribution of wealth, economic freedom, and social welfare (2:215, 59:7).
- promotes utmost respect to individuals (5:32).
- relates the quality of a society to the quality of individuals comprising it (13:11).
- recognizes and protects an individual's right to privacy (49:12).
- recognizes the right to the presumption of innocence and the right to confront the accuser (49:12).
- provides protection for witnesses (2:282).
- does not hold innocent people responsible for the crimes of others (53:38).
- protects the right to personal property (2:85,188; 4:29; exception 24:29; 59:6-7).
- discourages a non-productive economy (2:275; 5:90; 3:130).
- encourages charity and caring for the poor (6:141; 7:156).
- unifies humanity by promoting gender and race equality (49:13).
- values women (3:195; 4:124; 16:97).
- values intellect (5:90).
- offers peace among nations (2:62; 2:135-136, 208).
- considers the entire world as belonging to all humanity and supports immigration (4:97-98).
- promotes peace while deterring the aggressive parties (60:8,9; 8:60).
- pursues the gold-plated brazen rule of equivalence, otherwise known as retaliation with occasional forgiveness (42:20; 17:33).
- stands up for human rights and the oppressed (4:75).
- encourages competition in righteousness and morality (16:90).
- stands for peace, honesty, kindness, and deterrence from wrong doing (3:110).
- expects high moral standards (25:63-76; 31:12-20; 23:1-11).
- asks us to be in harmony with nature and the environment (30:41).
- No wonder that the only system/law approved by God is Islam (3:19,85).

2. Was the Byzantine Emperor you Quoted a Man of Peace and Reason?

You quoted Manuel II Palaiologus. Here is what Wikipedia Encyclopedia writes about him:

> "Manuel II Palaiologos used this period of respite to bolster the defenses of the Despotate of Morea, where the Byzantine Empire was actually expanding at the expense of the remnants of the Latin Empire."

Ironically, the English word "despot" is historically linked to "Despotates" after the Fourth Crusade, and your source falsely accuses Muhammad of promoting Islam through sword. I understand his aversion towards Muslims and Ottoman Empire, and I myself never condone the aggression of Ottoman empire just as I never condone Crusaders. However, it is unfair to blame Muhammad for the aggression and atrocities of kings and sultans who deviated from his message of peace, tolerance, justice and reason. Can we blame Jesus for aggression and atrocities committed by Crusaders, Despotates, Emperors and Popes?

When I read further about your source, I noticed that as the emperor of a declining empire, he did not share the typical arrogance of Crusaders:

> God is not pleased by blood - and not acting reasonably is contrary to God's nature. Faith is born of the soul, not the body. Whoever would lead someone to faith needs the ability to speak well and to reason properly, without violence and threats... To convince a reasonable soul, one does not need a strong arm, or weapons of any kind, or any other means of threatening a person with death..."

This is exactly what Muhammad preached through the Quran. The Quran always depicts polytheists as being belligerent and repressive against messengers and their supporters. Thus, as a messenger of God, Muhammad condemned violence and promoted peace and tolerance not only when he was weak but also when he became the victor at the zenith of power.

But later, I learned that Pope's Emperor did not utter those nice words when he had power. To the contrary, only when he lost everything and sought refuge in a monastery did he started writing about peace.

Gary Leupp, a Professor of History at Tufts University, in an article titled, "<u>Defender of the West, Scourge of Islam, The Crusade of Pope Rat</u>" sheds some light about the Pope's hero and asks the following question to the "Vicar of Christ": *Did the Byzantine emperors generally act according to "reason"---any more than their Persian, Turkish, or Arab contemporaries?*

Prof. Leupp then questions the "reason" of Manuel II, who asked for help from the Muslim Turks when he lost his throne to his brother in 1376. We are informed that Pope's model of peace and reason voluntarily paid tribute to the Turkish Sultan and lived as a "vassal" at the Turkish court! "But he rebelled in

325

1391, the very year that he wrote the above-quoted remark about God's nature while in the 'barracks at Ankara' mentioned by the Pope. Then, Leupp quotes Encyclopedia Britannica: "A treaty in 1403 kept peace with the Turks until 1421, when Manuel's son and co-emperor John VIII meddled in Turkish affairs. After the Turks besieged Constantinople (1422) and took southern Greece (1423), Manuel signed a humiliating treaty and entered a monastery." Here is an excerpt from Prof. Leupp's article:

> *And when did the Byzantine Empire ever tolerate a "dialogue of cultures" or apply "reason" to religious issues?*
>
> Seems to me that the Byzantine emperors, including the Palaeologan line from the thirteenth century, persecuted religious minorities, including Jews, Manichaeans and dissident Christians, during centuries in which the Islamic world showed relative tolerance. I've read the texts of *anathemas* that virtually everyone in some parts of the Empire was obliged to pronounce publicly in the sixth century: "I renounce Mani, Buddha his teacher," etc. On pain of death, basically. There was no division between church and state. Many Byzantine Jews welcomed the initial Muslim Arab advances, providing relief from Christian persecution.
>
> One increasingly expects historical distortion and hypocrisy in the speeches of Bush administration officials. The effort to depict the Terror War as a war on "Islamofascism" shows their desperation. They must be delighted to hear the pope conflate Christianity, the west, and Reason explicitly while implicitly linking Islam, violence, and irrational intolerance. How sweet that His Holiness's erudition should elliptically reference *Iran*, while the Bush administration prepares to attack it!

As it seems, Pope's pick for his ventriloquial preaching about peace and reason was neither a man of reason nor peace. Pope should be contrite for calling such a man "erudite."

3. Which One of these Committed More Violence: Muslims or Christians?

The word terror is used in a hypocritical way by Western media, including by those who promote Christian values. According to their propaganda, terror should not mean terrorizing civilians and killing innocent people, since the West or Christendom has outdone Muslims in murder of civilians and innocent people, perhaps by factor of 666!

For instance, the worst terrorist act in modern history occurred in Hiroshima and Nagasaki, which killed hundreds of thousands civilians including children and doomed millions to tribulations from immediate injuries and long-term effects due to radiation. Sure, the bomb was not made in the Vatican nor it was dropped by a bishop. But let's examine the previous trail of events to understand the influence.

After abusing its power for centuries, the Vatican was castrated through reformation, and all churches then lost most of their official power through the emergence of secular governments. However, to feed their thirst for human sacrifice, Catholic and Protestant leaders adapted to the change. Instead of direct involvement in bloodshed and aggression, they now manipulate governments through bloc votes that support religious leaders of secular governments. Going back to the Japanese cities, it is a fact that the bombs were made by a majority Christian nation, and the order to pick those two cities was given by a Christian president and supported by the prayers of Christians and Christian leaders such as Bill Graham. The perpetrator was a state, not a gang, and it has yet to apologize to humanity for its atrocities. To the contrary, it still tries to justify this historic crime through absurd excuses similar to the propaganda from authoritarian regimes. Ironically, the same terrorist state now demonstrates the audacity to preemptively bomb other countries who might dream of having a nuclear weapon!

The recent Israeli aggression and terror against Lebanon ruined its cities and bridges, killed thousands of Lebanese civilians, and injured many more. It terrorized the entire nation even though it was justified by the magical word "collateral damage." But the West preferred to label Hezbollah; they were terrorists who terrorized the poor state of Israel by "kidnapping" two poor Zionist Israeli soldiers having a happy potluck picnic on the other side of the border. Furthermore, the Western propaganda machine did not use the word "kidnap" to depict Israel as kidnappers of the democratically elected Palestinian members of congress. The Western media, which includes Christians and those manipulated by CAMERA, a Zonist organization aimed to force American media to autocensor, kept using the same label for Hezbollah who targeted the occupying Israeli soldiers and killed 150 Israelis, more than a hundred of them being Israeli soldiers.

So, when you, as "the Pope" in a holy robe and funny hat, accuse Muslims and their religions with violence, you deceive us all. While a reborn Christian president, as part of his Tenth Crusade, leads the world's biggest war machine through deception and lies to a war against one of the poorest countries ruled by one of their discarded despot puppets, you do not accuse Christians and their religions of deception, warmongering, and violence. When the American military, which received and still continues to receive the support and prayers of American churches and evangelical leaders, "shocked and awed" (code word for terror) millions of people living in Baghdad, killed tens of thousands Iraqi civilians, wounded hundreds of thousands, tortured thousands of their young men and women in Abu Ghraib and other prisons, created a torture industry by holding them in secret prisons in countries with horrible human rights records, massacred families, raped their women, destroyed their infrastructure, deliberately or recklessly instigated and inflamed sectarian fighting, wasted billions of dollars of American taxpayers' money while letting a few big corporations in the

327

so-called defense, oil, and construction industries rake in obscene profits — yes, when all these lies, atrocities, thefts, massacres, and terror were committed by Christians and supported by Armageddonite, Left-behind Crusaders, you did not criticize Christianity nor Evangelical and Protestant groups! Somehow you could not find a Byzantine emperor to speak for the truth!

Indeed, Muslims have become losers in science and technology although the West is destroying the earth with its consumerist wasteful lifestyle and capitalistic greed. We know that the Muslim world, despite the teachings of the Quran, have contradicted their mostly tolerant history and have become less tolerant to different religious and political ideas. However, almost all the authoritarian rulers in the Middle East, since the turn of the 20th century have been the puppets of USA-Inc and UK-Inc imperial powers — from Egypt's Sadat and Mubarak which gave birth to a violent strand of the Muslim Brotherhood, including Islamic Jihad lead by al-Zawahiri, to Iran's Shah which gave birth to Mullahs, to Saudi Kings that gave birth to Bin Laden and many other Wahhabi extremists, to General Musharraf whose regime gave birth to Talibans and a fanatic and angry new generation. We also know that the Muslim world have treated their women unjustly and deprived them from many blessings enjoyed by men (even though they got their misogynistic ideas and practices from your dogmas and medieval churches, which I document it in Manifesto for Islamic Reform, available at www.islamicreform.org, and even though women are abused and mistreated in the West differently).

Yes, Christendom leads the Muslim world politically, socially, economically, and technologically, but it also leads them militarily. For each drop of blood shed by Muslims, Christendom shed a gallon. If we conduct a body-count, Christians and Jews outnumber Muslims by far slaughtering humans. Just one look at the world map will show another ignored yet very striking fact. Virtually the entire Muslim world is under occupation, either militarily or covertly. The Western media has perfected its propaganda to hide atrocities committed by so-called civilized world, while using their cameras like a microscope to pick and focus on the angriest and ugliest faces among Muslims. These Muslim faces appear to be on the losing end of the clash of West and East, resembling the "barbarian American Indians" who experienced a similar problem in the past centuries.

Instead of directing a big portion of your criticism to state terrorism, imperialistic aggression, violent occupations, and covert operations, instead of chastising jingoist American Christians for switching the golden rule with the iron rule, instead of condemning the USA-Inc's bullying and its commitment to the worst of all rules "might makes it right," and instead of standing against the Western interferences that gave birth to small-gang terrorism and violence in traumatized societies — yes, instead of doing the right thing, you chose to condemn the victim for being angry and frustrated, you generalized the acts of the few extremists among them, you distorted the history and the message of Islam (that is, peace

328

and submission to God alone), and you attacked Muhammad through the words of an Byzantine emperor. This, again and again, shows one of the historical consistencies and patterns regarding your church: Unlike your idol Jesus, you side with the bully, you side with the emperor, and you side with the superman!

4.   Do these Biblical verses serve justice, and are they from God?

Here are a few examples of intolerance and cruel punishment attributed to God through Moses, for those who harbor differing opinions or choose different religious beliefs (The Quran refers to the distortions made in the Bible: 2:59; 2:79; 5:13-15; 5:41-44):

> "The Lord said to Moses: 'Take the blasphemer outside the camp. All those who heard him are to lay their hands on his head, and the entire assembly is to stone him. Say to the Israelites: If anyone curses his God, he will be held responsible; anyone who blasphemes the name of the Lord must be put to death. The entire assembly must stone him. Whether an alien or native-born, when he blasphemes the Name, he must be put to death.... Then Moses spoke to the Israelites, and they took the blasphemer outside the camp and stoned him. The Israelites did as the Lord commanded Moses." (Leviticus 24:13-16)

> "If your very own brother, or your son or daughter, or the wife you love, or your closest friend secretly entices you, saying, 'Let us go and worship other gods' ... Show him no pity. Do not spare him or shield him. You must certainly put him to death. Your hand must be the first in putting him to death, and then the hands of all the people. Stone him to death, because he tried to turn you away from the Lord your God, who brought you out of Egypt, out the land of slavery. Then all Israel will hear and be afraid, and no one among you will do such an evil thing again." (Deuteronomy 13:6-11)

> "Then shall thou bring forth that man or that woman, which have committed that wicked thing, unto thy gates, even that man or that woman, and shall stone them with stones, till they die." (Deuteronomy 17:5)

> "These are the statutes and judgments, which ye shall observe to do in the land, which the LORD God of thy fathers giveth thee to possess it, all the days that ye live upon the earth. Ye shall utterly destroy all the places, wherein the nations which ye shall possess served their gods, upon the high mountains, and upon the hills, and under every green tree: And ye shall overthrow their altars, and break their pillars, and burn their groves with fire; and ye shall hew down the graven images of their gods, and destroy the names of them out of that place." (Deuteronomy 12:2-4)

Do you think that these instructions to commit terror and violence were given by God? If not, then why do you still consider the Old Testament a divine book?

The Old Testament instructs a stoning-to-death penalty for various sins and crimes, including witchcraft; blasphemy, violation of the Sabbath, and murder:

> Leviticus 20:2. "Again, thou shall say to the children of Israel, Whosoever he be of the children of Israel, or of the strangers that sojourn in Israel, that gives any of his seed unto Molech; he shall surely be put to death: the people of the land shall stone him with stones."

> Leviticus 20:27. "A man also or woman that hath a familiar spirit, or that is a wizard, shall surely be put to death: they shall stone them with stones: their blood shall be upon them."

> Leviticus 24:16. "And he that blasphemes the name of the LORD, he shall surely be put to death, and all the congregation shall certainly stone him: as well the stranger, as he that is born in the land, when he blasphemes the name of the LORD, shall be put to death."

> Numbers 15:35. And the LORD said unto Moses, The man shall be surely put to death: all the congregation shall stone him with stones without the camp."

> Numbers 35:17. And if he smite him with throwing a stone, wherewith he may die, and he die, he is a murderer: the murderer shall surely be put to death."

> Deuteronomy 22:20-21. "But if this thing be true, and the tokens of virginity be not found for the damsel: Then they shall bring out the damsel to the door of her father's house, and the men of her city shall stone her with stones that she die: because she hath wrought folly in Israel, to play the whore in her father's house: so shalt thou put evil away from among you."

Exodus chapter 21 has many more stoning-to-death instructions. Even animals get their share of this stoning penalty:

> Exodus 21:28. "If a bull gores a man or a woman to death, the bull must be stoned to death and its meat must not be eaten."

According to the Old Testament, a rapist should be forced to marry the girl he violated. This rule punishes the victim to share the rest of her life with the violent and shameless man who violated her (Deuteronomy 22:28-30). How can these and many other unjust laws be imposed by a just and compassionate God?

5. **Do these Biblical verses Promote Peace and Justice, and are they from God?**

The Old Testament contains numerous instructions for violence and terror, which cannot be attributed to a benevolent and just God. They are mixed and introduced together with beautiful and constructive instructions:

> Exodus 32:27-28. "And he said unto them, Thus says the LORD God of Israel, Put every man his sword by his side, and go in and out from gate to gate throughout the camp, and slay every man his brother, and every man his companion, and every man his neighbor. And the children of Levi did according to the word of Moses: and there fell of the people that day about three thousand men."

> Joshua 6:21. "And they devoted the city to the Lord and they utterly destroyed all that was in the city, both man and woman, young and old, and ox, and sheep, and ass, with the edge of the sword."

> 1Samuel 15:3. "Now go and smite Amalek, and utterly destroy all that they have, and spare them not; but slay both man and woman, infant and suckling, ox and sheep, camel and ass."

Also see the following verses from the Old Testament:

> Exodus 22:18-19. Kill witches, perverts, polytheists.

> Leviticus 20:1-27. Stone to death anyone gave offspring to Molech. Kill anyone cursing father or mother. Kill the adulterers. Kill homosexuals. Kill and burn those committing incest. Kill those who commit bestiality and their animals. Kill the fortune-tellers.

> Leviticus 21:16-23. Lynch and stone the blasphemer to death.

> Leviticus 24:13-18. Stone the blasphemer to death.

> Numbers 15:32-36. Stone to death the man who collected sticks on the Sabbath.

> Numbers 31:1-18. Children of Israel killed all the males of Midianites and took all the women of Midian captives, their little ones, their property. Then burned all their cities, and killed all the little boys.

> Deuteronomy 13:6-10. Stone to death any of your relatives who serve the gods of other tribes.

> Deuteronomy 17:2-7. Stone to death man or woman who served other gods after two or three witnesses testifies against them.

Deuteronomy 20:16-17. Kill every living being in the cities of Hittites, Amorites, Canaanites, Perizzites, Hivites, and Jebusites, and utterly destroy their cities.

Deuteronomy 22:23-24. Stone to death the adulterers.

Deuteronomy 25:11-12. Cut off a woman's hand if she holds the balls of another man while her husband is fighting with.

Joshua 6:20-21. Joshua and his men utterly destroyed all that was in the city, both man and woman, young and old, ox, sheep and ass, with the edge of the sword.

Judges 1:4-12. Judah killed ten thousand men from Canaanites and Perizzites; and cut off the thumbs and toes of their leaders. Judah fought against Jerusalem and set it on fire. Then, Judah slew Sheshai, Ahiman,Talmai, and then attacked the inhabitants of Debir.

Judges 3:22-29. The people of the Israel were saved by an assassin who deceptively reached to the King Eglon of Moab and stabbed him to death. Ehud led a gang of Israelis to Moab and killed 10,000 of their men.

1 Samuel 15:3. God sent Samuel to smite Amalek and utterly destroy all they have, sparing nothing, slaying both men and women, infant and suckling, ox and sheep, camel and ass.

2 Kings 2:23-24. When the little children of Bathel called Elisha 'baldhead' he cursed them and soon two bears came out and mauled 42 of the children.

2 Chronicles 15:13. Whosoever would not seek the Lord God of Israel should be put to death, whether small or great, whether man or woman.

Psalms 58:10-11. The righteous shall rejoice when he sees the vengeance: he shall wash his feet in the blood of the wicked.

Psalms 137:9. Happy is he who dashes the infants of Babylon to the rocks.

Psalms 149:6-9. Praise God and execute vengeance with a two edged sword against heathens.

Isaiah 13:13-16. Their infants will be dashed to pieces before their eyes; their houses will be looted and their wives ravished.

Jeremiah 48:10. Whoever keeps his sword from bloodshed is cursed.

Jeremiah 51:10-24. Israel is God's battle axe and weapons of war. Ambush Babylon and destroy them to take vengeance. With Israel

God will break the nations in pieces, will break the man and woman, the old and young in pieces,

Ezekiel 9:5-6. Go to Jerusalem and kill, without showing pity or compassion. Slaughter old men, young men and maidens, women and children, but do not touch anyone who has the mark.

Ezekiel 23:25. Israel's God will direct his jealous anger against Babylonians, Chaldeans, Pekod, Shoa, Koa, and the Assyrians, and they will be dealt with in fury. Their noses and ears will be cut off, and they will fall by the sword. Their sons and daughters will be taken, and those who are left will be consumed by fire.

Zephaniah 3:8. The fire of God's jealous anger will consume the whole world.

The New Testament, however, contains a better teaching. Nevertheless, since the New Testament relies on many verses of the Old Testament and ambiguities exist regarding the degree of its validity for Christians, Christians have justified many barbaric acts, atrocities, and torture by using and abusing the verses of both Old and New Testaments. These include:

Matthew 5:17-18. "Think not that I am come to destroy the law, or the prophets: I am not come to destroy, but to fulfill. For verily I say unto you, Till heaven and earth pass, one jot or one tittle shall in no wise pass from the law, till all be fulfilled."

Matthew 10:34. "Think not that I am come to send peace on earth: I came not to send peace, but a sword."

1Peter 2:13-14. "Submit yourselves to every ordinance of man for the Lord's sake: whether it be to the king, as supreme; Or unto governors, as unto them that are sent by him for the punishment of evildoers, and for the praise of them that do well." (Following this instruction, many atrocities and wars were committed by Christians)

Below are other verses in the New Testament that have been used for justification of violence and many atrocities:

Mat 29-30;
Mat 19:12;
Mat 21:19;
John 15:6 (was abused by the church and used together with Exodus 22:18 to burn witches)

6. Were the Crusaders and their Popes good Christians?

You might justify Pope Alexander II giving papal blessings that started the Crusades against the advancing Muslim invaders, but what about Saint Augustine of Hippo's justification of use of force in the service of Christ? How does it differ from justifications given by Muslims? How do you explain the violence and atrocities committed by Crusaders against Muslims when they took Jerusalem during the Third Crusade, compared to the forgiveness and tolerance of Muslims who won under the leadership of Sultan Saladin?

What do you think about the atrocities of Crusaders against Orthodox Christians and Jews? What do you think of Pope Innocent III who considered the alleged Christian children's interest in joining the crusade as good news? What do you think about anti-Semitic legislations imposed by Pope Innocent III? Was he also "infallible" or "innocent" like all other Popes including you?

7. Was the Church Justified in Strangling and Burning Tyndale on the Stake?

For the crime of translating the Bible into English, in 1535, Tyndale was tried by the Catholic Church for heresy and treason and then strangled and burnt at the stake. Do you condemn the Pope who allowed Cardinal Wolsey to roast Tyndale? How can the Pope who approved such a religious verdict still be considered "infallible" by your religion?

8. Were the witch-hunters Christians?

Starting from the middle fourteenth until the beginning of eighteenth century, the Catholic Church terrorized Europe, especially its women population, through the witch craze. During that period, it is estimated that well above two hundred thousand people were burned, hanged, and tortured as witches. This was one the biggest acts of terrorism in human history.

> There was no possible piece of evidence that could show that the accused was not a witch. Once an accusation was made, no matter how flimsy the grounds for it, the accused was arrested. At this point, the accused was asked to confess to the charges. If the confession was not made, the accused was tortured. If a confession was still not made, the torture continued… There was no way out. If one confessed without torture to be witch, one was executed. If one did not confess at once, one was tortured until one did and was then executed. If one confessed and later recanted the confession, the torture started anew. To make matters worse for the accused, who might be willing to confess at once simply to escape torture, one was asked to name acquaintances who had engaged in witchcraft. If names were not forthcoming, they were extracted, again, under torture. These other individuals were then rounded up and tortured into confessing and naming still more

334

"witches," and so the horrible cycle went on. (<u>Pseudoscience and the</u> <u>Paranormal: A Critical Examination of the Evidence</u>, Terrence Hines, Prometheus Books, 1988, pp. 18-19).

Here is a description of some torture methods from Encyclopedia Wikipedia :

> "One of the most common forms of medieval inquisition torture was known as strappado. The hands were bound behind the back with a rope, and the accused was suspended this way, dislocating the joints painfully in both arms. Weights could be added to the legs dislocating those joints as well. Other torture methods could include the rack (stretching the victim's joints to breaking point), the thumbscrew, the boot (some versions of which crushed the calf, ankle, and heel between vertically positioned boards, while others tortured the instep and toes between horizontally oriented plates), water (massive quantities of water forcibly ingested–or even mixed with urine, pepper, diarrhea, etc., for additional persuasiveness), and red-hot pincers (typically applied to fingers, toes, ears, noses and nipples, although one tubular version [the "crocodile shears"] was specially devised for application to the penis in cases of regicide), although it was technically against church policy to mutilate a person's body. If stronger methods were needed, or death, the person was handed over to the secular authorities who were not bound by any restrictions."

This evil Church tradition might explain why the so-called reborn Evangelical Christian president of the US did not hesitate to permit the Military, CIA, and FBI to torture Muslim prisoners in Abu Ghraib, Guantanamo, and secret prisons in other countries, even though these prisoners were mostly innocent people held without charge and due process of law.

To learn more about torture and the creative torture machines invented by our preachers of love and peace, see the following websites:

> http://en.wikipedia.org/wiki/Torture
> http://www.antiwar.com/news/?articleid=8560
> http://www.lawbuzz.com/tyranny/torture/torture2.htm
> http://www.michiganatheists.org/events/caro/caro.html

9.   Were Hitler, Mussolini, Pope Pius XII, and their followers Christians?

In Mein Kampf, Hitler refers to the Bible numerous times to justify his actions. His supporters considered themselves Christians.

> "My feelings as a Christian points me to my Lord and Savior as a fighter. It points me to the man who once in loneliness, surrounded by a few followers, recognized these Jews for what they were and summoned men to fight against them and who, God's truth! was greatest not as a sufferer but as a fighter. In boundless love as a Christian and as a man I read through the passage which tells us how the Lord at last

335

rose in His might and seized the scourge to drive out of the Temple the brood of vipers and adders. How terrific was His fight for the world against the Jewish poison. To-day, after two thousand years, with deepest emotion I recognize more profoundly than ever before the fact that it was for this that He had to shed His blood upon the Cross. As a Christian I have no duty to allow myself to be cheated, but I have the duty to be a fighter for truth and justice... And if there is anything which could demonstrate that we are acting rightly it is the distress that daily grows. For as a Christian I have also a duty to my own people." - Adolf Hitler, in a speech on 12 April 1922 (Norman H. Baynes, ed. *The Speeches of Adolf Hitler*, April 1922-August 1939, Vol. 1 of 2, pp. 19-20, Oxford University Press, 1942)

It is claimed that Hitler was a Catholic and that he was never excommunicated by your church. I am not a historian who has the proper erudition and learning to study this claim on my own. However, we know that millions of Germans and the majority of Italy's population who supported Fascist aggression and atrocities called themselves Catholics. Mr. Ratzinger, if you know how to browse the Internet, which I doubt, please check the following links regarding the religious justifications and references made by Hitler:

> www.nobeliefs.com/hitler.htm
> www.infidels.org/library/modern/joh...onofhitler.html
> www.sullivan-county.com/nf0/hitler/hitler1.htm

History is filled with Christian leaders who professed deep religious conviction, yet were responsible from most horrendous crimes. Here is a short list of modern Christian racists, Christian fascists, Christian terrorists, and Christian warmongers:

Jefferson Davis (1808-1889): As a leader of the Confederacy, he enslaved a tenth of Americans and declared war on the other 60 percent. The Jefferson Davis Society's web page at Georgia's official state site brags about his Christian values: "May we never forget that Jefferson Davis, even though a leader of 'a cause that lost', as President of the Confederate States of America was indeed the commander-in-Chief of the Army, Navy, and several state militias of a government whose history proved to have fought one of the mightiest wars of modern time... The name Jefferson Davis will always inspire the hearts of young and old with patriotic thoughts, deeds of heroism, noble endurance, and Christian kindness, and will shine in the firmament of history to all generations to come."
http://www.state.ga.us/civilwar/davis.html

Hong Xiuquan (1814-1864): Christian Rebel who led an authoritarian sect and enacted atrocities costing the lives of millions in China.

Nathan Bedford Forrest (1821-1877): The Confederate general who became the first Grand Wizard of the KKK.

King Leopold of Belgium (1835 –1909): With the support of Christian missionaries, he pursued a colonialist and genocidal policy, killing an estimated 5 to 15 millions of Congo Africans. He turned the Belgian Congo into "a colonial regime of slave labor, rape and mutilation".

D.F. Malan (1874-1952): The Dutch-ordained minister, together with other Christian missionaries, helped in the creation of the Apartheid system in South Africa.

Pope Pius XII (1876-1958): Born as Eugenio Maria Giuseppe Giovanni Pacelli, this guy, according to some historians, supported Hitler in his rise to power. His representative Archbishop Cesare Orsenigo met Hitler personally in 1936 in Berlin. Papal Chamberlain and Roman Catholic priest Monsignor Joseph Tiso shook hands with Hitler in 1941. Pope Pius refused to publicly denounce Nazis in 1943. Even if the Pope whole-heartedly did not support Nazi's, it is clear that he acted cowardly and stood by complacently when Christians committed one of the biggest atrocities in history against Jews and other minorities.

Adolph Hitler (1889-1945): Supported by Protestant Germans and Catholic Italy, he committed genocide and horrendous atrocities against Jews, Gypsies, and other minorities. The Catholic Church remained silent.

Billy Graham (1918-?): This protestant evangelist who has prayed with ten successive U.S. presidents and received number 7 on Gallup's list of admired people for the 20th century. As one of the most prominent members of the Southern Baptist Convention, he baptized many aggressive wars and atrocities committed by the US government.

Rios Montts (1926-?): Evangelical Christian who became the dictator of Guatemala in 1982, he enacted his reign of terror with rapes, death squads and genocide, wiping over 400 indigenous villages.

Pat Robertson (1930-?): The influential televangelist who passionately supports the occupation of Palestine by the terrorist Zionist forces that have massacred tens of thousands of Palestinians and killed many of their young children. He also issued a fatwa for the assassination of Hugo Chavez, Venezuela's popular anti-imperialistic president.

If one tallies the number of dead and injured as the cause of just the above-listed Christians, and compares it to the number of dead and injured by Muslims, one will find that violence committed by Christians and their allies is at least greater by a factor of 666 than the violence committed by Muslims.

10. Do You Consider George W Bush and his Supporters Christians?

First let me briefly introduce George W. Bush (1946-2007). He is the grand-grand-son of Samuel Prescott Bush, who made a fortune in arms deals as one of the most prominent "Merchants of Death," the grand-son of Senator Prescott

Bush, who was implicated in profiting off slave labor and off the Auschwitz concentration camp, and the son of George H. W. Bush who started the first war against Iraq. He is an evangelical re-born Christian, and a Left-Behind, Armageddonite crusader. He adopted the iron rule — that is, "pre-emptive strike" — and waged war on Iraq based on lies and deception, causing the death of tens of thousands of civilians and the destruction of an entire nation who had not attacked the US. He supported Israel unconditionally even in the face of its fascist policy against Palestinians and its recent aggression and atrocities against Lebanon. He also ordered the torture of prisoners and tried to legalize torture and take many of the civil rights cherished by American citizens.

Now, why don't you condemn Bush and Company? Why don't you declare them warmongers, war-profiteers, terrorists, and irrational individuals? The Wahhabi Bin Laden caused the death of thousands of innocent people. On the other hand, the Evangelical Bush and his company deliberately deceived the American people and caused the death of hundreds of thousands of innocent people, thousands of which are the children of "lower class" Americans. Ironically, Bush's ardent supporters in his warmongering and torture-justifying policies have been the Evangelical Church and clergymen. Bin Laden might have duped a few thousand people to join his terrorist gang, but Bush and his company duped a superpower with 300 million people and hundreds of billions of dollars to join his terror and neocolonialism. From Bosnia to Chechnya, from Afghanistan to Iraq, from Palestine to Lebanon, many more Muslim children and innocent civilians are killed by the bombs and bullets of Christians and their allies than the other way around. It is no surprise that cruel occupations and atrocities committed by the so-called civilized terrorist states have given birth to gang terrorism in those lands.

So, if you indeed follow the teachings of Jesus, then shouldn't you have stopped using the double standard and raised your voice for justice and peace!

11. When did the world start rotating around the sun in the Vatican?

The Catholic Church, with its extensive hierarchy and powerful alliances, tried to suppress many different faiths, philosophies, and scientific ideas. The Church condemned any idea questioning its dogmas as "heresy," and tried to intimidate and eliminate the proponents of such ideas. It occasionally used extremely cruel and barbaric methods. For instance, Manicheans, Arians, Catharis, Waldenses, Hussites, Lutherans, Calvinists, and Rosicrucians were all targeted for their differing religious ideas and practices.

Starting with the ruling of Pope Gregory IX, a more systematic suppression of heresies was initiated in 1231. Life imprisonment, capital punishment, burning at the stake, and numerous sadistic tortures were carried out against "heretics." Furthermore, all the properties of the convicted heretics were confiscated by the Catholic Church. Thus, a significant portion of the Vatican's wealth is the spoil of those robberies and murders committed in the name of Jesus. The Spanish

Inquisition specially became notorious for its atrocities against converted Muslims, Jews and illuminists.

> "In 1231, Pope Gregory IX published a decree which called for life imprisonment with salutary penance for the heretic who had confessed and repented, and capital punishment for those who persisted. The secular authorities were to carry out the execution. Pope Gregory relieved the bishops and archbishops of this obligation and made it the duty of the Dominican Order, though many inquisitors were members of other orders or of the secular clergy. ... Penalties went from visits to churches, pilgrimages, and wearing the cross of infamy to imprisonment (usually for life, but the sentences were often commuted) and (if the accused would not abjure) death. Death occurred by burning at the stake, and it was carried out by the secular authorities. In some serious cases when the accused had died before proceedings could be instituted, his or her remains could be exhumed and burned. Death or life imprisonment was always accompanied by the confiscation of all the accused's property." (The Inquisition, http://galileo.rice.edu/chr/inquisition.html)

Galileo was one of the many who suffered the holy condemnation of the "infallible" Pope. In 1616, the consultants working for the so-called Holy Office declared the idea of Earth rotating around the Sun, to be "foolish and absurd in philosophy." After this ruling, The Revolution of Heavenly Bodies by Copernicus was listed in the Index of Forbidden Books. Galileo was threatened regarding his affirmation of the same ideas as Copernicus, and in 1633 he was tried by the Inquisition court for his scientific claims.

Before Galileo, another scientist, Italian philosopher Giordano Bruno was tortured and then burned at the stake as a heretic for speculating that there could be life in other worlds.

Do you think that the Popes who opposed Galileo and Bruno in the name of God were "infallible?" Who was the first Pope that accepted the reality that the Earth is rotating around the Sun, not the other way around? Who was the first Pope that accepted the possibility of extraterrestrial life? How could a religious teaching that follows science centuries behind be considered divine?

12. Was Your Great Hero Tertullian a Man of Reason?

Tertullian, the one who gave birth to the doctrine of the Christian Trinity in the 325AC Nicene Conference, wrote one of the fanciest defenses for dogmatism, bigotry and narrow-mindedness. He tried to banish reason by using lousy reasoning:

> "These are human and demonic doctrines, engendered for itching ears by the ingenuity of that worldly wisdom which the Lord called foolishness, choosing the foolish things of the world to put philosophy to shame. For

worldly wisdom culminates in philosophy with its rash interpretation of God's nature and purpose. It is philosophy that supplies the heresies with their equipment… After Jesus Christ we have no need of speculation, after the Gospel no need of research. When we come to believe, we have no desire to believe anything else; for we begin by believing that there is nothing else which we have to believe." (The Prescriptions Against the Heretics).

According to the 43 articles of your polytheistic Athanasian Creed, those who do not believe faithfully in your twisted math and logic which can be summarized as 1+1+1=1 cannot be saved. You define God and Man differently, yet you think that Jesus was at the same time fully God and fully man. No linguistic somersault and no holy mumbo jumbo will be able to make such an absurdity compatible with reason. Is it reasonable for a person who accepts a logical contradiction as the center of his faith to preach to others about reason? Is it reasonable for an institution considering a bigot named Tertullian as a holy man to preach reason?

13. What about Misogynistic Eunuchs, Celibate Pastors and Popes?

First, I would like present you the following two paragraph; from my notes on verse 42:21 in Quran: a Reformist Translation.

The religion that the so-called Muslims inherited from their parents and try hard to practice today has little to do with the system of surrendering to God alone, which was delivered by Muhammad through the Quran. These clergymen who arrogated themselves and falsely claimed to be the "*ulama*" (people of knowledge), polluted the message of islam with ignorance. They fabricated numerous *sharias* (laws), prohibitions, veils, beards, turbans, rules on how to clean one's bottom, rules on how to pee in the bathroom, toothbrushes, right hands, left hands, right feet, left feet, *hadiths*, *sunnas*, intercession, holy hair, holy clothes, holy teeth, holy feet traces, *hazrats*, lords, saints, *mawlas*, *mahdies*, innocent *emams*, orders, sects, rosaries, amulets, dreams, holy loopholes, prayer caps, circumcisions, shrines, extra prayers, extra prohibitions, and numerous Arabic jargon such as *mandup*, *mustahap*, *makruh*, *sharif*, *sayyid* and more nonsense. Thus, the religion of Sunnis and Shiites contradicts the divine laws in nature and scripture and condemns its sincere followers to misery and backwardness. The religious leaders and their political allies contribute greatly to the backwardness of the Muslim world. God Almighty now wants to reform us and open the path of progress with the message described as "one of the greatest" (74:30-37).

Similar distortion and corruption was inflicted upon the system of islam (submission to God in peace) by professional religious leaders. For instance, soon after Jesus, a Pharisee-son-of-Pharisee who claimed to have seen Jesus in his vision started preaching in the name of Jesus. His passionate, yet diabolic doctrine was rejected by the monotheists and muslims, but a majority of people were duped with his delusional passion and clever salesmanship. As a result, he made major changes, including transformation of monotheism into polytheism and coinage of the name *Christian* (Acts 11:26). Jesus never silenced women nor put them down with xenophobic teachings but St. Paul asked women to submit to men and hush (1 Timothy 2:7-15; 1 Corinthians 14:34-35; 1 Peter 3:7). Jesus never asked for money for preaching but St. Paul asked for money shamelessly and likened his audience to a flock of sheep to be milked by the holy shepherd! (1 Corinthians 9:7). He was a master of deceit as opposed to Jesus who did not twist the truth to gain followers. Paul made up anything he deemed helpful to increase the number of his milk-giving flock (1 Corinthians 9:22). See the Quran: 9:31; 33:67. Also, see 2:59; 3:45,51-52-52,55; 4:11,157,171; 5:13-15,72-79; 7:162; 19:36.

Now, please read the following paragraphs, which are also excerpts from my notes on verse 57:27:

According to a law attributed to Moses, eunuchs were not respected. "No one who has been emasculated by crushing or cutting may enter the assembly of the Lord" (Deuteronomy 23:1). However, Christians who later fabricated *hadith* attributing them to Jesus, turned castration or hermitic life into a righteous act: "Jesus replied, 'Moses permitted you to divorce your wives because your hearts were hard. But it was not this way from the beginning. I tell you that anyone who divorces his wife, except for marital unfaithfulness, and marries another woman commits adultery.' The disciples said to him, 'If this is the situation between a husband and wife, it is better not to marry.' Jesus replied, 'Not everyone can accept this word, but only those to whom it has been given. For some are eunuchs because they were born that way; others were made that way by men; and others have renounced marriage--because of the kingdom of heaven. The one who can accept this should accept it'" (Matthew 19:8-12). "These are they which were not defiled with women; for they are virgins..." (Revelation 14:4). St. Paul, the voice behind the Gospels of the Nicene Conference, praised hermitic life: "Now for the matters you wrote about: It is good for a man not to marry" (1 Corinthians 7:1).

Today, only the Catholic Church and some small sects are struggling to keep this innovation alive. However, as the Quran states, they do not follow their own fabricated practice of celibacy. Worse, their churches have become notorious for pedophilia and child abuse, and many rich churches have recently declared bankruptcy because of a series of litigations by abused children. The unnatural religious innovation in the name of God led many priests to engage in child abuse and sodomy, perhaps attracting homosexuals to the ranks of priesthood for various reasons. Some religious men with homosexual tendencies who thought celibacy to be a cure for their desires ended up getting more opportunity to spend time with altar boys in their churches. Perhaps some homosexuals picked the profession just to indulge in their perverted act behind holy curtains. This perversion was most likely going on for centuries, and it was kept a "holy secret" by the powerful and secretive Church. It is only in the last decades that children have more of a voice, and the Church's financial and social power to

341

keep the evil deeds of her priests as secrets behind the confession session is weakening.

The Catholic Church, which is also having problems recruiting priests, remains locked in a dilemma. If they adhere to their centuries-old celebrated rule, then they will continue to suffer from the perverted behavior of priests and a shortage in new recruits. If they amend their rules and abandon the practice, then their credibility and claims to infallibility will get hurt again. If history is a guide, the Church will resist until reality will force them to abandon it. They will always find a way to justify their blunders to their faithful, who consider reason and religion to be like ice and fire, with their eternally "infallible" teachings of their Popes! The popes who not only stole the power of forgiveness, infallibility, and the keys of heaven from God, but also stole the Biblical title of God, "holy father." According to the maxims of the Old, most of the New, and the Final Testaments, the Pope is no different than the Pharaoh, since he claims divine powers. According to the Quran, Catholics are mentally and spiritually enslaved by their Popes. Isn't it time to accept the truth so that truth will set us all free?

Now let's read a report about the sexual perversion endemic on the other side of the confession chamber, on the side where a eunuch pretending to be a representative of God on earth listens to the sinner's "Holy Father"!

John Jay Study Reveals Extent of Abuse Problem

Four percent of priests serving over last 50 years accused of abuse

By Agostino Bono

Catholic News Service

WASHINGTON (CNS) -- About 4 percent of U.S. priests ministering from 1950 to 2002 were accused of sex abuse with a minor, according to the first comprehensive national study of the issue.

The study said that 4,392 clergymen — almost all priests — were accused of abusing 10,667 people, with 75 percent of the incidents taking place between 1960 and 1984. During the same time frame there were 109,694 priests, it said.

Sex-abuse related costs totaled $573 million, with $219 million covered by insurance companies, said the study done by the John Jay College of Criminal Justice in New York. It noted, however, that the overall dollar figure is much higher than reported; 14 percent of the dioceses and religious communities did not provide financial data and the total did not include settlements made after 2002, such as the $85 million agreed to by the Boston Archdiocese.

...

342

The study listed the main characteristics of the sex abuse incidents reported. These included:

- An overwhelming majority of the victims, 81 percent, were males. The most vulnerable were boys aged 11 to 14, representing more than 40 percent of the victims. This goes against the trend in the general U.S. society where the main problem involves men abusing girls.
- A majority of the victims were post-pubescent adolescents, with a small percentage of the priests accused of abusing children who had not reached puberty.
- Most of the accused committed a variety of sex acts involving serious sexual offenses.
- The most frequent context for abuse was a social event, and many priests socialized with the families of victims.
- Abuses occurred in a variety of places with the most common being the residence of the priest.

http://www.americancatholic.org/News/ClergySexAbuse/

So, Mr. Ratzinger, why don't you allow your pastors, bishops, and all in between to get married and become normal human beings, the way God created them. You may be justified not to marry a woman or to show no interest in them. This is your personal choice and I respect it. You may even get a Darwin Award for taking your genes out of the multiplication pool. You may redeem yourself for one unwanted baby, out of millions who are born because of the unreasonable contraception prohibitions which have contributed to overpopulation. But, based on what REASON you are defending such an unnatural choice as a righteous act, and based on what REASON you are considering it as a requirement to serve in your church? Isn't it an unreasonable and ungrateful attitude to tacitly accuse your Creator for endowing you with a useless and harmful organ? As you see, many altar children have paid a high price for your unnatural rule and arrogant declaration, "I am so holy that I do not need Eve." Well, do I need to remind you how were you born?

A friendly advice to you Mr. Ratzinger:

I have no doubt that if you had the old glory and power, you would continue the inquisition rather than give lip service to dialogue, since you have yet to condemn Pope Innocent III, Pope Gregory IV, and all the other Popes who justified torture and swords against heretics. You cannot fool reasonable people that you do not hide the same holy virus in your genes without denouncing the tortures and the murderer Popes. To the contrary, you deem them to be "innocent" or "infallible" holy guys.

If you wish to serve humanity, you should discard all those Halloween or Santa Claus customs and cease all your silly rituals, as well as order your bishops and

343

pastors to resign from their positions and get real jobs. Stop pretending to be God's representative on earth, and go learn some skills besides preaching nonsense. Contribute to the society as a working man, not as an audacious leach assuming the right to milk the flock as was assumed by Saul (1 Corinthians 9:3-14).. The vast wealth and power your institution accumulated has generated plenty of holy lies, tragedies, irrational conflicts, wars, superstitions, misogyny, racism, slavery, inquisition, torture, and mental and financial exploitation. Return all the Vatican's wealth to the descendants of those that were massacred by Christians, and distribute all those billions of dollars you have collected from your gullible herd to the poor people of the third world countries, which have been occupied, bombed, terrorized, tortured, and destroyed by cross-carrying soldiers. Then, put your resume on monster.com and wait to find a real job, a beneficial job. You should not be interested in any teaching job since you do not qualify. You will contribute to the society much better if you pray in the opera or guide people to their seats in theaters or baptize fresh vegetables in a grocery store with a water spray in your hand. Remember that Moses was a shepherd, Jesus was a carpenter, and Muhammad was a merchant. Stop following the lead of Pharisees and the top Pharisee Paul, the mutated Saul! Get a life! This may be the only way you can redeem yourself in the sight of God.

3:71   "O people of the book, why do you dress the truth with false-hood and conceal the truth while you know?"

4:171   "O people of the book, do not overstep in your system, nor say about **God** except the truth. Jesus the son of Mary was no more than **God**'s messenger and the fulfillment of His word to Mary, and an inspiration from Him. So acknowledge **God** and His messengers, and do not say, 'Trinity.' Cease, for it is better for you. **God** is only One god, be He glorified that He should have a son! To Him is all that is in the heavens and what is in the earth. **God** is enough as a caretaker."

5:48   "We have sent down to you the book with truth, authenticating what is present of the book and superseding it. So judge between them by what **God** has sent down, and do not follow their desires from what has come to you of the truth. For each of you We have made laws, a structure. Had **God** willed, He would have made you all one nation, but He tests you with what He has given you, so advance the good deeds. To **God** you will return all of you, and He will inform you regarding that in which you dispute."

9:33   "He is the One who sent His messenger with guidance and the system of truth, to make it manifest above all other systems, even if those who set up partners hate it."

Approximately, four years after the publication of an article of mine titled *Triarchy*, America was hit by the worst terrorist attack in her history, costing the lives of about 3,000 civilians and total destruction of World Trade Center, partial destruction of the Pentagon and four airplanes, billions of dollars, massive unemployment, and an open-ended war against any country and group deemed to be at odds with the world's political and economic hegemons. The following article is the revised version of *Triarchy*.

From the Perspective of a former Radical Muslim Leader:
The Theo-Political Roots of "Islamic Terrorism"
November 2001

Narrated 'Ikrima: Some Zanadiqa (atheists) were brought to 'Ali and he burnt them. The news of this event, reached Ibn 'Abbas who said, "If I had been in his place, I would not have burnt them, as Allah's Apostle forbade it, saying, 'Do not punish anybody with Allah's punishment (fire).' I would have killed them according to the statement of Allah's Apostle, 'Whoever changed his Islamic religion, then kill him.'" (Bukhari, Volume 9, Book 84, Hadith Number 57)

Narrated 'Ali: Whenever I tell you a narration from Allah's Apostle, by Allah, I would rather fall down from the sky than ascribe a false statement to him, but if I tell you something between me and you (not a Hadith) then it was indeed a trick (i.e., I may say things just to cheat my enemy). No doubt I heard Allah's Apostle saying, "During the last days there will appear some young foolish people who will say the best words but their faith will not go beyond their throats (i.e. they will have no faith) and will go out from (leave) their religion as an arrow goes out of the game. So, where-ever you find them, kill them, for who-ever kills them shall have reward on the Day of Resurrection." (Volume 9, Book 84, Hadith Number 64)

Narrated Abu Burda: Abu Musa said, "I came to the Prophet along with two men (from the tribe) of Ash'ariyin, one on my right and the other on my left, while Allah's Apostle was brushing his teeth (with a Siwak), and both men asked him for some employment. . . Behold: There was a fettered man beside Abu Muisa. Mu'adh asked, "Who is this (man)?" Abu Muisa said, "He was a Jew and became a Muslim and then reverted back to Judaism." Then Abu Muisa requested Mu'adh to sit down but Mu'adh said, "I will not sit down till he has been killed. This is the judgment of Allah and His Apostle (for such cases) and repeated it thrice. Then Abu Musa ordered that the man be killed, and he was killed. Abu Musa added, "Then we discussed the night prayers and one of us said, 'I pray and sleep, and I hope that Allah will reward me for my sleep as well as for my prayers.'" (Volume 9, Book 84, Hadith Number 58)

In many so-called Muslim countries, clergymen (Mullahs, Ulamas, Khojas, Mawlanas, etc.) are usually either the sanctifying puppets of oppressive governments or the spiritual leaders of terrorist organizations. They use God's name

345

to justify discrimination, torture, and oppression. Their influence within the political sphere comes from their shared interests with kings, sultans, emirs, and totalitarian leaders of their countries.

Saudi's top clergymen, Abdul Aziz bin Ba'z, wrote a book claiming that the earth was flat and still. The book is full of references to hadith (narrations falsely attributed to the Prophet Muhammad) accompanied by murderous instructions:

> "If the earth is rotating as they claim, the countries, the mountains, the trees, the rivers, and the oceans will have no bottom and the people will see the eastern countries move to the west and the western countries move to the east. . . Those who claim that the earth is round and moving around the sun are apostates and their blood can be shed and their property can be taken in the name of God."[28]

This "authoritative" book was not published by a private publishing house but, by the Islamic University of Medina, a prestigious university in modern Saudi Arabia in 1975, years after men landed on the moon. You may see this as an example of harmless nonsense or amusement. Unfortunately, for those who live in Saudi Arabia or who dare to criticize such corrupt and oppressive religious teachings anywhere around the world, the issue is not amusing. When clerics are united, every corner of the planet might become the target of their fatwas. Let me give just one example:

In February 19, 1989 a group of scholars (38 members according to the newspaper reports) met in Saudi Arabia to discuss the issue of Salman Rushdie. When they issued their fatwa (religious decree) it became a headline news in Muslim countries, including my homeland, Turkey.[29] Their fatwa was that "both Rashad and Rushdie are apostate." The world knew Rushdie, but who was Rashad? Dr. Rashad Khalifa, a biochemist resident of Tucson, Arizona became a popular figure in Muslim countries after he discovered a secret mathematical system in the Quran via computer analysis in the early1970s.[30] The consequence of the

---

[28] Abdulaziz Bin Ba'z, Al-Adillatul Naqliyyati wal Hissiyati 'Ala Garayanil Shamsi wa Sukunil Ardi wa Imkanil Soudi Ilal Kawakibi (The Religious and Empirical Evidences that Sun is Moving and Earth is Still and the Possibility of Going to Planets), The Islamic University in Medina, Medina, 1975. (I have the original copy of the book in my library).

[29] Milli Gazete, the Turkish newspaper of a religious political party, gave an extensive coverage to the story. Nokta, a popular and secular weekly news magazine, made the "fatwa" against Rashad Khalifa its cover story in its April 16, 1989 issue.

[30] Rashad Khalifa, Ph.D., The Computer Speaks: God's Message To The World, Renaissance Productions, Tucson, 1981. Also see: Rashad Khalifa, Ph.D., Quran:

346

mathematical code was too difficult to be accepted by the Muslim clergymen.[31] Consequently, they issued fatwas calling for his assassination.

Although it was not as bold as Khomeini's fatwa, it sent a clear message to the fanatical followers of those clergymen that Rashad and Rushdie should be killed.[32] Rushdie is still alive, but the fatwa about Rashad Khalifa was executed in January 30, 1990. He was stabbed to death in the Tucson Masjid before the dawn prayer. For this task, a group of black Muslims named FUQRA (squads) were used by international terrorist forces operating from Pakistan and Saudi Arabia. The FBI discovered that the group "FUQRA" was a branch of the group that bombed the World Trade Center and that was receiving financial support from Pakistan.

Visual Presentation Of The Miracle, Islamic Productions, Tucson, 1982. I have argued the mathematical structure of the Quran in my books such as, The Prime Argument (with Dr. Carl Sagan) and Running Like Zebras (with Abdulrahman Lomax). Both books were published by Monotheist Productions International, Tucson in 1995. They can be found in my web site: www.moslem.org/yuksel.htm. The author's most recent Turkish book Uzerinde Ondokuz Var (On It Nineteen), an extensive evaluation and demonstration of the mathematical code, is currently in print.

[31] The mathematical code of the Quran required the rejection of other religious sources besides the Quran. Dr. Rashad Khalifa's biggest offense was to expose the corrupt nature of today's sectarian Islam and suggest reformation in religion (see: Quran: The Final Testament, Islamic Productions, Tucson, 1989, and Quran, Hadith and Islam, Islamic Productions, Tucson, 1982). By referring to the Quranic verses, he demonstrated that today's Islam has nothing to do with Muhammad's original message, but a religion concocted by scholars who traded the Quran with fabricated narration and medieval Arab culture (Hadith and Sunnah) falsely attributed to Prophet Muhammad two centuries after his departure. By incorporating their opinion with those medieval lies, Muslim scholars created various orthodox sects with thousands of contradictions, vicious and oppressive laws, and hundreds of regulations that can turn the daily life of a zealot to hell. For objective and extensive information on the mission of Khalifa I recommend the following book: Yvonne Yazbeck Haddad and Jane Idleman Smith, Mission To America: Five Islamic Sectarian Communities in North America, University Press of Florida, Gainsville, 1993.

[32] See: Chris Limberis, Terrorists in Tiny Town, Tucson Weekly, September 20, 2001, pp. 4-8. Mark Hosenball, Another Holy War Waged on American Soil, Newsweek, February 28, 1994, pp. 30-31. Also see: Tim Vanderpool, The No. 19 Murder, Tucson Weekly, January 19, 1994, cover story. Also see: Tucson Mosque slaying may be linked to sect, The Arizona Daily Star, October 12, 1992, first page. Most recently, this assasination was linked to Ben Ladin by CBS National News, Dan Rather, 10/26/2001 at 5:30 PM. Eye On America. Also visit: http://www.pbs.org/wgbh/pages/frontline/shows/binladen/upclose/elhage.html

Religious Muslims know very well that the teachings of the Sunni and Shiite sects demand capital punishment for apostates.[33] Guess who was the chairman of that international committee of clerics? It was Abdul Aziz b. Ba'z, the same Saudi religious leader who wrote a book declaring that the earth was flat and still.

Often, dissident priests use religion to promote international terrorism. Omar Abdurrahman, an Egyptian cleric who recently became popular in western media, serves as such an example. Egypt has never had a democratic system by Western standards, and its oppressive regime has produced a myriad of militant religious factions of the Muslim Brotherhood. Egypt's corrupt and totalitarian system has created many local and international heroes out of clerics such as Omar Abdurrahman. This Egyptian cleric who had immigrated to the U.S.A. did not hesitate to encourage his followers to agitate against the very country (U.S.A.) which provided refuge for him and some of his followers.

> "The obligation of Allah is upon us to wage Jihad for the sake of Allah. It is one of the obligations which we must undoubtedly fulfill. . . and we conquer the lands of the infidels and we spread Islam by calling the infidels to Allah and if they stand in our way, then we wage Jihad for the sake of Allah."[34]

Many blamed the U.S. immigration officials and procedures for letting the terrorists into the U.S.A. I believe that the real blunder occurred not in immigration but in the U.S.'s foreign policy. Supporting undemocratic or totalitarian regimes such as Iran's Shah or Egypt's current regime remains a myopic policy. It puts the security of US citizens, here and abroad, in great danger. How can the US expect security from international terrorism while it does not care about the security of people living under oppressive and corrupt governments?

Militant clerics, whether they are dissidents or collaborators with totalitarian regimes, should be taken seriously. Using the language of religion and proverbs from their forefathers, they can mobilize gullible masses into bloody conflicts. The best way to deflate the power of militant clergymen is (1) to support intel-

---

[33] The author of this paper was also declared to be an apostate in Turkey. See: Hulki Cevizoᵓlu, Edip Yuksel "Çöpe At" (Edip Yuksel 'Trash It'), Ad Yayincilik, Istanbul, 1997. Bahaeddin Saᵓlam, 19 Meselesi ve Edip Yuksel'e Cevaplar (The Issue of 19 and Answers to Edip Yuksel), Tebliᵓ Yayinevi, Istanbul, 1996. Sadreddin Yüksel (my father), Günümüz Meselelerine Kuran'dan Cevaplar (Answers From the Quran To Contemporary Issues), Madve, Istanbul, 1988. I was a bestselling author and a well-known political activist, but my rejection of my father's religion put my life at risk and forced me to immigrate to USA. I still receive death threats from orthodox and sectarian Muslims.

[34] Joseph Grinstein, Jihad and the Constitution: The First Amendment Implications of Combating Religiously Motivated Terrorism, 105 Yale L.J. 1347 (1996). (Quoting from a Nov. 21, 1994 television broadcast.)

lectuals who promote democracy and freedom, and (2) denounce and punish oppressive leaders without favoring one to another through international legal devices such as freezes of assets in foreign countries or trials in international tribunals during their reign or after removal from power.

Donna E. Arzt, Professor of Law at the Syracuse University College of Law, provides us with some recent examples of repression of religious dissidents, apostates, blasphemers, heretics, renegades, and infidels in so-called Muslim countries in a law review article. He groups the repression into three categories: "(1) officially state-sanctioned enforcement actions; (2) extra-legal enforcement of apostasy decrees issued by vigilante extremist groups; and (3) mixed cases."[35] Professor Arzt, concludes his article with the following caveat:

> "Throughout Muslim history, and particularly in contemporary Muslim states, much of the persecution of alleged apostates, heretics, and infidels, and other violations of international standards of religious human rights has been politically motivated, designed to benefit hegemonic, orthodox groups who have resorted to religious justifications to legitimize their abusive power. It is improper to conclude that Islam is inherently militant, violent, coercive, or intolerant."[36]

I agree with the author that "Islam" does not advocate violence, coercion or intolerance[37], but he is vague regarding the chronology and the source of the corruption. Religious justifications to legitimize political abusive power became an integrated part of traditional or contemporary Islam long ago. Repressive and oppressive religious instructions did not remain external or optional interpretations, but unfortunately were labeled as "Hadith" (alleged narrations from the prophet), "Sunnah" (alleged practice of the prophet), "Ijma" (consensus of leading scholars), and "Ijtihad" (opinion of sectarian scholars) and were incorporated as part of the original message, the Quran, as early as the Umayyad dynasty.[38] Today's sectarian Islam, with its volumes of hadith books (narrations falsely

---

[35] Donna E. Arzt, Religious Human Rights In Muslim States of the Middle East and North Africa, 10 Emory Int'l L. Rev. 139, 144. (Spring 1996).

[36] Id. at 160-161.

[37] The Quran repeatedly condemns compulsion in religion (see: 2:256; 10:99; 88:21,22), advocates perfect freedom of belief and expression (18:29), permits fighting for only self-defense (60:8,9), advises not to harm apostates except if they mobilize with arms against believers (4:90), and advises passive protest against those who insult and make mockery of God's revelation (4:140). A short article by Riffat Hassan, Professor of Religious Studies at the University of Lousville, provides some idea about the content of the Quran regarding human rights: Riffat Hassan, Religious Human Rights and The Quran, 10 Emory Int'l L. Rev. 85 (Spring 1996).

[38] See, supra note 13

attributed to Muhammad) and medieval sectarian jurisprudence, remains utterly incompatible with the standards of universal human rights as defined in the Quran. Without a reformation of traditional Islam, there will always be doors open for abuse by tyrants and corrupt clergymen.

Noticing this fact, Professor Arzt finishes his article with a genuine invitation:

> "Muslim dissidents and religious minorities in Muslim lands, however, do need and deserve more support from international human rights movements. The same is true for those within orthodox Muslim circles who are willing but for their fear of persecution to criticize abuses of human rights by their governments. Similarly, the international media must avoid giving undue prominence to violent Muslim militants, which in reality are small in number, and give proportional attention to liberal Muslim groups, albeit fledgling, who oppose violence, favor democratization and seek to promote accommodation and reform."[39]

I applaud this invitation and I believe that extending such international support to Muslim dissidents and reformers will hasten a paradigmatic change in the minds of people subjected to religious and political tyranny. The importance of religion in the lives of people cannot be ignored. Secular intellectuals might re-consider its positive power:

> "Modern human rights laws will provide no panacea to the world crisis in the next century, but they will be a critical part of any solution. Re-ligions will not be easy allies to engage, but the struggle for human rights cannot be won without them."[40]

The history of Muslim countries, especially those in the Middle East, are full of religious and tribal wars. Their textbooks usually distort and sanctify these bloody histories with virtually no criticism. As written, this history of the third world is a major source of national pride. This nationalistic pride is used by cor-rupt and failing governments as "opium for the masses." What can be expected from the next generation if their role models are those who knew nothing but the sword and did nothing but kill their opponents and conquer others' lands?

In this short paper I cannot provide references. If a person reads the high-school history textbooks of oppressive regimes, he will find repeated praises for the kings, caliphs and sultans who had oppressed their own people. Textbooks con-tinue to promote totalitarianism, fanaticism, animosity and racism. How can

---

[39]   Arzt, supra note 32, at 161.

[40]   John Witte Jr., Law, Religion and Human Rights, 28 Colum. Hum. Rts. L. Rew. 1, 2 (Fall 1996).

respect for human rights be expected from those who are "educated" by these textbooks?

A paper written by members of the Consultation Group on Religion and the Roots of Conflict, concluded with some reflections on religion and violence. Here is an excerpt from the conclusion:

> "An attempt to develop the resources of religious traditions against religious violence must deal with the phenomenon which some have termed the "reemergence of history" in the late 20th century. . . . Historical goals, now pursued with a militancy and mass-organizational character born of the modern ideology of nationalism, are supported by new communications and weapons technologies, and they are fostered by the complications of trying to build modern economies for modern states. Part of the irony of contemporary religious conflict is that religious factors in group life are at one and the same time among the most constructive and the most destructive forces in human affairs."[41]

We cannot expect elimination of terrorism in Muslim countries without knowing and acknowledging the negative impact of religious teachings and oppressive environment justifying aggression. Human rights institutions must cooperate with dissident intellectuals to push for reformation in Islam.

The real interest of the Western world lies not in the hands of puppet kings and tyrants in Muslim lands, but in the reign of democracy and freedom. Oppressive regimes create a toxic ecology that incubates and produces hate, hopelessness, and ignorance. Unfortunately, corrupt Muslim scholars, oppressive kings, and the foreign policy of Western world have all contributed in the production of so-called "Islamic Terrorism."

Muslims should abandon the backward teachings of clergymen and start following their only holy book, the Quran. American politicians should eliminate the antidemocratic influence of lobbies of big corporations and special interests in determination of American foreign policy and start seeking the interests of the American population.

---

[41]   Religion and Human Rights, eds: John Kelsay and Sumner B. Twiss, The Project on Religion and Human Rights, New York, 1994, pp. 15-16.

31 Flavors of Ice-cream, Yet Only Two Parties!

April 15, 2008

"We ain't right wing, we ain't left wing. We're trying to get the folks to see the problem ain't left vs. right; it's up vs. down. A Republican is a standard screw, a Democrat is a Phillips screw. So whichever way you vote, you get the screw." – Michael Chute (54) a leading member of Main Militia as reported by Christopher Ketcham, Time, November 16, 2009, p 8.

At Wal-Mart you may find half a dozen brands of bathroom tissues, at Home Depot a dozen brands of faucets, and at Baskin Robins you may find 31 plus flavors of ice-cream, yet in America's political market you have only two choices. Only two parties in the land of liberty and diversity. How ironic: a country, whose political leaders have been leading her to numerous wars under the guise of defending or exporting democracy is herself democratically challenged! Perhaps, has no democracy at all. We have a duopoly serving corporatocracy.

Why can't we vote a list of candidates in a preferred order so that when our top choices do not win sufficient votes they would count for the rest of the candidates in our list? Why can't we adopt the preferential voting and proportional representation methods? This way, by voting for our top choices we would not be worrying about helping worst of two evils. This way, third parties and independent candidates could get the votes of many people whose political views are not represented. Americans, a mosaic of people, deserve more diversity in political representation.

As a result of a conspiracy of the two parties, which has become almost identical twins, we are forced to play a political sea-saw every election cycle. They care less about people, and both are playing the tune of interest groups, big corporations, financial institutions, military industrial complex, and of course, compete with each other to please AIPAC. Our political system is rigged, and our government has become the government of corporations, by corporations and for corporations. No wonder whether we have small or big government, it works for big and bigger corporations.

Our choice should not be either big government or big corporations.

352

Your Children will be Ashamed of Your Support of NaZionist Atrocities!

7 January 2009

> "Israel's failure to properly investigate its forces' conduct in Gaza, including war crimes, and its continuing refusal to cooperate with the UN international independent fact-finding mission headed by Richard Goldstone, is evidence of its intention to avoid public scrutiny and accountability," said Donatella Rovera, who headed a field research mission to Gaza and southern Israel during and after the conflict... The scale and intensity of the attacks on Gaza were unprecedented. Some 300 children and hundreds of other unarmed civilians who took no part in the conflict were among the 1,400 Palestinians killed by Israeli forces... "The deaths of so many children and other civilians cannot be dismissed simply as 'collateral damage', as argued by Israel," said Donatella Rovera. *Impunity for war crimes in Gaza and southern Israel a recipe for further civilian suffering*, 2 July 2009, Amnesty International, Amnesty.org

All Americans and the entire world suffers because of your ignorance, delusions, hypocrisy, lies, distortions, hostility towards truth, injustice, lack of empathy, contradictions, and self-righteous arrogance. The world is tired of you blaming the victim, applauding the atrocities of a fascist military force, and preaching about human rights and democracy on your high asses and elephants!

You elected an Evangelist Christian warmonger not once but twice for the presidency. Now see what you have gotten — an unjust war against a nation that did not pose any threat to you. You unleashed your deadly war arsenal against that poor and small nation which suffered greatly from your pawn dictator. You caused more than a million dead civilians (I know you will blame your victim for that), along with millions of injured, displaced, and tortured people whom you were supposedly helping. This barbaric war has cost us about a trillion dollars and will continue to cost even more. You followed the lies and deception sold to you by the CAMERA-controlled American media, and all Americans ended up in a historical economic crisis. (Remember how a CAMERA NaZionist forced CNN;s spokeperson to apologize in public for objectively reporting the misery of a Palestinian family whose home was bulldozed in a Gaza concentration camp by NaZionists). It is a fact that the propaganda and the wars-on-borrowed money contributed to the current political and economic troubles we are in. Perhaps you might be incapable of connecting the dots between transforming 1 trillion ($1,000,000,000,000) plus dollars into bombs and the current

353

economic crises and millions of new hardened enemies. After 9/11 the world forgot our nasty deeds all over the world and cried with us for our losses. The day after 9/11, one million Iranians mourned for us. More than 90% of Turkish people supported America. But, after the criminal Bush government led us to a war through lies and deception — a war that was dictated by Israel — the world has turned against us.

Zionists are America's enemy. The foreign policy that they have dictated on both parties has only increased the number of our enemies, and only increased the amount of hatred felt against us. As long as we support their monstrous fascist policies, we will be in fear of national security, a fear that is destroying the future of our children. In fact, NaZionists are the enemies of Jews too. NaZionist bloodshed has unfortunately increased the amount of racism and anti-Semitism in the world. Jews should fight against Zionism for their own interests.

Poor Israelis Defending themselves against Palestinian Propaganda!

Now you are again supporting a bloodthirsty enemy of humanity, the NaZionist regime, and you fall again to their diabolic propaganda: "Poor Israelis are scared by Palestinian terrorists (they call the people in their concentration camps terrorist) and thus they are justified to kill their children and destroy their homes, hospitals, and schools. The NaZionist-controlled American media are focusing their cameras on a little hole allegedly created by Hamas rockets and showing the faces of scared Jewish people, while at the same time hundreds of children are slaughtered by the Zestapo in Gaza concentration camp. Their propagandists try to fool people by asking a deceptive question as we massacred Mexicans and Canadians, as if we starved them in concentration camps!: "What would America do if Mexico sends thousands of rockets to South California. Or what would America do if Canada sends thousands of rockets to Vermont? (This last question was asked by Sean Hannity on his radio program on December 7, 2008). Unfortunately, those who have lost their critical thinking abilities in churches as "flock of sheep," or in front of TV stations as "coach potatoes" were not be able to see the devil in the analogy.

Wake up from this hypnosis. Do not repeat the blunder of German and Italian Christians who were manipulated by Hitler's propaganda machine. Be brave; do not be afraid of being called "anti-Semitic" by the neo-fascist NaZionists. They are the real enemies of Semitic people. Stand up for truth and justice. Stand up for Jews and Palestinians as well. Be a human being! Claim your values, if you have any left besides capitalism!

Here are some SIMPLE yet PROFOUND facts which are kept hidden from average American people, from Joe the Plumbers. I have to remind you again, since because of the hypnotist, the CAMERA-controlled American media, you keep forgetting the following: Israel has one of the most powerful war machine in the world, it is a major arms merchant in the world, it is a racist state, it is a theocracy that believe the supremacy of Jewish race, it has acquired nuclear weapons in defiance of international law, and since its inception it is continuously increasing the number of its settlers in the lands grabbed from Palestinians. Israel has imprisoned Palestinians into several concentration camps divided by walls and Zestapo check points, and starves them whenever it can show a tiny excuse, a desire to live free, a teenager throwing rocks or primitive rockets to the Zoliath. Wake up from the AIPAC and CAMARE induced hypnosis and before reading the facts below, go read again the background facts listed above.

Check these Numbers and Stop Supporting Fascist Zionists

Here are some numbers from http://www.ifamericansknew.org/ which are substantiated by references and sources. You can verify each through various human rights reports. Between September 29, 2008 and December 3, 2009:

- 124 Israeli children have been killed by Palestinians
- 1,441 Palestinian children have been killed

- 1,072 Israelis have been killed
- 6,348 Pals have been killed

- 8,864 Israelis have been injured
- 39,019 Palestinians have been injured

- 65 UN resolutions against Israel
- Zero UN resolution against Palestinians

- 1 Israeli is being held prisoner by Palestinians
- 7,383 Palestinians are currently imprisoned by Israel

- 24,145 Palestinian homes have been demolished by Israel since 1967
- Zero Israeli home have been demolished by Palestinians

- 223 Jewish-only settlements and "outposts" built on confiscated lands.
- Zero Palestinian settlements.

- $7 million per day in military aid from the U.S. to Israil during in 2009.
- Zero in military aid to the Palestinians.

Let me insert a parenthetical paragraph here: After sharing those numbers with my email list, a hypnotized American, instead of reflecting on those numbers, directed me a stupid question accompanied with a stupid remark: "Are you supporting Hamas? Hamas was declared a terrorist organization by the Bush administration." Though the question was red-herring and stupid, the intention behind it was not. In fact, it is one of the common tactics used to justify apartheid regime, settlements, and concentration camps, killing of the children, bombing of schools, genocide and atrocities. The person who directed me the question wanted to intimidate me, to scare me. Well, he did not know that I do not worship American government, let alone it's most idiotic and bloody version, the Bush government. I am a monotheist and I was neither intimidated by the Turkish military, nor by the terrorist organizations. I appreciate the American constitution and every patriotic Americans know that the Bush administration betrayed many of its principles. So, I will not be intimidated by a betrayer, by terrorist governments. If Hamas is a terrorist organization, then Israel is terrorist state to the factor of 777. Furthermore, Israel was established by terror and has been the main source of creating gang terrorism as a reaction to its horrendous crimes against humanity.

Massacring Palestinian Children for Hypothetical death of a Jew

Even if we do not ask the crucial question why Hamas is throwing primitive rockets to their "peaceful Israeli neighbors who just want to left alone" (!), the following are the facts that happened during the last days of 2008 and the first day of 2009:

80 Hamas Rockets -------> one Israeli dea, and another Israeli COULD have died if he was not walking faster in the street, according to the three major American TV channels that I watched! The NaZionist propaganda machine has created a new justification for their genocide: Bombing Palestinian schools and hospitals and killing their children, men and women to retaliate the hypothetical death of Israeli citizens!

Seven days of Israeli air bombing campaign -------> More than 600 Arabs, about a quarter being children dead, and more than 4000 injured, SO FAR. These numbers is going to rise and they are not hypothetical dead people.

When I see the number of the dead on each side, I care less about speculations, which are mostly based on twisting the facts, fabricating polls, and doing propaganda. Even before Hamas was born, even before the enslaved Palestinians resorted to suicide bombing, even before the uprising of 2000 against the fascist Zestapo, Israeli colonialist forces were killing 25 Pals for each Israeli.

For one dead NaZionist <------> 25 dead Pals who are fighting for their liberty, usually with rocks and guns.

Who is occupying whose land? Israel is occupying the lands of Pals.
Who is creating more settlements on stolen lands? Israel is creating more settlements on Palestinian lands, every day, in violation of Geneva Convention.

Who is building walls around the towns and turning its people to prisoners? The
Israeli colonialists are.
Who is kidnapping Pals and putting them in prisons? Israel is kidnapping Pales-
tinians (when they call it with the magical word arrest, it is baptized by us).
How many Pals are kidnapped and tortured in Israeli prisons? More than 10,000.
How many Israelis are kidnapped and tortured by Hamas? One soldier.
Which country was the last to cut its relations with the Apartheid regime in
South Africa? Israel.
Which foreign country dominates American media through CAMERA and dic-
tates the American government through AIPAC and numerous corpora-
tions and organizations? Israel.

In 1990's, Israeli war machine killed 25 Palestinians (mostly teenagers and civilians) for EACH Israeli (mostly soldiers) and yet still played as victim while labeling their victims as terrorists. After the uprising of 2000, it still continued
killing 3 Palestinians for EACH Israeli soldier and continued crying: ARAB
TERRORISTS!

American Media is Used as a Propaganda Machine by the NaZionists

The shameless American media, which I watched the first day of 2009, such as
ABC; NBC, CBS and FOX gave more coverage to that "hypothetical death"
than the actual deaths of 600 plus Palestinians! They focused on the faces of
"poor Israelis" afraid of the sound of rockets coming from the concentration
camp called Gaza, while they glossed over the dead bodies of Palestinian children. Paranoid fear of an aggressive and arrogant NaZionists is used for justification for their atrocities and genocide against Pals.

Our news anchors, guests, spinners, and reporters tell us:

> Look my fellow idiot Americans, relax and trust us. You see those
> Arab and Muslim terrorists; they almost killed a Jew. Now you should
> not see 600+ Palestinians killed by Jews. Jews are chosen people. They
> have the right to occupy Palestinians' land, they have the right to settle
> there, to harass them, to put them under blockade, to deprive them from
> medicine, from necessities of life, to destroy their homes, to massacre
> them, to kidnap them and torture them. Jews are not only chosen peo-
> ple, they are perpetual victims. Jews our best allies in the oily Middle
> East. They do our dirty work better than we ever could; so we must
> continue our unconditional support. Jews have all the right to be scared
> from the terrorists. Do not use your brains, just accept what we are re-
> porting. Spell it: T-E-R-R-O-R-I-S-T-S. Arabs are terrorists. Muslims
> are terrorists. We are civilized. They want to take our freedom to inter-
> fere with their lives. We are chosen by our God to control them, to
> dominate them through our puppet dictators or supposedly elected

proxies. They are subhuman and they deserve what they get. We and our closest ally in the oily land may kill ten times more children than those terrorists do, but remember that we call our murdering "collateral damage." Make yourself belief that we do not enjoy killing them, we are the best killing machine the world has ever seen. When we transgress and take revenge, we call it retaliation. Spell it: R-E-T-E-L-I-A-T-I-O-N. Or we call it democracy, taking justice to them. But when they respond, we will call it revenge we will call it terror. It is how you frame it, how you present it. Remember, they are T-E-R-R-O-R-I-S-T-S and we are the good guys. When we kill thousands of children and women, young and old, call it collateral, but when they kill even a single person, even if it is our soldiers who are trained to kill, we will call it TERRORISM."

Learn Creepy Facts About Israel

Here are some accomplishments of Israel, which you might wish to absolve by blaming them for just being stupid for killing so many Palestinians and terrorizing the world's biggest concentration camp. You never blamed Israel for committing crimes against humanity, for being a terrorist state.

Israel is the ONLY state in the world that has been torturing its Palestinian prisoners, LEGALLY. (Recently, they worked hard through their embedded NaZionist agents in American media, universities and government to export their torture practice to the USA. Thank God, they so far failed to find popular support among Americans).

- Israel is the ONLY state that kills Palestinian teenagers with the arms and 10 Billion annual financial aid it receives from the USA.
- Israel is the ONLY state that has imprisoned several million people in concentration camps, separated by walls, towers, soldiers and fascist settlers.
- Israel is the ONLY state that was founded by the UN and has been repeatedly in defiance of the same UN resolutions. With the support of the hijacked USA government, it gets away with its crimes..
- Israel is the ONLY state that which was established upon terrorism, such as Irgun and Stern Gang.
- Israel is the ONLY state where six war criminals have been democratically elected as Prime Ministers: Begin, Shamir, Natanyahu, Sharon, Barak, and Olmert.
- Israel is the ONLY state that dominates American entertainment industry, media, financial institutions, and politics.
- Israel is the ONLY state that bombs neighboring countries and gets away with it.

358

- Israel is the ONLY state that has WMD in the Middle East.
- Israel is the ONLY state that by saying PEACE it really means GRABBING more Palestinian land and killing more Palestinians.
- Israel is the ONLY state demands pity from the world, for being the victim of Holocaust, but victimizes Palestinians.

And much more.

Israel is criticized by European media for not allowing them to report from Gaza, and the Israeli fascist government officials confessed the well-known fact: they want to CONTROL the news of their atrocities in Gaza concentration camp. Here is what the New York Times, "Israelis say the war is being reduced on television screens around the world to a simplistic story; American-backed country with awesome military machine fighting a third-world guerrilla force leading to a handful of Israelis dead versus 600 Gazans dead."

The Rapist Serial Killer who Expects our Sympathy

Yes, this is the simple story. The complicated one is even more heinous and troubling. Israeli's aggression, terror and genocide against Palestinians continue because of cowards, and ignorant people. Most of those who are bystanders of NaZionits' crimes are not evil themselves. But their fear of NaZionists turns them to Devil's little helpers.

If you are an intelligent person and have sense of justice, you cannot stay silent while NaZionist butchers are slaughtering innocent children. They use the cry and fear of "terrorists" to justify their terror and atrocities. Terrorism is just a buzzword, created and exploited by the imperialist forces and their stooges to justify the greater terror and horror.

NaZionists have the audacity to demand our sympathy for their crimes against humanity. It is like a rapist complaining from his victim trying scratching his face:

"Look world, you see this is a terrorist Palestinian. She is trying to scratch my face. I am scared of her nails. So, she deserves to be raped again! Look at her teenage son; he is throwing me pebbles. They almost hit me. I am scared. After I am done with her, I will roll over his son's body with my USA-donated truck. I am a poor victim of this terrorist family! Tell her to stop trying to scratch my face; tell him to stop throwing pebbles at me."

I rarely use the word, but it is the right place to use it: You are complaining of this or that country or group not recognizing you. Go to Hell! Soon the entire world will recognize your evil face and none will recognize your existence. You are a cancer for humanity. You are the enemy of Jews who are not infected with the virus called NaZionism.

Z-propaganda, Z-propaganda, Z-propaganda

The Zionist propagandist insults our intelligence by asking the following deceptive question while Israel is killing children and civilians in Gaza concentration camp in hundreds: "When was the last time Israel sent a child to bomb innocent people"?

I don't know. When was the last time a Palestinian bulldozed an Israeli home with people inside, razed an Israeli apartment building from an attack helicopter, or denied an Israeli citizen food, water, or the right to leave his town? When was the last time Palestinians bombed Israeli cities to the ground with most sophisticated fighter jets? When was the last time Palestinians forced Israelis out of their farms and homes and built settlements on the confiscated lands? When was the last time Palestinians divided Israeli towns and built walls around them? When was the last time Palestinians imprisoned millions of Israelis in concentration camps and harassed them in check points? When was the last time Palestinians targeted Israeli schools and hospitals? When was the last time Palestinians were denounced by the United Nations resolutions?

If Israel has been the victim, has been under terrorist attacks, why it has not yet invited the UN to its borders? Well, you might be surprised but the Palestinians frequently asked for the UN intervention, but Israel has always rejected the idea of UN intervention and help. Well, it might surprise you that Israel defied every UN resolution that would bring peace to the region through the USA-Inc's veto. If you were terrorized by your neighbor, would you reject the call for help from police? Think about it. At least once in your life when question involves Israel. (Israel seems finally accepting the presence of UN peace forces in the region. If history and the modus operandi of the NaZionists any indication, they will find a way to sabotage their mission.)

Do not believe anything you hear about the conflict without checking with non-Zionist sources. This will include another zpropaganda claiming that there was always bloodshed in the Middle East between Jews and Muslims, that it was Arabs that first attacked Israel in the war of 1967!

The world governments must cut political and economic relations with the Na-Zionist Israel. We must create a list of top 10 companies that financially support the NaZionist and terrorist state of Israel.

I strongly believe that the Nazionists will be the ultimate losers of this conflict. *Zulm* cannot sustain its agent forever.

360

Here is an American artist, Michael Heart's reaction to the most recent Zionist massacre, which I am sure will not be the last. Here his words and watch the pictures and let me know how long you can tone down my friend. "We will not go down!"

http://www.youtube.com/watch?v=dlfhoU66s4Y

And also make sure watching this award-winning documentary DVD: Occupation 101, which is sold at:

www.occupation101.com

And can be viewed online, though in low quality, at:

http://video.google.com/videoplay?docid=-2451908450811690589

You may look at these three sites, which I have not studied throughly; but they contain a lot of links and information:

http://www.amnesty.org
http://www.jewwatch.com
http://jewsvszionists.wordpress.com

And finally, you may look at the following books to get the facts in their historical and political context, without being distorted by Z-propaganda:

- Ali Abunimah, One Country
- Charles D. Smith, Palestine and the Arab-Israeli Conflict
- Donald Neff, Fallen Pillars
- George W, Ball & Douglas B. Ball, The Passionate Attachment
- Greg Philo and Mike Berry, Israel and Palestine: Competing Histories
- Ilan Pappe, The Ethnic Cleansing of Palestine
- Israel Shahak, Jewish Fundamentalism in Israel
- John Mearsheimer & Stephen Walt, The Israel Lobby
- John W. Mulhall, CSP, America and the founding of Israel
- Jonathon Cook, Blood and Religion
- Kathleen Christison, Perceptions of Palestine
- Mazin Qumsiyeh, Sharing the Land of Canaan
- Noam Chomsky, Fateful Triangle
- Norman Finkelstein, Beyond Chutzpah
- Nur Masalha, Expulsion of the Palestinians
- Paul Findley, They Dare to Speak Out
- Roane Carey, The New Intifada: Resisting Israel's Apartheid
- Robert John & Sami Hadawi, Palestine Diary 1914-1945
- Salman Abu-Sitta, Palestine Right of Return, Sacred, Legal, and Possible
- Sami Hadawi, Bitter Harvest
- Stephen Green, Taking Sides
- Virginia Tilley, The One State Solution

"Tone Down, Edip!"

Jan 9, 2009

"There [are] several Jewish organizations that are protesting against Israeli actions. You need to tone down your language, you sound like the usual angry Muslim mob we see in places like Pakistan. This type of emotional statement only diminishes any point you are trying to make peace." F.T.

Perhaps you are right my dear friend; I should not be angry when hundreds of Palestinian school children were massacred by Israeli jets donated by USA-Inc since they are far away from the comfort of my home in Tucson, Arizona. My children are secure and happy playing with their high-tech toys. After all, weren't wars helping our military industrial complex to make profits?

You are right my dear friend, I should tone down and indulge in my comfort and enjoy my junk food watching my favorite TV program when the 1.5 million suffocated and starved people in a crowded concentration camp get showered with deadly bombs — massacred, mutilated, and terrified — and are called terrorists deserving extermination. I should just ignore the terror and genocide for more land, and enjoy the diabolic propaganda day and night.

I should act like a heartless robot, or act as a stupid Joe-the-plumber, and watch another holocaust in the making. I should keep quiet. I should not offend our Zionist friends who enjoy another meal made of human flesh, bones, tears and blood!

I should act innumerate when I see the ratio between dead Israelis and Palestinians being 3 to 900+! I should act blind when I see a little hole created by peanut rockets thrown by the so-called dangerous terrorists in the concentration camp while the entire city is destroyed and burning under the bombings from poor Israeli soldiers. I should act deaf when I hear the terrifying sounds of heavy bombing of a city with a population of 40 percent children.

Yes, I should laugh and smile in the comfort of my home since I am a privileged American professor, and I should not care about the plight of the poor and ugly people out there in the middle of nowhere. I should just teach metaphysics, logic, and ethics without reflecting as a conscious being. I should discuss Socrates' Apology with my students without taking a lesson from it for myself. I should talk about John Rawl's "veil of ignorance" without trying it. I should talk about "life, liberty and pursuit of happiness" but act as if the powerful people deserve it. And, you wish me to adopt Thrasymachus.

My dear friend:

I am sick and tired of Zionist propaganda, and I cannot stay silent or emotionless when they massacre night after night and day after day helpless people and their children imprisoned in concentration camps, and yet show the audacity to blame their victims for their loss.

No, my dear friend, I will not tone down. I believe in the hereafter, the Day of Judgment, and I will not support the racist murderers for the sake of my interests in this worldly life.

I condemn murderers and warmongers, regardless of their race, religion and nationality, but Zionists will never condemn nor denounce the state of Israel, which is the biggest and the longest-lasting terrorist in the region. I will not hush to please Zionist murderers.

If I am going to lose my life for telling the truth, let be it. None will live here forever. How can I tone down when a serial rapist and murderer continues his crimes for decades with the help of misinformed people who are duped by a mixture of sophisticated propaganda and intimidation? The serial killer rapist is crying for our pity for the scratch on his face, and expects us to declare his victim as terrorists with long nails! Emotions are one way to fight back the propaganda, and I believe that this latest massacre in Gaza is going to break the spell. This has united many people around the world against the Zionist cancer.

No more do I believe that the Zionists have an iota of interest in peace. They are liars, and I will no more try to placate Zionists for the hope of a potential piece of peace granted by them and then taken back at whim. They have declared war against humanity and we cannot force ourselves to appease them. Our appeasement will not change their plan a bit. They will massacre and destroy Palestinians either way. But, our emotional condemnation of injustices and crimes might at least save our spirits and souls.

I strongly believe that the Nazionists will be the ultimate losers in this conflict. *Zulm* cannot sustain its agent forever.

Peace,
Edip

Militarist Evangelists vs. Taliban:
Look-alike Holy Rivals

23 October 2008

"So man's proneness to engage in war is still a fact. But wisdom born of experience should tell us that war is obsolete. There may have been a time when war served as a negative good by preventing the spread and growth of an evil force, but the destructive power of modern weapons eliminated even the possibility that war may serve as a negative good. If we assume that life is worth living and that man has a right to survive, then we must find an alternative to war. In a day when vehicles hurtle through outer space and guided ballistic missiles carve highways of death through the stratosphere, no nation can claim victory in war. A so-called limited war will leave little more than a calamitous legacy of human suffering, political turmoil, and spiritual disillusionment." Martin Luther King in his Nobel acceptance speech.

It is no secret that the war in Iraq was started to promote the geo-political interests of the American-Israeli alliance, with baptisal by big corporations. While the American weapon industry devours bloody profits from the destruction of Iraq, American construction giants pile up skyrocketing profits from its construction and oil companies are make lucrative profits from shortage speculations and future concessions received from the so-called Free Iraq's puppet regimes. War once again re-distributes the wealth in America, shifting it further from the poor and middle class to the filthy rich. All this is accomplished by utilization of our tax money, which 60 percent of American corporations contributed ZERO dollars towards.

In this war, the blood of poor people gets shed on both sides. Whether by accident or design, a son of a rich American enlists in military duty and ends up wounded on a battlefield, and the America Inc's media celebrates him program after program by telling the narrative of the Great American Hero. This makes poor Americans forget about their financial and health problems, prisons, debts, and joblessness while crying for this great hero. Poor and middle-class citizens are led to believe that rich people share the honor of snake-oil patriotism with them.

More than one million Iraqis were massacred as the direct or indirect consequences of this war. So far, about four thousand American soldiers lost their lives, and we got only one-and-a-half heroes — Lynch and Tillman. Their stories attracted the media's attention, since one was a woman and the other was a "potential" millionaire. The story of Jessica Lynch saved by brave American soldiers was revealed later to be fiction. To lure the daughters and wives of lower-class Americans in addition to their men to die for the aspirations of the big corporations, the media has always staged hidden propaganda campaigns. As for Tillman, he had an inspiring story. Yet a series of lies from the Pentagon raised suspicion about his death: Was he deliberately killed by warmongers to be used for militaristic propaganda? His family was disappointed in the Pentagon and lost their trust in the US government's account in relation to wars. His death was used to promote the right-wing's mantra "American values."

I am not talking about American values such as individual rights, freedom, innovation, optimism, and hard work. As for politicians who are hired and manipulated by big corporations and organizations, they almost always shed crocodile tears and get more votes from the exploited poor.

The enlisted military personnel mainly consists of Americans from the bottom 20 percent of the economic spectrum. Though many of them are financially FORCED to become hired guns, they are euphemistically called Volunteers. Besides the military service, the only two options for most of the enlisted "volunteers" are to join the homeless or prison populations. American soldiers have somehow "patriotically" picked the military, which seems to be a better option than being homeless or inmates. Ironically, when they become useless for the military, usually they end up on streets, prisons or mental hospitals.

After this introduction, I would like to present you with some facts about the deeds and words of two fanatic groups: Taliban, al-Qaida, or Army of the Mahdi VERSUS Crusaders, Fascist Evangelical Christians, or the Left-Behind-Armageddonites. The essence of the following statements are all gathered from the media, and can be verified. Aren't the similarities shocking?:

ZEALOT A: We destroyed and will continue destroying your SKYSCRAPERS.
ZEALOT Z: We destroyed and will continue destroying your HOMES and CAVES.
ZEALOT A: We will ATTACK and TERRORIZE you.
ZEALOT Z: We will first SHOCK and AWE you, then, we will F…K you!
ZEALOT A: This is a JIHAD
ZEALOT Z: This is unofficially a CRUSADE, officially your LIBERATION.
ZEALOT A: ALLAH is with us; He is on our FLAG.
ZEALOT Z: GOD is with us; He is on our MONEY.
ZEALOT A: MUHAMMAD is the best.
ZEALOT Z: JESUS is the best, forget the rest.
ZEALOT A: MUHAMMAD'S GRAND SON was killed because of our sins. In anniversaries, pretending to be sharing his agony, we SUFFER by BLEEDING ourselves.
ZEALOT Z: GOD'S FAVORITE SON was killed for our sins. In masses we enjoy drinking wine, pretending that it is his BLOOD, we eat

365

cookies pretending that it they are his flesh, and then we make heathens SUFFER.

ZEALOT A: We offer 10 kilogram GOLD for the head of IMPERIALISTS.

ZEALOT Z: We offer 50 million DOLLARS for the head of the TERRORISTS.

ZEALOT A: We will ENSLAVE the occupiers, especially their female soldiers.

ZEALOT Z: We will CAPTURE and IMPRISON the insurgents, especially their males.

ZEALOT A: We ENJOY abusing our HOSTAGES and SLAVES.

ZEALOT Z: We officially REGRET but unofficially ENJOY abusing and torturing the DETAINEES and PRISONERS.

ZEALOT A: Our countries are turned to HELL by ZIONIST and CHRISTIAN occupiers and their puppets, and we will go to HEAVEN while sending them to HELL.

ZEALOT Z: Our country is a great HEAVEN and we will occupy MUSLIM COUNTRIES in the holy and oily Middle East to maintain our HEAVEN.

ZEALOT A: We MOURN when our brothers and sisters killed by infidels. But we become MAD and DANGEROUS when the tombs of our DEAD idols are damaged.

ZEALOT Z: We MOURN when our heroes killed by insurgent thugs and terrorists. But we become MAD and DANGEROUS when the bodies of our DEAD heroes are mutilated.

ZEALOT A: When we are killed we will have 70 young VIRGINS in the HEAVEN.

ZEALOT Z: We do not care whether it is virgin or not. Perverts among us even do not care whether it is man or woman. While we are on EARTH we enjoy them in our BARS, HOTELS, PORNO SITES, and PRISONS.

ZEALOT A: We HATE our ENEMIES in our MOUSQUES and streets.

ZEALOT Z: We LOVE our ENEMIES in CHURCHES and we HATE them everywhere else.

God and Blood
The Theological Roots of ZionistViolence against Gaza Concentration Camp

Edip Yuksel
December 31, 2008

The current atrocities and crimes against humanity committed by Israel is neither first nor will be the last. It is worn to call this conflict a war, since there are no warring two parties. On one side there are millions of Palestinians who have been subjugated by Israel and treated like animals in concentration camps, and on the other side there is the world's most powerful military and killing machine. Those in concentration camps have been under blockade and deprived of food, medicine, and basic necessities by the fascist Israeli regime. They have been humiliated, harassed, arrested, tortured, assassinated, slaughtered daily and their homes are destroyed frequently to open more space for the "chosen" settlers.

Unfortunately the US media is an appalling accomplice of this genocide and they are distorting the facts to portray the fascist monsters as victims and the victims as monsters. Just this morning, while Israeli army was slaughtering hundreds of men, women, and children in a concentration camp called Gaza, the cameras of CBS, ABC and NBC all were zoomed on "Hezbollah's rockets", dramatizing the little hole they have opened in one of the buildings in Israel, and interviewing the "terrorized" poor Israeli settlers. The American media is shamelessly telling us that the blood of one Jew equals the blood of thousands Arabs! The American media is justifying and applauding the terrors, massacres, and atrocities committed by us or by our allies.

Before year 2000, the so-called mainstream American media were justifying Israeli's killing of 25 Palestinians for every 1 Israeli soldier. Then, the Palestinians had not resorted to uprising against the apartheid regime, they had not used a single suicide bombing, and they did not have Hamas. Then, the American media managed to portray the victim as deserving. Each time the manufactured an excuse and after 9/11 they are happy to use the magical word "terror" or "terrorist" to distort the facts, to lead us to unjustified wars, to lead us supporting brutal and fascist regimes.

Sure, only the gullible, uninformed, religiously delusional, jingoists, or neocons would be duped by such blatant bias and distortion. Unfortunately, more than one third of American population is gullible and uninformed about international issues.

Zionists are the greatest enemy of humanity and, more specifically, the Jews. Zionists are the main source of increasing anti-Semitism in the world. Progressive American Jews need to realize this fact and engage more actively in rejecting the Zionists as we muslims need to reject Al-Qaida and similar violent and regressive organizations. We should not let bloodsuckers and warmongers hijack our heritage, or name!

Those who have been terrorized tortured and massacred even before the inception of Israel, those who have been condemned to a hopeless and miserable life in concentration camps recently waited for six long months without any reaction to the injustices. But, they know by now that the "chosen people" have no mercy, have no intention to stop suffocating them. So, they did what every human under the same condition being should do: self-defense. Those in concentration camps do not have fighter jets, tanks, or any highly destructive missiles. Their crude rockets killed ONLY one Israeli, which provoked the Gestapo of the concentration camp to shower bombs on their heads, destroying their dilapidated streets, homes, schools, and rundown hospitals, and killing hundreds of them and injuring thousands.

The cause of this massacre, this gradual genocide, is not the democratically elected representatives of the Gaza Concentration camp, Hamas! Hamas did not exist several years ago. The Israeli Gestapo used every little excuse to kill as many Palestinians they could, destroy as many houses they could, and to grab as much land they could. Each time they did it with the support and blessing of the USA. They thumbed their nose to the United Nation's resolutions and the reports of Human Rights organizations.

How has Israel become the world's top weapon manufacturer and arms merchant? How has Israel become a terrorist state? Why does Israel consider itself a victim while it is the biggest bully in the Middle East? Why the children of the 20th century's greatest tragedy have now become the cause of great tragedies. For the answer, we need to look at the theological and historical background. Here are some samples of terrifying and bloody instructions found in The Old Testament. We recommend the reader to study them in their context:

> "The Lord said to Moses: 'Take the blasphemer outside the camp. All those who heard him are to lay their hands on his head, and the entire assembly is to stone him. Say to the Israelites: If anyone curses his God, he will be held responsible; anyone who blasphemes the name of the Lord must be put to death. The entire assembly must stone him. Whether an alien or native-born, when he blasphemes the Name, he

must be put to death.... Then Moses spoke to the Israelites, and they took the blasphemer outside the camp and stoned him. The Israelites did as the Lord commanded Moses." (Leviticus 24:13-16).

"Now kill all the boys. And kill every woman who has slept with a man. But save for yourselves every girl who has never slept with a man." (Numbers 31:18).

"And they utterly destroyed all that was in the city, both man and woman, young and old, and ox, and sheep, and ass, with the edge of the sword" (Joshua 6:21).

"Now go and smite Amalek, and utterly destroy all that they have, and spare them not; but slay both man and woman, infant and suckling, ox and sheep, camel and ass" (1 Samuel 15:3).

"And as David returned from the slaughter of the Philistine, Abner took him, and brought him before Saul with the head of the Philistine in his hand" (1 Samuel 17:57).

"Thus the Jews smote all their enemies with the stroke of the sword, and slaughter, and destruction, and did what they would unto those that hated them" (Esther 9:5).

"Why do the wicked prosper and the treacherous all live at ease?... But you know me, Lord, you see me; you test my devotion to you. Drag them away like sheep to the shambles; set them apart for the day of slaughter" (Jeremiah 12:1-3).

"A curse on all who are slack in doing the Lord's work! A curse on all who withhold their swords from bloodshed!" (Jeremiah 48:10).

Chapter 20 of LEVITICUS contains a list of very severe punishments for various sins. For instance, cursing one's own father of mother would prompt death penalty. A man marrying a woman together with her daughter must be burned in the fire. Homosexual men must be put to death. Those who commit bestiality must be put to death together with the animals. And many more death, burning penalties.

If you have not read the verses of Old Testament above, please go back and read them one by one. It will allow you to see the background virus that has transformed the victims of Nazi murderers into Nazionist murderers! The children of the victims of Nazi concentration camps are now torturing, terrorizing, killing and massacring Arabs in modern concentration camps called Gaza and West Bank.

It is our concentration camp, since it is maintained by American tax money, military, diplomatic and political support, and propaganda. It is the Palestinian holocaust, ironically created by those who demand pity from the world as victims of the Nazi holocaust.

Based on their theological culture, based on the superiority of Jews over all other races, the Zionists movement has turned the state of Israel into a machine of death and destruction. Any human being with a sense of justice cannot be a bystander of this horror, this modern tragedy. See it for yourself. Do not let the bloodsuckers fool you. Do not let them sell you their "terrorist Palestinians" and "poor victim Zionists"! Please see the following link to witness the modern concentration camp called Gaza:

http://www.youtube.com/watch?v=DSzn7XLLM7c#

Thank God, many Americans are now waking up to the naked truth. Here is a comment posted by Aaron Aarons:

"Why does Israel have a 'right to exist' as apartheid state? No other state I know of demands that anybody recognize its 'right to exist' as a condition for not being attacked by that state. And it especially takes a lot of chutzpah for the Zionists to demand that those who were ethnically cleansed from the land 'Israel' claims as its own should recognize that the racist state resulting from that ethnic cleansing has a 'right to exist'! It is Palestine, not Israel, whose right to exist needs to be recognized."

There are those who show the gullibility or audacity to ask Palestinians to get inspiration from Gandhi! No, acting like Gandhi would not work for Palestinians for multiple reasons:

1. The United Kingdom was over extended and India was not worth the trouble.
2. India had a big population.
3. Gandhi had an alternative: violent Indian nationalist groups.
4. The United Kingdom saw a bloody defeat in the end of the tunnel, and thus chose for a face-saving exit strategy.
5. British, even at the peak of its power in India, never treated its subjects as cruel and brutal as today's Nazionist Israel has been doing since its inception.
6. We know what happened to the Jews acting like lambs in the concentration camps; they were exterminated within several years.
7. Bullies and powerful majority do not grant the rights of minorities if they do not see that there is a price/cost to pay. For instance, the white majority would most likely not grant the dream of the singing King, if the same black minority did not give birth to Black Panthers, Nation of Islam, Malcolm X, street riots, etc... It is a matter of cost-benefit calculation... Morality is usually used by the

super and duper powers as a cover up. This might be a cynical way of evaluating the events, but unfortunately, we carry more the genes of Canes rather than of Abels.

What Palestinians are doing is so similar to what Rodney King, a black robbery parolee did. He was stopped by half a dozen police officers and subsequently struck as many as 56 times by officers wielding batons, kicked at least six times, and shot with a Taser electronic stun gun. As a normal reaction for survival he tried to stop the painful hits. Later, those defensive reflexes were cunningly used by the defense lawyers to accuse the victim of attacking the police. The incredible happened. The jury was duped.

(For how the jury was duped to confuse the brutal aggressors and the victim, please read this article at: http://www.yuksel.org/e/law/jury.htm)

Now an entire nation is beaten by the World's Super power's fascist ally in the region, over and over. When their victims show little reaction by slinging rocks and throwing primitive rockets that scratch the "chosen hands" of their slaughterers, the victims are depicted as terrorists, in turn, justifying another round of horrific beating.

Palestinian people were not much religious in the mid 20th century. The atrocities committed by the terrorist state of Israel year by year led them to resort in religion and become the prey of religious fanatics. Hamas was created by Israel's policies and atrocities in the region. In fact, there is evidence that Israel created or supported Hamas to divide PLO as the USA-Inc created or supported the Mujahids and Osama bin Laden to use against Russia.

Those who live by bombs, die by bombs. Israel will go down to history as the Nazi Germany did. And those who have supported the fascist state of Israel will be ashamed of themselves. Wait and see.

Though Sunni and Shiite Muslims cannot top the violence of the "Chosen Race", they too have their share of violence. Ironically, they too have baptized their violence through the fabricated instructions and stories falsely attributed to God and Muhammad. For those who are interested in our position on this issue, I recommend you reading the last sections of the Manifesto for Islamic Reform, where we direct heavy criticism against the followers of Sunni and Shiite sects:

http://www.islamicreform.org/

Also for facts on this issue, visit:

http://www.ifamericansknew.org/
http://www.jewishvoiceforpeace.org/

371

Skyscrapers vs. Caves:
The Unholy War Between Capitalist Crusaders and Feudal Mujahids
(This article was written in 2002)

After the diabolical terrorist attacks of September 11, 2001, Americans need to know the theological and political roots of terrorism and wars. This knowledge will help us to eradicate the religious, social, political, and economic factors that breed international terrorism and aggression, whether committed by groups or by states.

I am a muslim author/activist, and I have written numerous articles along with scores of books including Turkish and English translations of the Quran. I promote reformation in Islam. I was once a leader of a radical Muslim youth movement affiliated with Iran's Revolutionary Guard, Egypt's Muslim Brotherhood, and Afghanistan's Hizb-i Islami. After correspondances and discussions of theological issues with an Egyptian-American scientist, I later experienced a paradigm shift in my belief system and I denounced my religious and political ideology, becoming a target of my former comrades as an "apostate" or "betrayer."

The person pivotal to my conversion, Dr. Rashad Khalifa, was initially a popular scholar in the Muslim world. However, in January 1990 he was assassinated in Tucson, Arizona by Fuqra, a domestic terrorist group affiliated to Bin Laden, the leader of the international terrorist network Al-Qaeda, or The Base.

As a muslim who once was a leading member of the international network of anti-American radical Islam — a muslim who continuously receives death threats from Muslim fanatics, a muslim who lost his closest friend to the knives of Osama bin Laden's terrorists, a muslim who has dedicated himself to the promotion of human rights, freedom of expression, democracy, and islamic reform — I invite all Muslims to abandon man-made teachings besides the Quran. I invite Muslims to reform themselves under the light of the Quran alone. We should seek peace and justice for all. We should attain individual freedom by submitting ourselves to God's laws in nature and His scripture. We should use our reason rather than our superstitions. We should reject the teachings of clergymen which have doomed us to the darkness of ignorance and to the backwardness of medieval culture.

Muslims must join the islamic reformation movement. Otherwise, they will become extinct. Our movement's arguments rely primarily on theological and philosophical arguments, logic, critical analysis of history, and lessons learned from the backwardness of Muslim countries. The momentum of this monotheistic

372

movement is so powerful that it is going to change the social and political land-scape of Muslim countries.

Though the movement is in its embryonic stage, it is nevertheless receiving a surprisingly broad level of sympathetic support in Turkey, Malaysia, and North-ern Africa. Muslim populations living in Western countries also show interest in the message of the reformation movement. Monotheist, reformist, or progressive muslims are targets of oppressive and regressive religious governments and au-thoritarian regimes, ironically supported at times by the USA. Especially those who live in Iran, Pakistan, Malaysia, Saudi Arabia, and Egypt risk their lives. Sunni and Shiite clergymen have demonstrated their determination to fight fiercely against the monotheistic movement by labeling it as "apostasy" and "a Western and Zionist plot."

The loosely organized islamic reformation movement involves a radical princi-ple: all religious sources besides the Quran remain irrelevant for salvation and they should be dealt with like dinosaurs. By rejecting volumes of books of narra-tions, contradictory sectarian teachings, and numerous secondary sources, a new understanding of the Quran emerges. The islam based on the Quran is dramati-cally different than the "Islam" as propagated by Sunni or Shiite clergymen. First of all, according to the Quran, islam is not a proper name but a gerund meaning peacemaking and surrendering to God alone. Again, according to the Quran, promotion of freedom and peace did not start from Muhammad. It started from the first Homo Sapiens. Most importantly, the Quranic islam requires a paradigm change that emphasizes rational and empirical methodology over blind faith. It eliminates the reliance on fatwas of muslim clerics and rejects their power over individuals.

The ramifications of following the Quran alone cannot be exaggerated. It provides a paradigm shift regarding the roles of women, freedom of speech, democracy, positions against science and technology, the criminal justice system, international terrorism, and peace with other nations.

As an American citizen, I also invite American people to become more discern-ing regarding the foreign policies of the American government. The myopic American foreign policy, which primarily serves the interests of big corpora-tions such as weapons and oil industries, inadvertently helps the cause of reli-gious terrorists. Perhaps it is inaccurate to refer to the current Bush government as the US government, since it serves the interests of big corporations. It should be called the government of the United Incorporations of America.

For instance, in the early 1950's we alienated Iranian people by supporting an oppressive and corrupt monarchy against a popular prime minister (Mossadegh), thereby contributing to the success of mullarchy in Iran. We aided Saddam Hus-sein militarily and politically while using him against Iran, thereby participating in the destruction of hundreds of cities and millions of human lives. We did nothing when Saddam killed 5,000 Kurdish villagers instantaneously through chemical weapons in Halabja, but we brought the entire world together when an oil-rich Kuwait became occupied by the same Saddam. For more than a year we were bystanders when Serbs committed genocide and atrocities against Bosnian Muslims, and we kept sanctions banning Muslims from obtaining weapons for self-defence. The oppressive and racist Turkish government used our helicopters and weapons in its decade-long genocide against the Kurdish population. We backed the Turkish military whenever they meddled with Turkish democracy. Our economic sanctions intended to dethrone Saddam, our former ally, contributed to the starvation of millions of Iraqi children. Ironically, Saddam, a fascist, is now a hero in the eyes of starving people. We bombed a Sudanese medicine factory and killed many civilians by falsely declaring it to be a chemical weapon factory. Our TV stations did not interview the children and relatives of the employees we killed! We support the Saudi monarchy, one of the most oppressive and corrupt regimes on the face of earth, and we have therefore contributed to the creation of millions of oppressed and ignorant enemies. When they overthrow the Saudi King, they will surely chant, "Death to America!" We used Afghani people against Russia, our former arch-enemy, and we abandoned them after their economic, social, and political structure fell to ruins. We declared a futile war against drugs and thereby created a lucrative business for criminals and international terrorists. Our noble support of Jewish victims in their quest for their historical homeland unfortunately transformed into an unconditional support of racist and aggressive policies, leading to the creation of another victimized nation. By supporting Israeli terrorism and occupation, we have created millions of enemies and potential terrorists in Muslim world. Now, by invading Iraq and killing Iraqi civilians, destroying cities, and committing atrocities, we plant seeds for much bigger terrorist operations against America and its interests.[42]

Our warships expect friendly greetings in every foreign harbor, our bombers expect silent submissions from cities and their inhabitants, and our companies serve as the prime suppliers of weapons among many world nations and terrorists. We are the first nation to use the atomic bomb, and we killed record numbers of civilians in one day in the whole history of the human race. We are the main producer of biological and chemical weapons, and we sell our products for any price we choose. But, we want to fix the price of oil, and also the price for products sold by poor countries. We doom many countries to economic bankruptcy through the IMF and a myriad of financial institutions, and we stage mili-

---

[42]   [As of Dec. 2009, the Iraqi Death Estimator at www.justforeignpolicy.org/iraq estimates 1,339,771 Iraqi deaths due to the US-led invasion, which deliberately started civil wars to crush the uprising against the brutal invasion, massacres, and torture.]

tary coups via the CIA and support puppet governments in order to please our big corporations. Yet we wonder why so many people in other countries hate us. Ironically, we brag that we are a peace-loving, compassionate nation! We show our compassion by dropping food from one airplane and bombs from another!

During the outrageous sexual abuse and physical torture scandal, the Neocon-Zionist-Armageddonite coalition proved that the words "liberty and democracy" could be described by the Bush administration as killing, destruction, humiliation, and torture against Arabs and muslims. Israel, as the world's only government recognized by the United Nations that tortures prisoners LEGALLY, led the Neoconian USA government with their immense American political influence towards torture against political prisoners, or against those they call terrorists.

Israel and its influential Zionist lobbies exercise incredible amounts of influence on both major American parties. This is a fact known by every insider and by every outsider with average intelligence. For instance, James Bamford, an American intelligence expert, in his book A Pretext For War exposes the infiltration of Zionist gangs into the USA's key political positions. Time magazine reporter Michael Duffy wrote the following:

> "The Bush hard-liners had long believed that stability could come to the Middle East — and Israel — only if Saddam Hussein was overthrown andIraq converted into a stable democracy. Led by Deputy Defense Secretary Paul Wolfowitz, they were installed at various government, and nothing moved without their O.K. Bamford comes very close to stating that the hard-liners were wittingly or unwittingly acting as agents ofIsrael's hard-line Likud Party, which believed Israel should operate with impunity in the region and dictate terms to its neighbors. Such a world view, Bamford argues, was simply repotted by the hard-liners into U.S. foreign policy in the early Bush years, with the war in Iraq as its ultimate goal. Bamford asserts that the backgrounds, political philosophies and experiences of many of the hard-liners helped to hardwire the pro-Israel mind-set in the Bush inner circle and suggests that Washington mistook Israel's interests for its own when it preemptively invaded Iraqlast year." (One Expert's Verdict: The CIA Caved Under Pressure, Michael Duffy, Time, June 14, 2004, p.65).

The only point I disagree with is the depiction of the policy as "Israel's interest." I do not think at all that aggression, assassination, home destructions, elimination of hope for Palestinian youth pushed to become suicide bombers, massacres, erection of Jewish settlements on Palestinian lands, defiance of international laws and UN resolutions, dictation of will over its neighbours, commission of massacres in refugee camps, and deprivation of an entire nation of their liberty serve the interests of the Israeli people. What goes around comes around.

Thank God that many Jews with intelligence and heart remain aware of the fact that their country's policies are gradually transforming into Nazism itself. Hopefully, progressive and peace-seeking Jews will prevail over the extremist, racist and greedy ones.

After the collapse of communism, America Inc. is trying to create another nemesis confirmed by the blessings of Zionists and Evangelical Christians — this time islam and muslims — to distract us from corruption and plundering of resources. The powerful hormones of religion and nationalism are abused and manipulated to promote this agenda.

American foreign policy, Zionist racism, evangelical Christianity, and sectarian Islam are all incubators of religious terrorism. War against terrorism has two fronts: reformation in American democracy and reformation in the Islamic world. Unfortunately, the victims of these wars are mostly innocent poor people, whether they live in skyscrapers or caves.

P.S: For a list of American military interventions see: Zoltan Grossman's list in the following pages.

A Debate with a Jewish American on the Gaza Massacre

10 January 2009

MICHAEL: Hamas' overthrow of the more secular Fatah organization in Gaza in 2007 is part of a regionwide civil war between Islamists and modernists. In the week that Israel has been slicing through Gaza, Islamist suicide bombers have killed almost 100 Iraqis — first, a group of tribal sheiks in Yusufiya, who were working on reconciliation among Shiites, Sunnis and Kurds, and, second, mostly women and children gathered at a Shiite shrine. These unprovoked mass murders have not stirred a single protest in Europe or the Middle East.

Why not do somthing positive with your life. Try protesting this. . .

http://www.nytimes.com/2009/01/03/world/middleeast/03iraq.html?hp

Here's Thomas Friedman's complete article:

http://www.mercurynews.com/livechats/ci_11398931

EDİP: Dear Michael, first, I invite you to listen to this beautiful song by singer Michael Heart:

http://www.youtube.com/watch?v=dlfhoU66s4Y

And this song by Sami Yusuf:

http://www.youtube.com/watch?v=9-3VQmkq82A&feature=related.

Since now you are in good spirits, now you may give an ear to Congressman Ron Paul. It is short; trust me:

http://www.youtube.com/watch?v=4Z6vMAoFwf4

And, if you have some patience, you may also listen to the less exciting Congressman Kucinich:

http://www.youtube.com/watch?v=2X35OAb2wGo&feature=related

You know well that in the chaos and carnage created by the American invasion of Iraq, a lot of atrocities were committed. Under the smoke and dusts of military propaganda and covert operations, we may never be able to know the truth regarding some allegations. We have much evidence since Vietnam that the American military and government have become masters in fabrication of lies and deception. I also know that the American media serves as a much better official propaganda machine than the Russian media was before 1990.

377

Every atrocity committed under that brutal occupation — which for a while conducted major covert operations to divide the Iraqi people — remains the crime of the occupier! So, do not come up with silly propaganda diversions to blame the victim for the crimes of the murderers and torturers. If the USA was the subject of similarly atrocious and diabolic occupations by a country 20 times bigger than the USA, much worse could have happened among minorities in Los Angeles or New York.

I should not indulge in a silly response to your red herring. One thing you forget is that I teach logic and philosophy classes, and what you are doing is a classic case of red-herring, or irrelevant argumentation.

But, I will enjoy briefly playing with your little fish.

To the contrary of what you imply, I have in the past condemned Hamas and many Islamist terrorists for killing civilians, including Israeli civilians. If you wish, go check my articles. For instance, go read the end of the Manifesto for Islamic Reform. Or you may find my published articles on terrorism, such as "Militarist Evangelists vs. Taliban: Look-alike Holy Rivals." Besides, Hamas is the product of Israeli atrocities in Lebanon years ago. Before Hamas was born, there was the PLO, yet you declared their quest for freedom and justice as TERRORISM too. In fact, it is a well known fact that Hamas was initially supported by Israel to weaken the PLO. Perhaps you wished all Palestinians turn into Gandhis so that Zionists could grab all the Palestinian lands and banish them into the Dead Sea!

But you baptized the terrorism among Zionist forces obsessed in the creation of more and more settlements. (You may try to tell me that Israel once gave up its settlements. It is a fact on the ground that they have always increased the number of their settlements lying on the confiscated lands of the natives. They just once performed a gimmick by giving up a few settlements (2% of all) in Gaza. In return, they received several billions of dollars from the USA and built more settlements in better sections of Palestinian land.)

On the other hand, you never condemned Israel for killing multiple times more civilians and children than Hamas and PLO combined. Even if you wish me to do so, I do not believe that murderers have the right to kill and massacre innocent people when they wear uniforms or become state agents! If you are telling me that Israel does not really wish to kill Palestinian women, elderly individuals, teenagers, or children, or that they are all mistakes (propaganda word: collateral damage), then your Israel is an idiot who is incompetent and intoxicated, an entity which does not deserve to have a license even to drive a car in city traffic!

You never condemned Zionist forces for the bombing of an entire concentration camp, including schools and hospitals. You never condemned them for killing more than 1000 civilians and injuring more than 5000! Why?

Perhaps you are not honest in your claims for peace! Do you have a reasonable explanation for why you never condemn Israel, but you demand from us to condemn Hamas and the rest every day? It is now obvious to everyone in the world, except a few gullible ones, that Zionists follow the footsteps of Nazis. Go check the Internet and you will see that the world is waking up. They now see as clear as night and day that Zionists are the enemies of humanity.

You should not trust your Evangelical supporters so much. In reality, they hate Jews. They are just trying to use Israel to shed more blood in the region so that their Messiah will come back and save them through rapture. Then, "to hell with the Jews!" They will turn against you immediately. It will only take a dream and a new twist on fictional stories propagated through an evangelical leader.

Historically, Muslims were your closest friends. Before the Zionist cancer infected the region, you lived in peace with them. When you were massacred in Spain, it was they who opened their arms for you. It was not Muslims that committed genocide against you in the Holocaust; the corrupters were supposedly Christian Germany and supposedly Catholic Italy! But now they encourage you to repeat their criminal deeds so that you share the same crimes.

After witnessing what Israel has done to helpless people and children who have been starved and suffocated in concentration camps for years, I have dedicated myself to fight back against the injustices of these neo-Nazi-incarnates. They are so alike!

You have no idea what is going on now, dear Michael. God is JUST and has a system of establishing justice. You will see that Pharaohs and Hitlers of our time will fall on their faces. Arrogance and injustice cannot be sustained, even if the delusional people like you wish it so.

I am a friend of peaceful Jews. I urge my readers and contacts not to lash out angrily against Jews in their countries and neighborhoods. I advise them not to fall into traps of racism, and anti-Semitism. Unfortunately, you do not understand that the state of Zionist Israel does great harm to Jews around the world. Zionists have hijacked Jewish symbols and names and they will be drowned in the blood they have shed. Those who live by sword die the by sword, my friend! That is the maxim from the Torah!

If you have faith in the Merciful and Just God, you should repent for your sins, as you have supported a racist and violent state. Go ahead and ask help from God. Think and act as a member of the human race rather than as a member of a tribe. Get over your paranoia and fear. Fear is the one thing that leads you to justify horrendous atrocities and murders. If you submit yourself to God alone, you will have no fear.

PS: I am curious why you have not challenged my use of the term "concentration camp" for Gaza. If you wish, I can list my reasons why Gaza is a modern concentration camp. What do you think?

Muslims are not Angels of Death

Edip Yuksel
2003

I am appalled to see that an educated Turkish muslim nicknamed Zikr, in his recent post at 19.org under the title "Quran and 11 September," tried to justify and even praise the horrific September 11 attacks. Unfortunately, he abused the Quranic verses 104:1-9 and 9:109-111 to depict an act of terrorism as a holy war. He fabricated an unjustified implication. I agree that American foreign policy remains misguided and under the influence of a corrupt and arrogant cabal that do not care about the interests of average Americans nor the world, but I can never justify terrorist acts against non-combatant civilians.

Muslims might fight for self-defense against corrupt and oppressive forces, and during the course of the war they might unintentionally kill noncombatant civilians or children. However, muslims can never target them. Muslims are required to follow certain ethical principles, both during times of peace and times of war. One can find dozens of Quranic verses asking muslims to observe justice and to remain restrained during war. Here are two of them:

> 2:190 "You shall fight in the cause of God against those who attack you, but do not aggress. God does not love the aggressors."

> 5:32 "… anyone who murders a person who did not commit murder or horrendous crimes on earth, is as if he murdered all the people…"

In his simultaneous posting in the Turkish section of this forum, this person defended his position through examples of God's total destruction of groups that committed aggression in the past. He argued that even innocent people die in the course of divine retribution as well.

Indeed, in earthquakes many innocent people and children die together with ignorant people who rewarded corrupt contractors and governments in defiance of divine laws of gravity and tectonic motions. Indeed, a sexually transmitted disease may victimize many innocent people and children along with those who do not recognize limits in their sexual conduct. And obesity may kill thousands.

The author uses a fallacious analogy, since God grants life and ultimately takes the lives of His creatures. We cannot use God as our example in this case. If we take people's lives for reasons other than self-defense or civil defense, it is equivalent of claiming to be gods besides God, or at least angels of death!

Muslims, like all other people, are humans tested by God to follow certain divine principles. Mass murder or terrorism cannot serve as a muslim way of fighting against enemies. Muslims are neither gods nor angels of death.

Boycott What, Boycott How?

16 August 2009

"Boycott Israeli dates. Sometimes when I walk through the mall, I walk past some of these stores above M&S, Tesco, Sainsbury's, etc. I see Middle Eastern women wearing headscarves and men with big beards happily shopping away, buying grapefruits, oranges, and dates amongst many other things MADE IN ISRAEL. Agggggggggghh, it makes me so mad that I want to get a giant mallet and hit these stupid people on the head with it!" Eddy on Facebook.

This is a better campaign than the many other campaigns that I have witnessed so far. It directly targets Israeli goods. But this might not be the best product to target. It has little chance to succeed if it does not have a powerful team promoting it. Even if the campaign succeeds and the Israeli date companies suffer big losses, the public might not see the impact. Furthermore, I believe that targeting American and European companies assisting Israeli's fascist policies might have a more positive impact, both in the political and financial worlds.

I have seen invitations to boycott a list of 30-50 American or European corporations because they support Israel and Nazionism financially. The logos of major brands wink and blink at me. And unfortunately, it remains at that. Please forgive my language, but this is just stupid and wishful thinking since such a list has no chance of success. They are useless campaigns. As long as we do not think critically and scientifically, we will never succeed. Let me explain.

You can never pragmatically achieve anything through a black list targeting 30 or more major corporations. First, many of the products we are asked to boycott remain essential or semi-essential for modern life. Second and most importantly, only a few people will be able to remember the names of those brands. And very few people will be able to carry the black list in their pockets and check every item in the grocery store they intend to buy with the list.

So if we really want to accomplish something, we need to target an achievable goal. After we hit that target, we should move to the next one. In fact, after hitting a few targets successfully, the rest in the list will receive a serious warning, and even before they are put into the next blacklist they might stop their support for the Nazionist atrocities. Let's call this strategy SUCCESSFUL APPROXIMATION. That is, we will reach our ultimate goal to cut corporate support for Israel step by step.

For instance, we can pick no more than THREE corporations that we are sure are openly supporting Israel. Those corporations should not produce essential components or items such as computer chips or vital medicines, since the campaign against such a corporation will not ensure maximum success. They should not be very small companies like date producers either. We should choose these three corporations only after diligent research and deliberation.

Now we have picked our first target: three Nazionist companies that produce goods or services with competing or alternative brands.

A team of artists and thinkers should then combine these three brands in multimedia ads such as cartoons, billboard signs, video clips, songs, slogans, logos, jingles, etc. and flood the media and Internet with it.

...

Let's all Cry for Poor Zionists

17 August 2005

Let me first make it clear that by the word "Zionist" I do not mean Jew. Furthermore, I do not even include some of the early Zionists, who justifiably sought a land for the Jews subjected to genocide by racist Germans. Racism is a vile ideology that creates division and hostility among the Children of Adam. Unfortunately, in less than a century, some Jews have transformed and embraced their own racist ideology and policy, ironically stealing ideas from their former enemies.

It has been a week that Jewish settlers (that is land-grabbers, Jewish terrorists) have been seen on the headline news. They are forced by these conditions to end the 38-year old government-sponsored occupation. They are crying, weeping, sobbing, blubbering, sniveling, moaning, and whimpering. Some are grumbling, groaning, croaking, whining, moaning, bemoaning, wailing, bewailing, and scowling. Others are growling, squealing, screaming, screeching, bawling, bellowing, yelling, and roaring. Still others are mourning, lamenting, complaining, howling, and brawling. Their Rabbis covered in silly clothes hug strange objects and pray for divine intervention. Some young Zionists pound their chests and burn tires and cars. Sharon, the one who committed massacres, the one who destroyed many Palestinian homes and ordered many assassination attacks, tells the fanatics, "Attack me, I am responsible; do not attack the soldiers." And the world watches this silly and idiotic drama. They expect us to cry for their plight, for their bad fortune.

ABC, CBS, and NBC all provided news for them and demanded the audience to cry for poor Jews who are forced out from "their God-given land." The American mainstream media, the goddesses of objective reporting, objectively sneak into their report the word "EXODUS." Wow. Another Exodus! Palestinians must be the slave-owners!

I always wondered why Americans do not sympathize with the real victim in the region. Now I know why.

Ami Teibel, Associated Press

NEVE DEKALIM, Gaza Strip - Israeli troops dragged **sobbing** Jewish settlers out of homes, synagogues and even a nursery school Wednesday in a massive evacuation, fulfilling Prime Minister Ariel Sharon's promise to end Israel's 38-year occupation of the Gaza Strip.

Meanwhile, soldiers carried away worshippers still wrapped in their white prayer shawls. Men **ripped their shirts** in a Jewish **mourning** ritual. Women in a synagogue **pressed their faces against the curtain** covering the Torah scroll. Others **kicked** and **screamed** as they were loaded onto buses, as the **smell of burning garbage** rose in the air. ...

Troops also **scuffled** with protesters in the isolated settlement of Morag, while **irate** settlers at another outpost employed **Nazi**-era imagery — including stars of David on their T-shirts — to protest the military's actions.

One commander of a small army unit, identified only as Yitzhak, **tearfully hugged a settler** in Neve Dekalim. "It's not easy. **These are very special people**," he said. "But we have a mission and we will carry it out, and I think these people understand that."

A grizzled colonel, also with **tears** in his eyes, shook hands with a young father as he explained it was time to go.

Sharon called the scenes "**heartbreaking**" and praised the **restraint** of both settlers and soldiers. "It's impossible to watch this, and that includes myself, without **tears in the eyes**," he said. "**My heart is broken** when I see these things."

Sharon appealed to pullout opponents to avoid physical and verbal confrontation with the security forces. "**Attack me, I am responsible for this, attack me, accuse me,** don't attack the men and women in uniform," he said.

Some teenage activists showed fierce resistance. Troops dragged flailing protesters, some as young as 12, onto the buses. "**I want to die**," **screamed** one youth as he was hauled away. Several soldiers were hit by white paint bombs, and protesters **smashed** the window of the bus.

Settlers were being removed at a rapid pace, with soldiers bundling them onto buses one after the other. About 10 buses filled with protesters drove away, the army said.

A settler woman in Morag was arrested after lightly **wounding a soldier by sticking a medical needle into her**, the army said.

Hundreds of protesters gathered in Neve Dekalim's main synagogue for morning prayers early Wednesday, **clapping and singing songs** that expulsion would not happen. Several youngsters climbed onto the roof of the building, while others formed circles or milled about in the courtyard. "You should be ashamed at what you are doing," screamed a woman who was pushing a **baby** stroller.

At midmorning, the building remained packed with protesters. "I believe in the **messiah**," sang a group of teenage girls. Many **cried** as they pressed their faces to the curtain covering the Torah.

384

Veteran residents repeatedly doused the flames raging in **garbage** containers and complained that the young die-hards had no right to cause **trouble**.

In the Morag settlement, troops carried dozens of **worshippers** out of the local synagogue. Two soldiers escorted out a **crying** man covered by a **prayer shawl**.

Under Israel's plan to leave Gaza and four West Bank settlements, residents were given until midnight Tuesday to leave their homes or face forcible removal and the loss of up to one-third of government compensation. Officials said about half of Gaza's 8,500 settlers left before the deadline.

In Morag, soldiers encountered cement blocks and **burning garbage containers**, and briefly clashed with residents. But as the day dragged on, protesters gradually surrendered.

Several families at a nursery were escorted onto a bus that was headed out of the Gaza Strip as troops entered the community's synagogue to remove settlers.

A female soldier with **tears in her eyes held a toddler in her arms**, gave him some candy and implored, "**Where is his mother**?"

Soldiers also removed families from their homes. The women walked out under army escort, while the men let themselves be carried. One resident, Eran Hendel, lay on the floor, read a biblical psalm and **ripped his shirt collar in a sign of mourning** before being carried away.

In the **hardline** outpost of Kerem Atzmona, **irate settlers** employed Nazi-era imagery. As the soldiers arrived, settlers shouted at them: "**Nazi**!" "Refuse orders!" and "Jews don't expel Jews." ...

In Netzer Hazani, residents requested a 24-hour delay in the evacuation and were in negotiations with government officials. Anita Tucker, a spokesman for the settlement, said residents were seeking adequate short-term **housing solutions and assurances that they could leave in a dignified manner**. ...

The pullout is part of Israel's plan to "disengage" from the Palestinians. Israeli leaders say giving up Gaza, which is home to 1.3 million Palestinians, **will improve Israeli security**.

Palestinians have welcomed the evacuation but who also fear that **Israel is trying to draw borders without negotiations**.

Israel Admits Harvesting Palestinian Organs

by Ian Black
December 21, 2009
The Guardian/UK

Israel has admitted that pathologists harvested organs from dead Palestinians, and others without the consent of their families - a practice that it said ended in the 1990s, it emerged at the weekend.

The admission, by the former head of the country's forensic institute, followed a furious row prompted by a Swedish newspaper reporting that Israel was killing Palestinians in order to use their organs - a charge that Israel denied and called "antisemitic".

The revelation, in a television documentary, is likely to generate anger in the Arab and Muslim world and reinforce sinister stereotypes of Israel and its attitude to Palestinians. Iran's state-run Press TV tonight reported the story, illustrated with photographs of dead or badly injured Palestinians.

Ahmed Tibi, an Israeli Arab MP, said the report incriminated the Israeli army.

The story emerged in an interview with Dr Yehuda Hiss, former head of the Abu Kabir forensic institute near Tel Aviv. The interview was conducted in 2000 by an American academic who released it because of the row between Israel and Sweden over a report in the Stockholm newspaper Aftonbladet.

Channel 2 TV reported that in the 1990s, specialists at Abu Kabir harvested skin, corneas, heart valves and bones from the bodies of Israeli soldiers, Israeli citizens, Palestinians and foreign workers, often without permission from relatives.

The Israeli military confirmed to the programme that the practice took place, but added: "This activity ended a decade ago and does not happen any longer."

Hiss said: "We started to harvest corneas ... whatever was done was highly informal. No permission was asked from the family."

However, there was no evidence that Israel had killed Palestinians to take their organs, as the Swedish paper reported. Aftonbladet quoted Palestinians as saying young men from the West Bank and Gaza Strip had been seized by the Israeli forces and their bodies returned to their families with missing organs. The interview with Hiss was released by Nancy Scheper-Hughes, professor of anthropology at the University of California-Berkeley who had conducted a study of Abu Kabir.

She was quoted by the Associated Press as saying that while Palestinians were "by a long shot" not the only ones affected, she felt the interview must be made public, because "the symbolism, you know, of taking skin of the population considered to be the enemy, [is] something, just in terms of its symbolic weight, that has to be reconsidered."

Israel demanded that Sweden condemn the Aftonbladet article, calling it an antisemitic "blood libel". Stockholm refused, saying that to so would violate freedom of speech in the country. The foreign minister then cancelled a visit to Israel, just as Sweden was taking over the EU's rotating presidency.

Hiss was removed from his post in 2004, when some details about organ harvesting were first reported, but he still works at the forensic institute.

Israel's health ministry said all harvesting was now done with permission. "The guidelines at that time were not clear," it said in a statement to Channel 2. "For the last 10 years, Abu Kabir has been working according to ethics and Jewish law."

Will Americans Bomb Muslim Mosques in the USA?

3 July 2004

We know that more than a quarter of the American population belongs to Evangelical Christian movement that mostly care about issues related to genitals, such as abortion and gay rights. Through their preaching, church activities, publications, and TV and radio programs, the right wing of the Evangelists have made it clear that they have nothing to do with Jesus and his message on many vital issues including the following:

1. They do not devote themselves to the ONE GOD alone but to a false triune god with MULTIPLE PERSONALITES, a fabrication started with the distortion of Saint Paul (Saul), the "Pharisee son of Pharisee."

2. They do not care about the plight of the poor and underprivileged. To the contrary, they promote the greedy interests of the filthy rich, who were likened by Jesus to a fat camel not being able to pass through a needle eye.

3. They do not care about peace. To the contrary, they are screaming hallelujahs for wars and more wars. They are unholy activist warmongers. They support larger militaries, more nuclear weapons, more invasions, more landmines, more killing, and more destruction. They are against the UN, an institution that was established to promote peace and justice on earth.

4. They do not care about the environment or ecology. To the contrary, they support politicians who have sold themselves to polluting industries, such as the oil and automobile barons.

5. They do not care about justice. To the contrary, they support the racist Zionist regime in Israel that has killed civilians, mostly teenagers, twenty times over what the so-called suicide bombers have done. They care much less about the plight of the imprisoned, humiliated, impoverished, and oppressed Palestinian population.

6. They do not care about truth; to the contrary, all they care about is collecting more money and gathering more power.

7. They do not care about human rights and dignity; to the contrary, they were outraged at the outrage towards USA-Inc's systematic torture practices in its prisons in Afghanistan, Iraq, and Cuba, as well as the outsourcing of its torture to friendly countries with oppressive regimes.

8. For more details about the deeds and characteristics of right-wing Evangelicals, please see my article titled, "BEWARE: Priests are Singing Love, Again" at: http://www.yuksel.org/e/law/evilgelical.htm

Now these right-wing Evangelical Christians, or believers in the fiction-squared book series called *Left Behind* passionately promote a modern Crusade against Muslims in the hopes of bringing about their fictional Armageddon so that their Superman will take them to Heaven (fiction-squared, since the Left Behind books are fictional treatments of the fictional book, Revelation). Since such a Crusade will serve the interests of oil barons, weapons manufacturers, and other big American corporations along with the interests of Zionists, we see an odd coalition termed the Zionist-Capitalist-Crusaders Coalition.

In fact, jingoist Christians are no different than Sunni clerics or Shiite mullahs promoting violence and terror. The only difference is that they have more money, they can manipulate bigger and more sophisticated armies, they wear ties instead of turbans, they shave their beards, and they are masters of deception with smirks on their faces and with the word love on their lips. Since most of them are cowards and have no genuine conviction in what they preach, they use proxies, the children of poor Americans, to kill and destroy.

Now, I am expecting that the toxic feeding of the Zionist Capitalist Crusaders Coalition to finally give fruits in terms of American UNDERGROUND terrorist organizations (See the endnote below). These domestic terrorist organizations will be more fatal than the anti-government militias. I hope that my prediction is wrong, but a population fed with constant propaganda of "Christians are the saved ones, we are the super-duper-size great nation; and muslims are evil" will not wait too long to result in unofficial and underground terrorism that could exceed the acts carried out by Sunni or Shiite evil twins in the other part of the world. Perhaps, what stops them from such attacks is that they see their government is killing muslims by thousands and wrecking havoc in their lands.

PS: I consider it dishonest to distinguish uniformed killers from uninformed killers if both parties kill civilians. If soldiers fighting under the order of USA-Inc killed thousands of Iraqi children and civilians with bombs and bullets, what difference does it make if one calls dead and suffering people COLLATERAL DAMAGE? If the occupying Israeli military has killed many more children and civilians than Palestinian suicide bombers or freedom fighters, then how can we call them terrorists while we ignore and support the bigger terrorists?

A sample reaction and my response to the article above:

FUMUU: Werent you going to serve a prison sentence in Turkey and fled to the US? Now youre biting the hand that feeds you and gives a home. There is absolutely no appreciation of Allah so how would you be expected of being appreciative of anything else. "I will come to them from before them, and from behind them, and from their right, and from their left, and You will find that most of them are unappreciative." [7:17]

EDIP: Dear Fumuu; American domestic policy — thank God for American Jews, secular-minded citizens, and atheists — is not dominated by evilgelical Christians. Otherwise, I would be the subject of oppression and torture. Then, I would have to fight or to immigrate to another country.

If I immigrate to a country, does that mean that I have to accept and support all the policies of its governments? The land and oceans belong to God. Your mentality is the mentality of bystanders. I spoke my mind in the country where I was born and I left there just to be able to THINK and EXPRESS MYSELF FREELY. This was the ONLY reason for my immigration. Now, you want me to BETRAY that very reason for my immigration to the USA and SUPPRESS my mind, conscience, and principles?! Do you understand what you are asking from me? You ask me to sell my soul because a country saved me from Turkish prisons or potential assassination by radical Sunnis!

FUMUU: You may be concerned about muslims about the world being oppressed by the Christians, the same muslims who label you a heretic because of your Quran alone following. If you chose to live with either these muslims or amongst these Christians you are criticizing I know by fact you will choose live amongst the latter. Exactly where does your support lie and which of these two groups will be your ally?

EDIP: We are talking about American Inc's killings of millions of poor people and plunder of their resources via oppressive puppet regimes around the world in last century. Your logic is twisted and troubling. America Inc. has a DOUBLE STANDARD. It does not recognize the human rights which it recognizes for its citizens if it interacts with other nations. While I was in Turkish prisons, I was tortured by an American-ally military regime, and the torture tools were "donated" by America as the military aid!

Just because I received the privilege of being an American citizen, should I close my eyes to a corrupt government's horrendous acts around the world? As a taxpayer of that country, don't I have the right to question the so-called elected government? You want me to forget my right as a citizen, as a human, as a monotheist, just because I was not born in that country? I find your position appalling. It seems that if you are OK, you will not care about other people. And you shamelessly ask me to act the same way!

I recommend you go read some books, but perhaps a film would be easier for you. Go and watch Fahrenheit 9/11 and reflect on your position.

FUMUU: Since you are a big figure, here you are putting ideas into people's heads with no backing up of the Quran. My simple advice is disregard those who disbelieve. [53:29] You shall disregard those who turn away from our message, and become preoccupied with this worldly life.

EDIP: First, I do not consider myself a "big" figure as you think and I do not desire that anyone follow my opinion blindly because they perceive me as a leading figure. Occasionally, I deliberately try to sabotage my charisma and I sometimes act like a child just to wake up gullible people from being mesmerized by my reputation and charisma, of which I have plenty. When Turkish people call me with titles and words of respect, I ask them to call me by my first name alone, which makes the younger people accustomed to Turkish culture uncomfortable. People should not be persuaded by the signature or titles, but they should look at the ideas. So if anyone is swayed by my words because he or she thinks I am a big figure, I cannot help that person. They will always find some big figures to follow, and there are thousands of them out there who are seriously pretending to be big.

I do not mind losing monkeys as my supporters; in fact, I would be happy losing them to some other "big" guys. My audience involves those who can think for themselves and who are able to critically evaluate my assertions and opinions. Though I find you on the wrong side of this debate, I prefer you to the monkeys who would accept whatever I say because of my name.

Ironically, you think that by quoting a verse out of context you are BACKING UP your cowardly and selfish stand, your support of American Inc's destruction around the world? Do you really expect that by any verse you can justify American support of oppressive governments, such as Saudi Faisals, Egyptian Mubaraks, Israeli Sharons, former Saddams, etc? I do not need to quote a verse from the Quran to justify the statement that 2 times 2 is 4, that the tea I am drinking is delicious, or that destroying the cities of Hiroshima and Nagasaki is terrorism. Do you really need a verse to oppose an arrogant power roaming the earth, corrupting their culture, and destroying people's properties and lives?

By the way, I appreciate many good things about America and I have expressed them in many of my articles and correspondences. But, I cannot close my eyes to the unjustified wars and policies of a government, opposed and condemned by at least half of US citizens who have sense of justice.

FUMUU: Because you are suffering at the hands of these Christians you are trying to conjure up sympathy from 19 only followers by flooding them with politics. It is very sad indeed. Fumuu.

EDIP: I am not suffering at the hands of "these Christians" yet. But, millions of people around the world are suffering from their political decisions. Can you have a little concern about the plight of individuals other than yourself? Does your religion teach you to be selfish? Does your religion ask you to be a bystander when there is oppression? If your answer is affirmative, then you should question your religion, since it does not sound like the religion from a Benevolent and Just God. Peace.

The Bush Administration Always Told the Truth about Iraq

15 October 2007

"Simply stated, there is no doubt that Saddam Hussein now has weapons of mass destruction."
- **Dick Cheney**, August 26 2002

"Right now, Iraq is expanding and improving facilities that were used for the production of biological weapons."
- **George W. Bush**, September 12 2002

"We know that Saddam Hussein is determined to keep his weapons of mass destruction, is determined to make more."
- **Colin Powell**, February 5 2003

"Intelligence gathered by this and other governments leaves no doubt that the Iraq regime continues to possess and conceal some of the most lethal weapons ever devised."
- **Bush**, March 17 2003

"Well, there is no question that we have evidence and information that Iraq has weapons of mass destruction, biological and chemical particularly . . . all this will be made clear in the course of the operation, for whatever duration it takes."
- **Ari Fleischer**, March 21 2003

"There is no doubt that the regime of Saddam Hussein possesses weapons of mass destruction. As this operation continues, those weapons will be identified, found, along with the people who have produced them and who guard them."
- **Gen. Tommy Franks**, March 22 2003

"We know where they are. They are in the area around Tikrit and Baghdad."
- **Donald Rumsfeld**, March 30 2003.

"Iraq has trained Al Qaeda members in bomb-making and poisons and deadly gases."
- **Bush** in October 2002.

"Saddam Hussein aids and protects terrorists, including members of al Qaeda."
- **Bush** in January 2003 State of the Union address.

"Iraq has also provided Al Qaeda with chemical and biological weapons training."
- **Bush** in February 2003.

"We have removed an ally of Al Qaeda."
- **Bush** in May 2003.

Stated that the Iraqis were "providing bomb-making expertise and advice to the Al Qaeda organization."
- **Cheney** in September 2003.

"Saddam had an established relationship with Al Qaeda, providing training to Al Qaeda members in the areas of poisons, gases, making conventional weapons."
- **Cheney** in October 2003.

"[Saddam] had long established ties with Al Qaeda."
- Cheney in June 14, 2004.

"The reason I keep insisting that there was a relationship between Iraq and Saddam and Al Qaeda, because there was a relationship between Iraq and Al Qaeda."
- **Bush** in June 17, 2004

No, Saddam was not our friendly dictator in 1980s, he was our S.O.B. No, Rumsfeld did not shake his hands when Saddam committed his atrocities and gassed 5,000 Kurdish people in Halabja, Northern Iraq. Rumsfeld was just on a clandestine mission to secretly plant intelligence bugs in Saddam's pants. No, neither the US nor the UK enticed Saddam to declare war against Iran; Saddam was already loaded with our weapons and needed to dispose the old ones some-where. It happened to be our new enemy who disposed the Shah, our Persian-version S.O.B. Neither the US nor the UK supplied him with chemical and bio-logical weapons; he purchased them from the military industrial complex which is owned by private companies. It was just a false story that April Glasspie, the US ambassador to Iraq, declared in 1990 regarding that "it was not our business to interfere if Iraq is going to invade Kuwait." The Middle East has always been our business! The US did not set up Saddam to invade Kuwait in order to kick his butt and make multibillion-dollar-worth arms sales to oil-rich kingdoms while testing and advertising the so-called "smart missiles" in a realistic envi-ronment. Saddam was too smart for such a set-up! Unpatriotic people accuse the US for deliberately misleading Saddam to invade Kuwait so that the US could open new military bases in Saudi Arabia and other little kingdoms. Those kings were already our friends, lucrative customers, and suppliers of cheap oil.

The US government has been the most peaceful and fair government in the last century. We are the good guy, we are the superman, and we are the bastion of freedom and human rights. The only way is the American way. You are either with us or against us. George Washington was a great guy, so was Abraham Lincoln. We are a nation of great glory. We are not terrorists. Terrorists are bad, very bad. They want to get us. We need to be vigilant. Terrorists want to terror-ize us. They want to change our way of life, such as eating at Mc Donald's, our freedom to grow horizontally on double cheese burgers, our right to drink Coke, enjoy American Idol in peace, get pedicures for our poodles, and enjoy our free market economy that has increased the gap between the filthy poor and the pa-triotic rich! Those who terrorize us are terrorists. Terrorists are terrorists! Bad terrorists are really bad. They are barbarians. They kill children. They are out there to get us. Do not fear anything except the terrorists.

Do not listen to the propaganda of our enemies who make up too many false stories about us to demonize us. We are a compassionate republic! For instance, we did not intentionally evaporate two Japanese cities with nuclear weapons intentionally. We are not terrorists. Only terrorists intentionally attack civilians, kill hundreds of thousands people, and subject the rest to crippling and painful radiation. We are a peace-loving Christian nation. It was just a huge accident that happened in the sky. The bombs were intended to explode on top of two schools of sharks in the deep ocean. We wanted to protect Japanese people on the beaches from horrible shark attacks. However, due to some technical glitches in communication, our two pilots pushed the red button while they were on top of the two Japanese cities, Nagasaki and Hiroshima. This accident, however, inadvertently had a good outcome: the Japanese surrendered and we won the war!

Similarly we never supported terrorists or dictators in Latin America, Asia, Africa, or the Middle East. It was they that were supporting us, that is our military industrial complex and oil companies. So, Abacha of Nigeria, Hugo of Bolivia, Batista of Cuba, Botha of South Africa, General Humberto of Brazil, Vinicio of Guatemala, Roberto Cordova of Honduras, Alfredo of El Salvador, Ngo Dihn of Vietnam, General Samuel of Liberia, Duvalier of Haiti, King Fahd of Saudi Arabia, General Franco of Spain, Hassan II of Morocco, Ferdinand Marcos of Phillippines, Mobuto of Zaire, General Montt of Guatemala, General Noriega of Panama, Shah Pahlavi of Iran, Papadopoulos of Greece, Chung Hee of South Korea, General Pinochet of Chile, Pol Pot of Cambodia, Salazar of Portugal, Somoza of Nicaragua, Suharto of Indonesia, General Videla of Argentina, General Zia ul-Haq of Pakistan, Mubarak of Egypt — yes, all these and more have been our friendly S.O.B's. They helped us and we helped them. We are helping people. Helping is a family value. We are pro-family.

The US government has been subjected to the worst propaganda so much so that even some of its gullible citizens, especially those with Patriotic-Hormone-Deficiency-Syndrome, PHDS, tend to believe the propaganda. Let us focus on the most recent lies about Iraq.

LIE NUMBER ONE: Iraq did not Have Weapon of Mass Destruction
Iraq always had weapons of mass destruction. We know because we gave them to him when he helped us against the Iranian terrorist regime. Already more than three thousand American soldiers were destroyed by the enemy's weapons. Aren't the 4,000 martyrs enough to be considered a MASS? Obviously, to kill so many American soldiers they must have some left-over weapons of mass destruction. This mass destruction is causing a mass disruption in our effort to bring peace and freedom to the Iraqi people.

LIE NUMBER TWO: Iraq did not Have Ties with Al-Qaida
Our assertion regarding Saddam's ties with al-Qaida was a prophetic statement, which was fulfilled a few years after we invaded Iraq. Now there are al-Qaida fighters everywhere. Some claim that we just forced Iraqis to join them, but it is like blaming the victim instead of the terrorists.

LIE NUMBER THREE: Iraqi's didn't Welcome us with Flowers
In fact, according to our very intelligent intelligence sources, after learning our noble mission to free them, many Iraqis started growing flowers and roses in their gardens to welcome us. We have satellite pictures to prove that. But unfortunately, when we shocked and awed Baghdad, many of those gardens were destroyed as collateral damage. The remaining few rose gardens dried because of water shortages in the city. Many of those Iraqis who were killed during the early clashes had roses in their hands. The symbolic power of those red roses

swimming on the pools of their blood has been one of the best memories that keeps the morale of our troops so high.

LIE NUMBER FOUR: The US Troops Tortured Prisoners
The widely circulated picture shown that an American soldier pulling an Iraqi prisoner in Al-Ghraib with the leash was in fact innocent role-playing. The American soldier, a lovely lady, had missed her pet, and the friendly yet bored Iraqi prisoner just wanted to make her happy by acting like her pet. Another picture showing the prisoners making a naked pyramid was in fact a friendly dog-pile. It was another way of enacting an American sports game. The prisoners knew that American football players tackle and pile over each other. They just did not have the proper uniforms, so they celebrated with the American sport after they took a warm shower. Another picture showing an American soldier inspecting prisoner's genitals was another friendly gesture; the Christian American soldier was commending them for having circumcised genitals, unlike gentiles. Similarly, the news about us torturing prisoners in Gitmo is not true.

LIE NUMBER FIVE: The US Systematically Tortures Muslim Prisoners
That is not true. As the President Bush repeatedly stated, "We do not torture!" But our friends do. We outsource torture to our allies in Egypt, Afghanistan, Poland, and other backwards yet friendly countries. Excluding the few anecdotal torturers, we Americans have very tender hearts. We let bad people do the dirty work for us. So, it is true that the US does not systematically torture Muslim prisoners.

LIE NUMBER FIVE: The US did not Free Iraqi People
We did not claim that we would bring freedom and democracy to "all" Iraqis. We only freed or caused the freedom of about one million people. They attained perfect freedom from the miserable conditions following our invasion by being transported to another world. Can you imagine living in a very hot city with no water, electricity, security, or jobs? In our Christian faith, death is not the end, but a beginning for an eternal joy in heaven. Unfortunately, more than two million Iraqis escaped to the hell of Syria and Saudi Arabia and missed the opportunity to taste freedom and democracy through the hands and fingers of our great heroes.

LIE NUMBER SIX: Mission was not Accomplished
On May 1, 2003, indeed President Bush did declare the mission as accomplished. The mission was to invade Iraq and secure the building of the Ministry of Oil. We did accomplish that mission. The President did not *misunderestimate* the mission as some unpatriotic Americans claim.

As you can easily see, our enemies are working very well to weaken our goals to free the Iraqi people and other neighboring states. We must continue our support for our proud and great country, the United States of America. We are one nation under God, indivisible, for liberty and justice for all. God Bless.

The following section contains some
related news and articles written by others.

April 30th, 2009

Churchgoers more likely to back torture, survey finds

WASHINGTON (CNN) - The more often Americans go to church, the more likely they are to support the torture of suspected terrorists, according to a new analysis.

More than half of people who attend services at least once a week - 54 percent - said the use of torture against suspected terrorists is "often" or "sometimes" justified. Only 42 percent of people who "seldom or never" go to services agreed, according the analysis released Wednesday by the Pew Forum on Religion & Public Life.

White evangelical Protestants were the religious group most likely to say torture is often or sometimes justified - more than 6 in 10 supported it. People unaffiliated with any religious organization were least likely to back it. Only 4 in 10 of them did.

The analysis is based on a Pew Research Center survey of 742 American adults conducted April 14-21. It did not include analysis of groups other than white evangelicals, white non-Hispanic Catholics, white mainline Protestants, and the religiously unaffiliated, because the sample size was too small.

Falwell denied that many evangelicals opposed Iraq war

February 15, 2005
http://mediamatters.org/research/200502150011

Reverend Jerry Falwell erroneously denied that many evangelicals opposed the U.S.-led war in Iraq. Appearing opposite Sojourners editor-in-chief Reverend Jim Wallis on the February 11 edition of FOX News' Hannity & Colmes, Falwell called Wallis's claim that "evangelicals around the world were against the war in Iraq" "baloney" and remarked: "You could fit your [antiwar evangelical] crowd in a phone booth." After Wallis told Falwell that "there are evangelical Christians who don't share your pro-war views," Falwell replied, "I know -- you and William Sloane Coffin." Coffin is a longtime peace activist and former Yale University chaplain.

In fact, many evangelical leaders openly opposed the Iraq war, and a March 2003 poll by the Pew Research Center indicated that although most American evangelicals supported removing Saddam Hussein from power, less than half "favored the use of force if our major allies did not want to join us."

Prominent evangelicals to oppose the war in Iraq include the presiding bishop for the Evangelical Lutheran Church in America Reverend Mark S. Hanson, author and assistant professor of theology at the Garrett-Evangelical Theological Seminary D. Stephen Long, and -- as Wallis accurately pointed out on the program -- evangelicals from "Fuller Seminary [and] Wheaton College." Approximately 40 faculty members from the Fuller Theological Seminary -- "the largest evangelical seminary in the country" -- "signed a September 2002 letter opposing Bush's statements about a unilateral pre-emptive war in Iraq," the Pasadena Star-News reported on October 8, 2004. The faculty of Wheaton College -- who annually reaffirm "a summary of biblical doctrine that is consonant with evangelical Christianity" -- "passed a resolution opposing war in Iraq," according to the Student Peace Action Network.

According to a Pew Research Center poll taken March 13 through March 16, 2003, while 77 percent of white evangelicals "favored the U.S. taking military action to end Saddam Hussein's rule ... less than a majority -- 48% -- favored the use of force if our major allies did not want to join us."

The Washington Post reported on January 25, 2003, that, although five prominent evangelical ministers -- led by Reverend Richard Land -- signed a letter to Bush supporting the war, "most evangelicals leaders" were "ambivalent about the prospect of war with Iraq" while many were ambivalent about openly taking a position on the conflict:

"Since Land's letter ... few prominent evangelicals have spoken out for the war -- or against it.

"Such reticence suggests that most evangelical leaders, who strongly supported the Persian Gulf War a decade ago, are ambivalent about the prospect of war with Iraq, according to several evangelical theologians and scholars.

"They said some evangelical leaders question whether Saddam Hussein's regime poses the immediate threat to American security the Bush administration claims. And they said other leaders are fearful for the safety of hundreds of thousands of Christians in Iraq and thousands of missionaries working in Muslim-led countries around the world.

"Other observers say the silence of evangelicals does not necessarily mean that they do not hold strong positions on the president's policy. According to this view, evangelical leaders who favor military action are afraid that public statements to that effect will further inflame anti-American sentiment throughout the Muslim world -- while those against a war worry that they will be labeled as "liberals" because their arguments closely follow Protestant and Catholic leaders who oppose a U.S. attack."

PS by Edip Yuksel: The article above, though contains a good news about some Evangelical Christians, it attempts to sugarcoat the fact that 77% of Evangelical Christians stood for the worst of all moral rules, the Iron Rule (Preemptive Strike), which is adopted by paranoid jingoists. The article tries to emphasize 48% of Evangelical Christians opposing the war with the phrase "less than a majority". However, about half of them were reluctant to support the war not because of ethical or religious reasons; they were simply reluctant to support the war if the USA attacked Iraq alone. In other words, according to the survey, 77% of Evangelicals were warmongers, and 52% of them wished that the USA pressure other countries too to join her in the war against Iraq. This is much worse than the author of the article wishes us to believe.

It is no secret that the great majority of Evangelical Christians are right-wing jingoists and they voted for Bush for the second time, thereby approving his destruction of Iraqi cities, his killing tens of thousand of innocent Iraqis, maiming tens of thousands, implementing a systematic torture practice in prisons, inventing torture rendition, engaging in kidnappings, assassinations, covert operations to inflame sectarian conflicts that finally led to civil war, employing corporate terrorists and murderers, such as Blackwater, as contractors and mercenaries, and transferring billions of taxpayers' money to war-profiteers, oil and construction companies such as Haliburton, thereby causing one of the worst financial crisis and corporate robbery in American history.

This article originally appeared on Beliefnet in 2002.

The Rapture Factor

Why conservative Christians' love of Israel is intertwined with the Battle of Armageddon

Deborah Caldwell

Evangelical Christians have overwhelmed the White House switchboard in recent weeks with phone calls urging President Bush to continue supporting Israeli Prime Minister Ariel Sharon. In early May, more than 250 Christian leaders attended a prayer breakfast at the Israeli embassy. Last week, former Christian Coalition chairman Ralph Reed announced the formation of a Christian "Stand for Israel" campaign.

There have been many recent media reports of this "strange bedfellows" relationship between Jews--here and in Israel--and the conservative Christians who love them, especially since the relationship seems to be influencing government policy. Some have explained it as a result of the declining dependence on Arab oil, which meant leaders here needn't be as allied with Arab countries. Others suggest that after Sept. 11, Americans felt an immediate, gut-wrenching identification with Israelis, who have lived with the Muslim militant threat for decades.

But the least understood, and probably most important, reason has been missed by most secular analysts. Evangelicals support Israel because of biblical prophecy, including passages that tie the survival of Israel to the Second Coming of Jesus.

According to their reading of the Bible, God established a covenant with Abraham in the Book of Genesis. Essentially, says Beliefnet columnist Richard Land, a Southern Baptist leader with close ties to the Bush Administration, evangelicals support Israel because they believe "God blesses those that bless the Jews and curses those who curse the Jews. Consequently, we believe America needs to bless the Jews and Israel, because if we bless the Jews and support Israel, God blesses us. And if we don't, God curses us."

But it goes beyond that. The establishment--and continuation--of the State of Israel is essential to set the stage for the imminent return of Jesus. At the time of the Second Coming, these Christians believe, Jesus will descend from heaven, subdue all of Israel's enemies and take believers to heaven in what is known as the Rapture--literally, they will ascend to the clouds to be in heaven. This series of events ushers in the end-times. According to conservative Christians' reading of the Book of Revelation, this won't happen unless Israel exists in the Holy Land.

This belief is shared by most of the major evangelical leaders--among them Jerry Falwell, Pat Robertson, Ralph Reed, Beverly LaHaye, Jack Hayford, and Oral Roberts--all of whom are avidly pro-Israel. Even Billy Graham shares this

398

sentiment, despite the recent dust-up over his anti-Semitic remarks in the Nixon White House.

The evangelical view of the Book of Revelation, meanwhile, has gained widespread support among the American public because of the wildly popular Left Behind series by Tim LaHaye (husband of Christian activist Beverly LaHaye) and Jerry Jenkins, which has sold more than 30 million copies in the seven years since it was launched.

This view--though not new--is having an effect. It very likely explains why President Bush hasn't pressured Israel to curb its crackdown on Palestinians in recent weeks.

According to Land, evangelicals' relationship with Jews and Israel intensified after World War II, partly because of the Holocaust but mostly because the establishment of Israel seemed to evangelicals to prove the Bible's prophecies. By the 1950s and 1960s, Land said, affinity with Israel was an "essential part" of the Southern Baptist churches he grew up in around Texas. In fact, the late W.A. Criswell, the great pastor of First Baptist Church of Dallas, traveled to Israel in the early 1950s and met with David Ben Gurion. Later, he often preached that Jews' return to their land was the fulfillment of Biblical prophecy.

By the 1970s, Hal Lindsey wrote the best-selling book of the decade, The Late Great Planet Earth, which introduced this view of biblical prophecy to a wide audience. It was a kind of non-fiction forerunner of today's Left Behind series. Lindsey translated the "fire and brimstone" of the Book of Revelation into nuclear war and wrote that the 1960s upheaval showed the end was near.

So if evangelicals believe human history is following a predetermined divine script, and they and Israel are simply playing their assigned roles, why even bother to influence the outcome of Israel's fate?

As it turns out, evangelicals are somewhat opaque on this question.

According to Land--and most evangelical scholars--Israel's existence is critical. "We're one step closer to the end-times than we were before the Jews came back into their land because my understanding of biblical prophecy is that Israel is established in the land at the time that the events of the Second Coming take place," he says.

But he--and other evangelicals--nearly always add: "The Bible tells us no man knows the hour or the day of his coming."

So what happens if Israel is destroyed, perhaps in this latest round of conflict? First of all, Land says, that isn't likely. But if it happens? "My assumption would be that it means ... the Second Coming is coming later than some expected." ∎

Below you will find a partial list of US military interventions prepared by Zolton Grossman, faculty member in Geography and Native American Studies at The Evergreen State College. I am thankful for his permission to use his research, which surely will put the United States at the top of the Guinness Records book if there were a category for the most aggressive, militaristic, or violent nation. Ironically, right-wing Christian evangelists together with their Zionist allies have always been major supporters of militarism, occupations, wars, and massacres. So far their fruits! They sing peace in churches, yet they vote for more weapons and wars when they are out.

From Wounded Knee To Iraq:
A Century Of U.S. Military Interventions

by Dr. Zoltan Grossman
http://academic.evergreen.edu/g/grossmaz/interventions.html

The following is a partial list of U.S. military interventions from 1890 to 2009. Below the list is a Briefing on the History of U.S. Military Interventions. The list and briefing are also available as a PowerPoint presentation. This guide does not include:

- mobilizations of the National Guard
- offshore shows of naval strength
- reinforcements of embassy personnel
- the use of non-Defense Department personnel (such as the Drug Enforcement Administration)
- military exercises
- non-combat mobilizations (such as replacing postal strikers)
- the permanent stationing of armed forces
- covert actions where the U.S. did not play a command and control role
- the use of small hostage rescue units
- most uses of proxy troops
- U.S. piloting of foreign warplanes
- foreign or domestic disaster assistance
- military training and advisory programs not involving direct combat
- civic action programs
- and many other military activities.

Among sources used, beside news reports, are the Congressional Record (23 June 1969), 180 Landings by the U.S. Marine Corp History Division, Ege &

Makhijani in Counterspy (July-Aug, 1982), "Instances of Use of United States Forces Abroad, 1798-1993" by Ellen C. Collier of the Library of Congress Congressional Research Service, and Ellsberg in Protest & Survive.

Versions of this list have been published on Zmag.org, Neravt.com, and numerous other websites. Translations of list: Spanish French Turkish Italian Chinese Greek Russian Czech Tamil Portuguese. Quotes in Christian Science Monitor and The Independent. Turkish newspaper urges that the United States be listed in Guinness Book of World Records as the Country with the Most Foreign Interventions.

COUNTRY OR STATE	Dates of intervention	Forces	Comments
S. DAKOTA	1890 (-?)	Troops	300 Lakota Indians massacred at Wounded Knee.
ARGENTINA	1890	Troops	Buenos Aires interests protected.
CHILE	1891	Troops	Marines clash with nationalist rebels.
HAITI	1891	Troops	Black revolt on Navassa defeated.
IDAHO	1892	Troops	Army suppresses silver miners' strike.
HAWAII	1893 (-?)	Naval, troops	Independent kingdom overthrown, annexed.
CHICAGO	1894	Troops	Breaking of rail strike, 34 killed.
NICARAGUA	1894	Troops	Month-long occupation of Bluefields.
CHINA	1894-95	Naval, troops	Marines land in Sino-Japanese War
KOREA	1894-96	Troops	Marines kept in Seoul during war.
PANAMA	1895	Troops, naval	Marines land in Colombian province.
NICARAGUA	1896	Troops	Marines land in port of Corinto.
CHINA	1898-1900	Troops	Boxer Rebellion fought by foreign armies.
PHILIPPINES	1898-1910 (-?)	Naval, troops	Seized from Spain, killed 600,000 Filipinos
CUBA	1898-1902 (-?)	Naval, troops	Seized from Spain, still hold Navy base.
PUERTO RICO	1898 (-?)	Naval, troops	Seized from Spain, occupation continues.

GUAM	1898 (-?)	Naval, troops	Seized from Spain, still use as base.
MINNESOTA	1898 (-?)	Troops	Army battles Chippewa at Leech Lake.
NICARAGUA	1898	Troops	Marines land at port of San Juan del Sur.
SAMOA	1899 (-?)	Troops	Battle over succession to throne.
NICARAGUA	1899	Troops	Marines land at port of Bluefields.
IDAHO	1899-1901	Troops	Army occupies Coeur d'Alene mining region.
OKLAHOMA	1901	Troops	Army battles Creek Indian revolt.
PANAMA	1901-14	Naval, troops	Broke off from Colombia 1903, annexed Canal Zone 1914.
HONDURAS	1903	Troops	Marines intervene in revolution.
DOMINICAN REPUBLIC	1903-04	Troops	U.S. interests protected in Revolution.
KOREA	1904-05	Troops	Marines land in Russo-Japanese War.
CUBA	1906-09	Troops	Marines land in democratic election.
NICARAGUA	1907	Troops	"Dollar Diplomacy" protectorate set up.
HONDURAS	1907	Troops	Marines land during war with Nicaragua
PANAMA	1908	Troops	Marines intervene in election contest.
NICARAGUA	1910	Troops	Marines land in Bluefields and Corinto.
HONDURAS	1911	Troops	U.S. interests protected in civil war.
CHINA	1911-41	Naval, troops	Continuous occupation with flare-ups.
CUBA	1912	Troops	U.S. interests protected in civil war.
PANAMA	1912	Troops	Marines land during heated election.
HONDURAS	1912	Troops	Marines protect U.S. economic interests.
NICARAGUA	1912-33	Troops, bombing	10-year occupation, fought guerillas
MEXICO	1913	Naval	Americans evacuated during revolution.

DOMINICAN REPUBLIC	1914	Naval	Fight with rebels over Santo Domingo.
COLORADO	1914	Troops	Breaking of miners' strike by Army.
MEXICO	1914-18	Naval, troops	Series of interventions against nationalists.
HAITI	1914-34	Troops, bombing	19-year occupation after revolts.
DOMINICAN REPUBLIC	1916-24	Troops	8-year Marine occupation.
CUBA	1917-33	Troops	Military occupation, economic protectorate.
WORLD WAR I	1917-18	Naval, troops	Ships sunk, fought Germany for 1 1/2 years.
RUSSIA	1918-22	Naval, troops	Five landings to fight Bolsheviks
PANAMA	1918-20	Troops	"Police duty" during unrest after elections.
HONDURAS	1919	Troops	Marines land during election campaign.
YUGOSLAVIA	1919	Troops/Marines	intervene for Italy against Serbs in Dalmatia.
GUATEMALA	1920	Troops	2-week intervention against unionists.
WEST VIRGINIA	1920-21	Troops, bombing	Army intervenes against mineworkers.
TURKEY	1922	Troops	Fought nationalists in Smyrna.
CHINA	1922-27	Naval, troops	Deployment during nationalist revolt.
HONDURAS	1924-25	Troops	Landed twice during election strife.
PANAMA	1925	Troops	Marines suppress general strike.
CHINA	1927-34	Troops	Marines stationed throughout the country.
EL SALVADOR	1932	Naval	Warships send during Marti revolt.
WASHINGTON DC	1932	Troops	Army stops WWI vet bonus protest.
WORLD WAR II	1941-45	Naval, troops, bombing, nuclear	Hawaii bombed, fought Japan, Italy and Germay for 3 years; first nuclear war.
DETROIT	1943	Troops	Army put down Black rebellion.
IRAN	1946	Nuclear threat	Soviet troops told to leave north.

YUGOSLAVIA	1946	Nuclear threat, naval	Response to shoot-down of US plane.
URUGUAY	1947	Nuclear threat	Bombers deployed as show of strength.
GREECE	1947-49	Command operation	U.S. directs extreme-right in civil war.
GERMANY	1948	Nuclear Threat	Atomic-capable bombers guard Berlin Airlift.
CHINA	1948-49	Troops/Marines	evacuate Americans before Communist victory.
PHILIPPINES	1948-54	Command operation	CIA directs war against Huk Rebellion.
PUERTO RICO	1950	Command operation	Independence rebellion crushed in Ponce.
KOREA	1951-53 (-?)	Troops, naval, bombing , nuclear threats	U.S./So. Korea fights China/No. Korea to stalemate; A-bomb threat in 1950, and against China in 1953. Still have bases.
IRAN	1953	Command Operation	CIA overthrows democracy, installs Shah.
VIETNAM	1954	Nuclear threat	French offered bombs to use against seige.
GUATEMALA	1954	Command operation, bombing, nuclear threat	CIA directs exile invasion after new gov't nationalized U.S. company lands; bombers based in Nicaragua.
EGYPT	1956	Nuclear threat, troops	Soviets told to keep out of Suez crisis; Marines evacuate foreigners.
LEBANON	1958	Troops, naval	Marine occupation against rebels.
IRAQ	1958	Nuclear threat	Iraq warned against invading Kuwait.
CHINA	1958	Nuclear threat	China told not to move on Taiwan isles.
PANAMA	1958	Troops	Flag protests erupt into confrontation.
VIETNAM	1960-75	Troops, naval, bombing, nuclear threats	Fought South Vietnam revolt & North Vietnam; one million killed in longest U.S. war; atomic bomb threats in 1968 and 1969.
CUBA	1961	Command operation	CIA-directed exile invasion fails.
GERMANY	1961	Nuclear threat	Alert during Berlin Wall crisis.

LAOS	1962	Command operation	Military buildup during guerrilla war.
CUBA	1962	Nuclear threat, naval	Blockade during missile crisis; near-war with Soviet Union.
IRAQ	1963	Command operation	CIA organizes coup that killed president, brings Ba'ath Party to power, and Saddam Hussein back from exile to be head of the secret service.
PANAMA	1964	Troops	Panamanians shot for urging canal's return.
INDONESIA	1965	Command operation	Million killed in CIA-assisted army coup.
DOMINICAN REPUBLIC	1965-66	Troops, bombing	Marines land during election campaign.
GUATEMALA	1966-67	Command operation	Green Berets intervene against rebels.
DETROIT	1967	Troops	Army battles African Americans, 43 killed.
UNITED STATES	1968	Troops	After King is shot; over 21,000 soldiers in cities.
CAMBODIA	1969-75	Bombing, troops, naval	Up to 2 million killed in decade of bombing, starvation, and political chaos.
OMAN	1970	Command operation	U.S. directs Iranian marine invasion.
LAOS	1971-73	Command operation, bombing	U.S. directs South Vietnamese invasion; "carpet-bombs" countryside.
SOUTH DAKOTA	1973	Command operation	Army directs Wounded Knee siege of Lakotas.
MIDEAST	1973	Nuclear threat	World-wide alert during Mideast War.
CHILE	1973	Command operation	CIA-backed coup ousts elected marxist president.
CAMBODIA	1975	Troops, bombing	Gas captured ship, 28 die in copter crash.
ANGOLA	1976-92	Command operation	CIA assists South African-backed rebels.
IRAN	1980	Troops, nuclear threat, aborted bombing	Raid to rescue Embassy hostages; 8 troops die in copter-plane crash. Soviets warned not to get involved in revolution.

LIBYA	1981	Naval jets	Two Libyan jets shot down in maneuvers.
EL SALVADOR	1981-92	Command operation, troops	Advisors, overflights aid anti-rebel war, soldiers briefly involved in hostage clash.
NICARAGUA	1981-90	Command operation, naval	CIA directs exile (Contra) invasions, plants harbor mines against revolution.
LEBANON	1982-84	Naval, bombing, troops	Marines expel PLO and back Phalangists, Navy bombs and shells Muslim positions.
GRENADA	1983-84	Troops, bombing	Invasion four years after revolution.
HONDURAS	1983-89	Troops	Maneuvers help build bases near borders.
IRAN	1984	Jets	Two Iranian jets shot down over Persian Gulf.
LIBYA	1986	Bombing, naval	Air strikes to topple nationalist gov't.
BOLIVIA	1986	Troops	Army assists raids on cocaine region.
IRAN	1987-88	Naval, bombing	US intervenes on side of Iraq in war.
LIBYA	1989	Naval jets	Two Libyan jets shot down.
VIRGIN ISLANDS	1989	Troops	St. Croix Black unrest after storm.
PHILIPPINES	1989	Jets	Air cover provided for government against coup.
PANAMA	1989 (-?)	Troops, bombing	Nationalist government ousted by 27,000 soldiers, leaders arrested, 2000+ killed.
LIBERIA	1990	Troops	Foreigners evacuated during civil war.
SAUDI ARABIA	1990-91	Troops, jets	Iraq countered after invading Kuwait. 540,000 troops also stationed in Oman, Qatar, Bahrain, UAE, Israel.
IRAQ	1990-?	Bombing, troops, naval	Blockade of Iraqi and Jordanian ports, air strikes; 200,000+ killed in invasion of Iraq and Kuwait; no-fly zone over Kurdish north, Shiite south, large-scale destruction of Iraqi military.

KUWAIT	1991	Naval, bombing, troops	Kuwait royal family returned to throne.
LOS ANGELES	1992	Troops	Army, Marines deployed against anti-police uprising.
SOMALIA	1992-94	Troops, naval, bombing	U.S.-led United Nations occupation during civil war; raids against one Mogadishu faction.
YUGOSLAVIA	1992-94	Naval	NATO blockade of Serbia and Montenegro.
BOSNIA	1993-?	Jets, bombing	No-fly zone patrolled in civil war; downed jets, bombed Serbs.
HAITI	1994	Troops, naval	Blockade against military government; troops restore President Aristide to office three years after coup.
ZAIRE (CONGO)	1996-97	Troops	Marines at Rwandan Hutu refugee camps, in area where Congo revolution begins.
LIBERIA	1997	Troops	Soldiers under fire during evacuation of foreigners.
ALBANIA	1997	Troops	Soldiers under fire during evacuation of foreigners.
SUDAN	1998	Missiles	Attack on pharmaceutical plant alleged to be "terrorist" nerve gas plant.
AFGHANISTAN	1998	Missiles	Attack on former CIA training camps used by Islamic fundamentalist groups alleged to have attacked embassies.
IRAQ	1998-?	Bombing, Missiles	Four days of intensive air strikes after weapons inspectors allege Iraqi obstructions.
YUGOSLAVIA	1999	Bombing, Missiles	Heavy NATO air strikes after Serbia declines to withdraw from Kosovo. NATO occupation of Kosovo.
YEMEN	2000	Naval	USS Cole, docked in Aden, bombed.
MACEDONIA	2001	Troops	NATO forces deployed to move and disarm Albanian rebels.
UNITED STATES	2001	Jets, naval	Reaction to hijacker attacks on New York, DC

AFGHANISTAN	2001-?	Troops, bombing, missiles	Massive U.S. mobilization to overthrow Taliban, hunt Al Qaeda fighters, install Karzai regime, and battle Taliban insurgency. More than 30,000 U.S. troops and numerous private security contractors carry our occupation.
YEMEN	2002	Missiles	Predator drone missile attack on Al Qaeda, including a US citizen.
PHILIPPINES	2002-?	Troops, naval	Training mission for Philippine military fighting Abu Sayyaf rebels evolves into combat missions in Sulu Archipelago, west of Mindanao.
COLOMBIA	2003-?	Troops	US special forces sent to rebel zone to back up Colombian military protecting oil pipeline.
IRAQ	2003-?	Troops, naval, bombing, missiles	Saddam regime toppled in Baghdad. More than 250,000 U.S. personnel participate in invasion. US and UK forces occupy country and battle Sunni and Shi'ite insurgencies. More than 160,000 troops and numerous private contractors carry out occupation and build large permanent bases.
LIBERIA	2003	Troops	Brief involvement in peacekeeping force as rebels drove out leader.
HAITI	2004-05	Troops, naval	Marines land after right-wing rebels oust elected President Aristide, who was advised to leave by Washington.
PAKISTAN	2005-?	Missiles, bombing, covert operation	CIA missile and air strikes and Special Forces raids on alleged Al Qaeda and Taliban refuge villages kill multiple civilians.
SOMALIA	2006-?	Missiles, naval, covert operation	Special Forces advise Ethiopian invasion that topples Islamist government; AC-130 strikes and Cruise missile attacks against Islamist rebels; naval blockade against "pirates" and insurgents.
SYRIA	2008	Troops	Special Forces in helicopter raid 5 miles from Iraq kill 8 Syrian civilians

(Death toll estimates from wars can be found in the Historical Atlas of the 20th Century by alphabetized places index, map series, and major casualties .)

A Briefing on the History of U.S. Military Interventions

By Zoltán Grossman, October 2001-2009
(Published in Z magazine)

Since the September 11 attacks on the United States, most people in the world agree that the perpetrators need to be brought to justice, without killing many thousands of civilians in the process. But unfortunately, the U.S. military has always accepted massive civilian deaths as part of the cost of war. The military is now poised to kill thousands of foreign civilians, in order to prove that killing U.S. civilians is wrong.

The media has told us repeatedly that some Middle Easterners hate the U.S. only because of our "freedom" and "prosperity." Missing from this explanation is the historical context of the U.S. role in the Middle East, and for that matter in the rest of the world. This basic primer is an attempt to brief readers who have not closely followed the history of U.S. foreign or military affairs, and are perhaps unaware of the background of U.S. military interventions abroad, but are concerned about the direction of our country toward a new war in the name of "freedom" and "protecting civilians."

The United States military has been intervening in other countries for a long time. In 1898, it seized the Philippines, Cuba, and Puerto Rico from Spain, and in 1917-18 became embroiled in World War I in Europe. In the first half of the 20th century it repeatedly sent Marines to "protectorates" such as Nicaragua, Honduras, Panama, Haiti, and the Dominican Republic. All these interventions directly served corporate interests, and many resulted in massive losses of civilians, rebels, and soldiers. Many of the uses of U.S. combat forces are documented in A History of U.S. Military Interventions since 1890: http://academic.evergreen.edu/g/grossmaz/interventions.html

U.S. involvement in World War II (1941-45) was sparked by the surprise attack on Pearl Harbor, and fear of an Axis invasion of North America. Allied bombers attacked fascist military targets, but also fire-bombed German and Japanese cities such as Dresden and Tokyo, party under the assumption that destroying civilian neighborhoods would weaken the resolve of the survivors and turn them against their regimes. Many historians agree that fire- bombing's effect was precisely the opposite--increasing Axis civilian support for homeland defense, and discouraging potential coup attempts. The atomic bombing of Japan at the end of the war was carried out without any kind of advance demonstration or warning that may have prevented the deaths of hundreds of thousands of innocent civilians.

The war in Korea (1950-53) was marked by widespread atrocities, both by North Korean/Chinese forces, and South Korean/U.S. forces. U.S. troops fired on civilian refugees headed into South Korea, apparently fearing they were northern infiltrators. Bombers attacked North Korean cities, and the U.S. twice threatened to use nuclear weapons. North Korea is under the same Communist government today as when the war began.

During the Middle East crisis of 1958, Marines were deployed to quell a rebellion in Lebanon, and Iraq was threatened with nuclear attack if it invaded Kuwait. This little-known crisis helped set U.S. foreign policy on a collision course with Arab nationalists, often in support of the region's monarchies.

In the early 1960s, the U.S. returned to its pre-World War II interventionary role in the Caribbean, directing the failed 1961 Bay of Pigs exile invasion of Cuba, and the 1965 bombing and Marine invasion of the Dominican Republic during an election campaign. The CIA trained and harbored Cuban exile groups in Miami, which launched terrorist attacks on Cuba, including the 1976 downing of a Cuban civilian jetliner near Barbados. During the Cold War, the CIA would also help to support or install pro-U.S. dictatorships in Iran, Chile, Guatemala, Indonesia, and many other countries around the world.

The U.S. war in Indochina (1960-75) pit U.S. forces against North Vietnam, and Communist rebels fighting to overthrow pro-U.S. dictatorships in South Vietnam, Laos, and Cambodia. U.S. war planners made little or no distinction between attacking civilians and guerrillas in rebel-held zones, and U.S. "carpet-bombing" of the countryside and cities swelled the ranks of the ultimately victorious revolutionaries. Over two million people were killed in the war, including 55,000 U.S. troops. Less than a dozen U.S. citizens were killed on U.S. soil, in National Guard shootings or antiwar bombings. In Cambodia, the bombings drove the Khmer Rouge rebels toward fanatical leaders, who launched a murderous rampage when they took power in 1975.

Echoes of Vietnam reverberated in Central America during the 1980s, when the Reagan administration strongly backed the pro-U.S. regime in El Salvador, and right-wing exile forces fighting the new leftist Sandinista government in Nicaragua. Rightist death squads slaughtered Salvadoran civilians who questioned the concentration of power and wealth in a few hands. CIA-trained Nicaraguan Contra rebels launched terrorist attacks against civilian clinics and schools run by the Sandinista government, and mined Nicaraguan harbors. U.S. troops also invaded the island nation of Grenada in 1983, to oust a new military regime, attacking Cuban civilian workers (even though Cuba had backed the leftist government deposed in the coup), and accidentally bombing a hospital.

The U.S. returned in force to the Middle East in 1980, after the Shiite Muslim revolution in Iran against Shah Pahlevi's pro-U.S. dictatorship. A troop and bombing raid to free U.S. Embassy hostages held in downtown Tehran had to be aborted in the Iranian desert. After the 1982 Israeli occupation of Lebanon, U.S. Marines were deployed in a neutral "peacekeeping" operation. They instead took the side of Lebanon's pro-Israel Christian government against Muslim rebels, and U.S. Navy ships rained enormous shells on Muslim civilian villages. Embittered Shiite Muslim rebels responded with a suicide bomb attack on Marine barracks, and for years seized U.S. hostages in the country. In retaliation, the CIA set off car bombs to assassinate Shiite Muslim leaders. Syria and the Muslim rebels emerged victorious in Lebanon.

Elsewhere in the Middle East, the U.S. launched a 1986 bombing raid on Libya, which it accused of sponsoring a terrorist bombing later tied to Syria. The bombing raid killed civilians, and may have led to the later revenge bombing of a U.S. jet over Scotland. Libya's Arab nationalist leader Muammar Qaddafi remained in power. The U.S. Navy also intervened against Iran during its war against Iraq in 1987-88, sinking Iranian ships and "accidentally" shooting down an Iranian civilian jetliner.

U.S. forces invaded Panama in 1989 to oust the nationalist regime of Manuel Noriega. The U.S. accused its former ally of allowing drug-running in the country, though the drug trade actually increased after his capture. U.S. bombing raids on Panama City ignited a conflagration in a civilian neighborhood, fed by stove gas tanks. Over 2,000 Panamanians were killed in the invasion to capture one leader.

The following year, the U.S. deployed forces in the Persian Gulf after the Iraqi invasion of Kuwait, which turned Washington against its former Iraqi ally Saddam Hussein. U.S. supported the Kuwaiti monarchy and the Muslim fundamentalist monarchy in neighboring Saudi Arabia against the secular nationalist Iraq regime. In January 1991, the U.S..And its allies unleashed a massive bombing assault against Iraqi government and military targets, in intensity beyond the raids of World War II and Vietnam. Up to 200,000 Iraqis were killed in the war and its immediate aftermath of rebellion and disease, including many civilians who died in their villages, neighborhoods, and bomb shelters. The U.S. continued economic sanctions that denied health and energy to Iraqi civilians, who died by the hundreds of thousands, according to United Nations agencies. The U.S. also instituted "no-fly zones" and virtually continuous bombing raids, yet Saddam was politically bolstered as he was militarily weakened.

In the 1990s, the U.S. military led a series of what it termed "humanitarian interventions" it claimed would safeguard civilians. Foremost among them was the 1992 deployment in the African nation of Somalia, torn by famine and a civil war between clan warlords. Instead of remaining neutral, U.S. forces took the side of one faction against another faction, and bombed a Mogadishu neighborhood. Enraged crowds, backed by foreign Arab mercenaries, killed 18 U.S. soldiers, forcing a withdrawal from the country.

Other so-called "humanitarian interventions" were centered in the Balkan region of Europe, after the 1992 breakup of the multiethnic federation of Yugoslavia. The U.S. watched for three years as Serb forces killed Muslim civilians in Bosnia, before its launched decisive bombing raids in 1995. Even then, it never intervened to stop atrocities by Croatian forces against Muslim and Serb civilians, because those forces were aided by the U.S. In 1999, the U.S. bombed Serbia to force President Slobodan Milosevic to withdraw forces from the ethnic Albanian province of Kosovo, which was torn a brutal ethnic war. The bombing intensified Serbian expulsions and killings of Albanian civilians from Kosovo, and caused the deaths of thousands of Serbian civilians, even in cities that had voted strongly against Milosevic. When a NATO occupation force enabled Albanians to move back, U.S. forces did little or nothing to prevent similar atrocities against Serb and other non-Albanian civilians. The U.S. was viewed as a biased player, even by the Serbian democratic opposition that overthrew Milosevic the following year.

Even when the U.S. military had apparently defensive motives, it ended up attacking the wrong targets. After the 1998 bombings of two U.S. embassies in East Africa, the U.S. "retaliated" not only against Osama Bin Laden's training camps in Afghanistan, but a pharmaceutical plant in Sudan that was mistakenly said to be a chemical warfare installation. Bin Laden retaliated by attacking a U.S. Navy ship docked in Yemen in 2000. After the 2001 terror attacks on the United States, the U.S. military is poised to again bomb Afghanistan, and possibly move against other states it accuses of promoting anti-U.S. "terrorism," such as Iraq and Sudan. Such a campaign will certainly ratchet up the cycle of violence, in an escalating series of retaliations that is the hallmark of Middle East conflicts. Afghanistan, like Yugoslavia, is a multiethnic state that could easily break apart in a new catastrophic regional war. Almost certainly more civilians would lose their lives in this tit-for-tat war on "terrorism" than the 3,000 civilians who died on September 11.

Common Themes

Some common themes can be seen in many of these U.S. military interventions.

First, they were explained to the U.S. public as defending the lives and rights of civilian populations. Yet the military tactics employed often left behind massive civilian "collateral damage." War planners made little distinction between rebels

413

and the civilians who lived in rebel zones of control, or between military assets and civilian infrastructure, such as train lines, water plants, agricultural factories, medicine supplies, etc. The U.S. public always believes that in the next war, new military technologies will avoid civilian casualties on the other side. Yet when the inevitable civilian deaths occur, they are always explained away as "accidental" or "unavoidable."

Second, although nearly all the post-World War II interventions were carried out in the name of "freedom" and "democracy," nearly all of them in fact defended dictatorships controlled by pro-U.S. elites. Whether in Vietnam, Central America, or the Persian Gulf, the U.S. was not defending "freedom" but an ideological agenda (such as defending capitalism) or an economic agenda (such as protecting oil company investments). In the few cases when U.S. military forces toppled a dictatorship--such as in Grenada or Panama--they did so in a way that prevented the country's people from overthrowing their own dictator first, and installing a new democratic government more to their liking.

Third, the U.S. always attacked violence by its opponents as "terrorism," "atrocities against civilians," or "ethnic cleansing," but minimized or defended the same actions by the U.S. or its allies. If a country has the right to "end" a state that trains or harbors terrorists, would Cuba or Nicaragua have had the right to launch defensive bombing raids on U.S. targets to take out exile terrorists? Washington's double standard maintains that an U.S. ally's action by definition "defensive," but that an enemy's retaliation is by definition "offensive."

Fourth, the U.S. often portrays itself as a neutral peacekeeper, with nothing but the purest humanitarian motives. After deploying forces in a country, however, it quickly divides the country or region into "friends" and "foes," and takes one side against another. These strategies tend to enflame rather than dampen a war or civil conflict, as shown in the cases of Somalia and Bosnia, and deepen resentment of the U.S. role.

Fifth, U.S. military intervention is often counterproductive even if one accepts U.S. goals and rationales. Rather than solving the root political or economic roots of the conflict, it tends to polarize factions and further destabilize the country. The same countries tend to reappear again and again on the list of 20th century interventions.

Sixth, U.S. demonization of an enemy leader, or military action against him, tends to strengthen rather than weaken his hold on power. Take the list of current regimes most singled out for U.S. attack, and put it alongside of the list of regimes that have had the longest hold on power, and you will find they have the same names. Qaddafi, Castro, Saddam, Kim, and others may have faced greater internal criticism if they could not portray themselves as Davids standing up to the American Goliath, and (accurately) blaming many of their countries' internal problems on U.S. economic sanctions.

One of the most dangerous ideas of the 20th century was that "people like us" could not commit atrocities against civilians.

- German and Japanese citizens believed it, but their militaries slaughtered millions of people.
- British and French citizens believed it, but their militaries fought brutal colonial wars in Africa and Asia.
- Russian citizens believed it, but their armies murdered civilians in Afghanistan, Chechnya, and elsewhere.
- Israeli citizens believed it, but their army mowed down Palestinians and Lebanese.
- Arabs believed it, but suicide bombers and hijackers targeted U.S. and Israeli civilians.
- U.S. citizens believed it, but their military killed hundreds of thousands in Vietnam, Iraq, and elsewhere.

Every country, every ethnicity, every religion, contains within it the capability for extreme violence. Every group contains a faction that is intolerant of other groups, and actively seeks to exclude or even kill them. War fever tends to encourage the intolerant faction, but the faction only succeeds in its goals if the rest of the group acquiesces or remains silent. The attacks of September 11 were not only a test for U.S. citizens' attitudes' toward minority ethnic/racial groups in their own country, but a test for our relationship with the rest of the world. We must begin not by lashing out at civilians in Muslim countries, but by taking responsibility for our own history and our own actions, and how they have fed the cycle of violence.

A Message to President Obama:

Work with Western Muslims to Promote Stability and Peace in the Muslim World

Ruby Amatulla, President, Co-founder
Muslims for Peace, Justice and Progress (MPJP)

Dear President Obama,

This may be an extraordinary time in history, a formative period in which certain decisions can influence humanity's direction for generations to come. The entire world – facing enormous challenges and enormous possibilities – seems to be in a reflective and transformative mood, and waits for a visionary leader to set milestones towards a better world.

You have been elected as the president of the most influential nation in the world. Your election has raised hopes and aspirations around the world – even in the Muslim world, which has often maintained a confrontational relationship with the United States. This goodwill, a rare historic opportunity, should be captured and capitalized upon for the welfare of both the Muslim world and the West. This pursuit is an enormous responsibility.

American Muslims, along with other supporters around the world, feel that the United States should offer the leadership towards a better world – not because of our military strength or wealth, but because of the fundamental ideals upon which our nation was founded over 200 years ago: equality, dignity and liberty of all people.

The United States is a legitimate leader in the world due to the unparalleled strength and resilience this nation acquired in the struggles to actualize these ideals. Let us not allow the vested interests of the few degrade the esteemed position of the many.

America has not yet achieved this position in full. Many parts of the world – including many in the Muslim world – view the US with distrust and resentment. This failure has been enormously detrimental to our interests and to the interests of other nations. Due to the pursuit of short-term gains, our leadership has failed to achieve our long-term interests. Our taxpayers are paying an enormous price and are passing down an enormous burden of debt to the next generation.

If the US retained the trust and goodwill it once enjoyed with the Muslim world – over one-fifth of humanity constituting the majority in 56 different countries and controlling over 76% of oil reserves of the world – the US could have achieved many of its objectives at a fraction of the enormous price it has already paid.

416

One of the greatest challenges before us, therefore, is to regain the trust and goodwill between the two most vital camps of the world to make a better world.

Constructive Engagement

In this intensely interdependent world, the pursuit of self-interest through exploitation or subservience – as in the colonial and neo-colonial periods – should be forbidden in our modus operandi and erased from our mindsets. These ideas and actions are evil, and are also costly and counterproductive.

America should know the power of constructive engagement. This nation led the world towards higher standards of collective responsibility with the Marshall Plan, which rebuilt "enemy" countries – Germany and Japan – and reshaped Europe towards progress and prosperity after the devastation of World War II.

During the Cold War, America finally abandoned the ideology of proxy wars of 'containment' and achieved victory through the constructive engagement of 'détente.'

America reached out to China when she was a closed-door society and an utterly repressive regime during her 'Cultural Revolution, 'and helped her to become a global partner which benefited herself and the world enormously.

America's leadership has achieved much good, but it has failed to achieve the same success for the Muslim world. This is an utter failure. The policies toward this vast segment of humanity have remained narrow and self-defeating and have created one of the greatest liabilities for America herself. Our policies must change now.

Due to difficulties and long-suffering stress, the patience in the Muslim world runs thin. Time is running out, and the most dangerous possibilities are lurking on the horizon.

What America calls the "Muslim world" is actually a mosaic of different tribes, sects and cultures. In many places, this mosaic is becoming increasingly volatile due to conflicts, vested interests and wars created by both inside and outside forces. A vast and fast-growing young generation in the Muslim world – deeply frustrated by authoritarian and corrupt governments as well as by outside special interests – could potentially become bedrock of extremism. This situation necessitates a leadership which can generate an extraordinary speed of transformation.

An Effective Bridge-Builder

One powerful catalyst for change exists within America now: -- the American Muslims. We are the common denominator of the two polarized camps of humanity, and we are conversant with the mindsets and lifestyles in both camps. We believe we are in the right place in a critical time in history to become agents of change. A visionary leadership from among us could facilitate dialogue and diplomacy with the Muslim world.

Recently, the PEW report established that the majority of American Muslims – 65% – were born in foreign lands. These Muslim immigrants have close ties with Muslim-majority societies and have a strong understanding of their nuances. It remains advantageous to establish ties and trust among these societies using our experience and connections.

As the PEW survey discovered, we are educated and well-established people with moderate and mainstream ideas in America. Many of us are the "cream of the crop" from many lands with diverse backgrounds and cultures.

A dynamic and forceful leadership of mediation and dialogue could be raised from among American Muslims if your administration could reach out to us. We would like to work closely with your leadership.

Cures of the Dysfunctional State

Good governance is the solution for a dysfunctional state. An accountable, transparent and representative government stabilizes a society. The legitimacy of that governance increasingly builds up trust and confidence among its people and institutions to sustain a stable and consistent pattern of rule. A broad and impartial due process exerts a strong force of social integration based on the fundamental principles of equality, dignity and liberty for all citizens. Self-rule offers important incentives for a society to become stable and progressive. Through peaceful coexistence and constructive engagement, a society can prosper and its individuals can pursue their potential. Successful democracies have successfully demonstrated these ideas.

The challenge in our time is to achieve these goals in the volatile areas of the world in order to achieve stability and to facilitate constructive engagement.

American Muslims, as beneficiaries of self-rule and good governance, could be the most powerful proponents of these ideas.

A Powerful Diplomatic Agenda to Help Replace Military Engagements

In today's global society, a government-to-government relationship can work best when strong people-to-people understanding and dialogue exists. American Muslims could help generate this dialogue with many troubled parts of the Muslim world.

Governments need the power of persuasion through diplomacy to replace extremely costly and often unproductive military engagements. Vested interests and cynicism stand in the way of that persuasion. While we need the vision of the Marshall Plan, we need new ways to pursue that vision. The old methods of the Marshall Plan – nation-building under the wing of military occupation – might be counterproductive, as the mindset of humanity has changed substantially since the post-World War II period.

Multinational engagements would be very effective to promote constructive engagements and American Muslim leadership could be instrumental towards spearheading such an international movement.

Soul Searching

Soul-searching is long overdue. We need serious introspection in order to establish a mindset conducive towards reconciliation and progress. Why has a vast segment of humanity lost trust in our nation within the span of a few decades, even though it once had enormous trust and reverence for our nation?

Mistrust has become even more deep and widespread due to the obscuration, marginalization and ignorance of the effects of mistakes.

The world has witnessed how the CIA, under the secret persuasion of the British government and British Petroleum, ousted the democratically elected Prime Minister of Iran Mohammed Mossadegh in 1953. The world has seen how the US nipped a burgeoning democracy in the bud, thus destroying the possibility of self-rule and progress in the region – perhaps in the entire "Muslim world." The US further solidified this mistake by placing the Shah in power, supporting and sustaining his 25 years of repressive rule in the name of stability. Contrary to stabilization, America helped create a volatile region, the effects of which we are still enduring. Americans have forgotten this blunder, but for the Muslims in general and for the Iranians in particular this memory remains intact. Once the 1980s revolution deposed the Shah and instituted Khomeini, the hostage crisis enraged Americans. Vested interests capitalized upon this public outrage, and reached out to another puppet government in the neighborhood – Saddam Hussein – to conduct a proxy war with Iran for eight years. This war resulted in over a million deaths and enormous destruction for both countries. The region was further poisoned with bloodshed and conflict, and the Muslim world drifted further apart from America, bearing more and more distrust towards our country.

The US failed to institute proper damage control for these mistakes when it was possible. This sequence of events consequently took another wrong turn, as Saddam invaded Kuwait. America conducted the Gulf War, and Americans paid the price. In the name of sovereignty the tyrant – who held his nation hostage and conducted mass-murders of citizens – was not ousted. This inaction caused another 11 years of turmoil. Thousands upon thousands of Kurds and Shiites were slaughtered, and hundreds of thousands of children starved to death. Eventually, the US became awakened to the dangerous reality of years of pent-up frustration and anger, which manifested itself in the 9/11 attacks.

Again, vested interests took full advantage of the fear and anger Americans felt, legitimizing military intervention without adequate post-war planning in the most complex and disjointed regions of the Muslim world. Again, mishandling and blunders were made, and again, the horrendous suffering of the region continued. This time, the price became so high that our nation had to thrust the enormous burden upon the shoulders of Americans of future generations.

The American people have not been presented with the true account of the long chain of causes and consequences beginning with the dispossession of the Palestinian people and the destruction of a democratic government in Iran, and continuing with the failed strategies of tit-for-tat and finger-pointing.

Afghanistan is another example of our failed leadership in the 1990s. Afghan Mujahideen fought and defeated the Russians in 1989. When the job was finished, we left them and neighboring Pakistan out in the cold to deal with their region. This region overflowed with arms and ammunition in the absence of accountable political and social infrastructures and in the presence of a backward and narcotic-infested economy. Amnesty International and the US State Dept. warned of the dangers posed by the humanitarian crisis in Afghanistan. Was it surprising to find that the Taliban and al-Qaeda replaced the Russians during a decade of neglect? Could America blame the people of this region for distrusting America when their affairs were handled so carelessly and their lives were disrupted? Is it too difficult to see that terrorism would find a safe haven in this part of the world? The costs of these failed policies have remained incalculable.

The Deepest Source of Grievance: The Palestinian Suffering

Mr. President, the Palestinian issue remains one of the deepest sources of grievances and resentments, not just of Muslims but also of justice-loving people all around the world.

This history is like a great Shakespearean tragedy – all losers and no winner. The Palestinians lost their homes but retained their dignity in their struggles. The US lost its moral voice and leadership in the Muslim world, accrued a heavy burden of costs, and became a disingenuous promoter of peace, disliked and distrusted. The 13 million Jews of the world lost the benefit of goodwill and diplomacy with the 1.3 billion Muslims of the world, an incalculable loss for countless people indeed! Israel failed as a nation, as she failed to uphold either the dignity or the security of the Israelis, performing a terrible disservice to the true Jewish cause.

A people cannot claim dignity by denying dignity to other people. If a people live incarcerated in a tiny land – creating an ivory tower guarded by the military, unable to feel safe or to move around among neighboring people – these people are neither free nor secure. No amount of wealth or military power could offer them liberty. Israel defeated the true Jewish cause in Israel. This superpower became a super victim – its conscience paralyzed, its due process biased and infiltrated by vested interests and its leadership blindfolded. All these parties – the Palestinians, the Americans and the Israelis – have become victims, and all need to be emancipated from bondage of different kinds: the bondage of injustice, the bondage of lack of vision and leadership, the bondage of past ideas, and the bondage of cynicism that has frozen the soul of a nation. If wisdom fails to prevail, one million walls and one million troops cannot stop the verdict of history.

It is still possible to reclaim the situation, to reconcile seemingly irreconcilable differences, and to reinstate goodwill among the followers of three great religions who lived in peaceful coexistence for thirteen centuries before the state of Israel. The pursuit of peace and justice requires a new approach. God willing, it is achievable in our time.

We are faced with an unfortunate irony. The leaders and representatives of a great nation – a nation that proclaims the inalienable rights of all people, defines nationhood on the fundamental principles of equality, and advocates an impartial due process irrespective of ethnic or religious differences – consistently violates its standards by supporting a state that violates all these values and principles.

If we do not succeed, future generations will ask this question – how did America fail to convince Israel, its ally, to replace oppression with peaceful coexistence, when America successfully helped its arch-rivals, the Soviet Union and China, towards profound change?

History will not be kind to the forces responsible for such a derailment. They, individuals and institutions alike, will be discovered, and they will be exposed and targeted as culprits for generations to come.

Past Chances Missed, Future Opportunities Present

Many chances to harness forces for change came and left, and many opportunities for reconciliation knocked at our door and disappeared. We still kept our doors closed. America had many chances in the past to create a safer and better world, and to save herself from self-inflicted wounds. In 2001 and 2002, Iran helped America defeat the Taliban in Afghanistan. In spite of all the past grievances, Iran stepped forward in 2003 and offered a comprehensive proposal regarding reconciliation and long-term cooperation with the US. This proposal was truly visionary, and it gave the US the upper hand. This proposal was trashed and it was also kept hidden from the American public. We must stop these costly and detrimental ways of doing business.

As you pointed out repeatedly, we cannot hope to see a change until the old ways are changed.

How important is it for America to have a constructive partnership with the Muslim world? What direct bearing does a stable and prosperous Muslim world have on the interests, security and welfare of America? Aaron David Miller, a long-term Middle East negotiator and scholar, succinctly addressed these questions by stating, "The greatest threat to our national interest is not going to come from an ascending China or economically powerful Europe or former Soviet Union seeking to regain its glory. It is going to come from divided, angry and dysfunctional and conflict ridden Middle East and Arab and the Muslim world."

One great failure of global diplomacy involves the stereotype of America as a monolithic villain, with intent on intimidating, manipulating and dominating others through an enormous military presence. The world has failed to notice that America is not a monolithic nation. This is the most diverse, open, and pluralistic nation in the world. The world fails to realize that America is the most self-reflecting, self-critical and self-correcting society in the world. At any given time, and on any given issue, many good people struggle against evil. Unfortunately, we sometimes only see the final outcome of these struggles.

It pains us, the American Muslims and our supporters, to witness the confrontational relationship between our nation and the greater Muslim world community [the "ummah"] that we belong to. We, therefore, desire a win-win outcome. We can help you to end this confrontation.

A sincere and visionary leader like yourself can help dissolve these barriers, as you have a forceful national mandate as well as overwhelming international goodwill. We are counting on you, and you can also count on our sincerity and dedication to this great vision.

Sincerely.

***

Responding to the Ford Hood Tragedy

12 November 2009

Imam Zaid Shakir

This is my response to the Fort Hood tragedy and events both associated with it and ensuing from it. I begin by expressing my deepest condolences to the families of all of the dead and wounded. There is no legitimate reason for their deaths, just as I firmly believe there is no legitimate reason for the deaths of the hundreds of thousands of Iraqi and Afghani civilians who have perished as a result of those two conflicts. Even though I disagree with the continued prosecution of those wars, and even though I believe that the US war machine is the single greatest threat to world peace, I must commend the top military brass at Fort Hood, and President Obama for encouraging restraint and for refusing to attribute the crime allegedly perpetrated by Major Nidal Malik Hasan to Islam. We pray that God bless us to see peace and sanity prevail during these tense times.

For the full article please see:
http://www.newislamicdirections.com/nid/articles/responding_to_the_fort_hood_tragedy/

Published on Monday, November 30, 2009 by CommonDreams.org

An Open Letter to President Obama from Michael Moore

Dear President Obama,

Do you really want to be the new "war president"? If you go to West Point to-morrow night (Tuesday, 8pm) and announce that you are increasing, rather than withdrawing, the troops in Afghanistan, you are the new war president. Pure and simple. And with that you will do the worst possible thing you could do -- destroy the hopes and dreams so many millions have placed in you. With just one speech tomorrow night you will turn a multitude of young people who were the backbone of your campaign into disillusioned cynics. You will teach them what they've always heard is true -- that all politicians are alike. I simply can't believe you're about to do what they say you are going to do. Please say it isn't so.

It is not your job to do what the generals tell you to do. We are a civilian-run government. WE tell the Joint Chiefs what to do, not the other way around. That's the way General Washington insisted it must be. That's what President Truman told General MacArthur when MacArthur wanted to invade China. "You're fired!," said Truman, and that was that. And you should have fired Gen. McChrystal when he went to the press to preempt you, telling the press what YOU had to do. Let me be blunt: We love our kids in the armed services, but we f*#&in' hate these generals, from Westmoreland in Vietnam to, yes, even Colin Powell for lying to the UN with his made-up drawings of WMD (he has since sought redemption).

So now you feel backed into a corner. 30 years ago this past Thursday (Thanks-giving) the Soviet generals had a cool idea -- "Let's invade Afghanistan!" Well, that turned out to be the final nail in the USSR coffin.

There's a reason they don't call Afghanistan the "Garden State" (though they probably should, seeing how the corrupt President Karzai, whom we back, has his brother in the heroin trade raising poppies). Afghanistan's nickname is the "Graveyard of Empires." If you don't believe it, give the British a call. I'd have you call Genghis Khan but I lost his number. I do have Gorbachev's number though. It's + 41 22 789 1662. I'm sure he could give you an earful about the historic blunder you're about to commit.

With our economic collapse still in full swing and our precious young men and women being sacrificed on the altar of arrogance and greed, the breakdown of this great civilization we call America will head, full throttle, into oblivion if you become the "war president." Empires never think the end is near, until the end is here. Empires think that more evil will force the heathens to toe the line -- and yet it never works. The heathens usually tear them to shreds.

Choose carefully, President Obama. You of all people know that it doesn't have to be this way. You still have a few hours to listen to your heart, and your own clear thinking. You know that nothing good can come from sending more troops halfway around the world to a place neither you nor they understand, to achieve an objective that neither you nor they understand, in a country that does not want us there. You can feel it in your bones.

I know you know that there are LESS than a hundred al-Qaeda left in Afghanistan! A hundred thousand troops trying to crush a hundred guys living in caves? Are you serious? Have you drunk Bush's Kool-Aid? I refuse to believe it.

Your potential decision to expand the war (while saying that you're doing it so you can "end the war") will do more to set your legacy in stone than any of the great things you've said and done in your first year. One more throwing a bone from you to the Republicans and the coalition of the hopeful and the hopeless may be gone -- and this nation will be back in the hands of the haters quicker than you can shout "tea bag!"

Choose carefully, Mr. President. Your corporate backers are going to abandon you as soon as it is clear you are a one-term president and that the nation will be safely back in the hands of the usual idiots who do their bidding. That could be Wednesday morning.

We the people still love you. We the people still have a sliver of hope. But we the people can't take it anymore. We can't take your caving in, over and over, when we elected you by a big, wide margin of millions to get in there and get the job done. What part of "landslide victory" don't you understand?

Don't be deceived into thinking that sending a few more troops into Afghanistan will make a difference, or earn you the respect of the haters. They will not stop until this country is torn asunder and every last dollar is extracted from the poor and soon-to-be poor. You could send a million troops over there and the crazy Right still wouldn't be happy. You would still be the victim of their incessant venom on hate radio and television because no matter what you do, you can't change the one thing about yourself that sends them over the edge.

The haters were not the ones who elected you, and they can't be won over by abandoning the rest of us.

President Obama, it's time to come home. Ask your neighbors in Chicago and the parents of the young men and women doing the fighting and dying if they want more billions and more troops sent to Afghanistan. Do you think they will say, "No, we don't need health care, we don't need jobs, we don't need homes. You go on ahead, Mr. President, and send our wealth and our sons and daughters overseas, 'cause we don't need them, either."

What would Martin Luther King, Jr. do? What would your grandmother do? Not send more poor people to kill other poor people who pose no threat to them, that's what they'd do. Not spend billions and trillions to wage war while American children are sleeping on the streets and standing in bread lines.

All of us that voted and prayed for you and cried the night of your victory have endured an Orwellian hell of eight years of crimes committed in our name: torture, rendition, suspension of the bill of rights, invading nations who had not attacked us, blowing up neighborhoods that Saddam "might" be in (but never was), slaughtering wedding parties in Afghanistan. We watched as hundreds of thousands of Iraqi civilians were slaughtered and tens of thousands of our brave young men and women were killed, maimed, or endured mental anguish -- the full terror of which we scarcely know.

When we elected you we didn't expect miracles. We didn't even expect much change. But we expected some. We thought you would stop the madness. Stop the killing. Stop the insane idea that men with guns can reorganize a nation that doesn't even function as a nation and never, ever has.

Stop, stop, stop! For the sake of the lives of young Americans and Afghan civilians, stop. For the sake of your presidency, hope, and the future of our nation, stop. For God's sake, stop.

Tonight we still have hope.

Tomorrow, we shall see. The ball is in your court. You DON'T have to do this. You can be a profile in courage. You can be your mother's son.

We're counting on you.

Yours, Michael Moore MMFlint@aol.com MichaelMoore.com

P.S. There's still time to have your voice heard. Call the White House at 202-456-1111 oremail the President.[43]

Michael Moore is an activist, author, and filmmaker. See more of his work at his website MichaelMoore.com

---

[43] Edip Yuksel's note: Too late now, don't bother. Obama is now a Nobel Peace Prise Winner War President.

And a sample reaction of readers at Commondreams.org

NBob November 30th, 2009 5:46 pm

If anyone is disillusioned about Obama, he/she has not been paying attention to the many utterances he made during his campaign about Afghanistan. He was anxious to prove he was capable enough to "finish the job", whatever that means. American voters chose to see what they wanted to see. Those who are conciencious, know that the Afghan fiasco is about pipeline routes and not terrorism. It is about Empire. It is unfortunate that those who enlist in the army seems blind to the fact that they commit atrocities on behalf of the wealthy. As long as the image of Osama Bin Laden is dangled before dumb Americans, the corporate agenda is assured. If Osama bin Laden is still alive, why has it taken the mightiest army in the world in excess of eight years to capture him? This is mind boggling. Americans should also be asking themselves why the resistance to an impartial investigation into the 911 WTC tragedies? What is there to conceal? And from whom? Too many mysteries surround 911. This tragedy gave liscences to Governments around the world favorable to the US to invade any country and slaughter at the whims and fancies of leaders. Only awareness among the masses will bring an end to the many crimes being committed on the international scene. This, however is not possible until the Empire crashes because it has exhausted its wealth.

Mcoyote November 30th, 2009 5:24 pm

Strength in humility is a myth. Passive denial of the enormity of the problems that confront us and the radical solutions needed to address these, while understandable in light of all the devastation being visited upon the Earth by developers, corporate greed heads and a largely acquiescent populace, is still an indefensible and repugnant position.

As long as women and African-Americans were nice humble and passive what did they get? Nothing. Unless you count subjugation and servitude as something. Would those in power one day have awakened one day in a particularly genial and loving mood having experienced some psycho-spiritual transformation and said, "You are so nice and humble I'm going to allow you to vote, own property and while we're at it let's throw in equal pay?"

Dream on.

It took suffragettes and civil rights activists being insistent, unpleasantly arrogant, unrelenting and a willingness to risk what little they did have to attain the few freedoms that are "allowed" today. This meant laying their bodies on the line.

Those who are destroying our earth and our communities at breakneck speed are as humble and caring as barracudas, with all apologies to the more gentle piscine creatures, and will not easily or at all relinquish their stranglehold on the gasping planet or your neck.

What it will take is nothing short of large scale purposeful sustained direct actions that bring the system to a halt. This means tremendous sacrifice. This means discomfort. In this there is the inevitably of tremendous risk.

The only remedy will be when people begin to get interested in taking back active control of the processes that rule their lives and work with each other rather than crossing their fingers and heading off to the ballot box.

There is zero chance that our system can be fixed through the officially-approved mechanisms. Whether overtly recognized or not, there's a war going on — the US ruling class against all the rest of us. It's essentially a class war. The rulers want you to remain a Democrat, because the D's are a ruling-class institution, whose job is guiding the Dem half of the populace in paths that are safe for the rulers. To remain a Dem voter, and to swallow whatever slop the party dishes up, is to passively assent to this arrangement.

Therefore, your primary focus should be on resisting & criticizing the system, not on adapting yourself to it. You should be talking with your friends & family about the very real things that are wrong. You should be trying to make whatever contribution you can to elevating political consciousness. Accepting the slop of the Dem Party is the opposite of all that: it deadens political consciousness, & only makes your enemies stronger.

We need Latin American-style "socialist" revolution in the streets, complemented by effective traditional political organizing, social-class based. Genuine socialism is good. An honest look at history shows that it's what the global fascists truly fear.

Published on Tuesday, December 1, 2009 by The Guardian/UK

A Troop Surge Can Only Magnify the Crime Against Afghanistan

If Barack Obama heralds an escalation of the war, he will betray his own message of hope and deepen my people's pain

by Malalai Joya

After months of waiting, President Obama is about to announce the new US strategy for Afghanistan. His speech may be long awaited, but few are expecting any surprise: it seems clear he will herald a major escalation of the war. In doing so he will be making something worse than a mistake. It is a continuation of a war crime against the suffering people of my country.

I have said before that by installing warlords and drug traffickers in power in Kabul, the US and Nato have pushed us from the frying pan to the fire. Now Obama is pouring fuel on these flames, and this week's announcement of upwards of 30,000 more troops to Afghanistan will have tragic consequences.

Already this year we have seen the impact of an increase in troops occupying Afghanistan: more violence, and more civilian deaths. My people, the poor of Afghanistan who have known only war and the domination of fundamentalism, are today squashed between two enemies: the US/Nato occupation forces on one hand and warlords and the Taliban on the other.

While we want the withdrawal of one enemy, we don't believe it is a matter of choosing between two evils. There is an alternative: the democratic-minded parties and intellectuals are our hope for the future of Afghanistan.

It will not be easy, but if we have a little bit of peace we will be better able to fight our own internal enemies - Afghans know what to do with our destiny. We are not a backward people, and we are capable of fighting for democracy, human and women's rights in Afghanistan. In fact the only way these values will be achieved is if we struggle for them and win them ourselves.

After eight years of war, the situation is as bad as ever for ordinary Afghans, and women in particular. The reality is that only the drug traffickers and warlords have been helped under this corrupt and illegitimate Karzai government. Karzai's promises of reform are laughable. His own vice-president is the notorious warlord Fahim, whom Brad Adams of Human Rights Watch describes as "one of the most notorious warlords in the country, with the blood of many Afghans on his hands".

Transparency International reports that this regime is the second most corrupt in the world. The UN Development Programme reports Afghanistan is second last

428

- 181st out of 182 countries - in terms of human development. That is why we no longer want this kind of "help" from the west.

Like many around the world, I am wondering what kind of "peace" prize can be awarded to a leader who continues the occupations of Iraq and Afghanistan, and starts a new war in Pakistan, all while supporting Israel?

Throughout my recent tour of the US, I had the chance to meet many military families and veterans who are working to put an end to the wars in Iraq and Afghanistan. They understand that it is not a case of a "bad war" and a "good war" - there is no difference, war is war.

Members of Iraq Veterans Against War even accompanied me to meet members of Congress in Washington DC. Together we tried to explain the terrible human cost of this war, in terms of Afghan, US and Nato lives. Unfortunately, only a few representatives really offered their support to our struggle for peace.

While the government was not responsive, the people of the US did offer me their support. And polls confirm that the US public wants peace, not an escalated war. Many also want Obama to hold Bush and his administration to account for war crimes. Everywhere I spoke, people responded strongly when I said that if Obama really wanted peace he would first of all try to prosecute Bush and have him tried before the international criminal court. Replacing Bush's man in the Pentagon, Robert Gates, would have been a good start - but Obama chose not to.

Unfortunately, the UK government shamefully follows the path of the US in Afghanistan. Even though opinion polls show that more than 70% of the population is against the war, Gordon Brown has announced the deployment of more UK troops. It is sad that more taxpayers' money will be wasted on this war, while Britain's poor continue to suffer from a lack of basic services.

The UK government has also tried to silence dissent, for instance by arresting Joe Glenton, a British soldier who has refused to return to Afghanistan. I had a chance to meet Glenton when I was in London last summer, and together we spoke out against the war. My message to him is that, in times of great injustice, it is sometimes better to go to jail than be part of committing war crimes.

Facing a difficult choice, Glenton made a courageous decision, while Obama and Brown have chosen to follow the Bush administration. Instead of hope and change, in foreign policy Obama is delivering more of the same. But I still have hope because, as our history teaches, the people of Afghanistan will never accept occupation.

Malalai Joya is an Afghan politician and a former elected member of the Parliament from Farah province. Her last book is *Raising My Voice*

An excerpt from
The Catastrophe Al Nakba How Palestine Became Israel

(For the full article and its supporting references please visit, IfAmericansKnew.org)
July 9, 2008

.....

The Catastrophe

This growing violence culminated in Israel's ruthless 1947-49 "War of Independence," in which at least 750,000 Palestinian men, women, and children were expelled from their homes – half of them even before any Arab armies joined the war. At every point in this war, Zionist forces outnumbered Arab forces. This massive humanitarian disaster is known among Palestinians and others as 'The Catastrophe,' al Nakba in Arabic.

Zionist forces committed at least 33 massacres and destroyed 531 Palestinian villages and towns.

Zionist forces committed at least 33 massacres and destroyed 531 Palestinian villages and towns. Author Norman Finkelstein states: "According to the former director of the Israeli army archives, 'in almost every village occupied by us during the War of Independence, acts were committed which are defined as war crimes, such as murders, massacres, and rapes'...Uri Milstein, the authoritative Israeli military historian of the 1948 war, goes one step further, maintaining that 'every skirmish ended in a massacre of Arabs.'"

.....

Injustice Continues

Over the 60 years since Israel's founding on May 14, 1948, this profound injustice has continued. Palestinian refugees are the largest remaining refugee population in the world.

Palestinian refugee Mohamad Mahmoud Al-Arja, 80, still has the key from his house in Beer Al-saba, which is now inside Israel.

1.3 million Palestinians live in Israel as "Israeli citizens," but despite their status as citizens, they are subject to systematic discrimination. Many are prohibited from living in the villages and homes from which they were violently expelled, and their property has been confiscated for Jewish-only uses. In Orwellian terminology, Israeli law designates these internal refugees as "present absentees."

In 1967 Israel launched its third war and seized still more Palestinian (and other Arab) land. Israel also attacked a U.S. Navy ship, the USS Liberty, killing and injuring over 200 Americans, an event that remains largely covered-up today, despite efforts by an extraordinary array of high-level military officers and civilian officials to expose it.

Israel militarily occupied the West Bank and Gaza Strip – the final 22% of mandatory Palestine – and began building settlements for Jewish Israelis on land confiscated from Palestinian Muslims and Christians. It has demolished more than 18,000 Palestinian homes since 1967. In 2005 Israel returned Gazan land to its owners, but continues to control its borders, ports, and air space, turning Gaza into a large concentration camp, where 1.5 million people are held under what a UN Human Rights Commissioner described as "catastrophic" conditions. Approximately 11,000 Palestinian men, women, and children are imprisoned in Israeli jails under physically abusive conditions (many have not even been charged with a crime) and the basic human rights of all Palestinians under Israeli rule are routinely violated. A number of prisoners tortured by Israel have been American citizens.

....

430

Brainbow Press

Quran: A Reformist Translation
Translated and Annotated by: Edip Yuksel; Layth Saleh al-Shaiban; Martha Schulte-Nafeh. First Edition: Brainbow Press, 2007, 520 pages, $24.70. ISBN 978-0-9796715-0-0. Available also in **pocket size**.

Test Your Quranic Knowledge
Contains six sets of multiple choice questions and their answers. Edip Yuksel, Brainbow Press, 2007, 52 pages, $7.95. ISBN 978-0-9796715-5-5

Manifesto for Islamic Reform
Edip Yuksel, Brainbow Press, 2008, 209, 128 pages, $9.95. ISBN 978-0-9796715-6-2

The Natural Republic
Layth Saleh al-Shaiban (ProgressiveMuslims.org), Brainbow Press, 2008, 198 pages, $14.95, ISBN 978-0-9796715-8-6

Critical Thinkers for Islamic Reform
Editors: Edip Yuksel, Arnold Mol, Farouk A. Peru, Brainbow Press, 2009, 262 pages, $17.95. ISBN 978-0-9796715-7-9

NINETEEN: God's Signature in Nature and Scripture
A comprehensive demonstration of the prophetic miracle. Edip Yuksel, Brainbow Press, 2010, 456 pages. $19.95. ISBN 978-0-9796715-3-1

Peacemaker's Guide to Warmongers
Exposing Robert Spencer, Osama bin Laden, David Horowitz, Mullah Omar, Bill Warner, Ali Sina and other Enemies of Peace. Edip Yuksel, Brainbowpress, 2010, 432 pages. $19.95. ISBN: 978-0-9796715-3-1

Edip Yuksel's Upcoming Books in years 2010-2014

In the Name of Allah: My Journey from Radicalism to Reform (Provisional Title)
An autobiography.

Running Like Zebras
Edip Yüksel's debate with the critics of Code 19

19 Questions for Muslims, Christians, and Atheists
The first two sections are revisions of old booklets.

Purple Letters
A selection of correspondence on religion, philosophy, and politics.

From Faith to Reason: Inspiring Stories of Forty Converts
Inspiring stories of converts from Sunni, Shiite, Catholic, Protestant religions and Atheism to Islam.

The Bestest Teacher, Student and Parent:
57 Rules for Students, Teachers and Parents.

Twelve Hungry Men
A religious/political/philosophical comedy for a feature film

Edip's Record of Religious Odditiies:
A ranking of the bizarre beliefs and practices of world religions.

USA versus USA: The American Janus
A political mirror and x-ray of America's best and worst.

Muhammad: A Messenger of Peace and Reason
A script for an animated feature film about Muhammad's mission.

Join the Movement; Let the World Know!

The Islamic Reform movement is receiving momentum around the globe. We invite you to join us in our activities locally, internationally. Please contact us through the contact addresses posted at:

www.islamicreform.org
www.free-minds.org
www.mpjp.org
www.19.org

To study the Quran more diligently, you may visit 19.org for links to computer programs, searchable Quranic indexes, electronic versions of this and other translations, and various study tools. We highly recommend you the following sites for your study of the Quran:

www.quranic.org
www.quranix.com
www.openquran.org
www.studyquran.org
www.quranmiracles.org

****

www.19.org
www.yuksel.org
www.free-minds.org
www.islamicreform.org
www.quranmiracles.org
www.brainbowpress.com
www.groups.google.com/group/19org
www.deenresearchcenter.com
www.quranbrowser.com
www.openburhan.com
www.studyquran.org
www.quranix.com
www.quranic.org
www.mpjp.org

…and more

432

www.ingramcontent.com/pod-product-compliance
Lightning Source LLC
Chambersburg PA
CBHW062151270326
41930CB00009B/1500